The Brazilian-American Alliance

Frank D. McCann, Jr.

The Brazilian-American Alliance

1937–1945

Princeton University Press

LCC: 72-14030
ISBN: 0-691-05655-2

The following have appeared in somewhat different
form as follows:

Chapter 3, "Sigma and Swastika": "Vargas and the
Destruction of the Brazilian Integralista and Nazi Parties,"
The Americas, XXVI, 1 (July 1969), 15–34, copyright 1969
by Academy of American Franciscan History.
Chapter 6, "The Open Door": "La Lucha por El
Comercio Brasileño, 1935–1939," *Foro Internacional*
(El Colegio de Mexico), IX, 2 (1968), 182–193, copyright
1968 by *Foro Internacional*.
Chapter 8, "Airlines and Bases": "Aviation Diplomacy:
The United States and Brazil, 1939–1941," *Inter-American
Economic Affairs*, XXI, 4 (Spring 1968), 35–50, copyright
1968 by *Inter-American Economic Affairs*.

This book has been composed in Linotype Baskerville
Printed in the United States of America
by Princeton University Press, Princeton, New Jersey

With Love and Affection for
 Diane Marie
 Teresa Bernadette
 Katherine Diane and
 Our Brazil

Contents

Preface *ix*

Abbreviations *xiii*

Introduction *3*

1 Vargas' Brazil *11*

2 The Course *49*

3 Sigma and Swastika *77*

4 Security of the Western Hemisphere *106*

5 Toward Approximation *123*

6 The Open Door *148*

7 Crisis and Uncertainty *176*

8 Airlines and Bases *213*

9 An Uncertain Alliance *240*

10 No Turning Back *259*

11 Politics and Policy *291*

12 The Cobra's Pipe *343*

13 War and Development *378*

14 The Smoking Cobras *403*

15 End of an Era *443*

Note on Sources and Supplementary
Bibliography *487*

Index *509*

Preface

My INTEREST in Brazil and the study of Brazilian-American relations began rather suddenly in the late spring of 1962 during supper in the Graduate Residence Center at Indiana University. I was about to take a seminar in American diplomatic history with Robert Ferrell and was explaining to my friend George Fodor and three Brazilians from Minas Gerais, to whom he had recently introduced me, what I intended to write about. They let out cries of disbelief that I could consider a subject not dealing with their country. They insisted that Brazil was the most dynamic and important nation in Latin America and that I had to write about it. When I asked what topic they would suggest, they replied without hesitation relations between Brazil and the United States during the time of Getúlio Vargas and the Estado Nôvo. Over coffee they talked of Vargas' Brazil, and afterward Constancia Xavier de Lima, Iêda Dias da Silva, and Teresinha Souto Ward took me to the library to show me the Brazilian items. They were so earnest and determined that I could not say no. While the paper took shape (as a study of Brazil's entry into World War II) my four friends pursued me hawkishly discussing, arguing, and explaining. After that summer the direction of my academic career was set and now, four trips to Brazil later, this book is finished.

Its beginnings are important to me because they were not in the many dusty and dim archives that I would haunt in the next years but in the love of Brazilians for their land. I hope that this book repays in part the many kindnesses that they and their countrymen have shown to me and my family.

So many people have played a part in the research and writing of this book that I am certain I cannot assign each his proper due. But some feeble effort is necessary. Daniel McGuire, Bernard Williams, and Maury Baker gave great encouragement throughout the early years. Robert E. Quirk provided a scholastic standard that has served as a constant beacon, as did the energy and attention to detail of Robert Ferrell. With only a small research grant and a large NDEA loan to see us through what turned out to be an eight-month period of research in New York and Washington in 1964–1965, we would surely have gone broke if Richard Schroeder had not asked Mr. and Mrs. Joseph Virdone of Roslyn Heights, New York, to help us. They generously provided us with their friendship and a cottage on their property.

For the research in official United States files the help of the following people was indispensable: the late E. Taylor Parks and Arthur G. Kogan of the State Department's Historical Office; Wilbur J. Nigh and Thomas Hohmann of the National Archives' World War II Records Section and Patricia Dowling of the diplomatic files section; the staffs of the Office of the Chief of Military History, the Navy Library and Records, the Library of Congress, and the Franklin D. Roosevelt Library, especially Joseph Marshall and Robert Parkes. Judith A. Schiff at the Yale University Library granted access to the Henry L. Stimson Papers. And John C. Pirie, then Vice-President and Associate General Counsel of Pan-Amercian Airways, expedited research on the Airport Development Program. Special thanks are due Alberta Sankis for her assistance during my weeks in the Pan-Am Building.

The four trips to Brazil in 1965–1966, 1969, and 1970 were made possible by a Fulbright grant, my father's assistance, the cooperation of Colonels Amos Jordan and

Roger Nye of West Point, and a grant from the Penrose Fund of the American Philosophical Society. The hospitality and orientation of George Fodor, John and Marilou Schulz, Derek and Maria Lovell-Parker, William and Carmita Vance, Constancia Xavier de Lima, Iêda Dias da Silva, Rosa Marcôndes de Souza, and the Valladares, Flôres da Cunha, and Souto families was always delightful, and contributed greatly to my appreciation of Brazilian culture. Particular thanks for assistance are due Martha Maria Gonçalves, chief of the *Arquivo Histórico* of the Itamaraty; Seraphim José de Oliveira, charge officer of the *Arquivo da Fôrça Expedicionária Brasileira*; Charles Matthews of Natal; Antônio Flôres da Cunha; Cauby C. Araújo; Hélio Silva; João dos Santos Vaz and the *Clube dos Veteranos da Campanha na Itália*; Colonel Newton C. de Andrade Mello; General Willis D. Crittenberger; and General Vernon A. Walters. My debts to Marshals Estevão Leitão de Carvalho and João Baptista Mascarenhas de Moraes are indicated in the Note on Sources. If at times I have been critical of either, my presentation was motivated by a need for historical accuracy rather than by a lack of respect and admiration. Mascarenhas faced and overcame obstacles that would have destroyed a lesser man. He was, to use General Crittenberger's words: "the toughest little guy who ever wore boots!"

This book obviously would not be what it is without the graciousness of Alzira Vargas do Amaral Peixoto and Euclydes Aranha Neto, who in addition to the free use of the Vargas and Aranha papers gave liberally of their time to reminisce and to clarify areas of uncertainty.

Participation in the Rio Research Group during 1965–1966, and in the Interdisciplinary Seminar on Brazil at Columbia University from 1968 to 1971 greatly influenced my thinking. My colleagues and good friends Robert M. Levine and Neill W. Macaulay have given encouragement and advice from our days in Rio on. The manuscript owes much to Eugene Trani, David M. Pletcher, Judy R. Collins, Donn

Olvey, Stanley Stein, Jordan Young, Sérgio Buarque de Holanda, John Culver and Thomas Skidmore, who read various chapters and drafts with pencil in hand. I gratefully acknowledge the forbearance and good advice of Arthur S. Link, and the never-failing sense of perspective of David Hirst, while I prepared the final draft during my year with them at Princeton as a National Historical Publications Commission Fellow. Teresinha Souto Ward read through this and an earlier draft, trying to bring order to my chaotic accenting and Portuguese spelling. Kate Nicol typed several chapters with a very careful eye to spelling and style. Nancy Baldwin Smith deftly handled the copyediting. James Flagg, Robert Costa, and Marcia Walters read aloud each word, comma, and semi-colon of the galley proofs; and Marjorie Sherwood of the Princeton University Press oversaw the details of publication. Of course I am the only one responsible for any errors the book may contain.

I wish to thank my father, Francis D. McCann, Sr., for his steadfast confidence that somehow it was all worthwhile. But above all I thank my wife, Diane Marie Sankis, and daughters, Teresa Bernadette and Katherine Diane. In many ways this book is as much theirs as mine. Literally it determined the girls' birthplaces and has certainly shaped their world view. Diane has helped with the research, has thought and debated over ideas and approaches, read and reread every chapter and note, and throughout our travels preserved her sense of balance and good humor. A thousand thanks to all.

St. Patrick's Day, 1972   F.D.M.

Abbreviations

ADP	Airport Development Program
AFEB	Arquivo da Fôrça Expedicionária Brasileira (Ministério de Guerra, Rio de Janeiro)
AG	Adjutant General
AGV	Archive of Getúlio Vargas (Rio de Janeiro)
AHMRE	Arquivo Histórico de MRE (Itamaraty Palace, Rio de Janeiro)
BEF	Brazilian Expeditionary Force
CNO	Chief of Naval Operations
DA	Department of the Army
DAR	Division of American Republics (Department of State)
DBA	Division of Brazilian Affairs (Department of State)
DGFP–D	*Documents on German Foreign Policy,* U.S. Department of State, Series D
DSF	Department of State Files (Department of State Building, Washington)
EXP.	*Expedido*—outgoing MRE dispatch
EW	European War
FEA	Federal Economic Administration
FEB	Fôrça Expedicionária Brasileira
FDRL	Franklin D. Roosevelt Library (Hyde Park, New York)
Foreign Relations	*Foreign Relations of the United States, Diplomatic Papers (Department of State)*

JBUSDC	Joint Brazil-United States Defense Commission
MRE	Ministério das Relações Exteriores
NA	National Archives (Washington)
OAA	Oswaldo Aranha Archive (Rio de Janeiro)
OCIAA	Office of Coordinator of Inter-American Affairs
OCMH	Office of the Chief of Military History (Department of the Army, Washington)
OF	Official File (FDRL, Hyde Park)
OPD	Operations Plans Division (War Department)
PAA	Pan-American Airways
PPF	President's Personal File (FDRL, Hyde Park)
PSD	Partido Social Democrático
PSF	President's Secretary File (FDRL, Hyde Park)
PTB	Partido Trabalhista Brasileiro
SADATC	South Atlantic Division Air Transport Command
SLC	Standing Liaison Committee (State, War, Navy Departments)
UDN	União Democrática Nacional
USN	United States Navy
WPB	War Production Board
WPD	War Plans Division (War Department)
WWII RS	World War II Records Section (National Archives, Washington)

The Brazilian-American Alliance

Manaus

AMAPÁ

Belem

Fernando De Noronha

Fortaleza

MARANHÃO   CEARÁ   RIO GRANDE DO NORTE

PARÁ   Natal

AMAZONAS   PIAUÍ   PARAÍBA

                                                    PERNAMBUCO   Recife

ACRE   ALAGOAS

                                                          SERGIPE

                            GOIÁS   BAHIA

                                                    Salvador
                                                    (Bahia)

        MATO GROSSO

                            MINAS CERAIS

                                Belo   ESPÍRTO
                                Horizonte   SANTO

                            Volta   STATE OF RIO DE
            SÃO PAULO   Redonia   Petrópolis JANEIRO
                                    Niterói
                Sao Paulo   Rio De Janeiro

            PARANÁ

            SANTA CATARINA

        RIO GRANDE
            DO
            SUL   Pôrto Alegre

Introduction

VISIBILITY was zero. The cold, steady rain of the 10th and 11th continued to pour from the densely clouded sky on the morning of December 12, 1944. Two battalions of the Brazilian Expeditionary Force sloshed through the mud toward the German positions at Monte Castello. The war against Hitler's Third Reich was in its final six months. Arriving at Naples in August, the Brazilians had missed the early victories of the Italian campaign and were determined to make up the lost opportunities for glory. Their troops were stalled before Monte Castello—they had failed to carry the heights in three previous attempts, and they needed this victory to preserve the honor of Brazil. But without air and artillery cover because of the thick fog, and with supporting tanks immobilized in the mud, the Germans drove them back. Accepting the impossibility of fighting nature and German infantry at the same time, the Brazilians and the rest of the Fifth Army dug in for the winter. Under more suitable conditions on February 21 the Brazilians took Monte Castello, and neither the elements nor the Germans deterred their onward march thereafter.

The history of the Italian campaign is studded with many famous names and events. Although Brazil's combat participation was little noticed in the United States because of the more widespread activities of American troops, it was of considerable importance in the history of Brazil and of inter-American relations. It was the first time that Latin American soldiers had fought in Europe, and Brazil was the only Latin American nation to send ground troops into combat in World War II. The results were immediate and far-reaching. Brazil became the preeminent military power in Latin America and the Brazilian military gradually came to dominate national politics.

But Brazilian entry into the war had a greater importance in the outcome of that global conflict. Without Brazilian cooperation much that happened might have been different. Getúlio Dornelles Vargas' establishment of a dictatorship in late 1937 had cast an uncertain shadow on the future of democracy in the Western Hemisphere. From 1938 through 1940 official Washington was preoccupied with the specter of Brazil allying itself to, or at least cooperating with, Nazi Germany. Especially during the dreary days of 1940 when it seemed that Great Britain might collapse, American diplomats and military planners worked feverishly to secure Brazil. Even though the United States was still neutral, it was evident to the State and War Departments that the Americas had to be united. If Brazil joined the Axis fortress America would be vulnerable and the South Atlantic would be closed to allied shipping; it would be impossible to supply the beleaguered British in Egypt, and would give the Germans domination of North Africa and increased influence in the Middle East. From there to dividing South Asia with the Japanese would have been a logical step.

Fortunately Brazil eventually joined the allies, and the South Atlantic not only remained open but became the principal supply route to Africa and the Far East. American engineers turned Natal in Northeast Brazil into a trampoline that bounced supplies from American factories to the war fronts—"a trampoline to victory."

While Brazilian bases facilitated supply and Brazilian troops scored victories in Italy, Brazilian workmen, advised by American technicians, were installing the giant blast furnaces at Volta Redonda which were to provide the basis for Brazilian heavy industry. Wartime development efforts produced lasting changes in the Brazilian economy, not the least of which was to make São Paulo the greatest industrial park in Latin America and the fastest growing urban area in the southern hemisphere.

While the war undoubtedly increased Brazil's chances to realize its tremendous potential it also made it subservient, very nearly a dependency, to the United States. The growth of that dependency is an undercurrent that runs throughout the events discussed in this book. The war years brought to a peak the tendency in Brazilian foreign policy toward steadily closer approximation with the United States, which had begun during the foreign ministry of the Baron of Rio Branco (1902–1912). At that time Brazil made an unwritten alliance with the United States, as a step toward freeing itself from British domination and toward insuring its own hegemony in South America. In the 1930's and early 1940's, under the leadership of Foreign Minister Oswaldo Euclydes de Souza Aranha (1938–1944), Brazil cut its financial ties with the British Rothschilds in favor of Wall Street, and renewed and strengthened Rio Branco's alliance with the United States. This was done in the face of a German campaign to link Brazil with the Third Reich.

The drive toward closer union with the United States occurred largely on Brazilian initiative, with the northern republic taking a passive role until 1940. While it was true that Brazilian and American leaders could speak of a long friendship, that friendship was more verbal than substantive. Some five thousand miles of ocean and jungle separated the principal cities of the two nations, and the distance and slow transportation hindered contact. American interest in Brazil became greater when improvements in aviation began to reduce travel time.

Throughout the nineteenth century the United States was preoccupied with the trans-Appalachian west and, once the Panamanian route to the Pacific was firmly established, Americans showed little interest in the South Atlantic. They ignored the Argentine-Brazilian struggle over what is now Uruguay and the long war of the Triple Alliance against

Paraguay. At the same time, however, during the nine-teenth century the two largest and most powerful nations in the hemisphere were a republic and a monarchy, and they neither fought wars against each other nor engaged in important controversies.

Brazilians and Americans did not know each other except at second hand. With the collapse of the monarchy in 1889 the Brazilians entered the Western Hemisphere family of republics, but found that they had more to gain from ties with the United States than from alliances with their South American neighbors. The United States provided markets which the Spanish Americans did not, as well as a political and economic alternative to Britain.

Of the twenty-two independent countries in the Western Hemisphere eighteen were Spanish-speaking and their cultures were either Iberian or Indian. Language and culture separated Brazil and the United States from these countries. Africa had influenced Brazil's culture more than it did the culture of the rest of South America, and Brazil's Portuguese was only superficially similar to Spanish. Nor did the language and culture of the United States provide a common ground on which to meet Spanish-speaking peoples. In size and power, Brazil and the United States were the giants of the hemisphere, and as such were attracted to one another. So while it was true that their peoples had little direct contact or understanding, it was also true that their governments sought to maintain cordial relations.

The Brazilians were more aggressive in seeking ties. They pursued a policy of approximation with the United States which fell just short of formal alliance, as a means of off-setting the shifting alliances of the Spanish-speaking countries and Argentina's dream of rebuilding the colonial Vice-royalty of the Rio de La Plata. American support, real or imagined, was useful to Brazil in thwarting Argentina. Economically the United States provided an escape from British domination. The formula was Brazilian support of United States policies in the Caribbean, Europe, and Asia in return for American support of Brazilian preeminence in South America. Brazil often acted as intermediary between the other American nations and the United States, and provided a stable base for Washington's constantly changing Latin American policies.

American interest in Brazil increased during the 1930's for two reasons, the Good Neighbor Policy and the rise of Nazi Germany. Franklin Roosevelt's desire to create a Good Neighborhood in the hemisphere meant that the United States would renounce direct intervention in favor of more subtle forms of domination. In its post-Depression pursuit of markets the United States turned to Latin America as the logical area in which to recoup its losses in foreign trade elsewhere—indeed, the first reciprocal trade agreements were signed with Latin American republics. American officials talked in terms of equal opportunities for all in the Latin American market, but what they meant was equal opportunity based on American rules. Because United States businessmen could deal in hard currency while their German competitors could not, American insistence that the Germans use such currencies was tantamount to demanding that they withdraw from the market. The United States was seeking more than neighborliness, it was seeking economic and political hegemony. Brazilian leaders did not seriously oppose this hegemony, because they became convinced that they had more to gain than to lose by acquiescence. They were confident that Brazil could maintain its position in South America, and that they could maintain their positions in Brazil.

The Argentine government, on the contrary, was not at all pleased with Washington's desire for leadership of the Western Hemisphere. Active North American participation in hemisphere affairs would endanger Argentine plans to become the leader of Latin America. The Argentines did not trust American motives and did not believe that the new nonintervention policy would endure. They did not wish to depend on what they considered to be a fickle

United States and they suspected that the United States would favor Brazil. They complained bitterly that the United States was discriminatory in excluding Argentina's principle export—beef—while providing Brazil with the chief market for its coffee. If Argentina could not sell to the United States how could it buy from it? Argentine opposition to American proposals at the Inter-American Conference for the Maintenance of Peace at Buenos Aires in 1936 led the Roosevelt administration to see Brazil as a balance to Argentina. As American leaders became steadily more concerned over the growing strength of Nazism and Fascism in Europe and as they came to fear the spreading of these ideologies to South America, Washington sought closer relations with Brazil to offset Argentina's equivocal attitude toward the Axis powers.

The Roosevelt administration gave political, economic, and military aid to the government of Getúlio Vargas, even though after November 1937 that government was a dictatorship. Roosevelt followed the traditional United States policy of recognizing a *de facto* government regardless of its political composition or the way in which it came to power, but he added to the policy by supporting an undemocratic regime in Brazil. Because Brazilian stability was essential to the hemisphere defense plans of the United States and to American trade, Washington had no choice but to support Vargas. To weaken him would have aided the fascist-style Integralista party, the Nazi fifth-columnists, or militarists like Army Chief of Staff Pedro Aurélio de Góes Monteiro who favored a Bonapartist dictatorship. It was wiser to support the nonideological Estado Nôvo (New State) as long as it was cooperative and useful to United States interests. Vargas was deeply committed to developing his country, convinced of his ability to lead it to greatness, and secondarily concerned with the constitutions that supported his rule (those of 1934 and 1937). He was not interested in ideology but in moving Brazil in a conservative, steady fashion beyond the grasp of communists or Integralistas. In supporting Vargas the Roosevelt administration was pragmatic; Vargas was preferable to chaos—he held Brazil together and gave Brazilians a strong sense of national consciousness.

Brazilian policy was based on the premise that the nation's security must take precedence over other considerations. But there was a difference of opinion among Brazilian leaders as to the best means of obtaining security, and Nazi Germany's efforts to capture markets in Brazil provided another alternative to economic dependence on Britain, and also a means of preventing American trade domination. Some military leaders, such as Minister of War Eurico Gaspar Dutra and General Góes Monteiro, for a time favored Germany because they believed that the Reich would conquer Europe and the United States would accept the new European order. Others under Foreign Minister Oswaldo Aranha worked to eliminate the totalitarian façade of the Estado Nôvo and to ally Brazil with the United States because they feared Germany and the antidemocratic tendencies of the Brazilian military. The Aranha group believed that they could walk the tightrope between cooperation with the United States and American domination. Once Vargas realized that the American fear that Brazil would join or, at least, cooperate with the Axis equalled Germany's desire to detach Brazil from the Americas, he endeavored to obtain concessions from both sides. By late 1940 he was convinced that the United States could and would defend Brazil and that his position would be more secure if he cooperated with the Americans. Even so, he moved slowly, careful not to outdistance civilian or military opinion.

The role of the United States in Brazil's going to war was decisive—the nature of the relationship between the two nations made a choice imperative. Simple neutrality was impossible. Brazil had to choose between the Axis and the United States. Analysis of that decision affords a view of the diplomatic uses of economic and military aid which became features of diplomacy in the postwar years. It also provides insights on the influence of the military on foreign policy and into the functioning of Vargas' Estado Nôvo.

Throughout the prewar and war years Brazilian leaders sought to pursue policies based on national self-interest. They attempted to be pragmatic in securing the best possible position for their nation. It was not entirely their fault that approximation with the United States did not bring all the hoped-for benefits, and instead turned into economic, political, and military dependence. The uncertain fortunes of war limited their ability to perceive the long-range effects of their policies just as the fog and rain at Monte Castello made it difficult for the Brazilian troops to see victory ahead. For both politician and soldier visibility was zero.

"We will restore the nation . . . allowing it to construct freely its own history and destiny."[1]

1

Vargas' Brazil

AFTER A RAIN during the night and with a cloudy sky still threatening showers, Wednesday, November 10, 1937, dawned cool and breezy in Rio de Janeiro. The morning newspapers carried no mention of the manifesto read the previous day in the Congress, only a feature story on the new Minister of Justice, Francisco Campos. All appeared normal, and the city was outwardly calm despite the sudden closure of the Congress that morning. The old cog-railway carried its loads of tourists to the top of Corcôvado to see the view and to pose for photographs before the statue of Christ, while the tiny streetcars rattled their way from one end of town to the other. The ferryboats scurried back and forth across the bay between Praça Quinze and Niteroi, where the Fluminense soccer club was preparing for its match with Vasco da Gama, scheduled for the evening. The marquees in *Cinelândia* advertised the latest Hollywood films, starring the Marx brothers, Edward G. Robinson, Robert Young, and Claudette Colbert, and the Municipal Theater featured the opera "Rigoletto." The usual crowds bustled along the mosaic sidewalks of Avenida Rio Branco in the business district. At the General Staff School the director of instruction unveiled portraits of illustrious former professors before a gathering of generals. In the Guanabara Palace the presidential family enjoyed lobster at the mid-

1 Getúlio Vargas, *A Nova Política do Brasil* (Rio de Janeiro, 1938–47), V, 32.

day meal; and in the courtyard of the Itamaraty the swans glided over the reflecting pool.[2]

But ferment underlay the placid surface. Rumors of an impending coup had been gaining currency every day. As the president's daughter, Alzira Vargas, recalled: "No one knew for certain how, when, or who would effect it. The tension, the anguish, the expectation was perceptible in the very air one breathed."[3]

The politics of Brazil between 1930 and 1937 was fraught with tension, anguish, and expectation, but the republic presented to the world a calm façade, masking its political squabbles, social problems, and economic change. Always Brazil seems to have appeared outwardly tranquil while seething underneath. Perhaps this is what led Gilberto Freyre to call his country a tropical China—its great size allowed it to absorb shocks that would have crumbled a lesser state. It can appear as unshakable as the ancient crystalline rock that underlies the Brazilian highlands, even when its society is being shaken to its foundations. November 10, 1937, marked the culmination of seven years of political jockeying and the beginning of eight years of dictatorship. Because of the influence of domestic events on foreign policy a look at the Brazil of the 1930's will aid in understanding the processes of policy formation and implementation.

Since coming to power through an armed movement in 1930, Getúlio Dornelles Vargas had sought to construct a regime capable of supporting the changes that he saw as necessary to modernize Brazil; basically this came to mean a strong central government. While the initial provisional

[2] Based on *Jornal do Brasil* (Rio), Nov. 9 and 10, 1937; Estevão Leitão de Carvalho, *Memórias de um Soldado Legalista* (Rio de Janeiro, 1964), III, 305–306; Lourival Coutinho, *O General Góes Depõe* (Rio de Janeiro, 1956), p. 318. The Itamaraty Palace housed the Brazilian Foreign Ministry in Rio de Janeiro.

[3] Alzira Vargas do Amaral Peixoto, *Getúlio Vargas, Meu Pai* (Pôrto Alegre, 1960), p. 212.

regime allowed him to decree some progressive legislation, the factionalism of Vargas' Liberal Alliance, composed of old-time politicians and radical young military officers called *tenentes*, prevented strong unified effort. The various states balked at surrendering prerogatives that they had exercised since the fall of the monarchy in 1889. Federalism versus centralism, common to the histories of the American republics, produced in Brazil, as elsewhere, discord, violence, and civil war. In 1932 the rich and powerful state of São Paulo attempted to form a coalition with Minas Gerais and Rio Grande do Sul, to defend state autonomy and to resolve myriad local issues. Federal forces neutralized rebels in the two latter states and threw a cordon around São Paulo. The futile civil war had begun with a flourish of popularity among Paulistas on July 9, 1932. Women gave their golden wedding rings to finance the cause, but generosity could not put experience into the raw recruits who manned Paulista positions. By the end of the first week in October the dismal affair ended with São Paulo's surrender.

Vargas shrewdly adopted a policy of conciliation for the sake of Brazilian unity. There were no firing squads, though some two hundred of the rebellion's leaders sailed to exile in Portugal, and there were no harsh indemnities; on the contrary, the national government agreed to redeem the Paulista war bonds. But the problems that had sparked the revolt remained.

The coup d'état of 1930 had ended the "old republic" in a governmental sense, but it was no social revolution. Rather than destroying rural-based oligarchies and their urban business allies, it merely removed their representatives from political control. In the following years Vargas expended much effort absorbing the rural and commercial elites into his power base. He turned these former enemies into supporters—or at least neutrals. Vargas succeeded because he checked the radical *tenentes* and the authoritarian rightists within his regime, and eventually destroyed the communists and the fascistic Integralistas that threatened it. He showed the elites that they had more to gain from cooperation than from opposition.

Vargas wanted to modernize Brazil but to avoid the sweeping violence that characterized the Mexican and Russian revolutions. He adroitly escaped the embraces of both the extreme left and the extreme right. He proceeded like a Disraeli or a Bismarck, freely borrowing ideas and measures from the extremes in order to blur their authorship and to weaken their potency as rallying-points for radical action. His revolution, though conservative, painfully gradual, and lacking "even the embryo of a precise ideology,"[4] nevertheless merited the name revolution, because after 1930 it became obvious that "something profound had been changed in Brazil."[5] The country was at a crossroads in 1930 but, unfortunately, the route which Getúlio Vargas chose, while freeing Brazil from rigidly liberal orthodoxy, produced a situation which eventually resulted in an authoritarian military government.[6]

Getúlio, as he was called by everyone, was one of the most curious figures in Brazilian history. He was a short man with a determined and fatherly face which customarily wore a large and sympathetic smile. He dominated public opinion to a degree previously unknown, he achieved popularity without appearing to cultivate it, and he carefully avoided ostentation. He was a reserved and complex man whose daughter said that he hid his thoughts even from

[4] Nelson Werneck Sodré, *Orientações do Pensamento Brasileiro* (Rio de Janeiro, 1942), p. 13, as quoted in João Cruz Costa, *Contribuição a História das Idéias no Brasil* (Rio de Janeiro, 1967), p. 410.

[5] João Cruz Costa, *ibid.*

[6] For internal politics in the 1930's see Robert M. Levine, *The Vargas Regime, The Critical Years, 1934-1938* (New York, 1970); and for results of the era Thomas Skidmore, *Politics in Brazil, 1930-1964, An Experiment in Democracy* (New York, 1967) and Ronald M. Schneider, *The Political System of Brazil, Emergence of a "Modernizing" Authoritarian Regime, 1964-1970* (New York, 1971).

himself. His slow action in resolving controversies suggested discipline and nonpartisanship, as if his movements had mathematical precision. In crises he seemed serene, tranquil, even insensitive, always giving the impression that he had himself and the situation under control. He avoided displays of power, preferring to give at least the appearance of operating according to law. With self-discipline he allowed events to run their course before intervening. While usually attempting to rally a consensus before acting, he did not shrink from removing opponents or taking frank, decisive, even violent action. Whether he did this from temperament, intelligence, or cunning is difficult to say; he puzzled his family, friends, and contemporaries as well as the historian.

Vargas was a master of maneuver. His power rested on the armed forces, yet he was his own man, not subservient to the military; somehow he managed to be the final recourse in military as well as civil disputes. He did not hold grudges; if he needed a man, he used him, even if that man had fought against him in the past. But discard awaited those whose usefulness was spent. He balanced the power of one politician by that of another, one state with a second, one general with his rival. He was careful to see that no member of his administration achieved too much power, position, or popularity.

It might be useful to make some comparisons between Vargas and his contemporary in the United States, Franklin D. Roosevelt. Both were sons of traditional families, both squires of small rural towns—São Borja, Rio Grande do Sul, and Hyde Park, New York. The people of their native states are energetic and accustomed to assuming leadership in the affairs of their respective nations. Politics permeated the atmospheres in which Vargas and Roosevelt grew up: to them political office was as much a duty as a reward. Both men served apprenticeships in subcabinet or cabinet posts; both rose slowly through the ranks of their state political machines and took control after overcoming the party leadership. Vargas used the governorship of Rio Grande do Sul as a road to the presidency, Roosevelt used the governorship of New York State. Each headed a reform ticket—a violent revolution carried Vargas into power in 1930, and a peaceful one served Roosevelt just as effectively in 1932. In his own fashion each managed to put a reform program into effect. Indeed, in 1936 Roosevelt declared Vargas the co-author of the New Deal.

In governing they showed a remarkable similiarity. A 1937 cartoon depicted Vargas smiling while juggling all the major figures in Brazilian political life. Both Vargas and Roosevelt encouraged, even relished, rivalry among their subordinates. Each man enjoyed politics and the exercise of power, and within limits, each preferred to let problems resolve themselves rather than force a decision. Neither wanted to become involved in foreign affairs and turned attention abroad only when forced by events. They both were effective speakers who understood the value of an artful word or a graceful turn of phrase. Their concern was for their countries' welfare, and each felt that he was the man to solve his nation's problems. Each incurred the contempt of the rich and received the devotion of the common man. Each affected his nation's history, and gave his name to an era.

Vargas' Brazil was a rural nation, in spirit and in reality, that was only beginning to populate its vast 3,287,195 square miles of territory. Over 90 percent of its 41 to 42 million inhabitants clustered within two hundred miles of its 3,517-mile Atlantic coast, from French Guiana to Uruguay. Nearly 70 percent of its population lived in rural areas and only Rio de Janeiro and São Paulo could claim more than a million citizens. Poverty, malnutrition, and disease afflicted an interior dominated by one-crop agriculture—usually coffee, cotton, or cacao. Subsistence agriculture was a way of life for millions. These people and their neighbors on the great fazendas lived under the paternalistic exploitation of the traditional latifundia system. *Fazendeiros,* like medieval lords, controlled huge areas with hired gunmen. Rapid population increase, roughly 2.5 percent annually by 1940, caused a rural overflow that spilled into the cities. In addition, 4,190,837 immigrants streamed into Brazil between 1884 and 1943, most of whom settled in urban areas, particularly São Paulo, or in the southern states. Portuguese and Japanese predominated among the immigrants from 1914 to 1943, although German immigration reached its peak between 1924 and World War II; Italian and Spanish migration was heaviest before 1923.[7]

The combined currents of rural and foreign migrants placed severe strains on unprepared urban areas. This was especially true in the states of Rio de Janeiro, São Paulo, and Rio Grande do Sul, which accounted for more than half of the national agricultural and industrial production and possessed 50 percent of Brazil's railroads.[8] The rural poor became urban poor squeezed into the stinking *favelas* of Rio de Janeiro and São Paulo, untended by government or church organizations.

In Rio de Janeiro of the mid-1930's, the altimeter was "an unfailing index of social position; the higher you lived, the less important you were. Poverty perched on the hill-tops, where the black population lived in rags. . . ."[9] The rich landowner, now an urbanite, was just as impervious to human suffering in the city as he had been in the country. The Catholic Church can best be described as ultraconservative, with its leading cleric, Dom Sebastião Cardinal Leme (1882–1942), more preoccupied with such projects as erecting the famous statue of Christ on Corcôvado mountain

[7] Preston James, *Latin America* (New York, 1959), pp. 558–559.

[8] Joseph L. Love, "Rio Grande do Sul as a Source of Potential Instability in Brazil's Old Republic, 1909–1932" (Ph.D. Dissertation, Columbia University, 1967), pp. 10–12.

[9] Claude Lévi-Strauss, *Tristes Tropiques, An Anthropological Study of Primitive Societies in Brazil* (New York, 1968), p. 92. In addition to its anthropological importance this book contains a valuable record of rural Brazil in the 1930's.

than in alleviating the poverty below "The Redeemer's" outstretched arms.[10]

The Catholic Church, devoting itself to the spiritual needs of the rising urban middle class, left the poor blacks and *caboclos* to ease their lot in the ceremonies of the African cult and the fantasies of the Carnival Samba Schools.[11] The Church did not need to explain its existence; it simply was. Unlike the Church in North America it did not suffer the necessity of changing in order to survive.

Education barely existed in the Brazil of the 1930's. In his lengthy "state of the nation" message to the National Constituent Assembly in November 1933, Getúlio Vargas declared the hard truth that Brazil had never squarely faced the problem of education. He called the mass of illiterates "a dead weight" on national progress, a "disgrace of which we should be ashamed." Out of every 1,000 Brazilians, 513 never entered school. Of the 487 who matriculated, 110 soon dropped out, 178 attended first grade but did not learn to read well, 85 completed two years attaining superficial

[10] (Sister) Maria Regina do Santo Rosário, *O Cardeal Leme* (Rio de Janeiro, 1962), pp. 244–255. The statue of "Christ the Redeemer" was financed by contributions from the faithful in Rio de Janeiro and was dedicated on October 12, 1931. The people of Rio, the Cariocas, invented the story that when Getúlio rose to speak at the ceremonies he spread his arms like the statue as if to embrace the city below and declared: "The Gaúchos have arrived." See Alzira Vargas, *Getúlio*, p. 261.

[11] Only at Carnival would the blacks come swarming down from the *favela*s en masse, filling Rio with numbing rhythm and sweeping "all before them with the tunes they had picked out, on high, on their guitars." Lévi-Strauss, *Tristes Tropiques*, p. 92. The philosophy of carnival was expressed quite well in Vinicius de Morais' lyrics to Antônio Carlos Jobim's *Felicidade* (Happiness): "Sadness has no end, Happiness does; . . . The happiness of the poor appears with the morning of carnival. The people work the whole year for a moment of dreaming. . . ." The pathos of the celebration was captured beautifully in Marcel Camus' film *Orfeu Negro* (*Black Orpheus*, 1959). For a detailed study of the African cult see Roger Bastide, *O Candomblé da Bahia* (*Rito Nagô*) (São Paulo, 1961).

literacy, 84 went a bit further but failed to complete their studies, and only thirty finished the three years that comprised the elementary course.[12] Of those thirty, only those from relatively affluent families would be able to continue their education. The secondary schools were private in all but a few cases, acting as a sieve that kept the poor from reaching the universities. The universities themselves were new, formed from the government-sponsored, tuition-free *faculdades* after the Revolution of 1930. At the recently-founded University of São Paulo, the professors were "wretchedly paid" and forced to work at extra odd jobs to exist. The students, admitted after rigorous entrance examinations, were "hungry for the jobs" which their diplomas would bring. It seemed to Claude Lévi-Strauss, a member of the educational mission which France sent to assist the new university, that the students valued "the novelties of the day" more than serious learning—"for which they had neither the taste nor the methods." Obsessed with the need to prove that they were no longer country bumpkins, they disparaged the image of the Brazilian rustic, the *caipira* (hick) who made up the majority of Brazil's population. In part this was the normal reaction of the aspiring urbanite, but among the sons of thrifty, hard-working immigrants, especially Italians and Jews, who crowded the university it represented alienation from traditional Brazil. More determined and with more resources than native Brazilians, the immigrants had founded their own secondary schools or sacrificed to send their children to existing ones. Having gotten through the secondary school sieve they saw the University of São Paulo as a means of obtaining status and security. Its graduates entered Vargas' new civil service and in time would form a new elite.[13]

---

[12] Vargas, *A Nova Política*, III, 129.

[13] Lévi-Strauss, *Tristes Tropiques*, pp. 21, 106–107. Curiously the trend toward a predominance of immigrant offspring in the University of São Paulo student body continues; see Seymour M. Lipset, "Values, Education, and Entrepreneurship," in Seymour M. Lipset and Aldo

Perhaps the most striking feature of Brazil in the 1930's and 1940's was the tremendous gap between living standards in cities like Rio de Janeiro and in the rural interior. The Northeast (Maranhão, Piaui, Ceará, Rio Grande do Norte, Paraíba, Pernambuco, Alagoas, Sergipe, and Bahia) long had staggered under periodic droughts; those of 1930 to 1933 were especially severe. In Ceará, where the situation was the worst, seven refugee camps received some 105,000 persons.[14] Some of these took ship for the Amazonian rubber zone, while others crowded into slums from Fortaleza to São Paulo. Whether they stayed in the dusty, barren towns on the edge of the *sertão*, or joined the crab hunters in the mud at Recife, or reached the cacao groves of Ilheus exhausted and starving, or gathered boards and tiles to throw up a shack on a Rio de Janeiro hillside, they were disease-ridden, scrawny, dark-skinned reminders that Brazil was not predominantly white, urban, or comfortable. Ragged, barefoot, pot-bellied, dirty children with hacking bronchial coughs and ulcerated sores on their limbs, playing and fighting in the narrow feces-strewn alleys among the *favela* shacks, were like inhabitants of another world compared to the poised, immaculate, laughing children of the elite singing the traditional playsongs (*cantigas de roda*) as they whirled in dancing circles, one pink hand holding another under the watchful eyes of the white-uniformed, dark-skinned nursemaids (*babás*). While Cariocas spoke disdainfully of the rest of Brazil as the interior, the truth was that the interior could be seen on the hillsides and along the low swampy areas of Guanabara Bay.

The elite, and the middle class who aped their ways, lost itself in a continuous social whirl, insulated from annoying realities by servants and a basic belief in a society of classes.

Solari, eds., *Elites in Latin America* (New York, 1967), pp. 25–26. Only 22 percent of the students were of "purely Brazilian descent" at the end of the 1950's.

14 Vargas, *A Nova Política*, III, 101–102.

In Rio de Janeiro they built comfortable, even luxurious, homes in Botafogo, Urca, or Laranjeiras, sailed at the yacht club, joined friends for a set of tennis at the Country Club or a round of golf at Itanhangá. At night it was a candle-lit dinner party for a few friends, or a reception modeled on a Paris salon, highlighted by sparkling, witty conversation sprinkled with French or English phrases. The old imperial nobility preserved its social standing and a Bragança (the royal family) in attendance was a major coup for the hostess. The most striking feature for anthropologist Lévi-Strauss was the flippancy of it all; Rio seemed to him like "one huge drawing-room."[15]

Change was slow, but Brazil was changing in spite of all the obstacles that time-encrusted conservatism threw in its path. In 1922 came two symbolic blows at the established order: São Paulo's Modern Art Week, which sent shock waves through the Old Republic's cultural foundations, and the quixotic sacrifice of the Fort Copacabana rebels, which exposed the weakness of its political structure. Together they provided the spirit of change and the example of revolution. From 1923 to 1927 there were revolts of reform-minded young officers in Rio Grande do Sul, São Paulo, Rio de Janeiro, and in some northeastern cities, that culminated in the famous march of the Prestes Column.[16] The 1920's

[15] Lévi-Strauss, *Tristes Tropiques*, p. 89. The following will give some idea of the sharp contrasts: Jorge Amado, *Gabriela, Clove and Cinnamon* (New York, 1962) and *The Violent Land* (New York, 1945); Jacques Lambert, *Os Dois Brasís* (Rio de Janeiro, 1959); Roger Bastide, *Brasil, Terra de Contrastes* (São Paulo, 1964); Josué de Castro, *Geografia da Fome* (São Paulo, 1965) and his *Death in the Northeast* (New York, 1969), see especially "The Crab Cycle," pp. 128–130.

[16] Richard M. Morse, "São Paulo Since Independence: A Cultural Interpretation," *Hispanic-American Historical Review*, XXXIV (1954), 419-444; Glauco Carneiro and Osvaldo Tôrres Galvão, *História das Revoluções Brasileiras* (Rio de Janeiro, 1965), I, 223-309; Hélio Silva, *1922, Sangue na Areia de Copacabana* (Rio de Janeiro, 1964) and *1926, A Grande Marcha* (Rio de Janeiro, 1965); Adguar Bastos, *Prestes e a Revolução Social* (Rio de Janeiro, 1946).

In 1924 rebels from Rio Grande do Sul, under the command of Luís

and 1930's also saw the backlanders of the *sertão* from northern Minas Gerais to Ceará seeking their own solutions to ignorance, poverty, landlord oppression, and a government that usually meant police oppression rather than drought relief. If the average *caboclo* did not join Lampião's rampaging *cangaço* that attacked towns such as Água Branca in Alagoas (1922) and Mossoró in Rio Grande do Norte (1927) to the tune of "Mulher Rendeira," he sang about him and perhaps took quiet pleasure in seeing fear spread across a *fazendeiro's* face at the mention of the *cangaceiro's* name. Other northeasterners knelt under Padre Cícero's window in Juàzeiro, Ceará, to receive strength from his daily blessing. Still others gathered at Caldeirão, Ceará (1933–1935) for a religiously-oriented communal life under the *beato* José Lourenço, where they did for themselves what no government had been able to do, namely to elevate their existence from survival to life. Not surprisingly their houses, their cattle, their religious activities, their unity aroused suspicion, jealousy, fear, greed. Local police forced them to disperse, destroyed their settlement and turned their goods over to the municipality.[17] In 1928 Paulo

Carlos Prestes, linked up with another force retreating from São Paulo to form a column of nearly a thousand men who marched through the Brazilian interior as far north as Maranhão before heading west into asylum in Bolivia. They covered some 6,000 miles, fighting numerous engagements against the regular army, local police, and *fazendeiros'* gunmen. Their two-and-a-half year effort to keep the revolutionary spirit alive and to arouse the countryside failed, but their actions provided a symbol of the *tenentes'* revolutionary commitment. Prestes later became head of the Brazilian communist party.

[17] Luís da Câmara Casudo, *Dicionário do Folclore Brasileiro* (Rio de Janeiro, 1962), pp. 416–417; Maria Isaura Pereira de Queiroz, *O Messianismo, no Brasil e no Mundo* (São Paulo, 1965), pp. 264–267. *Cangaço* is a band of outlaws called *cangaceiros*. Of the many bands that terrorized the *sertão* during the period, Virgolino Ferreira da Silva or Lampião (lantern or light) headed the most famous and feared. His 23-year career ended in a fight in July 1938 in Sergipe. As used here a *beato* is a type of holyman without religious orders peculiar to the

Prado presented a melancholy portrait of Brazil as a "radiant land" with "sad people"—even so he sketched it with the confidence that the future "could not be worse than the past."[18]

But for the future to be better the economic underpinnings of the social order would have to change. Ironically Brazil's very underdevelopment may have lessened the direct impact of the Depression on most of its people; living by subsistence farming they were only marginally affected.[19] To millions of Brazilians the scorching sun and lack of rain were more to be feared than falling coffee or cacao prices. The difference between utter deprivation and mere poverty is hard to measure. Still, while Brazilian leaders could speculate that having millions beyond the reach of the world economy gave them time to modernize the country, they could hardly be proud of the fact.

Seventy percent of Brazil's exports consisted of coffee, two-thirds of which came from São Paulo. Nearly half of the beans which earned foreign exchange went to the United States, and two or three American firms dominated the Brazilian coffee export trade. As the principal importer of Brazil's principal crop, North America's ability to buy coffee affected the Brazilian economy, notwithstanding the "security" of the poverty-stricken *campesino*. A United States sunk in depression made itself felt in the coffee *municipios* of São Paulo, the cacao zone in Bahia, and in the various seaports. With no heavy industry and with the shaky light industry cowering behind foreign exchange regulations that tended to eliminate imported consumer products, Vargas needed to proceed so as to harness both the

---

Brazilian sertão. For the "saint" of Juàzeiro see Edmar Morel, *Padre Cícero* (Rio de Janeiro, 1966); and the excellent study by Ralph della Cava, *Miracle at Joaseiro* (New York, 1970).

[18] Paulo Prado, *Retrato do Brasil, Ensaio sôbre a Tristeza Brasileira* (Rio de Janeiro, 1928; 6th ed., 1962), pp. 3 and 183.

[19] Vargas, *A Nova Política*, iii, 30.

one-crop landlords and the budding industrialists. Strong government allied to the traditional latifundia and forward-looking industry seemed the only way to achieve development without adopting the Soviet model. Unfortunately Brazilian businessmen—cotton cloth manufacturers for example—tended to operate with unimaginative marketing policies that ignored the domestic market and the need to expand it by paying wages that would make the workers consumers as well as producers.[20]

Vargas kept the coffee plantations from the auctioneer's block by committing himself to a valorization scheme whereby the government purchased the entire national production, destroying whatever amount was necessary to keep the supply in line with market demand. The National Coffee Institute burned or dumped into the sea nearly eighty million sacks between 1931 and 1941, when the world market was never able to absorb more than fifteen million sacks annually.[21] These Brazilian efforts to support the world price had long-range benefits and disadvantages. To subsidize the chief agricultural sector of the economy via valorization the government was forced to borrow heavily abroad, consequently tying up foreign exchange in debt servicing and leaving little for purchases of finished goods. Whatever foreign exchange remained was needed for spare parts to keep the railroads, motor vehicles, and electrical equipment running. This unconscious pump-priming, to-

[20] Stanley J. Stein, *The Brazilian Cotton Manufacture: Textile Enterprise in an Underdeveloped Area, 1850–1950* (Cambridge, Mass., 1957), pp. 135–164. Stein describes the alliance between the Vargas regime and the cotton cloth producers, while pointing up the short-sightedness of the latter. For a contemporary discussion of the economy in the 1930's see Horace B. Davis, "Brazil's Political and Economic Problems," *Foreign Policy Reports*, xi, No. 1 (March 13, 1935), 2–12, passim.

[21] Caio Prado, Jr., *História Econômica do Brasil* (São Paulo, 1963), p. 297. From 1925 onward coffee production exceeded demand. The 80 million sacks destroyed in the 1930's totaled 4,800,000 tons, enough to supply the world for two years at the 1962 level of consumption.

gether with the Tariff of 1934 and the Reciprocal Trade Agreement with the United States (effective January 1, 1936) made Vargas the unexpected benefactor of the manufacturing interests in the Rio de Janeiro–Minas Gerais–São Paulo triangle.[22] Unfortunately it also made the world coffee market attractive to Colombian, Central American, and East Asian producers who grabbed much of Brazil's share of the market without making its sacrifices.

The obvious vulnerability of Brazil's agricultural export economy prompted demands for government action to achieve economic diversity and independence. This would mean creating a stronger executive authority than had existed during the Old Republic (1891–1930) and sacrificing the dual watchwords of the old order—state autonomy and economic orthodoxy. The latter held that Brazil was permanently cast in the role of raw-material supplier, and the former was the political mechanism that insured the position of those few Brazilians who benefited from this arrangement. Brazil's was a "penetrated political system" whose leaders cooperated with foreign interests, knowingly or unknowingly, to exploit the country's natural resources.[23] This

22 For a discussion of these trends in addition to Stanley Stein's work cited above see Celso Furtado, *The Economic Growth of Brazil* (Berkeley, 1963), p. 212; Donald W. Giffin, "The Normal Years: Brazilian-American Relations, 1930–1939" (Ph.D. Dissertation, Vanderbilt University, 1962), pp. 68–70. Vargas explained the complicated funding arrangements in his message to the Constituent Assembly, Nov. 15, 1933; see *A Nova Política*, III, 43–59. He was able to claim reduction of the national deficit from its 1929 level of 423.951:000$ to its 1932 mark of 178.279:000$. In 1929, 1.000$ (a Conto) equaled U.S. $118. and $71. in 1932. For currency equivalents 1920–44, see Levine, *Vargas Regime*, p. 193.

23 A penetrated political system is one in which "non-members of a national society participate directly and authoritatively through actions taken jointly with the society's members, in either the allocation of its values or the mobilization of support on behalf of its goals"; James N. Rosenau, "Pre-theories and Theories of Foreign Policy," in R. Barry Farrell, ed., *Approaches to Comparative and International Politics* (Evanston, Ill., 1966), p. 65. Carlos A. Astiz applies Rosenau's definition

foreign penetration helps to explain why the Brazilian elite tended to disparage the interior and look for guidance to Paris, London, New York, Rome, or Berlin.

Between 1930 and 1933 Vargas concentrated on consolidating his coalition and forming a popular following. This he could best do by appealing "to the urban sector's natural hostility to the traditional predominance of the rural oligarchy" and reiterating "promises made during his electoral campaign for social legislation to aid the working classes."[24] He established new ministries of labor and public works, government institutes that supervised social security and pension programs, and he reformed the civil service by creating the Administrative Department of Public Service (DASP). Though he did not seek public acclaim during these early years, he won the support of the urban working classes. The *tenente* elements who had joined his cause in 1930 in the hope of using him to revolutionize Brazil became embroiled within their own camp in factional disputes as to means and goals. Vargas used *tenentes,* such as Juracy Magalhães (Bahia), Joaquim Magalhães Barata (Pará), and João Alberto Lins de Barros (São Paulo) as federal *interventors* to replace ousted state governors. They tended to get enmeshed in state politics, dissipating their energies and turning their attention away from the national scene.

After the defeat of São Paulo in 1932 the federal army steadily grew stronger in relation to the military forces of the individual states. Because the Paulista crisis had in part been brought on by *tenente* ineptness in governing, Vargas was able to rely less on their political support and more on that of the federal forces, which were increasingly under the control of officers who owed their rise to him, especially General Pedro Aurélio de Góes Monteiro. This northeast-

to Latin American societies in his *Latin American International Politics: Ambitions, Capabilities, and the National Interests of Mexico, Brazil, and Argentina* (Notre Dame, 1969), pp. 10–12.

[24] Levine, *Vargas Regime,* MS, p. A-10.

erner from the small state of Alagoas had supported the
federal government against the *tenente* upheavals of the
1920's, switched in 1930 to serve as chief of staff of Vargas'
revolutionary forces, and went on to defeat the Paulistas in
1932. His influence on Vargas was great, and his Bonpart-
ist view of the role of the military in society left a lasting
impression on the Brazilian officer corps.

As *tenente* influence ebbed, Vargas "became increasingly
identified with conservative business and industrial spokes-
men who welcomed the growing trend to federal authority,
even at the expense of state independence." At the same
time agricultural groups "welcomed the new federal institutes for the development of such products as sugar, coffee,
vegetable oils, alkalis, and salt, and Vargas' commitment to
protectionism."[25]

The political atmosphere was extremely agitated from the
time of the calling of the Constituent Assembly in 1933 to
the declaring of the Estado Nôvo in 1937. In May 1933, the
first popularly elected constitutional convention in Brazilian
history convened in Rio de Janeiro. The delegates were to
consider and revise a proposed constitution developed by
an eight-man commission representing a variety of ideological positions. The draft was subjected to intense debate
that produced more than five thousand suggested amend-
ments. The hybrid result pleased no one. Vargas lamented
the constraints placed on presidential authority and, taking
advantage of a constitutional provision which approved
acts of the provisional government and exempted them
from judicial review, issued more than fifty executive decrees before the constitution took effect. The document contained ample social guarantees (including an eight-hour
work day, vacations with pay, pensions, minimum wages,
female suffrage, and prohibition of child labor); enumer-
ated cases in which the government could nationalize busi-
nesses; sanctioned establishment of political parties; limited

25 *Ibid.*, p. A-17.

the senate's authority; provided for federal supervision of state elections; made possible ownership of productive land after five years of uncontested occupation and expropriation of large estates; restricted inheritance; and permitted organization of labor unions under the guidance of the Ministry of Labor. In a feature reminiscent of the social encyclicals of Popes Leo XIII and Pius XI, and of Mussolini's Fascism, the Congress included fifty deputies representing classes and interest groups. Although this measure gave lobbyists seats in the legislature alongside the 350 state deputies, it tended to aid the president, since for the most part class deputies shared economic interests furthered by government programs. After transforming itself into the constitutional congress the assembly elected Vargas president by a vote of 175 to 63.[26]

Instead of giving Brazilians a period of calm, however, the coming of constitutional government unleashed a season of storms. The assembly had granted amnesty to political exiles, including the Paulista leaders, who returned determined to send Vargas and his Gaúchos home to Rio Grande. It was to be a struggle between the proponents of strong federal government and those of state autonomy, and by mid-1934 when state elections were held Brazil was caught up in a whirlwind of political activity. Some opposition parties won victories over Vargas forces. Uncertainty settled over the land as bitterness and acts of violence spread during 1935. The architects of the Revolution of 1930 began to fear that their victory would be undone. Oswaldo Aranha, close friend of Vargas and coordinator of the October 1930 Revolution, wrote from his ambassadorial post in Washington that Brazil's weaknesses resulted from its people's "ignorance, sickness, and lack of personal capacity," and that Brazil's destiny should not be left to its masochistic and sadistic politicians. He warned that Brazil's

[26] *Ibid.*, Chap. I; Hélio Silva, *1934, A Constituinte* (Rio de Janeiro, 1969).

disorganization would lead it down the trail blazed by Germany, Italy, and Russia.[27] Góes Monteiro was more afraid of anarchy; he worried that the Brazilians' seeming inability to govern themselves would lead to national decomposition, and saw an authoritarian regime as the solution.[28] This pessimism was justified. The politics of extremism seized control of Brazil's destiny. The conservative opposition, desiring a return to the pre-1930 order, became less important in the course of events than the far left and the far right. The Brazilian Communist Party, under the leadership of the near-legendary *tenente* Luís Carlos Prestes, posed what recent scholarship has shown to be an almost Quixotic threat.[29] But exaggerated threats are often not seen as such by contemporaries, and gun fights between communists and rightists were real enough to frighten many Brazilians into preferring security to democratic niceties. After their national front organization (National Liberation Alliance) was outlawed, the communists decided on a test of strength with the government in late November 1935. Uncoordinated risings in Natal, Recife, and Rio de Janeiro failed to gain popular support and government forces easily suppressed them, eventually capturing and jailing the leaders. The party went underground until the last days of Vargas' rule in 1945.

The government used the abortive revolt to silence or harass opponents. Vargas requested from the Congress, and received, a declaration of a "state of war," suspending constitutional guarantees that could directly or indirectly prejudice national security. This useful device was continu-

27 Aranha to Pedro de Góes Monteiro, Washington, Mar. 9, 1935, Oswaldo Aranha Archive, Rio (OAA); and Oswaldo Aranha to João Mangabeira, Washington, June 11, 1935, *ibid.* The Oswaldo Aranha Archive is in the possession of the Aranha family and is currently housed on their property in Cosme Velho, Rio de Janeiro.
28 Pedro de Góes Monteiro to Aranha, Caxambu, June 5, 1935, OAA.
29 Levine, *Vargas Regime*, MS, Chap. VI. This is by far the best study of the events of 1935.

ally renewed during the next two years to combat a communist threat that existed only in official propaganda.[30] With increased authority, Vargas' aides imposed stricter censorship, removed suspected elements in the military establishment, and restricted interstate travel. Intellectuals came under presidential fire for "poisoning the atmosphere, muddying the waters" by encouraging "evolutionary modification of universal values."[31] The trend of events became clearer. The Rio de Janeiro daily *O Imparcial* predicted ominously that Brazil was "on the road to military dictatorship."[32] Francisco de Assis Chateaubriand put the matter more pointedly in his *Diários Associados* column: "The recipient of all that Luís Carlos Prestes has lost is Getúlio Vargas."[33]

Among the most ardent supporters of Vargas' efforts to increase federal power and to fight communism were the Integralistas. Founded in 1932 by Plínio Salgado, a Paulista journalist, their organization was a Brazilian adaptation of European fascism. Claiming more than a million members, the extremely nationalistic greenshirts assisted Vargas by stressing the importance of being Brazilian. They condemned foreign penetration of Brazilian life and culture and urged their countrymen to study the works of national authors and poets. They sought an integrated nation, a unified Brazil capable of escaping foreign domination and international communism.

---

[30] For explanation of state of war see Pedro Calmon, *História do Brasil*, VI (Rio de Janeiro, 1959), 2238–39. During the 1930's a "state of war" usually applied to all Brazil, while states of siege or emergency applied to particular regions. A state of war allowed the national government to federalize state militias and to use federal troops to maintain order in the states.

[31] Vargas, *A Nova Política*, IV, 141.

[32] *O Imparcial* (Rio), Dec. 18, 1935; as quoted in Levine, *Vargas Regime*, MS, p. F-39.

[33] Francisco de Assis Chateaubriand, "A revolução hyperbólica," *Diário de Pernambuco* (Recife), Dec. 8, 1935; as quoted in Levine, *Vargas Regime*, MS, p. F-10.

The Integralista view of government was Authority with a capital A, to prevent, as their literature claimed, the powerful, foreigners, and selfish political groups from endangering Brazil's interests. Although their uniformed storm troopers took to the streets to fight communists, the Integralistas attracted members from all levels of society. Respectable Brazilians considered it a respectable organization.

The *Ação Integralista Brasileira* (AIB) was the only truly national party—certainly the only one, other than the defunct Communist party, which had a coherent body of doctrine and definite political aims. A major beneficiary and perpetrator of the red scare, the AIB increased its membership and by the election of 1937 seemed a force to be taken seriously.[34]

On September 7, 1936, the 114th anniversary of Brazilian independence, Getúlio set the tone for the fateful year ahead with an appeal to Brazilian patriotism. Warning that "the agents of subversion and disorder" were persisting in their "diabolical plans" to utterly destroy the Brazilian "fatherland, family, and religion," and to transform Brazil into a "colony of Moscow," the president asserted that it was "vital to maintain constant vigilance" against a "treacherous coup." Was he attempting dissimulation and falsehood, the very tactics he ascribed to the communists? Did his audience in Rio de Janeiro's Esplanada do Castelo detect some hidden meaning or did they accept Getúlio's words at face value? Historical experience had demonstrated, he declared, that "democracy is the form of government most suited to our people's nature and to their moral and material progress." But what did he mean by democracy? Brazilian democracy, he went on, could not be

[34] Plínio Salgado, *O Integralismo Brasileiro Perante a Nação* (Lisbon, 1946), pp. 17–26; Alzira Vargas, *Getúlio*, p. 214; Robert M. Scotten, Rio, Aug. 25, 1937, 832.00/1045, U.S. Department of State Files, NA; Frederico del Villar, "Life and Death of Brazilian Fascism," *The Inter-American Monthly*, II, No. 5 (June 1943), 16–19.

"structured in rigid and unchangeable formulas, shut off from the renovating action of time and existing realities; rather, it ought to vest itself in a plasticity capable of reflecting social progress, perfecting itself and . . . defending itself when threatened. . . ." Then, employing terminology remarkably similar to that of the 1964–1970 military dictatorship, he hinted at his concept of democracy by declaring: "Brazil is a country of order. Order and democracy mean discipline and liberty, conscious obedience and respect for the law. We will repel demagogic outbreaks just as we would not tolerate tyranny."[35]

Certainly Getúlio did not think of himself as a tyrant. Nevertheless, events and his view of the kind of government Brazil needed would lead him to establish a dictatorship. Of course, in the agitated atmosphere of the 1930's the appeal of strong central government was not limited to Brazil. Just before Franklin Roosevelt's inauguration in 1933, the American business journal *Barron's* thought that perhaps "a mild species of dictatorship will help us over the roughest spots in the road ahead."[36] The day after Roosevelt took office the German Reichstag gave Adolf Hitler absolute power, while in Italy Benito Mussolini's regime appeared quite successful. Obviously Roosevelt had been able to obtain reform and to increase presidential power without dictatorship, but it must be noted that the restraining tradition of constitutional government was immeasurably greater on Roosevelt than on Vargas. Although Roosevelt, during his 1936 visit to Rio, proclaimed Vargas the co-author of the New Deal, the milieus in which they operated were quite different. During the period in which the United States had lived under the constitution of 1789, Brazil had been a colonial viceroyalty, a kingdom equal with Portugal, an independent empire that experienced many governmental modifications, a republican dictatorship, a constitutional presidency based on a formula of big-state domination, and

[35] Vargas, *A Nova Política*, IV, 181–187.
[36] *Barron's*, XIII (Feb. 13, 1933), 12.

finally it had undergone the continuous changes between 1930 and 1937. Brazilian and American democracy were hardly the same.

Vargas had to perform a smooth juggling and balancing act to maintain control, not only of the country but of his own regime. Between October 1930 and November 1937, 42 men had held the nine cabinet posts, and 103 had been either appointed interventors or elected governors in the twenty-two states and the federal district and territory of Acre.[37] The states had militia and state police forces that often outnumbered the federal forces stationed within their borders. Political questions could all too easily find solution in tests of arms or acts of violence and terrorism—as happened in São Paulo in 1932, in Rio Grande do Norte, Pará, and Alagoas in 1935. Political conflicts between pro-Vargas and opposition groups occurred in almost every Brazilian state between the state elections in October 1935 and proclamation of the Estado Nôvo in November 1937.

By early 1936 Vargas apparently began seriously to contemplate staying in power even though the constitution contained a no reelection provision. But it is difficult to say exactly when contemplation turned into resolve. Those close to the president were either pessimistic about continuing electoral government or determinedly opposed to it. Oswaldo Aranha, Vargas' close friend and fellow Gaúcho, sounded the keynote from Washington—declaring that he no longer believed in elections and predicted that Brazil would have a dictatorship first.[38] Minister of Labor Agamemnon Sérgio Godoy de Magalhães had severely attacked old-fashioned presidential government at the 1934 Constituent Assembly. General Góes Monteiro had masterminded an unsuccessful plot during 1935 to discredit the Congress and to increase military influence. Francisco Campos, former Minister of Education and author of both the 1937

[37] Alzira Vargas, *Getúlio*, pp. 267–285. She lists their names, posts, and dates.

[38] Aranha to Ricardo Xavier, Washington, Apr. 21, 1936, OAA.

Estado Nôvo constitution and the Institutional Act of April 1964, steadfastly championed authoritarian corporatism as a barrier to the "Moscovite inundation." He believed that where power was diffused, instead of being concentrated in "one single Power," government did not exist because government was "one thought and one action."[39] Filinto von Strubling Müller, head of the regime's repressive police, maintained close ties with the Third Reich's embassy, while Minister of War Eurico Gaspar Dutra, also a Germanophile, disliked representative government and believed that Brazil needed a dose of discipline.

Even with such strong support for continuation, Getúlio proceeded indirectly, perhaps having decided to let events determine his course. The question of succession came to the fore when Armando de Sales Oliveira resigned the governorship of São Paulo to become a candidate for the presidency. Vargas did not welcome Armando Sales' action and attempted unsuccessfully to persuade him to reconsider. In his New Year's address to the nation in the first hour of 1937, Getúlio promised that the coming presidential campaign would be conducted "within the bounds of vibrant democracy, in a free and healthy atmosphere," and that he would collaborate to insure "that the name chosen effectively represented the will of the majority of the Brazilian people."[40] There would be no court favorite and, not unexpectedly, Getúlio's impartiality created an atmosphere of doubt.

Armando Sales, Paulista industrialist and son-in-law of Júlio de Mesquita Filho, publisher of the anti-Vargas *O Estado de São Paulo*, naturally attracted support among opposition elements throughout Brazil. His victory would bring to power the Paulista rebels of 1932, which could hardly be acceptable to the revolutionaries of 1930. Other politicians quickly followed Armando Sales' lead. Minister of Foreign Affairs José Carlos de Macedo Soares resigned

[39] Francisco Campos, *O Estado Nacional, Sua Estructura, Seu Conteúdo Ideológico* (Rio de Janeiro, 1941), pp. 62, 67.
[40] Vargas, *A Nova Política*, IV, 216; Alzira Vargas, *Getúlio*, p. 160.

so that he too might be eligible for the candidacy. José Antônio Flôres da Cunha, the spirited governor of Rio Grande do Sul, had been meddling in the politics of other states and mustering congressional opposition to the regime in a series of puzzling maneuvers, perhaps aimed at increasing his ability to play political broker or at securing the presidency for himself. What he secured was Vargas' distrust and the army's suspicion and opposition. To confuse the political scene even further, Oswaldo Aranha looked and acted like a candidate. A smooth-talking, popular figure, an old friend of both Vargas and Flôres da Cunha, Aranha could neither bring them together nor obtain their support for himself.[41]

After successfully testing his legislative support by unseating Antônio Carlos de Andrada of Minas Gerais as president of the Chamber of Deputies in April, Vargas turned his attention to the south and gave more authority to the federal commander of the Rio Grande do Sul military district, increased his troop strength, and ordered more coastal patrols to stop arms smugglers. Gôes Monteiro visited the south in May to survey the situation, as the general staff prepared contingency plans.[42] The Gaúcho governor purchased modern weapons in Europe, which reportedly included field-pieces and tanks, to improve the armament of his 26,000-man state Military Brigade and militia-like provisional units. The army, already anxious because of Argentina's military buildup, grew increasingly nervous over the possibility of an uprising in the border state. Clearly Flôres da Cunha had to go. But Vargas could not simply remove the governor, because this was not a Pará or Sergipe where the federal government could impose its will with a handful of troops. Rio Grande do Sul had a tradition of auton-

41 *Ibid.*, pp. 173–175.
42 Benedicto Valladares to Vargas, Rio, May 17, 1937; Gen. Emílio Esteves to Vargas, n.p., Apr. 25, 1937; Benjamim Vargas to Vargas, n.p., Mar. 5, 1937; all in Getúlio Vargas Archive, Rio de Janeiro. This valuable archive (AGV) is in the possession of Dona Alzira Vargas do Amaral Peixoto and is housed in her Flamengo (Rio) apartment.

omy. In the nineteenth century it had seceded from the empire and declared itself the "Rio Grande Republic." Ten years (1835–1845) and many lives were necessary to return it to imperial control. In the early 1890's and again in the 1920's civil war erupted in Rio Grande. Even a Gaúcho president had to proceed with caution.[43]

Vargas was an extremely cautious man. He knew that he was the key to the situation and that he could afford to wait —until he bestowed his support upon someone, there would be uncertainty. He continued to smile amicably at everyone and to make public statements complimentary to this one or that, always refraining from clarifying his position. Also, according to Getúlio's daughter Alzira—his longtime "confidante of political secrets"—he thought that it was a mistake for a president to impose an official candidate, preferring that the country's leaders make the choice.[44]

The governors and political chieftains met in Rio de Janeiro in late May 1937, under the chairmanship of Governor Benedicto Valladares of Minas Gerais, to choose the official candidate. Vargas unsuccessfully and inexplicably attempted to postpone the selection, but the convention chose José Américo de Almeida of Paraíba, a man closely associated with the 1930 revolution. Vargas then began a series of curious political maneuvers. He told an Integralista delegation, which came on June 14 to inform him officially of Plínio Salgado's candidacy, that he had no candidate and that he guaranteed the honesty of the coming elections. Four days later he wrote Aranha in Washington that José Américo's choice was a "truly happy" one and everything indicated that he would be victorious. In fact, he preferred to leave an American invitation to visit the United

[43] Scotten, Rio, Jan. 3, 1937, 832.00/1009, NA; Scotten, Rio, Jan. 6, 1937, 832.00/1010, NA; Alzira Vargas, *Getúlio*, pp. 175, 185–186. For a history of the state see Arthur Ferreira Filho, *História Geral do Rio Grande do Sul, 1503–1964* (Pôrto Alegre, 1965).

[44] Vargas to Aranha, Rio, Oct. 28, 1937, OAA; Alzira Vargas, *Getúlio*, p. 170.

States for his successor to accept. Early in July, he appointed a strong backer of José Américo as mayor of the federal district, thereby assuring him a majority of Rio's votes. But he refused to donate any money to the campaign fund or to make public statements favoring the candidate. And José Américo was not making it easy for him to do so; instead of taking issue with Armando Sales or Salgado, he was attacking the president and the policies of his regime. The official candidate was apparently more opposed to the government than was the opposition candidate. José Américo quickly made his continued candidacy unacceptable.[45]

The opposition was in no better condition, and Vargas was the cause of its difficulties. Lack of a strong party structure, like that of England or the United States, made election difficult for a man out of office. By fulfilling the constitutional requirement of being a private citizen for a year before the election, Armando Sales lost his chief political asset, the governorship of São Paulo: after the election of his successor, he gradually lost control of the state's political machinery. His position weakened when fellow-Paulista Macedo Soares, disappointed in his bid for the candidacy, returned to the Vargas cabinet as minister of justice.[46]

The situation in Rio Grande do Sul was crucial to the presidential campaign. Flôres da Cunha had given his backing to Armando Sales after discovering that his own chances were nonexistent. The army was nervous about Flôres da Cunha's open preparations for a showdown. The provisional units, which had been the basis of the independence of Rio Grande do Sul's caudillos, including Vargas in his provincial phase, had to be disarmed to bring the state under federal control. It was a difficult task requiring delicate handling; the provisionals were Gaúchos proud of their

45 Benedicto Valladares, *Tempos Idos e Vividos, Memórias* (Rio de Janeiro, 1966), pp. 134–145, 153–154; Scotten, Rio, May 22, 1937, 832.00/1032, NA; Vargas to Aranha, Rio, June 17, 1937, OAA; Scotten, Rio, June 19, 1937, 832.00/1038, NA; Scotten, Rio, July 10, 1937, 832.00/1040, NA.
46 Vargas to Aranha, Rio, June 17, 1937, OAA.

state's autonomy. Even a man like Oswaldo Aranha considered it the duty of every Gaúcho to defend the state's honor, the inheritance of 1835.[47] To demand their disarming could bring civil war; subtler methods were necessary. The "state of war" originally declared after the 1935 revolt had inconveniently expired, making it difficult for the federal government to act.[48]

At this juncture the army's general staff discovered a document, known as the "Cohen Plan," that supposedly outlined a communist plot to seize the government on October 30. The exact authorship of the plan was, and is, a subject of debate. It seems likely that Integralistas, possibly officers on the general staff, drew up the plan, probably with the knowledge if not at the order of the chief of staff, General Góes Monteiro. Whether the Cohen Plan was the work of communists, Integralistas, or General Góes Monteiro, it provided the basis for a new "state of war." The congress approved the suspension of constitutional guarantees for ninety days on October 2, thus giving the government the atmosphere it needed to remove Flôres da Cunha.[49]

[47] Aranha to Vargas, Washington, Oct. 27, 1937, OAA. The "inheritance of 1835" is Aranha's phrase and refers to the rebellion of Rio Grande do Sul against the Brazilian Empire from 1835 to 1845; it is sometimes called the Ragamuffins' War.

[48] See above, note 30.

[49] Góes Monteiro later claimed that he considered the Cohen document false from the start and that such items frequently were sent to the general staff, see Coutinho, *General Góes*, pp. 298–299. The subchief of the general staff, General Leitão de Carvalho and other high officers did not know of the Cohen Plan until later and they resented the name of the general staff being used to give weight to the document (Leitão de Carvalho, *Memórias*, III, 294–295, 302; Alzira Vargas, *Getúlio*, pp. 205–206). A recent account names the author as Captain Olímpio Mourão Filho, a member of the Integralista "historical department," who claims that he was drawing up a theoretical communist attack to be used by Integralista planners. According to him his document was altered before being published as the Cohen Plan. See John W. F. Dulles, *Vargas of Brazil, A Political Biography* (Austin, 1967), pp. 162–163.

General Manoel de Cerqueira Daltro Filho, the right arm of General Góes Monteiro, had gone to Rio Grande in August to take command of the military region. His orders were to disarm the provisional units at the first opportunity. Lacking sufficient troops, he had used the annual Independence Day parade on September 7 as a pretext to call in more army units. The "state of war" now authorized the general to place the state forces under his command. Faced with fighting or being humiliated before the nation, Flôres da Cunha hesitated and others seized the power of decision. Dissident elements in the state assembly worked feverishly to obtain a majority to impeach the governor. Rio Grande was splitting into factions. The commander of the state's Military Brigade voluntarily placed his troops under Daltro Filho, destroying any hopes Flôres da Cunha may have had. Finding himself alone, he resigned and flew to exile in Montevideo; with him went the presidential election. To avoid an inconvenient struggle for power within the state, Vargas appointed General Daltro Filho as federal interventor.[50] Aranha, while conceding that Flôres da Cunha had been "a promoter of conflicts, difficulties, and crises," and that his flight had ended the "comedy of miseries," was distressed at the intervention, which he termed a "brutal act." He realized that Getúlio had to maintain public order, but he could not understand why he had intervened instead of allowing Rio Grande to elect a new governor. Getúlio defended himself, claiming that after intervening the authorities had seized large supplies of arms located at strategic points throughout the state for use in the "sedition" that Flôres da Cunha had been preparing for months with military and Paulista elements. The president assured his ambassador that the danger had passed, and that there was such relief in Brazil that on the day after the intervention the interna-

[50] Alzira Vargas, *Getúlio*, p. 186; Coutinho, *General Góes*, pp. 296–300; Calmon, *História do Brasil*, VI, 2304; Leitão de Carvalho, *Memórias*, III, 302–304; Scotten, Rio, Oct. 2, 1937, 832.00/1053, NA; Vargas to Aranha, Rio, Oct. 28, 1937, OAA.

tional currency exchange reacted favorably. "Work now," he advised soothingly, "in a more confident and serene atmosphere."[51] Another of Aranha's correspondents, however, had described the situation more accurately when he wrote some weeks earlier that "Getúlio's strength merits a coup to end this foolishness. The navy is firm and dictatorial-minded; the army is the same. There will be no more constitutional solutions for Brazil."[52]

It is uncertain exactly when Vargas decided to stay in office. In his letters to Aranha during June 1937 he spoke of projects that should be left to his successor, such as the visit to the United States. In May he had ordered construction of an addition to his house on the estância Itú in São Borja; he even had books and other items sent there, presumably in preparation for his retirement from Guanabara Palace (the presidential residence). However, there must have been signs for close observers to read because Aranha's brother, Adalberto, had been writing him for more than a year of Getúlio's "imperious and deliberate intention" to continue in power.[53]

On October 1, Vargas wrote Aranha that the atmosphere was agitated, but that the horses were at the post and the race would be run unless some dogs crossed the track.[54] Perhaps he was trying to tell his old friend something, but if so Aranha did not understand. On October 18, he con-

[51] Aranha to Vargas, Washington, Oct. 27, 1937; and Vargas to Aranha, Rio, Oct. 28, 1937, both OAA.

[52] José Soares Maciel Filho to Aranha, Rio, mid-Sept., 1937, Maciel Filho Archive, as quoted in Levine, *Vargas Regime*, MS, pp. H-11-12.

[53] Vargas to Aranha, Rio, June 17, 1937, OAA; Alzira Vargas, *Getúlio*, p. 180. Adalberto Aranha to O. Aranha, Rio, Nov. 17, 1937, OAA.

[54] Vargas to Aranha, Rio, Oct. 1, 1937, OAA. In Portuguese the sentence read: "Os parelheiros estão em compostura e a carreira será corrida, a menos que os cachorros se atravessem na cancha." Aranha apparently said something like this to Vargas in 1930 and reportedly Vargas said the same thing to José Américo about the same time as his letter to Aranha. See Affonso Henriques, *Vargas, O Maquiavélico* (São Paulo, 1961), p. 401.

fidently told Undersecretary of State Sumner Welles that Vargas would not stay in office beyond his present term. In Rio de Janeiro on the following day, the minister of justice informed the United States Embassy that it would be difficult to continue the presidential campaign because of the public's lack of interest. He said that the government had come to the conclusion that the constitution was impractical and would have to be revised or replaced. The authoritarian-minded Mineiro lawyer Francisco Campos had been working with the president's tacit approval on a new constitution, based on those of Poland, Portugal, and Italy, that would strengthen the executive power and maintain Vargas in office.[55]

In the latter part of October, Governor Valladares met José Américo in Rio's Hotel Copacabana. The governor told the candidate that he did not like his attacks on Vargas and suggested that he make peace with the president. Flying into a rage, José Américo refused, whereupon Valladares decided to withdraw his support and seek an alternate. Vargas agreed in principle to accept a neutral Paulista, but Valladares' attempt to find one failed. The Mineiro leader then joined Góes Monteiro, Vargas, and Minister of War Dutra, in arranging a more revolutionary solution. After Naval Minister Admiral Henrique Aristides Guilhem agreed to go along, it only remained to apprise the governors of the situation. Valladares sent Mineiro Deputy Francisco Negrão de Lima to release the northern governors from supporting José Américo. He skipped Bahia and Pernambuco because their governors had incurred army and presidential displeasure by dealing with Flôres da Cunha; federal interventors would replace them. Valladares sent another emissary to Goiás and Mato Grosso, while Getúlio informed Paraná and Santa Catarina. There was no diffi-

[55] Memorandum by Sumner Welles of a conversation with Aranha, Washington, Oct. 18, 1937, 832.00/1065, NA; Scotten, Rio, Oct. 20, 1937, 832.00/1064, NA; Alzira Vargas, *Getúlio*, p. 216; Campos, *O Estado Nacional*, pp. 51, 54–56, 60–62, 67.

culty in abandoning José Américo. To avoid effective opposition, the governors of Pernambuco and Bahia were steadily undermined during the state of war and Valladares, after
calling up reserves to double his state militia, stationed
forces at Juiz de Fora and Poços de Caldas poised to move
on Rio de Janeiro and Campinas, in case of trouble in the
capital or if São Paulo resisted. The politicians and military
leaders considered Vargas' continuation in office as the
easiest and safest way to end the "political confusion and
military anarchy."[56] Getúlio was to stay.

In an attempt to prevent the projected coup d'état, Minister of Justice Macedo Soares requested a meeting of the
principal military chiefs in the office of the minister of war
so that he might present to them several proposals for constitutional changes that a majority of the Congress favored.
Macedo Soares could not persuade the generals to accept
the proposals, and after he departed General Dutra obtained the cooperation of those present to overthrow the
constitutional system. Afterwards Dutra sent coded telegrams to the regional commanders, nearly all of whom as-
sented. That same day Dutra and Góes Monteiro went to
the naval ministry to obtain the admirals' final consent to
the coup. The naval minister assured them that "as in 1889
and 1930" the navy would stand by the army.[57] With its sad
collection of creaking tubs and two aging cruisers that
scarcely had powder for ceremonial purposes, it could do
little more than declare solidarity with the generals. The
navy was not a center of decision.

The armed forces approved Vargas' staying in power because he promised funds to purchase equipment which they
greatly desired and needed. The candidates in the presi-

[56] Valladares, *Tempos Idos e Vividos*, pp. 153–181; Scotten, Rio, Nov.
6, 1937, 832.00/1083, NA. The phrase "political confusion and military
anarchy" reportedly was Getúlio's; see Coutinho, *General Góes*, p. 295.

[57] *Ibid.*, pp. 306–314. Two generals later withdrew their approval—
Manuel Rabello and Coelho Neto—placing themselves on the fringe
of the army.

dential race had obligations to interests and supporters; they would not be strong enough to take the only step which, in the opinion of the military, could make possible the increased expenditures of a rearmament program—suspension of service on the foreign debt.[58]

During mid-1937 Argentina was ominously increasing its military strength and seeking to extend its sway over Bolivia and Paraguay. The Brazilian government was uneasy. Ambassador Oswaldo Aranha, who usually counseled peace, urged Vargas to arm Brazil, regardless of the cost, because if he did not act immediately the country later would pay "much more, materially and morally."[59] Argentina's success in blocking the planned transfer of several old destroyers from the American to the Brazilian navy in mid-1937 deeply disturbed Brazilian leaders, and weakened their confidence in the sincerity of United States professions of friendship. A new warship had not been constructed in Brazil in nearly fifty years, the navy having been dependent on foreign shipyards, and the army was using a motley collection of French and German weapons, many dating from before World War I.[60] Vargas' pledge to change this situation insured military support of his continuation in power. Personal loyalty was also a factor; nearly all of the prominent officers had risen to their positions under Vargas. For his part, Vargas saw the military as the only means of putting down the political bosses who weakened the central government and of giving him the order and tranquility he needed to develop the country. Also he may have wanted to head off direct military dictatorship.[61]

[58] Charles A. Thompson, "News Letter on Brazil," Foreign Policy Association, Sept. 26, 1938, in 832.00/1232, NA.

[59] Aranha to Vargas, Washington, June 4, 1937, OAA.

[60] *Ibid.*, Nelson Werneck Sodré, *História Militar do Brasil* (Rio de Janeiro, 1965), p. 281.

[61] Vargas' speech of Jan. 14, 1938, at São Borja, Rio Grande do Sul, in Scotten, Rio, Jan. 19, 1938, 832.00, G. Vargas 10/47, NA. For Vargas' relations with the military see the following: Alzira Vargas, *Getúlio*, pp. 175–176, 190–191, 254; Sodré, *História Militar*, pp. 270–281; Heitor

The Integralistas were playing an important part in the now rapidly unfolding events. Vargas was using them to make the communist threat appear real so that he could change the constitution and stay in office. It was a dangerous tactic, demonstrating the tremendous self-confidence of a president certain that he could use the goose-stepping greenshirts to hold back the imaginary red hordes without surrendering to them his freedom of action.

Government representatives met secretly with Salgado, beginning in September 1937, seeking to gain his confidence and support. Speaking for Vargas, Francisco Campos requested Salgado's aid in the coming coup and asked for his comments on the new constitution. Campos told him that *Integralismo* would be the basis of the new order. All political parties would be abolished, but a National Union would be organized with the Integralistas forming its core, as a cultural and educational association. Salgado replied that the Integralistas would support the coup, because they considered the new constitution a step toward their dream of an organic democracy. Vargas later reaffirmed Campos' commitments.[62]

Thousands of Integralistas marched past Guanabara Palace to honor the president at dusk on November 1. Later that night Salgado renounced his candidacy in a radio address, saying that he preferred to be his country's adviser rather than president. Pledging *Integralismo*'s solidarity with Vargas, he declared that a new regime was necessary to save the institutions and traditions of Brazil. In the following days the Integralistas held two large, enthusiastic rallies in Rio under the sponsorship of military and naval

---

Borges Fortes, *Velhos Regimentos, Ensaio Sóbre a Evolução da Artilharia de Campanha Brasileira de 1831 a 1959* (Rio de Janeiro, 1964), p. 287; J. M. de Castro Silva to Aranha, June 24, 1938, "Assuntos Diversos," OAA. This last item is a report on the navy by a naval officer; Interview, Alzira Vargas do Amaral Peixoto, Rio, Aug. 10, 1969.

[62] Scotten, Rio, Nov. 6, 1937, 832.00/1083, NA; Salgado, *Integralismo*, pp. 81–105.

organizations. *Integralismo*'s prestige appeared to be soaring. The minister of war informed Vargas that of 4,000 army officers, 1,200 were registered members or Integralista sympathizers; the same was true for about half the naval officers.[63] The anti-communist drums beat louder by the day.

On November 8 Macedo Soares resigned his post as minister of justice, and the next day Francisco Campos replaced him. Macedo Soares had accepted the inevitability of Vargas' staying in office, but the generals did not trust him and demanded his removal.

The date for the coup was six days off—November 15, the forty-eighth anniversary of the republic—and all was going according to plan when the unexpected happened. Armando Sales issued a proclamation, read in the Senate and Chamber on November 9, calling on the military to guarantee the elections and accusing the president of trying to sabotage them. José Américo joined his opponent in attacking the plot. Vargas was visibly preoccupied; he hesitated, fearful that Armando Sales' move would provoke rebellion. Only after receiving word from the governor of São Paulo that Armando Sales was not speaking for him, his party, or his state did Vargas relax. But the manifesto was circulating in the army barracks and Dutra was worried. At the eleventh hour on November 9 Dutra, along with Francisco Campos, Agamemnon Magalhães, and Filinto Müller, met Getúlio in his small study on the second floor of the darkened Guanabara Palace. They urged immediate action and signified their determination by joining the president in signing the new national charter. Vargas instructed Dutra to close the Congress and ordered the constitution published in the *Diário Oficial*.

[63] Salgado, *Integralismo*, pp. 90–95; Scotten, Rio, Nov. 6, 1937, 832.00/1083 and Nov. 9, 1937, 832.00/1093, NA. The Integralistas claimed that 50,000 marchers took part in the November 1 parade but Vargas' agents counted only 20,000, convincing Vargas the movement could be dominated.

Before dawn on the 10th federal district police rode with carbines at the ready through Rio's rain-dampened streets to take positions around the Senate on Avenida Rio Branco and the Chamber of Deputies on Rua da Misericórdia. The Brazilian Congress would not reconvene until after World War II. The legislators docilely accepted the fact; eighty sent congratulatory messages. Only six expressed disapproval—but Armando Sales' deputies could not react because they were under house arrest. At eleven A.M. the cabinet met in the Catete Palace (the executive office building) so that the other ministers could add their signatures to the constitution of the Estado Nôvo. Only the Minister of Agriculture, Industry, and Commerce, a Mineiro, Odilon Duarte Braga, refused. He was immediately replaced by Fernando Costa, a Paulista who headed the National Department of Coffee. Early in the afternoon Minister Campos notified the newspapers that the government was issuing a new constitution, and that the president had dissolved the Congress and all state and municipal legislatures. The state governors, except those of Bahia and Pernambuco whom Vargas replaced with military interventors, had sent telegrams pledging their support.[64] The Foreign Minister called in American Ambassador Jefferson Caffery early that afternoon, before speaking to any other ambassador, to assure him that the day's events were necessary to forestall revolution. The new constitution would preserve democratic institutions, while giving additional power to the president and allowing him to continue in office for six more years. There would be no changes in foreign policy, and the government intended to "pursue a very liberal policy with respect to foreign capital and foreigners who have legitimate interests in Brazil." Caffery expressed skepticism to the

[64] Scotten, Rio, Nov. 20, 1937, 832.00/1111 and Nov. 20, 1937, 832.00/ 1106 (this last contains copy of Armando Sales' proclamation), NA; Adalberto Aranha to O. Aranha, Rio, Nov. 17, 1937, OAA; see photograph of police in Calmon, *História do Brasil*, VI, 2241; Dulles, *Vargas of Brazil*, pp. 168–171; Alzira Vargas, *Getúlio*, pp. 218–219.

State Department about the effective "preservation of democratic institutions" under the Estado Nôvo.[65]

Shortly before eight P.M. Getúlio Vargas walked through the corridors to the grand salon of Guanabara Palace to address the Brazilian nation via radio. Waiting for the signal to begin, he nodded and exchanged comments with the ministers of state, army officers, and functionaries who had crowded into the room. Then in slow, grave tones he explained that when circumstances demanded a decision which would profoundly affect the life of the country he could not flee from his presidential responsibilities; he must act. Political parties, instead of offering opportunity for growth and progress, were subverting order, threatening Brazil's unity and endangering its existence by polarizing rivalries and encouraging civil discord. They were carrying the contest of the ballot box to the field of combat. To prevent Brazil's disintegration he had decided to restore the national government's authority. He intended to correct the flaws which had marred Brazilian institutions since 1889. He outlined the country's economic and military needs— suspension of the foreign debt, construction of railways and highways into the interior, and reequipping of the armed forces. In order to adjust the government to the country's economic necessities, he was creating "a strong regime of peace, justice, and labor." Concluding, he declared that "when the means of government no longer correspond to the existing conditions of a people, there is no other solution than to change them, establishing other modes of action. The Constitution promulgated today created a new legal structure. . . . We will restore the nation . . . allowing it to construct freely its own history and destiny."[66]

After his speech, Vargas calmly took his family to dinner at the Argentine ambassador's residence, where he joked that he would like to tour the building in case some day he

[65] Caffery, Rio, Nov. 10, 1937, 832.00/1077, NA.

[66] Vargas, *A Nova Política*, v, 19–32; *Jornal do Brasil* (Rio), Nov. 11, 1937.

should need refuge. Quietly, without audible protest, the Brazilian people accepted the Estado Nôvo.[67]

For the next eight years Vargas' Estado Nôvo was the Brazilian government. It was an authoritarian regime based on Getúlio, not on ideology. It was not a one-man dictatorship but rule by consensus of a limited group of Brazilians. Foreign and domestic pressures shaped the Estado Nôvo—indeed the United States and Germany sought to influence Vargas in their favor, while he worked to maintain stability and to develop the country. While Vargas and the members of his government did not solve all of the country's problems—indeed they caused new ones—they laid the foundation for Brazil's subsequent industrial growth.

[67] Adalberto Aranha to O. Aranha, Rio, Nov. 20, 1937, OAA; Alzira Vargas, *Getúlio*, p. 218. Alzira Vargas, who opposed the coup, described the reaction of the Brazilian people in these words: "O golpe de 10 de novembro de 1937 foi como que um grande e profundo suspiro de alívio para a maioria do povo brasileiro. Não para todos, é claro."

"And now José?

You are marching, José!
José, to where?"[1]

2

The Course

FOREIGN REACTION to the new Brazilian regime
split largely along ideological lines—democratic and totalitarian. In Buenos Aires the press comments were unfavorable—*La Nación* stated that the new constitution signified
the end of democratic government in Brazil, *El Mundo* declared that the "soul of America cannot but feel alarmed,"
while *La Crítica* believed it an example of the fascist and
Nazi activities endangering South America.[2] Santiago de
Chile newspapers, *La Nación* and *La Hora*, denied the new
regime was fascist and took the position that it was a purely
political maneuver aimed at increasing Vargas' authority
and continuing him in office.[3] A Lima newspaper which
tended to favor fascism, *La Crónica*, concluded that the
new Brazilian constitution was "the first vibrant clarion of
functional democracy in America."[4] American correspondents described the attitude of German officials in Berlin as
one of suppressed elation. While cautious, German press
comment clearly evinced satisfaction with "the evolution
toward an authoritarian government in Brazil." Editorials

[1] Carlos Drummond de Andrade's poem "José"; see *Reunião Drum-*
mond (Rio de Janeiro, 1969), p. 70. "E agora, José? . . . você marcha,
José! José, para onde?"

[2] Alexander W. Weddell, Buenos Aires, Nov. 12, 1937, 832.00/1089,
NA.

[3] Wesley Frost, Santiago, Nov. 15, 1937, 832.00/1102, NA.

[4] Laurence Steinhardt, Lima, Nov. 12, 1937, 832.00/1104, NA.

carefully avoided giving any credit to German or Italian influence.[5] Domestic political and economic conditions were held responsible for the establishment of the new government. Fascism had nothing to do with it, they said. Brazil was merely readjusting the balance between the powers of the central government and those of the states.[6] The Italian press devoted much space to the events in Brazil. *Il Messaggero* (Rome) of November 13 carried a long editorial characterizing Vargas as one of the greatest and strongest contemporary statesmen. It declared that he had "ploughed the initial furrow for the new civilization and prosperity of his country in this Fascist century," and that the rest of Latin America would sooner or later follow Brazil's example.[7]

The press in the United States emphasized the supposedly fascist nature of the regime and implied that the change had some connection with the Axis. At the time there was a lull in the fighting in the Spanish Civil War and in the Sino-Japanese conflict, and American newspapers pounced on the events in Brazil as the subject of new headlines and alarmist editorials. Certainly there was interest in the Brazilian situation; *The New York Times* ran nineteen news items and two editorials on Brazil between November 11 and 29. The *Times* speculated that now Germany might gain a larger share of the profitable Brazilian market; and though admitting that the Brazilian variety might not be European-style fascism, the newspaper said it was still fascism.[8]

On the surface the new government did not seem to be causing official Washington much concern. The Department

[5] William E. Dodd, Berlin, Nov. 12, 1937, 832.00/1086, NA.

[6] Alfred Schneider, "Brazil's Course," *Wirtschaftsdienst* (Nov. 19, 1937), pp. 1624–1626, attached to 832.00/1145, NA.

[7] William Phillips, Rome, Nov. 13, 1937, 832.00/1090, NA.

[8] Aranha to Vargas, Washington, Nov. 24, 1937, OAA; *The New York Times*, Nov. 11–29, 1937; see especially Nov. 20, 1937, editorial entitled: "Fascism as a Neighbor."

of State had followed the events in Brazil dispassionately. Reports from the Rio embassy indicated that Vargas might continue in power if no way was found to break the political impasse, even though Ambassador Oswaldo Aranha repeatedly assured the department that the president would not stay in office. Aranha's assertions may have calmed the department because of the ambassador's long friendship with Vargas and because of his great rapport with Undersecretary of State Sumner Welles, who largely shaped Latin American policies.

Vargas considered the Washington embassy Brazil's most important diplomatic post. He had chosen Aranha to fill it because he was an old friend, and because he had the background, ability, and personality to be a successful ambassador. Vargas reportedly paid him $84,000 a year, the highest salary given a Brazilian official. From this amount Aranha paid for the lavish parties that made the Brazilian embassy a center of the Washington diplomatic corps' social life.[9] Aranha was not a crude Gaúcho from the cattle country of Rio Grande do Sul, but a polished diplomat. He had not learned his diplomacy in a foreign service school, but in practical politics. A graduate of Rio's aristocratic Colégio Militar, he had studied in Paris and was fluent in French. While practicing law in Rio Grande he entered politics and served as mayor of Alegrete, federal deputy, state secretary of interior affairs during Vargas' governorship, minister of interior, and minister of finance. He fought in defense of the legal government in the troubles of 1923 and 1926, sustaining wounds on both occasions. When he went to Washington in 1934, he was tall, erect, handsome with prematurely gray hair and boundless energy. His family, two sons and two daughters, was equally attractive. Unable to speak English when he arrived in the United States, he quickly mastered it. His memory for names, faces, and facts was

[9] Vargas to Aranha, Rio, June 17, 1937, OAA; *The Washington Post*, Jan. 24, 1938. Vargas also wanted the popular Aranha out of Brazil where he would not be a political threat.

extraordinary. Though he disliked crowds, in small groups he was at ease in conversation that could range from thoroughbred horses, which he raced in Brazil, to the latest scientific theories. The better to understand America, he traveled across it by automobile, making contacts that brought him speaking invitations from all over the country. He was probably the best-known Brazilian ambassador to serve in Washington.[10]

Aranha had discovered a similar spirit in Welles, who in 1937 was a career diplomat with twenty years of experience in dealing with the Western Hemisphere. Born to a wealthy and socially prominent east coast family, Welles attended Franklin D. Roosevelt's schools, Groton and Harvard. He became interested in Latin America while at the latter, where he studied economics and Hispanic literature. At twenty-eight, a few years after entering the Department of State, he became the youngest man ever named chief of the division of Latin American affairs. Later he served as commissioner to the Dominican Republic and arbitrated a civil war in Honduras. Falling out of sympathy with President Calvin Coolidge's Latin American policy, he left the foreign service to write *Naboth's Vineyard*, a history of the Dominican Republic that slashed at American policy.[11] Welles supported Roosevelt for the presidency with money and with ideas for the Good Neighbor policy, and in 1933 became assistant secretary of state. He was honest and precise, and dressed impeccably. He worked long hours and commuted to his Maryland estate in Oxon Hill; he liked reading history and cultivating flowers and was an excellent horse-

[10] Based on: "Biographical Sketch of Oswaldo Aranha," Oct. 1, 1934, OF Brazil 1933–1945, FDRL; variety of letters and newspaper clippings, OAA; interviews with Euclydes Aranha, Rio, Nov. 1965; also Carlos Delgado de Carvalho, *História Diplomática do Brasil* (São Paulo, 1959), pp. 268–269.

[11] Sumner Welles, *Naboth's Vineyard: The Dominican Republic, 1844–1925* (New York, 1928).

man.[12] He and Aranha formed a friendship that helped tie their nations together.

Welles told Washington correspondents on November 11 that he believed the Estado Nôvo was purely a Brazilian creation without European influence. To make certain that such was the case he instructed Ambassador Caffery to meet Vargas secretly to obtain assurances that the new government was not pro-Axis, and that the constitutional changes would not affect the "particularly close and friendly" Brazilian-American relations.[13] The United States was fortunate in having an excellent ambassador in Rio de Janeiro during the most critical years of its relations with Brazil. Caffery, a handsome forty-eight-year-old former assistant secretary of state who had recently taken over the Rio embassy, had the perfect temperament for dealing with Brazilians. A career diplomat, whose wide experience included assignments in Caracas, Stockholm, Madrid, Athens, Tokyo, Berlin, and Bogota, he was an exponent of the old style of diplomacy which operated without procedures; as he expressed it: "You just play it by ear."[14] He learned Portuguese and fired all the English-speaking servants at the embassy residence. He had married just before the Rio appointment and he and his wife made a serious effort to know and understand Brazil and Brazilians. During his nearly seven years in Rio he faced crises which would have overwhelmed a lesser man.

Realizing the danger in the Brazilian situation, Welles asked Caffery to hold a conference as soon as possible with American consular officers stationed in Brazil, to ascertain the general situation of the country and to arrange for con-

12 *Pathfinder* (Washington, D.C.), Jan. 24, 1942.

13 Welles, Nov. 12, 1937, as in *Foreign Relations, 1937*, v, 313–314.

14 Bryce Wood, *The Making of the Good Neighbor Policy* (New York, 1961), p. 356; Emb/Washington, Mar. 11, 1937, 104/407 (22), Ficha Confidential #1, "Jefferson Caffery," AHMRE (Itamaraty Palace, Rio).

tinuous reporting on the activities of Axis nationals in their areas.[15]

Brazilian officials were anxious to reassure the Americans. On the very day of the coup the foreign minister carefully outlined the official explanation for Caffery. After failing to find a compromise candidate, the government had come to the conclusion that the only way to prevent the presidential election from ending in bloodshed was for Vargas to proclaim a new constitution and to remain in office. The president also wanted to strike at the growing Integralista movement. According to the minister, the greenshirts were "clowns in the political circus" who would have no part in the new regime. He might have added that they had helped to create the atmosphere that made the Estado Nôvo possible, but that now their usefulness was ended. The minister assured Caffery that Brazil would continue its present foreign policy, especially its cordial relations with the United States, and he hoped that Washington would be sympathetic.[16]

When Caffery questioned Vargas about Axis influence on the Estado Nôvo, the president appeared surprised and said that it was laughable to suppose that the Germans, Italians, Japanese, or even Integralistas had any connection with the coup. The new constitution, he affirmed, was in no way Integralista, Nazi, or Fascist, and his government had no connection with the Axis powers. He emphasized that he wished to continue close relations with the United States. At the ambassador's urging he issued a statement to the press denying foreign influence.[17]

The Rio papers hailed the statement as opportune. *O Jornal* declared that Brazil wished to remain apart from

[15] Scotten, Rio, Nov. 29, 1937, 832.00/1124, NA. At a meeting held that day they agreed to submit regular reports. This practice contributed a large body of information on local events.

[16] Caffery, Rio, Nov. 10, 1937, *Foreign Relations, 1937*, V, 312–313.

[17] Caffery, Rio, Nov. 13, 1937, *ibid.*, pp. 314-315; *New York Times*, Nov. 14, 1937.

European questions that did not affect the Americas. Brazil had developed a foreign policy based on a Washington-Rio axis and the newspaper saw no reason to change. Although Brazil had friendly relations with Japan, Italy, and Germany, and although it was anticommunist, it would not sign the Axis-sponsored Anti-Comintern Pact, the objectives of which were outside Brazil's concerns.[18]

Actually, Vargas had not seen any objections to Brazil signing the Anti-Comintern Pact before Caffery indicated that such a move would disturb American opinion. The president, surprised on learning this, said he did not understand fascism and Nazism. He cared nothing for ideologies, political or otherwise, and was perfectly willing to use the Integralistas to maintain his power, even if he appeared a fascist. Vargas had assured Salgado that if the Integralistas supported him, he would not only take them into the regime but change the system of government to suit their ideas. If it would be helpful to sign the Anti-Comintern Pact he would sign, but this would not necessarily mean alignment with the Axis in other things. Vargas did not have the remotest intention of allowing anyone to dominate him or to impose conditions. When he realized that alignment with the Axis could hurt Brazil economically, and learned that the Integralistas were not as strong as they claimed, he felt secure enough to reaffirm publicly Brazil's traditional friendship with the United States and to suppress the Integralistas.[19]

Most of the minority of the population that actually participated in Brazil's political life quietly accepted Vargas' continuance in office. In the city of Rio de Janeiro there was an air of relief—the upper and middle classes had feared that the elections would end in fighting. They were content to accept dictatorship if it insured peace. The constitution of November 10 dissolved the national, state, and municipal

18 *O Jornal* (Rio), Nov. 18, 1937.
19 Caffery, Rio, Mar. 28, 1938, 832.00/1183, and Caffery, Rio, Mar. 7, 1938, 832.00/1171, NA.

assemblies and gave Vargas powers to issue decree-laws and to intervene in the states. He was to stay in office until he submitted the new constitution to a plebiscite. This meant that Vargas would rule Brazil as long as he wished, or until he was forced to step down. Even so the American embassy was optimistic. "In the hands of the usual run of Brazilian politicians these powers would be dangerous," wrote Embassy Counselor Robert M. Scotten, but Vargas was "extremely level-headed," did not persecute his enemies, and understood his people better than any other man in Brazil. The counselor expected important changes in the next several months.[20]

In the last days of November the major political problem confronting the government was what to do with the now disgruntled Integralistas. Vargas' address on November 10 surprised Salgado's cohorts because it contained nothing about *Integralismo*. After hearing the speech Salgado decided he had been mistaken from the beginning about Vargas' intentions. Immediately the government-controlled press began to attack and ridicule the mystical Supreme Chief and his greenshirts. The Integralistas, confused by being dropped so suddenly after the whirlwind courtship, spent uncertain and anguished days. General Góes Monteiro, who was sulking because Vargas had neglected to make certain changes that he had suggested in the state governments, made a vehement appeal to Salgado to preserve the movement. *Integralismo* had fulfilled a great mission by helping to establish the Estado Nôvo, and now, he said, it must protect true Brazilians in the midst of self-interest and hypocrisy. Abolition of the movement would be disastrous for Brazil. He insisted that Salgado speak with Minister of Justice Francisco Campos.[21]

[20] Getúlio Vargas, *A Nova Política do Brasil* (Rio de Janeiro, 1938–47), v, 96–98; for text of constitution see pp. 37–98; Scotten, Rio, Nov. 20, 1937, 832.00/1111, NA.

[21] Plínio Salgado, *O Integralismo Brasileiro* (Lisbon, 1946), p. 95; Alzira Vargas do Amaral Peixoto, *Getúlio Vargas, Meu Pai* (Pôrto

The minister told Salgado that he would receive a cabinet post if he disbanded the Integralistas. Salgado was shocked; he telephoned Góes Monteiro, who promised to speak with Vargas. *Integralismo's* sponsor in government circles, General Newton Cavalcanti, immediately went to Minister of War Dutra to seek his intercession with Vargas, and a meeting between the president and Salgado took place around the end of November.

Vargas was frank. He was about to outlaw all political parties but in order not to alienate the Integralistas Vargas offered Salgado the portfolio as minister of education, perhaps knowing he would not accept. Salgado said that he would reply after the government had issued the decree abolishing political parties, and the movement's leaders had studied it. Vargas was determined to crush the greenshirts, but he let Salgado think that the government would allow them to continue operations as a civil society wholly removed from politics.[22]

Vargas' purpose was to absorb individual Integralistas into the diverse groups supporting his regime and to forestall their opposition until he was ready to destroy them. He continued to lull the greenshirts. He reviewed an Integralista parade in front of the Catete Palace (the presidential office building on Rua do Catete in Rio) on November 25. Seven days later the promised presidential decree abolished political parties. Editorial comment universally supported the president's action. Curiously enough, the greenshirts docilely accepted the situation and quietly changed into a cultural society that managed to keep alive the spirit and aims of the movement.[23]

Alegre, 1960), p. 196; Lourival Coutinho, *O General Góes Depõe* (Rio de Janeiro, 1956), p. 314.

[22] Salgado, *Integralismo*, pp. 97–101; Scotten, Rio, Dec. 3, 1937, 832.00/1128, NA.

[23] Caffery, Rio, Nov. 26, 1937, 832.00/1109, NA; Scotten, Rio, Nov. 26, 1937, 832.00/1118, NA; the decree was dated Dec. 2, see Caffery, Rio, Dec. 3, 1937, 832.00/1119 and 832.00/1120, NA; Caffery, Rio, Dec. 4,

One of the principal reasons that Vargas had decided to crush the Integralistas was his realization that they were building a "shadow" government, and that unless he checked them they might soon constitute a danger. Shortly before he issued the decree several newly-appointed mayors in the state of Bahia had telegraphed their allegiance to Salgado. Vargas and his advisers also hoped that by sacrificing the Integralistas they would remove any suspicions the United States might have about ties between the Estado Nôvo and the Axis powers. Salgado lacked force and demagogic appeal, so Vargas' action removed the danger of the Integralistas coming to power through peaceful means. Salgado, of course, never entered the Vargas cabinet.[24]

In late November, Vargas converted all the state governors into interventors—except Benedicto Valladares of Minas, who continued with the title of governor in recognition of his role in the establishment of the Estado Nôvo. The two presidential candidates were treated according to their ability to hinder the new regime. José Américo returned to his position on the Federal Budget Tribunal, holding his tongue in check until safer days in 1945. Armando Sales was placed under house arrest, was later moved to sumptuous quarters in the Mineiro town of Nova Lima, and eventually accepted hints that he should seek exile abroad.[25] During September and October the war ministry had taken the precaution of shifting potential opponents in the officer corps to harmless posts, and afterwards several generals who objected to the coup were relieved of their commands. In Rio

---

1937, 832.00/1121, NA; Robert M. Levine, *The Vargas Regime, The Critical Years, 1934–1938* (New York, 1970), pp. 159–175 discusses the strange demise of Salgado and his greenshirts.

[24] Scotten, Rio, Dec. 6, 1937, 832.00/1135, NA; for full text of decree see *Correio da Manhã* (Rio), Dec. 4, 1937; also copy attached to 832.00/1135.

[25] Benedicto Valladares, *Tempos Idos e Vividos, Memórias* (Rio de Janeiro, 1966), p. 184; John W. F. Dulles, *Vargas of Brazil, A Political Biography* (Austin, 1967), p. 173; Coutinho, *General Góes*, p. 322.

de Janeiro the only officers of consequence in this category were General Pompeu Cavalcanti de Albuquerque, chief of coast artillery, and Colonel Eduardo Gomes of the army air service.[26] Whether Gomes asked to be relieved because of political scruples (as he would be credited with later) is perhaps questionable. According to Góes Monteiro, Gomes "had been wounded in his military dignity" and considered himself "humiliated" not by the coup but because General Newton Cavalcanti, the Integralistas' military advocate, had sent troops from his command at Vila Militar to surround Gomes' First Aviation Regiment at Campo dos Afonsos. Góes Monteiro, who was unable to persuade the stubborn aviator to return to his regiment, made him director of air routes attached to the general staff.[27]

At the end of November Brazil seemed resigned to its fate, but the Brazilian chancellery on Whitehaven Street in Washington was beset with uneasiness.[28] Although Ambassador Oswaldo Aranha worked hard to convince Americans that all was well in Brazil, he himself was not convinced. For about a year the ambassador's brother, Adalberto Aranha, had been saying in numerous and detailed letters that Getúlio wanted to continue as president, but Oswaldo apparently had believed, or at least had hoped, that he would not do so.[29] To be sure, Vargas had tried to give Aranha warning in his letter of November 8, which the ambassador received on November 15 when the events in Rio were already in American headlines. In a speech before a Cleveland convention on November 5—which received wide coverage in Brazil—Aranha had condemned authoritarian regimes as failures, regimes of both the right and the left.[30] Suddenly, he faced the embarrassing task of explain-

26 Scotten, Rio, Nov. 20, 1937, 832.00/1111, NA.

27 Coutinho, *General Góes,* pp. 322–323.

28 For a report on the political situation at the end of November see Scotten, Rio, Nov. 26, 1937, 832.00/1118, NA.

29 E.g., Adalberto Aranha to O. Aranha, Rio, Nov. 17, 1937, OAA.

30 E.g., *Diário de São Paulo,* Nov. 5, 1937, and *Diário Carioca* (Rio), Nov. 5, 1937.

ing Getúlio's rightist coup. In his letter of the eighth Vargas explained the coup on the grounds that the communists were again active and the army had insisted on a state of war to meet the grave danger. The constitution needed revision to safeguard Brazilian society and to strengthen the central government. His administration would stay on to make the reforms and would submit the results to a plebiscite. He asked Aranha "to dispel any apprehensions of the North American government as to the security of our policy of friendship with the United States, a policy that will and must continue."[31]

The new constitution so alarmed Aranha that he could not adhere to the Estado Nôvo. He telegraphed his "indeclinable" resignation to Getúlio, but being a good diplomat he preferred to be relieved of his post in Rio, so as to cause fewer repercussions in the United States. He would embark as soon as he received authorization from the foreign ministry.[32]

Vargas at first refused Aranha's resignation, saying that he needed his services in Washington. The change in government was necessary to preserve order, and it had general acceptance. He had counted on Aranha's collaboration because of their friendship, and because earlier in the year Aranha had remarked in a letter that Getúlio ought to continue in the presidency. Vargas pleaded with Aranha not to abandon a friend who needed his help.

But Oswaldo Aranha was a stubborn Gaúcho; he insisted on being relieved of his post. His defense of Brazil in the United States and his request to return to Rio before officially resigning were proof enough that he was not abandoning friend or country. His disagreement was not with Vargas but with the new constitution, which would not permit him to continue honorably as ambassador. Faced with

31 Vargas to Aranha, Rio, Nov. 8, 1937, OAA.
32 Aranha to Vargas, Washington, Nov. 15, 1937, OAA. The ministry sought to explain the situation in MRE to Emb/Washington, Rio, Nov. 13, 1937, #144, Exp. 3366, AHMRE.

Oswaldo's attitude, Vargas asked him to stay in Washington only until American confidence in the Brazilian government had been reestablished. In the meantime Aranha was to investigate the possibility of American financial cooperation in Brazilian development.[33] One of Vargas' principal objectives was to transform Brazil's "potential riches into effective resources" by modernizing port facilities and railroads, constructing new rail lines, opening new roads, equipping the merchant fleet, and extending air transport. He referred repeatedly in speeches and letters to the necessity of building a great steel mill "to forge the instruments of our defense and our industrial progress."[34] He also spoke of encouraging the search for petroleum and the production of coal, as well as reequipping the armed forces. To do all of this Brazil would need foreign capital. "American support," Vargas wrote Aranha, "would avoid [the necessity of] our accepting offers from other countries, which I have resisted and intend to resist."[35] They would solve the problem of the foreign debt moratorium, declared after the coup, by making a separate agreement with the United States. After obtaining information concerning financial assistance Aranha could return to Rio de Janeiro for "conversations."[36]

Adalberto Aranha, who had spoken frequently with Getúlio during the previous weeks, noted with apparent relief that the comedy was ended. He had come to accept Getúlio's staying in office as the only possible and acceptable way out of the electoral impasse. It was difficult for him to say which of the two candidates "displayed the greatest defects and errors," or which of the two would have been "the most disastrous for the country." He asserted that the audacious and cleverly-executed coup had received the "applause of nearly the whole nation." People were willing to

[33] Vargas to Aranha, Rio, Nov. 17, 1937, and Aranha to Vargas, Washington, Nov. 18, 1937, OAA.
[34] Vargas, *A Nova Política*, v, 122, 124.
[35] Vargas to Aranha, Rio, Nov. 17, 1937, OAA.
[36] Vargas to Aranha, Rio, Nov. 19, 1937, OAA.

accept the Estado Nôvo as the price of order and tranquility. Although there was some reaction against the idea of Getúlio's staying in power beyond a year or two, Adalberto did not think that it would be strong enough to change the situation. Everyone, he said, was waiting for Oswaldo's opinion.[37]

To sound him out, his brother Luís and Finance Minister Artur de Souza Costa telephoned the ambassador. He told them flatly that he did not agree with what was happening and that he was resigning. Souza Costa urged patience, saying that without him "it would be a disaster." Aranha said that he was "calmly defending" what they were doing, but that he could "not agree with a constitution written by an abnormal person [he was referring to Francisco Campos], without norms, without rules," which was "an affront to freedom." Souza Costa replied that he agreed, and handed the telephone to Luís Aranha who continued to argue against his brother's resignation. Oswaldo stated his position clearly: "I approve of a coup against the regime, but not of the constitution . . . I consider any matter with Getúlio a family matter, but I cannot agree to receive a writ of slavery." Luís answered "yes, but it was the only solution . . ."; Souza Costa chimed in plaintively: "We need you. . . ."[38]

Two days before Aranha had written Vargas a long letter; together with the transcript of the above conversation it could leave no doubt as to his attitude toward the Estado Nôvo. Firmly he wrote his old friend that the new constitution was "a revocation of Brazil," and would establish a regime incompatible with Brazilian traditions and Aranha's sentiments, but he had not despaired of Getúlio's "good

[37] Adalberto Aranha to O. Aranha, Rio, Nov. 17, 1937, OAA.

[38] Artur de Souza Costa, Luís Aranha, and Oswaldo Aranha, Rio de Janeiro–Washington, Nov. 26, 1937, transcript of conversation in AGV. The conversation lasted 25 minutes, from 5:14 to 5:39 P.M. and was recorded at Vargas' request. For a fuller version see Levine, *Vargas Regime*, p. 154.

sense" and was confident that his intelligence and patriotism would react against "carrying forward this attempt to reestablish slavery in Brazil." Aranha knew from his correspondence with friends and relatives in Brazil that Getúlio was the principal factor in the equation of power. Although he had moved with military support, he alone had taken responsibility for coldly throwing aside the federal constitution which a few short years before he had sworn solemnly to uphold. If Vargas had been willing to take such a drastic step and if it was true, as Aranha's brother believed, that the new constitution was made more for the president than for the nation that he governed, then perhaps Aranha could place his hopes on Vargas' good sense and on the possibility of influencing him. If so his task would not be simple, because Vargas' economic measures disturbed Aranha almost as much as did the constitution; to his mind they were clearly inopportune and contradictory. He especially disliked the moratorium on debt payments and various nationalistic restrictions on banks, securities, and mines, which he regarded as bordering on xenophobic. Brazil needed to attract capital, not scare it away.[39]

But Vargas was convinced that only drastic measures could save the Brazilian economy from ruin. Coffee, especially, was a problem; market prices fell as consumer demand decreased and competition from other countries increased. Through Brazil's valorization program the federal government insured coffee growers against loss by purchasing all that they grew, storing it for later sale on the world market. In effect, Brazil created an artificial price level that encouraged overproduction at home and competition abroad. Vargas disliked valorization, but for political reasons he had been forced to tolerate it. By 1937 the government was paying a higher price for coffee in Brazil than

[39] Aranha to Vargas, Washington, Nov. 24, 1937, OAA; Adalberto Aranha to O. Aranha, Rio, Nov. 12, 1937, OAA.

the product brought on the world market, so Vargas abolished valorization. The government had required coffee and cotton exporters to pay an exchange tax which with the lowering of world prices had become insupportable—Vargas revoked it. This tax had provided revenue for service on the foreign debt and without it the payments could not be continued, so the government declared a moratorium.[40]

Cancellation of payments on the foriegn debt brought immediate protests from England, France, and the United States. Aranha reminded the president that there were 250,000 holders of Brazilian bonds in the United States who were greatly alarmed at this action. Vargas excused the move as a necessity, not mentioning that Finance Minister Souza Costa had returned from a trip to Washington that summer with the impression that the United States would not take reprisals if Brazil stopped debt payments. In any case, the government was willing to brave European protests and to make a separate settlement with the Americans.[41]

His protests to Getúlio aside, Aranha proceeded cautiously and refrained from making critical public statements because he hoped that with time and reflection the president would realize his mistakes, and because he felt that their long friendship demanded careful consideration before taking a definite position. When he returned to Brazil he would try to make Getúlio see the error of his ways. He wrote whimsically that if he failed he would retire to a ranch and live in silence.[42]

Aranha's attitude towards the Estado Nôvo would determine his political future, which was crucial also for the fu-

---

[40] Vargas to Aranha, Rio, Dec. 6, 1937, OAA. The decision to stop payments was made on Nov. 20; see MRE to Emb/Washington, Rio, Nov. 20, 1937, #146, Exp. 3422, AHMRE.

[41] Aranha to Vargas, Washington, Nov. 24, 1937, OAA. For Brazilian debt question see Donald W. Giffin, "The Normal Years: Brazilian-American Relations, 1930–1939" (Ph.D. Dissertation, Vanderbilt University, 1962), pp. 175–229.

[42] Aranha to Vargas, Washington, Nov. 24, 1937, OAA.

ture of Brazil, and until it was settled Brazilian relations with the United States were in a state of latent crisis. Aranha symbolized Brazilian democracy and close ties with the United States; without his influence both would be in danger. His antagonist in the debate over the direction which the regime would take was Francisco Campos, the learned, opportunistic, and somewhat shy minister of justice, who was trying to shape the government in a totalitarian mold.[43]

In a newspaper interview Campos affirmed that Brazil should be included in the list of corporative states and that democracy in Brazil was impossible because of the ignorance of the masses. Besides, there was a worldwide tendency to strip parliaments of their powers—he cited as an example the Roosevelt administration's legislative program.[44] Undersecretary Welles visited the Brazilian embassy on November 30 to tell Aranha that Campos' remarks were especially deplorable at that time. Roosevelt was faced with a rebellious Congress, still smarting from his attempt earlier in the year to pack the Supreme Court; he did not need Campos' description of him as a usurper of parliamentary prerogatives. Aranha complained to Vargas that many Americans were behaving as if the Brazilians had the plague, and that the last thing Roosevelt wanted was to be identified with dictatorial government. The ambassador accused Campos of trying to cause a break with the United States, whose government, he reminded Vargas, was "the only ally . . . on whose cooperation we can count." The American press was calling Campos the inspirer of the

[43] Caffery, Rio, Mar. 28, 1938, 832.00/1183, NA; Luiz Vergara, *Fui Secretário de Getúlio Vargas* (Rio de Janeiro, 1960), p. 144. Vergara wrote: "Francisco Campos tinha uma antiga e manifesta atração pelos regimes de fôrça e de molde totalitário."

[44] *Correio da Manhã* (Rio), Nov. 28, 1937. Discussed in Aranha to Vargas, Washington, Nov. 29, 1937, OAA. These statements appeared in American newspapers on the 29th, see *New York Times*, Nov. 29, 1937. Also in Francisco Campos, *O Estado Nacional* (Rio de Janeiro, 1941), pp. 32–68.

coup, and because he had written the new constitution his words received wide coverage. Aranha was in basic disagreement with Campos' view of Brazil's problems. Democracy had floundered, not because the people were ignorant but because the Brazilian elites were incapable of leadership. All the fuss puzzled Vargas, who had attributed little importance to his minister's statements. He was ideologically neutral and content to let Aranha and Campos fight for their respective ideals until he could determine the proper course. He was in no rush to give the Estado Nôvo definite form. Aranha reassured the Washington press corps that the new Brazilian government had no ties with the Axis powers, that it was not fascist, and that Vargas did not intend to rule as dictator but as constitutional president under the charter of November 10, which would be submitted to a plebiscite. Apparently after reading the constitution he was beginning to think that it could be lived with. He reaffirmed Brazil's independence, saying that it would not tolerate infiltration, much less domination by other peoples, "even of Americans."[45]

Plebiscite scheduled for 1943

Aranha's popularity in Washington, his reputation as a democrat and friend of the United States gave his assertions a strength that otherwise they probably would not have had, and the consistently pro-American tone of the Brazilian press during November and December seemed to indicate that he was right. A typical editorial ran as follows: "It is necessary to raise, over the Atlantic from north to south, a spiritual wall that will spare us the diseases prevailing in Europe. . . . Dictatorships, Communist or Fascist, let us keep rigorously out of our path. . . . Identity of interests suggests identity of policies. Let us look then to the United States. From there we shall see good examples, which we shall follow sooner or later."[46]

On December 6, in a speech at George Washington Uni-

[45] Aranha to Vargas, Washington, Nov. 29, 1937, and Nov. 30, 1937, and Vargas to Aranha, Rio, Nov. 30, 1937, OAA.

[46] *Fôlha da Manhã* (São Paulo), Nov. 17, 1937.

versity, Welles publicly threw the support of the Roosevelt administration behind Vargas. He criticized the press and the politicians for making derogatory comments about the coup before the facts were known. He declared that a salient principle of the Good Neighbor policy was "to refrain from minding your neighbor's business for him."[47] Aranha reported that the administration intended the speech to be a public confirmation of its friendly attitude toward Brazil.[48] The reaction in Rio de Janeiro was jubilant; the foreign minister expressed Vargas' gratitude to the American embassy, while newspapers carried the speech as headline news and praised it in editorials. *O Jornal* was typical: "Friendship between the United States and our country is something outside of changes of governments and regimes. . . . No government, whatever its ideology, could change the orientation of our international policy. . . ."[49] This was exactly the reaction Washington desired; it was anxious to maintain friendly relations with Brazil.

But a mood of uncertainty in the United States was affecting business and producing an atmosphere of hesitation in Washington. Faced with a hostile Congress, with slipping public support during 1937, and with increasingly volatile situations in Europe and Asia, the Roosevelt administration had decided, according to Aranha, to place renewed emphasis on Pan-Americanism to regain domestic prestige and to insure a secure base for United States foreign policy. Pan-Americanism allowed the United States to take the stance of defender of "democracy, peace, and happiness" in the hemisphere, while at the same time giving its people pleasant and harmless "international fantasies" to cultivate. Invigoration of the Good Neighbor crusade would be Roosevelt's salvation, "because it had something of the Red

47 State Department Press Release, speech by Sumner Welles, Dec. 6, 1937, at George Washington University, "On the need for a Spirit of Tolerance in Inter-American Relationships." Copy in 832.00/1126, NA.

48 Aranha to Vargas, Washington, Dec. 7, 1937, OAA.

49 *O Jornal* (Rio), Dec. 8, 1937.

Cross, the Salvation Army, Rockefeller Foundation, religious philanthropy, and expansionist Puritanism which is the heart and soul of this country." With the Latin American republics securely aligned, Roosevelt would be better able to confront Germany and Japan. For this effort Brazil would be the "axis and even the stage," because without that country Roosevelt's hemispheric policy would fail. Fortunately, however, Brazil was a traditional friend and an ardent supporter of Pan-Americanism, and offered an effective counterweight to Argentina's unfriendly influence in Latin America. In practice this meant United States support of Getúlio Vargas. Finance Minister Souza Costa, while in Washington in June to negotiate a loan program, had surmised that such an attitude was developing. Though the establishment of the Estado Nôvo troubled the Roosevelt administration, it refused to do anything that might alienate Vargas and push Brazil into the Axis orbit. Roosevelt's policy aimed at preserving Brazilian friendship and at Americanizing, or at least Pan-Americanizing Brazil, before it could be "completely Europeanized, Hitlerized, or Mussolinized."[50]

This policy of approximation meant that Vargas could expect American aid for his development plans; the president of the Export-Import Bank was ready to go to Rio de Janeiro to discuss financing arrangements whenever Vargas wished. Welles told Aranha that the United States "felt it a duty to give practical aid to Brazil" because the American government was convinced that Vargas would reciprocate.[51] Aranha passed this on to his chief, with the information that the United States had a "secret fund of $100,000,000 for the acquisition and formation of a stockpile of raw materials for war" and that his embassy was seeking to arrange purchases of Brazilian products such as manganese and vegetable oils.[52] He also thought that Brazil could

---

[50] Aranha to Vargas, Washington, Nov. 24, 1937, OAA.
[51] *Ibid.*   [52] *Ibid.*

sell unlimited quantities of corned beef to American dog-food producers, who could absorb more beef than the whole Brazilian population. Argentine beef was then being imported into the United States in large quantities, but opposition to it was growing because the Argentine exporter was government-controlled and represented only by a commercial attaché. The Brazilian president was pleased with the American position. He assured Aranha that he would follow the ambassador's wishes concerning the United States. Close friendship with the northern republic was the traditional axis of Brazil's foreign policy and coincided perfectly with its present interests.[53]

Now that the United States was committed to supporting Vargas politically and economically Aranha decided to return to Brazil. In spite of his positive statements to the contrary, he was filled with doubt when he sailed on the *Western Prince* from New York on Saturday, December 11, 1937.

Shortly before Aranha arrived in Rio, Campos asked German Ambassador Karl Ritter if the Reich government would send to Brazil an anti-Comintern exhibit like the one shown in Germany. He also wanted to send some Brazilian officials to Germany, for instruction in combating the Comintern and to establish permanent contact with Berlin's Anti-Comintern Bureau. Campos wished to strengthen the relations established earlier that year, when the head of the Brazilian secret police had visited Germany as Heinrich Himmler's guest, to study the Gestapo's anticommunist techniques. Ritter urgently recommended that his government send the exhibit, because he considered Campos the most important person in the administration next to the president. "It would be of great value to us to fulfill his wish quickly . . . and thereby win his cooperation with Germany in other matters. . . ." The possibility that Aranha would enter the cabinet made it all the more desirable for the Germans to win over the minister of justice. The German gov-

[53] Vargas to Aranha, Rio, Dec. 6, 1937, OAA.

ernment duplicated the exhibit and sent it to Brazil in November 1938, but by that time Campos had lost his primacy to Aranha.[54]

A small boat bearing General Góes Monteiro met the *Western Prince* as it sailed into Guanabara Bay late in the evening of December 23. Speaking for the president, Góes Monteiro told Aranha that he had three choices: he could continue as ambassador in Washington, go to London in the same position, or become foreign minister. According to the general, Aranha was tired, disillusioned, and seemingly determined to return to his Rio Grande law practice.[55] He told the numerous friends and reporters who were on the dock to greet him that he had returned to examine the situation so that he might better defend Brazil's interests in Washington. He denied that he was returning to take a high position. Asked about suspension of the foreign debt, he said that there was "no greater error than to repudiate the payment of debts. . . ." Not to pay was to lose credit, to frighten capital, and to abolish confidence. Brazil would find a way to pay its debts. The newspapers headlined his comments, and reported his arrival on page one with many photographs.[56] His remarks upset the military chiefs, and may have caused the subsequent absence of news concerning him. The censor received orders to prohibit the publication of any remarks Aranha might make about the regime or about payment of the foreign debt.[57]

On the evening of December 27 the Aranha clan gathered at Oswaldo's home in the Urca section of Rio, to hear his views on the situation and to decide what attitude the family should adopt. The Aranhas were a tightly-knit group headed by their spirited elderly mother, Luiza de Freitas Valle Aranha, who wielded tremendous influence over their

[54] *DGFP–D*, v, 816–819. Ambassador Ritter's request was made on December 23, 1937.
[55] Coutinho, *General Góes*, p. 325.
[56] *Correio da Manhã* (Rio), Dec. 24, 1937.
[57] Caffery, Rio, Jan. 3, 1938, 832.00/1160, NA.

public and private affairs. Oswaldo did not want to return to Washington. His brothers tried to convince him that his presence in the United States was necessary for the good of Brazil. They feared that his withdrawal from the government would lower its prestige abroad and weaken its stability. But Oswaldo was determined; he would remain in Brazil.[58]

President Vargas flew to Pôrto Alegre on the morning of January 6 and did not return to the capital until January 20. Meanwhile, the ambassador's future remained a question mark. Vargas realized that if he allowed Aranha to withdraw from the government he ran the risk of having his old friend become a focal point of opposition. And during these uncertain days Aranha was under heavy pressure to oppose Getúlio; he listened to various proposals but refused to commit himself. He was downcast and depressed.[59]

Campos had been doing his best to make Vargas uncertain of Aranha's loyalty, and to persuade him to reinforce the Estado Nôvo with a single political party molded on fascist lines. The minister of education, Gustavo Capanema, Campos' collaborator in an attempt to establish a fascist legion in Minas Gerais after the 1930 revolution, was encouraging Vargas to establish a youth movement of fascist type. And General Dutra, sometime Germanophile, was unhappy about Aranha's pro-American attitude.[60]

Fortunately, events during January nullified these efforts to cast a shadow on Aranha. While Vargas was in Rio Grande do Sul, state authorities called his attention to Nazi

---

[58] Adalberto Aranha to Luiza de Freitas Valle Aranha, Rio, Dec. 30, 1937, OAA.

[59] Alzira Vargas, *Getúlio*, pp. 231–235; for dates see Caffery, Rio, Dec. 27, 1937, 832.00/1156, NA; interview, Euclydes Aranha, Rio, May 16, 1966.

[60] Caffery, Rio, Mar. 28, 1938, 832.00/1183, NA; Vergara, *Fui Secretário*, p. 145; Alzira Vargas, *Getúlio*, pp. 235–236; Coutinho, *General Góes*, pp. 336–337; DGFP–D, XI, 311. The German ambassador listed Generals Dutra and Góes Monteiro, and police chief Filinto Müller as being pro-German in document dated October 17, 1940.

activities among Germans in the southern states. In the latter part of December, the federal government had returned the state police forces to state control. Authorities in Rio Grande do Sul applied the decree abolishing political parties to the Nazis, and were busily turning up information on a variety of questionable activities. The interventor, General Daltro Filho, died during Vargas' visit to Rio Grande. The general's successor was his chief of staff and director of the anti-Nazi campaign, Colonel Oswaldo Cordeiro de Farias, former member of Góes Monteiro's staff and a friend of Oswaldo Aranha.[61]

Upon his return to Rio de Janeiro, the president consulted Góes Monteiro and Campos about Nazi activities. They decided to take energetic measures to eliminate the Nazis' formidable organization in Brazil. Currently engaged in dismembering the Integralistas, they were not about to allow the more dangerous German National Socialist Party to exist.[62]

Although Góes Monteiro had flirted with the Integralistas, he saw that Vargas was determined to destroy them and accepted the decision rather than share their fate. An admirer of totalitarian regimes, Campos was willing to deal with the German ambassador to obtain his help in fighting communism, but he could not tolerate foreign political parties functioning in Brazil. He and the other men in the Vargas regime were Brazilians, not Quislings. None were willing to see foreigners—Germans or Americans—control Brazil. It was now clear to Vargas that Aranha would be useful, and he laid aside any doubts he may have had about his old friend. Campos' desire for an *estadonovista* party would endanger Vargas' principal aim—unity of Brazil.

---

[61] Scotten, Rio, Mar. 4, 1938, 832.00/1170, and Dec. 23, 1937, 832.00/1155, NA; Aurélio da Silva Py, *A 5a Coluna no Brasil, A Conspiração Nazi no Rio Grande do Sul* (Pôrto Alegre, 1942), pp. 1–8, 60–142. Silva Py was state chief of police in Rio Grande do Sul. For a more detailed discussion of the problem see Chapter 3 below.

[62] Scotten, Rio, Mar. 4, 1938, 832.00/1170, NA.

The symbolic burning of state flags in November had not destroyed the centrifugal forces at work in the country, and Vargas was convinced that a single party would "immediately split into factions and uselessly agitate and disturb the country's life." Free from factional politics, Vargas could better achieve economic development. He also pigeonholed the plan for a fascist type of youth movement; two years later a less dangerous version was established.[63]

Aranha had reservations about the constitution of the Estado Nôvo and argued long hours with Vargas almost daily after the latter's return from the south. Although Aranha could not persuade the president to alter the regime, he agreed to take charge of the foreign ministry (the Itamaraty). Apparently he now understood that Getúlio considered the constitution as only so many words, whose sole importance was that they allowed him to create a strong central government. Aranha also realized that he would have no influence outside the government, but as head of the Itamaraty he might be able to keep Brazil out of the clutches of the Axis, and moderate Campos' influence on Vargas.[64]

Aranha's swearing-in as Chancellor of the venerable Itamaraty, on March 15, 1938, was "the most important political development since the November 10th coup d'état," and it took place before the largest audience ever to attend such an event. There was a feeling of relief and satisfaction in Brazil, even on the part of Aranha's former political foes. He immediately began taking every opportunity to impress upon the public that democratic traditions were inherent in the Brazilian character, and that the government would

[63] Alzira Vargas, *Getúlio*, pp. 226, 235–236; Vergara, *Fui Secretário*, p. 145.

[64] Vergara, *Fui Secretário*, pp. 145–147; interview, Euclydes Aranha, Rio, May 16, 1966. On Vargas' attitude toward the constitution see Alzira Vargas, *Getúlio*, pp. 246–252. Scotten summarized Aranha's situation saying that he would probably become foreign minister; see his Jan. 28, 1938, 832.00/1164, NA.

utilize every means to prevent fascist and communist infiltration.[65] Germany's absorption of Austria in mid-March
was a forceful warning that Nazi activities among Brazil's
Germans could have serious consequences. On March 24,
in a short-wave radio broadcast beamed to the United
States, Aranha linked Brazilian economic development and
approximation with the United States as the dual aims of
his chancellorship. He quoted Vargas as having said that
Brazilians welcomed all who wished "to cooperate in our
progress, but never those who want to force their peculiar
doctrines upon us." They would not allow importation of
alien "ideas, practices, ideologies or political regimes."
Aranha told Americans that "in this grave moment for man-
kind, your country, more than any other, is the hope of millions of men and women who long for peace in the world.
. . . In this hour of universal confusion and distress, Brazil
is, as it ever was, at your side . . . I wish to tell you in the
name of my government and in my own name that more
than ever the Americans are welcomed [sic] in Brazil." The
principal Brazilian newspapers gave his remarks prominent
space the next day, and the *Diário Carioca* and the *Correio
da Manhã* praised them in leading editorials. In the opinion

[65] Scotten, Rio, Mar. 11, 1938, 832.00/1176; Caffery, Rio, Mar. 16,
1938, 832.00/1174; Scotten, Rio, Mar. 25, 1938, 832.00/1182, all NA. The
distinguished career diplomat Mário de Pimentel Brandão, who had
served as foreign minister from November 1936 to March 1938, was
named to replace Aranha as ambassador in Washington. The American
chargé noted that Pimentel Brandão had been "a consistent and valued
friend of this Embassy"; Scotten, Rio, Mar. 11, 1938, 832.00/1176, NA.
A member of the diplomatic corps since 1912, he had served in Asunción, Brussels, at the League of Nations, Paris, Ankara, and La Paz.
See story in *Brazil* (American-Brazilian Association), x (May 1938), 6.
Pimentel Brandão stayed in Washington only until December 1938,
when Aranha found it necessary to transfer him to Tokyo because of
"the unfortunate situation created by the presence of a certain lady in
Washington." Quotation from Welles to F. D. Roosevelt, Washington,
Dec. 8, 1938, OF 11 Brazil 1933–1939, FDRL. Carlos Martins Pereira de
Sousa, then ambassador in Brussels, replaced Pimentel in the United
States.

of Counselor Robert M. Scotten of the American embassy, Aranha was "unquestionably having a most salutary effect upon the Estado Nôvo."[66]

Several days earlier, in his first letter to Welles since leaving Washington, Aranha explained the Brazilian situation. He asserted that Brazil would always be democratic. The form of government, he said, was not as important as the "sentiment, spirit, tendency, and life of the people." And the people had chosen "the present solution in an almost electoral manner," as the only means of avoiding civil strife and extremist control of the government. The regime was liberal, and could only be so with Getúlio Vargas at its head: his entire political life had been an example of tolerance in power. He always exercised authority in an atmosphere of ample discussion, never doing anything without first allowing free examination and general debate within the government. He did not use his power for personal, family, factional, or regional gain but for the good of Brazil. His continuation was imperative and the friends of Brazil should accept it.

Although certain parts of the constitution were distasteful, they would be corrected peacefully, much as the United States had reformed its constitution. He assured Welles that he could have confidence in the new order of things in Brazil, and that Brazil would continue to be the "most friendly, the most faithful, and the most impartial of the brothers of the American Union." In the Itamaraty Aranha would be better able "to serve the union and friendship" of Brazil and the United States, "the foundation of hemispheric peace and prosperity."[67]

The months between November 1937 and March 1938 were fraught with danger for the traditional Brazilian-American friendship. This friendship, which at times

[66] *Diário Carioca* (Rio), Mar. 25, 1938; *Correio da Manhã* (Rio), Mar. 25, 1938; Scotten, Rio, Mar. 25, 1938, 832.00/1182, NA.

[67] Aranha to Welles, Rio, Mar. 9, 1938, OAA. Aranha's words were: "o povo . . . optou, por forma quasi plebicitaria, pela solução actual. . . ."

amounted to an alliance, was the cornerstone of Brazilian foreign policy and of Washington's Pan-American efforts. A hostile or an obstructionist Brazil would have made impossible Roosevelt's invigorated Good Neighbor policy. Oswaldo Aranha's influence assured that instead of radical departures in foreign policy, Vargas' Brazil would move closer to the United States. Approximation, not divergence, would be the goal of Brazilian policy.

*"South America is Latin, and will
continue to be Latin."*[1]

*"Our friendship is older than our existence; it is
a family tradition, . . . I do not see . . . how this
occurrence . . . could be reason for your removal."*[2]

3

Sigma and Swastika

IN THE MONTHS after the establishment of the
Estado Nôvo, Vargas destroyed two organizations that had
contributed to the excited atmosphere in which the events
of November 10 occurred: the Brazilian branch of the German National Socialist Party (NSDAP) and the *Ação Integralista Brasileira*. Vargas attacked the first because it was a
threat to Brazilian security and sovereignty, the second because it was a danger to his regime. Although Vargas apparently was never serious in his ostensive flirtation with
the green-shirted Integralistas, he did welcome their support until he consolidated control. Integralista sympathy for
and possible links with Nazi Germany precluded Getúlio's
allying himself with the movement but not from using it. He
sought to destroy the Nazi Party because it tended to preserve German nationalism among German immigrants and
hindered their Brazilianization.

The Germans in Brazil were numerous and respected for
their achievements, but the government expected them to
become Brazilians—not to remake their portions of the
country in a German mold. The immigrants were faced

[1] Statement of Italian ambassador to Brazil as quoted in Robert
M. Scotten, Rio, Apr. 22, 1938, *Foreign Relations, 1938*, v, 412–413.

[2] Vargas to Aranha, Rio, July 1, 1938, OAA.

with a conflict between the demands of their homeland and their adopted country. To increase its population Brazil had encouraged immigration during the nineteenth century. Movement was light until 1890, when a surge began that brought some 3.8 million Italians, Portuguese, Spanish, Germans, Japanese, and others to Brazil by 1942. While many immigrant groups tended to assimilate—to learn Portuguese and marry into Brazilian families—the Germans remained aloof. The German government encouraged them to consider themselves not as immigrants but as Germans living abroad, part of a greater Germany. As for citizenship, Imperial Germany sanctioned "double nationality status," and so did the Weimar Republic. Hitler retained and perfected the policy. At the Stuttgart meeting of "Germans Living Abroad," in August 1937, Foreign Minister Konstantin von Neurath proclaimed that "whoever lives abroad is a German first, working primarily in the interest of the German Fatherland."[3]

Although the Germans in Brazil represented less than 5 percent of the total immigration, they and their descendants assumed a place in Brazilian life out of proportion to their numbers. The so-called German element totaled more than a million persons as of 1942, and there were 220,000 German-born residents in Brazil in 1938.[4] They were concentrated in the three southern states of Rio Grande do Sul, Santa Catarina, and Paraná, with smaller but important groups in São Paulo. These were relatively temperate areas of expanding settlement with most of the people attached to the land in small, prosperous, independent farms. Since government patronage was sporadic, the credit of establishing successful settlements belongs to the German immigrants. Generally located in isolated areas, the new com-

[3] Quoted in Whitney H. Shephardson, William O. Scroggs, *The United States in World Affairs, 1940* (New York, 1941), p. 325.

[4] William N. Simonson, "Nazi Infiltration in South America, 1933–1945" (Ph.D. Dissertation, Fletcher School of Law and Diplomacy, 1964), pp. 74–75.

munities preserved German traditions and language. They built churches and schools, importing ministers, priests, and teachers to staff them. They formed numerous sporting, cultural, and other types of associations, all of which helped maintain the mother tongue. An example of the degree to which Germans retained their language was that the seventy-five to one hundred American missionaries, who served in German towns in Rio Grande do Sul and Santa Catarina in 1939, preached and taught in German and knew practically no Portuguese.[5]

In the 1930's well over 50 percent of the Germans and German-Brazilians were engaged in agricultural pursuits. They held about 0.43 percent of the country's cultivated land, produced an estimated 8 percent of Brazil's total agricultural output—in the three southern states it was 24 percent. They also made inroads in the commercial and industrial sections of the economy. Just before World War II, Germans controlled 10 percent of Brazilian industry and 12 percent of commerce. Breweries, cigar factories, textile mills, and mining companies were the main areas of activity.[6]

After Germany fell under Hitler's domination in 1933 "the German citizens of Brazil . . . formed National Socialist associations to express their solidarity with the fatherland."[7]

[5] *Ibid.*, p. 91. As late as 1965 Protestant missionaries came from the United States to work in these communities knowing only German and English, with the idea that Portuguese would not be necessary; conversation of author with minister from Michigan en route to Brazil, Apr. 13, 1965. An interesting fictional account of the German problem is found in Clodomir Vianna Moog, *Um Rio Imita O Reno* (Pôrto Alegre, 1948). It is the story of a young Brazilian engineer's isolation and hardships in a German community in southern Brazil.

[6] Simonson, "Nazi Infiltration," p. 92. By 1965 German ranked second to English as the foreign language most used in business circles in Rio de Janeiro; interview, George Fodor, Director, *Lar Financeira, Banco Lar Brasileiro* (Rio de Janeiro), December 5, 1965.

[7] Reinhard Maack, "The Germans of South Brazil: A German View," *The Quarterly Journal of Inter-American Relations*, I, No. 3 (July 1939) 5–23. Author was a German geographer.

To insure complete and universal conformity Nazi agents worked to bring Nazism into all aspects of the lives of the more than a million people of German descent in Brazil. Not only were *Reichsdeutsche* (those born in Germany) encouraged to join the Brazilian branch of the National Socialist Party, but the German government waged a persistent campaign to promote cultural affinity between *Reichsdeutsche, Volksdeutsche* (Germans born abroad), and the Fatherland.[8]

Hitler included Brazil, indeed all of South America, in his plans for world dictatorship. Hermann Rauschning, Nazi leader in Danzig and a personal friend of Hitler, gave an interesting account of the Fuehrer's plans in *The Voice of Destruction*:

> He was specially interested in Brazil. "We shall create a new Germany there," he cried. "We shall find everything we need there. All the pre-conditions for a revolution were there, a revolution which in a few decades, or even years, would transform a corrupt mestizo state into a German dominion. . . . We shall give them . . . our philosophy. . . . If ever there is a place where democracy is senseless and suicidal, it is in South America. . . . Let us wait a few years, and in the meantime do what we can to help them. But we must send our people out to them. . . . We shall not land troops like William the Conqueror and gain Brazil by the strength of arms. Our weapons are not visible ones. Our conquistadors . . . have a more difficult task than the original ones, and for this reason, they have more difficult weapons."[9]

Hitler's conquistadores were the German diplomatic and consular service; the foreign organizations of the NSDAP and other party agencies; and cultural, economic, and educational associations. Nazi policy toward Brazil had as its ob-

[8] Simonson, "Nazi Infiltration," p. 95.

[9] Hermann Rauschning, *The Voice of Destruction* (New York, 1940), pp. 61–67. He broke with Hitler in 1934 and went into exile in England.

jectives the complete regimentation of German-speaking communities, promotion of cordial relations with Brazil and stimulation of governmental and popular attitudes favorable to Hitler's foreign policy, closer trade relations, and the infiltration of Nazi agents and sympathizers into key positions in the government, armed forces, and economy. The ultimate aim was Nazi conquest and domination to fulfill the Fuehrer's dream of world dictatorship.[10]

In 1936 the Nazi Party established a new organization to overcome the disunity that existed in Brazil among the numerous groups maintaining separate ties with the Fatherland. Named the *Federação 25 de Julho* in honor of the first German settlers who arrived in Brazil on July 25, 1824, it was composed largely of German-Brazilians (*Volksdeutsche*). According to a German embassy report its purpose was to promote "in a nonpolitical manner *Deutschtum* and cultural ties with Germany among German-Brazilians," and to place German-Brazilians in useful political positions.[11] Nazi officials such as the party chief in Brazil, Hans Henning Von Cossel, ostensibly the cultural attaché of the German embassy, closely supervised the organization. The involvement of federation leaders with the Integralistas and their participation in plotting against the Vargas regime led to the arrest of several of them in June 1938. Their arrest became an issue in Brazilian-German relations and will be discussed below.[12]

The Nazis in Brazil were remarkably successful in gaining control of German societies, clubs, and associations. By 1937 they controlled an overwhelming majority of the nearly 2,300 German organizations of all types in the country. As early as 1935 the Nazis had taken over the important German organizations in São Paulo state: fifty-two societies with a combined membership of 15,000, all of whom belonged to a statewide league under the leadership of the São Paulo district chief, Karl Spanaus, and affiliated—con-

[10] Simonson, "Nazi Infiltration," pp. 144–145.
[11] *DGFP*–D, v, 860.   [12] *Ibid.*, pp. 860–863.

trary to Brazilian law—with the League of German Societies Abroad in Berlin.[13]

Increasingly, Nazi activities posed a threat to Brazil's sovereignty and an affront to Brazilian nationalism. The Vargas government, especially after Germany absorbed Austria, could no longer tolerate the situation. In Rio Grande do Sul, under the supervision of Colonels Oswaldo Cordeiro de Farias, chief of staff of the military region, and Aurélio da Silva Py, state chief of police, the state authorities began to move against Nazism in December 1937. They prohibited the wearing of Nazi insignia and the publication of newspaper propaganda favoring National Socialism. They ordered the Nazis to close all their organizations directly connected with foreign headquarters, which included some German-language schools, and instructed all other foreign schools to begin the intensive teaching of Portuguese.[14]

During Vargas' visit to Rio Grande, in January 1938, Colonel Cordeiro de Farias called his attention to Nazi activities in the southern states. Vargas was so impressed with the colonel and his work that he made him federal interventor in Rio Grande to give him a freer hand in dealing with the situation. After consulting with Army Chief of Staff Pedro de Góes Monteiro and Minister of Justice Francisco Campos, the president decided upon an immediate and energetic program to eliminate Nazi activities.

Riograndense authorities closed the state's Nazi headquarters in late February 1938, arrested Ernst Dorsch, the

13 Simonson, "Nazi Infiltration," pp. 290–291.

14 Scotten, Rio, Dec. 23, 1937, 832.00/1155, NA. Unless noted otherwise, all correspondence of the Department of State in this chapter will be from the 832.00 grouping and will be identified only by slash number. There was no immediate public reaction in Germany. The Brazilian ambassador in Berlin, José Joaquim de Lima e Silva Moniz de Aragão, suggested the MRE cite Switzerland, which had also closed German schools, as a precedent; Moniz de Aragão, Berlin, Feb. 19, 1938, #17, AHMRE.

chief Nazi agent in the state, and instituted deportation proceedings. Reich Ambassador Karl Ritter protested immediately. He told the current foreign minister, Mário de Pimentel Brandão (November 1936–March 1938), that the anti-Nazi campaign was a direct slap at Hitler, and that the minister should remember that the ambassador was primarily the representative of the Fuehrer and the Nazi Party and secondarily of Germany. Brazilian-German relations would be impaired seriously if the campaign continued because the question transcended all other problems between the two countries.[15]

Not satisfied with the foreign minister's response, Ritter went to Petrópolis to see Vargas at the Rio Negro Palace, his summer residence. In his anger Ritter took an almost threatening attitude, insisting that the "persecutions" were illegal because the government's decree abolishing political parties specifically referred to Brazilian parties, not foreign ones. He heatedly demanded that the NSDAP be allowed to function in Brazil. Vargas replied sharply that he would not tolerate Nazi activities in the country. At this Ritter softened his tone and pleaded as a friend of Brazil, but the president coolly told him to submit his complaints in writing and ended the audience.[16] Proceedings against Dorsch were halted, but the anti-Nazi campaign continued.

The Integralistas posed a more delicate problem. Their leader had withdrawn from the presidential campaign in November 1937, and they had encouraged Vargas in establishing the Estado Nôvo in the belief that *Integralismo* would be the ideology of the new regime. They learned too

[15] Jefferson Caffery, Feb. 25, 1938, *Foreign Relations, 1938*, v, 408–409. For biographical data on Pimentel Brandão see Chap. 2, note 65.

[16] Caffery, Rio, Feb. 27, 1938, *Foreign Relations, 1938*, v, 409. Vargas sent Aranha down to Rio from Petrópolis to tell Caffery of Ritter's remarks with the request that they be passed on to President Roosevelt. At the same time Aranha told him that he would become foreign minister and that Pimentel Brandão would go to the United States as ambassador.

late that they had been wrong. Getúlio organized a personalist government, with himself firmly in command, that ruled by the consensus of a limited number of Brazilians. He did not need *Integralismo* or its adherents.

For practical political reasons Vargas could not allow the Integralistas to continue; they were a threat to his rule because he could not control them. The *Ação Integralista Brasileira* was the only political party organized nationally according to a coherent body of doctrine and motivated by definite political goals. The organization had the trappings of fascism: green shirts and armbands decorated with the Greek sigma, parades, rallies, and the fascist salute used with a Tupi-Indian word (*anauê*) as a greeting. In 1937, it claimed to have a million members from all levels of Brazilian society. In Integralista parades ladies of the best families marched side by side with laborers, poets, sailors, lawyers, priests, army officers, and small businessmen. The movement had the support of wealthy Brazilians, and it was rumored that it received advice and financial aid from the German and Italian embassies. Although its storm troopers fought their enemies in the streets, such activities did not prevent names of respectable families from appearing on its membership rolls.

In the few years since Paulista journalist Plínio Salgado had founded the movement in 1932, the Integralistas had created a shadow state in anticipation of the day when they would govern Brazil. As Supreme Chief, Salgado headed a hierarchy of leaders and governing bodies at municipal, state, regional, and national levels. In some areas the movement maintained its own courts, medical clinics, milk dispensaries, schools, libraries, and militia. It marketed cigarettes, published two newspapers (*A Ofensiva* and *O Povo*) and a review (*Anauê*) in Rio de Janeiro, and had the support of newspapers in several states. It also kept extensive files on members and enemies. The importance of the party steadily increased after the communist revolt of 1935 and by late 1937 *Integralismo* was clearly a force to be taken into account.[17]

News of Germany's absorption of Austria strengthened Vargas' determination to continue his anti-Nazi and anti-Integralista campaign. From the end of December 1937 police continually raided Integralista centers in various parts of Brazil. The Department of Press and Propaganda closed the Integralista newspapers in Rio de Janeiro, and each week there were new arrests and reported discoveries of arms caches. In early March, a series of incidents indicated that the Integralistas were feeling heavily pressed and were plotting a counterattack. In Recife a group of greenshirts greeted with the illegal party salute three Brazilian submarines which had been purchased in Italy. Nearly all the officers and men of the vessels returned the salute. The incident so angered Vargas that he declared he would not approve the scheduled promotions of the submarines' officers. The naval minister, Admiral Henrique Aristides Guilhem (1930–1945), threatened to resign, as did other high-ranking admirals. And one night in the midst of Carnival, while Vargas was considering the matter, the battleship *São Paulo* and several cruisers and destroyers anchored off the Rio naval base began getting up steam. When the chief of police inquired the reason the fleet commander curtly replied that it was none of his business. Vargas naturally approved the promotions.[18] Meanwhile, in Pôrto Alegre a

[17] Plínio Salgado, *O Integralismo Brasileiro Perante A Nacão* (Lisbon, 1946), pp. 17–26; Alzira Vargas do Amaral Peixoto, *Getúlio Vargas, meu Pai* (Pôrto Alegre, 1960), p. 214; Scotten, Rio, Aug. 25, 1937, /1045 NA; Frederico del Villar, "Life and Death of Brazilian Fascism," *The Inter-American Monthly*, II, No. 5 (June 1943), 16–19. For the development of *Integralismo* see Robert M. Levine, *The Vargas Regime: The Critical Years, 1934–1938* (New York, 1970); and Stanley E. Hilton, "*Ação Integralista Brasileira*: Fascism in Brazil, 1932–1938," *Luso-Brazilian Review*, IX, No. 2 (December 1972), 3–29.

[18] Scotten, Rio, Mar. 7, 1938, /1172, NA. The submarines were the *Tupi*, *Tamoyo*, and *Tymira*. For detailed reports of the Austrian situa-

large shipment of arms and ammunition mysteriously disappeared. The crates arrived safely at the regional army headquarters but they contained only rocks. Arrests and feverish investigation produced nothing.[19]

The government announced on March 18 that it had discovered and disarmed a plot to overthrow the regime, involving Integralistas, which had ramifications in Pernambuco, Bahia, Minas Gerais, São Paulo, Paraná, and Rio Grande do Sul. In a raid several days before, on the home of an Integralista leader in Rio de Janeiro, police found a large store of machine guns, small arms, and ammunition. They also discovered two lists, one of persons to be assassinated, including Vargas, the cabinet, and many prominent Brazilians, and another of army officers loyal to the Integralista cause. The officers, including some generals, were arrested, as were many civilians all over Brazil. The jails and army barracks were so crowded that concentration camps for political prisoners were set up in Minas Gerais and on the island of Fernando de Noronha. The press gave great publicity to the plot and popular feeling ran high against the greenshirts.[20]

In mid-March, just after taking charge of the foreign ministry, Aranha refused a strongly-worded note from the German ambassador concerning the arrest of Nazi agents. In one of several unfriendly encounters between Aranha and Ritter the German became so abusive that the minister, ordinarily an extremely gracious individual, nearly threw him

---

tion and Germany's military preparations see Ambassador Moniz de Aragão's reports in the AHMRE: e.g. Mar. 12, 1938, #28; Mar. 14, 1938, #29; Aug. 15, 1938, #87.

[19] Scotten, Rio, Mar. 14, 1938, /1179, NA.

[20] Caffery, Rio, Jan. 3, 1938, /1160; Scotten, Rio, Jan. 28, 1938, /1164; Scotten, Rio, Mar. 4, 1938, /1170; Scotten, Rio, Mar. 11, 1938, /1176; Scotten, Rio, Mar. 14, 1938, /1179; Caffery, Rio, Mar. 14, 1938, /1466; Caffery, Rio, Mar. 18, 1938, /1178; Scotten, Rio, Mar. 18, 1938, /1181; Scotten, Rio, Mar. 25, 1938, /1182, all NA.

bodily out of his office.[21] Berlin considered Aranha pro-American and unalterably opposed to its policies, and instructed its embassy in Rio de Janeiro to do everything to bring about his downfall.[22] The Germans were correct in assuming that Aranha was pro-American, but this did not mean that he was controlled by the Americans. He favored the United States because of Washington's traditional policy of supporting Brazilian hegemony in South America and because he did not believe the United States posed a threat to Brazilian sovereignty or security. While he was a personal friend of Undersecretary of State Sumner Welles and maintained extremely close, cordial relations with American Ambassador Jefferson Caffery, he was his own man—determined to preserve Brazilian independence and freedom of action. Aranha's accession to the foreign ministership was important to the United States and hailed as such in newspaper columns and in the halls of the State Department. This was not because Aranha was an American puppet but because he was a disciple of the Baron of Rio Branco. He believed that Brazilian-American unity meant peace and security for the hemisphere, and would assist Brazil in achieving its predicted greatness.

Throughout March the Brazilian government was carefully drafting a decree forbidding political activity by foreign organizations. Apparently there was considerable discussion within the government as to content and timing. The German population, after all, was generally peaceful and on amicable terms with their Brazilian neighbors—the unpleasant situation had been caused by the aggressive tactics of the Nazis. A clumsy move against German organizations might bring a break in diplomatic relations, or worse, a naval bombardment of Brazil's exposed seaports.

[21] Drew Pearson, "Merry-Go-Round," *Washington Post*, Feb. 11, 1939. Pearson and Aranha became friends during the latter's ambassadorship in Washington and carried on a lively correspondence until Aranha's death. See Drew Pearson file in OAA.

[22] Caffery, Rio, Mar. 18, 1938, /1178, NA.

The Department of State's attitude was one of caution and concern, not interference. It welcomed detailed information from Brazilian officials on Nazi activities, but avoided giving advice because it was a purely Brazilian affair. Undersecretary Welles, indeed, even refused to comment on the timing of the decree, so German accusations that the United States was responsible for their problems gave the American authorities undue credit. The Americans generally avoided mixing in internal matters, outside the economic sphere. This was wise because Brazilian leaders would not have tolerated such interference, no matter how well intentioned.[23]

While the decree was being prepared the Germans aggravated the situation by an article, on March 21, in the *Deutsche Diplomatische Korrespondenz*, news organ of the German Foreign Office (Wilhelmstrasse), sharply criticizing the Brazilian government for its repressive measures. The article, acknowledged by German officials as expressing the government's thought, produced intense reactions against the Reich in Brazilian press and official circles; Rio newspapers strongly condemned this "interference" in Brazil's internal affairs. The general theme of editorial comment was that immigrants were welcome, but there could be no minority groups. The article also caused strong anti-German reactions in the press of Uruguay, Argentina, and Chile, which expressed alarm over the extent of Nazi infiltration in Brazil and condemned the undiplomatic attitude of the Reich's official representatives. Their comments were headlined in Brazilian newspapers.[24]

At the end of March, Vargas felt that the situation was secure enough for him to leave the capital for a rest at the

[23] *Ibid.*; Caffery, Rio, Mar. 7, 1938, *Foreign Relations, 1938*, v, 411–412; Sumner Welles to Caffery, Rio, Mar. 21, 1938, /1178, NA; Oswaldo Aranha to Getúlio Vargas, Rio, Mar. 29, 1938, OAA.

[24] Scotten, Rio, Mar. 25, 1938, /1182, NA; Simonson, "Nazi Infiltration," p. 470; Moniz de Aragão, Berlin, Mar. 22, 1938, #32; Mar. 25, 1938, #35; Mar. 26, 1938, #36, AHMRE.

spas of Minas Gerais (Poços de Caldas and São Lourenço). He was quite content with the course of events, and spent much of his time playing golf, which he had recently taken up. He remarked to a reporter: "my luck at golf . . . and other things . . . has been very good."[25] Chancellor Aranha's luck had been good, too. Since entering the government his strength had grown rapidly. Other cabinet ministers reportedly consulted him before every major decision.[26] His influence was important in the formulation of the anti-Nazi decree of April 18, 1938, which declared illegal all foreign political organizations and provided a thirty-day period in which they were to disband. It allowed foreign cultural, educational, and aid societies to continue under the close supervision of the Ministry of Justice. Ambassador Ritter made an immediate oral protest to Justice Minister Campos, and in a report to the Wilhelmstrasse recommended that the German press treat the decree as "a consciously unfriendly act against Germany attributable to the influence of the United States."[27]

An article in the newspaper *Essener National Zeitung* voiced one of the more moderate German press reactions and was quoted in Rio's *O Jornal* on May 1: "We do not understand the reasons which motivated this action, nor can we understand what benefit Brazil can derive from it. . . . the friendship . . . between Brazil and Germany has been disturbed. . . . No government on earth can promulgate laws prohibiting to us Germans the expressions of our feelings."[28]

In late April, the Rio press carried the text of another article appearing in the *Berliner Boersen Zeitung*, which criticized American press attacks against "supposed Nazi

[25] Scotten, Rio, Apr. 1, 1938, /1186, NA.

[26] *Ibid.*; Aranha to Vargas, Rio, Mar. 29, 1938, OAA; Scotten, Rio, Apr. 4, 1938, /1187, NA.

[27] *DGFP*–D, V, 833; Scotten, Rio, Apr. 22, 1938, *Foreign Relations, 1938*, V, 412–413.

[28] *O Jornal*, Rio, May 1, 1938.

ambitions" in Brazil. The article attributed these attacks to American concern over the growth of Brazilian-German trade: "We understand very well this so-called idealism. Germany, right from the start, has been one of Brazil's best customers for Brazilian cotton, and the Yankee planters found themselves in the position of losing their markets."[29] Brazilian authorities took several other measures to curb Nazi infiltration and activities. In April 1938, for example, the governments of Paraná, Santa Catarina, and Rio Grande do Sul issued instructions reorganizing foreign-language schools within their borders, requiring that instruction be given in Portuguese, prohibiting foreign subsidies, and otherwise providing for the Brazilianization of these institutions.[30] In addition, police in the south raided the homes of Nazi agents, which led to the discovery of large quantities of Nazi literature printed in Germany, and to the arrest and deportation of several important party functionaries.[31]

The measures against foreign political activity and foreign-language schools affected other nationalities besides the Germans. The government forced Italian Fascists to shut down their operations among Italian immigrants, who were especially numerous in São Paulo. The Italian ambassador and consular officials gave up their customary black shirts and Fascist emblems without the blustering of their Nazi colleagues. The ambassador stated his country's attitude when he said: "South America is Latin, and will continue to be Latin."[32] The Italians knew that futile protests would only harden the Brazilian position, and besides their schools apparently were not molested. Being Latin and Catholic, the Italians had a rapport with the Brazilians that neither the Germans nor the Americans could achieve, and they would not endanger it. The German Foreign Office

29 Quoted in Simonson, "Nazi Infiltration," p. 472.
30 *Ibid.*
31 Scotten, Rio, Apr. 22, 1938, /1191, NA.
32 Scotten, Rio, Apr. 22, 1938, *Foreign Relations, 1938*, V, 412-413.

rather enviously asked its ambassadors in Brazil, Argentina, and Chile to investigate Italy's experiences in the field of the cultural struggle and the organization of the Fascist Party abroad, since "we can perhaps make use of them in the present situation."[33]

On May 10 Ritter handed a written protest to Aranha, arguing that the German National Socialist Party, unlike political parties in other countries, was a state party entrusted with official functions and, therefore, the April 18 decree struck at "an organ of administration of the German state." The Nazi Party, he insisted, was strictly forbidden to intervene in the affairs of host countries, and he protested against the "systematic campaign of press agitation against Germany and everything German" in Brazil.[34] His timing could not have been worse, for that night shortly before one A.M. a group of Integralistas and Vargas opponents made a last futile bid for power.

The greenshirts were far from the center of attention as darkness settled over Rio de Janeiro on May 10, 1938. The day had passed without incident, save for the disappointing news from Europe that Argentina had purchased a large quantity of arms in Czechoslovakia, thereby breaking its agreement with Brazil and Chile not to increase its military strength. After a conference with General Góes Monteiro and Minister of Finance Artur de Souza Costa, Vargas had retired for the night. At midnight the only lights in the Guanabara Palace were in the residential wing. Suddenly shots shattered the stillness of the palace gardens. Integralistas in marine uniforms, joined by the commander of the palace's own marine guards, opened fire on the presidential quarters and on a handful of loyal guards. Four of the latter were killed, but fortunately another kept the rebels out of the interior courtyard by refusing to unlock the heavy wrought-iron gate. Only by a frontal assault across the open

[33] *DGFP–D*, v, 852–853. Document dated May 12, 1938.
[34] *Ibid.*, p. 833, note 4.

garden could the attackers reach the palace, and because of confused instructions, a lack of courage, or poor leadership they never made the effort.

Inside, the defenders included Vargas, his wife, his daughter Alzira, and a few members of the president's staff who slept in the palace. They were armed only with pistols and one machine gun. After some time the shooting became desultory, the defenders unable to get out and the attackers unable to get in. So it went through the night until help finally arrived shortly before dawn.

The military reacted cautiously. Minister of War Dutra, still in civilian clothes after a celebration at the Ministry of Justice commemorating the Estado Nôvo's sixth month, eluded some would-be attackers and gathered a handful of troops from Fort Leme. While he was placing them in blocking positions before the palace an Integralista bullet grazed his ear. Despite the greenshirts he managed to reach the entrance and inform those inside that help was on the way. Then as police began to join his men he commandeered a motorcycle to scurry across the city to police headquarters, where he found Filinto Müller and Colonel Oswaldo Cordeiro de Farias. Sending the colonel to Guanabara Palace to coordinate the rescue, Dutra went on to the office of the First Military Region and ordered artillery into position, ready to fire on the naval ministry which Integralista naval personnel had seized. Though the minister of war had managed to approach the palace, other would-be rescuers hesitated. General Francisco José Pinto, chief of the president's military staff, declined to send aid from among the guards at the Catete, alleging that they were untrustworthy and too few to protect the executive office building let alone undertake relief missions. In a comic-opera scenario soldiers under Cordeiro de Farias and João Alberto Lins de Barros waited a considerable time in the Fluminense Football Club, on the opposite side of the palace from the garden, without making a serious attempt to attack the Integralistas by way of the street in front or to force open the locked door between the palace and the club. Apparently they were looking for the key![35]

At the naval ministry across the city Integralistas had set up machine guns on the two top floors. Artillery fire from the naval arsenal on the Ilha das Cobras, several hundred yards across the channel in front of the ministry, eventually dislodged them. Four were killed and many wounded in the shooting, and the new ministry building was damaged severely. An attempt to seize the destroyer *Bahia* failed, as did a plan to take over the Panair do Brasil facilities at Santos Dumont airport. In Rio's business district there was fighting at the Esplanado do Castelo. Surprise attacks on the residences of the minister of war, chief of staff, commander of Vila Militar, and the commander of the military police were unsuccessful. At dawn it was all over: loyal troops had captured most of the rebels.[36]

The American and German ambassadors displayed different points of view in reporting the results of the abortive revolt. Ambassador Caffery said the general public reaction was one of strong feeling against the Integralistas, and of extreme sympathy with the president. A personal attack of this nature was foreign to Brazilian revolutionary technique; it produced indignation and unquestionably enhanced Vargas' popularity. His bravery was acclaimed, as was his calmness in the morning when he walked unguarded down Rua Paissandu from the Guanabara to Catete Palace to carry on affairs of state as usual. He smiled and nodded to the applauding crowds on the way.[37]

[35] Alzira Vargas, *Getúlio*, pp. 115–133; Lourival Coutinho, *O General Góes Depõe* (Rio de Janeiro, 1956), pp. 348–353; Caffery, May 16, 1938, Revolutions/607, NA; Hélio Silva, *1938, Terrorismo em Campo Verde* (Rio de Janeiro, 1971), pp. 197–233.

[36] Caffery, Rio, May 12, 1938, Revolutions/604, NA; for an unofficial account see Jay Rice to Evan Young, Rio, May 12, 1938, Cauby C. Araújo Papers (Rio de Janeiro). Rice, Young, and Araújo were Pan-American Airways executives. One Panair captain was arrested as a subversive.

[37] Caffery, Rio, May 12, 1938, Revolutions/604, NA; Alzira Vargas,

Ambassador Ritter saw the situation differently. He assured Berlin that the events of May 10–11 had caused the Vargas regime to "become even more unpopular . . . than before." Vargas would have to enforce his dictatorship more severely in order to remain in power. He admitted that rumors of German involvement would cause "the feeling toward everything German" to "deteriorate further." Ritter commented caustically that such a poorly-executed revolt and sloppy response was "possible only in a country like Brazil." In view of Brazil's unfriendly attitude toward German interests, Ritter urged that the German press give the insurrection sensational treatment—to make the Brazilians realize that their position on the German question was impractical. Emphasis should be on popular discontent with "Vargas' complete submission to the orders of the United States of America" and with his "betrayal of the Integralist movement." In view of the dictatorial rule in Brazil, he declared it was "no less than grotesque for North America and other American countries continually to hold up the example of democratic government to the European countries with authoritarian governments."[38]

Ritter apparently did not take the trouble to report the demonstration of popular support that took place on May 13 in front of the Catete. Vargas addressed a large crowd and received such an ovation that he had to make a few additional remarks after concluding his prepared speech. He condemned the Integralistas for abusing the invocations dearest to the Brazilian heart—God, country, family—by committing treason. They would be punished. Declaring that this vulgar episode should be turned into "a point of departure of a new order," he called upon the Brazilian people to defend the nation. In this speech and later ones at Vila Militar and the naval academy, he praised the

---

Getúlio, pp. 130–131; for a summary account with documents and interviews, see Hélio Silva, *1938, Terrorismo Em Campo Verde.*

[38] *DGFP*–D, v, 837–839.

armed forces and promised to continue their rearmament. His vocation, he asserted, was to serve Brazil, and he preferred death to ceding a line of the Estado Nôvo's program for national reconstruction.[39]

Arrests of Integralistas and Germans took place immediately. The authorities took nearly 1,600 into custody, a third of whom turned out to be enlisted men and noncommissioned officers in the various services, an embarrassing fact for the government. Police arrested the greenshirts' ruling Council of Forty, and Vargas retired ten officers of the Federal District's police force.[40] A knowledgeable foreign observer commented that the events of May marked "the death knell" of the Integralista movement, while "the Government now emerges stronger than ever before"; and he predicted that a companion reaction would probably "be a tendency toward further curbing of Nazi influence."[41] On cue the Brazilian press began connecting Germans with the plot and implied that high officials of the Reich embassy were involved. Vargas was quoted as saying that the plotters had "help from the outside."[42] Although he may have been referring to money from Flôres da Cunha, the Germans were paranoiac enough to assume that he meant them.

The German press heatedly charged Vargas with using Germans in Brazil as scapegoats to divert public attention from American domination and economic penetration. According to one newspaper, the *Deutsche Allgemeine Zeitung*, the anti-German campaign increased appreciably

[39] Getúlio Vargas, *A Nova Política do Brasil* (Rio de Janeiro, 1938–47, V, 211–213; Caffery, Rio, May 16, 1938, Revolution/607, NA; Vargas, *Nova Política*, v, 219–221, 233–235 (Vila Militar on May 15, 1938 and Escola Naval on June 11, 1938); Caffery, Rio, May 19, 1938, Revolutions/610, NA. In view of the circumstances of Vargas' suicide in 1954, the comment about preferring death to surrender would seem to be more than mere rhetoric.

[40] Caffery, Rio, June 10, 1938, Revolutions/602, NA; Levine, *Vargas Regime*, 164.

[41] Jay Rice to Evan Young, Rio, May 12, 1938, Araújo Papers.

[42] *DGFP–D*, v, 841.

after the appointment of Aranha as foreign minister; an appointment made, it said, at the wish if not the order of the United States.[43]

After much investigation the Brazilian government announced that evidence indicated that a group of Integralistas had organized the plot in conjunction with sympathizers in the navy. They hoped to kill Vargas and several cabinet members and seize power in the resultant confusion. The Integralistas were convinced that they would be able to obtain the full support of the navy and that the army would accept the *fait accompli*. The official report freed German diplomats of suspicion, even though Aranha told Ambassador Caffery that the president, the minister of war, and the chief of the general staff all thought that the German representatives not only knew and sympathized with the plotters but took part in the planning.[44]

The correspondence of the Reich embassy in Rio de Janeiro indicates that these suspicions were unfounded, at least as far as Ritter was concerned. However sympathetic he may have been with the plot, owing to the clash of personalities between the Brazilians and himself, he does not seem to have known of the affair in advance. Even so the ambassador's attitude had a negative influence on Brazilian-German relations. He was convinced of the supremacy of the Reich and impatient with the twists and turns of Brazilian politics. In conversations and diplomatic notes he was often blunt and discourteous to the point of being offensive. He was a perfect example of a crisp, dedicated Prussian diplomat of the type depicted in Hollywood films, though he was sometimes ruffled when Nazi agents acted without his knowledge.[45]

Ritter continually protested the arrest of German nationals and the suppression of the Nazi Party. He com-

---

[43] Prentiss B. Gilbert, Berlin, May 17, 1938, *Foreign Relations, 1938*, v, 415; Moniz de Aragão, Berlin, May 16, 1938, #62, AHMRE.

[44] Caffery, Rio, May 21, 1938, *Foreign Relations, 1938*, v, 417.

[45] *DGFP–D*, v, 861–862.

plained repeatedly about the regulations forbidding the use
of German in schools and churches, and requiring all text-
books to be in Portuguese. These laws he insisted were due
to American influence.[46] On May 13, 1938, Ritter delivered
a protest to the Brazilian foreign ministry against the arrest
of German citizens supposedly connected with the Integralista *Putsch,* and repeated his violent protest of May 10
against the anti-Nazi decree. Aranha coolly told him that
if Germans had been arrested there was undoubtedly good
reason, and that the government would not modify the decree of April 18.[47]

That same day in Berlin the state secretary of the German foreign office, Ernst Weizsäcker, who was apprehensive that a break was about to occur, called in the Brazilian
ambassador, José Joaquim de Lima e Silva Moniz de
Aragão (June 1936–October 1938), and emphatically told
him that Brazil's measures against Germans "had caused
great excitement in Germany," and might permanently
damage relations between the two countries. He urged the
ambassador to persuade Rio to rescind its anti-German
measures, to release those whose guilt could not be firmly
established, and to end the inflammatory newspaper campaign against Germany. Moniz de Aragão replied that he
hoped he could obtain what the state secretary wished.
Weizsäcker notified Ritter of this conversation, and told him
that the steps he had taken in Brazil had the "full approval"
of the foreign office, and that he could further sharpen the
tone of his demarches; the state secretary reminded him,
however, that Germany had "no means of pressure available." Nevertheless the importance of preserving the German colony in Brazil required "plain speaking."[48]

Ritter realized the weakness of his position and sought
permission from the Wilhelmstrasse to use threats: either

[46] *Ibid.,* p. 833, note 4.

[47] Caffery, Rio, May 13, 1938, *Foreign Relations, 1938,* v, 414–415.

[48] *DGFP*–D, v, 839–840; Moniz de Aragão, Berlin, May 17, 1938, #63;
May 18, 1938, #64, AHMRE.

his own departure or severance of diplomatic relations if his demands were not met. However, his report of May 14 that Vargas had "precise information" regarding foreign intervention caused the foreign office to hesitate. If, as the result of "bungling," Germans were actually involved in the May 11 affair it could be very embarrassing, and the foreign minister wanted to be sure of his ground before taking energetic action. Relations with Brazil were too important to make mistakes. Ritter assured the foreign office that no Germans had bungled or made mistakes, and that he was now convinced the Brazilians had no proof of German involvement.[49]

Meanwhile, the Nazi Party had decided on a strategic retreat in Latin America. The head of the *Auslandsorganization* (AO) sent a circular telegram on May 18 to all German missions in the area saying that the situation required avoidance of open activity and concentration on internal indoctrination: dismissal of *Volksdeutsche* from the party, the German Labor Front, and sponsored organizations; withdrawal of German nationals from *Volksdeutsche* political groups, and the formation of their own groups under party leadership.[50]

Also on May 18 the Brazilian ambassador in Berlin persuaded the foreign office that German press attacks on Vargas should be stopped in return for a similar calming of the Brazilian press. He pointed out that even in the worst days of the crisis the Brazilian press, though accusing Germans of involvement, had not attacked Hitler personally. The ambassador agreed to recommend to his government the immediate release of all Germans whose guilt was not indisputably established, and to urge the issuance of a communiqué absolving Germany of any suspicion of participation in the May 11 plot. The Brazilian government released

---

[49] *DGFP–D*, v, 840–843.

[50] *Ibid.*, p. 843. For effect of these instructions in Brazil see *Delegacia Especial de Segurança Política e Social* (DESPS), Boletim Informativa: "Frente Alemã do Trabalho," May 9, 1939, OAA.

a statement on May 21 to the effect that it had no "evidence
. . . that German firms and German nationals participated
in or lent support to the events of May 11."[51] In addition,
the Brazilian ambassador in Berlin officially informed the
foreign office that no German nationals were involved in the
fiasco. The German press immediately expressed satisfaction and changed its tone, describing the Brazilian announcement as "in line with the farsightedness of the Chief
of State of the great South American Republic," and noted
that it created an atmosphere conducive to the solution of
other questions.[52]

The German embassy in Rio, however, was not behaving
in a manner conducive to preserving such an atmosphere.
The head of the Nazi Party in Brazil, Hans Henning von
Cossel, left for Germany in the week of May 20 by special
plane. Before he went Ritter had taken him to see Filinto
Müller, Federal District chief of police, to obtain a statement that there were no complaints or suspicions against
him, but his hurried departure was more likely to arouse
suspicion than to ease it.[53]

During a visit to the foreign ministry on May 21, Ritter
turned down Aranha's invitation to attend a social function
a few days later. He told Aranha he did not consider it "appropriate . . . to dance at a ball of the foreign minister as
long as German nationals were under arrest on the entirely
unfounded suspicion of having somehow taken part" in the
recent revolt. This statement produced a rather heated exchange in which Aranha said he would instruct his ambassador in Berlin not to accept any more invitations from the
German government. Ritter shot back that this would not
be necessary as the Brazilian ambassador would "receive
no more invitations from the German government in any
case, as long as the NSDAP was forbidden" in Brazil. Aranha

---

[51] *DGFP–D*, v, 843–844, 845, note 5.

[52] Hugh R. Wilson, Berlin, May 27, 1938, *Foreign Relations, 1938*,
v, 418–419.

[53] Caffery, Rio, May 20, 1938, *ibid.*, p. 416.

was very angry and abruptly ended the conversation. In this incident Ritter had acted without the prior approval of Berlin, which led to a strong reprimand from the Wilhelm-strasse and instructions to tell Aranha that there was no so-cial boycott of the Brazilian ambassador in Germany.[54] This affair appears to have convinced Aranha that Ritter, whom he personally disliked, had exceeded the limits of proper diplomatic behavior and that Berlin should replace him.

While the suspicion of German involvement in the at-tempted coup distracted the foreign ministry and Rio de Janeiro's diplomatic community, Brazilian politicians and military men were absorbed in observing the political situa-tion resulting from the affair. Rumors of plots still circu-lated in the capital and Vargas' position was difficult at best,[55] but during the week of June 10 the Brazilians' fanati-cal love of *futebol* suddenly "killed all rumors and interest in politics."[56] The Brazilian team's unexpected victories in the international soccer matches in France stirred Brazilian patriotism, and the press devoted most of its space to the team's activities. The American ambassador commented that it was "no exaggeration to state that this subject tran-scended all others in every walk of Brazilian life . . . so much so that politics and the rumors of weakness of the Vargas regime were a dead issue. . . ." The *futebol* "inter-lude" was "very helpful for President Vargas."[57]

The German ambassador's position was further weak-ened in late June 1938 when police arrested several Ger-man-Brazilians and Nazi Party members closely associated with von Cossel's Nazi infiltration activities. According to Ritter, the authorities found compromising documents in the possession of some of these individuals. One document

---

[54] *DGFP–D*, v, 853–854; O. Aranha to Moniz de Aragão, Rio, May 21, 1938, #50, Exp. 1463, AHMRE.

[55] Caffery, Rio, May 16, 1938, Revolutions/607, NA.

[56] Caffery, Rio, June 24, 1938, Revolutions/627, NA. These were Góes Monteiro's words to Caffery on June 20.

[57] Caffery, Rio, June 17, 1938, /1199, NA.

was a detailed plan for an Integralista uprising in southern Brazil and another directly linked the embassy and the ambassador with Nazi political activities in the country. These developments forced Ritter to grant asylum in the embassy to two party "comrades" and to request safe-conduct permits from the foreign ministry for their departure from Brazil.[58]

Without warning, on June 26, Foreign Minister Aranha became personally involved in the aftermath of the May 11 affair. His brother, Captain Manoel Aranha, a member of General Góes Monteiro's staff, and several other general staff officers aided the leader of the assault on Guanabara Palace, ex-Lieutenant Severo Fournier, to obtain asylum in the Italian embassy. Captain Manoel had no Integralista sympathies, but Fournier's father was a friend and had begged him to help his son because he had heard the police would not take him alive. The officers were arrested and Minister of War Dutra demanded that Vargas retire them from the service, or he would resign. A crisis ensued. General Góes Monteiro submitted a *pro forma* resignation which Vargas refused. The Aranha family held a meeting chaired by the dowager, Luiza de Freitas Valle Aranha, at which they decided that all members of the clan should withdraw from the Vargas government. Oswaldo Aranha was dispirited as he wrote Getúlio that he could not continue as chancellor, that he had to "respect the reaction" of his "old and sainted mother."[59] But Vargas refused to replace him, saying:

> Our friendship is older than our existence; it is a family tradition. . . . We worked together in Rio Grande and on the national scene; our loyal comradeship, frank collaboration, mutual support during long years . . . were always a motive of constant and reciprocal satisfaction.

[58] *DGFP–D*, v, 860–863.

[59] Aranha to Vargas, Rio, June 26, 1938, OAA. Aranha wrote: "terei que respeitar a reação de minha santa e velha mae. . . ."

. . . I was accustomed to seeing you as a sort of a younger brother . . . now . . . you resolve, in consequence of the unhappy event in which your brother Manoel took part, to ask dismissal. I do not see . . . how this occurrence . . . could be reason for your removal. . . . You well know I am profoundly and sincerely sorry for what happened to your brother. . . . It was a case of conscience and not of family. . . . It was my duty to do what I did . . . rest a little and return to work . . . I will not accept your resignation.[60]

Whether personal or political reasons were uppermost in Getúlio's mind in this instance is not known. Possibly he was afraid to allow Aranha to leave the government because his great popularity could easily make him a center of the opposition. He did all in his power to keep Oswaldo in the cabinet. The president's aged father, General Manoel do Nascimento Vargas, telegraphed Senhora Aranha the elder from Pôrto Alegre asking her to change her mind. Dona Darcy, Getúlio's wife, made several visits to Aranha's wife seeking her support. Getúlio, appealing to Oswaldo's sense of Gaúcho solidarity, said the Paulistas and Mineiros were saying that once they got the Gaúchos out of power they would see to it that they never returned. In the end, Aranha's mother gave in and consented to his remaining in the government. Aranha and Dutra exchanged *abraços* and explanations of their misunderstanding. Fournier left the Italian embassy, accompanied by his father and two Brazilian army officers, to surrender to police. The affair ended to the satisfaction of everyone—except perhaps Fournier, who went to jail.[61]

[60] Vargas to Aranha, Rio, July 1, 1938, OAA.

[61] Caffery, Rio, June 29 to July 15, 1938, Revolutions/621–636, NA. Fournier's fear of being shot by police may have had some basis. Góes Monteiro claimed that several of the captured Integralista attackers were executed on the spot; Coutinho, *General Góes*, pp. 353–355. Ambassador Ritter mentioned police brutality and suspected that the secretary of the *Federação 25 de Julho* was murdered by his jailers; *DGFP*-D, v,

From late May to late September 1938 the Brazilian ambassador in Berlin repeatedly intimated to the foreign office that it would be "very convenient for German-Brazilian relations" if Ritter were replaced. He also suggested that von Cossel, who had left Brazil in May for consultations in Germany, should not return. The Wilhelmstrasse persistently ignored Brazil's wishes. Von Cossel returned to Rio de Janeiro as cultural attaché in early July, and was later promoted to counselor for cultural affairs. And Ritter, who had gone to Germany to attend *Auslandsorganization* conferences and the annual party rally at Nuremberg, was to return to Brazil in late September. At a meeting with Nazi Party chiefs and officials of the Ministry of Economics, Ritter, who had previously lauded Brazil in public on several occasions, declared that it was urgent for Germany to initiate a new policy of close friendship with the republic. The German leaders were so impressed with his presentations that they determined to ignore Brazilian objections and to keep him at the Rio post. Before leaving for Genoa, where he was to embark for Brazil, Ritter told Moniz de Aragão that he hoped to remain in Rio only until the following April, when he would transfer to a post at home. He appeared, as Moniz de Aragão cabled Aranha, "disposed to collaborate with the Brazilian Government in a spirit of frank cordiality."[62] Aranha would have none of it. On the afternoon of September 21 he telephoned Berlin and instructed his ambassador to attempt once again to secure

---

860–863. As a result of the May 11 affair Vargas amended the Constitution of November 10, 1937, to provide the death penalty for crimes of treason, especially for violence against the regime or the president (Law 1, May 16, 1938). But the measure was not made retroactive so it did not apply to the May 11 rebels; Caffery, Rio, May 19, 1938, Revolutions/609, NA. Hélio Silva concluded that eight or nine were shot after they surrendered but *not* on orders from Vargas or Dutra, rather the Special Police took instant action; see *1938, Terrorismo em Campo Verde*, pp. 234–239.

[62] Moniz de Aragão, Berlin, Aug. 29, 1938, #90; Sept. 20, 1938, #101, AHMRE.

Ritter's replacement, and, failing that, to inform the foreign ministry that Ritter was *persona non grata*. The ambassador took pains to explain that his government desired cordial relations and increased trade with Germany but that Ritter had proven himself unsuitable as ambassador and his presence in Brazil was harmful.[63] The main complaint against Ritter was that he "had not complied with the usual formalities of courtesy"; once, he had sent "such an impolite note to the Brazilian government that he himself had later withdrawn it."[64] The Germans refused to be graceful about it and forced the stronger, more distasteful alternative, insisting that Ritter had done his duty and merited the Reich government's full confidence. He returned from Genoa and —an apparent indication of the government's esteem—became head of the foreign ministry's economic section. In retaliation Aranha, at the beginning of October, publicly ordered Moniz de Aragão's departure. Berlin attempted to obtain a statement that the withdrawal of ambassadors was not occasioned by evidence of German complicity in the affair of May 11, but agreement on a text proved impossible.[65] Chargés d'affaires handled diplomatic business in the two capitals from October 1938 until June 1939.

The rapid deterioration of Brazilian-German relations between January and October 1938 was primarily the result of Ambassador Ritter's ineptitude in dealing with Brazilian leaders. He displayed no understanding of Brazil or its people, he ignored the most basic necessity for doing business in the country, namely the need for friends. He alienated all but the most ardent Germanophiles and was consequently hamstrung. Berlin subsequently came to understand that

[63] *Ibid.*, Sept. 21, 1938, #102; Sept. 22, 1938, #103, AHMRE.

[64] *DGFP–D*, v, 873.

[65] Moniz de Aragão, Berlin, Oct. 1, 1938, #111; Oct. 3, 1938, #113; Oct. 6, 1938, #114, and other documents bound with these in AHMRE. See also comments in Themistocles Graça Aranha (Chargé d'Affaires), Berlin, Feb. 18, 1939, #920 (42) (81) and stamped received Mar. 7, 1939, AHMRE; *DGFP–D*, v, 868, 872–874.

the Brazilians would not tolerate open Nazi activity and the new ambassador, named in mid-1939, was a man who knew how to function in Brazil. When the final break with Germany came in January 1942 it would not be the result of the acrimonious behavior of Reich diplomats but of a resolution of the Rio Conference.

While the Estado Nôvo was an authoritarian dictatorship it was not subservient to the Axis powers, as some American observers feared at the time. Vargas' willingness to face German displeasure demonstrated his independence. Nor did he intend to be an American puppet. He was primarily interested in the well-being of his country and would not tolerate foreign interference from any quarter. His actions against the Nazis and Integralistas eliminated groups that were a threat to Brazil and to his regime. Vargas showed himself throughout to be more interested in establishing a personalist government that would advance Brazilian development than in any form of fixed ideology.

*". . . to readjust our friendship . . . giving to
Americans the security of our aid in any
international circumstances and to Brazilians
the tranquility necessary to allow them to work
without . . . criminal threats to their destiny."*[1]

4

Security of the Western Hemisphere

THE INCREASING German interest and activity in
Brazil and Spanish-America in the late 1930's caused anxiety in Washington. Gradually, during 1938 the United
States prepared diplomatically for a confrontation. It re-
vamped the Latin American section of the State Department, it attempted to develop a workable arms-supply
policy, and it sought to strengthen hemispheric unity. The
Vargas government reacted strongly against Nazi activities
in Brazil, even while the Brazilian army purchased weapons
in Germany. Chancellor Aranha proposed that Brazil and
the United States cooperate in defense, and that the Pan-
American conference scheduled to meet at Lima in December discuss a hemispheric security pact. Although Argentine opposition made a pact impossible it served to push
Brazil and the United States closer together.

While the State Department was working to maintain the
American position in Brazil, it sought to improve relations
with the other American republics. In recognition of the increasing importance of Latin America, Secretary of State
Cordell Hull ordered reorganization of the department's
Latin American sections. He established a Division of American Republics in May 1938 that absorbed the former Divi-

[1] Aranha to Welles, Rio, Nov. 8, 1938, OAA.

sions of Latin American and Mexican Affairs. By the end of that year the division consisted of fourteen officers, who concerned themselves with commodity problems, Axis economic and political activities, Inter-American conferences, military and naval cooperation, and trade agreements. They placed emphasis on research in connection with policy planning, spending nearly a fifth of their time in that activity. The division cooperated with other government agencies to promote good will between the United States and Latin America.[2]

President Roosevelt took the first step in marshaling the government's resources in February 1938, when he appointed an interdepartmental committee to formulate a policy for international broadcasting aimed at countering Axis shortwave propaganda. In May he ordered the Departments of State, War, and Navy to form a second interdepartmental committee to study the promotion of closer relations with Latin America, and in July approved the creation of the Division of Cultural Relations in the Department of State to foster intellectual cooperation. Shortly, a program for improving cultural relations began to take shape. The Federal Communications Commission granted permission to major American networks to transmit shortwave programs to Latin America in Portuguese and Spanish. These featured music and news and were devoid of overt propaganda. In June Congress authorized the loan of radio experts to other governments, and Welles discussed with Brazilian Ambassador Mário de Pimentel Brandão the possibility of sending such technicians to Brazil. Several years earlier Brazil had suggested that the two countries exchange broadcasts, but at the time no American network had been technically prepared. At the end of 1938 the National Broadcasting Company and the Columbia Broadcast-

[2] Graham H. Stuart, "The New Office of American Republics Affairs in the Department of State," *The American Political Science Review*, xxxiv, No. 3 (June 1945), 483–484.

ing System were ready if Brazil was still interested.[3] With a government subsidy Moore-McCormack Lines inaugurated regular passenger steamship service to Rio de Janeiro and Buenos Aires with the refitted and rechristened *Argentina, Brazil,* and *Uruguay,* comfortable vessels which offered accommodations comparable to the Axis ships plying South America's eastern coast. The company offered special fares to teachers and students who would spend a year in the country of destination.[4] These programs were the basis for the later operations of the Office of the Coordinator of Inter-American Affairs. And they played an important role in United States relations with Brazil and Spanish America by reinforcing the growing influence of American news services, music, and films.

Developing stronger cultural ties would pay long-term dividends, but the Axis threat was immediate; the United States had to be prepared in the eventuality that a coup d'état or civil strife provided an excuse for Axis intervention. The Spanish Civil War was an obvious warning, as was the presence of German officers in the Bolivian army in the recent fighting in the Chaco. The United States Army had few contacts with its Latin American counterparts. It was a small force (Greece and Bulgaria had larger armies) and did not command respect in Latin America. As of January 1938 it had six military attachés stationed in the other American republics; Mexico, Cuba, and Brazil had full-time attachés, while the remaining three officers covered two or more countries. Likewise there were only two army missions—a four-man group in Brazil and a one-man mission in Guatemala. This limited contact reflected the deliberate policies of avoiding intrusion into Latin American mil-

[3] Memorandum of Conversation Between Welles and Mário de Pimentel Brandão, June 8, 1938, *Foreign Relations, 1938,* v, 408.

[4] Whitney H. Shepardson, William O. Scroggs, and Walter Lippmann, *The United States in World Affairs, 1938* (New York, 1939), pp. 271–275.

itary affairs (to the extent of discouraging American manufacturers from selling arms), while limiting the army's mission to the defense of the continental United States and its possessions.

Secretary Hull, alarmed by expanding Nazi activity, requested an interdepartmental conference to discuss extending military aid to the Latin American states. As a result of the meeting, held on January 10, 1938, the State Department urged increasing military assistance in order to strengthen United States ties in the hemisphere, to lay the foundation for close military and naval cooperation, and to counter the efforts of the Axis nations. The Department proposed five modest measures of cooperation: training Latin American military personnel in United States service schools; frequent demonstration flights of American aircraft and visits by naval vessels; inviting high-ranking Latin American officers to tour the United States; providing armed forces publications for military libraries; and appointment of additional military and naval attachés in the area. The army and navy agreed and took steps to implement these suggestions. The War Department added two important proposals: encouraging American commercial aviation in Latin America, and active promotion of American arms sales.[5]

After several months a policy began to emerge. Secretary Hull then requested the president to create a standing committee, composed of the second-ranked officers of the Departments of State, War, and Navy, to coordinate and supervise the departments' activities. Under the guiding

[5] Stetson Conn and Bryon Fairchild, *The Framework of Hemisphere Defense* (Washington, 1960), pp. 173–174. Other countries also followed the practice of assigning an attaché to cover two or more countries. For example, the German naval attaché in Rio de Janeiro was also accredited to Buenos Aires, while the Japanese military attaché was assigned to Argentina, Brazil, Chile, and Peru. In 1938, Germany did not have a military attaché in Brazil.

spirit of Sumner Welles, the Standing Liaison Committee (SLC), from its first meeting in May 1938, concerned itself with hemispheric defense and development of policy.[6]

Welles explained the new American military policy to Ambassador Pimentel Brandão on June 8, 1938. The United States would make available to Brazil and other American states such assistance in military and naval training as law permitted. He stated that if one American republic accepted military assistance from another instead of from outside the hemisphere it would serve inter-American solidarity. All the republics could expect military aid.[7]

But on the important subject of arms supply, which was the key to Brazilian military cooperation, serious problems hindered an effective policy: restrictive legislation, the inability of American industry to offer prices and terms of payment competitive with German proposals, the Brazilian government's desire to obtain the most weapons for the least price, and Argentine opposition. In January 1937 Vargas had proposed that the two countries discuss all forms of military and naval cooperation, including construction of a naval base in a Brazilian port for American use in the event of a war of aggression against the United States.[8] The suggestion came to nothing, because the United States was not prepared to go that far at the time. Ironically less than

[6] Mark S. Watson, *Chief of Staff, Prewar Plans and Preparations* (Washington, 1950), pp. 90–91. See also SLC, Minutes, Vol. I, Items 4–6, WWII RS. There are two sets of SLC minutes available, one in the army files and another in the State Department records. The committee was composed of the Under-Secretary of State, the Army Chief of Staff, and the Chief of Naval Operations.

[7] Memorandum of Conversation Between Welles and Pimentel Brandão, June 8, 1938, *Foreign Relations, 1938*, v, 408.

[8] Welles to Franklin D. Roosevelt, Washington, Jan. 26, 1937, PPF 4473 (Vargas), FDRL. This contains Vargas' message to Roosevelt. He also said that if the United States were attacked "the vital interests of Brazil would necessarily be involved." And he raised the possibility of the United States "utilizing some other portion of Brazilian territory as a means of safeguarding the eastern approach to the Panama Canal."

two years later Washington was seeking desperately the co-operation which Brazil had offered freely in 1937.

Unable to meet American prices and conditions of payment the Brazilians turned to Europe, ordering artillery in Germany, infantry weapons in Czechoslovakia, and naval vessels in England and Italy. From the United States they ordered only some airplanes and matériel to construct a few destroyers in Brazil.[9]

The Brazilian army gave the Krupp interests an order for $55,000,000 for artillery pieces and accessories in March 1938, with further orders under consideration. American officials feared that German military advisors would follow these purchases and expressed concern that, because the weapons would be paid for largely in compensation marks, the purchases would tend to continue and expand Brazil's restrictive trade arrangements with Germany. This trade, which will be discussed in Chapter 6, was an elaborate barter arrangement utilizing blocked compensation marks in such a way as to exclude third parties from participation. Brazil was planning to spend $100,000,000 on a five-year arms program, the money to come from savings accumulated from the cessation of foreign debt payments, increased trade with Germany and Italy, and credits from the United States. Brazil was to receive 50,000,000 Reichsmarks' worth of supplies from Germany each year for five years, approximately five-sixths payable in compensation marks and the balance in free currencies. This agreement committed Brazil to the German compensation trade for at least five years.[10] Militarily the arrangement proved to be

[9] Aranha to Welles, Rio, Nov. 8, 1938, OAA.

[10] Scotten, Rio, Aug. 11, 1938, 832.24/146; Charles A. Thomson, "News Letter on Brazil," Foreign Policy Association, Sept. 26, 1938, 832.00/1232, NA. For a discussion of compensation trade see Chapter 6 below. Vargas followed economic issues carefully. The only cabinet minister with whom he met every day was Finance Minister Souza Costa; see Alzira Vargas do Amaral Peixoto, *Getúlio Vargas, Meu Pai* (Pôrto Alegre, 1960), p. 184. Much of Getúlio's correspondence with his am-

an error, because when war broke out in Europe Brazil was able to obtain only a part of the Krupp artillery order, and then at the expense of a near-rupture of relations with Great Britain. A confusing variety of arms handicapped the Brazilian army in organizing and training for war, and in the end it was forced to turn to the United States for weapons.

In 1938, however, the Brazilians saw the matter in another light. A difference of opinion existed between Brazil and the United States concerning military assistance to Latin America. The divergence was important because it indicated that Washington and Rio viewed their mutual relations differently. Brazil considered itself the preeminent nation in South America, the mediator of disputes among its Spanish-speaking neighbors. In the Brazilian view, relations with the United States were based on an unwritten alliance, in which Brazil pledged its support of the United States in all international questions in return for support of Brazilian preeminence in South America. More than a century of experience, Aranha wrote Welles, had demonstrated that this policy "brought only benefits to both . . . countries and peace for the rest" of South America. "To it, and only to it, do the American peoples owe the peaceful solution of their problems." Brazil had never abused American assistance and would never do so, because it was a "satisfied nation" with territory enough for centuries of growth. But, he said, there were dissatisfied nations in the Americas who wished to expand and who threatened to break the peace and harmony of the continent. The Brazilian government could not understand the American policy concerning mili-

---

bassadors concerned economic questions; see, for example, Luiz Sparano to Vargas, Rome, Jan. 21, 1939, and Feb. 7, 1939, AGV. Italian purchases of Brazilian coffee, cotton, skins, leather, meats, oils, and various extracts rose steadily in 1938, and payment was being made in currencies of Brazil's choosing.

tary assistance. "We are convinced," wrote Aranha, "that indiscriminate military and naval assistance to the American countries will bring a political atmosphere of fear, of suspicion."[11]

Brazil had been shocked when the United States bowed to Argentine protests against the transfer of three old destroyers from the American to the Brazilian navy in mid-1937. Brazilian military and government officials felt that the United States had deserted Brazil, and the incident caused the Brazilian military to distrust American intentions. Convinced that only a strong, well-armed Brazil could insure tranquility in South America, they had turned to Europe for military and naval equipment. These purchases did not indicate a change in Rio's view of Brazilian-American unity, but they did show that Brazil was willing to act alone to effect its defense and to enable it to continue the "historic function of mediator" in South America.[12]

The news in May 1938 that Argentina was buying large quantities of arms in Europe and the frightening discovery that Brazil had only enough gasoline and oil to fight an eight-day war increased Rio's determination to reequip and modernize its armed forces.[13] The Czechoslovakian crisis and the disappointing showing of Britain and France at Munich in September 1938 strengthened this resolve. Public opinion had been solidly anti-Nazi during the crisis, but after the capitulation at Munich Brazilians began to wonder about the future of Brazil in the event of Nazi domination

[11] Aranha to Welles, Rio, Sept. 14, 1938, OAA; the phrase Brazilian "preeminence in America" is from Aranha to Vargas, n.d. (Cilate, 1938), OAA.

[12] *Ibid.*; the AHMRE records for 1937 and 1938 contain extensive documentation on the destroyers dispute. For summary of the American position see Donald W. Giffin, "The Normal Years, Brazilian-American Relations, 1930–1939" (Ph.D. Dissertation, Vanderbilt University, 1962), pp. 329–333.

[13] Lourival Coutinho, *O General Góes Depõe* (Rio de Janeiro, 1956), pp. 340–341, 348–349.

of Europe. The American embassy in Rio thought that the crisis had caused German prestige to rise at the expense of the French and British.[14]

Concern for Brazil's security dominated editorial comment on the crisis. *Diário da Noite* observed that Hitler's victory signified "at least the possibility of an attack against the territorial integrity of Brazil." Several papers referred to Hitler's previous remarks concerning an *Alemanha antártica*. The *Correio da Manhã* favored buying arms to strengthen Brazil, because the recent events in Europe had shown the folly of depending exclusively on alliances. *O Jornal* summed up the general feeling by saying Brazil could not leave solely to the United States the task of defending the Americas. "It is necessary," it said, "that we all contribute to this defense, and that we be prepared to do so. . . . We counsel the government . . . to continue . . . , in spite of the sacrifices which this will cost us, the program of equipping our armed forces."[15]

On the first anniversary of the Estado Nôvo President Vargas declared that Brazil would not tolerate any diminution of its sovereignty. No sacrifice was too great and no vigilance too excessive to defend the Brazilian flag, language, and traditions. The "spectacle of threats and intimidations" which the world was witnessing required the strengthening of national institutions. "Disciplined, we will be strong, and united we will have nothing to fear."[16] Later, he explained to reporters that Brazilian foreign policy was based upon abstention from interference in European affairs. Taking a neutral position ideologically, he said that every nation had the right to organize itself according to its own desires; Brazil was "not interested in the regimes of

[14] Scotten, Rio, Sept. 23, 1938, 832.00/1227, NA.

[15] *Diário da Noite*, Rio, Sept. 29, 1938; *Correio da Manhã*, Rio, Oct. 5, 1938; *O Jornal*, Rio, Oct. 9, 1938.

[16] Getúlio Vargas, *A Nova Política do Brasil* (Rio de Janeiro, 1938–47), VI, 74–75.

other countries or in criticism of the doctrines which they choose to adopt."[17]

A few days later President Franklin Roosevelt linked the security of the United States to that of the whole hemisphere. "As a result of world events," he told reporters, the "orientation of this country in relation to the continent . . . from Canada to Tierra del Fuego . . . has had to be changed." The American Republics, he said, were determined to maintain the continental solidarity established at Buenos Aires in 1936, and were concerned about threats to any part of the hemisphere.[18]

While German prestige may have increased, the Nazi triumph at Munich did not cause Brazil to become pro-German. The chargé d'affaires of the Reich embassy reported to Berlin in late October that Brazilian sentiment was decidedly anti-German. He attributed this to the work of "the Democratic-Jewish element, Catholicism, and North America," as well as to a constantly growing fear of powerful Germany. Rather puzzled, he observed that "one would think that this fear would lead the Brazilians to strive for better relations with Germany. Owing to the influence of North America, however, this is not true, but rather the opposite can be observed. Government circles are still trying to keep economic relations with Germany out of the conflict since these are clearly needed. Politically . . . they are obviously following more and more in North America's wake."[19]

Earlier in the month, just after the untoward behavior of the Reich envoy had caused a mutual recall of ambassadors, the German economics ministry cautioned against further deterioration of relations because Brazil was economically "the most important country in South America." A growing shortage of foreign exchange increased Brazil's significance because there the Germans could deal in compensation

[17] Scotten, Rio, Nov. 10, 1938, 832.00/1233, NA.
[18] Press Conference 500, Nov. 15, 1938, FDRL.
[19] *DGFP*–D, v, 881–882.

marks. This was especially true after the annexation of the "Sudeten-Germans" made it necessary for Berlin to supply Sudeten textile mills with cotton.[20]

Although Aranha assured the German chargé that Brazil desired to maintain good relations with both Europe and North America, the chargé was convinced that the chancellor was "a hireling of North America" and "our greatest opponent in Brazil."[21] Actually Aranha did not think that the German government wanted to cause trouble—in his opinion Brazil had to fear only some impetuous act by pro-Nazi German-Brazilians. His desire to eliminate the Nazi movement and the German language in southern Brazil was because of his nationalism, not his suspicion of Germany. That was his view until late October 1938, when Brazilian authorities uncovered an alleged Nazi plot to foment rebellion in Brazil, Uruguay, and Argentina. Aranha then told the American chargé that he had become convinced that the danger was real and was directed from Germany.[22]

Intercepted documents indicated that the Nazis were considering three courses: open rebellion to justify intervention similar to that in Spain; and/or gaining control of the German-populated areas by an "anschluss across the Atlantic"; or, if these proved impossible, obtaining political concessions which would allow Nazi organizations to operate freely until they could seize power. Diplomatic and consular missions directed agents who were preparing and organizing plots in the three countries. Aranha was now convinced that Germany, possibly in conjunction with Italy, Poland, and Japan, wanted to divide the rich, largely unpopulated and unguarded South American continent into colonies. This solution to Germany's desire for territory had some chance of success, he thought, because it would be acceptable to European opinion.[23] Aranha notified the

[20] *Ibid.*, pp. 874–875; see Chapter 6 below.   [21] *Ibid.*, pp. 881–882.

[22] Scotten, Rio, Nov. 4, 1938, *Foreign Relations, 1938*, v, 419–420.

[23] Aranha to Welles, Rio, Nov. 8, 1938, OAA. The German documents have not revealed such a plot, and stories (such as the one in the

United States government and arranged for a regular exchange of information. Also he asked Welles to have the Federal Bureau of Investigation send an agent to Rio de Janeiro to help organize a special secret service.[24]

In this state of mind Aranha prepared for the Eighth Inter-American Conference at Lima in December 1938. The chancellor was not going to Peru, because the Itamaraty did not want to turn each Pan-American meeting into a foreign ministers' conference; such meetings it felt should be called only to handle extraordinary matters. The Argentines were of like mind, and their foreign minister, José María Cantilo, planned to attend only the opening session and would leave immediately thereafter.[25] The Brazilian and Argentine position did not alter Secretary Hull's plans to attend; later Hull ignored the fact that he had been forewarned, and complained bitterly that Cantilo "had run away from the conference in order to kill it."[26]

Boston Herald, Feb. 19, 1939) that German Ambassador Hans Heinrich Dieckhoff was directing Nazi revolutionary activities in southern Brazil from Washington are not supported by known evidence. See Alton Frye, *Nazi Germany and the American Hemisphere, 1939–1941* (New Haven, 1967), pp. 108–117. The papers which Aranha referred to in his conversation with Scotten, and in his letter of Nov. 8, 1938, to Welles, could not be identified in the oaa. There are, however, numerous reports of antigovernment plots, such as the one dated Jan. 13, 1939, in folder "Informações Políticas," which gave names of Integralista air force officers at Campo de Marte in São Paulo, outlined their antiregime activities, and summarized police reports of seizures of arms caches. It is possible that Aranha could have been trying to scare the Americans into giving Brazil more support and thereby enhancing his own position in the regime. But it seems likely that he believed the rumors and stories of German-directed plots.

[24] Welles to FDR, Washington, December 10, 1938, OF 11 Brazil 1933–39, FDRL. Roosevelt approved sending an agent in a penciled note: "S.W. Yes.—it should be done. Very important. FDR." This special secret service was to be unknown to, and operate separately from, the existing Brazilian secret police.

[25] Aranha to Welles, Rio, Sept. 14, 1938, OAA.

[26] Cordell Hull, *The Memoirs of Cordell Hull*, 2 vols. (New York, 1948), I, 605.

Vargas instructed the distinguished Brazilian delegation, headed by former Chancellor (1930–1933) Afrânio de Melo Franco, to collaborate closely with the United States representatives. The Itamaraty exchanged views with the Argentine government in an effort to resolve all differences, so that they could avoid opposing one another as they had at Buenos Aires in 1936.[27]

German plans for subversion had convinced Vargas and Aranha that a collective security pact, turned down by Argentina in 1936, was urgently needed. Brazil was determined to cooperate with its neighbors to turn aside threats to their sovereignty and their peace; Brazil felt that the American republics had to demonstrate that they would resist all attempts made against them. Aranha wrote Welles that the hour had come "to readjust our friendship on the basis of provident cooperation, capable of giving to Americans the security of our aid in any international circumstances, and to Brazilians the tranquility necessary to allow them to work without . . . criminal threats to their destiny." Vargas was determined to prevent Axis intervention in South America. Would the United States aid Brazil? And Aranha, modifying the Brazilian position on American military assistance to Latin America, declared that the republics needed United States help to arm themselves.[28]

While Aranha was sincere in his request that the United States support a Brazilian-sponsored pact at Lima and give military assistance to the republics, he also saw the situation as an opportunity to breathe new life into the unwritten Brazilian-American unity pact. To arm Brazil was to prepare the defense of half of South America and to aid the security of the rest. Preparation of Brazil, the chancellor observed, would be the best way of avoiding ostensive United States participation in Latin American defense, making it less direct and less onerous. Brazil had decided

27 Aranha to Welles, Rio, Sept. 14, 1938, OAA.
28 *Ibid.*, Nov. 8, 1938, OAA.

to make sacrifices to obtain matériel required for its defense and the defense of its neighbors. It was procuring this matériel in Europe because of price and conditions of payment and would welcome American aid. It had the manpower to fill the ranks of the armed forces, but it needed coast artillery, airplanes, and ships. Argentina would also have to receive weapons to maintain the military balance, and the Argentines would be helpful in raising a defensive barrier from the Guianas to Tierra del Fuego. But Aranha saw Brazil as the leader of the continent, using its arms to defend itself and the peace of South America—Brazil the mediator, the peacemaker. Its peace efforts in the Chaco dispute and in the bitter struggle between Peru and Ecuador over their Amazonian boundaries had earned Brazil this distinction. Speed was necessary; the United States must act to make hemispheric defense a reality before the Axis could snatch away South American independence.[29]

While declaring Brazilian-American cooperation a keystone of United States foreign policy, Washington's reaction to Aranha's proposals was mixed. The weakness of the hemisphere's southern flank made War Department officials uneasy, and at their urging Roosevelt asked Congress to approve the manufacture of weapons for Latin American forces. Unfortunately, isolationist opposition blocked passage of the necessary legislation until the German invasion of France jarred the Congress into action,[30] a delay which prevented effective military cooperation until late 1940 and nearly forced the Brazilians into the arms of the Germans. The State Department considered a security pact desirable, but impossible of achievement; the department's objective was to prevent discord at Lima, to present a seemingly united front.[31]

[29] *Ibid.*

[30] Welles to Aranha, Washington, Nov. 29, 1938, OAA. The Pittman Resolution (Public Resolution 83, 76th Congress, 3rd Session) was signed by FDR on June 15, 1940.

[31] Welles to Aranha, Washington, Nov. 29, 1938, OAA.

The Brazilian government gave up hope of arranging a pact when it learned that Argentina was stubbornly opposed. Such a pact would mean reliance on the United States, and the Argentines were unwilling to subject themselves to the vagaries of what they felt to be an unstable American foreign policy. Also they were certain that dependence on the United States would mean Brazilian domination of South America. Only a sharp warning from Aranha prevented the Argentine foreign minister from condemning the proposal in his address at Lima. The Argentines did what they could to be uncooperative during the conference, while Vargas and Aranha instructed their delegation to cooperate fully with the Americans.[32] Perhaps the Argentine-Brazilian rivalry was the main reason for Argentina's opposition to American proposals at the conference, rather than the frequently cited Argentine-American competition for leadership of the hemisphere. It appears likely that Argentina was more concerned about its position in South America than its position in the hemisphere; its position relative to Brazil was of more immediate importance than its position relative to the United States. The Argentine attitude during the Lima meeting gave warning of the uncertain attitude the Plata country would maintain throughout the prewar and war years.[33]

The main issue at Lima was the implementation of the Buenos Aires declaration of 1936, which stated that any act susceptible of disturbing the peace of the hemisphere was of concern to all, and justified consultation. The United States delegation, headed by Secretary Hull, hoped to ob-

[32] Hull, *Memoirs*, I, 604–605; Afonso Arinos de Melo Franco, *Um Estadista da República, Afrânio de Melo Franco e seu tempo*, 3 vols. (Rio de Janeiro, 1955), III, 1581–1582.

[33] The usual explanation is Argentina's rivalry with the United States for leadership of the hemisphere; see for example, Samuel Guy Inman, *Inter-American Conferences, 1826–1954: History and Problems* (Washington, 1965), pp. 182–187; and Harold Peterson, *Argentina and the United States, 1810–1960* (New York, 1964), pp. 393–397.

tain approval of a declaration that an attempt by a non-American state to disturb the peace of an American nation was of concern to all, and that they would take steps for joint resistance. The Argentines considered Pan-American solidarity a reality: in the face of danger the republics would naturally join together in common defense—special pacts were not required. The pact already existed, according to Foreign Minister Cantilo, in the common history of the Americas; they would "act with one and the same impulse . . . under one flag . . . , the flag of liberty and justice." Secretary Hull conceded that Cantilo was "a good deal more cooperative" than he had expected, but his proposed declaration was weak and did not mention the real and imminent dangers to the hemisphere.[34]

The regular sessions of the conference were serene scenes of unity, but in corridors and hotel rooms the delegates held heated discussions in an effort to resolve the differences between Argentina and the United States. The Argentines accepted the principle that an attack on one was an attack on all, but wanted the declaration to refer to aggression by both American and non-American states. Hull maintained that there "should be a difference in attitude and treatment for an American state as against a non-American state." He instructed the ambassador in Buenos Aires to explain the American view to President Roberto M. Ortiz. Brazil, to the delight of its diplomats, played the role of mediator. Melo Franco arduously sought to find common ground between the American and Argentine arguments; the Itamaraty studied both sides and expressed its opinion that the divergences were not fundamental; and Vargas appealed to President Ortiz to remove obstacles to accord. Argentina gave in, and on December 24 the conference unanimously approved the Declaration of Lima. It affirmed the determination of the American republics to help one another if foreign intervention or subversion endangered

[34] Hull, *Memoirs*, I, 603–605.

their peace, security, or territorial integrity; they would consult to choose the proper response.[35]

Secretary Hull was satisfied that the Axis powers would understand the intention of the declaration—although not everything he desired, it was close enough. Most important, unanimity was preserved, which was always his aim in Pan-American conferences.[36] As for Aranha, although he had not obtained a security pact, Brazilian-American efforts resulted in a declaration that made enforcing the Monroe Doctrine the responsibility of all the American republics. As a consequence of this work and of points Aranha raised in his letters to Welles, Roosevelt asked Vargas to send his foreign minister to Washington to discuss questions of interest to both governments. These conversations would set the general direction of relations between the two countries for the next several years.[37]

[35] *Ibid.*, pp. 602–608; Melo Franco, *Estadista*, III, 1583–1588; Jayme de Barros Gomes, *Exposição Sucinta dos Trabalhos Realizados Pelo Itamaraty nos Últimos Doze Mezes, 1938–1939* (Rio de Janeiro, 1940), p. 10.

[36] Hull, *Memoirs*, pp. 608–609. Hull explained that a declaration was preferable to a treaty because it could contain stronger language; it did not require ratification by national legislatures and entered into effect at once. For the text of the declaration and a contemporary evaluation see Samuel F. Bemis, *The Latin American Policy of the United States* (New York, 1943), pp. 359–360.

[37] Carlos Delgado de Carvalho, *História Diplomática do Brasil* (São Paulo, 1959), p. 310; Hull, *Memoirs*, I, 608; Barros Gomes, *Exposição Sucinta*, p. 15.

*"My dear fellow, you simply don't begin
to know how much everything has to do with
the Army at the present time."*[1]

*"These people understand that they must aid
us. . . . There is a clear field for great
possibilities in all departments."*[2]

*"They do not want to know if our government
is liberal or not. . . ."*[3]

5

Toward Approximation

A SERIES OF high-level conferences between Brazilian and American officials followed the close cooperation
at Lima. Foreign Minister Aranha arrived in the United
States in February for a five-week stay. The new American
army chief of staff, George C. Marshall, went to Brazil in
May and returned home with General Góes Monteiro as his
guest. Out of the exchange of views came the beginning of
wartime cooperation, though the process was slow and at
times seemed impossible of achievement. The changing European situation and isolationist sentiment in the United
States adversely affected Roosevelt's efforts to prepare the
nation for possible war, while Brazilian insistence that their

[1] Aranha to an American visitor, in Norbert A. Bogden to Laurence
Duggan, Apr. 24, 1939, 033.3211 Aranha 71, NA.

[2] Aranha to Vargas, Washington, Feb. 14, 1939, AGV.

[3] Luiz Simões Lopes to Vargas, Washington, Feb. (n.d.), 1939, AGV.
Simões Lopes was a member of the Aranha Mission, sometime civil
service administrator, and long-time Vargas supporter. During such
foreign missions, Vargas normally corresponded with more than one
member to obtain a variety of views.

principal defense efforts be in the south rather than the northeast delayed joint defense measures.

Welles telephoned Aranha on January 6, 1939, to say that Roosevelt would like to ask Vargas to send the chancellor to Washington to discuss matters of mutual interest. Vargas and his cabinet approved; Aranha notified Welles; the invitation was extended, accepted, and arrangements were soon concluded.[4] Vargas requested a proposed agenda from the American embassy so that each cabinet minister could give Aranha a statement relative to the interests of his ministry. Topics were arranged in two groupings; those Aranha should take up with the State Department, and those he should discuss with treasury officials. First on the list was American cooperation in Brazil's defense program. Other items covered trade, economic development, shipping, air mail, radio, refugee problems, settlement of the Brazilian debt, private investment, and establishment of a central bank.[5]

While Aranha was en route to the United States on board the steamer *New Amsterdam*, President Roosevelt held a secret conference on January 31 with members of the Senate Military Affairs Committee in which he expressed his views on the post-Munich world. He told the senators that his efforts to preserve peace had failed and that the world was faced with an aggressive alliance of Germany, Italy, and Japan. The first lines of American defense were the island bases in the Pacific and the "continued independence of a very large group of nations" on the Atlantic. Regrettably, many of these would soon lose their independence to "this wild man" Hitler. In discussing the possible directions of new Nazi thrusts, he said that in conjunction with Musso-

[4] Aranha to Vargas, Washington, Mar. 27, 1939, "Missão aos EUA—1939," OAA; Roosevelt to Vargas, Washington, Jan. 9, 1939, 033.3211 Aranha 4, NA, copy also in AGV; Vargas to FDR, Rio, Jan. 13, 1939, 033.3211 Aranha 3½, NA.

[5] Welles to Scotten, Washington, Jan. 16, 1939, 033.3211 Aranha 6, NA.

lini they might go west and south into the Netherlands and toward the Mediterranean. If Britain and France yielded, the smaller countries would "drop into the basket" with little effort, and Africa would fall automatically because it was 95 percent colonial. With Europe under Nazi control "next would come Brazil," where they already had a nucleus and "an organization which probably on pressing a button from Berlin, would be put into operation and would constitute . . . a very serious threat to the Brazilian government. After Brazil, the same thing, of course, would be possible in other places."[6] American concern for hemispheric security was underlined soon thereafter, when General George C. Marshall asked the Army War College to examine secretly the steps necessary to safeguard Brazil.[7]

The Rio de Janeiro afternoon daily, *O Globo*, saw that the Aranha visit was connected to the German threat. It predicted the formation of a "Rio-Washington Axis" against "extra-continental interference" around which the American republics would rally.[8] Hopes were high that the talks would produce tangible benefits. Shortly before Aranha embarked the Vargas government announced an ambitious "Special Five Year Plan for Public Works Development and National Defense." In addition to rearmament, the plan called for development of the São Francisco River Valley along the lines of the Tennessee Valley Authority, the building of a national steel industry, and the refitting of the national shipping line, Lloyd-Brasileiro. Press, business, and military circles thought Aranha would return with aid commitments.[9]

[6] Conference with Senate Military Affairs Committee, White House, Jan. 31, 1939, PPF 1-P Box 262, FDRL.

[7] Marshall to Lt. Gen. John L. DeWitt, Washington, Feb. 6, 1939, and attached papers, War Plans Division (WPD) 4115-4 to 7, WWII RS, NA.

[8] *Baltimore Sun*, Jan. 16, 1939.

[9] *New York Times*, Jan. 21, 1939; *Gazeta de Notícias*, Rio, Jan. 25, 1939.

Brazil was clearly in need of aid. Up to December 1938 it had defaulted on its dollar bonds to the extent of $357,071,745. At the end of January, Brazil had a favorable balance of trade with the United States of about $36,000,000, but its worldwide trade had practically balanced in 1938, affording no foreign exchange to renew payments on the foreign debt. At the time of the Washington talks, Brazil was somewhere between $10,000,000 and $20,000,000 in arrears on payments for current imports of American products, and was unable to provide dollars for an estimated $10,000,000 of profits accruing to American enterprise in the country. And it had only about $33,000,000 in gold reserves. Since late 1937 the Vargas government had maintained tight exchange controls, to keep Brazilian trade from collapsing and to insure sufficient exchange for arms purchases abroad. At times payments were held up for three or four months, because imports had slipped ahead of exports and the supply of exchange was insufficient. In February 1939 payments reportedly were running about a month behind.[10]

The day before his ship docked in New York Aranha wrote Vargas, summarizing his intentions and the missions' prospects. He planned to be frank about Brazil's economic and military needs and the impossibility of satisfying them without help. The result of the mission should be a "practical accord of reciprocal assistance between the two countries" which recognized that the United States must assist Brazil immediately so that Brazil would be able to reciprocate in the future. He would have to convince the Americans that their future well-being depended on aiding Brazilian development. Analyzing American policy, he termed the New Deal internally a positive program but internationally "a negative policy," which pretended that individual leaders were nations to be dealt with on the basis of "im-

[10] *Journal of Commerce*, New York, Feb. 14, 1939; *The Wall Street Journal*, New York, Feb. 10, 1939.

mortal principles." Everything indicated, he thought, that the European and Asian situations had convinced the Roosevelt administration that it would have to abandon the "puritan policy of the good neighborhood" for the creation of markets and strong allies in the Western Hemisphere, because if it did not do so "Brazil will have to accept [the aid] of one or another of the industrial countries that . . . are offering us the elements required by our undelayable economic and military preparation."[11] A few days later he enthusiastically informed Getúlio that: "These people understand that they must aid us. In my view, everything now depends on the form in which we transmit our requests. There is a clear field for great possibilities in all departments."[12]

For five weeks after Aranha arrived in Washington on February 9 the Brazilian mission met with representatives of the Departments of State, Treasury, Agriculture, Commerce, War, and Navy, and with the presidents of the Financial Reconstruction Corporation, the Federal Reserve Bank, and the Export-Import Bank. Conferences were held daily—morning, noon, and night. While talks were in progress, Aranha renewed old friendships, attended more than a dozen official dinners, and spoke to such groups as the Washington Press Club, the Foreign Relations Council, and the Brazilian-American Association. He had several conversations with President Roosevelt and long talks with Hull and Welles.[13]

In the midst of these discussions Aranha reported to Vargas that "the attitude of Roosevelt and the public is definitely favorable to our pretensions . . . [and] in favor of the policy of continental [hemispheric] cooperation and

---

[11] Aranha to Vargas, on the *New Amsterdam*, Feb. 8, 1939, AGV.

[12] Aranha to Vargas, Washington, Feb. 14, 1939, AGV.

[13] Aranha to Vargas, Rio, Mar. 27, 1939, "Missão aos EUA—1939," OAA. This document is a long official report drawn up by Aranha upon his return.

association starting with Brazil."[14] The press was giving the mission front-page coverage and lauding the Vargas regime. Speaking of the great esteem in which Welles and Roosevelt held Getúlio, another member of the mission assured the president that "they do not care to know if our government is liberal or not. . . ."[15] Getúlio recognized that the Americans' good will and desire to aid Brazil would be reduced by the difficulties of implementation, but that American cooperation had become even "more necessary and urgent" to effect the partial liberation of exchange, to set up the Central Bank, and to arrange a large credit to finance purchases in the United States. Both countries' economies would benefit from American assistance. But he cautioned Aranha that in any joint plans it was "incumbent that the Brazilian Government have control."[16]

The arrangements which emerged, though largely economic, were also politically important. The Export-Import Bank agreed to arrange credits to finance purchases in the United States and to loan Brazil $19,200,000 to pay off its arrears. The administration promised to send technicians to help develop Brazil's ability to export such things as rubber, manganese, iron ore, nickel, chrome, quinine, vegetable oils, and tropical fruits, and to request congressional approval for a $50,000,000 gold loan to capitalize the proposed Brazilian central bank. The Export-Import Bank opened a credit to encourage importation of Brazilian products. In return Aranha promised that Brazil would regulate the German compensation trade, and would relax foreign exchange controls so the American dollar would not com-

[14] Aranha to Vargas, Washington, Feb. 23, 1939, AGV.

[15] Luiz Simões Lopes to Vargas, Washington, Feb. (n.d.), 1939, AGV. For some sample news stories see: *Washington Post*, Feb. 5, 1939; *Wall Street Journal*, Feb. 10, 1939; *New York Herald Tribune*, Feb. 12, 1939; *New York Times*, Feb. 14, 1939 and Mar. 10, 1939; *New York World-Telegram*, Mar. 10, 1939; *Newsweek*, Mar. 10, 1939.

[16] Aranha to Vargas, Rio, Mar. 27, 1939, "Missão aos EUA—1939," OAA.

pete with uncontrolled compensation marks. He agreed that
his government would treat American investors as it treated
Brazilians, and that it would arrange a permanent payment
plan on American-held Brazilian bonds. He also pledged
that Brazil would develop its rubber production, to free the
United States from dependence on the vulnerable East
Indies. He talked with State, War, and Navy officials about
Brazilian-American defense cooperation and suggested that
their respective military people continue the conversations.
He did not ask financial assistance for rearmament.

When Aranha sailed from New York on March 10 he was
certain that the accords signed the preceding day would
add economic collaboration to the ties already binding the
two nations and would contribute to the well-being of their
peoples and to hemispheric peace. Sumner Welles told reporters that the agreements were mutually advantageous
because they would free trade between the two countries
from harmful restrictions, and would form the basis for developing commerce in noncompetitive products.[17]

American editorial comment echoed Welles' optimistic
assessment of the Aranha mission. The *New York Times* saw
the commitment to relax exchange controls as a blow at the
German compensation trade, while creation of a central
bank would tie Brazilian currency to the American dollar.[18]
Brazil's difficulties in providing sufficient exchange to cover
its export-import trade and foreign debt payments had led
to the severing of ties with the English Rothschilds and to
closer links with American banks. The Washington accords
consolidated the trend toward approximation in the financial sphere, thereby adding an economic pillar to the edifice
of Brazilian-American unity that Aranha was carefully constructing. According to Walter Lippmann, the Brazilian
agreements were the most constructive measures yet taken

---

[17] *Ibid.*; Jayme de Barros Gomes, *A Política Exterior do Brasil,
1930–1942* (Rio de Janeiro, 1943), pp. 206–210.
[18] *New York Times*, Mar. 10, 1939.

"to restore peace and prosperity in the world," because Washington had demonstrated that it understood that gold had "some function beside that of being buried in Kentucky." The United States was keeping a gold hoard worth over fourteen billion dollars—out of twenty-six billion dollars of monetary gold in the world; this was the greatest single supply of purchasing power in existence, but it was useless in Fort Knox's vaults. Lippmann wrote that if there was nothing the United States wished to buy, "the only sane thing to do" was to lend the gold to someone who would spend it, make a profit, and repay the United States with interest. The Brazilian agreements would inaugurate a movement to revive normal world trade.[19] Summarizing the general mood, the *New York Times* declared that the accords "marked the successful culmination of one of the most important missions conducted by a South American stateman [sic] for many years."[20]

The contrast between the American and Brazilian reactions to the accords was striking. When Aranha arrived in Rio de Janeiro the war and navy ministers were not at shipside to greet him, and Góes Monteiro, who was to make a speech of welcome, managed to be out of town. When the foreign minister had left for the United States many thought that he would return with "tangible political benefits" which vaguely took the form of cruisers, airplanes, coast artillery, etc., or, as the American embassy expressed it, "something for nothing." After the agreements were made public on March 11, there was general disappointment. High-ranking officers saw curtailment of military spending in the promise to resume foreign debt payments. Press and business circles were unenthusiastic. Aranha's enemies spread the rumor that the accords were more advantageous to the United States than to Brazil. Minister of Finance Souza Costa referred to them as "literature," and

19 *Ibid.*; Walter Lippmann, "Today and Tomorrow," *New York Herald Tribune*, Mar. 14, 1939.
20 *New York Times*, Mar. 10, 1939.

Francisco Campos spoke sarcastically of Aranha's sojourn in the United States.

The cabinet met in Petrópolis on March 30 to hear Aranha's report. Afterwards an aide gave out an extremely brief statement to the effect that the president had thanked the foreign minister and had ordered publication of the Washington accords. The administrator of the foreign debt settlement, Valentim Bouças, told the counselor of the American embassy that if the government should resume payment, it would be only a token one to save face in the United States.[21]

The press was reserved, limiting itself to publishing the text of the accords and the official statement released at Petrópolis. The *Correio da Manhã*, which was extremely friendly toward the United States and Chancellor Aranha, said there was talk of increasing exports to the United States but no concrete data indicating what form the increase would take. Brazil had "a very real commercial relationship with certain European countries," which the *Correiro da Manhã* did not think it should abandon in "exchange for vague promises."[22]

It was clear to the military that the proposed central bank would tie Brazil's currency to the dollar, to the detriment of the compensation trade with Germany, and that a decline in that trade would adversely effect Brazil's ability to pay for German weapons. In conversation with an American, Aranha mentioned that he would like to have United States help in organizing a central bank, but that it was difficult to convince army leaders. When the American asked what the central bank had to do with the army, Aranha replied pathetically: "My dear fellow, you simply don't begin to know how much everything has to do with the army at the present time."[23]

[21] Scotten, Rio, Apr. 10, 1939, 832.00/1255, NA.

[22] *Correio da Manhã*, Rio, Apr. 9, 1939.

[23] Norbert A. Bogdan to Laurence Duggan, Apr. 24, 1939, 033.3211 Aranha 71, NA.

Vargas may have encouraged the lukewarm reaction to Aranha's mission in order to deflate the foreign minister's rising political prestige. Aranha was a logical candidate to succeed the president and Vargas was always careful to prevent any one minister's popularity from becoming overwhelming, thereby denying potential rallying points to the opposition. And Aranha's enemies, such as Campos, were eager to whisper harmful rumors in the president's ear. One rumor had Getúlio taking a leave of absence and handing the government over to Aranha.[24]

From the foregoing it should not be surprising that implementation of the accords was slow and spotty. Exchange was freed on April 10, and payment of commercial arrears began shortly. But the central bank remained a much-discussed dream. Strong opposition to closer regulation of the German compensation trade prevented action until August 10, when the Bank of Brazil ordered that the compensation mark fluctuate with free currencies. Actually the uncertain European situation did more to inhibit German-Brazilian trade than any action of the Rio government. Aranha met the strongest resistance to his pledge to renew debt payments; no one in the government supported his position. The army especially was insistent that available exchange be used only to cover current purchases. Largely by force of personality Aranha obtained Vargas' agreement that $1,000,000 would be deposited in New York on July 1, as a token of good faith, while a permanent plan was worked out.

Aranha was more successful in bringing to a happy conclusion the effort he had made in the military sphere. In February 1938, the German high command had invited Góes Monteiro to visit Germany and to command a division during Wehrmacht maneuvers in Silesia. A full European tour quickly took shape, with visits to England, France, and

[24] Raul Azambuja to Aranha, Pelotas, Rio Grande do Sul, Apr. 26, 1939, OAA.

Italy. To offset the possible adverse results of the journey and to effect approximation in military relations Aranha suggested to American officials that their chief of staff visit Brazil and invite Góes Monteiro to return to the United States with him. Aranha sounded out Getúlio, who replied that his government would be honored to receive the American chief of staff but asked if the purpose of the visit was military or "purely political." Aranha telegraphed that the objective was political, and that the United States had never sent such a mission before or invited one such as it wished to receive from Brazil. Any military ends "are ours to initiate" through direct, personal contact "between the chiefs and officers of our armies." After the first contacts the "development and extension will depend logically on our will and our military program."[25]

United States army leaders readily accepted the suggestion because in recent months they had come to view Brazil as the key to hemispheric defense. If Hitler gained control of Europe, Africa would fall easily, and it was only some 1,400 miles and eight hours by air from Dakar, French West Africa (Senegal), to Natal in northeast Brazil. In March 1939 an Army War College study concluded that Brazilian forces were not strong enough to safeguard the Natal "Bulge," and only the United States could provide the necessary defense forces.[26] Brazilian war plans, on the other hand, called for troop concentrations in the southern states in readiness for the ever-expected conflict with Argentina. There had been no serious threat to the northeast since the expulsion of the Dutch in 1654, and Brazilian officials did not see the strategic situation in the way the Americans saw

[25] Aranha to Vargas, Washington, Feb. 13, 1939; Vargas to Aranha, Rio, Feb. 20, 1939; and Aranha to Vargas, Washington, Feb. 21, 1939, all AGV. See also Forrest C. Pogue, *George C. Marshall, Education of a General* (New York, 1963), p. 338; Lourival Coutinho, *O General Góes Depõe* (Rio de Janeiro, 1956), pp. 357–360.

[26] "Special Study, Brazil," Mar. 29, 1939, Army War College, WPD 4115–7, WWII RS, NA.

it. They thought a transatlantic invasion unlikely, while the German population in the south was a potential source of subversion and disorder.

In consequence of this strategic view, the 2,500 miles of sandy coast line north of Rio de Janeiro was defenseless in 1939. Belém, Natal, Recife, and Salvador had excellent harbors, but a handful of troops, some garrisoned in forts of the colonial era, defended them, and they had no long-range artillery to repel invaders. The best equipment of this sort was concentrated around Rio de Janeiro, and the one "first-class" battery there was a generation old and had a scant 23-kilometer range and no powder. The other two direct-fire batteries of major caliber were equally antiquated, and supplied only with brown prismatic powder of pre-1900 vintage. Antisubmarine defenses were "nothing plus": all mines were over twenty years old and their ability to function was doubtful. One modern battleship could have sailed into Guanabara Bay, leveled Rio's forts, and easily destroyed the Brazilian navy's antiquated and motley collection of vessels. Joint army and navy action was unheard of, and except for a few machine guns there was no antiaircraft defense in all Brazil.[27]

The northeastern cities were islands isolated from one another and from the south by wasteland and mountains. Troops could be sent to the northeast only by sea, and only with considerable effort; and once there an enemy with sea power could easily cut off their logistical support. While naval invasion was unlikely as long as friendly powers controlled the seas, the development of air power and of the airway across the South Atlantic made an air attack feasible. The Brazilian air force in 1939 was engaged largely in airmail activities and had no modern combat planes to repulse an air assault. Such an attack, combined with a Nazi and Integralista fifth-column movement, might overthrow Vargas or plunge Brazil into civil war, thus producing a sit-

[27] Memo on Brazilian Coastal Defense, WPD 4115-3, *ibid.*

uation inimical to the interests of the United States and the other American republics.[28]

The Axis threat to Latin America was taken seriously in the United States, allowing the Roosevelt administration to stress the area's defense without incurring isolationist opposition. Concern for hemisphere defense was a small and logical extension of defense of the United States itself. The Monroe Doctrine "gave to that defense such anti-European color as not to stir the isolationists' fear of foreign entanglements."[29] Security of the hemisphere provided Roosevelt with the means by which he could begin to prepare the United States for the inevitable conflict without endangering his political stature. The United States badly needed preparation, for in early 1939 the American army consisted of nine divisions, not one of which was at full strength. At the same time Japan had fifty divisions in China, Germany could put ninety into the field, and Italy boasted forty-five.[30]

American military planning from 1939 until 1942 emphasized the exposed nature of the Brazilian bulge and the War Department's desire to garrison it with United States troops. The American army's plans at this stage specified particular and short-term objectives, mostly aiming at stationing its forces in the northeast, not at the acquisition of permanent bases in Brazil. One of the earliest evaluations of the situation—the Army War College Study of March 29, 1939—called for sending troops to the region, but insisted that provision be made "for the immediate evacuation of Brazilian territory as soon as the desired results have been obtained."[31] Brazilian military authorities, however, con-

---

[28] This situation was remedied somewhat in 1941 when all Brazilian aviation activities, civilian and military, were placed under the new Ministry of Aeronautics. "Historical Resumé of the Military and Naval Airmails," Burden File, Private Papers of Cauby C. Araújo (Rio de Janeiro); see Stetson Conn and Byron Fairchild, *The Framework of Hemisphere Defense* (Washington, 1960), p. 266.

[29] Pogue, *Marshall*, p. 336.   [30] *Ibid.*

[31] "Special Study, Brazil," Mar. 29, 1939, Army War College, WPD 4115-7, WWII RS, NA.

sistently rejected American offers to send troops, preferring to build up the strength of their own forces. The objective of the Brazilian army, from 1939 on, was to improve and increase its ground units to enable it to defend the country without American assistance. Because Brazil was dependent on foreign armaments, American army leaders concluded that if they could supply the Brazilians with weapons and equipment the latter would drop their objections to stationing American forces in the northeast. Prior to Pearl Harbor, however, Brazilian military planners were willing to accept American air and naval support because they conceded the impossibility of modernizing their air force and navy, but they continued to reject ground support in the northeast. Thus from 1939 to 1942 the basic problem in Brazilian-American military relations was the method of conducting a ground defense of the Brazilian bulge—in 1942 the changed military situation allowed a solution in accordance with Brazilian desires.[32]

But on May 25, 1939, when the USS *Nashville* arrived at Rio de Janeiro bearing George C. Marshall, newly appointed chief of staff, and his party, the stalemate on ground troops was still in effect. The reception on the quay and along Avenida Rio Branco, bedecked with American and Brazilian flags, was extremely friendly, and the warm applause from the crowds surprised even the Brazilian officers. Vargas' military aide, General Francisco Pinto, remarked to the president and Ambassador Caffery: "Our people are generally undemonstrative and somewhat indifferent to foreign state visits. . . . I was surprised and delighted with the size of the crowds and their applause."[33] Caffery was so pleased with the reception, and with Gen-

[32] Conn and Fairchild, *Framework*, p. 267.

[33] Caffery, Rio, May 26, 1939, 832.2011/19, NA. Many clippings are attached to this dispatch. Marshall was "Chief of Staff Designate" at the time of the trip and for a couple of months after his return; the incumbent chief of staff, Malin Craig, was merely filling out his time until retirement.

eral Marshall, that he reported immediately that the general had made an excellent impression; that his dignity and personality would win him friends on all sides, and that his mission would be an unqualified success. As indeed it was.

The next twelve days were a crowded mixture of festivities, conferences, and inspections, because the object of the trip combined good will and military business. Among the social engagements in Rio de Janeiro was a reception at Guanabara Palace for Countess Edda Ciano, Mussolini's daughter, whom *Time* termed Italy's attractive answer to America's "humdrum" Marshall.[34] When the Brazilian and American chiefs of staff were presented to the countess, she was cold to Marshall and extremely warm to Góes Monteiro. It was as if two jealous suitors were meeting in the presence of the desired one—the United States and Italy being the suitors and Brazil the prize.[35]

Marshall held secret talks with Generals Dutra and Góes Monteiro seeking military cooperation with Brazil in event of war. Then he set out on a festive tour of the country, with visits to Curitiba, Pôrto Alegre, Santos, São Paulo, and Belo Horizonte. Flag-waving children, parades, speeches, confetti, receptions, champagne, balls, and enthusiastic crowds greeted him along the way. Pôrto Alegre, capital of Rio Grande do Sul, outdid the rest of the nation with its extravagant welcome, thanks to the efforts of Interventor Oswaldo Cordeiro de Farias and regional military commander Estevão Leitão de Carvalho. They were engaged in a resolute campaign against Nazi activities in the state and used the Marshall visit to emphasize their position.[36]

In Curitiba, Paraná, Marshall distributed 200 pounds of candy at an orphanage and in a single stroke captured the

[34] "Brazil Visitors," *Time*, xxxiii, No. 29 (May 22, 1939), 29; "Picture of the Week," *Life*, vi, No. 26 (June 26, 1939), 20.

[35] Coutinho, *General Góes*, p. 361.

[36] Pogue, *Marshall*, p. 339. Both Marshall and his hosts were impressed with the reception. Estevão Leitão de Carvalho, *A Serviço do Brasil na Segunda Guerra Mundial* (Rio de Janeiro, 1952), p. 14.

hearts of thousands of Brazilians. The general kept a meticulous record of the receptions so that the welcome accorded Góes Monteiro in the United States would not fall short of Brazil's hospitality. He asked the War Department to inform the chief of ordnance that the Brazilians served champagne and cakes in the middle of a shell factory.[37]

In Rio, from the first of June on, the receptions and inspections continued, along with conversations on ways and means of assuring closer cooperation, especially in defense of the northeast. En route to Brazil Marshall had told his staff, which included Colonel Lehman W. Miller, an old Brazil hand and later chief of military mission, and Major Matthew B. Ridgway, the War Department's chief Latin American planner, that he wanted to get definite information on Brazil's military capabilities, establishments, and problems, the physiography of its strategy, its air bases, and aviation difficulties. He explained to Brazilian officials that the United States wished to construct air bases, complete with munitions and supply depots, in the northeast. They would be part of the Panama Canal defenses and would enable the United States to protect Brazil and the hemisphere from Axis invasion. Land defense and protection of coastal navigation would be Brazil's responsibility unless it were attacked, in which case United States air and naval forces would come to its aid. If this happened the American navy would need a port at which to base its ships.

General Góes Monteiro asserted that in the event of war Brazil's principal concern would be defense of the south against invasion and against subversive activities among the German colonies. Current Brazilian policy was to develop a field army capable of supporting that strategic view. The talks continued on board the *Nashville* en route to the United States and during Góes Monteiro's visit there.[38]

[37] Pogue, *Marshall*, pp. 339–340.
[38] *Ibid.*, p. 341; Leitão de Carvalho, *Serviço do Brasil*, pp. 58–61. The author was formerly First Sub-Chief of the general staff, and at the time of the visit was commander of the Rio Grande do Sul military

While on board ship, as Góes expressed it between the "sky and the sea," he wrote Aranha that: "Your American friends are very amiable and have been all attention, within their customs and mentality." The general was worn out from "mental gymnastics"—trying to give a "flattering impression of our internal affairs," and exchanging ideas on arms acquisition in the United States and the eventual development of Brazilian industries applicable to weapons production. Nothing concrete had been arranged because weapons purchases depended on Brazil's financial situation, which Góes quipped did not permit them "to bathe in running water." While hoping that God would help them, he asserted that "everything depends on confidence in our political stability and on the strength of the regime."[39]

On July 7 Góes wrote Vargas about his luncheon with Roosevelt, whom he described as very friendly and ready to facilitate Brazilian arms purchases. He expressed annoyance that the American press was insinuating that he favored Nazism, when he was actually working toward approximation with the United States. He warned Getúlio that he had no doubt whatever that if the United States failed to get Brazil's assent to an alliance it would seek Argentina's, and he was certain that Argentina would accept. Góes thought Marshall had formed a low impression of "our military potential," which was another reason why the United States might switch to Argentina where it already had an air mission. He expressed confidence that Vargas

---

region. He gives a summary of the Rio conversations. Góes Monteiro to Aranha, USS *Nashville*, June 16, 1939, OAA; Coutinho, *General Góes*, p. 361. The *Nashville* departed Rio, June 6, stopped at Recife, arrived Annapolis, Md., June 20. Góes Monteiro's staff was composed of Colonel Canrobert Costa, Major José Machado Lopes, Major Aquinaldo Caiado de Castro, Captain Orlando Eduardo da Silva, Captain Ademar Alvares da Fonseca, as listed in Jayme de Barros Gomes, *Exposição Sucinta dos Trabalhos Realizados Pelo Itamaraty nos Últimos Doze Meses, 1930–1939* (Rio de Janeiro, 1940), p. 20.

[39] Góes Monteiro to Aranha, USS *Nashville*, June 16, 1939, OAA.

would arrange solutions most beneficial to Brazil and that the policy of "approximation with this extraordinary country" would solve "our capital problems."[40]

Although conceding the need to defend the northeast, Góes Monteiro insisted that if Brazil were involved in armed conflict, or if such a conflict appeared imminent, its geographic position and "its situation in the South American concert of countries required preventively the concentration of its principal Forces in the Southern Sector of the country." The assumption was that in the event of war the Brazilian forces had to be prepared to face an Argentine offensive. The integrity of the northeast would be guaranteed by American naval and air force units, protecting the sea lanes from bases to be built by Brazil at locations such as Natal and Fernando de Noronha Island. Góes requested that the United States provide the technical data required to construct suitable bases. He promised to organize new coast artillery units, antiaircraft, and motorized elements to provide ground defense of the proposed sites; indeed a full army division was to be stationed permanently in the area. But he repeated again and again that everything would depend on the degree of material assistance that the United States provided. He submitted a list of military equipment that the Brazilian army considered of "first [and] indispensable urgency," insisting that American prices and terms of payment must not be "less advantageous for Brazil than those which until now have been agreed upon and proposed by Germany and other Nations." Though representing only a third of Brazil's total military needs, the list was considerable; the first priority items included 156 heavy artillery pieces, 196 antiaircraft guns, 41 tanks, 252 armored cars, and 722 automatic weapons. Brazilian authorities wished to exchange raw materials, such as manganese, for most of this equipment. Later, when Góes returned to Rio, he wrote Marshall that Vargas was

[40] Góes Monteiro to Vargas, Washington, July 10, 1939, OAA.

pleased with the results of the mission and had authorized him to continue conversations toward "eventual cooperation." But the Brazilians were worried that the political situation in the United States would prevent the Americans from fulfilling their part of the proposed agreement. The Brazilian government wanted "to know with absolute certainty if, in virtue of the attitude of the American Congress in the question of revocation of the Neutrality Law and in not permitting the furnishing of armament to foreign countries, there would be future obstacles to our possible acquisitions in the United States."[41]

Summarizing the conversations for General Marshall, Major Ridgway noted that the crucial factor would be arms supply. If the United States could furnish the arms (though the War Plans Division thought the requests larger than Brazil's needs), it would be "relatively easy" to place American troops in the northeast. The problem was that the army could not legally provide the matériel from its arsenals, and private manufacturers could not match the terms of the Krupp interests. Ridgway urged that the American government seriously consider the arms supply problem, that the United States provide technical training for Brazilian military officers, and that, in the meantime, the American army and navy develop plans for a joint expeditionary force to defend the northeast in an emergency.[42]

Góes Monteiro returned to Rio de Janeiro in early August 1939 with the basis of an agreement for military cooperation, but nearly three years passed before it was signed, largely because of American slowness in supplying arms. The exchange of visits had mixed results. Marshall made an

41 Góes Monteiro to Marshall, Rio, Aug. 8, 1939, AGV. There are copies of the Góes-Marshall correspondence and lists of the Brazilian arms requests in WPD 4224–7 to 13, WWII RS, NA. And a summary of the Brazilian strategic view in Welles, Washington, May 8, 1940, *Foreign Relations, 1940*, V, 40–42.

42 Memo, Matthew B. Ridgway to Marshall, June 17, 1939, WPD 4224–11, in Conn and Fairchild, *Framework*, pp. 268–269.

excellent impression on the Brazilians, and he and his staff obtained much important data about Brazil's defense capabilities, plans, and attitudes. His visit strengthened the determination of pro-American elements in the Brazilian armed forces to avoid ties with the Axis and gave a much-needed public indication of American concern for Brazilian security.[43] In the United States the exchange of visits focused attention on hemispheric defense, helping to get Americans thinking in terms of active rather than passive measures for national security—"in terms of raising fighting forces rather than filling sandbags."[44]

Góes Monteiro's visit prevented him from going to Germany—he stayed so long in the United States that war broke out before he could go to Europe. After the general returned to Brazil, Aranha frankly told Vargas: "The visit of an Army Chief of Staff to another nation is a highly political act. . . . We do not have, at this time, immediate political interests that justify a visit of our Chief of Staff to any of the European countries." He noted, however, that the European invitations had been extended in terms that made refusal difficult, and that the best Góes Monteiro could do was to conduct himself in such a way as to avoid "the least indication of sympathy."[45] The German invasion of Poland ended the matter.[46]

[43] Coutinho, *General Góes*, p. 365; see the following editorials: *Diário de Noticias, Jornal do Brasil, O Jornal, Diário Carioca*, all Rio, May 25, 1939.

[44] Pogue, *Marshall*, p. 342.

[45] Aranha to Vargas, Rio, Aug. 18, 1939, OAA.

[46] Caffery reported at the beginning of June that Góes Monteiro had decided against going to Germany and would return to Brazil in the Flying Fortresses offered by the U.S.: Caffery, Rio, June 6, 1939, 832.20111/20, NA. See Donald W. Giffin, "The Normal Years: Brazilian-American Relations, 1930–1939" (Ph.D. Dissertation, Vanderbilt University, 1962), p. 413; and Pogue, *Marshall*, p. 341. For Góes Monteiro's statements on the matter see Coutinho, *General Góes*, pp. 364–365; and Góes Monteiro to Aranha, Washington, June 20 and July 10, 1939, OAA. Góes Monteiro intended to go to Germany but agreed to return to Brazil first, so as not to embarrass the U.S.; because of his heart con-

Góes Monteiro returned from the United States "like Radames, victorious and half enamoured, not with Aida but with American organization."[47] The American reception greatly impressed him, from the air escort of six Flying Fortresses and thirty-five pursuit planes that met the *Nashville* off the Virginia Capes, to his talks with Roosevelt, and his grand tour of American military installations.[48] But, as he commented to Marshall and Roosevelt, the American army did not appear ready for war. He refused to commit his country definitely to agreements that could later prove detrimental. He believed American industry capable of supplying arms for both countries, but as long as isolationist sentiment prohibited such action—as exemplified by the administration's inability to get Congress to pass legislation authorizing military assistance to Latin America—Brazil must not antagonize a possibly victorious Germany.[49]

Would there be war? Themistocles da Graça Aranha, counselor of the Brazilian embassy in Berlin, observed in mid-August that the situation depended almost exclusively on Hitler, who unfortunately was adamant concerning Danzig and the Polish corridor. But he saw reason for hope that peace might be preserved, because "with the exception of certain Nazi elements and a small fraction of army officers all the population of Germany is frankly against war, whose result certainly would be disastrous for this country

---

dition he declined the plane trip and returned by steamer. He was scheduled to embark from Rio for Europe on a ship called the *Neptunia* on August 29, and as late as mid-August the Itamaraty was making plans, but, because of the international situation the trip was canceled on August 28; MRE to Emb/Berlin, Rio, Aug. 12, 1939, #54, Exp. 2734 and Aug. 28, 1939, #58, Exp. 2997, AHMRE.

[47] Ambassador Martins to Aranha, Washington, July 14, 1939, OAA.

[48] Góes Monteiro to Aranha, Washington, June 20 and July 10, 1939, OAA. There are several telegrams and letters dealing with the trip in the Góes file in OAA. See also Pogue, *Marshall*, p. 341; Coutinho, *General Góes*, pp. 362–364.

[49] Coutinho, *General Góes*, p. 363.

which can not count very much on the military efficiency of Italy."[50]

War broke out in Europe on September 1, 1939, and early that morning Oswaldo Aranha drove to the Itamaraty where he met with his bureau chiefs to decide on measures to protect Brazilian citizens in the war zone. He had already sent instructions to the embassies and legations in Europe concerning the repatriation of Brazilians. On September 2, the day the new Brazilian ambassador, Cyro de Freitas Valle, presented his credentials to Hitler, Vargas outlined regulations establishing strict neutrality. Two months earlier Aranha had advised him that he expected a clash between the totalitarian and democratic states and that Brazil should remain neutral. Because it was likely to be a long war, victory would go to the side controlling the seas, and Aranha was certain that the democracies would maintain naval supremacy. As in the "Great War" it would be difficult to maintain permanent neutrality, and, he said, the government should decide what Brazil's attitude would be when it became necessary to abandon neutrality. He urged preparation of public opinion and of the economy. In the following weeks the Brazilian government quietly removed functionaries who had suspicious relationships with German elements.[51]

After the outbreak of fighting in Europe Brazil was doubly anxious to obtain American weapons, because it would now be difficult to obtain the arms ordered in Germany. But the Pittman Resolution (authorizing the Ameri-

50 T. da Graça Aranha, Berlin, July 10, 1939, #51, AHMRE.

51 Barros Gomes, *Exposição Sucinta*, p. 24. For first reports from Europe, see Brazilian "Green Book," MRE, *O Brasil e a Segunda Guerra Mundial* (Rio de Janeiro, 1944), I, 53–54. For neutrality decrees, *ibid.*, pp. 69–80; Aranha to Vargas, Rio, June 29, 1939, OAA; same document in MRE, *Brasil e a Segunda Guerra*, I, 9–10; Cauby C. Araújo to Evan Young, Rio, Oct. 26, 1939, Private Papers of C. C. Araújo. Araújo was Brazilian representative of Pan-American Airlines and Young was PAA Vice-President (N.Y.) in charge of the airline's relations with foreign governments.

can army and navy to assist their counterparts in Latin America) still languished in Congress, so General Marshall sought to preserve Brazilian confidence by offering surplus coast artillery, seventy-five old field guns and some antiaircraft cannon, at nominal prices. Meanwhile President Roosevelt became alarmed at reports that the Germans planned to seize the island of Fernando de Noronha, a Brazilian possession lying about 215 miles off the Natal bulge, and turn it into a submarine base. The Brazilian authorities assured Washington that the island was secure, but they urged speed in supplying their forces. President Roosevelt now gave their requests his personal attention and backing.[52]

During the summer of 1939 the War Department had arranged for American Flying Fortresses to visit Rio on the occasion of the fiftieth anniversary of the Brazilian republic (November 15, 1939). Major General Delos C. Emmons, commanding officer of the Army Air Force, who led the flight, carried a letter from Roosevelt to Vargas reaffirming Brazilian-American friendship and solidarity.[53] The flight gave the United States an opportunity to display its splendid new aircraft, to make an aerial survey of routes to the Brazilian bulge, and to examine the Natal area as the possible site for a major air base. Major Ridgway accompanied the flight and together with Colonel Allen Kimberly, chief of the United States Military Mission to Brazil, discussed problems of arms supply and strategy with Góes Monteiro. They repeated the offer to sell surplus coast artillery pieces and gave the Brazilian chief of staff a list of stragetic materials that the United States needed. The State Department had vetoed the Brazilian proposal that payment for American arms be made in raw materials. Simple as that would be, a direct barter arrangement would violate the liberal

[52] For Pittman Resolution see above Chapter 4, note 30; Marshall to Góes Monteiro, Oct. 5, 1939, AGV. Copy also in WPD 4224–19, WWII RS, NA.

[53] FDR to Vargas, Hyde Park, Nov. 7, 1939, OF 11 Brazil 1933–39, FDRL.

trade policies of the American government, and the State Department would not allow the exigencies of war to drive the United States into adopting Nazi trade practices. Instead the department proposed that purchases in both directions be in cash—the exchanges to equal one another as far as possible. The Brazilians agreed, and designated three artillery officers to return with General Emmons to inspect the materials offered.[54]

Meanwhile the United States took its first step toward abandoning neutrality. During the invasion of Poland the president called a special session of Congress, which after long and heated debate repealed the embargo on the exportation of arms to belligerents. Officially, Washington was still neutral, but it was neutrality in favor of Britain and France. The United States could not accept allied defeat because that "would leave the western hemisphere between the jaws of a victorious German Empire in a conquered Europe and a triumphant Japanese Empire in a subjected Asia."[55]

While Congress was meeting in Washington, representatives of the American republics gathered in Panama City (September 23 to October 3, 1939) to insulate the New World from the contagion raging in Europe. They issued the Declaration of Panama, demarcating a neutral zone that extended hundreds of miles from the shores of the American continents. It had little practical effect on the belligerents, and its violations produced reams of diplomatic protests, but it was a further step in the development of hemispheric solidarity. More important, it allowed Roosevelt to launch naval patrols in the Atlantic under a cloak of legality.[56]

[54] Conn and Fairchild, *Framework*, pp. 269–270.

[55] Samuel F. Bemis, *The Latin American Policy of the United States* (New York, 1943), p. 363.

[56] Carlos Delgado de Carvalho, *História Diplomática do Brasil* (São Paulo, 1959), pp. 390–391; for text see MRE, *Brasil e a Segunda Guerra*,

The round of visits and conferences during 1939 set the direction of Brazilian-American relations for the next years. Continuously, if fitfully, the two countries moved toward closer economic, military, and political cooperation. Their mutual problems—defense of the northeast and arming Brazilian forces—were not immediately resolved because of Brazil's insistence on defending the south rather than the northeast and American inability to supply arms. The most important and far-reaching event of the year was the signing of the Aranha accords, which marked the end of Great Britain's long domination of the Brazilian economy, weakened Germany's trade position, and laid the basis for economic collaboration between Brazil and the United States during the Second World War.

pp. 33–37; Bemis, *Latin American Policy*, p. 366; Cordell Hull, *The Memoirs of Cordell Hull*, 2 vols. (New York, 1948), II, 945–946.

*"The Brazilian economy is
export-oriented to a
remarkable degree."*[1]

6

The Open Door

TRADE WITH the United States had long been an important factor in the Brazilian economy, but the great depression made it imperative for Brazil to expand its markets; it could not diversify its economy and at the same time be totally dependent on North American consumption of its exports. There was no demand in that market for Brazilian cotton and textiles, nor much for sugar and its derivative products. The Vargas government thus became committed to industrial development in order to transform Brazil from an exporter of raw materials to a consumer of its own natural resources.

In the second half of the 1930's, however, Germany competed strenuously with the United States for the Brazilian market. Hitler's Germany wanted to renew the active trade that the First World War had weakened and the depression disrupted, and this provided Vargas and his commercial supporters with a foil to keep the American government and American business at a safe distance. The Brazilians wanted economic independence, but having only recently eased themselves from John Bull's clutches they were not anxious to be grabbed by someone else. They attempted to maneuver in such fashion as to increase trade, particularly exports, with both the United States and Germany, while avoiding dependence on either. Unfortunately events made such a balance impossible.

[1] Henry W. Spiegel, *The Brazilian Economy, Chronic Inflation and Sporadic Industrialization* (Philadelphia, 1949), p. 117.

With passage of the Reciprocal Trade Agreements Act in 1934 the Roosevelt administration began a concerted effort to maintain trade supremacy in Brazil. As the war drew closer and the struggle for the Brazilian market increasingly took on ideological overtones and greater strategic significance, it might be asked whether that struggle contributed to Germany's paranoiac claustrophobia? Was the American vision of equal opportunity for all, of an open door in Brazil, interpreted in the same way in Berlin, Rio de Janeiro, and Washington? No; the Americans attempted to write the rules of the game to emphasize their strengths and their rivals' weaknesses. The Americans demanded that the Germans deal in hard currencies, although this would force them out of the Brazilian market and generally restrict German economic recovery and expansion. And Brazil, like Germany, was hampered in trading according to American rules by a lack of internationally acceptable currencies. Barter deals and compensation arrangements made good sense to Brazilian authorities, with their abundance of raw materials, and they decided it was best to do nothing about American demands for tighter control of German trade. As a policy, doing nothing produced a tolerable balance that only war was able to upset. If the American-German struggle for the Brazilian market was ideological, it would seem that the ideology involved was neither totalitarianism nor democracy but economic nationalism.

The United States hoped to use reciprocal trade agreements to reopen outlets for American agricultural and industrial surpluses. The president was to negotiate executive agreements with foreign countries, which would include lowered United States tariff schedules. The negotiations instituted with the Brazilian government resulted in an agreement signed in February 1935, effective on January 1, 1936.[2] It was the first reciprocal trade agreement that the United States concluded and, like those that followed,

[2] See Hugh Gibson (U.S. Ambassador), Rio, Aug. 23, 1935, in *Foreign Relations, 1935,* IV, 300–321.

it contained the unconditional most-favored-nation principle. The United States pledged to maintain coffee on the free list and decreased its duty 50 percent on Brazil nuts, castor beans, and manganese ore. For its part Brazil accorded advantages to imports of American automobiles, machinery, spare parts, newsprint, wheat, and oatmeal.

Mutual need was the basis of trade arrangements between Brazil and Germany. The Germans sought raw materials and a market for their industrial goods, and the Brazilians wanted to dispose of the former and buy the latter. The situation seemed ready for joint concessions, but the Germans wanted to avoid using their scanty supply of internationally acceptable currency. So instead of paying for Brazilian cotton, coffee, unfinished and finished woods, tobacco, rubber, tropical fruits, iron ore, skins, and hides with such currency, they gave *aski* or compensation marks. *Aski* was the abbreviation for *Aüslander-Sonderkonten für Inlandszahlungen* (Foreigners' Special Accounts for Inland Payments), a system set up in 1934. Brazilian banks would open special accounts in German banks, and German importers, after having obtained the necessary permits from an import control board, would deposit their payments, in Reichsmarks, in these accounts to the credit of the Brazilian seller. The *aski* accounts or marks, as they were usually called, could be used by the Brazilians only to purchase German goods for export abroad. Once the deposit was made, the Brazilian exporter would arrange through the Bank of Brazil to sell his *aski* marks to a Brazilian importer wishing to purchase German products. The German exporter would be paid by the German bank that held the *aski* account on instructions from the Brazilian bank. The system tended to increase trade between Brazil and Germany because, as Brazilian exports to Germany multiplied, the Bank of Brazil found itself with large amounts of *aski* marks which it could unload only by lowering the selling rate. "This tended to reduce the prices of German goods for

Brazilian importers, thereby leading to an increase in German exports to Brazil."[3]

These increasing commercial relations with Brazil were one of the most effective methods of establishing Nazi influence. Shortly after coming to power in 1933, Hitler began an active trade program in South America aimed at overcoming the adverse effects of the depression on the German economy. The success of this program and the resulting increase in German trade "contributed significantly to a strengthening of a pro-German attitude" in Brazil, indeed in all South America, and "to the fulfillment of Nazi political objectives in the Western Hemisphere."[4] Naturally the commercial ties which had existed between the two countries for several decades prior to 1933 facilitated Nazi economic activities. German bankers, merchants, traders, and financiers occupied prominent positions in the Brazilian economy. The German businessman's willingness to settle permanently in the country, together with his industriousness and commercial acumen, enabled him to become firmly entrenched in Brazilian business and foreign trade circles. The prosperity of the German communities in southern Brazil (e.g., Blumenau, Santa Catarina, and Nôvo Hamburgo, Rio Grande do Sul) contributed to the overall growth of that region and increased German prestige.

The complementary nature of Brazilian-German commerce—manufactured goods in exchange for primary ma-

[3] Margaret S. Gordon, *Barriers to World Trade, A Study in Recent Commercial Policy* (New York, 1941), pp. 179–181; quotation from p. 181. See also study by Economic, Financial, and Transit Department of the League of Nations, *International Currency Experience, Lessons of the Inter-War Period* (League of Nations, 1944), pp. 177–181; and Cleona Lewis, *Nazi Europe and World Trade* (Washington, 1941). *Aski* marks were also called compensation marks and the names are used interchangeably in this chapter.

[4] William N. Simonson, "Nazi Infiltration in South America, 1933–1945" (Ph.D. Dissertation, Fletcher School of Law and Diplomacy, Tufts University, 1964), p. 320.

terials—led to a large trade prior to World War I. In 1913 Germany ranked third in the Brazilian market, behind Great Britain and the United States. The First World War temporarily forced Germany out; it returned during the 1920's to recapture its position, only to see it slip away again in the depression. The Nazis adopted energetic measures to promote the economic recovery of Germany and to establish the framework for attaining Hitler's basic economic and political aim—*Lebensraum*.[5] Under the Nazi system the state dominated and controlled foreign trade in order to support political objectives, operating through a highly complex and elaborate mechanism of exchange controls, bilateral trade balancing, compensation and clearing agreements, barter arrangements, and export subsidies.

The most objectionable feature of Brazilian-German trade in American eyes was the employment of the *aski* mark system, which subjected every transaction to the regulation and approval of a German government agency. The *aski* system allowed the Third Reich to control its export and import trade, buying only essential products, excluding those that were not necessary to the economy, and enabling Germany to obtain raw materials from Brazil while assuring a market for German manufactures.

In the latter part of the 1930's Germany wanted to negotiate a bilateral compensation and clearing agreement with Brazil further to facilitate trade. Between 1935 and 1939 several German trade delegations visited the country and the German embassy, consular staffs, and banks concerned themselves to a large extent with trade matters. Representatives and salesmen of German firms toured Brazil in great numbers. Before leaving Germany these people reportedly attended special courses to study National Socialism so they could faithfully represent the Reich while selling its goods.[6]

[5] George N. Holm, *Economic Systems: A Comparative Analysis* (New York, 1951), pp. 330–358.

[6] Simonson, "Nazi Infiltration," pp. 332–333.

In June 1935 the Brazilian government made an informal compensation (*aski*) arrangement with Germany, in spite of having signed the reciprocal trade agreement with the United States in February of the same year. Finance Minister Artur de Souza Costa, in defending this move, stated that certain Brazilian commercial interests depended on the compensation system to export their products to Germany, while others used it to import German goods. He implied that the Bank of Brazil, which handled the necessary accounting in Brazil, would adopt measures to protect other trading partners. The Department of State protested fruitlessly that the arrangement would place American traders at a disadvantage.[7]

In April 1936 Brazil announced it was considering negotiation of a provisional commercial agreement with Germany that would establish a quota system for Brazilian-German trade. The main purpose was to be the disposition of surplus Brazilian cotton in Germany. The United States immediately took the position that American commerce with Brazil would be affected adversely because Brazilian traders would utilize the *aski* system; moreover, such an accord would run counter to the spirit, if not the letter, of the 1935 reciprocal trade agreement. The matter was especially touchy because the United States also sold cotton to Germany, but for hard currency, and obviously Germany would benefit if it could obtain Brazilian cotton via the *aski* system. Berlin pressed energetically for an early signing, at times assuming a "very truculent and threatening attitude"; even Hitler himself reportedly took part in the negotiations.[8]

The Germans rejected out of hand the Brazilian sugges-

---

[7] George A. Gordon (Chargé), Rio, June 19, 1935, *Foreign Relations, 1935*, IV, 376–378; Hull, Washington, June 21, 1935, *ibid.*, 379; Gordon, Rio, June 22, 1935, *ibid.*, 379–381; Robert M. Scotten (Chargé), Rio, July 31, 1935, *ibid.*, 381–382.

[8] Gibson, Rio, May 30, 1936, *Foreign Relations, 1936*, V, 257–258.

tion that certain items which Brazil normally imported from the United States should be excluded from the agreement. Secrecy surrounded the talks, and the American ambassador in Rio had considerable difficulty obtaining exact information about the proposed accord. The Germans and their Brazilian friends attempted to have the agreement signed before the matter had been fully discussed within the Brazilian government, and before the United States had time to declare its opposition. Only by great effort was the American ambassador able to secure a guarantee that the Brazilians would not sign until the United States government had expressed itself. American insistence that the proposed arrangement contravened the 1935 reciprocal trade agreement and Brazil's professed policy of nondiscrimination resulted in the Vargas government's abandoning its intention of signing a formal trade agreement with Germany. Instead it secretly concluded an informal understanding that was essentially the same.[9]

When the "understanding" came up for renewal in early 1937 the Department of State outlined its objections in an *aide-memoire*, again stressing the hardships resulting for American traders. It urged Brazil to renounce the compensation (*aski*) arrangement and to replace it with a formal trade agreement on liberal lines, providing for merchandise payments in free currencies, reciprocal reductions of tariffs and quantitative restrictions, and especially elimination of German *aski* mark and subsidy procedures.[10] The German government embarked on a high-pressure campaign, offering attractive inducements for increased imports of Brazilian products, to obtain a favorable decision from the Vargas regime. Pressure from German and Brazilian sources alike became tremendous; nevertheless, the Brazilian government, as a concession to the United States, notified the German embassy that the "understanding" would be ex-

[9] *Foreign Relations, 1936*, v, 257–273.

[10] Francis B. Sayre (Asst. Secy. of State) to Scotten, Washington, May 12, 1937, *Foreign Relations, 1937*, v, 323–326.

tended only for three months, while it studied the American objections.[11]

At the suggestion of Oswaldo Aranha, then Brazilian ambassador to the United States, Finance Minister Souza Costa went to Washington in mid-June to discuss economic relations in general and the Brazilian-German compensation arrangement in particular. Berlin protested vehemently against this "unwarranted and unfair interference" by the United States in the Reich's trade relations with Brazil.[12] At the end of the discussions Aranha, in the name of his government, pledged the complete execution of the reciprocal trade agreement of February 1935 in "letter and in spirit." Brazil would not accept goods which were subsidized directly by the German government if they competed with American exports. But the Brazilians held firm on the key issue—the *aski* system. Compensation, Aranha insisted, was a necessary, but temporary, expedient and the Brazilian authorities would regulate it to prevent the dislocation of trade with countries operating in free currencies. In order to improve the operation of their reciprocal agreement he agreed to the creation of two committees, one in New York and the other in Rio de Janeiro, composed of businessmen from both countries; the committees would study trade problems and make recommendations.[13] In exchange for these pledges, though not officially so stated, the United States agreed to sell up to $60,000,000 in gold to Brazil over a five-year period, and to furnish foreign exchange against it. The Germans promptly accused the United States of using gold credits "to gain influence over the form of Brazil's trade with other countries."[14]

[11] *Ibid.*, pp. 326–331.

[12] *Ibid.*, pp. 331–332; Welles to Hans Heinrich Dieckhoff (German Ambassador in Washington), July 21, 1937, 632.6231/225A, NA.

[13] Aranha to Hull, Washington, July 14, 1937, *Foreign Relations, 1937*, v, 334–335; see also Artur de Souza Costa file in OAA for related documents.

[14] *New York Times*, July 20, 1937; American-Brazilian Association

When the three-month extension of the Brazilian-German compensation understanding neared expiration (on September 5, 1937), Germany strongly urged Brazil to renew it for an additional year with no limitations on the value of German purchases. Germany envisaged a substantial increase in the mark values allotted in its new quota schedules for Brazilian products. Brazil, however, desired quotas with value and quantity limitations, because the existing arrangement only limited purchases by quantity and allowed Germany to control the flow of compensation marks into the Brazilian economy by increasing the prices paid. This method served to keep Brazil in an overbought position, and artificially balanced trade in Germany's favor.

Several months of negotiations followed, during which verbal agreements from time to time extended the compensation arrangement. The negotiators were faced with the triple difficulty of securing a formula acceptable to both parties—and also to the United States under the terms of the 1935 agreement and the Aranha note of July 1937. The Brazilians, with the State Department pressing them at every turn, sought to obtain Germany's promise not to subsidize exports and to regulate their commerce so as not to dislocate trade between Brazil and countries using hard currencies. The Germans were willing to guarantee that the Reich government would not directly subsidize exports, but they would not include reference to indirect or private subsidies.[15] According to Washington's interpretation, the contributions of German industries which financed the German subsidy program were obligatory, though Berlin claimed that such contributions were voluntary. While it was nominally true that the Reich government itself was not granting subsidies, a government-controlled organization

---

(New York), *Brazil*, Vol. 9, No. 106 (August 1937), 6–7; John M. Blum, *From the Morgenthau Diaries: Years of Urgency, 1938–1941* (Boston, 1965), p. 493.

[15] Hull to Caffery, Washington, Sept. 9, 1937, *Foreign Relations, 1937*, v, 342–343.

administered the so-called voluntary fund. The German government had demonstrated its ability to assume responsibility for the voluntary fund organization in 1936, when Berlin gave Washington assurances that "no public or private subsidies would be paid with respect to German exports to the United States."[16] The State Department desired a similar guarantee for Brazil, but the Germans refused.

As 1937 came to a close it was apparent that the temporary extensions of the Brazilian-German arrangement were serving as well as a formal long-term accord. Although both Germany and the United States were increasing their share of the Brazilian market at the expense of other trading nations, Germany was edging ahead in percentage terms and cutting into the profits of American concerns.[17] Members of the American business community in Brazil declared that the *aski* trade had nullified any benefits resulting from the Reciprocal Trade Agreement, which they termed a failure. The complaints of these businessmen and consular reports from Brazil continually reminded the State Department of the importance of its efforts to protect American commerce from what they considered unfair competition.[18]

The Brazilians, unable to find a formula acceptable to both their number one and number two trading partners, tried a new tack. Ambassador Aranha suggested that the crux of the problem was not German subsidy of exports but the undervaluation of the *aski* mark by the Bank of Brazil. The government, he said, planned gradually to raise the

---

16 Welles to Caffery, Washington, Nov. 3, 1937, *ibid.*, pp. 345–346.

17 Banco do Brasil, *Relatório, 1938*, pp. 276, 281.

18 For reports on the status of American trade and the economic situation in Brazil see the following in State files in NA: 1) Report of Norbert A. Bogdan of J. Henry Schroeder Banking Corp., Jan. 10, 1938, in Duggan to Herbert Feis, Jan. 15, 1938, 832.00/1168; 2) Scotten, Rio, Jan. 26, 1938, 832.00/1163 (this is a study of the economic and political situation by the Rio embassy); 3) Report on Brazil by Bankers Trust Company of New York in H. V. Johnson, London, May 9, 1938, 832.00/1168; 4) Memo; Groves to Hawkins, Feb. 2, 1938, 611.3231/1168, all NA.

cost of the mark, relating it directly to the dollar so that it would fluctuate in value like hard currency. The State Department commented that while Brazil's efforts to control the value of the *aski* mark would be helpful, the department was "more immediately concerned" with the question of subsidized trade.[19]

After the new Reich ambassador, Karl Ritter, arrived in Rio de Janeiro in December 1937, the German position stiffened. Ritter refused to sign any agreement in connection with "indirect subsidies" and made his government's position clear—Germany need not, necessarily, buy Brazilian coffee and cotton, and if Brazil interfered in the operation of the *aski* mark arrangement, the Reich would buy coffee and cotton elsewhere.[20] Germany thereupon demonstrated its importance to the Brazilian economy by reducing cotton purchases. Immediately the Itamaraty and the Ministry of Finance were flooded with letters from Brazilian businessmen protesting the government's German trade policy. Faced with German stubbornness and with opposition at home the Brazilian government apparently resolved to maintain the *status quo*—it seems to have been an axiom of Brazilian administrative policy that when faced with an awkward situation the wisest thing was to procrastinate until events had run their course. And in this case a policy of doing nothing was likely to be successful. The members of the Souza Costa mission to the United States in mid-1937 had assured themselves that Washington would not retaliate if Brazil continued the compensation procedure with Germany.[21] And because the United States brought no economic pressure to bear, Brazil frankly considered "all the many arguments . . . put forth throughout the past several

[19] Walter F. Donnelly (Economics Section Rio Embassy) to Caffery, Rio, Jan. 28, 1938, 632.6231/239, NA; Caffery to Aranha, Rio, Feb. 19, 1938, OAA; Hull to Caffery, Washington, Feb. 3, 1938, *Foreign Relations, 1938*, V, 389–390.

[20] Caffery, Rio, Jan. 11, 1938, *ibid.*, pp. 382–383.

[21] Caffery, Rio, Feb. 25, 1938, *ibid.*, pp. 392–393.

years as 'pure literature.' "[22] In September 1937 Aranha had described United States foreign policy as "weak and lamentable"; he thought that the American government would not protect the "very interests of the country." Moreover, after Vargas established the Estado Nôvo, the Roosevelt administration had committed itself to supporting the new regime.[23]

The State Department objected to the Itamaraty, in February 1938, that "Brazil was not playing ball . . . on this subject." Although it made the Brazilians uncomfortable, American representatives told them that "Brazil was entirely too much afraid of the attitude of the Germans, and that should Brazil actually bring herself to the point of taking action in this matter she would find that the Germans considered the Brazilian market to be just as important as the Brazilians considered the German market to be."[24] Faced with Brazilian determination not to give in to American demands, Ambassador Caffery recommended that Washington adopt a firmer stance. But Undersecretary Welles flatly rejected coercive action. In his view there had been several favorable developments, particularly the Brazilian ambassador's statement that his country would not sign a new, formal compensation accord with Germany; this led Welles to conclude that the current American policy had produced "certain definite results," so there was no need to change it.[25] Perhaps he thought that strong economic pressure would endanger Brazilian-American approximation and reinvigoration of the Good Neighbor Policy. At any rate, the Brazilians decided not to negotiate a new trade agreement with Germany. They were certain that they could continue their German trade under the *aski*

[22] Caffery, Rio, May 6, 1938, *ibid.*, pp. 344–347.

[23] Aranha to Vargas, Washington, Sept. 24, 1937 and Nov. 24, 1937, OAA.

[24] Memo: Scotten (Counselor of Embassy), Rio, Feb. 23, 1938, *Foreign Relations, 1938*, v, 390–392.

[25] Welles to Caffery, Washington, June 2, 1938, *ibid.*, pp. 347–349.

system without running the risk of losing their American market—they merely continued to operate under the existing arrangement on a "temporary" basis until the war halted all trade.

The United States had prevented the signing of a new agreement, but it had not achieved its goals, namely preventing the use of compensation practices and the expansion of German-Brazilian trade, and insuring equal opportunity for American exporters in the Brazilian market.[26] Both the United States and Germany saw Brazil as a source of raw materials for their industry and as a market for their manufactures. Brazilian economic development was of interest only in proportion to its potential for increasing their share of the market, or for its political value. For both powers Brazil was a neocolonial state, governmentally independent but economically dependent on whatever powers controlled the lion's share of world trade. Brazilian leaders were in the jaws of the beast because their greatest exchange earners were raw cotton, a variety of minerals, and the desert crops—coffee, cacao, tobacco. Only by increasing their sales of these products could they hope to obtain sufficient exchange to finance development projects, such as hydroelectric plants.

The Vargas government hoped that electrification would reduce coal imports (in 1938 coal was the principal import from Germany) but of course the turbines, generators, transformers, booster equipment, and wiring would all have to be imported. In the initial stages development would merely raise the sophistication of the imported products from coal to electrical equipment. But while development would not immediately end dependence on foreign sources of manufactured items it would drastically alter

[26] Donald W. Giffin, "The Normal Years: Brazilian-American Relations, 1930–1939," (Ph.D. Dissertation, Vanderbilt University, 1962), pp. 312–324. Giffin gives a detailed, day-to-day account of Brazilian-American negotiations up to 1939 based upon Department of State papers.

Brazil's internal political structure. As the government's dependence on a particular crop as exchange-earner (for example, coffee) was reduced by increased sales of other crops (cacao, then cotton), new segments of society accumulated capital, prestige, and political power. Diffusion of power would allow the government more room to maneuver politically, so in a sense development would bring the ruling group, at least as long as it was able to maintain control, a feeling of increased independence.

Brazilian policy, therefore, aimed at enlarging and broadening foreign sales. In so doing the Vargas regime hoped to increase Brazil's economic independence, while assisting in the growth of new power-groups within the country. Such economic nationalism was intended to preserve the Brazilian nation and to fend off the political penetration which the economic policies of both Germany and the United States tended to encourage under various guises; for example, joint committees to suggest ways to facilitate binational trade. Brazilian and American policies were necessarily in conflict, as long as United States diplomacy sought reduction of Germany's share of the Brazilian market and Brazilian diplomats worked to increase their nation's sales to the Reich.

The Brazilians wished to trade wherever possible, on whatever terms were agreeable; they were less concerned with trade mechanisms per se than in securing markets and moving goods. Indeed, Washington's pleas for liberal trade policies based on purchases in hard currencies were not eagerly received: the Brazilians lacked such currencies and what little they had were needed to back up the *Mil-réis* (replaced in 1942 by the *cruzeiro*), pay off foreign holders of Brazilian bonds, remit the profits of foreign companies, and finance purchases in the United States. To obtain dollars, for example, the Brazilians had to sell to the United States, but their principal exchange-earner in that market was coffee, which was meeting increasing competition from Central American, Colombian, and Venezuelan producers.

That was why Germany was so attractive; it offered a chance to expand exports and purchase finished goods without expenditure of hard currency. Moreover, Germany provided an outlet for Brazilian cotton, wool, and fruits such as oranges, that had no market in the United States. The fact that Brazilian and American cotton exporters were competitors in the German trade naturally aroused Brazilian suspicions that Washington's commercial policies were not as disinterested as the United States professed.

While the Brazilians had to guard against the United States securing undue influence over Brazil's trade policies, they had to be careful of the Germans, too. In 1937 Brazil had ranked eighth among the countries selling to Germany. The next year German buyers increased their purchases, raising Brazil to sixth place, and Brazilian officials thought that they might reach fourth or fifth place in 1939. For 1938–1939 Brazil's exports to Germany represented 16.5 percent of Brazil's total exports (by comparison 34.2 percent went to the United States). That being the case, an examination of the principal exports to Germany in 1938 would be useful. While coffee was the most important product in Brazil's sales to the United States, cotton was the most important in its trade with Germany. In 1938 Germany imported 1,211,182 bales of raw cotton, of which 466,364 came from Brazil, 200,170 from the United States, 136,953 from Egypt, and the remaining 407,695 from miscellaneous sources. Since the cotton producers' lobby in the United States prevented importation of the Brazilian fiber, the Vargas regime looked with considerable favor on the cotton sales to Germany. Brazil's coffee exports to Germany were likewise sizable. Of the 197,419,700 kilos which Germany imported in 1938, Brazil supplied 41 percent or 91,789,700 kilos. And it had reason to hope, because of Berlin's reduction of the Colombian and Venezuelan quotas, that it could gain a larger share in the future. In the same year 14 percent of Germany's tobacco came from Brazil, which was a substantial increase over the previous year

(14,382,500 kilos in 1938 as against 13,883,900 in 1937) and the Brazilians expected further increases at the expense of their nearest competitors, Greece and the Dutch East Indies.[27]

The story was the same in cacao, Brazil's third most important export. Of the 127,887 tons of cacao which Brazil exported in 1938, 10,599 tons went to Germany. And since Germany was the third largest consumer of that product, after the United States and Great Britain, the Brazilians were excited at the prospect of "a newly conquered market," to which the Brazilian embassy in Berlin recommended "permanent attention."[28] For two other products Germany was Brazil's chief market—rubber and wool. Though Brazil's production of raw rubber declined from 14,792 tons in 1937 to 8,819 tons in 1938, of the latter figure 6,715 tons or 77 percent went to Germany. Even though Brazil's portion of the total German rubber market was small (7.2 percent) the sales obviously were of tremendous importance to the limping Amazonian producers.[29] The same was true of wool; though Brazil supplied only 2,177,000 kilos of Germany's total imports of 75,436,600 (1938), these equaled 40 percent of all the wool Brazil sold that year. The fact that this was a decline from 88 percent in 1936 and 93 percent in 1937 emphasized Germany's importance to Brazilian wool producers.[30]

The Brazilians were rapidly becoming dependent on the German market for the sale of certain products—cotton, rubber, wool—and being tempted by possibilities of in-

[27] The foregoing is based upon Carlos Alberto Gonçalves (2d Secy. of Embassy), Memo: "O Intercâmbio da Alemanha com o Brasil," in Themistocles da Graça Aranha (Counselor of Embassy), Berlin, Apr. 27, 1939, #152, AHMRE.

[28] Gonçalves, Memo: "O Cacau na Alemanha," in Graça Aranha, Berlin, Aug. 9, 1939, #282, AHMRE.

[29] Gonçalves, Memo: "A Borracha no Mercado Alemão," in Graça Aranha, Berlin, June 20, 1939, #210, AHMRE.

[30] Gonçalves, Memo: "A Lã na Alemanha," in Cyro de Freitas Valle (Ambassador), Berlin, Sept. 9, 1939, #197, AHMRE.

creasing sales in others—coffee and cacao, as indicated above, but also finished and unfinished woods, tropical fruits, skins and hides, iron ore, and butter.[31] And because most of these purchases were made in *aski* marks, the more Germany bought the more marks Brazil accumulated and the more it could buy from German producers. Use of the *aski* system allowed the Germans to offer more favorable prices than their American and British competitors. In May 1938, for instance, *aski* marks enabled Brazilian importers to buy German goods at a price 24 percent less than the goods would have cost in Reichsmarks. And government subsidies and controls also allowed German exporters to extend attractive terms which their less flexible competitors could not match. It might be argued that this created an exclusive trading situation that was harmful to world trade, but the fact was that enough Brazilian businessmen were profiting to make it politically inexpedient for the Vargas government to undermine the trade. Other countries, such as the United States, were unhappy because their exports were hurt by the German methods. They complained not only that the *aski* system restricted trade, but also that it did not contribute foreign exchange, which Brazil sorely needed to pay the holders of Brazilian bonds (who happened to include a large number of Americans), traders operating in free currencies, and interest due on various foreign loans. Within the Brazilian government counsels were divided sufficiently to insure the trade's continuation for want of an equally functional substitute.[32]

[31] For a detailed review of Brazil's export trade with Germany see Gonçalves, Memo: "O Intercâmbio da Alemanha com o Brasil" cited in note 27.

[32] Ambassador Caffery argued in favor of using economic pressure to force Brazil into line, observing that "the Brazilians are completely happy to do business with Germany on a compensation basis and have not the slightest desire to give up this trade unless they are forced to do so. As long as it is money in their pocket, our arguments from the long-range point of view of dislocation of markets, free triangular trade versus bilateral trade, removal of trade barriers, et cetera, have a

This was the heart of the American-German conflict over the Brazilian market. Ostensibly the Americans did not object to Brazilian sales of rubber and wool to the Reich, though they were concerned about Brazilian cotton competition—what they objected to was that Brazil's sales obligated it automatically to buy German products that competed with American ones. This aspect of Brazilian-German trade worried the Brazilians as well. In 1938 Brazil was the principal non-European consumer of German products, and ninth (as determined by the value of its purchases) among all of Germany's customers. Brazil was buying coal, yarn, cotton and artificial silk threads, wire and tubing, various types of cloth (including cotton and wool), prepared skins and cured hides, textile looms and other machines, cement, wood pulp, fertilizers, malts, paper products, steam locomotives, glass, prepared rubber, copper articles, optical goods, agricultural implements, chemical and steel products. The raw materials for some of these products, such as the skins, hides, rubber, cotton, and wool, probably came at least partly from Brazil, underscoring the economy's low level of industrial development. But somehow it was particularly ironic that the country which had dominated sugar production in the seventeenth century should at the end of the third decade of the twentieth century import 45,400 kilos of sugar and 9,800 kilos of *aguardente* (a strong drink made from sugar) from Germany.[33]

The extensive German purchases in 1938 were a mixed blessing: while they stimulated sectors of the economy they also caused the Bank of Brazil to accumulate a huge stock of *aski* marks, because Brazilian importers could not buy German goods rapidly enough to maintain a balanced ex-

---

purely abstract significance which carry but little appeal to those directing the policies of Brazil today" (Caffery, Rio, May 6, 1938, *Foreign Relations, 1938*, v, 344–347). Aranha outlined the Brazilian position in a letter to Welles; Rio, Sept. 14, 1938, OAA.

[33] Gonçalves, Memo: "O Intercâmbio Teuto-Brasileiro," in Graça Aranha, Berlin, May 15, 1939, #177, AHMRE.

change. In June the bank, attempting to check and reduce its overbought position, adopted several measures restricting exports to Germany. Also the bank insisted that all German cotton purchases be made in hard currencies. The Germans, apparently determined to keep the bank overbought, shifted to cacao and purchased 300,000 bags at higher prices than other buyers were offering. By the end of the year Germany had imported 10,598,600 kilos (valued at 4,049,000 marks) as against 1,086,100 kilos (valued at 655,000 marks) in 1937, for an increase of 975 percent.[34] Of course, these purchases might have been part of the Reich's stockpiling in preparation for war.

Whatever the policy motivations, the Bank of Brazil found itself with an excess of approximately 30 million *aski* marks and, desiring to reestablish "equilibrium between these exports and our imports," the bank decided unofficially and without public announcement to refuse further authorization of exports against *aski* marks.[35] The German Ministry of Economy expressed its willingness to study any Brazilian proposals for ways of reestablishing the trade balance, but after waiting nearly three weeks without result it announced on July 13 that because of the bank's measures it was impossible for Germany to continue buying in the Brazilian market. Moreover, the ministry said, because it had to supply its population, augmented by the annexation of Austria, it was forced to turn to other countries that operated in compensation marks and offered the same products as Brazil, particularly coffee. Foreign Minister Aranha attempted to use the impasse to force Berlin to remove Ambassador Ritter, who was creating, in Aranha's words, "obstacles, irritations and misunderstandings" (Chapter 3). Ritter's replacement was to be the "preliminary condition to prepare a favorable atmosphere in which

[34] Gonçalves, Memo: "O Cacau na Alemanha," in Graça Aranha, Berlin, Aug. 9, 1939, #282, AHMRE.

[35] MRE (Oswaldo Aranha) to Emb/Berlin, Rio, June 24, 1938, #67, Exp. 1790, AHMRE.

to carry on negotiations." Aranha emphasized that the Vargas government was disposed to enter into an "ample and frank understanding" and to conclude "a commercial accord that takes into account the needs of the two countries," but he was reluctant to do this while the present German ambassador remained in Rio. The Germans firmly refused to withdraw Ritter and seemed determined to trade elsewhere. Berlin held the trump card and played it skillfully. Brazil could not afford to lose the German market, so on July 20, 1938, the bank announced its willingness to deal in *aski* marks again.[36]

Berlin was pleased with its victory, especially since it apparently saw the hand of the United States in the Brazilian maneuver. The director of the Wilhelmstrasse's commercial section assured Ambassador Moniz de Aragão that, although the ministry had received proposals from Brazil's competitors to supply Germany with coffee, tobacco, and cotton, it had not made any agreements because it hoped to reach a "rapid understanding" with Brazil. Furthermore, Germany would be greatly pleased to see their "commercial understanding" officially renewed, if possible for a minimum period of two years, so that the compensation system could be arranged to avoid future imbalances.[37]

Although Brazil had been forced to back down, and Ritter was still annoying Aranha, the Bank of Brazil had been able to reduce its overbought position considerably (from 22,000,000 *aski* marks on June 22, 1938, to 5,000,000 on July 20) before Berlin stopped German purchasing. The prob-

[36] J. J. Moniz de Aragão (Ambassador), Berlin, July 1, 1938, #81; July 13, 1938, #82; MRE to Emb/Berlin, Rio, July 14, 1938, #69, Exp. 1960, AHMRE.

[37] Actually American influence seems to have been marginal in the Bank of Brazil's decisions to stop dealing in *aski* marks and then begin again. Ambassador Caffery discussed the situation in a series of telegrams; see, for example: June 2, 1938, *Foreign Relations, 1938*, v, 394; June 15, 1938, *ibid.*, 394–395; June 22, 1938, *ibid.*, 350; July 22, 1938, *ibid.*, 353. The paragraph is based on Moniz de Aragão, Berlin, July 22, 1938, #85, AHMRE.

lem of maintaining a reasonable balance of trade in *aski* accounts was not adequately solved during the remaining months of 1938 which, as indicated earlier, witnessed a remarkable growth in commerce between the two nations. Nor was it solved in the following year. Throughout 1939, however, the Germans sought to intensify their trade with Brazil, much to the frustration of Washington, which continued to protest its unfairness.

Early in the year, Aranha went to the United States to attempt to resolve Brazilian-American differences, particularly to obtain admittance of a greater quantity of Brazilian products into the American market. Instead, the United States provided credits to finance exports to Brazil without substantially increasing Brazilian exports to the United States. Although the Export-Import Bank offered a line of credit to American importers, the United States quota arrangements for coffee and cacao did not allow expansion, and cotton continued to be excluded.[38] Germany, however, encouraged continuous expansion of Brazilian imports. The United States appeared to be seeking to stifle certain aspects of the Brazilian economy by selling more than it bought, by dealing in hard currencies, by giving loans and credits that were tied to purchases in the American market, and at the same time protesting that the Brazilians were not paying on hard-currency bond issues and debts, and that they were utilizing a system that tended to link sectors of the Brazilian and German economies to the exclusion of American competitors. The Brazilian military, in particular, was irritated when Washington objected to arms purchases in Germany made with mixed hard-currency and compensation marks, but offered no alternative source of armament.

American arguments for liberal trade policies, for an open door in Brazil, seemed hollow indeed when Washington sponsored an international conference on cotton in early

[38] The Aranha Mission was discussed in Chap. 5 above.

1939 with the object of getting producing countries to limit their output. Both Brazilians and Germans saw self-interest behind the façade of American concern about overproduction. Germany could not get enough cotton to satisfy its domestic (and expanding military) requirements and was annoyed when the United States refused to sell it three million bales in late 1938, forcing expanded purchases in Egypt, Iran, Turkey, and Brazil, using the *aski* system.[39] The Brazilian embassy in Berlin reported that the Reich needed four million bales a year for the normal functioning of its industries; in 1938 Brazil had supplied 30 percent of Germany's cotton imports, and the decrease in United States sales to Germany, as well as problems with the cotton harvests in Egypt and India, would in all likelihood enable Brazil to step up its cotton exports.[40] Both the United States and Brazil had favorable balances of trade with Germany for 1938, but Brazilian-American trade was tipped in favor of the United States.[41] Therefore the Brazilian authorities were as interested as were the Germans in stepping up the pace and extent of their commerce.

The Wilhelmstrasse and the Ministry of Economy had come to see Brazil as such "an indispensable source [of supply] for the German economy" that they were willing to reduce Nazi party activities there as the price of greater economic ties. The Brazilians used Germany's economic needs as a shield to protect themselves from Nazi political penetration. Foreign Minister von Ribbentrop and other leaders eventually recognized that they had committed an error in tact in regard to party activities in Brazil. As early as July

[39] Graça Aranha, Berlin, Jan. 30, 1939, #42; Feb. 2, 1939, #7, AHMRE; Welles to Aranha, Washington, Feb. 27, 1939, OAA. Latter discusses world cotton situation.

[40] Graça Aranha, Berlin, June 19, 1939 [signature date: June 15], #209, Report: "Mês económico no. 4–5, Abril–Maio 1939," AHMRE.

[41] For 1938 trade balances see charts in Graça Aranha, Berlin, Apr. 19, 1939, #144, Report: "Intercâmbio da Alemanha com o continente americano," AHMRE.

1938 German diplomats in South America had recommended making Nazi political goals subservient to economic considerations.[42] But the dispute over Ambassador Ritter had delayed implementation of such a policy toward Brazil until early 1939. By that time German officials were willing to admit that they had trampled needlessly on Brazil's sovereignty, and that they had not given sufficient consideration to the facts that Brazil was a "declared enemy of communism, without any contact with Russia" and that, again like Germany, she was not a member of the League of Nations. Certainly they could find ways to take advantage of their similar points of view. They even gave ground on the school question, admitting that the Brazilians were acting correctly in protecting their nation from foreign influences. This remarkable enlightenment was generated by the desire to increase purchases of coffee, cotton, cacao, tobacco, manganese, wool, fruits, and a variety of other products. They were even willing to consider paying for a desired million-sack increase in coffee imports with 50 percent or more in hard currencies and the remainder in *aski* marks. And they agreed to a Brazilian request to raise the quota on oranges from 200,000 crates a year to 250,000 in 1939.[43]

42 *DGFP–D*, v, 863–864. German diplomats from posts in Argentina, Brazil, Chile, and Uruguay met in Montevideo in July 1938. They predicted that the anti-German measures, which South American governments were then enacting, would continue in force for several years. They noted that these governments were worried that Germany was pursuing "aims of power" in South America; and that to achieve economic success Germany should "clearly repudiate such [political] intentions . . . and confine herself to economic and cultural aims." They also recommended ways to avoid open political conflict, and to ease the effect of restrictions against the Nazi party and German organizations while at the same time subtly promoting the Third Reich's political objectives in the area. In all, their recommendations underscored the importance of trade in Germany's foreign policy. See *ibid.*, pp. 830, 874–875, 880–882, 886–889, 891–893.

43 Graça Aranha, Berlin, Feb. 18, 1939, Private Memo on Economic-Political Relations, no number [rec'd. MRE Mar. 7, 1939 and stamped

The Germans contrasted their willingness to open their borders to Brazilian exports with the hesitancy of the United States to lift restrictive quotas and other barriers. They accused the United States of betraying the world economy and refusing to recognize that the exchange of goods was the alpha and omega of economic traffic between peoples.[44] The Minister of Economy and president of the Reichsbank, Walther Funck, asserted that the German and Brazilian economies were naturally complementary because Brazil was extremely rich in primary materials, while Germany, though highly industrialized, was poor in natural resources. He argued that the two countries needed one another but, while Germany's necessities were acute, the Reich did not desire a commercial monopoly but only "fair competition" to secure a share of Brazil's exports and imports. Germany wanted an open door in Brazil as much as the United States did, but Funck declared that the American attacks on the compensation trade could destroy German-Brazilian commerce. "If the efforts against compensation should be crowned with success," he warned, "Brazil will lose a highly receptive market and an important support for its national economy." He pointed out that Germany's 90 million people (1939) and dominant position in Central Europe made it an important and developing market, which could be a major factor in Brazil's future without necessarily prejudicing third parties. The minister went on to characterize Brazil's policy as seeking "to maintain its economic independence, in order not to be subject to particular states or groups of states," an objective which he said compensation trade with Germany strongly aided. Moreover, Germany was disposed to do everything it could

---

03815]; Graça Aranha, Berlin, June 7, 1939, #200, AHMRE. As a point of reference 100,000 crates of oranges were worth RM 450,000.

44 "El comercio exterior del Brasil," *El Observador del Reich* (Berlin), June 23, 1939, copy in Graça Aranha, Berlin, June 23, 1939, #217, AHMRE.

to cooperate and to assist Brazilian development as laid out in Vargas' Five-Year Plan.[45]

The Brazilians were, of course, aware that development would affect the nature of German-Brazilian commerce, indeed Brazil's international trade generally. As Brazil's coal mines increased production and as the electrification of the railroads went forward the demand for foreign coal would be reduced. Likewise iron and steel imports would decline with the establishment of a national steel industry; the same thing would happen to pharmaceutical and chemical imports as those industries developed. Brazilian officials hoped that such import reductions would result in tremendous savings. In 1938, Brazil paid Germany alone about 100,000 contos de réis (roughly $5,000,000 with 1 conto equaling $50) for sundry iron and steel products—bars, laminated steel, plates, etc.—and some 40,000 contos de réis (about $2,000,000) for pharmaceuticals. But Brazil would continue to need other products that it would be unable to produce for the foreseeable future, such as anilines, optical equipment, motors, industrial machines, porcelains, and other items made from patented processes.[46]

So on the eve of World War II Brazil was firm in its resolve not only to continue trade with Germany, but to expand it, in spite of United States opposition to the methods employed and of Aranha's pledges to reduce use of the *aski* mark system. On September 2, 1939, the new Brazilian ambassador, Cyro de Freitas Valle, presented his credentials to Adolf Hitler. German troops were rapidly smothering Polish resistance and the world teetered on the brink of global war. In the next days as it became clear that Great Britain and France would engage Germany, Brazil's trade with the Reich appeared more and more vulnerable, espe-

[45] From *Berliner-Börsen-Zeitung*, Berlin, June 16, 1939, clipping and commentary in Graça Aranha, Berlin, June 19, 1939, #207, AHMRE.

[46] Graça Aranha, Berlin, May 15, 1939, #177, AHMRE. This is a detailed memo on German-Brazilian trade in 1938 with comments on the possible effects of Brazilian economic development on that trade.

cially since commerce in *aski* marks could leave Brazil with useless paper if a blockade prevented the actual exchange of goods. In the second week of the war the Bank of Brazil had some 17 million marks deposited in Germany for the use of Brazilian buyers, while in Brazil the bank was holding 80 million marks. In order to keep up the Brazilians' confidence, high officials at the Wilhelmstrasse assured them that Germany intended to receive, pay for, and store in Brazil all the cotton that it had contracted for, and it was ready to make an agreement "convenient to both countries" regarding the unused surpluses in the *aski* accounts. However, the Reichsbank would keep its surplus on deposit with the Bank of Brazil so as to be ready to resume purchases immediately after the war. All conversations between the Brazilian embassy and German officials indicated that they believed the war would be short and that their main interest was to prepare the way to reopen normal trade.[47]

But as the weeks dragged on into months the Brazilians began to worry. There seemed to Ambassador Freitas Valle

[47] Freitas Valle, Berlin, Sept. 2, 1939, #304; Sept. 14, 1939, #132, AHMRE. Freitas Valle's presentation took place in Hitler's office in the Reich Chancellery in Foreign Minister Ribbentrop's presence. Hitler asked about Vargas, talked knowledgeably of German-Brazilian problems, offered the ambassador his assistance if needed, and ended the interview with comments indicating his "consternation" at the necessity of making war. Apparently Hitler had not slept for the previous forty-eight hours and appeared drained. More than a month passed before Ribbentrop called the ambassador in for the traditional first conversation (and then after Freitas Valle complained to foreign ministry officials of being ignored). At that meeting, on November 9, Ribbentrop was so cordial that he told the ambassador to come to see him as often as he liked and went to the extreme, in Freitas Valle's estimation, of praising his German, which, as the ambassador commented to Aranha, "Your Excellency knows, is very bad." Freitas Valle, Berlin, Nov. 21, 1939, #364, AHMRE. Actually Freitas Valle had had an opportunity to practice his German before going to Berlin, because as part of his preparation for the assignment he had toured the German settlements in Paraná, Santa Catarina, and Rio Grande do Sul in June 1938; see MRE to Emb/Berlin, Rio, June 28, 1938, #39, Exp. 2190, AHMRE. Freitas Valle was a cousin of Aranha.

to be "no enthusiasm" for the war among the German people. Everything was well organized and the Germans accepted the rationing of gasoline and other essential items without complaint, but at the same time there was little display of enthusiasm. People, he said, did not seem happy at the announcements over the radios in the cafés. They wanted the fighting ended as soon as possible, but did their stoic attitude indicate recognition that it probably would continue for a long time? The Brazilian army grew steadily more concerned that it would not be able to transport its extensive purchases of German artillery safely to Brazil. By mid-October, the embassy in Berlin still had not received funds from Rio to pay its staff for August and September. And Britain's ability to enforce a passport system (called Navicert) to prevent neutrals from shipping proscribed goods to Germany had an unsettling effect, as did the British censorship at Gibraltar of Brazilian mail bound for the embassy and consulates in the Reich. Also disturbing was the German suggestion that if the British disrupted the flow of trade the neutrals should band together "to threaten Great Britain and impose conditions on it." Freitas Valle observed dryly that "the argumentation is infantile, but it is popular here." At the end of October, an aide at the consulate in Berlin told a Brazilian reporter "that the situation was very grave." Growing lack of confidence in an early German victory as the fighting entered the "phony war" stage, and the awareness that they might lose their German markets for the duration caused the Brazilians to hedge their bets. In early November 1939 the Commission for the Defense of the National Economy directed the Itamaraty to explore possibilities of selling a long list of products in the American market, especially items which the United States then obtained in Africa or Asia.[48]

[48] Freitas Valle, Berlin, Sept. 30, 1939, #315, Memo: "O Primeiro Mês da Guerra, Visto do Berlim"; MRE to Emb/Berlin, Rio, Sept. 15, 1939, Exp. 3456; Freitas Valle to Graça Aranha, Berlin, Oct. 13, 1939, no number; MRE to Emb/Washington, Rio, Nov. 14, 1939, Exp. 4540;

American diplomacy had been unable to secure application of classic open-door principles in Brazilian foreign trade. Brazilian leaders rightly believed that if they conducted international commerce solely in hard currencies, when their own currency had depreciated 71.3 percent between 1928 and 1938, they would face further depreciation at home and greater debts abroad. Brazil had simply been running out of money. The Vargas government had been forced to suspend debt payments at the start of the Estado Nôvo, and had to pursue trade methods that did not necessitate the outflow of cash and gold reserves.[49] American arguments that this hurt American interests had fallen on deaf ears because the *aski* account system was helpful to Brazilian interests.

Brazilian policy aimed at achieving an equilibrium between American and German interests in the national economy so that it would not be entirely dependent on any one foreign country. Unaligned with either, Vargas sought to obtain something of benefit from both.[50]

Freitas Valle, Berlin, Nov. 27, 1939, #375; Freitas Valle, Berlin, Oct. 31, 1939, #195; MRE to Emb/Washington, Rio, Nov. 7, 1939, Exp. 4404, all AHMRE.

[49] Aranha to Vargas, Rio, Feb. 8, 1939, Memo: "O Problema da Divida Externa," AGV.

[50] For Vargas' attitude see his speech at the Army Arsenal on Mar. 24, 1939, in his *A Nova Política do Brasil* (Rio de Janeiro, 1938–47), VI, 191–192; and DESPS (*Delegacia Especial de Segurança Política e Social*) report on reaction to speech in Alvaro Baptista Teixeira, n.p., Mar. 28, 1939, AGV.

"There are certain hopes for peace . . . the war already is materially impossible. It will cost so much in raw materials and human material that no one has the courage to begin a real offensive."[1]

7

Crisis and Uncertainty

THE WAR gave a new dimension to Brazilian foreign relations. If victorious Germany confronted a weak and neutral United States in the Western Hemisphere, Brazil would be at the mercy of the Reich. With Axis forces sweeping all before them in Europe, the strategic situation and Brazil's weakness combined to impose cautious neutrality. Argentina's attitude was uncertain, demanding extensive preparations in the south despite American warnings about the vulnerability of the northeast. Unassimilated immigrant groups of questionable loyalties caused the government considerable worry, while a shaky economy and poor transportation and communications systems made control difficult. The armed forces were strong enough to keep Getúlio Vargas in power, but they were not adequate to defend Brazil's thousands of miles of coastline. With good reason, Brazilian officials maneuvered during the months of 1940 to increase their bargaining power with both Germany and the United States, hoping to follow a course that would place them on the right side no matter who won the war.

Brazilian-German relations had all but collapsed during 1938 because of Reich Ambassador Karl Ritter's unreasonable demands that the Vargas government allow the Nazi party to function freely in Brazil. When Aranha and Vargas

[1] Aranha to Vargas, Rio, Mar. 11, 1940, OAA.

refused to tolerate Ritter's presence any longer and forced a mutual recall of ambassadors the Germans realized that their hard-line tactics were not profitable and adopted a friendlier attitude. At the same time the Brazilians endeavored to show that they wanted cordial relations with Germany, as long as the Reich did not meddle in Brazil's internal affairs, and both countries worked toward a rapprochement in the first half of 1939. General Góes Monteiro accepted an invitation to attend army maneuvers in Germany. A Brazilian arms-purchasing commission established itself at Essen near the Krupp works, and a group of aviation officers inspected German air force facilities and laid wreaths at German war monuments. The anti-Nazi tone of the Brazilian press softened, and Vargas sent his eldest son, Luther, to study for six months at the Medical School of the University of Berlin, which the Germans took as a gesture of regard. His other son, Getúlio Jr., was studying chemical engineering at Johns Hopkins. Thus he sent a prince to each camp, but neither was a hostage.[2]

The friendly atmosphere prompted the German chargé to comment that "there were no serious fundamental differences between the two countries and that it ought to be possible to overcome the ill feeling" which Ambassador Ritter had caused. When the Itamaraty proposed a new exchange of ambassadors Germany agreed, and in June 1939 Kurt Max Prüfer was named Reich envoy to Brazil. Though a militant Nazi and a friend of Hitler, he was a tactful career diplomat of extensive experience, having served in a variety of Near Eastern posts, including Ethiopia and, most recently, as chief of the foreign ministry's personnel service. He enjoyed "general esteem in the Wilhelmstrasse" where he was considered "completely the opposite" of Ritter. Brazilian Chargé Graça Aranha believed that Prüfer's party connections and friendship with the Fuehrer, rather than being prejudicial, could facilitate "approximation between

2 *DGFP*–D, v, 891; Themistocles da Graça Aranha (Chargé d'Affaires), Berlin, Jan. 30, 1939, #5, AHMRE.

the two countries," and in fact indicated Hitler's desire to improve relations. After his appointment Brazilian-German relations did steadily improve, and the Reich Foreign Ministry explicitly stated that it wanted the affair of the ambassadors forgotten.[3]

At the same time German diplomatic and consular officials in Brazil actively publicized German victories, and worked to maintain cohesion among the German communities which Vargas' Brazilianization program was seriously weakening. Ambassador Prüfer acquired luxurious quarters for his embassy and entertained lavishly. Important Brazilian military officers, including the minister of war and chief of staff, received German decorations in May 1940. The success of their forces caused jubilation among German diplomats, who frequently predicted early victory for the Reich. Germans in Brazil carelessly talked of what "will take place here later on," and the embassy adopted a somewhat arrogant tone in notes to the Itamaraty. In Berlin, Marshal Goering invited the chiefs of the diplomatic missions and their military attachés to see a film entitled "Baptism of Fire," showing the use of German air power in the Polish campaign. Goering asserted that his pilots would be equally damaging against France and England.[4]

The Brazilians sought to measure the situation. They knew that Roosevelt, taking advantage of Italy's fear that continued hostilities would only result in enormous sacrifice of life and the weakening of civilization, had encouraged Mussolini and the Pope to use their good offices to obtain peace. Roosevelt feared that Russia would be the sole victor, and Brazilian diplomats were aware that he believed it would be possible to restore at least partly the

3 *DGFP–D*, v, 891; Graça Aranha, Berlin, May 21, 1939, #33; May 24, 1939, #183; Aug. 18, 1939, #64, AHMRE.

4 William N. Simonson, "Nazi Infiltration in South America, 1933–1945" (Ph.D. Dissertation, Fletcher School of Law and Diplomacy, 1964), pp. 492–493; Caffery, Rio, May 24, 1940, *Foreign Relations, 1940*, v, 42–43; Cyro de Freitas Valle, Berlin, Apr. 6, 1940, #76, AHMRE.

countries which Germany had conquered, in exchange for a more agreeable distribution of natural resources. They also knew that the Italians hoped the American republics, under United States leadership, would use their leverage as producers of raw materials to convince Great Britain that further prosecution of the war did not serve its interests, because the British could not achieve victory without destroying the world economy.[5] Aranha told Vargas that the war was reaching a stalemate and would end soon. The British blockade could succeed if it prevented petroleum and iron ore from reaching Germany, but Rumania and Sweden were supplying the Reich abundantly with those products. And there was the possibility that a prolonged blockade would only strengthen Germany's conviction that autarky was a defensive necessity. Entry of other nations into the war on the Allied side seemed doubtful. Hesitation was spreading through the world's chancelleries, neutrals were increasing pressure on the belligerents to end the fighting, and Sumner Welles was touring European capitals in search of peace. In Berlin the press noted his arrival coolly, with a five-line announcement. A high official in the foreign office told a Brazilian diplomat that Welles' journey was an admission that Roosevelt had been wrong in withdrawing his ambassador from Germany. And Aranha, though grateful for the information that Welles was giving to Brazilian embassies on the Continent, thought that Roosevelt's hope for a "moral peace" was a "Puritan fantasy without proximate or remote possibilities." Aranha was also inclined to believe that England would not fight on indefinitely because the British preferred regular business to good wars. Still, there was confidence in the Itamaraty that England's pertinacity, naval superiority, and history would carry it through. At any rate, it was clear to Aranha that this war would have a solution different from those of previous conflicts and that it would destroy the "equilibrium of nations and ideas." In the face of the European situation,

5 Freitas Valle, Berlin, Jan. 22, 1940, #18; June 7, 1940, #160, AHMRE.

Aranha advised Vargas that the Brazilian government should endeavor to be prudent and cautious "in order to avoid the inevitable anarchy that will result from this unprecedented conflict."[6]

Vargas' efforts in the first half of 1940 pointed toward economic development, inter-American cooperation, and neutrality vis-à-vis the European war. In speeches during visits to Santa Catarina, Rio Grande do Sul, São Paulo, and Minas Gerais he stressed national progress and the importance of being Brazilian. At Blumenau, the heart of Santa Catarina's German colony, he warned: "Brazil is neither English nor German. It is a sovereign country that demands respect for its laws and defends its interests. Brazil is Brazilian."[7] Repeatedly, he mentioned plans for a national steel industry, a port at Laguna, Santa Catarina, and a railroad (the Teresa Cristina) to transport coal to the steel mills. He praised a new packing-house in Pôrto Alegre and the construction of the Rio-Bahia highway. Despite a report that officers on the regional commander's staff were plotting an attempt against Vargas, his relations with the military appeared cordial when he witnessed army maneuvers at Saican, Rio Grande do Sul, in mid-March 1940. He told the assembled troops that Brazil was not a warlike nation, but preferred pacific understanding to violent solutions. The government was doing all it could to equip the army and navy, and he asserted that during these uncertain days the nation was looking to the military to guarantee national peace, dignity, and progress.[8]

In March and April the ministers of war, navy, and finance were negotiating with Italian Ambassador Ugo Sola

[6] Aranha to Vargas, Rio, Mar. 11, 1940; Mar. 20, 1940, OAA; Freitas Valle, Berlin, Feb. 14, 1940, #32, AHMRE.

[7] Getúlio Vargas, *A Nova Política do Brasil* (Rio de Janeiro, 1938–47), VII, 198.

[8] Estevão Leitão de Carvalho, *A Serviço do Brasil na Segunda Guerra Mundial* (Rio de Janeiro, 1952), pp. 19–20; Vargas, *A Nova Política*, VII, 257–259.

to put into operation a January agreement that called for Italy to supply the federal government and the state of São Paulo with some $26,000,000 (U.S.) worth of military and other equipment, to be paid for in currency of international acceptance. But the payments were to go into a special Italian account in the Bank of Brazil, which could be used only to buy Brazilian products. Among the military equipment requested were three submarines (*Tupi* class) for immediate delivery and three to come later, 175 armored cars of various types, and 250 "Breda" machine guns along with fabrication rights—so that this model, which Dutra considered the best ever offered to Brazil, could be made in the country. As part of the same package the state of São Paulo requested a bid from an Italian consortium for locomotives, rolling stock, stations, and transformers needed to electrify 140 kilometers of the Sórocabana Railway. Such purchases and the method of payment would not only mollify the military and those holding an interest in the Paulista railway but would generate sales in the agricultural sector.[9]

During his May tour of Minas Gerais Vargas reaffirmed Brazilian neutrality. At a banquet in Belo Horizonte, possibly as a response to recent German brashness, he said the government would not "permit extremist elements . . . which cultivate violence to live and flourish in Brazilian society." He declared that if Brazil took any action in regard to the European conflict it would do so in accord with the other American nations. For the present, "like cautious Ulysses, we should keep our eyes and ears turned away from the enchantments and lure of the sirens which roam our seas, in order that our thoughts may be free to concen-

[9] Aranha to Vargas, Rio, Apr. 11, 1940, and attached memo from Ugo Sola (Italian Ambassador) to Aranha, Rio, Apr. 4, 1940, both OAA. Brazilian sales to Italy of coffee, cotton, skins, leather, meats, oils, and extracts had been rising since 1938; see letters of Brazilian ambassador to Rome, Luiz Sparano, in AGV. For example, Luiz Sparano to Aranha, Rome, Jan. 21, 1939, AGV, analyzes trade increases in late 1938. There are also detailed reports in AHMRE.

trate . . . on Brazilian interests. . . ."[10] Those interests apparently included placating the United States with resumption of payments on the foreign debt, even though this action displeased army leaders. The German press happily saw the Belo Horizonte speech as indication that Brazil would maintain its neutrality.[11]

Brazil's internal situation tended to impose such a course. It had joined Pan-American protests to Great Britain over the *Graf Spee* and *Wakama* incidents.[12] But when Germany invaded the Low Countries and Uruguay suggested that the American republics protest, the Brazilian military authorities opposed it. Germany was delivering weapons which army officials were convinced they could not obtain elsewhere; they were reluctant to do anything that might make the Germans stop shipments. Also they feared repercussions in Brazil in the event of German victory and were apprehensive of Nazi fifth-column activities in connivance with the Integralistas. With difficulty Aranha overcame their opposition and obtained Brazil's adherence.[13]

German reaction to the protest was based on the rationale that the Monroe Doctrine excluded Europe from affairs in the American hemisphere and likewise precluded American interference in Europe. Moreover, Berlin regarded the publication of the protest as anti-German propaganda which cast doubt on the sincerity of the American republics' neutrality. In Washington officials at the Department of State were pessimistic as to the outcome of the European struggle. Wild rumors were about—the King of England was going to flee, like a latter-day Dom João VI, to Canada;

---

[10] Vargas, *A Nova Política*, VII, 319–320.

[11] Freitas Valle, Berlin, May 14, 1940, #126, AHMRE.

[12] MRE, *O Brasil e a Segunda Guerra Mundial* (Rio de Janeiro, 1944), I, 39–50. The *Graf Spee* affair is well known. The *Wakama* was a German merchantman halted by British warships fifteen miles off the Brazilian coast and scuttled by her crew on February 12, 1940.

[13] Caffery, Rio, May 18, 1940, 832.00/1286, NA. Interestingly enough, the Brazilian "Green Book" omits mention of the protest against the invasion of the Low Countries.

Germany had captured the English fleet; society ladies in England were practicing with rifles to fight paratroopers. The bloodletting in Europe assuredly had demonstrated that the United States was not properly equipped for war. American military authorities were especially nervous over the efficiency of German aviation. They feared American warplanes were inferior to those of the *Luftwaffe*.[14]

Welles gave Brazilian Ambassador Carlos Martins some disturbing information on May 24. The French Foreign Office had received a report from its ambassador in Buenos Aires that a Nazi-supported coup was in preparation in Argentina, with ramifications in Chile and Brazil. Four Argentine generals were said to be conspiring with the Reich ambassador, with leftist elements in Chile, and with Nazis in southern Brazil. Welles said the rebellion would erupt when Germany attacked England, after gaining the expected victory over France. If the report were true, the future of Great Britain and South America were intertwined. Ambassador Martins aptly summed up the situation by saying that all was confusion before the spectacle of a world going to pieces and the establishment of a "new order of things" whose true nature no one could divine.[15]

Italy caused new worries. German armies had invaded the Low Countries on May 10, outflanking France's Maginot Line; eighteen days later the British were evacuating remnants of their expeditionary force from the beach at Dunkirk. The Somme was crossed on June 5, and the Germans were on the road to Paris. Speculation was rife that Italy would join the conflict, and Ambassador Caffery be-

[14] Freitas Valle, Berlin, May 27, 1940, #143, AHMRE; Martins to Aranha, Washington, May 3, 1940 and May 24, 1940, OAA.

[15] Martins to Aranha, Washington, May 24, 1940, OAA. Rumors of pro-German plots in Argentina had some basis in fact in that opposition toward the Ortiz government among conservatives and army officers was on the upsurge in April and May 1940. But the plots resulted more from discontent in Argentine right-wing circles than from German stimulation. It seems the Germans offered little more than encouragement. See discussion in Simonson, "Nazi Infiltration," pp. 570–571.

came deeply concerned because the Italian population in Brazil was second only to the Portuguese in size. Many people, including Aranha, said that Brazilian sentiment was 90 percent in favor of the Allies, but that it was unorganized.[16]

Back in October 1939 Hitler had requested that Italy enter the war if Great Britain and France refused his peace proposals. Count Ciano, the Italian foreign minister, opposed such action; instead he favored a peace conference with the European powers and the United States participating. But Hitler prevailed and Mussolini's intentions were clarified on May 31, when his ambassador in Rio asked Brazil to assume responsibility for Italy's interests in France and Great Britain in the event of war. Aranha's acceptance underlined Brazil's precautionary policy.[17]

Ten days later Italy declared war on a crumbling France. An enraged Franklin Roosevelt accused Mussolini of plunging a dagger into his neighbor's back while Hitler was attacking from the front. The speech, on the evening of June 10 in Charlottesville, Virginia, caused a sensation, and the rapid change in American public opinion amazed the Brazilian ambassador. For months no one had dared think of intervention in the war, because isolationist sentiment dominated American opinion. But as French resistance dissolved before the German onslaught, the Gallup Poll reported that 65 percent of the Americans questioned thought that the United States would enter the war; the figure had been 32 percent in February.[18] Suddenly most politicians lacked the courage to be unconditional isolationists. Not only was the government permitting all types of

---

[16] Caffery, Rio, May 27, 1940, *Foreign Relations, 1940*, v, 615; for a report of the diplomatic reaction in Berlin see Freitas Valle, Berlin, May 10, 1940, #121, AHMRE.

[17] MRE, *Brasil e a Segunda Guerra*, I, 95–96; Freitas Valle, Berlin, Oct. 4, 1939, #164, AHMRE.

[18] Whitney H. Shepardson and William O. Scroggs, *The United States in World Affairs, 1940* (New York, 1941), p. 308, contains a digest of the 1940 Gallup Poll.

war matériel to go to the Allies, but it was stripping its own forces to supply them and it was increasing arms production. The new army secretary, Henry L. Stimson, advised war, and the isolationist Senator Arthur Vandenberg radically modified his position and applauded aid to the Allies. Mayor Fiorello La Guardia of New York, idol of Italian-Americans, said in a vehement address that the country was closer to war than it had been after the sinking of the *Lusitania* in 1915. Everything indicated, Ambassador Martins reported to Aranha, that the United States was marching toward an extreme decision in the face of the Axis threat.[19]

Suddenly, on June 11, Vargas muddied the turbulent international waters even more with a speech entitled "On the Threshold of a New Era," delivered at Navy Day ceremonies on the battleship *Minas Gerais*. He referred to the chaotic world situation, saying that "old systems and antiquated formulas" were disappearing, and the world was forming a new economic, social, and political organization. It was not the end of civilization but "the tumultuous and fruitful beginning of a new era." He spoke of the need of understanding the times, of removing "dead ideas and sterile ideals." Economic democracy based on the will of the people must replace political democracy based on private wealth. There was no longer room for regimes founded on privilege and class distinctions. He concluded: "Happily in Brazil we have established a regime which is adequate for our necessities without imitating or affiliating ourselves with any of the current ideologies."[20] The speech was an

19 Martins to Aranha, Washington, June 11, 1940, OAA.

20 Vargas, *A Nova Política*, VII, 331–335. For an English translation of the questionable portions of the speech see Caffery, Rio, June 11, 1940, *Foreign Relations, 1940*, V, 616–617. Brazil announced that it was taking charge of Italy's interests in Britain and France; see MRE, *Brasil e a Segunda Guerra*, I, 96; Hull to Caffery, Washington, June 12, 1940, *Foreign Relations, 1940*, V, 619. The *New York Mirror* carried a story on Brazilian consulates being responsible for Italian interests entitled: "Brazil a Pal," mentioned *ibid.*

excellent demonstration of Vargas' middle-of-the-road policy. It was peppered with just the right amount of fascist-style phraseology, but included enough kernels of democratic thought to placate Washington.

Against the background of the shocking events in Europe, some thought the address rabidly fascist. The *New York Times* carried the headline: "Vargas Backs The 'Virile'; Predicts New World Order. Attack on 'Sterile Demagogy of Political Democracy' by Brazil's President Seen as Divergence from Roosevelt."[21] Other headlines were similar. In Buenos Aires, *La Crítica* ran the streamer: "Vargas, with Fascist language, justifies the aggression of the barbarians." Argentina and Paraguay reportedly strengthened their frontier garrisons.[22] The comments in the German press and in radio broadcasts were decidedly favorable. Newspapers printed the speech with captions such as: "Brazil At The Front of the New Peoples"; "Old Systems Abandoned." Vargas' statements were "clear and courageous," and had special significance coming as they did just after the Italian attack on France. Overnight the president was the darling of German news commentators, who pointed to the June 11 address as proof of his receptivity to the Axis point of view.[23]

Secretary Hull, mindful of the secret Brazilian-American military talks then in progress in Rio de Janeiro, stressed the friendship between the two countries and told reporters that the Department of State did not make a practice of commenting on speeches by heads of other governments to their own people. Even so, he kept the wires to Rio busy with requests for information and clarification from Caffery. The ambassador thought that Italy's entrance into the war had increased Vargas' concern

21 *New York Times*, June 12, 1940.

22 Hull to Caffery, Washington, June 12, 1940, *Foreign Relations, 1940*, v, 619.

23 Freitas Valle, Berlin, June 12, 1940, #183; June 15, 1940, #189; July 2, 1940, #233, AHMRE.

about the large German and Italian populations in Brazil, and his speech, while praising Pan-American ideals, included portions which were "manifestly sops to those groups."[24] Sumner Welles, after reading a long telegram from Caffery, assured Roosevelt that there was "nothing whatever in the speech except one or two ill-chosen phrases" to justify the heated attack of the American press on Vargas. It was clearly a speech intended for domestic consumption, and in all of his references to political systems Vargas was "talking solely about the Brazilian Government and in no sense about the German or Italian dictatorships."[25]

The violent press reaction in the United States disturbed Vargas, and he hastened to assure Roosevelt that he did not intend to contradict the Charlottesville speech, of which he had known nothing at the time, but was issuing "a warning, a call to reality, addressed to Brazilians." Roosevelt should not be concerned, he added, because Brazil would "not fail him in loyalty."[26] Vargas played the same tune in a different key for the German ambassador, to whom he emphasized his intention of maintaining neutrality and, in reference to the Navy Day talk, his personal sympathy for the authoritarian states and his aversion to England and the democratic system.[27] It was Vargas' familiar maneuvering on an international scale.

The attitude of the Brazilian army was a key factor in Vargas' action. On the afternoon of June 10 General Góes Monteiro remarked to Colonel Lehman W. Miller, new chief of the American military mission, that the United States had been talking for a year about military coopera-

[24] Caffery, Rio, June 11, 1940, *Foreign Relations, 1940*, v, 616.

[25] Welles to F. D. Roosevelt, Washington, June 12, 1940, *ibid.*, p. 620; Martins, Washington, June 12/13, 1940, #178 and June 13, 1940, #179, AHMRE.

[26] Vargas to F. D. Roosevelt, Rio, June 13, 1940, OF 11 Brazil 1940–45, FDRL; Martins to Vargas, Washington, June 18, 1940, AGV. Martins described the U.S. reaction.

[27] *DGFP–D*, IX, 659.

tion and as yet not a gun, not a round of American ammunition, had reached Brazil. Instead of arms, the United
States sent "cases of whiskey and cartons of Lucky
Strikes."[28] And, in a heated argument at a social gathering
on June 11, several pro-German members of General Dutra's staff took the position that a German victory over Britain could have only advantages for Brazil. English power,
they said, had dominated the world for centuries, and Germany was the savior of countries like Brazil which lived
"without possibility of liberation, under a colonial regime
imposed on its economy by the great democratic powers."[29]
Indeed, had not the United States government denied Brazil a few destroyers a couple of years before because of
Congressional opposition and Argentine pressure, but only
recently had ceded fifty of them to Britain without even a
Congressional hearing?[30] Could the Americans be trusted?
Germanophiles argued that they could not, and saw Vargas'
words as agreement with their views. But were they? General Leitão de Carvalho, then commander of the Rio
Grande military region, thought the president's previous
anti-Nazi attitude contradicted such an interpretation.[31]
Quite probably Vargas had not foreseen any external reper-
cussion because he had not discussed the address with his
cabinet, or even with Aranha, as he usually did in questions
of international importance. Caffery had heard that Vargas
believed the Good Neighbor policy would probably prevent the United States from interfering with a movement
against his regime by Germans and Italians in Brazil, if it

[28] Caffery to Welles, Rio, June 10, 1940, 832.20/203 1/3, NA; Memo:
"Political Attitude of General Góes Monteiro, Brazilian Chief of Staff
and His Relations with President Vargas," Oct. 10, 1940, DAR, 832.00/
1317, NA.

[29] Leitão de Carvalho, *Serviço do Brasil*, p. 22.

[30] The Germans were quick to point out the difference between the
American treatment of Brazil and Britain; see Freitas Valle, Berlin,
Apr. 5, 1940, #80, AHMRE.

[31] Leitão de Carvalho, *Serviço do Brasil*, p. 24. He said of Vargas:
"Sua atitude posterior o desmente."

appeared to be a purely Brazilian affair. He was merely seeking to appease those groups and the pro-German officers in the Brazilian armed forces.[32]

The speech incensed pro-allied elements, who spoke against Vargas' apparent position. The president's opponents, who had been quiet since November 1937, began plotting again. Vargas, in an effort to defend himself and against the advice of Aranha and Caffery, made another speech on June 28 emphasizing two points: first, his Pan-Americanism; second, his belief that the form of a government had nothing to do with Pan-Americanism. Brazil had been a monarchy until 1889, and each American state was free to adopt any system of government it wished. That was his interpretation of the Monroe Doctrine.[33]

Aranha counseled "the necessity of the greatest prudence and of the greatest parsimony" in the use of gestures that might indicate Brazil's preference for one side or the other. Definition of Brazil's position should wait for the Havana Conference or for the result of the fighting between England and Germany.[34]

The American embassy appeared outwardly unconcerned by all this discussion. Góes Monteiro gave an address on June 22 at a luncheon honoring the retiring chief of the American military mission, General Allen Kimberley, which was interpreted in Rio as very Pan-American. It was, the embassy reported, a further effort "to correct the unfortunate impression" which the June 11 speech had created. But Góes Monteiro pointedly said that it was the duty of those members of the Pan-American brotherhood most capable of doing so to give the other republics the instruments to make their solidarity effective and efficient—he was reminding the United States that Brazil needed and

[32] Caffery, Rio, June 11, 1940, *Foreign Relations, 1940*, v, 616.

[33] Caffery, Rio, June 17, 1940, *ibid.*, pp. 623–624; and Caffery, Rio, June 28, 1940, *ibid.*, p. 625; and Caffery, Rio, June 29, 1940, *ibid.*, pp. 625–626.

[34] Aranha to Vargas, Rio, June 28, 1940, OAA.

wanted arms. Ambassador Caffery reported that Vargas' speech of June 28 was simply a reply to his critics, a reaffirmation of his Pan-Americanism and of Brazil's right to select its own form of government.[35] German Ambassador Prüfer gave the speeches a different interpretation. They meant, "despite protestations of friendship, a rejection of North American policy by the Federal President in anticipation of England's defeat and the resulting weakening of Roosevelt, and orientation of Brazilian policy toward trade with Germany and Europe."[36]

With the collapse of French resistance on June 17, England stood alone against Hitler. While the ladies of Rio society offered a votive Mass in the Candelária church for the salvation of their beloved Paris, General Góes Monteiro, once the prize student of the French military mission to Brazil, fumed at their useless gesture and predicted complete victory for the Axis by September. A similar conviction existed in Germany. The Brazilian embassy reported that the Germans hoped to appropriate the French fleet to strengthen their attack on England, and were declaring that Roosevelt's efforts to bolster British morale were useless because Reich forces would overcome all resistance. Yet beneath the German determination, Freitas Valle noted a "great preoccupation to end the war quickly."[37]

Vargas indicated his attitude when he secretly called in the German ambassador on June 21 to tell him that he saw Brazil's salvation in the continuation of trade with Germany, and he requested agreements. Prüfer said that at the end of the war Germany was prepared to purchase Brazilian products, especially coffee and cotton, and would sign purchase contracts immediately. The Reich was ready to build the all-important steel mill and to agree in principle

---

[35] Randolph Harrison (2d Secretary), Rio, June 24, 1940, 832.20/209, NA; Caffery, Rio, June 29, 1940, *Foreign Relations, 1940,* v, 625–626.

[36] *DGFP–D,* x, 101.

[37] Leitão de Carvalho, *Serviço do Brasil,* pp. 24–25; Freitas Valle, Berlin, June 17, 1940, #193, AHMRE.

to accept products in payment. Vargas was pleased and asked Prüfer to convey his thanks to Berlin. He promised to "redress abuses and encroachments by local officials" against German nationals and German-Brazilians in the South. "The agitation against the fifth column," Vargas reportedly said, "was due to foreign propaganda of lies which was carried on particularly by Jewish emigrants . . . which he would not tolerate."[38] But, to be sure, Vargas ordered the Itamaraty to send two of its staff to investigate German allegations that immigrants were being mistreated. They found that most complaints were groundless.[39]

Prüfer reported this turn of events to Berlin, and ironically former Ambassador Karl Ritter, currently head of the economic section of the foreign ministry, wrote the response. The Reich, he said, was in favor of an intensive exchange of goods, despite the disappointments which Germany had suffered in Brazil in the past. The Reich was especially willing to collaborate in developing Brazil's great natural resources. As the result of recent events, he noted, Greater Germany had grown from 65 million producers and consumers to 90 million. This new Germany would buy more Brazilian products and supply more finished goods. After the war Germany would turn toward countries which guaranteed the stable and uniform development of economic relations, "without being influenced by the political bias of individuals." The Reich was not interested in long, tedious discussions; it insisted that negotiations be conducted without interruption and concluded quickly, and that agreements be permanent.[40]

German efforts sought to counter English and American influence, but Berlin cautioned diplomats against giving the impression that they had "to run after the Brazilians because of anxiety over these influences." They were to convince Brazilian leaders that continued trade was important

---

[38] *DGFP–D*, IX, 598–599, 659. Quotation is in Prüfer's wording.
[39] MRE to Emb/Berlin, Rio, Aug. 19, 1940, #229, Exp. 4765, AHMRE.
[40] *DGFP–D*, X, 41–42.

for Brazil, and to emphasize that England and the United States would not fill the void if Germany withdrew from the Brazilian market. To make their point they offered to purchase 30,000 tons of cotton while the war was forcing England and France to decrease their purchases. German commercial representatives began accepting orders at discount prices for goods to be delivered in September. Underlying the entire arrangement was the condition "that no substantial change" be made "in the present state of Brazil's neutrality."[41] But trade depended on the ability to transport goods. And the British blockade was adversely affecting Brazil's trade, not only with Germany but also with the Scandinavian countries. For example, in mid-1940 the Finnish vessel *Atlanta*, loaded with Swedish cellulose and paper, could not pass from the Baltic to the Atlantic because the British had mined the Skagerrak and German naval authorities were reluctant to allow merchant ships to use the Kiel canal. When the Brazilian ambassador proposed that the Germans allow Sweden to ship to Brazil, via the Kiel or German ports, 20,000 tons a month of cellulose and paper products in return for a like amount of coffee, Ritter said that "because of his love for Brazil" he would consider it, but noted smilingly that the Brazilians wanted him to authorize delivery of paper to be used by newspapers which attacked Germany. In the same mood Ambassador Freitas Valle replied that no one knew if all the coffee would be drunk in Sweden.[42] Indeed, the course of the war would determine whether Swedes and Germans would drink coffee at all.

Despite the intensity of their campaign the Germans regarded trade with Brazil as a temporary expedient. The coming Nazi victory would give Germany a colonial empire in the tropics comprising the old German colonies in Africa,

41 *Ibid.*, IX, 630–631. The Itamaraty contrasted this German activity with the "apathy of North American commerce"; see MRE to Emb/Washington, Rio, Aug. 5, 1940, #155, Exp. 3801, AHMRE.

42 Freitas Valle, Berlin, June 11, 1940, #175, AHMRE.

the Belgian Congo, French Equatorial Africa, and possibly British Nigeria. After a decade of intensive development these colonies could supply Germany with cocoa, coffee, tea, tobacco, cotton, rubber, woods, and tanning extracts. Trade with Brazil would "undergo certain changes and a contraction." Reich exports would then decline, but the German colonial empire and German currency areas would provide new markets. The Nazi government even planned to invite Germans and their descendants living in Brazil to move to the colonies.[43]

The Brazilians were naturally interested in Germany's postwar intentions. In a fascinating dispatch on the Reich's plans for the reorganization of Europe and for global spheres of influence, Ambassador Freitas Valle noted that German plans called for a distribution of power based on the formula: "Europe for Berlin, the Americas for Washington and Oriental Asia for Tokyo." In this scheme the Germans would use Russia to counterbalance the United States and Japan. The ambassador thought it was too early to be concerned with such things and implied that the Germans would do better to concentrate on the war.[44] But where would Brazil fit into the grand design? If a victorious Germany intended to leave Brazil in the American sphere of influence would not Brazilian leaders be wise to solidify ties with the United States?

Throughout July and August, Vargas and Finance Minister Souza Costa carried on secret negotiations with Prüfer. At the core of the discussions was the Krupp offer to build a steel mill. At the same time Brazil was conducting similar negotiations with the United States.

During the Aranha mission to Washington the United States government had promised to cooperate in Brazil's development program. Vargas sent Edmundo de Macedo Soares e Silva to discuss the establishment of a steel industry with American interests in May 1939 and, as a result, the

43 *DGFP–D*, IX, 499–501.
44 Freitas Valle, Berlin, July 3, 1940, #238, AHMRE.

United States Steel Corporation sent a group of experts to Brazil. The State Department, aware of these developments, took no part beyond expressing interest and willingness to be of assistance. The United States Steel group reported that there were no technical obstacles to a Brazilian steel industry; it even denied the long-held belief that Brazil lacked usable coal, asserting that the Santa Catarina variety was adequate. The report created expectations among Brazilian leaders that the company would cooperate, and they were greatly disappointed when the company's board of directors decided against participation. Vargas considered American aid "a most important test of the good-neighbor policy," and indicated that if American assistance was not forthcoming "he would turn in other directions." He was under heavy pressure from the military to show that cooperation with the United States would bear some fruit, and he was committed to industrial development as a means of establishing Brazil's economic independence.[45]

While the Department of State unsuccessfully attempted to get United States Steel to reconsider, the Brazilian government decided against participation by any American steel company. It would raise funds in Brazil to cover local costs and use credits conceded in the Aranha agreements of March 1939 to purchase machinery in the United States. On the last day of May 1940 Secretary Hull notified Caffery that Federal Loan Administrator Jesse Jones had agreed to lend the necessary funds, with the understanding that such a commitment would become effective when he and the Brazilian authorities had agreed upon a plan for construction and operation. The news delighted Vargas, who named a commission to handle the details in the United States. The Brazilian government hired the Arthur J. McKee Company

[45] Memorandum on Conversation of Ambassador Carlos Martins with Secretary Hull by Advisor on International Economic Affairs (Herbert Feis), Washington, Jan. 22, 1940, in *Foreign Relations, 1940*, v, 600–601 and note 28.

of Cleveland to make preliminary studies and supervise construction.[46]

Conversations and negotiations between the two governments during mid-1940 covered a variety of topics, from military and naval cooperation to debt settlement, an international coffee agreement, and agricultural assistance. The Brazilian embassy in Washington was so busy with visiting delegations that Ambassador Martins called it "a general Brazilian offensive."[47] But events in Europe during the crucial month of June 1940 caused Vargas to hedge his bets by also opening negotiations with the German embassy.

Ambassador Caffery reported in early July that Krupp's agents were working hard, and with some success in army circles, to make Vargas accept their attractive offer to build the steel mill. He emphasized that arms supply and financing of the steel project were intimately connected with "the possibility of Brazil's falling altogether into the German orbit." In Caffery's opinion, there were only two ways of "combatting the increasing German menace," arms credits and liberal financing arrangements for the mill. If the Germans supplied the arms or the mill or both, the United States could not hope to maintain its position in Brazil. The time had come, Caffery declared, for Washington to decide whether keeping Brazil out of German control was worth these steps.[48]

Aranha wrote Welles on July 24 that a commission headed by Brazilian industrialist Guilherme Guinle had sailed that day for the United States to negotiate a financing agreement. No other undertaking was more vital than the establishment of basic industries, which would "mark the

[46] Caffery, Rio, May 22, 1940, *ibid.*, pp. 605–606; Hull to Caffery, Washington, May 31, 1940, *ibid.*, p. 607; Caffery, Rio, June 1, 1940, and July 8, 1940, *ibid.*, p. 608.

[47] Martins to Aranha, Washington, Mar. 21, 1940, OAA; for the topics mentioned see *Foreign Relations, 1940*, v, 40–52 (defense), 380–407 (coffee), 559–599 (debt).

[48] Caffery, Rio, July 8, 1940, *ibid.*, p. 608; Caffery, Rio, July 16, 1940, *ibid.*, pp. 49–50.

true economic independence of Brazil," and, he reminded Welles, they were "counting on the frank and decided aid of the Government of the United States."[49]

On the same day Welles cabled Caffery that Federal Loan Administrator Jones would make an arrangement as soon as the Brazilian representatives arrived. Welles emphasized to Jones the "utmost importance" for the United States of the steel project, and reminded him that the government had committed itself in early 1939 to cooperate "in every way possible in the Brazilian development program." Failure to assist would result in Brazil's immediate acceptance of the German offer, and assure Germany's predominance in Brazil's economic and military life.[50]

The negotiations which Vargas had initiated with the Germans in June had come to a halt. On July 10 the Wilhelmstrasse had urged Ambassador Prüfer to press the discussions to a conclusion prior to the Inter-American Conference, scheduled for Havana on July 21–30. Germany was prepared, after the war, to import 300 million Reichsmarks' worth of Brazilian products a year instead of the previous total of 170 million Reichsmarks, and 30 percent of the imports' total value was to be in coffee and cotton.[51] Prüfer's reply on August 7 revealed that the attitude of the Brazilian authorities toward Germany had shifted when Reich forces failed to achieve a quick victory over England. He had communicated the latest German offer to Finance Minister Souza Costa, and said that the minister had received it favorably. But negotiations had not progressed in the interim, and Souza Costa was avoiding further conversation on the matter. Vargas and other members of the government "had obviously counted on a quicker blow against England," and that part of the cabinet "which reckoned on

[49] Aranha to Welles, Rio, July 24, 1940, OAA.

[50] Welles to Caffery, Washington, July 24, 1940, *Foreign Relations, 1940,* v, 608–609; Welles to Jesse Jones, Washington, Aug. 7, 1940, *ibid.,* pp. 609–610.

[51] *DGFP–D,* x, 177–178.

a longer duration of the war [had] won more ground." The ambassador included the finance minister in this group, which felt an agreement with Germany inadvisable: it might prove a hindrance if the war continued and if the United States made more attractive offers to buy surplus Brazilian export products. But even so they hesitated to close the door on a German arrangement. A week later the ambassador reported to Berlin that the finance minister "stated orally" that the government agreed "in principle to our comprehensive offer." And Aranha also, he said, wanted "a general conclusion" with Germany.[52]

In Washington, a tentative agreement had been worked out, but action was delayed because Congress had not passed a bill increasing the funds of the Export-Import Bank and removing a $20,000,000 limitation on the bank's loans. Aranha on September 4 told Caffery that Krupp had made another attractive offer to construct the steel mill.[53] A few days later the German ambassador cautioned Berlin that Brazil's attitude toward an agreement depended on the war and prospects for its end, and that in the meantime the need to find markets was necessarily forcing Brazil into the economic sphere of the United States. Moreover, the German-Italian assault on Gibraltar, predicted for early August, had not materialized, perhaps indicating to the Brazilians that the Axis had reached its high-water mark on the western front.[54]

The exchange of notes between Federal Loan Administrator Jones and Brazilian representative Guinle decided the question on September 26. The Export-Import Bank would lend Brazil $10,000,000 immediately, and as the work progressed would increase the sum to a total of $20,000,000, dependent on a Brazilian investment of mil-réis equal to

[52] *Ibid.*, p. 426, note 5.

[53] Hull to Caffery, Washington, Aug. 30, 1940, *Foreign Relations, 1940*, v, 610; Caffery, Rio, Sept. 5, 1940, *ibid.*

[54] *DGFP*-D, x, 426, note 5 (document was dated Sept. 9, 1940); Fernando Nilo de Alvarenga, Berlin, July 25, 1940, #292, AHMRE.

$25,000,000. The bank gave Brazil ten years to repay the loan, payments to begin three years from the first advance of funds. The rate of interest was set at 4 percent. The United States insisted upon concurrence in the appointment of managerial officers, engineers, and contractors. Brazilian and American officials would jointly approve all plans and specifications. American managers and engineers would run the steel mill until Brazilians were trained and experienced.[55]

Satisfaction in Brazil was general. Aranha declared that the agreement clarified the true meaning of Brazilian-American friendship and would deepen the intimacy between the two nations. Vargas received congratulatory telegrams from all over the country and spoke enthusiastically of what the project meant for Brazil's future.[56]

The question of where to locate the mill was both technical and political. Minas Gerais had some of the largest and purest iron ore deposits in the world; in fact, there were whole mountains of the mineral. A steel plant already existed at Sabará (*Siderúrgica Belgo-Mineira*), a short distance from Belo Horizonte, and Governor Benedicto Valladares expected the new plant to be built in Minas. It would be a political asset. But the coal fields were in Santa Catarina, and the fuel had to come by ship from the port of Laguna to Rio, about 700 miles, and then by rail to the mill. Therefore it was expedient to choose a site in the State of Rio de Janeiro at Volta Redonda. Politically the choice struck a balance between the Paulista industrialists and Governor Valladares. Technically it was simpler to haul coal ninety miles from the Rio docks to Volta Redonda over the existing Rio-São Paulo railroad, which ran on a

[55] Hull to Caffery, Washington, Sept. 25, 1940, and Hull to Caffery, Washington, Sept. 26, 1940, *Foreign Relations, 1940*, v, 612–613. Contains text of Jones-Guinle notes. See also report of Carlos Martins, Washington, Sept. 26, 1940, #275, AHMRE.

[56] Aranha to Welles, Rio, Oct. 15, 1940, OAA; Caffery, Rio, Oct. 4, 1940, *Foreign Relations, 1940*, v, 614–615.

fairly level railbed once it crossed the *Serra do Mar,* than to haul it over mountains to Minas Gerais. Trains were deadheaded up to ore sites at Lafaiete in Minas (2,700 ft. elevation) and returned to Volta Redonda (1,800 ft.) loaded with iron ore, manganese, and limestone over a 250-mile "downgrade."

Plans called for completion of the mill by 1944, but because of wartime shortages, construction difficulties, and administrative red tape in both countries production did not begin until 1946. Volta Redonda was the symbol of Brazil's "industrial coming of age" and tangible proof of Vargas' assertion that if given order he could bring progress.[57]

Conclusion of negotiations for the mill affected Brazilian-American relations in other areas and also affected the attitude of Brazilian officials toward Germany. The Brazilian government gave Pan-American Airways permission to fly directly from Belém to Rio, via Barreiras in western Bahia, shortening the time from the United States by two days and bringing to a close eight months of intense effort by Pan-American representatives.[58] On October 1 the Press and Propaganda Department (DIP) suspended for five days the German-subsidized newspaper *Meio Dia,* after the American embassy protested an article attacking a pro-allied speech by Welles. DIP director Lourival Fontes had prom-

[57] "War Projects in Brazil," *Fortune,* XXVI, No. 5 (November 1942), 218; "Brazil's Transition," *Business Week,* No. 725 (July 17, 1943), 46; *Brazil,* XIII, No. 146 (January 1941), 9; Aranha to Welles, Rio, July 24, 1940, OAA; *Jornal do Brasil,* Rio, Apr. 17, 1966. Starting with an initial capacity of 270,000 tons of ingot steel Volta Redonda had increased production to more than 1,200,000 tons by 1965. Though small by American and European standards it is the largest steel mill in South America. For more on Volta Redonda see John D. Wirth, "Brazilian Economic Nationalism: Trade and Steel Under Vargas" (Ph.D. Dissertation, Stanford University, 1966).

[58] Araújo to Young, Rio, Sept. 20, 1940, Brazil Folder 3, Pan-American Airways Archive (New York); Randolph Harrison, Rio, Aug. 29, 1940, 832.20/220, NA.

ised in mid-September to stop such anti-American attacks, but this was the first indication that he intended to do so. The embassy reported that the action would have "a salutary effect in preventing future press attacks against the United States."[59] The trend culminated in the shelving of any agreement with Germany on postwar trade. On October 17 Ambassador Prüfer aptly described the situation in a report to the Wilhelmstrasse:

> The approaching presidential election in the U.S.A. is showing its effect here in the increasing nervousness of government circles that are friendly to us, the President, the military, and the police. The anticipated re-election of Roosevelt is expected to bring about an intensification of his extortionary policy toward President Vargas, who in particular would be forced to dismiss his pro-German followers. Police Chief Filinto Müller said yesterday in a conversation that the Minister of War, the Chief of the General Staff, and he could be saved only by a dazzling German victory over England and a consequent waning of Roosevelt's prospects.
>
> The slackening of Brazilian resistance is shown also in the far-reaching toleration of pro-Roosevelt propaganda in the press while attacks on him and even objective criticism are suppressed as unneutral.[60]

The most the Germans were able to obtain was agreement that the Brazilians would make regular payments to the German account at the Bank of Brazil for armaments ordered from the Krupp works. These funds could be used only for the purchase of products which Brazilian authorities would select and store in Brazil until the war's end, when they would ship them to Germany. In late November

---

[59] Memorandum: Walter N. Walmsley to Paul C. Daniels, DAR, Oct. 8, 1940, 832.918/27, NA, and attached dispatch Harrison, Rio, Oct. 1, 1940. The offending article was "Solidariedade Defensiva," *Meio Dia*, Rio, Sept. 30, 1940.

[60] *DGFP–D*, XI, 311.

1940, Aranha told the American chargé d'affaires that Germany was not allowed to use this account to purchase goods for shipment by air to Europe or to finance propaganda activities. The Germans were flying out diamonds, but the chancellor promised that he would stop the practice.[61]

The steel-mill agreement also aided the military conversations which were held throughout 1940. American officers had long stressed the importance to hemispheric defense of the Brazilian bulge, indeed the War Department's earliest contingency plan, Rainbow I (August 1939), placed defense of that area at the top of the list of tasks for the United States armed forces. General Delos Emmons' air reconnaissance of South America in November 1939 emphasized that the Natal area was "of critical and utmost importance in the defense of the continental United States and the Panama Canal against a possible coalition of European nations."[62] The army's air board in 1939 used the hypothetical problem of dislodging a hostile air force from the northeastern bulge to determine the strength of army air units assigned to hemispheric defense. During the fall and winter of 1939–1940, army and navy planners worked out detailed plans for sending a joint expeditionary force to northeast Brazil, although they did no more than plan until German forces invaded western Europe.[63]

President Roosevelt on April 30, 1940, ordered Admiral Harold R. Stark, Chief of Naval Operations, to arrange for immediate conversations with Brazil concerning the security of Fernando de Noronha Island, located off the Natal bulge (3' 50' x 12' 50'). The USS *Helena* had surveyed the

[61] William C. Burdett (Counselor), Rio, Nov. 27, 1940, and Nov. 27, 1940, *Foreign Relations, 1940*, v, 635–637, 638–639. Burdett replaced Scotten as embassy counselor in July 1940.

[62] "Report on Brazil Flight," Col. Robert Olds to Maj. Gen. Delos C. Emmons (CG, GHQAF), Dec. 1, 1939, WPD 4185–2, WWII RS, NA.

[63] Stetson Conn and Byron Fairchild, *The Framework of Hemisphere Defense* (Washington, 1960), pp. 272–273. Such an expeditionary force was suggested in Army War College, "Special Study–Brazil," Mar. 29, 1939, WPD 4115–7, WWII RS, NA.

island's defenses in mid-January and reported them inadequate to repulse a surprise attack. It would be a logical way-station for an Axis air invasion of northeast Brazil. The president wished to make certain that no European nation would use the island, and indicated two emergency courses of action: American occupation of the island, or destruction of the airfield.[64]

After consultation, Admiral Stark and General Marshall notified Welles of the president's directive, and the undersecretary instructed Caffery to talk with Chancellor Aranha about the island's defenses and American use of northeastern bases. In 1939 General Góes Monteiro had offered the use of bases in the Natal area, including Fernando de Noronha, in return for American protection of coastal communications, but without success. Now the United States wished to make a formal agreement embodying such an arrangement.[65]

Immediately after Germany launched its western offensive, Góes Monteiro sent word to Marshall that collaboration between the United States and Brazil was vitally necessary because both were confronted with "real and imminent danger." If the Germans won, as Góes Monteiro thought they would, the dictator countries would inevitably combine to attack the Americas. It appeared that the way was clear for intimate Brazilian-American military collaboration.[66] But by mid-May the conquest of the Low Countries and the German forces' precipitous advance into France created a new situation. Roosevelt ordered his military advisors to broaden the planned conversations with Brazil into defense discussions with most of the American repub-

[64] F. D. Roosevelt to CNO, Apr. 30, 1940, WPD 4224-86, WWII RS, NA; see copy in Elliott Roosevelt, *F.D.R.: His Personal Letters, 1928–1945* (New York, 1950), II, 1016.

[65] Conn and Fairchild, *Framework*, pp. 175, 273; Welles to Caffery, Washington, May 8, 1940, *Foreign Relations, 1940*, V, 40–42.

[66] Burdett to George C. Marshall, Rio, May 17, 1940, 832.00/1289 ½, NA.

lics.[67] United States authorities now realized that seeking individual agreements would take time, and meanwhile the United States must prepare to take drastic action to protect the "vital and vulnerable Brazilian bulge."[68] When the State Department learned, during the last week in May, that pro-Nazi officers were plotting a coup d'état in Argentina, and the British Admiralty passed on reports that the Germans might be preparing to launch an attack in the direction of Brazil, American concern for Brazilian security took tangible, albeit impractical form.[69]

On orders from President Roosevelt, and over one weekend (May 25–27), the army developed the *Pot of Gold* plan for rushing a 100,000-man force to various points from Belém to Rio de Janeiro. The Brazilian high command, however, although sufficiently alarmed by reported Nazi plots to seize control of Montevideo to send 5,000 rifles from its own stocks to the Uruguayan army, was not alarmed enough to permit American troops to occupy the Brazilian coastline north of Rio. Unfortunately, it took the War Department a long time to realize this fact, and American plans for defense of the Brazilian northeast continued to turn on stationing United States forces there. The State Department agreed to send consular officials to Natal, and to instruct consuls in other areas to obtain information for planning the move of American troops to Brazil.[70]

The war plan drawn up in mid-June (Rainbow IV) projected northeast Brazil as a theater of operations in the event England fell. In July the war plans divisions of both

[67] Conn and Fairchild, *Framework*, pp. 175–176.

[68] *Ibid.*, p. 273.

[69] Martins to Aranha, Washington, May 24, 1940, OAA; Conn and Fairchild, *Framework*, p. 33.

[70] *Ibid.*, pp. 273–274; Cordell Hull, *The Memoirs of Cordell Hull* (New York, 1948), I, 820–821; William L. Langer and S. Everett Gleason, *The Challenge to Isolation* (New York, 1952), pp. 611–614. For an example of the consular reports see "Certain Characteristics of the Pernambuco, Brazil, Consular District," Walter J. Linthicum (Vice-Consul), Recife, July 15, 1940, 810.20 Defense/202, NA.

the army and the navy believed it highly probable that, if England were defeated, German forces would drive through Africa and across the South Atlantic to Brazil. Actually no such German plans existed, but during the summer of 1940 American military leaders acted as if an invasion of the Western Hemisphere were imminent. Washington understood that no plan for operations in Brazil could be successful without the cooperation of the Brazilian armed services. To make arrangements the army chose Colonel Lehman W. Miller, Corps of Engineers, who had served on the military mission in Brazil and was going to Rio de Janeiro to become its chief. Both Caffery and Góes Monteiro had requested his appointment, and the War Department hoped to promote Colonel Miller to general-officer rank to increase his prestige and to emphasize Washington's concern for Brazilian security.[71]

Miller arrived in Rio to find the Brazilian government alarmed over events in Europe and dubious of American ability to protect Brazil or to help Brazil protect itself against Nazi aggression. At a meeting in the Itamaraty on June 12, Miller and Caffery attending for the United States and Aranha, Dutra, and Góes Monteiro for Brazil, Aranha declared the "preliminary question" to be the arming of Brazil. Once that was achieved there would be no reservations as to cooperation with the United States, even to the extent of "joint action" outside the hemisphere. He made clear that Brazil did not desire free arms, but needed credit to permit purchases in the United States where arms were extremely expensive. Speaking for the military, Góes Monteiro lamented that it had not been possible—"despite the good will manifested by his American colleagues"—to reach a practical conclusion in regard to Brazilian-American military cooperation.[72]

[71] Conn and Fairchild, *Framework*, pp. 274-275. Rainbow IV was dated June 17, 1940.

[72] "Conferência de 12 de Junho de 1940," report dated June 17, 1940 in file "Assuntos Políticos e Comerciais," OAA.

Miller wrote Marshall that the situation in Brazil was extremely delicate because of "increasing Nazi influence." The majority of the Brazilian people were, he thought, strongly pro-American, but the government was "trying to keep on the fence." Hemispheric defense plans were contingent on the solution of matériel problems. The Germans were promising delivery of armaments in September and giving generous terms—ten years for payment and 75 percent of the total acceptable in raw materials. The Brazilian Army was convinced that the Germans could fulfill their promises, and the question of arms supply was the principal reason for Brazilian efforts to stay on good terms with the Reich. If the United States was to combat the growing Nazi influence in Brazil, Washington "must quickly find means to render effective help to Brazil under most favorable terms." Otherwise, Miller was sure, the United States would not obtain Brazilian cooperation. The German victories, instead of creating fears, were "raising hopes of greater possibilities for Brazil."[73]

In a conversation with Caffery, on June 18, Aranha declared forcefully that if the United States did not find means to assist Brazil in obtaining armament, the Brazilian military authorities would turn to Germany at the end of the war and acquire arms there at little or no cost. He added that if Brazilian weapons came from Germany, German military instructors would most probably replace American instructors. The same day Aranha received word that a new shipment of German artillery had arrived at Genoa for transport to Brazil—the British were then reluctantly permitting German arms delivered to Brazilian authorities in Italy to pass through the blockade.[74]

[73] Lehman W. Miller to George C. Marshall, Rio, June 17, 1940, and Miller to Caffery, Rio, June 21, 1940, WPD 4224–101, WWII RS, NA.

[74] Caffery, Rio, June 18, 1940, *Foreign Relations, 1940*, V, 48–49; for listings of equipment sent via Genoa on the Lloyd-Brasileiro ships *Santarem* and *Raul Soares* in late 1939 see: Freitas Valle, Berlin, Sept. 14, 1939, #134; Sept. 15, 1939, #135; Sept. 21, 1939, #139; Sept. 27, 1939, #151; Oct. 2, 1939, #159; Oct. 9, 1939, #173; Oct. 9, 1939, #206, AHMRE.

In the midst of the confusion and anguish after the German defeat of France, the United States strove to construct a new balance of power to contain the Axis. The chief of the War Department's intelligence section, in a memorandum on furnishing military information and equipment to the other American republics, stated that the question facing the American government was whether it was going in "unreservedly for hemisphere defense, and thereby adopting the Latin American countries as full-fledged allies."[75] Brazil's request for arms became the vehicle for determining a general Latin American arms-supply policy. Colonel Matthew B. Ridgway, presenting the problem for decision, reiterated the views of Colonel Miller and Ambassador Caffery: future relations with Brazil depended upon American willingness to supply armament and to finance the steel mill. Caffery warned that unless Washington acted promptly Brazil would slip under German control.[76] After much discussion, the War Department defined its Latin American objective as the securing of "better mutual understanding" by impressing Latin American officers with United States military preparations and with its determination to uphold the Monroe Doctrine. The objective did not include using Latin American forces as active allies in war.[77] The Army War Plans Division and the State Department worked out the final form of a national policy on arms supply to Brazil (and the other Latin republics) which President Roosevelt approved on August 1. It provided arms for Brazil—on financial terms the Brazilians could meet—to insure its ability to defend itself against an Axis attack or an internal disorder until the United States could send assistance. It also called for "adjusting the economic relations between the United States and Latin American states to insure the lat-

[75] Brig. Gen. Sherman Miles to Brig. Gen. George V. Strong (Asst. Chief of Staff), WPD, July 1, 1940, WPD 4115-23, WWII RS, NA.

[76] Conn and Fairchild, *Framework*, p. 276; Caffery, Rio, July 16, 1940, *Foreign Relations, 1940*, V, 49–50.

[77] Conn and Fairchild, *Framework*, p. 179.

ter's political cooperation," and declared that any financial losses should be accepted as a charge against the national defense. On August 2 Welles told Caffery to inform General Dutra that the Brazilians could procure all their arms within three years, and that within the next few months they would receive some aviation and automotive equipment.[78]

Several days later the War Department authorized Colonel Miller to continue the conversations with Brazilian military authorities, which had been adjourned in mid-July to await the Havana Conference. To prevent the Germans from seizing European possessions in the New World, the American republics approved the temporary occupation of those possessions; and, in an obvious vote of confidence in the United States, they sanctioned individual action in an emergency. The Havana meeting did not affect Brazilian-American negotiations, except that it committed both nations to closer Pan-American ties. Colonel Miller's task was to work out a plan for collaboration with the Brazilian army for "the maintenance in Brazil of a government, both determined and able, to preserve its territorial integrity and freedom from European control, and to cooperate fully with the United States in hemispheric defense."[79] This meant supporting the Vargas regime as long as it fulfilled those requirements. Miller emphasized in his talks with Brazilian military authorities the American concern for security of the northeastern bulge. He reached no agreement because in the latter part of August General Marshall invited Góes Monteiro to attend a conference of Inter-American chiefs of staff in Washington scheduled for October, and Góes Monteiro indicated his preference for negotiating an agreement directly with the War Department.[80]

[78] Memo: "Proposed National Policy re Supply of Arms to American Republics," Washington, July 27, 1940, *Foreign Relations, 1940*, v, 12–13; Welles to Caffery, Washington, Aug. 2, 1940, *ibid.*, p. 50.

[79] Conn and Fairchild, *Framework*, pp. 276–277.

[80] Marshall to Góes Monteiro, Washington, Aug. 23, 1940, WPD 4224–100, WWII RS, NA; Conn and Fairchild, *Framework*, p. 276.

Reports at the end of August from the Brazilian embassy in Washington were optimistic that negotiations for the steel mill would work out in Brazil's favor. As the days passed it became increasingly clear that the Third Reich would not humble Britain and that ties with Germany would not aid Brazil. Vargas called a meeting of the service chiefs and Chancellor Aranha on September 22 to discuss Brazilian-American military cooperation. They decided that in case of aggression all of Brazil's resources should be placed on the side of the United States. Soon thereafter, Góes Monteiro asked Colonel Miller to send Washington a draft of the agreement the Brazilian authorities wanted.[81]

Although the Vargas government was nominally committed to cooperation with the United States from the end of 1940 on, close military collaboration was not immediately achieved. Nearly two years elapsed before the two countries attained the cooperation forecast by the military conversations of 1940, because of American inability to supply Brazil with arms and the unwillingness of the Brazilian military to allow American troops on national soil before those arms were received. As a point of pride, the Brazilians wanted to deal with the Americans as equals. They wanted to participate in hemispheric defense measures, not merely to acquiesce in them, and possibly they thought that only a strong, modern Brazilian army could insure that once American forces were in the northeast they would not stay forever. Meanwhile the strategic situation changed when Germany attacked Russia; danger of a Nazi invasion of Brazil faded, but so did any chance for early shipment of arms from the United States. Secretary of War Stimson was convinced, at the end of 1940, that "Hitler's so-called fifth-

---

[81] Paulo G. Hasslocker (Brazilian Embassy Staff) to Aranha, Washington, Aug. 29, 1940, OAA. Hasslocker was a personal friend of Aranha who provided the minister with an unofficial view from Washington. Caffery, Rio, Sept. 23, 1940, *Foreign Relations, 1940*, v, 51; Caffery, Rio, Sept. 24, 1940, *ibid.* For text of draft see memos dated Sept. 21 and Oct. 9 in WPD 4224-101, WWII RS, NA.

column movements in South America" were merely "attempts to frighten us from sending help where it would be most effective."[82] In allocating war planes the secretary thought that none should go to Latin America because there was no war in the Western Hemisphere, and equipment should go "only where the war was raging."[83] The secretary's attitude was one factor delaying arms shipments to Brazil.

As a footnote to the Brazilian-American military conversations, it is curious that in late 1940 the United States was considerably more successful in getting German weapons into Brazil than American ones. When war broke out the Brazilians had just begun to receive the Krupp artillery ordered in 1938. The British allowed several shipments to reach Brazil via Italy between September 1939 and June 1940, and then via Portugal after Italy entered the war. They permitted the last vessel to pass through the blockade with the "understanding" of no further shipments. The Itamaraty, with the support of the British Foreign Office, petitioned the blockade committee in October for permission for a Lloyd-Brasileiro vessel, *Siqueira Campos*, to carry a portion of the Krupp order from Lisbon to Brazil. The blockade authorities said no, and Rio indignantly ordered the vessel to sail. The Royal Navy stopped it off the Portuguese coast and escorted it to Gibraltar.[84]

To put it mildly, the Brazilian authorities were angry. Aranha termed the British action brutal and told the American embassy he was staking his position as chancellor against the British releasing the vessel. If Brazil failed to get the matériel, he would resign and permit the designation of a foreign minister with antidemocratic views. The

[82] Henry L. Stimson and McGeorge Bundy, *On Active Service in Peace and War* (New York, 1948), p. 319.

[83] Stimson Diary, entry for Dec. 23, 1940, Yale University Library.

[84] MRE, *Brasil e a Segunda Guerra*, I, 159–160; for a listing of some of the equipment aboard see Freitas Valle, Berlin, Sept. 30, 1940, #383, AHMRE.

continuation of Brazil's pro-allied, prodemocratic policies and attitudes were in the balance. Góes Monteiro and other generals called for breaking relations, and there was even wild talk at the cabinet level of going to war with Britain. The government drew up decrees for expropriation of British-owned enterprises, and forbade all pro-British items in newspapers and motion-picture newsreels. Brazilian-British relations had reached their nadir.[85]

Welles was deeply concerned and told the British ambassador so, "most directly and vigorously." General Marshall made clear to the British that it was essential for the *Siqueira Campos* to reach Brazil, particularly because the Brazilian Army planned to use the weapons in defense of Natal. The British were creating an embarrassing situation for the United States government. At a time when Washington was giving Britain every consideration in arms supply, the British were making things impossible for Brazil, in whose defense the United States was interested.[86]

Against the advice of the Admiralty and the Foreign Office, the blockade committee maintained that, if it made this exception, other neutrals such as Argentina and Japan, which had made similar purchases in Germany, would demand similar treatment. The Brazilians insisted that the arms were not "enemy goods," but Brazilian government property purchased before the war. In fact the Germans had insisted that the Brazilians sign a declaration that the arms were "destined exclusively for the Brazilian army and could not be sold or ceded to a third power." And, ironi-

[85] Burdett, Rio, Nov. 1, 1940, *Foreign Relations, 1940*, v, 626–627; Burdett, Rio, Nov. 22, 1940, *ibid.*, pp. 628–629; Burdett, Rio, Dec. 10, 1940, *ibid.*, pp. 650–651; Burdett, Rio, Dec. 14, 1940, *ibid.*, pp. 654–655; Burdett, Rio, Dec. 3, 1940, *ibid.*, p. 643. Caffery was in Washington for consultations and in Aranha's opinion: "Your help has allowed us to consider you as our ambassador at the State Department"; Aranha to Caffery, Rio, Dec. 7, 1940, OAA.

[86] Welles to Burdett, Washington, Nov. 25, 1940, *Foreign Relations, 1940*, v, 629–631; memo of a conversation between Welles and British Ambassador Lord Lothian, Dec. 3, 1940, *ibid.*, pp. 641–642.

cally, when the *Siqueira Campos* was seized the Germans suspected that the Brazilians were transferring the arms to Britain. Even though the Brazilians had not compromised their pledge, Freitas Valle foresaw, as he said, "with profound sadness, the complete suspension of the furnishing of war matériel to the national army."[87] The Germans, though still demanding scheduled payments, put the remaining equipment in storage until after the war. The Brazilian officers could not understand the Anglo-Saxon logic involved in impounding the vessel. War Minister Dutra thought the British obsession with self-defense was blinding them to the rights of neutrals—a perennial British failing—and to the obvious fact that if the arms were in Brazil Britain's enemies could not use them.[88]

Finally, on December 18, the British bowed to American insistence and released the *Siqueira Campos*. The incident served to heighten Brazilian-American friendship—indeed Dutra declared that Washington officials were behaving more like brothers than friends. But the damage to British relations with Brazil was severe and long in being forgotten. Brazilian coolness toward Great Britain lasted throughout most of the war. In an important speech before a large group of army and navy officers Vargas fired the closing salvo in the incident. He warned "that the war matériel which we ordered is ours, and was bought with our money. To impede its arrival to our hands would be a violation of our rights, and whoever attempts to do so cannot expect from us acts of good will or a spirit of friendly collaboration."[89]

[87] MRE, *Brasil e a Segunda Guerra*, I, 160–163; Freitas Valle, Berlin, Sept. 21, 1939, #139; and Dec. 1, 1940, #463, AHMRE.

[88] Eurico Dutra to Vargas, Rio, Nov. 28, 1940, OAA. There is a full file in OAA on the *Siqueira Campos* incident.

[89] Burdett, Rio, Dec. 31, 1940, 832.00/1321, NA; Vargas, *A Nova Política*, VIII, 241. He gave the speech on Dec. 31. For other documents concerning the incident see the following: MRE, *Brasil e a Segunda Guerra*, I, 157–171; *Foreign Relations, 1940*, V, 626–658; Aranha to Vargas, Rio, Jan. 6, Jan. 13, Jan. 16, 1941, and Marshall to Aranha,

The Brazilian government cautiously cast its lot with the allies. As it became certain that Britain would not surrender and that the United States was committed to defending Brazil, the attraction of Germany faded. The year 1940 was the most critical in twentieth-century Brazilian-American relations and marked the turning-point in Washington's efforts to prevent German domination of Brazil. Vargas continued to move slowly and carefully, but after 1940 he did so more because of internal pressures than because of danger from the Axis. Those pressures were formidable and kept Brazilian-American relations in a state of uncertainty until 1942, but they were not sufficient to reverse the trend toward cooperation begun in 1940.

Washington, Jan. 6, 1941, OAA; Standing Liaison Committee discussion in SLC, Vol. 1, and Marshall–Góes Monteiro correspondence in AG 386.3 Brazil, both in WWII RS, NA. The British had angered the Brazilians even more by seizing two other ships, the *Buarque* and the *Itapé*. They removed twenty-two German passengers from the *Itapé* who were en route to Brazil; see MRE to Emb/Berlin, Rio, Dec. 9, 1940, #22, Exp. 6302, AHMRE.

"Without the air bases Brazil permitted us to construct on her territory victory either in Europe or in Asia could not have come so soon."[1]

8

Airlines and Bases

A PRINCIPAL OBJECTIVE of United States foreign and military policy from late 1938 to December 1941 was to prevent the establishment of Axis bases in the Western Hemisphere. The rapid development of aviation in the late 1930's made such an eventuality possible, and, together with the volatile world situation, forced American leaders to consider the aerial defense of the hemisphere. They worked to eliminate Axis-controlled airlines in Latin America, to obtain strategic bases, and to station American troops in northeast Brazil. They met with success in the first two instances but, as we have seen, were unable to persuade the Brazilian government to request American defenders.

The northeastern tip of Brazil, closer to French West Africa than to the nearest of the Antilles, was the one point in the hemisphere vulnerable to large-scale aerial attack or invasion. The area was undefended, inaccessible by land to Brazilian forces concentrated in the south, and beyond the range of American aircraft stationed in the Caribbean. To make the Brazilian bulge defensible the United States Army arranged with Pan-American Airways (PAA) to construct two chains of airfields leading from North America to northeastern Brazil. Although Brazilian leaders would not allow large numbers of American troops to garrison the re-

[1] Cordell Hull, *The Memoirs of Cordell Hull* (New York, 1948), II, 1423.

gion, they cooperated in the elimination of Axis airlines and in the construction of the airfields. These programs were conceived individually but were intimately connected to hemispheric defense and later to the prosecution of the war.

, It was fortunate that, when the world situation forced the United States to take an interest in Latin American aviation, Pan-American together with Panagra already circled South America and flew routes in Central America and the Caribbean.[2] The airline had been in Brazil since the late twenties. It operated an international service from Miami to Belém, near the mouth of the Amazon, thence to Rio de Janiero via the coastal cities of Natal, Recife, and Salvador; from Rio its clippers flew to Pôrto Alegre in southern Brazil and on to Buenos Aires. It maintained another route from Rio de Janeiro to Asunción, Paraguay, via Curitiba and Iguaçu Falls. Its subsidiary, Panair do Brasil, S.A., flew a variety of internal routes and acted as the feeder line for the parent company.[3] Pan-American pioneered many advances in aviation in Brazil, as elsewhere, setting up the first meteorological stations and ground-to-air communication system to safeguard its flights. Company engineers laid out many of the republic's airfields. Its innovations and pioneering spirit won the admiration and respect of many Brazilians, as well as the enmity of ultranationalist military officers and interests linked to Germany's Lufthansa and the German-con-

---

[2] Panagra, which was jointly owned by PAA and Grace Lines, operated on the west coast of South America.

[3] Panair was a wholly-owned subsidiary whose president was Brazilian—as were all of its pilots by the end of 1938—and whose business manager was Pan-American's senior representative in charge of operations in Brazil, Uruguay, Paraguay, and Argentina. Beginning in 1944 PAA sold Panair stock to Brazilians, gradually making the firm an independent Brazilian airline. Panair was responsible for all construction and maintenance of Pan-American's facilities in Brazil. On subsidiaries see William A. M. Burden, *The Struggle for Airways in Latin America* (New York, 1943), pp. 12–13, 27, 29–40.

trolled Brazilian lines—Condor, Varig (*Viação Aérea Rio Grandense*), and Vasp (*Viação Aérea São Paulo*).

In a memorandum to Foreign Minister Aranha in early 1939 Sumner Welles stressed the importance of PAA in Brazilian-American relations. Only air travel could reduce the great distance between the two countries. It took fourteen days to go by ship from New York to Rio de Janeiro and five days by air (in 1940 the introduction of the DC-3 and the use of a new route through central Brazil cut the travel time to three days). Washington wanted to maintain Pan-American's preeminence in international aviation and to assist it in meeting competition from non-American airlines. The company's position had "an important bearing upon questions of aerial defense" in which both countries were interested.[4] In September 1939 the United States adopted as a national policy the promotion of American or bona fide local ownership of feeder airlines in Latin America. But little was done to carry out the policy until the critical summer of 1940.[5]

Before the war three airlines connected South America to Europe: Lufthansa, Air France, and the Italian Lati (*Linea Aeree Transcontinentali Italiane*); all were government-controlled. In Europe Lufthansa and Air France collaborated in arrangements. In Brazil the original land facilities at Natal and Salvador—Pan-American flew seaplanes—belonged to Air France. Condor was a fully owned Lufthansa subsidiary, and the Brazilian Varig and Vasp were German-controlled with close links to Lufthansa. Competition had been lively between these companies and Pan-American/Panair before September 1939, but afterward larger interests were at stake in the control of Brazilian airways. Outbreak of hostilities forced Lufthansa to discon-

[4] Memo: "Aviation," Welles to Aranha, Feb. 27, 1939, Welles Letters, OAA.

[5] Stetson Conn and Byron Fairchild, *The Framework of Hemisphere Defense* (Washington, 1960), pp. 240–241.

tinue its transatlantic run, and Air France ended operations with the collapse of French resistance in June 1940. Lati increased its flights to take up the slack. It carried few passengers, mostly Axis agents and officials, but provided a useful means of communication beyond the reach of allied censorship, and a way to avoid the British blockade by flying light strategic goods, such as industrial diamonds, to Europe. The continually increased schedule, from the original two trips a month to weekly flights in the summer of 1941, indicated that it was a lucrative enterprise. Prior to the war Lufthansa and Condor had used German air-force pilots on a rotation basis to familiarize them with South American terrain and flying conditions. Condor continued to expand, receiving equipment from blockade runners; it spread its network into the strategic northeast. Lati pilots radioed the location of allied vessels in the Atlantic to lurking submarines and raiders, and assisted German and Italian merchantmen to run the British blockade.[6]

In the second half of 1940, the United States embarked on an effort to remove Axis influence from Latin American airlines. Both Undersecretary Welles and Juan T. Trippe, president of Pan-American Airways, considered the Brazilian aviation situation the most important in South America. At the department's urging Pan-American began to eliminate Germans from its Brazilian operations as the first step in this program. Washington's concern may have been exaggerated, but Pan-American did remove some individuals from sensitive positions and regions, and began to give thought to nationalizing Panair do Brasil by encouraging investment of Brazilian capital.[7]

[6] Burden, *Struggle for Airways*, pp. 12–13, 63–68, 75–76; *Foreign Relations, 1940*, v, 658–669; Nelson A. Rockefeller to FDR, Jan. 22, 1941, 813B, FDRL; Charles Murphy, "Letter from Recife, Intrigue on the Bulge," *Fortune*, XXIII, No. 6 (June 1941), 36. The stranded Air France personnel at Natal grimly collected landing fees ($12.50 or 250 cruzeiros) each time a Lati craft landed; see History SADATC, Part I, II, 89.

[7] Welles to Caffery, Washington, July 30, 1940, *Foreign Relations, 1940*, v, 658–660; Memo of Conversation between Ellis O. Briggs (DAR)

In mid-1940 Vargas was maneuvering between the Axis and the United States and again, as in other areas of Brazilian-American relations, the question of eliminating German influence and control over Brazil's airlines depended on the resolution, on the Brazilian scene, of the steel mill and arms-supply problems, and internationally on the outcome of the Battle of Britain. As these questions were resolved, Brazilian-American difficulties disappeared. In early October 1940 Vargas ruled that only native citizens could pilot Brazilian-registered aircraft, thus eliminating the Germans who had taken out citizenship after an earlier decree which required all pilots to be Brazilian citizens. Because of a lack of trained Brazilian pilots, Condor had to suspend routes which Brazilian aviation authorities transferred to Panair. And they asked Pan-American to increase its Rio-Buenos Aires services.[8]

Condor refused to give up. The Vargas government, while desiring to cooperate with the American-sponsored "degermanization" program, was unwilling to cancel Condor's services completely because Panair lacked sufficient planes to absorb all its routes. That Condor's continued existence was detrimental to the allied war effort was obvious. In mid-1941 Condor flew a crew from Rio to Belém for a German freighter (*Norderey*), which was lying in the Amazon port loaded with rubber awaiting a chance to slip across the Atlantic. En route they landed at coastal airfields where Pan-American's Airport Development Program and the American Army Air Force's ferrying operations were under way.[9]

---

and Juan Trippe, Aug. 21, 1940, *ibid.*, pp. 660–661; Interview, Cauby C. Araújo, Rio, Oct. 15, 1965.

[8] Caffery, Rio, Oct. 6, 1940, *Foreign Relations, 1940*, v, 661; Burdett, Rio, Oct. 22, 1940, *ibid.*, p. 663; Burdett, Rio, Oct. 31, 1940, *ibid.*, p. 665; Burdett, Rio, Nov. 11, 1940, *ibid.*, pp. 666–667; Walker (U.S. Consul), Belém do Pará, Dec. 22, 1941, 832.00/1449; Walker, Belém, Feb. 24, 1942, 832.00/1453½, NA.

[9] Caffery, Rio, Oct. 24, 1941, *Foreign Relations, 1941*, VI, 525–526;

The Brazilian position was that Condor, the oldest airline in Brazil, had rendered excellent services to the republic and would continue to do so. Moreover, Brazilian aviation authorities suspected that the United States wanted to destroy Condor to create a monopoly for Panair do Brasil. This was the view held by General Eduardo Gomes, the most important and most formidable figure in Brazilian aviation, air commander in northeast Brazil (2d Air Zone) at the time, and Director General of Airways in the new Ministry of Aeronautics. Gomes was the bane of Panair do Brasil's existence. Through the army airmail service, which he founded and directed, he pioneered air routes to the remotest sections of his vast country. He dreamed of the day when Brazilian civil aviators would replace his men, and he opposed nearly every extension of Panair because he considered it an American rather than a Brazilian company. Apparently he regarded Condor as more Brazilian than German and less of a threat to the fulfillment of his dreams.[10]

The United States denied any intent of creating a monopoly for Panair, and was prepared to call upon Pan-American to cancel extensions of service which had resulted from cessation of Condor flights. This attitude was in line with Washington's decision not to make Pan-American a government-controlled line or accord it monopolistic rights as the sole American-flag airline abroad, and with its policy

Young to Araújo, New York, Jan. 19, 1940, and Mar. 12, 1941, Araújo Papers; Araújo to Alice R. Hager (Civil Aeronautics Board), Rio, Jan. 15, 1942, *ibid.*; Charles Murphy, "Letter from Recife, Intrigue on the Bulge," *Fortune*, XXIII, No. 6 (June 1941), 36.

[10] Caffery, Rio, Feb. 3, 1942, *Foreign Relations, 1942*, V, 767–768; Frederico del Villar, "Brazilian Air Chief," *The Inter-American Monthly*, II, No. 8 (August 1943), 15–17; Alzira Vargas do Amaral Peixoto, *Getúlio Vargas, Meu Pai* (Pôrto Alegre, 1960), p. 240; interview, Cauby Araújo, Rio, Oct. 18, 1965. In 1964, while serving as minister of aeronautics, Eduardo Gomes presided over Panair's dismemberment.

of encouraging international aviation generally.[11] But
Washington desired the elimination of all German influence
in Condor, Vasp, and Varig. Early in 1941 it developed the
policy of offering aircraft, financial credits, and technical
assistance in return for "degermanization." Vasp had dis-
missed all its German personnel by August 1941 without receiving this *quid pro quo*—Varig followed suit. But Condor
still presented a problem because the Rio government in the
beginning of 1942 believed that the line had been thoroughly reorganized and was now Brazilian. General Gomes began to supply it with gasoline from army stocks, because the
airline, which was on the so-called black list, could get none
from the regular American suppliers. He got Condor planes
into the air by giving them military assignments and allowing reserve officers to pilot them.[12]

Vargas became annoyed at United States interference in
what he considered an internal matter; he felt that he was
perfectly competent to decide what was harmful to Brazil
and what was not. With his approval Condor continued flying, even though the War Department suspected that Axis
agents used the airline's radio facilities to follow the movement of United States military aircraft through Brazil.[13]
In spite of its suspicions the American government made
arrangements with Finance Minister Souza Costa to sell
Condor seven new aircraft at reasonable prices. Utilization

[11] Hull to Caffery, Washington, Feb. 5, 1942, *Foreign Relations, 1942*, v, 769–770; Memo: Rockefeller to FDR, Dec. 30, 1940, and attached unsigned, undated, Memo on proposed Pan-American monopoly, Box 12, July-Dec. 1940, OF 249, FDRL; Welles to Caffery, Washington, Oct. 10, 1942, *Foreign Relations, 1942*, v, 785. Welles said: "The Department . . . has no intention of taking any steps to block an international air service desired by the Brazilian Government."

[12] Caffery, Rio, Aug. 15, 1941, *Foreign Relations, 1941*, vi, 523; Welles to Caffery, Washington, Feb. 23, 1942, *ibid., 1942*, v, 772; Memo: Walmsley, Mar. 28, 1942, *ibid., 1942*, v, 778.

[13] Caffery, Rio, Mar. 13, 1942, *ibid.*, p. 774; Welles to Caffery, Washington, Mar. 14, 1942, *ibid.*, p. 775.

of American equipment would make the airline dependent on the United States for spare parts, and would weaken actual or potential German influence.[14]

American officials continued to prod, and, after Brazil entered the war in August 1942, the Vargas government also became anxious to remove German influence from all quarters. Condor then liquidated its indebtedness to Lufthansa to avoid any postwar links, and the United States removed the airline, completely Brazilianized under a new name, *Serviços Aéreos Cruzeiro do Sul*, from the proscribed list.[15]

The problem of Lati was also solved satisfactorily. The Italian airline was dependent on American-owned Standard do Brasil for gasoline and lubricants, but Foreign Minister Aranha was extremely reluctant to see the Lati service interrupted, because it was the only effective means, aside from cable, of communicating with many of Brazil's representatives in Europe and Africa. He even considered helping the Italians get gasoline and oil. Out of deference to the chancellor's wishes Washington did not press for immediate suspension of operations; it was concerned, however, because it knew that Lati planes were carrying mica, industrial diamonds, and platinum to Europe. The United States was eventually able to obtain exclusive procurement of such strategic materials in Brazil, and American officials hoped that Lati would die a natural death. Instead the Italians began constructing facilities at Natal, across the field from where Panair was building the Parnamirim air base for the American air force. The United States government arranged to underwrite for Pan-American the cost of opening a route from New York to Lisbon via Belém, Natal, and West Africa, and the Brazilian minister of aeronautics agreed in principle to the elimination of Lati. After Pearl Harbor, American officials demanded as a matter of mili-

[14] Souza Costa to Vargas, Washington, Feb. 8, 1942, and Vargas to Souza Costa, Petrópolis, Feb. 9, 1942, AGV.

[15] Hull to Caffery, Washington, Nov. 14, 1942, *Foreign Relations, 1942*, V, 787–788.

tary necessity that Lati's services be suspended. Sixteen days after war came to the Americas the Brazilians closed all Lati facilities, and Vargas ordered their expropriation. At Natal, the departing Italians thoroughly angered Americans working on the Parnamirim air base by flying back and forth, obviously photographing what became one of the world's largest and busiest military airfields.[16]

The American "degermanization" policy was slow in achieving success because of the great need for air transport in Brazil. Once the United States was able to provide equipment to replace German aircraft, and Pan-American Airways took over some of the cancelled international routes, the Brazilians cooperated in removing Axis influence and control in Varig, Vasp, and Condor. This policy established a truly national airways system in Brazil and eliminated a potential danger to hemispheric security and to the important supply routes which the Airport Development Program (ADP) created.

The ADP was Pan-American's principal contribution to hemispheric defense and to allied victory in the Second World War. Under a secret contract with the War Department, Pan-American built a string of some fifty-five airfields and bases stretching from the United States like the jaws of pincers—one running through Panama, Colombia, and Venezuela and the other through the West Indies and the Guianas—converging on Natal in northeast Brazil, the area eight hours by air from Dakar that had long caused nervousness in Washington. Natal became the "springboard to

16 Hull to Caffery, Washington, Apr. 7 and 14, 1941, *ibid.*, 1941, VI, 517–518; Caffery, Rio, Apr. 9, 1941, *ibid.*; Memo for the foreign minister from member of his staff, Nov. 8, 1940, "Assuntos Políticos e Comerciais," OAA; Hull to Caffery, Washington, Oct. 13, 1941, *Foreign Relations, 1941,* VI, 524; Caffery, Rio, Oct. 24, 1941, *ibid.*, 525; Hull to Caffery, Washington, Dec. 11, 1941, *ibid.*, 527; Caffery, Rio, Dec. 23, 1941, *ibid.*, 528; Harold Sims, Natal, Sept. 22, 1941, in "Official History," SADATC, Part I, Chap. II, 87–116; Interview, Charles Matthews, Natal, May 24, 1965. Matthews worked at the Parnamirim base from the start of construction until 1946. He has lived in the Natal area since the mid-1930's.

victory" that sent a steady stream of men, aircraft, and equipment to the battle fronts. In November 1942 *Fortune* magazine declared that the earlier situation was reversed, that it was Natal that was dangerously close to Dakar.[17]

During the defense planning of 1939 and 1940, United States authorities came to the conclusion that if the government undertook construction of the airfields, while the American republics were neutral, it would be necessary to negotiate numerous treaties that might never be ratified or, at best, might involve delays fatal to hemispheric defense. The December 1939 report on General Delos C. Emmons' flight to Brazil stated: "The economic and military value of the Panagra–Pan American Airways System to the United States in . . . hemispherical defense cannot be over-estimated. . . . The concentration . . . of Air Force units from North America to South America will depend solely . . . upon the full utilization of Panagra–Pan American Airways facilities. . . . It is mandatory that certain existing facilities of the Pan American System be augmented along the east coast of South America to insure the rapid concentration of American Air Forces in the defense of the critical Natal area."[18] After considering various alternatives, Washington chose construction and improvement of the airfields by Pan-American as "the most practical method of achieving the desired results."[19] Army officials wanted to conceal the hand of the United States government to avoid arousing anti-American sentiment.

The Military Appropriation Act of June 13, 1940, enabled the president to authorize secret projects without a public

[17] Memo to Manager PAA News Bureau, May 24, 1945, ADP, PAA Library (NY); "Brazil: The New Ally," *Fortune*, XXVI, No. 5 (November 1942), 106; Harold Sims, Natal, June 8, 1942, 832.00/4202, NA. For background on the ADP see Conn and Fairchild, *Framework*, pp. 249–252, and History SADATC, Part I, II.

[18] "Special Strategical Report on Brazil Flight," Col. Robert Olds to Maj. Gen. Delos C. Emmons, Dec. 1, 1939, WPD 4185-2, WWII RS, NA.

[19] Welles to Secretary of War, Washington, Oct. 24, 1940, WPD 4113-37, *ibid.*; see also Conn and Fairchild, *Framework*, p. 253.

accounting of funds. The War Department negotiated a contract with the Pan-American Airports Corporation, a special PAA subsidiary, to carry out the Airport Development Program. General Marshall emphasized the program's importance when he wrote the Secretary of War that "the immediate conclusion of the PAA contract is now more essential to our national defense than any other single matter."[20] The contract, signed in November 1940, stated that the facilities were to "be available for such use by United States Army, Navy, Marine Corps, and Coast Guard aircraft as may be authorized by the respective countries in which such airports are located. . . ."[21]

On December 2 Evan Young, an ex-foreign service officer in charge of PAA's relations with foreign governments, informed company representatives that they were to prepare to negotiate agreements that would include such items as government assistance in procurement of land, exemption from taxes on imported equipment and on the completed airfields, employment of local labor, installation and operation of radio equipment, charging of landing fees, and free use by all United States military and naval aircraft. Also, in order "to protect the investment incurred by the Company in establishing and providing of these modern airports," its agents were to seek operating rights for PAA aircraft for a twenty-year period.[22] This last was desirable for two reasons: first, no one was certain when or under what conditions American military forces would be able to utilize the airfields, so it was necessary to insure some degree of American control and, equally important, experienced maintenance; second, for much of the previous decade one of

[20] Memo, Chief of Staff, for Secretary of War, Sept. 7, 1940, as quoted in Conn and Fairchild, *Framework*, p. 252; History SADATC, Part I, II, 75.

[21] "War Dept-Pan American Aviation Contract for Latin-American Aviation Facilities," Nov. 2, 1940, WPD 4113-3, WWII RS, NA.

[22] Young to PAA Representatives, Memo: "Heads of Agreement," New York, Jan. 6, 1941, copy in Araújo Papers.

PAA's central preoccupations had been the securing of new air routes which the airline was naturally interested in preserving.

In Brazil the brunt of the work would fall on the airline's Brazilian representative and also the general counsel for Panair do Brasil, Cauby C. Araújo, who wrote Young suggesting that a hurried trip to New York might be in order to obtain "first-hand knowledge of our company's as well as Washington's viewpoint on this important matter, prior to formally contacting the Brazilian Government authorities." Meanwhile, Araújo was "discreetly surveying government circles" to determine how best to conduct negotiations.[23] At the beginning of January he flew to New York to discuss the program with the home office. One detail of great importance was who would actually build the Brazilian fields. Elsewhere in Latin America the Pan-American Airports Corporation directed the work for "the Sponsor," as PAA officials referred to the army; but Araújo convinced his superiors that the Vargas regime would not tolerate ADP operations unless they were carried out in the name of Panair. He argued that even Panair was suspect in nationalist eyes but, though owned by PAA, at least it was a Brazilian-flag line. From hard experience in seeking new routes, such as the one to Asunción in 1937 and more recently the Barreiras "cut-off" from Belém to Rio, Araújo had learned that success in obtaining concessions depended on not stirring up those nationalists who opposed operation of foreign aircraft over Brazilian territory. To avoid delays it should appear as if the airfields and related facilities were primarily for the use of Panair and secondarily for PAA. No public mention was to be made of possible foreign military use, but company officials authorized Araújo to use his discretion as to how much information to give to individual Brazilian leaders. Understandably, they were concerned lest the company's close ties with the United States Army,

[23] Araújo to Young, Rio, Dec. 18, 1940, Araújo Papers.

in a project that could easily appear as disguised imperialism or worse, damage the airline's position in Brazil. The war would not last forever, and afterward Pan-American would have to deal with the Brazilians without "the Sponsor." The American army, concerned with the war, did not always appreciate the company's long-term view.[24]

Araújo, returning to Rio, met on January 18 with Góes Monteiro, to whom General Marshall had written concerning construction of the bases. The next day with Góes' approval Araújo went to Petrópolis to confer with Vargas at his summer residence, the Palácio Rio Negro. He explained the program, including the United States government's role. After some hesitation Vargas gave his approval, explaining that he could not immediately issue a decree authorizing construction because of the uncertain attitude of the army. The president's military aide, General Francisco José Pinto, present during the conversation, added that "nazista" sentiment was strong in the officer corps and that it was necessary to proceed slowly. Work could begin, but Panair had to submit a formal application seeking a decree.[25] Although the regime was dictatorial it followed bureaucratic procedures, and pressure groups within and without the government shaped decree-legislation. If there was no substantial opposition, and if the desired law did not conflict with the regime's definition of national interest, the concerned parties literally could write their own decree, but when, as in this case, powerful elements such as nationalist military officers, rival airlines, and foreign governments were involved, the procedure became slow and cautious, with commissions and agencies submitting studies and position papers.

At the beginning of 1941 Vargas was engaged in a struggle to check the army's power. During the *Siqueira Campos*

---

[24] F. P. Powers (Panair's Business Manager) to Young, Rio, Dec. 18, 1940, "ADP," Araújo Papers; History SADATC, Part I, II, 79; Interview, Cauby C. Araújo, Rio, Oct. 4, 1965.

[25] *Ibid.*

affair, when it appeared that Britain would not give in and Aranha might leave the cabinet, Vargas had decided to reduce the generals' influence. The army had been seeking the creation of an aeronautics ministry under an army officer, to control all Brazilian aviation activities, civil and military, but the navy was unwilling to turn its air arm over to an army-controlled ministry. Vargas' solution—naming a civilian to head the new ministry—satisfied the navy and weakened the army. One Sunday morning General Pinto had interrupted Vargas' game of golf to deliver the army's protest. After finishing his round unusually badly, the president went off by himself for a long time and then calmly told Valentim Bouças, his golf partner and economic adviser, that the next day, January 20, he would appoint a close friend of Oswaldo Aranha, Joaquim Pedro Salgado Filho, as Minister of Aeronautics. Having thus overruled the army, he shifted pro-German generals to positions where they would be harmless. There was some talk in army circles of not turning over the planes, but after some delay they did so. Vargas had come out on top again, but perhaps not without a price in the long run. Years later Góes commented on the Salgado Filho appointment, saying that Getúlio consistently "employed every means to keep the Armed Forces weakened or divided, acting towards them as if they were a political body or a party. . . . what he intended, separating Aeronautics from the Army and from the Navy, was to weaken the Armed Forces—an evil [act] that would cost him dear. . . ."[26]

The new ministry presented a different sort of problem for Panair because the men who controlled it were under Lufthansa's influence. To avoid submitting Panair's ADP application to the new ministry Araújo backdated it to January 20, the day Vargas had signed the decree establishing

[26] Burdett, Rio, Jan. 20, 1941, 832.00/1325; Burdett, Rio, Jan. 23, 1941, 832.00/1330; Burdett, Rio, Feb. 5, 1941, 832.00/1337; Caffery, Rio, Feb. 10, 1941, 832.00/1338; see also clippings attached to A. W. Childs, "New Air Ministry," Jan. 22, 1941, 832.00/1332, all NA.

the ministry. This allowed him to send it to the National Security Council via the Ministry of Transportation and Public Works, which continued to supervise aviation until the new air ministry was functioning. General Pinto, who was secretary-general of the security council, gave it his personal care and protection. This stratagem effectively precluded any successful opposition.[27]

With Vargas' verbal permission, Araújo spent most of the following months in an airplane, flying from one site to another to obtain the necessary local permits, licenses, and land. The Department of Civil Aviation (DAC) or the army owned the sites at Belém, Camoçim, Fortaleza, and Recife; Air France's subsidiary *Cia. Aéropostal Brasileira* owned the landing fields at Natal, Maceió, and Salvador. Araújo bought Aéropostal outright and negotiated agreements with the DAC and the army. In some cases he purchased additional properties, or the government confiscated them and turned them over to Panair. These were tiring, difficult days.[28]

Six months passed before the machinery of the Brazilian government turned out the authorizing decree, and then Araújo drew up the basic document. Even though the airfields were under construction, opposition delayed approval. And in June Vargas, always careful to keep himself and his country from an inescapable position, held a series of secret meetings with the German ambassador that kept alive in Berlin the impression that Brazil was "the bulwark against the inclusion of South America in Roosevelt's anti-German policy."[29] Prior to the cabinet meeting which gave final approval in late June 1941, Vargas asked Aranha to

[27] Interview, Cauby C. Araújo, Rio, Oct. 4, 1965; Petition to Minister of Transportation and Public Works, Jan. 20, 1941, "Requerimento 30/31"; and "Requerimento 28/41 ao Presidente, Conselho Superior de Segurança Nacional," Jan. 20, 1941, both in "ADP," Araújo Papers.

[28] Powers to Young, Rio, Dec. 18, 1940, "ADP," Araújo Papers; Interview, Cauby C. Araújo, Rio, Oct. 4, 1965.

[29] *DGFP–D*, XII, 994, see also 924–925, 974–975, 993–995.

place his signature on the decree below his own. But just before the meeting Aranha noticed that someone had removed the president's signature, leaving only his own and those of a couple of other ministers. The military had yet to sign. Aranha angrily produced a photostatic copy of the original document bearing Vargas' signature, and heatedly told the president that he would not stand alone before the army as the advocate of the United States. With a sly smile Vargas signed the document again and it was published in the *Diário Oficial* forthwith.[30] Official sanction was not merely a formality; if the Brazilians had not issued the decree the United States would have been compelled "to occupy Northeast Brazil by force of arms" to insure the security of the new airfields.[31]

The decree specified that Panair submit plans, specifications, and cost estimates to the Brazilian government for approval. Upon completion of the facilities Panair was to turn them over to the Brazilian authorities for ownership, maintenance, and operation. When Panair transferred the airfields, it was to receive a twenty-year prepaid lease at an annual rate of 1350 contos, or $67,500 (1 conto was worth $50). Over the twenty-year period this would amount to $1,350,000, the 1941 estimate of the airfields' cost. Panair thereby would obtain free use and operating control of the airfields. This arrangement later gave rise to charges that PAA and Panair had used ADP funds for selfish commercial gains.[32] But these charges came long after the United States Army Air Force's Air Transport Command was firmly established at the ADP sites and the tense atmosphere of the early war years had disappeared.

[30] Interview, Euclydes Aranha, Rio, Nov. 15, 1965; Decree-Law 3462 (July 25, 1941), *Diário Oficial*, July 26, 1941, copy in Araújo Papers.

[31] History SADATC, Part I, II, 71.

[32] C. C. Araújo to Samuel F. Pryor (Vice President PAA and Assistant to Juan Trippe), Rio, Oct. 14, 1944 and July 25, 1945, both Araújo Papers. As late as the mid-fifties charges of self-interest were aired, see *New York Post*, June 29, 1956.

The reasons behind the provision that the Brazilian government lease the fields to Panair were largely practical. Brazil lacked an organization capable of running or maintaining the sophisticated facilities. Araújo was afraid that the Brazilian authorities would let them "go to seed," and that when the United States needed them they would not be usable. He also wanted to establish a measure for reasonable compensation in case the regime expropriated them. Araújo added the lease provision to the decree after the aeronautics minister requested that the radio and meteorological equipment, buildings, landing rights, and other accessory facilities be turned over to the government along with the runways and ramps. As Araújo wrote in a sworn statement in 1943: "I suggested the lease and rental in order to insure control of the facilities insofar as this was possible and in order to insure reimbursement from the Brazilian Government in the event that the facilities were for any reason taken over by the Government."[33] As we have indicated, however, airline officials were interested in keeping acquired air routes. It should be noted that the ADP bases, south of Belém, were along the coast and, while they were useful to Panair, PAA itself had shifted its international operations away from the coast, where it had employed amphibian craft, to an interior route, from Belém south to Rio via Barreiras in western Bahia, over which it used land planes. So it would appear that if commercial motives were involved in the lease arrangement they were more in Panair's interest than in PAA's. But Araújo steadfastly maintained that at the time commercial interests were not uppermost in his mind.[34]

During the first half of 1941, Pan-American was under constant pressure from the War Department to expedite the work to the very utmost. General Erwin Rommel's desert units were sweeping through North Africa, and Natal was

[33] Cauby C. Araújo, sworn statement on ADP, July 19, 1943, copy in Araújo Papers.

[34] Interview, C. C. Araújo, Rio, Oct. 7, 1965.

the main link in the supply route to the beleaguered British forces. Because of Brazilian neutrality it was necessary that work on the airfields proceed with no publicity or litigation. It had to be handled as a strictly civilian, commercial activity without diplomatic assistance or intervention. Panair officials resented criticism that they were proceeding too slowly, for they felt that their critics ignored the realities of the Brazilian situation.[35]

Nor were they engaged in child's play. In mid-1942, Araújo was suddenly arrested and held for trial in a military prison on trumped-up spy charges. Apparently an officer of the general staff had been passing information about ADP to former Condor officials who in turn passed it to the Germans. The star-chamber methods of the secret police forced a suspect to implicate Araújo, who was then president of Panair do Brasil. The charges were obviously absurd, but headlines calling for the death penalty emphasized the seriousness of the situation. Góes Monteiro pointed out that Araújo was the principal figure in the Brazilian ADP and had access to much more secret and important documents than the one which the police informant had in his possession—a document outlining Brazilian air policy. That Araújo was arrested, imprisoned, and tried, even though Vargas, Aranha, Góes Monteiro, and American officials were certain that the charges were false, indicated the uncomfortable influence that the Axis fifth-column exercised in Brazil, even after the country entered the war in August 1942. Fortunately the Supreme Military Tribunal acquitted Araújo of all charges in early 1943, and Pan-American Airways invited him to the United States for a well-earned six-month rest.[36]

[35] Young to Araújo, New York, June 24, 1941, Araújo Papers; Araújo to Samuel F. Pryor, Oct. 14, 1944, "ADP," *ibid.*

[36] Interview, C. C. Araújo, Rio, Oct. 7, 1965; Araújo to Panair Director, Rio, Feb. 12, 1943, Araújo Papers; Moesia Rolim, "Defesa do Dr. Cauby da Costa Araújo," Supremo Tribunal Militar, Conselho de Justiça da 1ª Região Militar, Rio de Janeiro, 1943, copy in *ibid.*; Luiz Vergara, *Fui Secretário de Getúlio Vargas* (Rio de Janeiro, 1960), p. 172.

From the start delays hampered the Airport Development Program. They resulted from poor communications in the northeast, slowness in obtaining various permits and equipment, the lack of standard construction methods and materials, such as bricks, plumbing, and electrical fixtures, and, in the beginning, the paucity of field engineers who could make on-the-spot decisions instead of having everything approved in New York. The need for rushing the work forced Pan-American to hire and send to South America many non-company men who were not put through the usual "familiarization" schooling regarding the company, its activities, and the basic "picture" in Brazil. Some of these men were poorly qualified, while others were entirely unsuited to working and living in the northeast. In one instance, in early 1942, local ADP officials spirited an American worker out of the country after he struck a Brazilian general during a drunken brawl in Natal's Grande Hotel.[37]

Probably of greatest importance was the difference between American and Brazilian ideas of speed and magnitude of construction which, combined with the language problem, did much to slow the program. All these deficiencies, coupled with lack of understanding of the dangerous European situation by Brazilians and Americans alike, constituted the most important factors producing delay in construction. The fact that it took five months after the initial survey merely to clear the ground for one of the runways as Parnamirim (Little River) field at Natal indicated the extent of the delay.[38]

At Natal the survey of the base area was conducted in late April 1941 but it was July before workers from the surrounding region were set to clearing the land. Panair's ADP staff hired an American Baptist missionary, Charles Matthews, who had lived in the region for several years, to

[37] Araújo to Young, Rio, July 23, 1941; Young to Araújo, New York, July 23, 1941; Araújo to Young, Rio, May 12, 1942, Araújo Papers. Interview, Charles Matthews, Natal, May 22, 1965.

[38] History SADATC, Part I, III, 104.

select many of the initial 250 laborers. During the week the workers stayed at the site; on Saturday afternoon they were taken home by truck and returned the same way Monday morning, each man with his week's provisions in a sack—farinha, rice, beans, and dried meat. The food went into the common pot of the various work-gangs, each of which appointed cooks from among their number. At night they slung their hammocks in large sheds and entertained one another with jokes and songs. It was rather picturesque but painfully primitive and slow.

Finally in September the first heavy equipment—graders, bulldozers, heavy trucks—arrived with their operators from the States. The same month saw work begin on several Panair facilities, such as the generator and radio shacks, a building to store oil drums, and a much-needed well. As might be expected there was a fair amount of local graft and profiteering in the sale of land and the supplying of services and materials. Araújo had been anxious not to arouse suspicions regarding the purpose of the construction, so he had paid $12,500 (250 contos) to a "Widow" Machado for the central tract of 494 acres. The land was probably not worth that much and the owner might have accepted a good deal less, because her late husband had given land free to Air France some years before. Panair unwittingly paid overly high rates for stone and clay to men who posed as owners of property containing those materials, when actually they had rented the land for that purpose. If Panair had rented the land itself it could have eliminated unnecessary and costly middlemen. In one case a contractor arranged to sell clay from his rented plot and got ADP personnel to clear the land, strip the soil, and pile the clay in rows.[39] The more money that flowed into the region, however, and the wider its distribution the less likelihood there was of opposition.

[39] Charles F. Matthews, "Sidelights on the History of Parnamirim Field," Report to Historical Office, SADATC, n.d.; and Matthews to Col. Wold, Natal, Dec. (n.d.) 1942, both in Charles Matthews Papers, Natal.

There were some efforts at organized agitation and sabotage, and considerable fear of a sudden German commando or aerial attack. At the end of August 1941 a supposed Integralista, an ex-army officer, went to the base site at Fortaleza, Ceará, on a Sunday, distributed bottles of liquor, and gave an inflammatory speech calling on the imbibing workers to kill the construction engineer and destroy the facilities "with dynamite and fire" because it was the work of traitorous Brazilians who had sold out to Americans. The lone, unarmed guard could do nothing, but the poor laborers were not about to endanger their opportunity to obtain cash by burning the hand that offered it.[40] The agitator was arrested later, but such incidents made all concerned nervous, and throughout the year American military authorities sought to station Marine guards at the sites. After Pearl Harbor security consciousness naturally increased, and Vargas acceded to Roosevelt's request that Brazil permit uniformed Marines to be stationed at Belém, Natal, and Recife. Not surprisingly, there was considerable opposition to such action among Brazilian military officers, notably General João Batista Mascarenhas de Moraes, army commander of the northeastern region and later head of the Brazilian Expeditionary Force to Italy, and Brigadier Eduardo Gomes, regional air force commander. Foreign Minister Aranha likewise was against admitting armed foreigners, but accepted in principle the Americans' need to send service personnel to operate the developing ferry route to Africa. As a compromise three Marine companies were allowed to come in uniform but with their arms crated and kept in storage. The Marines made the ADP staff feel safer but they were amazed at seeing them carrying short clubs instead of rifles.[41] These Marine guards were an open-

[40] J. E. C. Bahiana (Resident Engineer) to Araújo, Fortaleza, Sept. 2, 1941, Araújo Papers. Report was forwarded to Gen. Pinto and the National Security Council two days later.

[41] Memo of Conversations Between Welles and Ambassador Martins, and Welles and F. D. Roosevelt, Dec. 17, 1941, 810.20 Defense/1791

ing wedge—in the months thereafter the numbers of American navy and air corps personnel in the region slowly increased. But even Marines did not deter sabotage completely. In February 1942 a worker put sugar in the gas tanks of a B-17; it crashed shortly after takeoff and all nine men aboard were killed.[42]

As late as August 26, 1942, PAA officials in the United States were disturbed at reports of Clippers being left unguarded, and ordered "rigid control" of aircraft and cargoes.[43] But with only slightly over four hundred American officers and enlisted men at Natal in mid-1942 and no sizable Brazilian defense units, the establishment of tight security was difficult. The dispersion of facilities at Natal made the situation worse. PAA's activities were centered at its landing ramp on the Potengi river in town, as were the naval rescue operations. The airbase was located southwest and inland, at the end of a tortuous, dusty seventeen-mile road. The only communication between the two areas was by motor car or a temperamental telephone line that often did not function for hours at a time. A 1941 American military intelligence study had warned that "landings are possible throughout practically the whole coast line of the Natal region," and that it "would be the initial objective of an European thrust at the eastern coast of South America."[44] However, little could be done until Brazil was in the war and the United States had open control of the base.

Meanwhile, in May 1941, Washington asked Pan-American to utilize the ADP sites, which were still raw landing

⅔, NA; Aranha to Vargas, Rio, Feb. 16, 1942, OAA; Matthews, "Sidelights . . ." cited above in note 39.

42 Matthews, "Sidelights . . . ," *ibid.*; and interview, Matthews, Natal, May 23, 1965. The suspected saboteur fled into the interior and returned to Natal only in the early 1960's. He was never arrested or tried.

43 John C. Leslie (Mgr. Atlantic Division) to Business Mgr. PAB, North Beach, Aug. 26, 1942, "Brazil: Airport-Natal 1942," PAA Archive.

44 U.S. War Dept., "A Survey of the Natal Region of Brazil," May 14, 1941, I, 35 as in History SADATC, Part I, II, 72.

strips, to ferry aircraft to the British in Africa. Rommel's forces had pushed the British back into Egypt and London requested transports to carry supplies from Bathurst, British Gambia, and Takoradi, Gold Coast, to Cairo. Since the British did not have spare crews and the United States Air Corps officially could not fly outside the country, PAA set up another dummy subsidiary, Atlantic Airways, Ltd., whose crews would ferry the planes. The air corps, however, sent some of its pilots along as far as Natal to familiarize them with the route, and each of the ten aircraft in the first flight carried a British navigator from PAA's navigation school in Miami. The problem was how to get the Brazilians to permit passage over their territory. Major General Harold Arnold, air corps chief, instructed his liaison officer with the Brazilian air force to invite the Brazilian deputy chief of staff to cocktails and, waiting until after the planes would be well out from Miami, "diplomatically inform him as to the action that is being taken . . . explaining the reason for the rush. . . ."[45] The result was, as Brigadier General Carl Spaatz of the air general staff put it, "confusion and embarrassment in Brazil."[46] It seems that by mistake the planes' registry had been transferred to Britain before they reached Brazil, so the Brazilians found themselves being forced to allow belligerent aircraft to fly over their territory and be serviced there. Aside from that faux pas the mission successfully inaugurated the South Atlantic ferrying route and indicated the chief purpose of the ADP sites. Henceforth, however, all aircraft carried United States markings and papers until they reached Africa. So six months before Pearl Harbor and fourteen months before Brazil entered the war the ADP airfields were part of the allied supply system. By the end of the war literally thousands of aircraft would utilize them, especially the fields at Belém and Natal.

In mid-1942 Natal's Parnamirim field had two 6,000-foot runways, a group of tents for the navy, marine, and air transport people, a small operations office and control tow-

45 History SADATC, Part I, II, 96.   46 *Ibid.*, p. 97.

er, a tiny Panair passenger building, the old Air France hangar, and the Lati hotel. The American officers took over the hotel and provided transient pilots with meals and a night's lodging, as well as all the local beer and *guaraná* (a tropical soft drink) that they could drink, for $2.50. The overflow from the Lati hotel, the only advantage of which was its location beside the field, went into town to the Grande Hotel, where the food was termed "unfit for consumption" in a PAA report and which the American military would eventually declare off-bounds because of the unsanitary condition of its kitchen. Others more fortunate, or better advised, went to the *Casa Branca*, a boarding-house run by an Englishwoman where $2.00 paid for room, board, and laundry. Later on, when the American military were quartered almost entirely at the air base and services in town deteriorated further, PAA built a staff house to quarter its own personnel because "no other satisfactory housing and messing facilities" were available.[47] At the field the sandy soil, stripped bare by construction crews, blew about in clouds that irritated the men and fouled the planes' engines. Enlisted men subsisted on cans of Spam, complained of the lack of milk, and dreamed of baked goods. Barracks were being constructed gradually but as yet lacked screens; although the steady ocean breezes kept malarial mosquitoes away, flies swarmed over the garbage, open-pit latrines, and the casual defecation of the workers. Diarrhea and amoebic dysentery were a scourge that few escaped. And with no movies, post-exchanges, or other simple amusements in those early days, the men drank a great deal and sampled the pleasures of the local whorehouses, which in Natal, as elsewhere along the line of bases, multiplied rapidly.[48]

With hundreds of Americans from a variety of organizations suddenly descending on Natal in late 1942 and early

[47] E. R. Littler to Executive Assistant (N.Y. Office), Natal, Aug. 17, 1944, "Brazil: Airport-Natal, July–Dec. 1944," PAA Archive.

[48] History SADATC, Part II, IV, 77–78.

1943, discipline became a serious problem. Since few spoke Portuguese, PAA's local representative suggested providing each man on arrival with the airline's "Air Traveler's Dictionary" to enhance the "enjoyment and interest" of his visit. Asking for 5,000 copies, he wrote excitedly that: "The potential good for interdivisional relations and understanding among USA citizens and Brazilians is thought-provoking in the extreme. . . ."[49] In 1942, troops in Natal appeared sloppy and bored. In addition to the military there were civilians attached to ADP, PAA, the PAA ferrying operations, Trans-World Airways, which flew from New York to Cairo, Standard Oil, and a constant stream of transients.[50] In one case three transient American officers went on a "binge" and frightened several people by waving knives and shouting threateningly; they topped off their drunken performance by kicking in the door of a warehouse belonging to the brother of the state governor. At that time the officer in charge of the base was a Captain, who could hardly deal on an equal level with Brazilian officers and officials who out-ranked him. Of course, such problems were not limited to Brazil but in this case they led to a minor dispute regarding legal jurisdiction, in which the Americans refused, in the words of Ambassador Caffery, "to turn over members of our armed forces to the Brazilian authorities to try." A head-on clash was averted because the Brazilians, while reserving the right of jurisdiction over foreign troops who violated local laws, yielded in practice to American authorities. Such questions took on greater importance in 1944 and 1945 as the United States army attempted to preserve access to the Brazilian bases after the war. The Brazilians, however, declined to include, in the June 1944 agreement that agreed to a continued American presence, an ar-

[49] Robert C. Hallet to Traffic Mgr., Rio, Dec. 12, 1942, "Brazil: Airport-Natal, 1942," PAA Archive.
[50] For a May 1942 enumeration see History SADATC, Part II, IV, 13, FN 27.

ticle surrendering Brazilian jurisdiction over American personnel.[51]

In 1943, with Brazil officially in the war, Washington arranged for the United States Engineering Department (part of the Army Corps of Engineers) to assume charge of further construction. Panair's ADP personnel continued to be involved but under the Engineering Department's supervision.[52] The road into Natal had been paved, and was known as the "Pista Americana," and a pipeline beside it carried fuel from tankers in the Potengi river to the air base. The next two years saw the base grow to 3,301 acres containing some four hundred buildings, including a two-hundred bed hospital, several large mess halls, open-air and roofed theaters, two pleasant officers' clubs, a NCO club, extensive hangars and repair shops, control tower, and headquarters. With the physical improvements morale was less of a problem and recreation facilities offered movies, USO shows, a GI study program, an extensive sports program, and trucks to carry swimmers back and forth to Natal's Ponta Negra beach. If it had not been for the constant drone of aircraft, the soft warm breezes and the clear blue sky would have made it difficult to remember that war was raging across the ocean.

Parnamirim air base was the focal point in the air transport system stretching north through Belém and the Guianas to Miami, and east via Ascension Island and Africa to the China-Burma-India theater. It was proudly and rightly called the trampoline to victory for without it supply problems during 1942 and 1943 might have been insurmountable. If Vargas and the Brazilian military had not cooperated the United States might well have seized the region by force, which probably would have caused serious and constant fighting in Brazil. Through the Airport Devel-

---

[51] Caffery, Rio, June 24, 1944 as in *Foreign Relations, 1944*, VIII, 600; see also 600–603.

[52] Asst. Engineer to District Mgr., Recife, Apr. 29, 1944; George Rihl (Vice Pres.) to District Engineer, May 5, 1943, both in Araújo Papers.

opment Program the United States obtained a military air transport system in Latin America in the easiest and cheapest manner. The forty-one ADP airfields, six seaplane, and eight blimp bases stretching from the United States through Brazil made possible immediate reinforcement of the Panama Canal defenses in December 1941, and the launching in 1942 of a successful antisubmarine campaign in the Caribbean and South Atlantic. And, most important, the War Department's prewar alliance with Pan-American Airways, provided a basis for military collaboration with Brazil.[53]

[53] Conn and Fairchild, *Framework*, pp. 258, 264. The ADP construction costs by 1945 reached $90,000,000 and the army paid PAA more than $10,000,000 for maintenance. More than half of the money was spent on the Brazilian fields.

"One more good-will mission and Brazil will declare war on the U.S.A."[1]

9

An Uncertain Alliance

VARGAS' DECISION to permit the ADP to function in Brazil was one of the key factors in the republic's eventual entry into the war on the allied side. But in early 1941 it was not clear that events were moving in that direction. The same weekend that Vargas gave Cauby Araújo verbal approval for the construction program the military asked the president to close the important Rio de Janeiro newspaper, the *Correio da Manhã*, because it had refused an army request to publish anti-British items. The *Siqueira Campos* and other such incidents hurt the pride of Generals Dutra and Góes Monteiro, who were backing an anti-British press campaign. The *Correio da Manhã* carried a British advertisement on January 19 stressing England's ties with Brazil, and the *Diário Carioca* ran an editorial indirectly warning the military to stay out of civilian affairs. Góes Monteiro and Dutra urged Vargas to suspend the *Diário Carioca* temporarily and to close the *Correio da Manhã* indefinitely. But Vargas, who had decided to place the new air ministry under a civilian instead of an army officer, took the opportunity to strike another blow at the military. He refused to close the *Correio da Manhã*, alleging that such an arbitrary act would be too unpopular, but, as a concession, he ordered the Press and Propaganda Department to suspend the *Diário Carioca* for a few days. Góes Monteiro reportedly quipped that they had gone hunting for a lion (*Cor-*

[1] Oswaldo Aranha quoted in "The Wooing of Brazil," *Fortune*, xxiv, No. 4 (October 1941), 100.

reio) but instead had gotten an alley cat (*Diário*). The American chargé d'affaires thought the incident revealed Dutra's pro-German bias and hurt his prestige. On the other hand, the chargé considered Góes Monteiro pro-American in spite of his violent antipathy toward the British.[2]

Officers who were anti-British were not necessarily anti-American or pro-German. Many ardent admirers of Hitler's war machine would side with the United States in a conflict between North America and the Reich. By the spring of 1941 Italian reverses were causing doubts in pro-Axis circles, a trend stimulated by the emphatic statement of the chief of the Brazilian arms-purchasing commission, Colonel Gustavo Cordeiro de Farias, recently returned from Essen, that German defeat was inevitable. But since American policy turned on aid to Britain, at the expense of being unable to provide Brazil with arms, the anti-British attitude of the Brazilian army was a constant worry to Washington.[3] To smooth relations with the army authorities Welles negotiated with the British to allow the Brazilians to ship their German artillery, which Krupp was still supplying, from Portugal to the United States and thence reship it to Brazil. And Roosevelt, in an attempt to tighten relations, tried unsuccessfully to get Vargas to visit the United States, but Getúlio felt that the situation was too unsettled—it was not safe for him to leave Brazil. Vargas told James A. Farley, who visited Brazil in early March 1941 while on a business trip to South America for Coca-Cola, that "unreserved collaboration with the United States constituted the corner stone of his government's foreign policy." If the United

2 Burdett, Rio, Jan. 22, 1941, 832.00/1333, NA; John Gunther gave a version of the episode in his *Inside Latin America* (New York, 1941), p. 385; as did John W. F. Dulles, *Vargas of Brazil* (Austin, 1967), pp. 216–218; Góes Monteiro was silent on it in Lourival Coutinho, *O General Góes Depõe* (Rio de Janeiro, 1956).

3 Caffery, Rio, Feb. 11, 1941, 832.00/1339; Caffery, Rio, Mar. 31, 1941, 832.00/1346; Caffery, Rio, Apr. 3, 1941, 832.00/1347; Welles to Caffery, Washington, Apr. 4, 1941, 832.00/1347, all NA.

States as a result of its assistance to Great Britain came to declare war on Germany, Vargas promised that Brazil would not remain neutral but would take its place at the side of the Americans. Vargas seemed less antagonistic toward the British than did his generals.[4]

Washington's concern for the security of the northeast—more important now with the ADP underway—flared anew in May when Vichy made a tentative agreement with the Reich permitting the use of Dakar as a German submarine base. General Marshall hurriedly sent Colonel Matthew B. Ridgway to Rio (for earlier negotiations see Chapter 7) to secure immediate Brazilian agreement to joint defense planning and to the dispatching of United States Army forces to the northeast.[5] A small number of well-equipped Brazilians and Americans could hold the area against a strong attack; and Axis forces from Africa could not safely bypass the Brazilian bulge and attack another portion of South America. The northeast was the key to the hemisphere's Atlantic defenses. Once the Brazilian flank was secure the United States could prepare the bulk of its forces for action in the decisive European theater. But again the inability of the United States to supply sufficient arms to insure equality in joint operations precluded entry of American troops. An American request to participate in planned

---

[4] For Welles' efforts see Carlos Martins to Vargas, n.p. (Washington), June 24, 1941, AGV. On the nature of artillery equipment and problems in dealing with the Germans see transcript of telephone conversation with Essen Commission, Mar. 5, 1941, AGV. Roosevelt to Vargas, Washington, Jan. 4, 1941–Apr. 26, 1941, AGV. Aranha to Carlos Martins, Rio, Mar. 5, 1941, OAA; also, Memo: "Brazilian Cooperation," DAR, May 20, 1941, 711.32/143, Item I, NA; on Farley's tour see James A. Farley, "It's Time We Got Practical in South America," *Brazil*, XIII, No. 148 (April 1941), 1off.

[5] United States Navy, Office of Naval Intelligence, *Fuehrer Conferences on Matters Dealing with the German Navy*, 1941, I, 76. Report dated May 22, 1941; Julius W. Pratt, *Cordell Hull*, XII–XIII in Robert H. Ferrell, ed., *American Secretaries of State and Their Diplomacy*, XIII (New York, 1964), 375; Stetson Conn and Byron Fairchild, *The Framework of Hemisphere Defense* (Washington, 1960), pp. 284–286.

Brazilian maneuvers in order to get United States forces into the country led to cancellation of the maneuvers. It was probably fortunate, because using "a wolf in sheep's clothing . . . [was] very dangerous and capable of producing a very unfavorable reaction in Brazil."[6] Under conditions existing in 1941, Vargas' approval of such a plan could well have caused the Brazilian army to withdraw its support of his regime.

At this juncture the War, State, and Navy Departments in Washington were working at cross-purposes. The army was endangering the stability of the Vargas government and Brazil's friendly relations with the United States by urging entry of American troops. The other two departments opposed the army's proposal, but for different reasons. Former Integralistas and pro-Axis officers were becoming bolder, and a conspiracy reportedly was afoot to oust Vargas and replace him with a pro-Axis president. That would have been a calamity for the United States, and the State Department was attempting to shore up Vargas by constantly recommending that arms be sent to Brazil.[7] The navy was unwilling to aid the army because early in 1941 it obtained permission to station naval observers in Brazilian ports, and to use Recife and Salvador as unrestricted supply ports for its South Atlantic units. And President Roosevelt, without saying so, did not favor the army's proposal, so it never got beyond the planning stages.[8]

Roosevelt had another approach in mind. In early July he wrote Vargas, explaining the nature of the agreement with Iceland that permitted United States forces to take over the island's protection from the British. He saw Ice-

[6] Report of Lehman Miller, Aug. 8, 1941, quoted in Conn and Fairchild, *Framework*, p. 288; Caffery, Rio, July 31, 1941, 832.20/281, NA.

[7] Memo: Laurence Duggan to Dean Acheson, May 29, 1941, 832.00/1359, NA.

[8] United States Navy, "Commander, South Atlantic Force," Vol. XI in "Administrative History Atlantic Fleet" (by Prof. Charles E. Nowell), pp. 8, 10, 21. Hereafter cited as USN, South Atlantic Force. Conn and Fairchild, *Framework*, p. 289.

land and Greenland as the "last lines of defense of our hemisphere in the North Atlantic." His aim was to prevent a German pincer movement across the north and south Atlantic, and with the north now secured he was turning his attention south. He told Vargas he was afraid that if Germany suddenly occupied West Africa and the Cape Verdes it would then be "in position to launch an attack by air and sea against Natal almost immediately." He was studying the possibility of negotiating with the Netherlands for temporary use of air and naval patrol facilities in Dutch Guiana, and wanted to know if Brazil would be willing to cooperate and to send troops to "complement the forces of the United States." Also, he wanted to know—in the event Portugal were invaded and Salazar asked for American or Brazilian help in protecting the Cape Verdes—whether Brazil would be ready and willing to act? Quite obviously, once the two armies were operating together on foreign territory it would be simpler to persuade the Brazilians to let American forces into Brazil. Vargas sought the reactions of his military ministers. Dutra said that the army was not ready, and wondered why the Americans considered the Brazilian forces capable of carrying out foreign operations but incapable of defending their own territory. Aeronautics Minister Salgado Filho thought that Brazil ought to cooperate in defense of the continent, but insisted that deficiency in military equipment would "not permit, at the moment, any collaboration outside of our frontiers." Brazil had only twenty-seven fighter aircraft "without adequate armament and without ammunition," and should not consider foreign operations until the United States delivered the equipment they had requested. Otherwise, embarking on such foreign adventures without sufficient military strength, and without a clear and definite aggression or threat to repel, would have disquieting effects on Brazil's internal situation.[9]

[9] Roosevelt to Vargas, n.p., July 10, 1941; Joaquim Pedro Salgado Filho to Vargas, Rio, July 23, 1941, AGV.

There the matter lay; to gain closer cooperation and admittance for its forces the United States would first have to arm the Brazilians.

Vargas softened the tone of the Brazilian position by replying to Roosevelt that the mixed general staff commissions, then being set up, would arrange the manner of cooperation, knowing full well that the Brazilian army had no intention, at that time, of participating in such operations. He took the opportunity to reassure Roosevelt that "Brazil continues disposed to lend complete collaboration to the United States, employing all its forces and means at its disposal to insure the common defense of the American Continent."[10]

Even as Washington attempted to mount a defense and was putting pressure on Vichy to prevent German occupation of Dakar, Roosevelt moved elements of the American fleet to the Atlantic and increased naval patrols in the narrows between Brazil and Africa. Meanwhile, the Brazilians made gestures toward reorganizing and increasing their garrisons in the northeast. The Vargas regime allowed American army doctors to conduct a medical survey of the northeast (which the Americans used in part to gather intelligence on the region) and, perhaps more important for its long-range effects, agreed that only the United States would be allowed to obtain strategic Brazilian materials—diamonds, manganese, nickel, mica, tungsten, rubber, etc.—thus keeping them from the Axis.[11] But the War Department was still hopeful that it could implement Rainbow IV's provision for sending more than 60,000 troops to the bulge without large arms transfers to the Brazilian forces. The army was willing to pare the figure depending on an

[10] Vargas to Roosevelt, n.p., July 26, 1941, AGV.

[11] Cordell Hull, *The Memoirs of Cordell Hull* (New York, 1948), II, 945; Pratt, *Hull*, XIII, 375; Memo: Welles to FDR, May 29, 1941, Box 75, PSF Brazil, 1941, FDRL; Caffery, Rio, May 28, 1941, 832.20/267, NA; Memo: "Brazilian Cooperation," DAR, May 20, 1941, 711.32/143, NA. For negotiations on strategic materials see *Foreign Relations, 1941*, VI, 538–551.

improved strategic situation, but it continued to seek the entry of thousands of troops.[12] Although the army unsuccessfully attempted to use joint staff planning as a device for getting troops into Brazil, it did obtain much valuable data for correction and elaboration of earlier war plans, and prepared the way for the military improvement of the ADP air bases in early 1942. The joint staff agreement signed on July 24, 1941, served as an important diplomatic link between the two armies, but expressly stated that Brazil alone would determine when, where, and for how long military assistance would be needed. Invited American forces would act only as "an element of reenforcement."[13] Even so, officers in the War Department continued to work under the misconception that Brazil would agree to the entry of American troops under circumstances different from those specified in the July agreement.

Ambassador Caffery repeatedly cautioned Washington that both America's friends and enemies would oppose such efforts. "They are adamant on this issue," he warned. "Our troops can be sent to Natal, but the region can be occupied against the will of the Brazilians only by force of arms. It is a mistake for our military authorities to proceed . . . with anything else in mind." The United States would lose Brazilian cooperation if it pursued an unrealistic policy based upon "wishful thinking."[14] But the ambassador made little impression on American military planners. The new Rainbow V plan, drawn up between October and December 1941, called for the deployment of two divisions of ground and air troops numbering 64,000 to the vicinities of Belém, Natal, and Recife. After Pearl Harbor this was basically the plan the army wanted to follow.[15]

Meanwhile the United States was waging a propaganda

12 Conn and Fairchild, *Framework,* pp. 290–291.
13 "Term of Agreement," July 24, 1941, *Foreign Relations, 1941,* VI, 507–509.
14 Caffery, Rio, Sept. 4, 1941, 832.20/304, NA.
15 Conn and Fairchild, *Framework,* p. 293.

campaign on a grand scale under the supervision of Nelson A. Rockefeller's Office of the Coordinator of Inter-American Affairs (established in August 1940).[16] Waves of goodwill ambassadors broke over Brazil in 1940 and 1941. Earnest and energetic Americans poured into Rio de Janeiro from Pan-American clippers and Moore-McCormack ships. Douglas Fairbanks, Jr., arrived as a personal representative of President Roosevelt to look into the Brazilian film industry, only to find that Hollywood had a near-monopoly. Two women from Washington's Children's Bureau turned up to help organize one in Brazil. Two plane-loads of men from the National Research Council inspected Brazil's laboratories and talked of Brazilian-American scientific cooperation. A representative of the United States Weather Bureau arrived to study Brazil's meteorological methods and equipment. Arturo Toscanini directed a symphony in Rio's ornate Municipal Theater. A sculptor came to do a bust of Getúlio Vargas. Even the Boys' Club sent a "short-pants ambassador." Chancellor Aranha, who received nearly all of these people, wearily joked: "One more good-will mission and Brazil will declare war on the U.S.A." He may have been jesting but Vargas was cautious; he allowed the secret police to infiltrate and spy on American and British agencies in Rio de Janeiro. Police chief Müller passed the word to the president that Douglas Fairbanks was not only Roosevelt's representative but was also a propaganda agent for the British, and would extoll the success of the blockade and emphasize the certainty of Britain's eventual victory.[17]

16 For activities of OCIAA see Coordinator of Inter-American Affairs, OF 4512, FDRL.

17 "The Wooing of Brazil," *Fortune*, XXIV, No. 4 (October 1941), 100. The secret police (*Delegacia Especial de Segurança Política e Social*) reported to Müller, who sent summaries of their activities to Vargas, see e.g., Felisberto Batista Teixeira to F. Müller, Rio, Jan. 17, 1941, AGV. This made quite clear that DESPS agents were "infiltrados nos meios norte-americanos e inglêses desta capital." On Fairbanks: F. Müller to Benjamim Vargas, Caxambú, Apr. 30, 1941, AGV.

Almost invariably, the American missions, experts, and investigators were on their way to or from Buenos Aires, sweeping around the continent, "doing" all of South America in one whirlwind trip. The sudden and breathtaking courtship was not altogether flattering—Brazilians were only too aware that the United States was paying the same attention to their Spanish-speaking neighbors. They felt that Brazil should receive special treatment, because of its size and importance and because of its old friendship with the United States. Despite the long diplomatic friendship, knowledge of each other scarcely existed beyond the portals of the Itamaraty and the Department of State. Until 1940 no history of the United States was available in Portuguese in any Brazilian public library; of course, there were few public libraries and the literacy rate was low.[18]

Few Brazilians had visited the United States, while Americans frequently confused Buenos Aires and Rio de Janeiro. The huge distance, the expensive means of transportation, and the time necessary limited travel to the rich. The common Brazilian conception of the United States was derived from the extremely popular Hollywood films, and unfortunately Americans could only surmise from the same source that Brazilian men were sharp, witty little fellows like Walt Disney's "Zé Carioca," and the women were all Carmen Mirandas. And any educated American knew they spoke Spanish in Brazil, and that the tango was the national dance, or was it the conga?[19] Probably more lasting and effective results would have been obtained if the northbound traffic had been heavier than that going south. An American staying a week to ten days in Rio—they rarely went into the interior—contributed little to Brazilian un-

[18] Ruth E. McMurry and Muna Lee, *The Cultural Approach: Another Way in International Relations* (Chapel Hill, 1947), p. 218.

[19] John Nasht, "Hollywood's Carioca Fans," *The Inter-American Monthly*, ii, No. 9 (September 1943), 28–30; John Nasht, "Brazil's Year of Change," *The Inter-American Monthly*, ii, No. 5 (May 1943), 29.

derstanding of Americans, and in that length of time could hardly have learned much himself.

The Coordinator of Inter-American Affairs, through the American Council of Learned Societies, began in 1941 to stimulate the translation of American books into Portuguese and Brazilian books into English.[20] Several Portuguese grammar and phrase books appeared in the United States, and some colleges and universities began to offer Portuguese, although frequently it was the language of Portugal rather than of Brazil. The best that can be said is that the feverish efforts of the 1940's laid the basis for later serious study.

Perhaps more successful were American efforts to counter Axis propaganda and to explain shortages of such things as newsprint and gasoline after the United States entered the war. The coordinator's office provided news items and feature articles, and through "judicious needling" the Rio embassy obtained publication of news and editorials favorable to the United States. The embassy established an indirect subsidy program to encourage a friendly press, and thus kept in business some newspapers which had previously depended upon Axis subsidies or advertising. Efforts to produce motion pictures about the United States for Brazil and vice versa were less successful, and the State Department was lukewarm to proposals to organize a program "glorifying Brazil in the U.S."[21] Even so, propaganda did much to prepare Brazilian public opinion for events ahead, and public opinion frequently ran in advance of government policy. In the end it would be the Brazilian people who would lead the republic into war.

20 McMurry and Lee, *Cultural Approach*, p. 219.

21 Caffery, Rio, May 2, 1941, 832.00/1355; Memo: William Wieland to Michael McDermott, Mar. 9, 1942, 832.911/11½; Memo: Wieland to McDermott, May 11, 1942, 832.9111/24½; Memo: John C. Dreier to L. Duggan, Oct. 28, 1942, 832.91211/4 all NA; Hernane Tavares de Sá, *The Brazilians, People of Tomorrow* (New York, 1947), has section on propaganda, pp. 229–236.

In a speech commemorating the fourth anniversary of the Estado Nôvo (November 10, 1941), at a celebration appropriately enough in the war ministry, Getúlio warned that the government would punish invaders and fifth columnists. Brazil was committed to continental solidarity and would take part in the common defense of the Americas.[22] Leading Brazilian newspapers praised the speech; Secretary of State Hull expressed his "deepest appreciation"; and Roosevelt cabled Vargas that the United States joined him in reasserting the necessity of common defense of the hemisphere.[23] Twenty-seven days later the Japanese fleet attacked Pearl Harbor, and the long-feared war enveloped the New World.

In Rio, on December 8, Vargas called together his cabinet, which declared solidarity with the United States and approved steps to silence the many clandestine Axis radio stations operating in Brazil. Aranha gave all the Latin American diplomats accredited to Brazil "pep talks," affirming that the attack on the United States was an attack on all and urging that their republics respond unanimously.[24]

In the busy weeks that followed the American republics organized the Third Foreign Ministers Conference, held at Rio de Janeiro January 15–28, 1942. Washington prevented attempts to transfer the site elsewhere (Santiago, Panama, or Washington), because Hull and Welles thought the "psychology" created by holding the meeting in Rio would be favorable to the Allied cause, and because there Oswaldo Aranha would preside over the conference.[25]

The *Jornal do Brasil* summed up the Brazilian reaction to Pearl Harbor when it declared: "Brazil was neutral, but

[22] Getúlio Vargas, *A Nova Política do Brasil* (Rio de Janeiro, 1938–47), IX, 127–134.

[23] Simmons, Rio, Nov. 12, 1941, 832.00/1413, NA; Secy. Hull's Press Conference, Nov. 12, 1941, State Dept. Press Release 542, in 832.00/1428, NA; FDR to Vargas, Washington, Nov. 19, 1941, PPF 4473 (Vargas), FDRL.

[24] Caffery, Rio, Dec. 8, 1941, *Foreign Relations, 1941*, VI, 73–74.

[25] Welles to Caffery, Washington, Dec. 14, 1941, *ibid.*, p. 128; Welles to Caffery, Washington, Dec. 15, 1941, *ibid.*, pp. 128–129.

now neutrality is past. . . . We are in the war. . . ."[26] Not quite, but events steadily swept Brazil in that direction. At Rio the American delegation, headed by Undersecretary Welles, sought severance of diplomatic relations with the Axis by all the republics. Although United States military authorities preferred a Pan-American declaration of war, the State Department, knowing this to be impossible, worked instead for a complete break.[27]

The atmosphere in Rio was charged with excitement as the world watched to see how the Americas would react to aggression. Posters throughout the city showed Vargas and Roosevelt dining together during the latter's 1936 visit to the Brazilian capital. Crowds gathered around Tiradentes Palace to cheer the delegates as they entered for the opening session. The Cariocas, especially the students, spared no efforts to indicate their anti-Axis feelings, even though the government was painfully slow in permitting pro-Allied demonstrations. Welles told the delegates that the greatest danger since independence confronted their peoples. Washington's solution was for all the republics to break diplomatic relations; thirteen of the twenty-one states had already done so, and ten had declared war. To many of the ministers the subsequent arguments must have appeared somewhat academic. In the sweltering heat of the Brazilian summer the delegates moved from one session to another in the lazy, tropical atmosphere that characterizes Rio at that time of year.[28]

The old cleavage that plagued Secretary Hull's efforts in Latin America quickly appeared—after an encouraging be-

26 *Jornal do Brasil* (Rio), Dec. 16, 1941.

27 Minutes, SLC, Jan. 3, 1942, NA; Conn and Fairchild, *Framework*, p. 193, gives a full quotation from army copy of SLC minutes.

28 Memo: Adolf A. Berle to FDR, Jan. 27, 1942, PPF 4473 (Vargas), FDRL; for student opinion and activities: Interview, Euclydes Aranha, Rio, May 20, 1966 (the Chancellor's son was a leader of the *União Nacional dos Estudantes* [UNE] in 1942); *Jornal do Brasil* (Rio), Jan. 16, 1942.

ginning it was evident that the United States and Argentina were at loggerheads. Washington wanted a declaration breaking relations with the Axis, and sentiment in the State Department favored letting Argentina go its own way rather than compromise on the strong wording of the proposed American text. Prior to the conference Vargas and Aranha had secretly expressed approval of the American position.[29] Hull and Welles thought Paraguay, Uruguay, Bolivia, Ecuador, and Peru would follow Brazil; they were confident those states would break relations regardless of what Argentina or Chile did. They forgot that Brazilian policy in South America was traditionally predicated upon closeness with Chile as a counterpoise to Argentina. Moreover, Brazil always avoided directly opposing Argentina. In Rio, Welles found the situation not as certain as it had appeared from Washington. He was forced to compromise on the declaration's language in order to obtain not only apparent unanimity, but also Brazil's adherence and thereby the adherence of its smaller neighbors.

When it became certain that Argentina would not accept a declaration calling for a break in relations, even one that allowed subsequent ratification by Buenos Aires, the immediate reaction among the foreign ministers was that if Argentina would not go along they would go on without it. This attitude faded quickly. The feeling in Chile and elsewhere was that a severance of relations was "equal to a declaration of war."[30] Brazil received dire warnings from Berlin that a "rupture of diplomatic relations would provoke reprisals." Already the Germans were accusing Brazil of violating neutrality by permitting American planes en route to Africa to fly via the northeast. Italian Ambassador Ugo Sola, who was very sympathetic toward Brazil, wrote Aranha that a break in relations would be viewed in Axis

[29] Caffery, Rio, Dec. 31, 1941, 710. Consultation 3/148, NA.

[30] Welles to Hull, Rio, Jan. 22, 1942, *Foreign Relations, 1942*, v, 33–34; Bowers to Hull, Santiago, Jan. 23, 1942, *ibid.*, 34; Hull, *Memoirs*, II, 1147.

capitals as a step toward war; he pointed to Brazil's "entirely Latin and totally Catholic" nature, which considered Rome the birthplace of its civilization, as reason not to take such a drastic course. The Japanese ambassador, Itaro Ishii, asked Aranha and Dutra to use their influence to prevent an alteration in Brazilian-Japanese relations. Aranha, who sent Getúlio copies of these notes, wrote on the Japanese one: "Now the winds come from the Orient; we are in the midst of a tempest."[31] Indeed, Brazil was the center of the storm which swirled around the Rio Conference.

Secretary Hull had taken Vargas and Aranha's professions of solidarity as statements of national policy (as had Welles before going to Rio), without taking into account the domestic obstacles, political and military, that had to be overcome. The concessions Welles made were absolutely necessary, despite Hull's arguments to the contrary. Hull did not understand the Vargas government's situation or the delicate nature of Argentine-Brazilian relations. He wrongly assumed that the United States could bully its way ahead and that Brazil would docilely support it. He viewed diplomacy as based on principles rather than on the exchange of concessions and the development of mutual interests. Welles' solution at Rio—the only one acceptable to Vargas—caused the subsequent dispute and further estrangement between Hull and Welles.[32]

Aranha was doing his best to force Getúlio to take an unequivocal stand, which accounted for the apparent certainty of the foreign minister's messages to Washington. But the president was the most equivocal of men, and he refused to move ahead of the consensus of the regime—he would withhold his consent until the last moment. His wel-

---

[31] Coutinho, *General Góes*, pp. 378–379; for Axis threats that break would mean war see MRE, *O Brasil e a Segunda Guerra Mundial* (Rio de Janeiro, 1944) II, 19, 26, 31. Ugo Sola to Aranha, Rio, Jan. 16, 1942; Itaro Ishii to Dutra, Rio, Jan. 17, 1942, and to Aranha, Rio, Jan. 17, 1942, all AGV.

[32] Hull, *Memoirs*, II, 1145.

coming address, indeed, was bland enough to encourage the Italian ambassador. And while he told the press on January 17 that Brazil had ceased being neutral when war reached the Western Hemisphere, he did not elaborate.[33] Aranha placed his prestige behind an immediate break with the Axis, putting himself in direct opposition to Minister of War Dutra and Chief of Staff Góes Monteiro, who were convinced that such a step would "immediately and inevitably carry us to war" and that the armed forces were not "sufficiently equipped to insure the defense of our territory."[34] As always, the army's position was pivotal.

When Buenos Aires refused to accept the declaration calling for general severance of relations, Welles went to see Vargas to ascertain what Brazil would do. Vargas told him that the Brazilian military authorities were firmly convinced that in a war with the Axis, in which Argentina was neutral, Brazil's southern frontiers could not be guaranteed. Brazil would not break relations unless "the Conference could find some formula that the Argentine government would support."[35] Aranha and Welles consequently bent their efforts toward achieving a compromise acceptable to Argentina. After much debate the delegates finally accepted, on January 23, the Argentine formula "recommending" that the republics sever relations, a procedure which allowed the Argentines to vote in favor of the resolution knowing that they did not have to follow it. At least the appearance of unanimity was preserved.[36] But approval of

[33] Vargas, *A Nova Política*, IX, 190–198, 199–204; for Italian ambassador's reaction to speech see MRE, *Brasil e a Segunda Guerra*, II, 25.

[34] Góes Monteiro to Dutra, Rio, Jan. 24, 1942, and Dutra to Vargas, Rio, Jan. 24, 1942, AGV. See also Estevão Leitão de Carvalho, *Memórias de um Soldado Legalista* (Rio de Janeiro, 1964), III, 437.

[35] Sumner Welles, *Seven Decisions that Shaped History* (New York, 1951), pp. 110–111.

[36] Welles to Aranha, Washington, Feb. 3, 1942, and Aranha to Vargas, Rio, Feb. 18, 1942, both OAA; Welles to Hull, Rio, Jan. 23, 1942, *Foreign Relations, 1942*, V, 34–35; Eric Sevareid, "Where Do We Go From Rio?" *Saturday Evening Post*, 214, No. 39 (Mar. 28, 1942), 59.

the declaration did not necessarily insure Brazil's break with the Axis either. From January 23 to January 28 Aranha fought one of the most difficult battles of his political and diplomatic career. Although Brazil and the other republics had recommended to themselves to sever relations, Aranha knew that if Brazil did not do so before the end of the conference while world attention was focused on Rio, stubborn opposition in military circles would cause endless procrastination. And Brazil's example would surely set the pace for the other republics.[37]

On January 24 Dutra wrote Vargas that he knew the president was "not unaware of the state of unpreparedness" in which the armed forces found themselves. He did not blame Vargas for this—the situation, he noted, had certainly resulted from circumstances beyond the government's control—but he reminded him that in "repeated reports, messages, and letters" he had explained the army's needs. The war had interrupted delivery of the German purchases, so that most of the Brazilian army's new equipment was still stored in Germany. Naturally, Dutra was disturbed at the possibility of losing these arms altogether, especially since for two years they had been seeking an alternative source in the United States of "the most indispensable war matériel . . . without obtaining to date anything concrete."[38] And Góes Monteiro, lunching at the Copacabana Hotel with Caffery, Welles, Alzira Vargas, and Ernani Amaral Peixoto, said that Dutra was considering resigning.[39] Although the war minister's mood changed and he decided to see it through, Vargas knew that he had to strike a balance be-

[37] See 710. Consultation 3 File in NA; *Foreign Relations, 1942*, V, 6-47; Hull, *Memoirs*, II, 1143-1150; Welles, *Seven Decisions*, pp. 94-122. These imply that once the compromise was arranged there were no other obstacles to Brazil severing relations.

[38] Dutra to Vargas, Rio, Jan. 24, 1942, AGV. As an example of the "repeated reports, messages, and letters" on the needs of the army see Dutra to Souza Costa, Rio, Nov. 4, 1940, AGV, protesting cut in army budget.

[39] Interview, Alzira Vargas do Amaral Peixoto, Rio, Aug. 5, 1969.

tween the desires of the United States and the needs of Brazilian national security. If Brazil was going to war it would have to strengthen its forces, and the only source of equipment was the United States. Vargas had given Welles lists of material that the Brazilian armed forces wanted and the undersecretary had promised to help obtain the arms; he was convinced that Vargas had gone as far as he could without American concessions to justify his policy to the generals. The Brazilian military had to be certain of American assistance in case Brazil broke relations and Argentina did not.

Dutra's personal feelings were obscure. He had a reputation within the government and in the army of being pro-German. The courier who brought him the message in 1940 that Paris had fallen reported that Dutra and his family had cheered at the news. According to American intelligence reports, as late as December 1942, his wife, though possibly without his knowledge, plotted with pro-German officers against Vargas.[40] But most probably he, like many professional soldiers, admired the German war machine while giving little consideration to the ideology of the Nazi regime. Certainly he had little reason to have confidence in the United States and, understandably, he did not want the responsibility for a Brazilian defeat. He was coldly realistic as to Brazil's state of readiness and was, within the framework of his code of honor, doing his duty by seeking a course of action that would best safeguard Brazil and its interests.

Vargas, too, probably would have preferred to wait until the direction of the war was clearer, until he could be certain that his decision would not unduly endanger Brazil externally or internally. As in 1930 he preferred to let events decide the most suitable course—and as in 1930 Oswaldo Aranha forced a decision. He told Getúlio flatly that

40 Interview, Euclydes Aranha, Rio, Nov. 20, 1965. The foreign minister's son was the courier; for a report on Senhora Dutra's activities see Simmons, Rio, Dec. 9, 1942, 832.00/4331, NA.

if Brazil did not break relations immediately he would publicly resign, after the conference, and tell the world why—
because Brazil had signed a declaration it did not intend to
keep.[41]

The days dragged by painfully as Aranha awaited
Getúlio's decision; January 25, 26, 27—the final session was
put off until the 28th to allow more time to resolve the Peru-
vian-Ecuadorian border dispute, giving Aranha an extra
day. He prepared his speech for delivery on the evening of
January 28. The Itamaraty drew up telegrams to Brazilian
representatives in the Axis capitals ordering the break: the
diplomats should notify the respective foreign ministries at
6:00 P.M. on January 28. They did not meet that deadline.[42]
When Aranha left his house for the final session of the conference on the evening of January 28, he still had not received Getúlio's approval. Literally at the last moment
word arrived from the president.[43]

With much emotion Aranha addressed the delegates. He
declared the conference to be a decided victory for democracy and "the greatest historical affirmation" of its "immor-
tality." Amidst applause and *vivas*, he announced that Brazilian relations with the Axis were severed. Even in this
moment of glory there was a reminder of what Aranha's
victory had cost; Dutra had not yet reconciled himself and
the chair reserved for him was empty.[44]

In view of what happened at the Rio Conference, Secretary Hull's angry condemnation of Welles for committing
the United States to "an unwise agreement" that compro-

[41] Interview, Euclydes Aranha, Rio, May 16, 1966. See also unsigned,
undated document in pencil on official Itamaraty stationery, in "Assuntos Políticos e Comerciais," OAA.

[42] MRE, *Brasil e a Segunda Guerra*, II, 22, 28, 33.

[43] Interview, Euclydes Aranha, Rio, May 16, 1966.

[44] For description of closing session, see *Jornal do Brasil* (Rio), Jan.
29, 1942. Speech is in MRE, *Brasil e a Segunda Guerra*, II, 14–17. Aranha
later said that Dutra did not attend "as a public sign of his disapproval of Brazil's decision"; Aranha to Welles, Vargem Alegre, May
24, 1945, OAA.

mised an "all important issue" and made the conference a
disaster can hardly be justified.[45] Welles' "compromise" was
a great achievement that prevented a disaster instead of
causing one. In Aranha's words it served "to preserve the
unity of America."[46] Without a compromise Brazil would
not have supported a declaration that isolated Argentina,
and would have maintained relations with the Axis.[47]
Welles' pledge of arms would not in itself have persuaded
the Brazilian military to confront both Argentina and the
Axis. Even after this commitment to the Allied cause, however, Brazilian authorities tolerated the activities of Nazi
agents, who continued to broadcast maritime and other information from clandestine radio stations in Rio de Janeiro
and its environs.[48] The situation remained cloudy until the
United States convinced the Brazilian military that it would
supply them with arms and equipment, and German submarines forced them to see that they had no choice but to
collaborate with the Americans.

[45] Hull, *Memoirs*, II, 1149; Pratt, *Hull*, XII, 710.

[46] Aranha to Welles, Rio, Feb. 12, 1942, OAA.

[47] For the estimate of an informed observer see Eric Sevareid, "Where
Do We Go From Rio?" *Saturday Evening Post*, 214, No. 39 (Mar. 28,
1942), 27ff., especially 57.

[48] Estevão Leitão de Carvalho, *A Serviço do Brasil na Segunda Guerra
Mundial* (Rio de Janeiro, 1952), p. 79.

". . . the friendship between Brazil and the
United States has never before been as close as
it has now become."[1]

"It would be most unfortunate for us if anything
should happen to President Vargas at this time."[2]

10

· No Turning Back

BRAZIL'S DECISION to break with the Axis had
been contingent on Argentina's adherence to the Rio declaration and Sumner Welles' promise that the United States
would supply arms. Vargas had committed the nation
against the advice of his minister of war and general staff.
His continuance in power was dependent on his ability to
show that his decision would benefit Brazil: if the United
States provided military and economic assistance he would
be the darling of the military, if not, the game would be up.
Security and development were the keys to the "Land of the
Future" (as contemporaries referred to Brazil) and Vargas
strove to hold them in his hands.

During the first week in February 1942, he sent Finance
Minister Artur de Souza Costa to the United States to col-
lect on the American promises. Before his arrival Roosevelt
instructed presidential aide Harry Hopkins to see that Brazil received the arms. But when the minister arrived in
Washington the War Department said it could not increase
or speed up deliveries because of heavy demands from its

[1] Welles to Aranha, Washington, Feb. 3, 1942, OAA.
[2] Welles referring to Vargas' automobile accident of May 1, 1942 at
meeting of Standing Liaison Committee, see SLC Minutes, May 20, 1942,
NA.

own forces and those of the British and Russians. All the allied nations were seeking weapons in the United States, and American industry was barely able to provide their basic requirements. At the same time the Army Air Force Ferrying Command wished to increase the number of men stationed at the ADP bases and to obtain blanket clearance for unlimited flights through Brazil. Welles, however, refused to submit the air force requests to Vargas until the War Department fulfilled the Brazilians' minimum needs.[3]

Reports from Argentina, meanwhile, indicated that the Ramón S. Castillo government had decided that to follow the Rio Conference's recommendation to break with the Axis would be bowing "to North American impositions" and would jeopardize Argentine sovereignty. Ignoring popular opposition, the pro-Axis nationalists among the Argentine military pushed the La Plata nation toward the lonely course it was to pursue during the war. Buenos Aires became the principal center of Nazi espionage and intrigue in South America. The effects of events in Argentina will be discussed in more detail in the next chapter; here it suffices to say that the Argentines attempted to disrupt the traditional Brazilian-Chilean alliance and to establish domination over Paraguay, Uruguay, and Bolivia. Such behavior alone would have been enough to cause nervousness in Rio de Janeiro and Washington, but the Argentines also began reinforcing their garrison along the Brazilian border.[4] The implied threat, though motivated more by the Argentine military's desire to increase its power domestically than by any plan to attack Brazil, drove the Americans and the Brazilians more firmly together.[5] And it gave Vargas additional

[3] Welles to Aranha, Washington, Feb. 3, 1942, OAA; Stetson Conn and Byron Fairchild, *The Framework of Hemisphere Defense* (Washington, 1960), pp. 315–316.

[4] Augusto do Amaral Peixoto, Jr. (Naval Aide) to José de Paula Rodrigues Alves (Brazilian Ambassador to Argentina), Buenos Aires, Feb. 26, 1942, AGV.

[5] Apparently the Argentine military feared that German immigrants

leverage to tighten the screws on the United States: he telegraphed Souza Costa to use news of the Argentine troop movements "to speed delivery of our war material."[6]

The Brazilian mission seemed to be in an excellent position to wring a great deal out of the Americans. Even without the Argentine "danger" the Brazilian bargaining position was strong, because the Americans wanted concessions from Brazil that were extraordinary for a belligerent to expect from a neutral. Rumors of German agents disguised as clergymen spying on Brazilian military installations in the south caused the American army to ask permission to station military observers throughout Brazil—the American navy already had observers in several ports—but understandably the Brazilians took this as an indication of lack of confidence in their ability and good faith. Aranha told Caffery that he did not oppose the observers from conviction, but that every now and then he had to give in to the military on some small things and this was one of them. He pointed out that if the War Department had followed his advice and never mentioned sending troops to Brazil, the Brazilians would have asked for them after severing relations with the Axis. To solve the problems between the two armies he proposed establishment of mixed military commissions rather than enlargement of the United States military attaché's staff.[7] Welles wrote Roosevelt that the "crux of the problem" was to give the Brazilian army concrete

---

in south Brazil might link up with pro-German elements in Argentina. Vargas' ambassador in Buenos Aires wrote that even though the military knew that "this fear is more a fantasy than a real possibility they are exploiting it . . . to facilitate the acquisition of war material, and the increase of effectives [troop strength] which always bring promotions and other material advantages." Rodrigues Alves to Vargas, Buenos Aires, Mar. 7, 1942, AGV.

[6] Vargas to Souza Costa, Petrópolis, Feb. 9, 1942, AGV.

[7] Welles to FDR, Washington, Feb. 19, 1942, PSF Brazil 1942, FDRL; Caffery, Rio, Feb. 18, 1942, enclosed in *ibid.*; Caffery, Rio, Feb. 21, 1942, 832.20/345, NA; Aranha to Vargas, Rio, Feb. 18, 1942, OAA.

evidence that the United States was going to furnish arms. Once they did that, and if they exercised tact in stating their needs, Welles was certain they would obtain what they wanted in Brazil.[8]

The War Department was impatient to enlarge its ferrying operations, and Secretary Stimson appealed to Roosevelt to bypass the State Department and write directly to Vargas. "I cannot tell you," he wrote the president, "how important I think this Natal danger is. With the redoubled necessity of planes for Burma and China; with the French fleet moving in the Mediterranean; with subs in the Caribbean, we can't allow Brazil, who is not at war, to hold up our life line across Africa." The army accompanied this plea for action with a more generous proposal for future arms deliveries under the lend-lease programs,[9] and Roosevelt sent a message to Vargas reaffirming his promise to order the immediate delivery of all the equipment that Brazil had requested.[10]

Souza Costa was to seek a new lend-lease agreement covering army, navy, and air force equipment, material for construction of Volta Redonda, rails and rolling stock for the Central do Brasil railroad, financing for the production of strategic materials (such as iron ore and rubber), and arrangements for their purchase. Paramount was the question of army supply. Getúlio said that the delivery of war material was "very urgent" and would prove "if it is worthwhile or not to be the friend of the United States."[11]

Vargas' correspondence during this period shows great preoccupation with Brazil's military preparedness. He repeatedly reminded Souza Costa that he was to be energetic and totally frank with the Americans. "We can't lose time,"

[8] Welles to FDR, Washington, Feb. 19, 1942, PSF Brazil, 1942, FDRL.

[9] Henry L. Stimson to FDR, Feb. 19, 1942, quoted in Conn and Fairchild, *Framework*, p. 316.

[10] Aranha to Vargas, Rio, Feb. 18, 1942, OAA. Aranha referred to Roosevelt's message.

[11] Vargas to Souza Costa, Petrópolis, Feb. 14, 1942, AGV.

he wrote, "we can't let ourselves be deluded with parties or demonstrations of good will. We have people ready and able to fulfill their duty. We only lack material. . . . This is the moment to arm Brazil."[12] His telegrams and letters to Souza Costa were extremely detailed and probing, and displayed a keen grasp of a wide variety of problems. He discussed the suitability of different credit and payment schemes, the types and quantity of weapons desired, and suggested arguments to buttress various development programs. He was anxious to have as many purchases as possible included under lend-lease because Brazil would have to pay for only 35 percent of the total cost.[13]

Vargas understood that Brazil was a key factor in United States defense plans and that the Americans would pay a high price to keep Brazilian cooperation. He may have needed American aid to justify to his generals the exposure of Brazil to Hitler's wrath, but he knew that the Americans feared a Brazil without him and would seek to keep him in power. Whether he expected this attitude to endure after the war is uncertain—though he does seem to have regarded his relationship with Roosevelt as a special one. Unhappily, Souza Costa was an overly cautious emissary who did not press his advantage to the fullest. After the Rio Conference the man of the hour was Oswaldo Aranha. With his great prestige, forceful personality, and known closeness to Getúlio he could have negotiated in hard-nosed fashion, but two factors mitigated against his being sent to Washington: first, the military's disappointment with the results of his 1939 mission; and second, Getúlio's practice of maintaining an equilibrium of power and prestige among the members of his government. If Aranha followed the achievement at Rio with a successful mission to the United States his prestige might well become overpowering. Getúlio chose Souza Costa because he had confidence in his

12 Vargas to Souza Costa, Petrópolis, Feb. 23, 1942, AGV.

13 Letters and telegrams between Vargas and Souza Costa, Feb. 10 through Mar. 9, 1942, AGV.

ability and because, unlike Aranha, he did not aspire to the presidency.[14]

But instead of moving energetically to squeeze the Americans for Brazil's benefit, Souza Costa adopted a conservative, passive approach to the negotiations. Even though he had a talented group of experts with him, they never sat down to plan their presentations or to unify their ideas. One of the mission's members, Valentim Bouças, a long-time economic advisor and golf partner of Vargas, did not hesitate to write the president of his dismay and frustration with Souza Costa's methods of diplomacy. Bouças explained that there were two currents of thought in the United States government; that of the New Dealers who genuinely wanted to help Brazil and that of the "dollar-a-year" men on leave from Wall Street who, even in wartime, thought of profits and of exploiting raw materials in such fashion as to leave Brazil with "holes in the ground and without industries." He cited Nelson Rockefeller's rubber plan as a typical example of the exploitative approach. While the Brazilians wanted to develop the Amazon, Rockefeller's suggested program would be concerned only with rubber production; and besides, the sparse initial financing with a $5,000,000 credit would be nothing in such a vast region. The program called for operational costs to be divided equally, but although the Brazilians would have the corporation presidency the post would be without executive authority because the Americans would administer services and money. Such an approach, Bouças said, would do little to help Amazonia, did not take Brazilian interests into account, and "could be classified as American Imperialism." It exemplified a tendency not to aid Brazil's industries—on the contrary, to dominate them.[15]

[14] In his message of Feb. 23, 1942, Getúlio said: "Sua missão aí grande responsibilidade. Escolhi-o pela confiança tenho sua capacidade." Vargas to Souza Costa, Petrópolis, Feb. 23, 1942, AGV.

[15] Valentim Bouças to Vargas, New York, Feb. 23, 1942, AGV.

To sidestep such efforts, Bouças proposed to Souza Costa that they tell the Americans that the Brazilian government would establish an official agency to direct the development program, and wanted only American technical assistance and loans to buy equipment. Souza Costa responded negatively, forbade Bouças to present the idea, and said tartly that they were "authorized to receive proposals not to make them."[16] Bouças, not satisfied with this and certain of his ground, took his case to American officials he trusted. With his long experience in dealing with American businessmen and his deep knowledge of the American scene, he was confident that he could outmaneuver the Wall Street clique who were trying "to orient the general policy of the country contrary to the reality of the modern world." As he wrote to Vargas: "Happily, for us, the men of the government, notably President Roosevelt, the Department of Agriculture and of State, do not accept this antiquated policy of domination and subjugation."[17] On the morning of February 17, without Souza Costa's knowledge, Bouças explained his objections to the Rockefeller plan and outlined his own proposal in a meeting with Laurence Duggan, Thomas K. Finletter, and Emilio Collado at the State Department. At lunch that day Welles repeated Bouças' plan as if it were his own, suggesting to Souza Costa that it would be a good idea if Brazil set up a corporation with Brazilian directors to oversee a comprehensive Amazonian program and that the United States would provide an initial credit of $100,000,000. But even then Souza Costa acted as if the idea were new to him, insisting that the Americans make detailed suggestions.

One is tempted to say that Souza Costa exemplified the dependent mentality of a traditionally colonial people, but instead it may be that his approach was that of a debtor nation's minister of finance who habitually dealt cautiously with creditors. But, as Bouças told Vargas, the minister's

16 *Ibid.*   17 *Ibid.*

methods suited a time of peace, and "we are in the midst of a state of war. Our military requirements demand prompt decision." It could be, as Alzira Vargas thought, that Getúlio sent Bouças along to smooth the way for Souza Costa and to see that the right things got done.[18]

A curious sidelight on the negotiations was the apparently easy access the Americans had to Brazilian government communications. Throughout his chancellorship Aranha showed Caffery intracabinet memoranda and telegrams to and from Brazilian diplomats. For example, he let Caffery read a message from Dutra to Vargas commenting adversely on the American request to place military observers in Brazil. Obviously, he was trying to emphasize the impossibility of acceding to the War Department's wishes. On another occasion he told Caffery that Vargas had asked Souza Costa to explain to Washington officials that his government deeply resented the apparent lack of confidence that some United States departments displayed toward Brazilians, especially the inclination of American officers to look down upon Brazilian military valor and efficiency. But beyond such deliberate leaks it is surprising how rapidly Washington learned the contents of messages between the Brazilian embassy and Rio de Janeiro. There is evidence suggesting that the Americans were monitoring the international cable—if so the Brazilians were at a decided disadvantage in their dealings with the United States.[19]

[18] *Ibid.*; interview, Alzira Vargas do Amaral Peixoto, Rio, Aug. 14, 1969. She called Souza Costa Brazil's greatest minister of finance. Bouças later wrote that Souza Costa's term as minister "será assinalada pela posteridade como sendo das mais profícuas. Foi ele um dos mais honrados, capazes e brilhantes gestores das finanças nacionais." Valentim Bouças, *Estudos Econômicos e Financeiros, Meio Seculo de Trabalho*, 3 vols. (Rio de Janeiro, I and II, 1953; III, 1955), I, 11.

[19] Welles to FDR, Washington, Feb. 19, 1942, PSF Brazil 1942, FDRL; Caffery, Rio, Feb. 21, 1942, 832.20/345, NA; Welles to FDR, Washington, Feb. 18, 1942, PSF Brazil, 1942, FDRL. This latter document was a copy of Vargas to Souza Costa, Petrópolis, Feb. 16, AGV. There is no indication that it came from a Brazilian source.

The Washington Accords, as they were called, perhaps did not give Brazil everything it might have obtained through more energetic, demanding diplomacy, but they did represent the most comprehensive military and economic assistance program the United States had ever attempted in Latin America. They insured Brazilian cooperation and Vargas' continuance in power, and tied Brazil firmly to the United States economy for the next decade—but they were no display of altruism. In different measure they gave each side what it wanted—immediate security, psychologically and physically. But clearly both governments were making a mockery of Brazilian neutrality. In asking Brazil, whose interests in Europe were not yet in jeopardy, to aid the American war effort, the United States was invoking the unwritten alliance, which pledged Brazil to support it in extrahemispheric matters in return for support of Brazilian preeminence in South America. The Brazilians, therefore, naturally expected the United States to build up their military power in order to guarantee their regional hegemony.

The Brazilian arms requests discussed during Souza Costa's mission included: equipment for the nucleus of an armored division (205 light tanks, 75 medium tanks, 500 quarter-ton trucks, and a variety of other trucks totalling 1,000); complete material for the new division's engineer battalion; road construction materials; small arms, machine guns, and ammunition; guns for two antiaircraft battalions and four antitank units; and chemical products and drugs to set up a pharmaceutical laboratory. This equipment was to be delivered by July 1942. Intense negotiations with the State and War Departments reduced the list to proportions acceptable to the Americans. The compromise, which Vargas termed reasonable, involved immediate delivery of twenty light tanks, in addition to those which the army had already promised, four antiaircraft guns (removed from the New York harbor defenses for this purpose), and the drafting of a new lend-lease agreement. The agreement called for the eventual delivery of $200,000,000 worth of military equipment, or double the amount provided in the Brazilian-American Lend-Lease Agreement of October 1941. The War Department also promised to deliver before the end of 1942 100 medium tanks, 205 light tanks, and a number of antiaircraft and antitank guns. These pledges did much to satisfy the Brazilian army.[20]

Souza Costa and Welles signed the lend-lease agreement and several others on March 3. The latter included a $100,000,000 loan for developing production of strategic materials, a $14,000,000 loan for development of the Itabira iron deposits and the Vitória-Minas railroad, the establishment of a $5,000,000 fund to improve the quality of the raw rubber produced in the Amazon, and a like amount to finance a health and sanitation program in the rubber-producing regions. To encourage production, the Americans obligated themselves to pay a fixed basic price for rubber and a premium for everything over certain tonnages. The premiums were to be placed in a fund to be used to encourage the establishment of rubber plantations. Although rubber was native to the Amazon basin it grew wild, and efforts, such as those of the Ford Company, to establish profitable plantations had failed. On the American side the rubber program would be overseen by the Rubber Reserve Company (later called the Rubber Development Corporation), and on the Brazilian by the Rubber Credit Bank (Banco de Crédito da Borracha). The latter's capital was to be 60 percent Brazilian and 40 percent American, and the bank would have a mixed board of directors. The United States also committed itself to buy all of Brazil's surplus manufactured rubber products (principally tires and tubes). In addition it promised to purchase Brazilian strategic materials, such as iron ore, timbó, mica, quartz, dia-

20 For the Brazilian requests see Eurico Dutra, "Boletim Especial Secreto, #10," Rio, Mar. 23, 1942, "Neutralidade 1940," OAA; Souza Costa to Vargas, Washington, Feb. 10, 1942, Feb. 11, 1942, and Vargas to Souza Costa, Petrópolis, Feb. 14, 1942, AGV; Conn and Fairchild, *Framework*, pp. 315–316; History SADATC, Part I, III, 131.

monds, fibers, and various oil-producing nuts, seeds, and palms. All the purchasing agreements were to run for five years. And to ease Brazil's dependence on coastal shipping and eliminate complaints that American military bases in the northeast were absorbing the area's scant food supply, Washington granted $2,000,000 to develop local agricultural programs. The United States thereby committed itself to underwriting the Vargas government militarily and economically for the duration of the war.[21]

The Rio press praised the accords. *A Manhã* predicted that their execution would place Brazil in a position of "incontestable power" in the postwar world. The *Diário Carioca* commented that the government, by endeavoring to assure practical results from its collaboration with the allies, was showing "good sense and prudence."[22] Vargas promptly approved several "exceedingly broad requests" for increasing the number of American maintenance personnel at the ADP bases, construction of military and naval installations, and blanket permission for American aircraft to pass through Brazil. Caffery later observed: "From that moment his attitude was definitely changed for the good; he had made his decision; he was on our side."[23] On March 11 the Brazilian chiefs of staff (army, navy, and air force) and Chancellor Aranha agreed on the draft of a joint defense agreement which Brazil then proposed to the United States.[24]

[21] Jesse H. Jones to Welles, Washington, Feb. 25, 1942, 711.32/111A; State Department Press Release 88, Mar. 3, 1942, 711.32/110A, NA; *The Inter-American Monthly*, I, No. 5 (May 1942), 36; for lend-lease see OF 4193, FDRL; Bouças, *Estudos Econômicos*, II, 11-23, 30-33, 43-93; Frederic W. Ganzert, "Agriculture," in Lawrence F. Hill, ed. *Brazil* (Berkeley, 1947), pp. 238-247.

[22] As quoted in John F. Simmons, Rio, Mar. 6, 1942, 711.32/111, NA.

[23] Caffery, Rio, Feb. 6, 1943, 832.00/4349, NA. This report reviews much of Caffery's dealings with the Vargas regime from 1937 to 1943. Vargas approved the American requests on Mar. 9. Conn and Fairchild, *Framework*, p. 317; History SADATC, Part I, III, 129-130.

[24] Caffery, Rio, Mar. 11, 1942, 832.20/355, NA.

While the War and Navy Departments were giving the Brazilian proposal their urgent consideration, Brigadier General Robert Olds, commander of the ferrying command, went to Brazil to arrange details of the expanded American military activities in the northeast. In Rio de Janeiro Generals Dutra and Góes Monteiro were most cooperative, but Aranha made clear that Olds needed the approval and good will of Brigadier General Eduardo Gomes, air commander of northeast Brazil, to carry out his plans effectively. While touring the ADP bases Olds cultivated Gomes, invited him to go to the United States to inspect American war activities, and promised to provide the Brazilian air force with thirty bombers and thirty pursuit planes. In the United States the War Department made every effort to impress Gomes with the sincerity of its desire to assist the Brazilian armed forces. Before returning home he inspected six B-25's and six P-40's lined up at Washington's Bolling Field, ready to take off for Natal. Olds had correctly assumed that Gomes' cooperation would be more enthusiastic if he received some of the promised aircraft immediately. The way was now clear for enlarging United States air operations. American civilian and military personnel could travel by aircraft without entry visas to and from the war zones, a concession which allowed the War Department to set up the South Atlantic Wing of the Air Transport Command by the end of May.[25]

Washington approved the Brazilian draft of the proposed joint defense agreement and instructed two army colonels and the chief of the American naval mission to conduct negotiations in the Brazilian capital under the guidance of Caffery and Aranha. Now that the army had obtained all the concessions it wanted for its ferrying activities it cautioned the colonels not to mention stationing large numbers

[25] Welles to Caffery, Washington, Mar. 21, 1942, 832.20/359, NA; History SADATC, Part I, III, 133–137; Part II, IV, 4–5; Carlos Martins Pereira e Souza to Hull, Washington, May 4, 1942, reproduced in History SADATC, Part II, V, Appendix.

of American troops in the northeast. The War Department said that its objective was an agreement establishing one or (as the Brazilians wished) two joint defense commissions, and fixing basic policies for their guidance. These commissions would work out specific measures for joint defense similar to those in effect between the United States and Great Britain. Much to the surprise of the American representatives the Brazilians readily accepted the various changes that Washington wanted, and by April 18 both sides had agreed on a final text. Indeed, Colonel Henry A. Barber, who had succeeded Matthew B. Ridgway as the army's principal Latin American planning officer, remarked that he was "entranced" when the Brazilians accepted the draft; he had expected them at least to demand Brazilian command of the troops of both nations in the northeast.[26] The United States would certainly not allow foreign troops under foreign command on its soil. Brazilian agreeableness in permitting the opposite did not increase American respect. Several times during the negotiations the Brazilians wanted the Americans to be more specific about the wording and meaning of various articles. Caffery had commented to Aranha that "all this depends on mutual good faith, doesn't it?" Aranha had agreed and the Brazilians did not press further.[27] Such trust and openness worked well in the prewar years when a small group of men, who understood the rules of the game, were involved, but on the American side the players increased so rapidly after Pearl Harbor that they had no time to learn the rules. They mistook as weakness what the Brazilians intended as cooperation. Caffery and Aranha did not sign the agreement until May 27, because of the Navy Department's last-minute misunderstanding of certain articles. This procrastination did not produce any textual changes, but it did embarrass American officials who had a hard time explaining the delay.[28]

[26] Caffery, Rio, Apr. 22, 1942, 832.20/374, NA.
[27] Caffery, Rio, Apr. 24, 1942, 832.20/376, NA.
[28] Conn and Fairchild, *Framework*, p. 318; Admiral F. J. Horne to

The new defense agreement provided for joint commissions, one in Washington and one in Rio, and outlined the policies that were to guide their work. The Washington commission was to draw up a defense plan for northeast Brazil, and make such other recommendations for joint action as the terms of the agreement and the changing strategic situation required. The Rio commission was to work with the American military and naval missions to improve the combat readiness of the Brazilian armed forces.[29] Negotiation of the agreement coincided with an important change in the War Department's policy toward Brazil. Since 1939 it had been trying to place United States forces in the northeast to ward off Axis invasion. It now sought to collaborate in the preparation of Brazil's defense by training and supplying Brazilian forces. The War Department intended to make every effort to maintain the flow of lend-lease material,[30] and the Brazilian army's strategic thinking appeared to have changed as well. The May agreement specified the north, northeast, and Rio de Janeiro as areas of "prime importance" and called for the concentration of Brazilian forces in them.[31] The agreement dissolved the Joint Board for the Defense of Northeast Brazil, which the

---

Welles, Mar. 20, 1942, Serial 94517 (SC) A16-1/EF12, Dept. of the Navy Records, US Naval Archives; Welles to Caffery, Washington, Mar. 21, 1942, 832.20/359, NA. For the initial Brazilian draft see Caffery, Rio, Mar. 12, 1942, 832.20/357, NA; Caffery, Rio, Apr. 15, 1942, 832.20/367 and other items through to Caffery, Rio, Apr. 28, 1942, 832.20/378; and Hull to Caffery, Washington, May 14, 1942, 832.20/389; and Caffery, Rio, May 27, 1942, 832.20/402, all NA.

[29] Conn and Fairchild, *Framework*, pp. 318–319; History SADATC, Part I, III, 137–140.

[30] Conn and Fairchild, *Framework*, p. 319; Góes Monteiro to Marshall, n.d. (probably end of April), in "Política Exterior do Brasil" file, and Marshall to Góes Monteiro, May 12, 1942, in "Correspondência," both OAA. There are also copies in WWII RS, NA but as of 1970 they were classified even though they are exactly the same as the copies in OAA.

[31] Caffery, Rio, Mar. 12, 1942, 832.20/357, NA; History SADATC, Part I, III, 139.

two countries had set up the previous year to formulate the defense plan for the bulge. The board had not been very successful, but its existence had led to the appointment of Estevão Leitão de Carvalho as Inspector-General of the north and northeast and to his nomination as commander of the "Northeast Theater of Operations."[32] A distinguished officer, Leitão de Carvalho had trained in Germany prior to World War I and had served on the Brazilian delegation to the League of Nations and on the Chaco peace commission. Recently, as commander of the Rio Grande do Sul military region, he had greatly improved the training and readiness of the troops there. He was an excellent choice for commander of the northeast.

The Brazilian high command's show of interest convinced Washington that it could now concentrate on preparations for the great offensive against the Axis, confident that the Brazilian flank was secure. Unfortunately, it was a classic case of deception. War Minister Dutra did nothing to reinforce or improve the troops in the northeast. In fact, he increased the forces in Rio Grande do Sul, prevented Leitão de Carvalho from actually taking command of the northeast "theater," and undermined his position as Inspector-General. The defense plan that Leitão de Carvalho drew up was not put into effect, and later, when Vargas assigned the general as chief of the Brazilian delegation on the Washington defense commission, Dutra did his best to ignore the commission.[33] Although the United States did not realize it,

[32] Caffery to Aranha, Rio, May 30, 1942, 832.20/408, NA; and Estevão Leitão de Carvalho, *A Serviço do Brasil na Segunda Guerra Mundial* (Rio de Janeiro, 1952), p. 53. This Caffery item was not found in OAA. Aranha's papers contain surprisingly few Caffery items and Caffery's communications with State rarely mention his sending letters to the foreign minister. Though there may be some messages in the closed files of the Itamaraty it is likely that Caffery conducted most of his business via telephone or in private conversations.

[33] The practice of deceptive façade is known in Portuguese as "para o inglês ver," for the English to see. Since 1942 it has gradually become "para o americano ver." Leitão de Carvalho, *Serviço do Brasil*, pp. 109–

the May agreement did not change the Brazilian army's orientation toward the south or help to prepare the ground defense of the northeast prior to Brazil's entry into the war. American officials did not understand this immediately, because of their preoccupation with air and naval operations in the South Atlantic.[34]

Vargas' approval of the expansion of ferrying operations and Gomes' cooperation cleared the way for eventual American army control of the ADP bases. Since late 1941 the navy, in the person of Vice-Admiral Jonas H. Ingram, had been carrying on a diplomatic campaign to base naval forces in northeastern ports in order to facilitate patrol of the Atlantic narrows. Ingram had carefully cultivated regional political leaders and his counterpart in the Brazilian navy. A flag-officer well before the war, Ingram "had the right combination of tact, energy, and firmness to get things done; and he comported himself with a native vigor and a certain magnificence that both pleased and impressed" the Brazilians.[35] The portly admiral commanded the South Atlantic Force (designated United States Fourth Fleet in March 1943), a small force of light cruisers and destroyers with a wide field of operations and a variety of duties. It escorted convoys, intercepted blockade runners en route from Japan to Europe, and searched for enemy submarines and surface raiders; it protected the long Brazilian coast north of Salvador and the American garrison on lonely Ascension Island in the mid-Atlantic. Navy seaplanes had begun patrols from Brazilian bases in December 1941, and in

---

113, 117–144, 151–158, 170; Memo: "A Defesa Nacional nas Mãos da 5a Coluna," Um Chefe Militar to Aranha, Bahia, May 23, 1942, "Neutralidade 1940," OAA.

[34] Marshall wrote Welles on May 10, 1942: "It becomes increasingly apparent that the Brazilians are not seriously cooperating with us to secure that vital area [northeast Brazil], sea and air, against Axis aggression," in 832.20/403½, NA.

[35] Samuel Eliot Morison, *The Battle of the Atlantic* (Boston, 1947), p. 383.

1942 land-based amphibians operated from the ADP bases at Natal and Recife.[36]

German submarines sank four Brazilian steamers off the United States coast in February and March 1942, causing great concern in Brazil. With nearly the entire Brazilian merchant fleet committed to the essential run between Brazil and the United States, Vargas feared it would all end up on the bottom. There were two alternatives: either Washington arranged convoys and provided artillery pieces for Brazilian merchantmen or he would order the ships into port. After the *Cairú* went down (March 9) he resolved to suspend navigation to the United States until the Americans took defensive measures.[37]

When the United States failed to act Vargas kept his word, and in April he placed an embargo on Brazilian shipping. It was an effective measure—the United States needed every vessel it could get and the cargoes coming from Brazil were essential to American war industries. The Brazilian economy, of course, needed coal and petroleum from the United States, but Vargas was certain that his drastic action would force Washington to provide adequate protection quickly. It may even be that he did not demand as much as the Americans would have been willing to give.

[36] Commander Task Force 23, May 15, 1942, "Report of Operations in South Atlantic Area, February 5, 1942–May 15, 1942," 0026; and Office of Naval Intelligence, "Post-Mortems on Enemy Submarines," 250-G:Serial 8, both US Naval Archives; USN Administration in World War II, Commander in Chief, Atlantic Fleet, Vol. XI, "Commander South Atlantic Force," 46–51. Hereafter cited as USN, "Commander South Atlantic Force." This is a typewritten history of the USN in the South Atlantic written by the then Lieutenant Charles Nowell (Prof. Emeritus, University of Illinois). USN, Bureau of Yards and Docks, *Building the Navy's Bases in World War II* (Washington, 1947), II, 43–47; this contains photographs and descriptions of American naval facilities in Brazil.

[37] Vargas to Souza Costa, Petrópolis, Mar. 9, 1942, and Mar. 11, 1942, AGV. For a listing of Brazilian losses up to October 1943 see Ministério da Marinha, *Subsídios Para a História Marítima do Brasil*, vol. XII (Rio de Janeiro, 1953), 11–12.

The first Brazilian ship to go down was the *Buarque* (February 16, 1942) just out of Belém do Pará with a cargo of raw rubber, Brazil nuts, and other Amazonian products. American concern for the Amazon and its products was such that Washington might well have parted with some war and merchant ships, or at least have allocated to the Brazilian merchant marine some of the Liberty ships that were sliding down the ways. But Getúlio's demands were simpler; he only asked for protective convoys and artillery.[38]

In the last days of April Admiral Ingram made one of his periodic visits to Rio de Janeiro. Vargas, who was vacationing at the spa of Poços de Caldas in Minas Gerais, asked the admiral to come to see him. The two men, who had not met before, liked each other instantly. After a friendly talk in which Ingram described the steps he was taking to protect neutral shipping, Vargas asked if he would be willing to assume responsibility for the protection of Brazilian vessels. The admiral said yes, with a proviso: Vargas must understand that he could not guarantee complete success. In convoy operations the risks were mutual, though Ingram realized that the United States would bear the blame for mishaps. The important thing was to get the ships to sea.[39] Vargas appreciated Ingram's clear analysis of the situation and his forthright manner. He agreed to lift the embargo, and calling Ingram his "Sea Lord" asked him to act as his secret naval advisor. The president opened all ports, repair facilities, and airfields to the American navy, and instructed Brazilian air and naval forces to operate according to Ingram's recommendations. In effect Ingram was now responsible for Brazil's nautical defenses. In return, the admiral promised to expedite delivery of naval equipment and to train Brazilian personnel.[40]

[38] For a report on the *Buarque* and reaction to its sinking see Jay Walker, Pará, Feb. 24, 1942, 832.00/1453½, NA.

[39] USN, "Commander South Atlantic Force," pp. 48–50.

[40] USN, War Diary, Commander South Atlantic Force (SOLANT), Apr.

This was a private arrangement between President Vargas and Admiral Ingram, made without the prior knowledge of other officials. Possibly Vargas knew that, regardless of commitments to station troops in the northeast, the Brazilian generals would insist on giving top priority to the southern frontier. In effect he was accepting their strategic estimate that Argentina and the southern immigrant colonies were a more immediate danger than an Axis invasion of the north. At any rate his secret pact with Ingram did more to protect Brazil and to solidify military cooperation in the months ahead than any other action of the two governments. Ingram took his advisory role seriously, and from time to time sent Vargas evaluations of Brazilian naval operations and requests for presidential action in particular cases. He provided the United States Navy with a direct line to Vargas that the American army did not have. Vargas trusted him, and a review of naval records suggests that his trust was well placed. Ingram made a point of stressing his loyalty; for example he ended one memorandum to Vargas by saying that "his sea lord" was doing his best for Brazil.[41]

Brazilian merchantmen returned to the sea lanes with guns on their decks. The German Naval High Command thereupon issued orders to its submarines and raiders on May 16, 1942, to attack without warning all armed South American ships, except those of Argentina and Chile. Between May 1 and June 1 four Brazilian vessels went to the bottom. At the end of the month the Brazilian air ministry announced that its planes had attacked Axis submarines and would continue to do so. At a conference with his admirals on June 16, Hitler decided to launch a submarine blitz against Brazil. The German government believed that Brazil's cooperation with the United States and the activities of its navy and air force indicated that Brazil was no

---

28, 1942, A12/Serial 0025; and Commander Task Force 23, Report of Situation in Brazil, Apr. 22–26, 1942, Serial 0018, US Naval Archives.

[41] Jonas A. Ingram to Vargas, n.d., 1942, AGV.

longer neutral but in a state of war, and that when the nation was organized and prepared it would make a formal declaration against the Reich. Ten submarines left French ports for the South Atlantic—to arrive off the Brazilian coast during the first week of August.[42] Hitler warned Brazil in a radio broadcast that its actions would have dire consequences. His threat to destroy the air base at Natal produced panic in that city: residents fled into the interior; General Gomes ordered a blackout; ADP personnel and the few American marine guards dug slit trenches and mounted machine guns around the field.[43] The expected air attack never came, but German submarines torpedoed four more Brazilian vessels off Puerto Rico and Trinidad.[44]

In the meantime President Vargas had been seriously injured in an automobile accident on May 1—he had a dislocated hip and a broken jaw. At the most critical time since 1930 he was confined to bed and unable to speak, and a political crisis ensued. Important government business was at a standstill, and pro-Axis agitators began whispering that Vargas was no longer capable of governing the country.[45] The defense agreement with the United States was signed, but the Brazilian army did little to fulfill its commitments. The Department of State was worried. Welles told the Standing Liaison Committee that it would be most unfortu-

[42] Karl Doenitz, *Memoirs, Ten Years and Twenty Days* (Cleveland, 1959), p. 239; USN, Office of Naval Intelligence, *Fuehrer Conferences on Matters Dealing with the German Navy*, pp. 89–90; International Military Tribunal, *Trial of the Major War Criminals Before the International Military Tribunal* (Nuremberg, 1948), V, 276; XIII, 480; XIV, 122–123; XVIII, 423.

[43] Charles F. Matthews, "Sidelights on the History of Parnamirim Field," Report to the Historical Office SADATC, n.d., C. F. Matthews Papers, Natal; interview, C. F. Matthews, Natal, May 24, 1965.

[44] One was sunk on June 26, the other three were attacked on July 26; Ministério da Marinha, *Subsídios Para História Marítima do Brasil*, Vol. XII (Rio de Janeiro, 1953), 12.

[45] Caffery, Rio, May 1, 1942, 832.001 Getúlio Vargas, 10/99; May 3, 1942, 832.001/100; May 6, 1942, /104; May 9, 1942, /105, NA.

nate for the United States "if anything should happen to President Vargas at this time."[46] May and June passed with Getúlio in bed, while pro-allied and pro-Axis groups carried on a silent struggle against each other.

At the end of May Mexico had declared war, after Axis submarines torpedoed two of its ships. Brazil at that point had lost eight vessels, and on June 1 and 26 German torpedoes claimed two more. Even so, the police repeatedly refused permission for university students in Rio de Janeiro to hold public demonstrations supporting the allies. Vargas apparently knew nothing of the requests or felt unable to grant them. Finally his son-in-law, Ernani do Amaral Peixoto, interventor of the State of Rio de Janeiro, sponsored a huge pro-allied demonstration in Niteroi on June 29. Shortly thereafter, possibly through the intercession of his daughter Alzira, Vargas met with student leaders and gave his permission for a rally in the federal capital.[47]

As German forces swept into Russia in late June the situation in Brazil worsened. Emboldened by German victories, the pro-Axis elements were growing more active and daring every day. They claimed that the German army was invincible and that it would destroy the Russians before the end of the summer. High-ranking army officers warned Vargas not to identify himself any more closely with the United States and quietly plotted to remove him from office.

Vargas fell into a deep depression. Ambassador Caffery complained that the pro-Axis elements would not have been so daring if the president had not been "in bed with his foot suspended in the air."[48] The inability of the United States to keep Brazil supplied with gasoline and coal or to make

[46] SLC, Minutes, May 20, 1942, NA.

[47] Interview, Euclydes Aranha, Rio, May 16, 1966. The chancellor's son was a student leader and much involved in pro-Allied agitation. For a contemporary report see Caffery, Rio, June 30, 1942, 832.00/4207, NA.

[48] Caffery, Rio, July 15, 1942, 711.32/126; July 17, 1942, /128; July 20, 1942, /132, NA.

deliveries of lend-lease equipment because of German submarines cast doubt on the value of cooperation. Axis agents intensified their activities. Numerous clandestine radio transmitters broadcast the movement of vessels in and out of Guanabara Bay, and Federal District Police Chief Filinto Müller did nothing to stop them. The crisis reached its peak when Interventor Amaral Peixoto sent his police from the state of Rio de Janeiro into the capital to apprehend Axis agents and to silence their radios. Müller had to go, but Vargas did not feel strong enough to oust him without some concession. So on July 17 he accepted the resignations of Müller, Minister of Justice Francisco Campos, and Director Lourival Fontes of the Department of Press and Propaganda. Campos and Fontes had long since sided with the allies, much to the discomfort of Axis supporters. The immediate reaction in many circles was that Getúlio was weakening and would not last long. A few days later Müller joined the staff of the minister of war.[49]

Vargas filled the vacated posts with Lieutenant Colonel Alcides Gonçalves Etchegoyen as police chief, Alexandre Marcondes Filho as minister of justice, and Major José Coelho dos Reis as director of the Press and Propaganda Department. The appointments represented a gain for the pro-allied camp, which was especially pleased with Etchegoyen, a friend of Aranha and a loyal Vargas man since 1930. Müller's people had left Rio's police headquarters a shambles, and the new chief had a difficult task choosing personal aides whom he could trust. But after Axis submarines attacked three more Brazilian ships off Trinidad on July 26 and 28 the situation suddenly improved. Dutra and Góes Monteiro began "making friendly passes" in Ambassador Caffery's direction, and the minister of war said

[49] Leitão de Carvalho, *Serviço do Brasil*, p. 160; Walter N. Walmsley to Welles, Washington (DAR), July 18, 1942, 832.00/4219; Caffery, Rio, July 20, 1942, 711.32/132; Simmons, Rio, July 28, 1942, 832.00/4230, all NA; Vargas to Lourival Fontes, Rio, July 17, 1942 and Vargas to Vasco Leitão da Cunha, Rio, July 17, 1942, AGV.

that he was as pro-American as Aranha and ardently desired an allied victory, but complained that Aranha had wanted Brazil to go to war when it was totally unprepared. Dutra, counseling caution, maintained that the United States was in no condition to prepare Brazil to take part in hostilities, and therefore the Brazilians should limit their cooperation to measures short of war. On July 28 the Rio newspapers gave prominent publicity to Fourth of July telegrams exchanged between Brazilian and American military leaders. Despite Dutra's hesitancy the alliance was preserved.[50]

One area of consistent difference of opinion, however, between Brazil and the United States was the latter's treatment of Argentina. Since early June Aranha had been complaining that in spite of Brazil's cooperation and Argentina's foot-dragging the United States was penalizing Brazil and mollifying Argentina. Areas of friction were currency control, shipping, and allocations of coal and oil products. According to Aranha, after Brazil placed controls on currency American money began flowing toward Argentina, and he felt that the La Plata republic was receiving more coal and oil than it deserved. The imposition of gasoline rationing in Brazil in mid-July, soon after a decree prohibiting the use of private automobiles, and the sinking of Brazilian ships while Argentine vessels sailed relatively unmolested, increased pressure on the government to show that approximation with the United States was benefiting Brazil and not merely imposing a crown of thorns. Ambassador Caffery said Aranha kept referring to all the favors Brazil had granted, for which he had to produce results. The ambassador responded as best he could, "but," he said, "we are going to have a hard time keeping him quiet."[51]

[50] Walmsley to Welles, Washington (DAR), July 18, 1942, 832.00/4219; Caffery, Rio, July 23, 1942, 711.32/136; Caffery, Rio, July 20, 1942, 711.32/132; July 27, 1942, 832.00/4224; July 28, 1942, 4225; July 28, 1942, 4226, all NA.

[51] Caffery, Rio, June 8, 1942, 711.32/114, NA. Martins to MRE, Wash-

Welles forcefully answered Aranha's complaints, saying that in July the War Shipping Administration had assigned six times as much tonnage to Brazil as to Argentina. Washington was also trying to persuade Great Britain to have its ships from India stop in Brazil, and the British and Americans were attempting to coordinate their economic policies to facilitate the flow of goods. Moreover, the United States was putting pressure on Argentina through discriminatory allocations of export licenses and shipping space. When Washington authorities prepared estimates of the needs of the American republics they applied the same formula to each, and then arbitrarily cut Argentina's allocations by 50 to 70 percent, while Brazil's needs and requests received special consideration. Petroleum supply offered a striking example of how this weighted allocation system functioned. The last petroleum shipment to Argentina in allied vessels had been in April. Since then, except for some oil carried in Argentine tankers, no petroleum had been sent to Argentina. In the same period shipments to Brazil had been regular. Brazil's estimated requirements for July and August, based on 40 percent of 1941 consumption plus 100 percent for essential industries, amounted to 450,000 barrels of refined oil and 385,000 barrels of crude. On July 1 Brazilian stocks had totaled 471,000 barrels refined and 249,000 barrels crude, and delivery schedules called for 456,000 barrels refined and 646,000 barrels crude to reach Brazil by late August. And, to emphasize their attitude, the American navy turned over a tanker to the Brazilians to help supply their armed forces.

Brazil's struggle with Argentina for domination of Bolivia prompted Aranha to complain when the United States could not produce the promised rails for the Santa Cruz–Corumbá railroad, which would connect the principal town

---

ington, July 20, 1942, AGV. For a news story on gasoline rationing see *Correio da Manhã*, Rio, July 12, 1942. The quotation is from Caffery, Rio, June 12, 1942, 711.32/115, NA.

of lowland Bolivia with the Brazilian border in Mato Grosso. The American army was insisting that all available rails be kept for use in war zones and that for the near future railroad construction in Brazil should be limited to the strategic coastal regions. As it was, the United States was discriminating against the rest of Latin America in favor of Brazil. In the third quarter of 1942 only 15,000 tons of rails were assigned to all of Latin America and 13,000 of those were for the Central do Brasil. Naturally the State Department wanted to avoid publicizing such favoritism. Welles gave assurances that the United States was as interested as Brazil in removing Bolivia from Argentina's influence, and that its plans called for building roads and eventually railroads linking Bolivian centers with Brazil. But for the present they must bow to the demands of the war effort. Having thus documented his case, Welles asserted that the Brazilian complaints were "utterly unwarranted and unjustified." There was no country in the Western Hemisphere that had "received such preferential treatment from the United States during the war period as Brazil." He instructed Caffery to emphasize at every opportunity the American government's whole-hearted "desire to afford Brazil every possible form of cooperation notwithstanding the war situation."[52]

For the time being the matter faded into the background, as Brazil's entry into the war approached. It was not surprising, however, since the basis of the relations of the two nations with Argentina differed, that their policies also differed. The United States needed Argentina's tungsten, quebracho, zinc, hides, and wool and so was unwilling to boycott the republic completely. Moreover, it was interested in building up its economic position in the Argentine at Great Britain's expense. While the Brazilians wanted the United States to commit itself completely to them in case of

[52] The previous paragraphs are based on Welles to Caffery, Washington, July 14, 1942, 711.32/126A, NA.

conflict with Argentina, Washington would agree to support Brazil only if the feared Argentine aggression was "sympathetic to, or instigated by, the Axis powers." In that case the United States would furnish such assistance to Brazil as was "necessary for its national security and maintenance in power of the present government."[53] In the meantime United States policy aimed at preserving Brazilian friendship without fully alienating Argentina. A year later the American attitude would change drastically.

But in 1942 the Americans hoped to win Argentina over to their cause. They attempted to put on pressure by refusing to supply arms and munitions unless the Argentine navy joined allied convoy operations in the South Atlantic. Argentina refused, accusing the United States of employing its war policies to dominate Latin America. The reasons for Argentine hostility toward the United States were complex and of long standing, but they may perhaps be reduced to four basic ones: 1) past Argentine-American rivalry for leadership of the hemisphere; 2) Argentine antagonism toward Brazil and irritation at its steady adherence to the United States; 3) the strength of Argentine conservative forces favoring totalitarianism; 4) Argentina's geographic location outside the probable route of a German attack on the Western Hemisphere.[54] And Brazilian policy, of course, sought to sow suspicion of Argentina in the minds of American leaders so that they would continue to support Brazil. But it must be understood that this was not just a diplomatic tactic, the Brazilians genuinely feared Argentina.

In early July a different sort of problem arose. A correspondent of the *Chicago Daily News* wrote Secretary of the Navy Frank Knox that an "aide" of Vargas had told him that Caffery was "personally antipathetic" to the president, and that Aranha had been trying to get him replaced with a "big name" ambassador. The secretaries of war and the

[53] Welles to Norman Armour (U.S. Ambassador to Argentina), Washington, July 7, 1942, 832.20/418, NA.

[54] Martins to MRE, Washington, July 22, 1942 and July 23, 1942, AGV.

navy used the letter as a pretext to complain to Roosevelt about the ambassador, with whom they had been dissatisfied for some time. Welles defended Caffery. It was true that he had "not gone to the President of Brazil nor to the other high officials of the Brazilian Government and pounded the desk demanding that the desires of the War Department be immediately granted." This apparently was what the army believed he should have done. He had, however, obtained "every single thing that the War Department considered essential," and he had done it in such a way as not to injure Brazilian susceptibilities or to arouse the antagonism and ill will of the Brazilian army. Welles considered Caffery "a singularly successful ambassador." Vargas told Welles in January that he had complete confidence in Caffery, and that "the United States had never had an ambassador in Brazil who had shown greater tact or more knowledge of how to deal with Brazilian officials and with the Brazilian people. . . ."[55] Aranha and Vargas had not made uncomplimentary statements about the American ambassador; on the contrary he and his wife were well liked and unusually popular.[56] Vargas himself settled the issue when he wrote Roosevelt that he had only high praise for "this illustrious diplomat," who "practices diplomacy as it ought to be practiced: with the sole preoccupation of uniting, deepening, increasing the friendship of the people in whose midst he lives for the people whose government he represents."[57] Perhaps a measure of Caffery's success was

[55] Welles to Roosevelt, Washington, July 1, 1942, OF 884 Jefferson Caffery, FDRL.

[56] U.S. Army files contained uncomplimentary statements by army officials about Caffery but I found none by Brazilian officials. See as example History SADATC, Part I, III, 143. The Dept. of the Navy also was impatient with the ambassador's insistence that he was the chief American official in Brazil and should coordinate all U.S. activities. But Caffery apparently got on well with Navy officers on the scene; see Jonas H. Ingram to Caffery, Recife, Nov. 29, 1942, 832.30/477, NA.

[57] Vargas to Roosevelt, Rio, July 30, 1942, AGV.

a German broadcast beamed to Brazil from Hamburg that asked: who "runs Brazil—Getúlio Vargas or that man Caffery."[58]

Even so the State Department called the ambassador home for a general review of Brazilian-American relations at the end of July, taking him temporarily out of Brazil on the eve of the republic's entry into the war. He went to see Vargas on July 30 and found him in an excellent humor but looking worn and weak. Vargas was taking a few steps a day supported by canes, and expected to be getting round more actively in a month. He felt that he had the situation under control and that there was no longer any danger of his being overthrown. He believed that the turning-point in the crisis had been his appointment of the new police chief, who was now working closely with the embassy in counter-espionage. He asked Caffery to assure Roosevelt that Brazil was more determined than ever to continue cooperation with the United States. But Brazil was suffering from the submarine attacks, having lost twelve ships by July 20, among them some of the merchant fleet's largest and best units. Vargas was convinced that convoys between Brazil and the United States would counter German efforts to halt the flow of supplies. But he was disappointed that American authorities had not been able to provide the eight to ten torpedo boats and submarine chasers that he had hoped to use to protect coastal shipping. He asked Roosevelt to give the matter his personal attention, confident that as always the president would be "solicitous and vigilant in Brazil's favor."[59] One of Caffery's aides prepared a list of some of the "rabbits" which the Brazilians expected him to "pull out of the hat for them." The list included more shipments of coal, fuel oil, newsprint, radio tubes, and gasoline. "And outside

[58] Memo: Summary of Translation of German Broadcast, July 20, 1942, 711.32/134, NA.

[59] Caffery, Rio, July 30, 1942, 711.32/140, NA; Vargas to Roosevelt, Rio, July 30, 1942, AGV.

of a million other products that is practically all they want."[60]

Meanwhile, the ten German U-boats, silently made their way toward Brazilian waters. In Belém, *A Vanguarda* reported that a local yacht, unfortunately named *"Brasil,"* had been seen provisioning two submarines near Maracá Island off Amapá.[61] Between August 15 and 19 the U-boats struck at Brazilian coastal shipping, attacking in rapid succession six vessels off the coast of Sergipé and Bahia—*Baependi, Anibal Benévolo, Araraquara, Itagiba, Arará,* and *Jacira*—and leaving Brazil with only one possible course of action —belligerency.[62]

In five days the Germans had cut Brazil's maritime communications with the northeast and had achieved what United States diplomacy had succeeded in doing only superficially—they united Brazil against them. Even the army cried out for blood. The *Baependi* carried to the bottom 250 men and seven officers of the Seventh Artillery Group, along with two batteries of guns and other equipment.[63] Another ship was carrying pilgrims to a Eucharistic Congress in São Paulo. All Brazil shuddered in revulsion. Throughout the country people took to the streets seeking revenge from anything or anybody of Axis origin or sympathy. In Salvador mobs stoned German and Italian establishments. Crowds in Recife attacked thirty pro-Axis firms and, unobstructed by police, carried off signs and metal for the Brazilian navy scrap campaign. In Pôrto Alegre the American consul reported that all around the consulate Brazilians were demolishing stores. Police were powerless to control the mobs in Fortaleza as they looted and burned

[60] Memo for Caffery, Rio, Aug. 13, 1942, 832.00/4264, NA.

[61] *A Vanguarda*, Belém, July 30, 1942; History SADATC, Part II, IV, 89–90.

[62] Ministério da Marinha, *Subsídios Para História Marítima do Brasil*, pp. 11–12; Hélio Vianna, *História Diplomática do Brasil* (São Paulo, 1958), pp. 200–201; Leitão de Carvalho, *Serviço do Brasil*, p. 142.

[63] *Ibid.*

Axis-owned shops. Vitória, Manaus, Belém, Belo Horizonte —all across Brazil the reaction was the same. Finally the students gave voice to the thoughts of all; in São Paulo and Rio they called for war.[64]

Roosevelt wrote Vargas that the Axis mistakenly thought the sinkings would intimidate Brazil into discontinuing its "collaboration in defense of the Hemisphere." But to make sure he ordered two sub-chasers immediately turned over to the Brazilian navy, and promised that others would follow "at the very first opportunity." And to ease the growing economic pressures on the Vargas regime Roosevelt authorized Ambassador Caffery to purchase unexportable surpluses of coffee, cacao, and Brazil nuts.[65]

The prowar campaign mounted as Brazilians took to the streets chanting anti-Axis slogans and waving Brazilian and American flags. In Rio on the morning of August 18 they raided the offices of the pro-Axis *Meio Dia* and *Gazeta de Notícias*. Later in the day they swept under the Imperial palms of Rua Paissandu to Guanabara Palace where thousands of voices demanded "*O Presidente*," and thundered "We want war!" Vargas appeared at a window leaning on his wife's arm. Below him as far as he could see were his countrymen, their hands raised high in the victory sign, shouting for war. He told them he understood their anger; that the government would seize Axis ships and property, and would give fifth columnists, spies, and other traitors picks and shovels and send them into the interior to open new roads. The crowd moved on to other parts of the city; some groups favoring an immediate declaration of war demonstrated in front of the Itamaraty and the American embassy.[66]

[64] Castleman, Bahia, Aug. 18, 1942, 832.00/4235; Leo J. Callahan, Recife, Aug. 18, 1942, /4236, and /4239; Walker, Belém, Aug. 18, 1942, /4244; Simmons, Rio, Aug. 18, 1942, /4238, and Aug. 19, 1942, /4245, and /4247, and /4249, all NA.

[65] Roosevelt to Vargas, Washington, Aug. 20, 1942, AGV.

[66] Simmons, Rio, Aug. 18, 1942, 832.857/94, NA; the scene was de-

The next evening thousands watched a bonfire of Axis flags on the steps of the Municipal Theater and then marched again to Guanabara Palace, where Amaral Peixoto urged them to continue demonstrating because Vargas needed their support. Inside the ornate palace the cabinet was trying to reach a consensus on the form of retaliation. All agreed that Brazil had to take forceful measures against the Axis, but there agreement stopped. The army wanted to hang a lot of Germans; some ministers preferred a protest that would not take Brazil into the conflict; Dutra reminded them that the country was practically defenseless, that they had received very little equipment so far from the United States; the minister of education urged a declaration of war; and Aranha contended that recognition of the existence of a state of war would be in keeping with Brazil's tradition of never having declared war. A few weeks earlier he had given a speech proclaiming peace to be the basis of Brazilian foreign policy. Brazil would never enter an armed struggle, he said, unless forced to defend its honor, its territory, or its ideals. Vargas sent his ministers home to think and the following day summoned them again. They decided to enter the conflict, but were divided on whether to declare war or to recognize its existence.[67]

On the evening of August 21 Vargas received a delegation of sailors from the Brazilian merchant marine who had come to express their solidarity with the government. The Germans, he said, were trying to intimidate Brazil, but the nation had never retreated from a chosen path and would not do so now. The sea was a symbol of liberty, and Brazil

scribed in "Brazil: The New Ally," *Fortune*, xxvi, No. 5 (November 1942), 210; for Getúlio's speech see his *A Nova Política do Brasil* (Rio de Janeiro, 1938–47), ix, 227–228; for photographs see Manuel Thomaz de Castello Branco, *O Brasil na II Grande Guerra* (Rio de Janeiro, 1960), p. 62; and Pedro Calmon, *História do Brasil* (Rio de Janeiro, 1959), vi, 2260.

[67] Caffery, Rio, Aug. 28, 1942, 832.00/4268; Simmons, Rio, July 21, 1942, /4227; and Aug. 19, 1942, /4247, NA.

would defend it. That night the Itamaraty gave its diplomatic missions advance warning of what was about to occur, and Aranha alerted the American embassy. The lights burned throughout the night in Guanabara Palace. The next afternoon the cabinet met to approve a declaration recognizing the existence of a state of war with the Axis. Brazil was in the war; there was no turning back.[68]

[68] Vargas, *A Nova Política*, IX, 233–234; Simmons, Rio, Aug. 21, 1942, 832.00/4254, NA; MRE, *O Brasil e a Segunda Guerra Mundial* (Rio de Janeiro, 1944), II, 188, 191–192; Aranha to Raimundo Fernandez-Cuesta y Merelo (Ambassador of Spain), Rio, Aug. 21, 1942, OAA. The note to Germany went via the Spanish embassy in Berlin, while the note to Rome was delivered by the Swiss.

*". . . if we let the present historic moment go by . . .
without raising ourselves from the baby's crib to
acquire a solid and ample position on the Continent,
I believe that we risk losing all the rest."*[1]

*". . . to introduce the use of United States material in
the Brazilian Navy in order to promote American
trade. . . ."*[2]

11

Politics and Policy

BRAZIL'S DECISION to go to war against the Axis
was far-reaching in its consequences. Most immediately it
rallied opposition elements around the Vargas regime and
forced Brazil's neighbors to choose between neutrality and
belligerency, while in the long run it loosened Brazil's ties
with Europe and linked it still closer to the United States.
It may also have caused Brazil to avoid the kind of political
turmoil that rocked Argentina in the next years.

Brazil had been following a policy that went beyond
benevolent neutrality in favor of the United States. Even
before American entry into the war Brazil had assisted the
United States Navy in replenishing its vessels, and had permitted disguised construction of military air bases and passage of armed planes over its territory. Germany, however,
preferred a flawed, imperfect Brazilian neutrality to bel-

[1] Góes Monteiro to Aranha, Montevideo, Apr. 3, 1944, OAA.

[2] Memo: Background of Naval Mission Functions, Enclosure A (Functions USN Mission-Brazil), NS, ND, QC/EF12, A14-5, Documents US 4th
Fleet, Naval History Division, Dept. of the Navy. This memo was probably written some time in 1943. The Mission operated during the war
under a contract signed May 7, 1942.

ligerency, because as long as Brazil was officially neutral Berlin could hope to influence its policies. It would be wrong to say that unwarranted German aggression forced Brazil into the conflict—the Germans merely pushed Vargas' policies to their logical conclusion. Brazil had started down the path to war when Vargas allowed the Airport Development Program to begin construction. But very probably, if the Germans had not attacked, the Brazilians would not have mobilized, sent troops to Europe, or aligned themselves unreservedly with the Allies.

President Roosevelt called the Brazilian cabinet's decision "courageous," and rather grandly said that it "hastened the coming of the inevitable victory of freedom over oppression, of Christian religion over the forces of evil and darkness."[3] In Argentina the reaction was profound and evidently sincere. The Brazilian embassy received expressions of sympathy from all sides. Former President General Agustín Justo, who some years before had been made an honorary general in the Brazilian army, applauded Brazil's action and offered to fight with its forces.[4] The congress in Buenos Aires passed a resolution protesting the attacks on Brazilian vessels, and the government of Ramón S. Castillo recognized Brazil as a nonbelligerent and declared itself ready to concede all facilities in accord with the various Inter-American resolutions. The Brazilian ambassador in Buenos Aires, José de Paula Rodrigues Alves, wrote Vargas that if so many pro-Axis men had not surrounded Castillo he believed the president would have taken stronger action. After the Rio Conference, Castillo had told Rodrigues Alves: "If Brazil comes to be attacked our position will be different, [that is] complete and absolute solidarity and cooperation."[5] Argentine politics prevented Castillo from

[3] Roosevelt to Vargas, n.p., Aug. 22, 1942, PPF 4473 (Vargas), FDRL.

[4] Augustín Justo (President of Argentina, 1932–38) to Vargas, Buenos Aires, Aug. 25, 1942, AGV.

[5] José de Paula Rodrigues Alves to Vargas, Buenos Aires, Aug. 25, 1942, AGV.

joining Brazil, and his statement emphasized the complexity of the Argentine scene during the war years.

Júlio Prestes, the Brazilian president-elect who had been prevented from taking office by the revolution of 1930, wrote to a friend that they should not be concerned with the form of the government that was defending Brazil. "We need to be united," he said, "and to suffocate and repress any resentments in order to strengthen the chief of the government, to fortify Brazil."[6] Such an attitude among opposition leaders gave Vargas more flexibility and authority to act than he had previously enjoyed.

A day or two after Brazil's entry into the war the senior officers of the Brazilian naval, air, and army forces in the northeast met with Admiral Ingram. They agreed that naval defense was paramount and that the Brazilian navy would serve under Ingram's direction, that the air force would function independently but in accord with the Fourth Fleet's joint operations plans, that the army would set up shore defenses, and that in an emergency all would cooperate fully. The Brazilian attitude "exceeded the most optimistic expectations" of the United States Navy, whose officers professed to be very encouraged.[7]

At the end of August Vargas issued a decree declaring a state of war throughout Brazil, thereby widening the government's interventive powers. A few days later the Ministry of Aeronautics asked commercial airlines not to carry Axis nationals, and requested that pilots cooperate with submarine patrols during coastal flights.[8] Then, on September 9, the American Naval Attaché, Captain E. E. Brady, and a Commander Paul Foster, met with Vargas at Guanabara Palace. They explained their plans for convoys be-

6 Júlio Prestes to Adolpho Konder, Itapetininga, Aug. 31, 1942, ACV.

7 A. D. Struble (Office of Chief of Naval Operations) to Dept. of State, Aug. 25, 1942, 832.20/434, NA.

8 Lt. Col. Dulcidio Cardoso (Minister of Aeronautics' chief of cabinet) to Cauby C. Araújo (President of Panair do Brasil), Rio, Sept. 8, 1942, Araújo Papers.

tween Montevideo and Trinidad, and Ingram's problems in handling such operations, and also coastal defense, with a divided command. The Brazilian air force, navy, and army all had separate headquarters and, although they cooperated, better results could be obtained if overall control were concentrated in Admiral Ingram's hands. Ingram felt that they needed a more definite understanding as to relative authority and responsibility. Brady and Foster emphasized Ingram's cordial relations with Brazilian army commanders in the area, and said that he had no desire at present to bring American troops to guard the air fields or other installations. After deliberation Vargas agreed to give Ingram full authority over the Brazilian navy and air force, and complete responsibility for defense of the entire Brazilian coast. He asked that Washington extend Ingram the necessary authority and reinforcements,[9] an action which would amount to de facto American control of the Brazilian navy. So it was not surprising that naval historian Samuel E. Morison considered Brazil's entry into the war "an event of great importance in naval history." Without it, it would have been impossible to close the "Atlantic Narrows" to German and Japanese blockade-runners.[10]

For some time the American army had wanted to move its ferrying command headquarters from British Guiana to Natal or Recife, and had chafed at Caffery's insistence that as ambassador he should coordinate all United States activities in Brazil.[11] But the Brazilians were hesitant to allow

[9] Cpt. E. E. Brady to Caffery, Rio, Sept. 10, 1942, 740.0011 E.W. 1939/24344, NA.

[10] Samuel Eliot Morison, *The Battle of the Atlantic, 1939–1943* (Boston, 1964), p. 376. Morison went on to say that: "If the Axis, with the collaboration of Pétain and Laval, could control the Atlantic Narrows between Cape San Roque and the Cape Verde Islands, it would be able to cut off the foreign and much of the domestic trade of Brazil. . . . The dependence of Brazil on coastwise shipping recalled that of the United States before 1850" (p. 377).

[11] See Memo: D. D. Eisenhower to Marshall, n.p., May 14, 1942, OPD 381 Brazil in History SADATC, Part II, Appendix.

the American army to expand its ferrying activities or establish headquarters in their territory. With some 18,600 troops, only fifty-two guns larger than .30 caliber, and just thirty combat aircraft to cover the region from Belém to Salvador, the Brazilian army was too weak to insure that foreign forces would leave when the emergency passed.[12] But Ingram and the United States Navy were different. The two navies had preserved close relations since the First World War, when Brazilian officers had seen duty on American warships in the South Atlantic, and the United States had maintained an effective naval mission in Brazil since the early 1920's. But the most important factor was Admiral Ingram. His ardent wooing and open personality completely won over Vargas and the Brazilian naval authorities. In his wake the United States Army eventually secured permission to establish two commands in Brazil; the South Atlantic Wing of the Air Transport Command at Natal and the United States Armed Forces, South Atlantic, at Recife. Both were under Brigadier General Robert Walsh.

Secretary of the Navy Frank Knox had not been privy to the Fourth Fleet's private dealings with the Vargas regime, and initially he reacted negatively to Ingram's assuming responsibility for Brazil's defense. Knox was in Rio de Janeiro for an inspection tour when Vargas called Ingram to the palace on September 29 to offer him official command of Brazilian forces, and he told the admiral that no self-respecting country would take such a step and therefore the Brazilians were not serious and somehow were making a stooge of him. In a heated discussion Ingram explained that he had already held a preliminary conference with the chiefs of the Brazilian armed services, and that if their plans for joint operations could not go through they should be told immediately, but in that case he would be

[12] For Brazilian army strength and distribution in the northeast see *ibid.*, Part II, IV, 82; and Eurico G. Dutra to Ministers of State, Rio, Sept. (n.d.) 1942, AGV.

compelled to resign his command. After Caffery assured the secretary that Vargas was serious and that the president considered the step necessary to unify the efforts of his forces, Knox relented.[13]

The incident pointed up the different ways the Brazilians and the Americans looked at military cooperation. If Vargas had suspected that his action would cause a decline in American respect for Brazil he would never have taken it. He was realistic about Brazil's weakness and, as one imbued with the "patron" outlook, he believed that the weak should stand in the shadow of the strong, and, conversely, that the strong should protect the weak. Most probably he also knew that the army had not even prepared its war plans, and that after Secretary Knox arrived in Rio and his aides asked for a meeting with Brazilian military officials to discuss joint operations, Góes Monteiro, to avoid embarrassment, had thrown together in an all-night session a set of "plans" for presentation the next day to the Americans. While the ruse fooled Ingram and Knox it did not strengthen Brazil's defensive posture.[14] Vargas knew there would be a price for American protection but, because it was in the interest of the United States to have Brazil safely on its side, he assumed that he could keep the accounts reasonably balanced.

[13] U.S. Navy Administration in World War II, Commander in Chief, Atlantic Fleet, Vol. XI, Commander South Atlantic Force, 82.

[14] Lourival Coutinho, *O General Góes Depõe* (Rio de Janeiro, 1956), pp. 382–384. Góes recalled: "Naquela emergência, era imprescindível salvar as aparências. Tornei-me audacioso. . . . A minha agonia foi grande durante essas horas e as demais que se seguiram. O amor próprio nacional me impelia para, com o máximo de vigor, encobrir as nossas falhas e debilidades. . . . Elaborei, então, um esquema meio artificioso, que seria o programa de guerra brasileiro. . . . Afinal, à hora marcada no dia seguinte, pude, na reunião dos oficiais brasileiros e norte-americanos, apresentar um trabalho que, embora de afogadilho, trabalho de fortuna, era, entretanto, perfeitamente razoável e aceitável naquela contingência" (pp. 382–383).

On September 16 he ordered a general mobilization, and by the month's end Góes Monteiro was talking of calling up two million men and of sending an expeditionary force abroad.[15] Vargas received regular reports concerning military cooperation from General Leitão de Carvalho, whom he had sent to Washington to serve on the Joint Brazil-United States Defense Commission. He carried on similar correspondence with ambassadors and lesser officials in Washington, London, Lisbon, Montevideo, Buenos Aires, and Santiago, thus avoiding total dependence on his ministries for information.

Having just handed over the nation's defense to the American navy, he put pressure on Washington to keep the construction materials flowing to Volta Redonda, regardless of the cost. Alzira Vargas wrote Ambassador Martins that "*O Patrão*" wanted him to tell the Americans that "the steel mill can not stop." "Every sacrifice" would be made for the continuation of the work because it was "essential for Brazil."[16]

Meanwhile, Aranha and Sumner Welles had been corresponding regarding postwar reorganization. Back in June 1942 Welles had written to Aranha and seven other Latin American leaders, to arrange an informal exchange of ideas regarding a future world organization. He believed that "when the war ends the Western Hemisphere will be immeasurably the strongest entity left on earth." And the American republics "must take the lead jointly when the time comes and must not permit, as they did in 1919, their effective influence to be dissipated and to be largely nullified. . . ." In mid-1941, Roosevelt had the State Department create a confidential committee of selected government officials and private citizens to formulate recommendations

15 History SADATC, Part II, V, 101. General Walsh was in Rio at the end of September and submitted a report dated Oct. 5, 1942. The mobilization decree was No. 10,451 and a copy is in OAA.

16 Alzira Vargas to Carlos Martins, Rio, Sept. 28, 1942, AGV.

for postwar reconstruction and for a world organization to insure peace. So far the committee's incomplete studies had not been discussed with other governments, but, because Welles was profoundly convinced that "when the time comes for the creation of a new world order the initiative and the lead should be taken by the twenty-one American Republics," he wanted to send Aranha and the other Latin American leaders regular reports of the committee's deliberations so that they could give him the benefit of their thoughts.[17] His exchanges with Welles prodded Aranha to consider Brazil's postwar role and encouraged him to think that it would be an important one. They alerted him to the fact that the United States was determined to create and to join a world organization, and that it was willing to finance reconstruction. There was no excuse for the Brazilians not to plan their participation, and if they failed to secure their desired position they would bear a large burden of responsibility. A prerequisite to obtaining a strong postwar position was to secure a voice at the peace table and, later, a permanent seat on the council of the world organization. Brazil had left the League of Nations in 1926 when it was denied a permanent council seat; and Aranha, remembering that one of the Baron of Rio Branco's basic foreign policy goals was the securing of international prestige, could not help but make membership in the inner circle of the world organization one of Brazil's wartime objectives. It would be included in a cogent statement of wartime aims that he would send Vargas on the eve of the Natal conference, which will be discussed below.

So far Brazil's war was still in the proclamation and speechmaking stage. Its naval units knew the reality of seeking out a lurking, dangerous enemy, but life for the rest of the country went on much as it had before August 22. The shortage of gasoline and the imposition of rationing caused

[17] See for example: Welles to Aranha, Washington, June 1, 1942 and Aug. 28, 1942; Aranha to Welles, Rio, Oct. 26, 1942, all OAA; Francisco Cavalcanti Pontes de Miranda to Aranha, n.p., Aug. 9, 1942, AGV.

grumbles, and forced more people in Rio de Janeiro to depend on the rattling *bondes* (streetcars) to take them to *Cinelândia*, or to movie houses in Copacabana to see Walt Disney's Zé Carioca teach Donald Duck to dance the samba and drink *cachaça*. After the movies people might walk along Avenida Atlântica, enjoying the roar and smell of the foaming surf while trying the new taste treat that had just hit the market—*Kibon* ice cream—one of the pleasanter results of the war. An American company that the Japanese had forced out of China resettled in Brazil, and began selling *Kibon* (from *que bom*, how good!) to an eager clientele.[18] Other people with more expensive tastes, crowded around the roulette tables at one of the fashionable casinos —Atlântico, Copacabana, or Urca. Although newspapers, such as the *Correio da Manhã, Diário de Notícias,* and *Diário Carioca* attacked them as a waste of the public's money and a detriment to morals, the casinos flourished until the end of the Vargas regime. Blackouts, however, beginning in early September, reminded the city that there truly was a war. Lights on top of Corcôvado, Urca, and Sugar Loaf were visible for miles out to sea, as was the clock tower of the Mesbla department store. But blackouts, the arrests of hundreds of suspected Axis agents, and even the display of green-dyed chickens tagged with the Integralista sigma in birdcages in public squares, soon became pale stuff before the news reports from the fighting fronts. As we shall see in Chapter 12 the Brazilians by the end of 1942 became determined to see action.[19]

[18] "Ice Cream in Brazil," *Business Week* (November 21, 1942), p. 24. The company was the Cia. U.S. Harkson do Brasil, owned by Ulysses S. Harkson of Portland, Oregon, and Kent Lutey of Butte, Montana.

[19] The foregoing is based on: "Brazil: New Ally," *Fortune* xxvi, No. 5 (November 1942), 214ff.; "Night and Day in Wartime Rio," *The Inter-American Monthly*, I, No. 11 (November 1942), 26–29; Simmons, Rio, Sept. 4, 1942, 832.20/437; Caffery, Rio, Sept. 7, 1942, /440; Memo for State Dept. from Navy Dept., Aug. 30, 1942, /435, NA. This last is a USN Observer's report of events in Florianópolis.

Even so Admiral Ingram complained to Vargas that the war effort was progressing too slowly. In spite of the danger of wholesale starvation in the north if shipping stopped for any appreciable length of time, the "sea lord" wrote to his chief that "only with the greatest difficulty do port officials recognize that there is a war on." Still worse, the "antiquated" Brazilian naval procurement and supply system was not functioning, and Brazilian naval units were not getting materials to keep their forces operating. "This is going to be a hard war," Ingram warned, "and money must be spent for material and supplies."[20]

Vargas did what he could to prod his people onward and to procure sufficient supplies. He made good use of Brazil's increasingly favorable balance of trade, which rapidly built up the nation's reserves for the first time since the Depression. In 1942, Brazil's expanding exports were valued at approximately $388,000,000, giving it a favorable balance of $148,000,000, more than twice the 1941 level. By the end of the year the republic's gold reserves had risen from a 1939 figure of $40,000,000 to $121,000,000. Brazilian manufacturers, especially in textiles, were finding a ready market in Argentina and South Africa. It was becoming obvious that Brazil stood to benefit financially from the war.[21]

Starting with his speeches commemorating the fifth anniversary of the coup d'état of November 10, 1937, Vargas began referring to his government as the Estado Nacional (National State), to improve the regime's image and to erase the unsavory, fascist-tainted connotations of the Estado Nôvo. Between the lines he seemed to be saying that actions were more important than names and forms. In his principal address on the 10th, in Rio's Municipal Theater, he said that he considered it "mere Byzantinism" to inquire whether the regime was or was not democratic. The old

[20] Ingram to Vargas, n.p., n.d., 1942, ACV. Most probably written in late October 1942.

[21] "Brazilian Trends," *The Inter-American Monthly*, II, No. 7 (July 1943), 43–44.

oligarchies, while calling themselves democratic, were regimes of privilege. They had used power to benefit a small portion of the population. Brazilian experience in the past five years had shown that "true democracy" benefited "the people as a whole," and the "supreme interests of the *Pátria*, over the impositions of groups, clan, or region." He went on to hint that the regime was preparing to normalize its status. The present task, he said, was "to perfect the politico-administrative apparatus, completing the constitutional organs, preparing the country for the normal succession of its leaders within the formulas of functional democracy that we instituted." He then sketched the regime's efforts to reform, develop, and provide security for Brazilian society, and declared that he was pursuing a labor policy which would protect workers even in the current economic crisis. While maneuvering to maintain and strengthen the military's support of his regime, he was also seeking wider support among the proletariat to broaden the basis of his power.[22]

He may have been attempting to offset the efforts of a small group of officers, attached to General Dutra's staff, who were plotting under the "benevolent eye" of Senhora Dutra, supposedly without her husband's knowledge. This group, which included the former chief of police Major Filinto Müller, were known to be pro-German, and their conspiratorial efforts were apparently aimed at regaining control of the police. Such subversive activities indicated that Vargas had to keep a watchful eye on his subordinates,

---

[22] The quotations are from "O Primeiro Lustro do Estado Nacional," Nov. 10, 1942, in Getúlio Vargas, *A Nova Política do Brasil* (Rio de Janeiro, 1938–47), IX, 311–317. The portion referring to normalizing the regime reads: "O que nos cumpre agora é aperfeiçoar o aparelho político-administrativo, completando os órgãos constitucionais, preparando o país para a sucessão normal dos seus dirigentes dentro das fórmulas da democracia funcional que instituímos" (p. 313). A few days before Caffery had reported that Brazilian authorities in a "somewhat inconspicuous fashion" had begun to use Estado Nacional instead of Estado Nôvo; Caffery, Rio, Nov. 6, 1942, 832.00/4314, NA.

and that an atmosphere of trust did not exist in or around the government.[23] Vargas would replace the chief of police four times in the next three years, to thwart such factional plots—self-preservation for a coalition dictator necessitated such maneuvers.

In late December Brazil began to thaw its heretofore cool relations with Great Britain. The British community in Rio held a luncheon in Aranha's honor and he gave a decidedly friendly speech. Brazil's policy was American-oriented, he said, because it was part of the American continent, but Brazilians followed "England's fate with the same sentiments, anxieties and hopes that we follow the fate of the North American commonwealth and of all America. . . ."[24] Such public sentiments gave cooperation with the allies a unified appearance, but in fact Ingram saw to it that British warships stayed on the African side in the Atlantic patrols, and the United States Embassy in Rio maintained a certain reserve toward the British.[25] While the Brazilian army still resented British interference with the arms shipments from Germany (see above, Chapter 7), Aranha was trying to swing Brazilian foreign policy back toward a center point, perhaps already beginning to fear too great a dependence on the United States. Although he would continue to argue forcefully for his approximation policy, he was too Brazilian not to maintain some caution and to preserve a way out. His objective, since his stint as minister of finance, was to shift the focus of Brazilian foreign relations from London to Washington and New York, but he was not out to alienate the British completely, or to replace dependence on them with dependence on the Americans. He was seeking inde-

[23] See Simmons, Rio, Dec. 9, 1942, 832.00/4331, NA.

[24] The full speech was published in *Jornal do Comércio*, Rio, Dec. 19, 1942.

[25] Walmsley, Memo: "Apparent Improvement of Brazilian Government's Attitude Toward Great Britain," DAR, Jan. 4, 1943, 832.002/210, NA.

pendence, and understood that he could play the British and the Americans against each other.

As 1942 drew to a close Vargas was urging Brazilians to have confidence "in the prophetic voice of Franklin Roosevelt, the great leader of the American Continent," with certainty that they were not in the war to "guarantee privileges and increase monopolies but to establish peace with justice and security of a better life for all."[26] To the chiefs of the armed forces, however, he spoke more frankly at a luncheon on December 31. The previous months had been "a dangerous phase" in national life, full of events with "profound and grave repercussions." It was impossible to tell how the war would develop, or where it would take Brazil. The nation should not limit itself to supplying strategic materials, or to serving as a way-station for troops and equipment en route to North African and Asian battlefields; rather it should prepare to intervene outside the hemisphere with large numbers of well-trained and equipped forces. He said that his government was striving to move the country forward socially and economically "to assure our efficiency in the war and our progress in the peace," and called on the officers to preserve their faith with each other and with the regime. Warning them that divergences of opinion and dispersion of effort would weaken their unity of action, he reminded them that in the present emergency they embodied "national honor and the very future of the *Pátria*."[27]

Vargas' purpose was twofold—to increase Brazil's military participation in order to secure a stronger international position, and to envelop the armed forces in defense activities to keep them out of politics. National policy and personal ambition merged conveniently. Vargas was turning the proletariat into supporters of his regime and appeared intent on remaining in power indefinitely. But to

[26] Vargas, *Nova Política*, x, 316–317.
[27] *Ibid.*, pp. 323–327.

realize his ambition he had to distract and depoliticize the armed forces, and what better way to do so than with a war![28]

In a New Year's message, Roosevelt told Vargas that 1943 would be "a fateful year for Brazil, the United States, and the continent," and "one in which the statesmen of our two countries, continuing their traditional collaboration, will draw the blueprint for the new and lasting peace."[29] The Brazilians had every reason to think that Aranha's policy of approximation was succeeding admirably.

Aranha himself was confident, as he penned a long letter to Getúlio analyzing Brazil's foreign policy and giving a thoughtful defense of the American alliance. Vargas was about to fly to Natal for a secret meeting with Roosevelt, who was returning from the Casablanca Conference. The traditional Brazilian policy of "supporting the United States in the world in exchange for its support in South America," Aranha argued, as he had many times before, should be continued "until the victory of American arms in the war and until the victory and consolidation of American ideals in the peace." The United States would be the peacetime leader of the world and Brazil should be at its side; to do otherwise would be a grave error. Brazil should continue its diplomatic collaboration because without it "Pan-Americanism would not be possible and the United States would not be able to count, in this war, on the unanimous support of the hemispheric peoples. . . ." Aranha saw Brazil and the United States as "cosmic and universal" nations, whose futures could only be continental and worldwide. Realistically, he knew that Brazil was still "a weak country economically and militarily," but he had no doubt that with the capital and population which would come from the country's natural growth, or would flow to it after the war, it would be "inevitably one of the great economic and politi-

[28] For a review of the political-military situation at the beginning of 1943 see Caffery, Rio, Feb. 6, 1943, 832.00/4349, NA.

[29] Roosevelt to Vargas, n.p., Dec. 24, 1942, PPF 4473 (Vargas), FDRL.

cal powers of the world"—it already was second in the Americas. He cautioned Getúlio against adopting an overly nationalistic economic policy, because the flight of American and British capital would be fatal for Brazil. The Brazilians should subject themselves without reserve to the war economy, so that by "ceding in war" they would "gain in peacetime" reciprocal arrangements that would take into account the interests of both Brazil and the United States. Brazil's postwar economic policies should include the liberalization of international trade, the intensification of American cooperation with the "Vargas program" of industrialization, and the free movement of immigration and capital to Brazil.[30] Aranha was aware that such complete cooperation with the United States carried grave risks, but a weak Brazil was at the mercy of stronger nations and without a powerful ally "the future of Brazil will be everyone's, except the Brazilians."[31]

Though Aranha did not believe that it was then necessary to send Brazilian soldiers to Africa or Europe, he allowed that the course of the war might make it in Brazil's interest to do so later. He urged Vargas to question Roosevelt as to future allied operations and plans for European occupation and reconstruction, so that they could better plan their moves. Mixed commissions already regulated their military relations, but Aranha thought that the two governments should maintain intimate contact and a continuous exchange of ideas at the ministerial level. At any rate, Brazil should not wait on events but should prepare militarily as if it were to enter combat immediately, because "this preparation by itself, without our being called to battle, will be counted as one or more victories at the peace table." Aranha went on to urge adherence to the Atlantic Charter and the United Nations Declaration, as well as participation in all the study committees of the United Nations, and he wanted a place for Brazil in the supreme military councils. The fu-

[30] Aranha to Vargas, Rio, Jan. 25, 1943, OAA.
[31] Aranha to Dutra, Rio, Aug. 11, 1943, OAA.

ture of European colonies and mandates was of interest in two areas—the Portuguese territories and the Guianas. If Salazar did not change his policies an allied victory would mean the collapse of the Portuguese empire; in that event Brazil should demand American support of whatever policies Brazil adopted "in defense of a patrimony that is hereditarily Brazilian." All the European colonies in the Americas should be eliminated, some by absorption, the rest by being given independence. Brazil intended to play a key role in whatever was to be done. It was especially interested in French Guiana because of the security of the Amazon. As regards Africa, which also had great influence on Brazilian security, Brazil should demand a voice in deliberations concerning the colonial continent's future. Aranha doubted that Anglo-American unity would outlast the war because Great Britain's war-inflicted poverty would force it into an aggressive program of economic reconstruction. And, because Anglo-American economic competition could only serve to benefit Brazil, Brazil should not take sides. In conclusion Aranha listed eleven consequences that Brazil should seek from World War II:

1) an improved position in world politics;
2) consolidation of its preeminence in South America;
3) a more confident and intimate solidarity with the United States;
4) greater influence over Portugal and its possessions;
5) development of maritime power;
6) development of air power;
7) development of heavy industries;
8) creation of war industries;
9) creation of industries—agricultural, extractive, and light mineral—which would be complementary to those of the United States and necessary for world reconstruction;
10) extension of Brazil's railways and highways for economic and strategic purposes;
11) exploration for essential combustible fuels.

With these "hurried and general lines" Aranha hoped that his chief would be better prepared to deal with Roosevelt at Natal.[32]

On the evening of January 27 Vargas, and a party of Americans that included Admiral Ingram and Ambassador Caffery, disembarked from an American "Stratoliner" at the Parnamirim air base, and drove into Natal, via what was known locally as the "Pista Americana," to quarters aboard the American destroyer *Jouett* where they spent the night. Brazilian authorities did not know of Vargas' presence, indeed few people in the country knew where he was, because it was generally assumed that he was in São Paulo with his son, Getúlio Jr., who had contracted infantile paralysis shortly before. (The boy died on February 2.) It was as if the Americans had spirited Vargas away to a meeting that had the atmosphere of an audience more than that of a conference between chiefs of state. They were in Brazil, yet Vargas appeared to be Roosevelt's guest instead of the reverse. Getúlio, ever the realist, showed no sign that he resented the arrangements, which certainly mirrored the realities of the situation. Afterward, however, he did make a point of mentioning at a press conference that he had gone to Natal the night before Roosevelt arrived because "the host should await the visitor."[33]

Roosevelt's PanAm *Dixie Clipper* arrived from Africa shortly before eight on the morning of January 28 and the president went immediately to the USS *Humboldt*, a seaplane tender anchored in the Potengi River. Later in the morning Caffery briefed him on the situation in Brazil and the questions Vargas would want to discuss. Because Aranha had let the ambassador read his letter to Vargas outlined above, Caffery was able to be quite exact. Vargas came aboard at 11:45 A.M. and the two presidents, who had not met since Roosevelt's 1936 visit to Rio, greeted each other warmly. After posing for photographers on the deck,

32 Aranha to Vargas, Rio, Jan. 25, 1943, OAA.
33 Caffery, Rio, Jan. 30, 1943, 740.0011 EW 1939/27590, NA.

they had lunch in Roosevelt's cabin and then went on a tour of local military installations. Naturally they were recognized and cheered. Only the local Brazilian army commander expressed resentment at not being forewarned. Roosevelt charmed Vargas, giving him his cane because Getúlio was still suffering from the effects of his May automobile accident, and joking that their jeep would probably collapse under Admiral Ingram's weight. Vargas was especially pleased when Roosevelt said that he would like to have him at his side during the peace conference.[34] After visiting the extensive and impressive Parnamirim base, they dined on the *Humboldt* with Caffery and presidential assistant Harry Hopkins.

Conversing in French, Roosevelt discussed the progress of the war, American industrial production, Anglo-American relations, the Russian front, some of his postwar hopes and plans, and the future of France's colonies. He thought Dakar should become a trusteeship, with commissioners from the United States, Brazil, and some other American republic. Then they talked in a general way about Brazilian industrial development and postwar immigration. Vargas expressed willingness to adhere to the United Nations and to send troops to the Portuguese Azores and Madeira, but he reminded Roosevelt that "we need equipment from you for our military, naval, and air force."[35] This aspect of their exchange will be dealt with more fully in Chapter 13. Finally they drew up a statement for the press, emphasizing that West Africa could "never again under any set of circumstances be permitted" to become a threat to the Americas. "Brazil and the United States seek to make the Atlantic Ocean safe for all."[36]

[34] Caffery to Roosevelt, Rio, Feb. 9, 1943, PSF Brazil, FDRL.

[35] Caffery, Rio, Jan. 30, 1943, 740.0011 EW 1939/27588, NA.

[36] Press Release, Natal, Jan. 30, 1943, in folder "Política Exterior do Brasil, 1938–44," OAA. Aranha's attached note said that this was the original document.

Everyone seemed pleased. The *Diário Carioca* proclaimed that "the Natal meeting was held at the threshold of a new era." Many newspapers called Natal the logical consequence of the Casablanca Conference. Commentator J. S. Maciel Júnior said in *A Noite* that if Brazil had had forces in combat there would have been a Brazilian delegate at Casablanca. And *A Manhã* summed up the general reaction, saying that Natal marked the "high point of our alliance with the United States and shows the absolute solidarity which unites us."[37]

Vargas was in high spirits when he returned to Rio, confident that he could trust Roosevelt and delighted at the prospect of taking part in the peace conference. Roosevelt had invited him to come to the United States so that he could entertain him at Hyde Park. Roosevelt's papers do not reveal what he thought of Vargas, but his feelings certainly were not negative. Getúlio had great respect for the American president, and Brazilians generally seemed to regard Roosevelt as a superpatron. Indeed, no American leader had ever captured the hearts of Brazilians as Roosevelt did.

The Americans were pleased with Vargas' obvious enthusiasm for the allied cause. They attributed much of their success in Brazil to Admiral Ingram's work, which Welles termed a "remarkable job." At a Standing Liaison Committee meeting Admiral Frederick J. Horne quipped, "I think they want to turn the Army over to Admiral Ingram."[38]

Natal apparently increased Brazil's prestige among the American republics. Caffery commented to Roosevelt that "at this moment all Latin America (except the Argentine), and this perhaps is one of the principal results of the Natal

[37] These are all Rio newspapers. The quotes were taken from "News Summary For Week Ending Feb. 4, 1943," 832.9111/34, NA; and "Natal," *Brazil*, 17, No. 172 (March 1943), 19.

[38] SLC Minutes, Feb. 8, 1943, NA.

meeting, look to Brazil as the spokesman for and champion of the Americas with and under you."[39] Natal reassured the Brazilians of the wisdom of their policy of approximation and stiffened their determination to achieve continental preeminence.[40]

With Argentina's internal situation becoming more uncertain and with its apparent determination to maintain relations with the Axis, Brazil found ready response to its overtures toward close ties with Paraguay and Bolivia. In January, Brazil conceded to Paraguay free port privileges in Santos, and in May Paraguayan President Higínio Morínigo journeyed to Rio de Janeiro to return Vargas' 1941 visit to Asunción. The Brazilians had opened a branch of the Bank of Brazil in the Paraguayan capital, and Aranha and Vargas had been working to strengthen ties via student scholarships in Brazilian schools, training programs for Paraguayan officers at Brazilian military installations, the signing of a trade and navigation treaty, donation of a radio station to develop communication between the two countries, and discussion of extending the São Paulo railway to Concepción. During Morínigo's visit they declared Paraguay's debt to Brazil, resulting from the War of the Triple Alliance (1865–1870) to be "nonexistent." Although largely a symbolic gesture, this indicated Brazil's wish to cultivate

[39] Caffery to Roosevelt, Rio, Feb. 9, 1943, PSF Brazil, FDRL.

[40] In addition to the citations above, the account of the meeting at Natal was based on the following: "Log of the Trip of the President to the Casablanca Conference, 9–31 January 1943," pp. 44–49, USN Office of Naval Records and Library; Pan-American Airways, *Wings Over the World*, Annual Report for the War Year 1942, p. 3; History SADATC, Part III, VII, 80–86; "Historic Conference Off Natal," *Brazil*, XVII, No. 172 (March 1943), 5ff.; *Foreign Relations, 1943*, V, 653–658; Roosevelt to Vargas, n.p., Feb. 24, 1943, PPF 4473 (Vargas), FDRL. Roosevelt sent Vargas the photograph of the two presidents and Ingram in the jeep, with the inscription: "For my old friend President Vargas from F.D.R." Later an artist, Raymond R. R. Moore, did an oil painting from the photograph which is periodically displayed at FDRL.

a benevolent image in Paraguay.[41] In June the president of Bolivia, General Enrique Peñaranda, came to Rio to enjoy Vargas' hospitality. Since Bolivia had declared war on the Axis, the Brazilians could attempt to use their status as allies to undermine Argentine predominance in Bolivian affairs. Brazil had completed about one-fourth of a rail line from the border town of Corumbá to Santa Cruz de la Sierra, which when finished would give Bolivia access to the Atlantic via Santos.[42] A revolution in December 1943 would overthrow Peñaranda and disrupt Vargas' courting of Bolivia, but Brazil had managed to make its actions appear less motivated by self-interest than were Argentina's strenuous efforts to dominate its northern neighbor.[43]

Meanwhile, pressures were building up for change in the Brazilian political system. On January 30 the cabinet approved joining the United Nations, and the prodemocratic elements (defined at the time as those who wanted elections) increased their activities in such groups as the "Friends of America." This organization included seventy-year-old General Manoel Rabello, as president, Chancellor Aranha, as first vice-president, and among its members such notables as Ambassador Caffery, Minister of Communications General Mendonça Lima, the mayor of Rio, Henrique Dodsworth, Brigadier Eduardo Gomes, diplomat Afrânio de Melo Franco (d. January 1943), and several of the *tenente* group.[44] The incongruity of a dictatorship fighting

[41] Vargas, *Nova Política*, x, 45–48, 65–67; "Brazil and Paraguay Collaborate," *The Inter-American Monthly*, ii, No. 7 (July 1943), 44; "Brazil Denounces Fascism," *ibid.*, p. 7; "Toward a National Type," *ibid.*, ii, No. 12 (December 1943), 6–7.

[42] Vargas, *Nova Política*, x, 91–105; for Vargas' 1941 trip to Paraguay see *ibid.*, ix, 53–73.

[43] For a careful study of Bolivia during this period see Herbert S. Klein, *Parties and Political Change in Bolivia, 1880–1952* (New York, 1970).

[44] "Friends of America in Brazil," *The Inter-American Monthly*, ii, No. 2 (February 1943), 4.

a war against totalitarianism increasing bothered such men in and out of the government. It was certain that something would have to be done to regularize the government and to provide for an orderly succession. Vargas had no vice-president, and his accident in May 1942 had given pause to many.

In mid-1943 the cabinet seems to have been divided as to whether to follow Aranha, who insisted that elections should be held immediately, or Minister of Justice Marcondes Filho, who advised that nothing be done until the war ended. Vargas, as indicated in his speech of November 10, 1942, agreed that the regime had to be legalized but was uncertain as to when to hold elections. He was extremely cautious and, as one analyst observed, his sense of self-preservation was sensibility itself, which prompted him to grind "out his stuff with the slowness of the mills of the Gods."[45]

Another knowledgeable observer, Walter N. Walmsley of the State Department's Division of American Republics (DAR), visited Brazil in early 1943 and returned with the correct impression that there was no serious plan to hold elections during the war. And because Vargas had captured the deep affection of so many Brazilians a palace revolt or a repetition of the Paulista rising of 1932 would stand little chance of success. By holding the lid down on political reform until the war ended, Walmsley feared that Vargas might unintentionally produce a "turbulent situation which may seem to justify Army leaders directly seizing control."[46]

[45] Simmons, Rio, Aug. 4, 1943, 832.00/4435, NA. For other reports on possibility of elections see Caffery, Rio, Apr. 22, 1943, 832.00/4383; July 31, 1943, /4428; Aug. 10, 1943, /4439, NA.

[46] Walmsley, Memo: DAR, May 8, 1943, 832.00/4383 and May 17, 1943, /4397, NA. As regards São Paulo he said (my paraphrase): that the Paulista plutocrats would very much like to regain control of the central government, but they had too little influence over the masses or in the army to successfully carry off a conspiracy. The Paulista elite had been making money for so long that its sons were not attracted to

What was Vargas up to? On May 1 he addressed the annual labor rally in Vasco da Gama stadium, saying that his principal task was to achieve the well-being of the entire population and to that end he was reshaping the government and its processes. He asserted that his labor policies did "not divide, nor discriminate," but on the contrary joined and conciliated potentially divergent interests. Praising the patriotism and nationalism of the workers, he said he knew he could count on them to increase production, and, of course, to support the government. To make that easier, he outlined some new decrees being prepared that would improve their working and living conditions and provide educational opportunities via vocational schools for their families. Significantly, volume ten of his speeches, which appeared in October 1944, skipped from December 31, 1942, where volume nine ended, to May 1, 1943, thus allowing the first address to be this statement of labor policy.[47]

In early June Getúlio issued a decree bringing all municipal, state, and quasi-official civil servants under the jurisdiction of the federal civil service (DASP—Administrative Department of Public Service) thereby tightening his control of all public jobs.[48] The political importance of Brazil's bloated civil service was very great because, given the general illiteracy of the population, the civil servants comprised a large percentage of those who could pass the literacy test for voting. Moreover, Getúlio deliberately waited until November 10, 1943, to give federal civil servants a long-overdue salary increase. Prices had risen tremendously

---

military careers, and Walmsley did not know of a single active-duty general officer in the army from São Paulo.

[47] The speech was entitled: "The Patriotism of the Brazilian Worker and the Labor Policy of the Government," *Nova Política*, x, 27–37.

[48] For DASP see Gilbert B. Siegel, "The Vicissitudes of Governmental Reform in Brazil: A Study of the DASP," (Ph.D. Dissertation, University of Pittsburgh, 1964).

since their last pay boost in 1936. Labor had had several increases but the federal service was paid so little that Rio's rapidly growing city government was luring competent workers away from the federal offices by offering higher wages.[49] Yet Getúlio had chosen not to quiet the grumbling because he had expected the war to end soon, in which case he intended to hold elections, employing strategic pay raises at proper intervals to boost his popularity. To be prepared he called in the author of the 1937 constitution, Francisco Campos, to discuss ways of legalizing the regime.[50] He may have expected pressure for elections to become irresistible if the war in Europe ended before November 1943, when his six-year term under the 1937 constitution would end.

His speeches had a steady nationalist theme; his May 1st labor address recalled the Integralista conspiracy of 1938 as an example of false patriotism. The greenshirts came under heavier fire two weeks later, on the anniversary of their attack on the presidential palace; mass meetings were held, the ministers of war and navy visited the graves of the soldiers and marines who had died in the fighting, movie houses presented free showings of anti-Nazi films, and a popular tribunal tried Plínio Salgado in absentia and sentenced him to death.[51] In a speech at Volta Redonda, Vargas declared that the country's natural resources must be kept in Brazilian hands. He was not an *exclusivista*, nor would he counsel repudiation of foreign capital in developing Brazil's industries, but he favored limiting foreign participation to loans, the providing of certain services, and short-term concessions. But the iron and steel industry, hydroelectric energy, and the railroads were too closely linked to national defense to permit their alienation.[52] Obvi-

[49] Simmons, Rio, July 7, 1943, 832.00/4412, NA.

[50] Simmons, Rio, July 23, 1943, 832.00/4424, NA.

[51] "Brazil Denounces Fascism," *The Inter-American Monthly*, II, No. 7 (July 1943), 6.

[52] Vargas, *Nova Política*, X, 55–56.

ously, he was balancing the ever-closer American alliance against heightened nationalism, which had great appeal among the workers, middle-class civil servants, and military officers.

To strengthen his grasp even further he replaced the head of the Department of Press and Propaganda, Major Coelho Reis, who was a Dutra man, with an army officer loyal to himself, and he increased the intensity of proregime radio propaganda—which was useful in mustering support among illiterates.[53] As events turned out this campaign to maintain adherence among labor, civil servants, and nationalists was not needed to support Vargas' reelection in 1943, because Marcondes Filho and Benjamim Vargas, the president's brother, persuaded him to postpone elections until after the war. This disappointed many of Getúlio's supporters, including Aranha, because they thought he would be confirmed by an overwhelming majority in an open election.[54] As it became certain in September and October 1943 that elections would not be held, the old opposition, including such men as former President Artur Bernardes; Virgílio and Afonso de Melo Franco, sons of the deceased ex-foreign minister; Odilón Braga, former minister of agriculture; Pedro Aleixo, former majority leader in the Chamber of Deputies; Affonso Pena, Jr., the son of a former president, and others drew up a manifesto addressed to the people of Minas Gerais which was released in Belo Horizonte on October 24. It said that because Brazilians were fighting against fascism and for the restoration of liberty and democracy in Europe, political rights and guarantees should be reestablished at home.[55] Mysterious

[53] Simmons, Rio, July 15, 1943, 832.00/4420, NA.

[54] Caffery, Rio, Nov. 5, 1943, 832.00/4495, NA.

[55] "Ao Povo Mineiro," Belo Horizonte, Oct. 24, 1943, OAA. Other signers were Bilac Pinto, José de Magalhães Pinto, Milton Campos, and Luiz Camilo de Oliveira Neto. There is a copy and commentary on the Minas Manifesto in Walter C. Dowling (2d Secy. of Emb.), Rio, Oct. 29, 1943, 832.00/4489, NA. Its origins, preparation, and results are discussed in

telegrams referring to uprisings disturbed the sleep of a few officials, student agitation in São Paulo resulted in the arrest of the president of the students' union, and the military and police went on alert status.[56] But the regime was not in immediate danger.

The wind out of Minas died away, but it forced Vargas to play his trump card and raise wages and salaries on November 10. In announcing a military pay boost he assured the army that while it was shedding its blood to defend the nation, he would "not vacillate in repressing any attempts at useless perturbation." It was a time for unity, which he would preserve with "energetic measures." In the war emergency the government must maintain order and safeguard the collective welfare. Later the same day he told an audience of civil servants and labor that the nation's readjustment to a war economy was causing hardship, but that the Brazilians' "admirable capacity for adaptation" made him confident that all obstacles would fall before their cooperation and good will. He praised them for not striking and agitating, and promised that "when the war ends . . . we will readjust the political structure of the nation." Moreover, organized labor would have a central part in that reorganization. The prime leadership positions would "fall to those that work and produce" and not to those professional politicians who cultivate public activity to their own advantage. He also said he would consult the representatives of youth, who were preparing themselves in the schools, factories, and barracks "to construct the future of the *Pátria*."[57]

Getúlio was mustering the new political forces that would run Brazil in the years ahead, but he was careful not to alienate the business interests represented by such men as Roberto Simonsen and Euvaldo Lodi, who supported his

Carolina Nabuco, *A Vida de Virgílio de Melo Franco* (Rio de Janeiro, 1962), pp. 134–153.

[56] Caffery, Rio, Oct. 30, 1943, 832.00/4490; Nov. 3, 1943, /4485, NA.

[57] Vargas, *Nova Política*, x, 165–169, 175–179.

regime for their own reasons. In the next months he continued his efforts with speeches to various groups emphasizing themes tailored to each one. He told journalists and teachers in São Paulo that because their salaries were always the lowest, he had established an agency to assist the "intellectual worker" (*Serviço de Assistência ao Trabalhador Intelectual*); he said the Paulista farmers had shown themselves to be true descendants of the *Bandeirantes*; and he lauded the Brazilian Academy of Letters as responsible for Brazil's "cultural emancipation." To the army he declared that the expeditionary corps they would soon send abroad would open a new period in the history of Brazil. On January 18 he made a formal call on the Archbishop of Rio, Dom Jaime de Barros Cámara, in what observers considered an unusual demonstration of his solidarity with the Church. It was a deft display of political know-how that gathered sufficient popular support to guarantee Getúlio's continuation in power until the end of the war.[58]

Even so the question of political reorganization remained in the foreground and, understandably, was a matter of considerable concern in government circles. From his exile in Buenos Aires, Armando Sales de Oliveira, the 1937 presidential candidate, issued a manifesto criticizing the regime.[59] This may have prompted Minister of Justice and Labor Alexandre Marcondes Filho to ask the American embassy for an estimate of the probable end of the war, because, he explained, Vargas had charged him with preparing a plan for restoring legal government.[60] Shortly there-

[58] *Ibid.*, pp. 195–201; 207–208; 213–215; 236–237; 243–245; *Correio da Manhã*, Rio, Jan. 19, 1944.

[59] Photocopy of manifesto dated Dec. 10, 1943 in Simmons, Rio, Feb. 25, 1944, 832.00/4536, NA.

[60] Marcondes talked with Simmons, who was Chargé d'Affaires during Caffery's absence in the US, on Jan. 16. See his report: Simmons, Rio, Jan. 17, 1944, 832.00/4523, NA. In his memoirs Vargas' secretary, Luiz Vergara, described his own role in the discussions. He felt that Marcondes procrastinated unduly and gave the impression that Getúlio did not

after the army intelligence service reported that the old politicians in São Paulo had succeeded so well in marshaling opinion against the regime that the agents asserted: "We do not have the least doubt that 90% of the people of São Paulo are hostile to the Federal Government. . . ." However, the evidence of hostility which the agents cited was limited to factory owners who objected to a new tax on "extraordinary profits," and to students in bars shouting *vivas* for democracy and death to His Excellency the President.[61] Since the report did not sample workers' opinions its 90 percent estimate was doubtful, but it did indicate that the army was sniffing the political winds. Its usual watchdog for this sort of thing, Góes Monteiro, was in Montevideo in early 1944, having left the general staff to represent Brazil on the Emergency Advisory Committee for Political Defense set up after the Rio Conference.[62] He wrote Aranha and Vargas that the president should take firmer control of the government and the course of events, implying that Vargas was letting things coast too much. Góes said it was time to replace the deadwood in the government with "a more active group of our people of 1930, less reactionary and less corrupted—people on whom you can count in the difficult moments," not opportunists like those currently in various positions who would "abandon the chief at the first sign of danger." Góes predicted that the war, or the peace that followed, would "degenerate into a profound social revolution"; and perceiving that time was running out for the renovating movement of 1930, he urged reform of the political structure, of governmental administration, of the

---

want to wait on Marcondes' suggestions. See Vergara, *Fui Secretário de Getúlio Vargas* (Rio de Janeiro, 1960), pp. 151–165.

[61] Report of 2d Section (Intelligence), Estado Maior Regional ao Ministério da Guerra, [in] Boletim de Informações No. 1, até Jan. 29, 1944, copy in OAA.

[62] For the committee's work see *Foreign Relations, 1943*, v, 2–39 and *ibid., 1944*, VII, 1–26; and Coutinho, *General Góes*, pp. 398ff.

armed forces, and of "our customs and inveterate bad habits."[63]

In view of Góes' role in deposing Vargas in October 1945, his comments about him in a private letter to an old friend twenty months earlier are most interesting. Getúlio was, Góes wrote, "an exceptional man" and he would "die satisfied if his work succeeded in organizing and fortifying the cohesion of Brazil." Further, "by his virtues and even by his defects," Vargas was the man to lead Brazil during the "historic moment" in which the victors would decide the fate of the world.[64]

But other forces in and out of Brazil would determine who would shape its fate. Aranha, who had been seriously ill in mid-1943, was on a course that would take him out of the government in August 1944. His loss would have as great a negative effect on Brazil's future as the resignation of Sumner Welles in August 1943 had on United States foreign policy. Welles had written Aranha a letter, before news of his forced withdrawal from the State Department was made public, saying simply "I do not have to tell you what this means to me nor do I have to explain to you the circumstances involved." Aranha certainly knew of his long conflict with Cordell Hull and that Hull resented Welles' great diplomatic abilities and his closeness to Roosevelt. He may have also known of the rumors of homosexuality, but he was more tolerant than the Puritan wolves in Washington whose lust for blood befogged their reason. Welles was the architect of the reinvigorated Good Neighbor policy of post-1937 and, with Aranha, was chiefly responsible for the "Brazilian-American understanding" which he considered "not only a corner-stone in the edifice of inter-American solidarity itself, but also one of the most vitally important factors in assuring stability and peace in the world of the future."[65]

[Handwritten margin note: Forced resignation of Sumner Welles]

[63] Góes Monteiro to Aranha, Montevideo, Feb. 24, 1944, OAA.
[64] *Ibid.*
[65] Welles to Aranha, Washington, Aug. 22, 1943, OAA; James Mac-

Without Welles' steadying hand and with the subsequent disappearance from the scene of Aranha, Caffery, Hull, and Roosevelt, United States policy would gradually shift from alliance with, to domination of, Brazil.

In mid-1943, Welles had become alarmed at news of Aranha's illness and sent a message via Caffery that "we need him in the best possible state of health more than ever during the months to come." And a little later he added, "I can conceive of nothing more important from the standpoint of our New World during the war period and during the period thereafter than that you should be your usual vigorous and outstandingly able self."[66] Aranha reassured him, observing philosophically: "You know how fatalistic we are. I am therefore convinced that, God willing, we will keep in good shape not only during the months to come but until our jobs are thoroughly and completely done."[67] Unfortunately, God proved unwilling, or perhaps preoccupied with matters elsewhere on the war-torn globe.

Throughout the Second World War the Argentine Republic was a problem for Brazil and the United States. Though its foreign minister had voted at the Rio Conference to recommend that Argentina break relations with the Axis, the government of Ramón Castillo, despite constant pressure from Washington, could not bring itself to take the action. In June 1943 the military deposed Castillo and, as general followed general in the *Casa Rosada* (the presidential palace), Argentina marched determinedly toward political confusion.

The Brazilians were nervous because the officer clique behind the revolt had issued a proclamation specifying Brazil as Argentina's rival for domination of South America. To

---

Gregor Burns, *Roosevelt, The Soldier of Freedom, 1940–1945* (New York, 1970), p. 350. Burns makes clear Roosevelt's unhappiness at being forced to let Welles go.

[66] Caffery to Aranha, Rio, May 28, 1943; Welles to Aranha, Washington, June 7, 1943, OAA.

[67] Aranha to Welles, Rio, May 31, 1943, OAA.

insure that Argentina win out, they seized power—to make their republic "stronger than all the other countries in South America combined," and to force alliances on their neighbors. "With Argentina, Paraguay, Bolivia and Chile united it will be easy to pressure Uruguay. Then the five united nations will easily attract Brazil due to its form of government and the great colonies of Germans there. With Brazil fallen, the South American continent will be ours." It was ominous that their model was Germany.[68]

From Montevideo, in early 1944, Góes Monteiro urged creation of bases of operations in the southern states and in Mato Grosso. He did not think the Argentines would attack but it would be prudent to take precautions. Góes also worried over Brazil's future if England continued its economic support of Argentina, and if the United States failed to help Brazil develop in such fashion as to "assure our military supremacy on the continent."[69]

It did appear throughout 1944 that the Argentine military, now with Juan Perón at its head, was up to something. Perón increased the army's size. He graduated cadets from the military academy early to fill the vacancies in the service—so many officers now occupied government posts formerly held by civilians. He justified the military buildup with references to territorial expansion. Military parades were a daily occurrence, and reservists in Corrientes and Entre Ríos provinces held weekly exercises.[70] Brazilian agents reported that nearly 5,000 Axis officers and technicians were assisting Argentina to mobilize its armed forces and industries. Argentina reportedly had between 800 and

[68] Circular Distributed Among Officers of the Argentine Army on May 3, 1943 and issued as a proclamation when the revolt took place on June 4, 1943, copy in file entitled "Posição Internacional da Argentina," OAA.

[69] Góes Monteiro to Aranha, Montevideo, Mar. 8, 1944, and Apr. 21, 1944, OAA.

[70] Clarimundo Flôres to Aranha, Buenos Aires, Aug. 10, 1944, OAA. Flôres was Brazilian Consul-General in Buenos Aires.

1,000 airplanes of all types and the factory in Córdoba, which turned out two aircraft a week, was about to increase production to ten a week. For these craft the Argentines had a reserve of 1,000 motors. With German advisors, they had been mounting tanks on tractor chassis for the past three years, and had completed roughly 500. They had extended duty tours of conscripts, called up reservists, and ordered border units to maintain a constant war footing.[71] The Brazilian Consul-General in Buenos Aires observed that because of the large-scale military activities "the people are led naturally to think that the country is preparing for war."[72] An analyst in the Itamaraty noted the rehabilitation of Juan Manuel de Rosas (1829–1852), who had attempted unsuccessfully to recreate the colonial Viceroyalty of the Rio de La Plata in the 1830's and 1840's. He warned that revival of this Argentine dream would turn into a nightmare for Brazil.[73]

Góes Monteiro feared that "if *o Deus brasileiro* (God the Brazilian) abandons gigantic Brazil to its evil congenital paralysis" Spanish America would unite to trounce Brazil. Leaving no doubt as to the seriousness of the situation, he wrote Aranha that "if we let the present historic moment go by—this latest opportunity which the war offers us—without raising ourselves from the baby's crib to acquire a solid and ample position on the Continent, I believe that we risk losing all the rest."[74]

[71] Memo: "Mobilização na Argentina," n.d., not signed [appears to have been written by Clarimundo Flôres], in "Posição Internacional da Argentina," OAA.

[72] Clarimundo Flôres to Aranha, Buenos Aires, Aug. 4, 1944, OAA.

[73] Luiz Augusto de Rego Monteiro, "Relatório sôbre os problemas sociais da Argentina, do Chile, e do Uruguai," Feb. 12, 1944, OAA. The classic *Rosista* foreign policy called for defense against Brazilian imperialism by extending Argentina to its "natural frontiers," which included Uruguay, Paraguay, and Bolivia. Ramón Doll gave it contemporary expression in his *Acerca de una Política Nacional* (Buenos Aires, 1939).

[74] Góes Monteiro to Aranha, Montevideo, Apr. 3, 1944, OAA.

Everything depended on the continuance of United States assistance. In January 1944 Hull and Roosevelt had exchanged memoranda on checking Argentina's plans for South American domination. Roosevelt was disturbed, and believed Argentina had been involved in the coup d'état in Bolivia, was plotting against Paraguay, and had done "a great deal of preliminary work" in Uruguay, Chile, and Peru. He thought that "this trend should be nipped in the bud and that we should proceed with the Argentine in strong ways." The United States should move at once to build up Brazil's strength. "This," he wrote, "should cover American arms and munitions and possibly more Army instructors, so as to give Brazil an effective fighting force near the Argentina border such as two or three divisions of motorized regiments."[75]

At the same time Washington decided to increase pressure on Buenos Aires to break relations with the Axis. In addition to the State Department's threat to reveal Argentine involvement in the Bolivian coup, to freeze Argentine assets in the United States, and to curtail all exports to the republic, Admiral Ingram steamed to Montevideo in his flagship, the cruiser USS *Memphis*. The Argentines' nerve weakened and they severed relations with the Axis on January 25, 1944.[76]

Argentina's neutrality had been based on the army's intense admiration for the German military organization, which it copied minutely, and on the agricultural elite's estimate that, as in the First World War, they would profit by selling beef and grain to the combatants and to Europe after the war. With military power and control of scarce

[75] Cordell Hull, *The Memoirs of Cordell Hull* (New York, 1948), II, 1390–1391. The exchange took place on Jan. 8 and 12, 1944. *Foreign Relations, 1944*, VII, 567–568, printed the same memoranda deleting reference to placing Brazilian forces on the Argentine border.

[76] *Foreign Relations, 1944*, VII, 228–240; and Luiz Augusto do Rego Monteiro, "Relátorio sôbre os problemas sociais da Argentina, do Chile, e da Uruguai," Feb. 12, 1944, OAA.

foodstuffs the Argentines thought that they could afford to be arrogant and stubborn.[77] They weakened when they thought Britain would join the United States in a trade embargo, but, when the Perón clique discovered this was not the case, they forced General Pedro P. Ramírez to turn the presidency over to his vice-president and minister of war, General Edelmiro J. Farrell.[78] The United States succeeded in severing relations between Buenos Aires and Berlin, but tension remained between Argentina on the one hand and the United States and Brazil on the other.

While Argentina's attitude tended to drive Brazil and the United States into closer cooperation on the military level, economically and politically it created divergences. Thus when the United States restricted trade with Argentina to essential items related to public health and war industries, Brazil joined Great Britain, South Africa, and several Latin American countries in supplying items that the United States had cut. While Brazilian officials thought that Argentina should be dealt with firmly politically, they wished to avoid offending Argentine dignity and forcing the republic into a position where its leaders would feel compelled to attack Brazil. Brazilian policy dictated caution and military preparedness, but was predicated on the belief that persuasion was better than force and trade better than embargo.

Aranha, who was not particularly drawn to Hull, missed the link that Welles had provided between the Itamaraty and the State Department. As the Brazilian generals prepared the expeditionary force for embarkation the man who was principally responsible for Brazil's Americanist policy and for Brazil's participation in the war found his prestige

[77] Rego Monteiro, "Relátorio . . . ," *ibid.*; and report entitled "Impressões sôbre o caso argentino em face da política americana," Montevideo, Mar. 22, 1944, unsigned, OAA. For an Argentine view see Nicolas Repetto, *Política Internacional* (Buenos Aires, 1943). Repetto said (p. 128) that Argentine leaders considered the war ended when France fell and therefore shipped their grain crop to Europe.

[78] *Foreign Relations, 1944*, VII, 251–254.

declining both in Brazil and outside it. His very success and vibrant personality made him a political threat to his friend Getúlio, if and when a free electoral system were established. In the meantime, as he did not represent a specific organized constituency, but instead enjoyed general popularity and respect, he was apparently expendable. Since Marcondes Filho had entered the cabinet, he and Aranha had come into conflict, both personally and ideologically, while struggling for preeminent influence. Marcondes was aligned with Dutra, Benjamim Vargas, and the new police chief, appointed at the end of July 1944, Coriolano de Araújo Góes, in what appeared to be maneuvers to keep Vargas in office. In mid-1944 Aranha was steadily losing ground against the Marcondes group and was becoming increasingly unhappy about it. Long periods passed without his seeing the president and the wellsprings of his political influence, his ability to distribute patronage, dried up.

The deterioration of Aranha's prestige within the regime was paralleled by Hull's failure to consult him as frequently as Welles had. Aranha once told Getúlio that the United States could do nothing in Latin America without Brazil. When the Roosevelt administration was uncertain of its position in the area it was only too happy to have Aranha run interference for it. Welles had understood that if, in Pan-American councils, a Brazilian expounded a policy that Washington wanted, it had a good chance of acceptance, but Hull, fancying himself a superior diplomat who enjoyed great prestige in Latin America, preferred to conduct his diplomacy directly without Brazilian mediation. Generally speaking, the State Department after Welles' departure did not appear to comprehend the nature of the Brazilian-American understanding (as Welles called it), and seemed bent on unilateral, interventionist policy in Latin America that sought to make permanent the region's wartime dependence on the United States. Moreover, on March 21, 1944, the Department of State issued a statement outlining the basis of United States foreign policy which said there would "no longer be need for spheres of influence, for alliances, for balance of power or any other of the special arrangements."[79] Where did this leave Brazil and the United States?

In April 1944 Aranha complained to Caffery that the United States was keeping Brazil in the background. Thereupon Hull sent a telegram saying that American cooperation with China, Great Britain, and the Soviet Union was the *sine qua non* to win the war and to preserve the peace, but that it did not weaken in any way "our obligations within the Hemisphere, and most especially to Brazil . . . ," and that the improvement of Inter-American relations was the cornerstone of United States foreign policy. Moreover, Hull asserted that the "well-being and security of the United States are indissolubly linked to the well-being and security of the other American Republics."[80]

Hull's telegram and the March 21 policy statement troubled Aranha. He wrote Hull that his "declarations seemed to reduce the force and cohesion of the traditional North American Brazilian policy." He was troubled as to how to interpret the reference to "spheres of influence and alliances" because "interdependence and cooperation were and ought to be the best basis of our continental life." It was not possible, he said, to substitute the "Code of the Good Neighborhood" for any other international agreement. He pointed out that only unlimited confidence in the integrity of American leaders and their fidelity to the basic principles of the United States could justify Brazil's unprecedented "policy of cooperation, of concessions, and of open doors." Since the Empire (1889), the friendship between the two nations had been based on reciprocal and "vigilant cooperation in defense of the North American position in the world," and on "our historic and natural preeminence, increasingly more necessary, in the political affairs of the

[79] Bulletin No. 69, American Embassy, Rio, Mar. 21, 1944, in folder "Política Externa do Brasil," OAA.

[80] Hull to Aranha, Washington, Apr. 20, 1944, OAA.

South American peoples." The preservation of this policy, Aranha observed, was "the governing principle of Brazil's attitudes."

Hull's hard line toward Argentina also disturbed Aranha. It was beyond doubt, he declared, that the Argentine revolutionaries desired to do more than simply to seize control of their government: their object was to reconstruct the Viceroyalty of the Río de La Plata under their own control. Certainly the Argentines were striving to extend their influence in the surrounding countries, as their role in the Bolivian coup d'état indicated. But he argued cogently that Washington, by refusing recognition to the Bolivian regime and by withdrawing ambassadors, was only forcing the Bolivians to look to Buenos Aires. Furthermore, he disagreed with Hull's denial of recognition to the Argentine government, and maintained that neither nonrecognition nor selective economic boycott would have favorable results. With accredited representatives in Buenos Aires and La Paz they would be able to influence the two governments toward cooperation. He observed that "Argentina will be able to accustom itself to live without us, while we can not do without its commerce and its products." Nor did he regard the current Argentine regime as radically different from its predecessors or, by implication, Nazi. "The fashion of dress and the brusque and somewhat spectacular manner are the only differences that we note between those that used to govern and those that now govern Argentina."[81]

The alarmed reaction to Aranha's letter by an official of the State Department's Division of American Republics clearly indicated that Aranha's suspicions were correct about a new mood having settled on Washington after Welles resigned. While admitting that he was not familiar with earlier exchanges, the DAR official urged "extreme caution to avoid committing ourselves in any way to any such proposition as the support of a form of Brazilian hegemony

[81] Aranha to Hull, Rio, May 17, 1944, OAA.

in South America in return for Brazilian support of our foreign policy in general." Washington's interest lay in promoting Inter-American cooperation among all the republics and not in acquiescing in a balance of power arrangement which "would align the United States and Brazil against the other American countries of Spanish origin. . . . This is a fundamental issue on which we must proceed with the greatest care if we are to avoid finding ourselves entangled in the subtle web of Mr. Aranha's 'balance of power' politics."[82]

At the same time the United States was revamping its lend-lease arms-supply program so as to insure American hegemony over the entire Western Hemisphere, including Brazil. In late 1943 a Navy memorandum listed the following among the functions of its naval mission in Brazil: "to assist in suring [*sic*] the predominance of the United States in Brazilian and Western Hemisphere affairs; . . . to introduce the use of United States material in the Brazilian Navy in order to promote American trade and to standardize the requirements of material and spare parts for United States and Brazilian ships operating together in time of war; . . . to prevent the establishment of any other foreign Naval Mission in Brazil; to demonstrate to other Latin American countries by successful functioning of the Naval Mission to Brazil the desirability of similar Missions in their own countries." The memorandum ended with the statement: "It is the policy of the United States Government to maintain the Naval Mission in Brazil after the war for the purposes set forth above."[83] In September 1943 the Joint Army and Navy Advisory Board on the American Republics sent a report on lend-lease revision to the service secretaries, admitting that during the dark days of 1940 and 1941 commitments

---

[82] Eric C. Wendelin, Memo, DAR, June 10, 1944, 832.00/5-3144, NA.

[83] Memo: Background of Naval Mission Functions, Enclosure A (Functions USN Mission-Brazil), NS, ND, QC/EF12, A14-5, Documents US 4th Fleet, Naval History Division, Dept. of the Navy. This memo probably was written sometime in 1943.

had been made which were not "warranted under later improved strategical situations"; and that because the Western Hemisphere was no longer in danger and because "many of the United Nations, armed neutrals and Axis Powers" would attempt to dispose of their surplus military equipment after the war at low prices or via barter, "to establish an influence of a military character throughout the Western Hemisphere," it recommended that sufficient equipment be shipped to Latin America to enable military and naval missions to keep the various republics interested in American equipment and methods "to the exclusion of non-American material and influences." The board further recommended the furnishing of armament "best designed to maintain internal security in those countries exporting vital strategic materials to the United Nations and whose governments continue to support the United States."[84] The Acting Secretary of State, Edward R. Stettinius, Jr., United States Steel's contribution to the federal government's war bureaucracy, agreed that, since the Latin republics had to import their armament, "military considerations," such as weapons' standardization to facilitate joint operations, dictated that the United States should supply it.[85]

The proposed disposal of American surplus equipment in a manner that would weaken European influence in Latin America and would tie the area closely to the United States economically and politically was partly intended to avoid the unscrupulous arms sales that had taken place after the First World War.[86] But primarily its aim was to prevent the reintroduction of European trade and influence. After the First World War the United States had lost the ground gained during the war, and its planners did not want to face that situation again. To implement the arms disposal policy the United States initiated military staff con-

[84] *Foreign Relations, 1944*, VII, 87–92. Memo dated Sept. 13, 1943.
[85] *Ibid.*, p. 93.
[86] See Adolf A. Berle Memo printed in *ibid.*, p. 100.

versations with the Latin American republics (except Argentina) in mid-1944. Their objective was the negotiation of individual bilateral agreements that made each republic separately dependent for supplies and training on the United States. Instead of an Inter-American alliance, which could have permitted the Latin Americans to unify and thereby balance North American power, these agreements were one-to-one arrangements that kept the republics separate and dependent. Naturally in such a conception of power dispersion the need for Brazil to serve as United States proconsul in South America was reduced, if not eliminated.

Even though Aranha may have suspected that something basic had changed in United States policy he continued to argue for closer approximation. In June 1944, despite previous denials and public pledges that no United States military personnel would remain at Brazilian bases after the war, the two countries signed an aviation agreement that would permit a continued United States military presence in Brazil. Aranha saw the air base agreement as "a proof of alliance" between the two countries and insurance of American assistance in repelling aggression against Brazil.[87] And when in the following month the United States asked for general staff conversations "to guarantee the military security of the hemisphere in the post-war period,"[88] Aranha viewed the request as an opportunity to obtain all that would be "necessary and indispensable to the security and the political, economic and military aggrandizement of Brazil." He warned Vargas that after the war, even with the

[87] MRE (Aranha) to Vargas, n.d. (but between June 14 and July 30, 1944), OAA. It read: "que o acôrdo de cooperação para conservação de bases aéreas . . . era . . . um penhor de aliança entre os Estados Unidos da America e o Brasil . . . mais do que tudo, assegurava ao Brasil o concurso norte-americano para defesa contra quaisquer agressões aos nossos territorios." For the agreement see *Foreign Relations, 1944*, VII, 543–566. It was signed June 14, 1944.

[88] Caffery to Vargas, Rio, July 10, 1944 in *ibid.*, pp. 124–125.

Brazilian wartime buildup and the expeditionary force's combat experience, Argentina would still "have more resources, strength, and means than Brazil." He obviously saw the American proposal for discussions as the result of the policy of "supporting the United States in International questions in exchange for the assistance to our internal progress, our external security and our preeminence in South America." Aranha did not know that the United States was negotiating identical pacts with all of Brazil's neighbors except Argentina and Bolivia.[89]

From Montevideo Góes Monteiro reinforced Aranha's position, warning that Perón was mounting a great war machine with popular and military backing. And because the United States and the Soviet Union would regulate their respective hemispheres after the war, Góes believed that the only road open to Brazil was the one Aranha had set it on. Góes' caution that the *gente que habla* (italics in original) were "working to disorient us" indicated that he saw their situation in terms of the traditional rivalry between Portuguese-speaking Brazil and its Spanish-speaking neighbors.[90]

These ancient enmities did not trouble the Washington policy-makers for whom Latins were Latins, and the differences between Portuguese and Spanish were unimportant. As presidential candidate Wendell Willkie supposedly commented (when someone corrected a reference to Brazilians speaking Spanish), Brazilians had better learn Spanish because everyone else in South America spoke it. The Americans were playing a two-faced game. They knew that the Brazilians regarded themselves as being in "a category apart" from the rest of Latin America and "would highly resent any endeavor to put them in the same category with

[89] MRE (Aranha) to Vargas, n.d. (but between June 14 and July 30, 1944), OAA.

[90] Góes Monteiro to Aranha, Montevideo, July 10, 1944, OAA. "Gente que habla": "People who speak" (Spanish). The Brazilians use *falam* (from *falar*, to speak), Portuguese.

other Latin American countries. . . ."[91] When it suited American interest, as in the case of Argentina, Washington would stress the "Brazil is different" theme, but when it was a question of Brazil's interests vis-à-vis the United States it suddenly became a part of Latin America to be dealt with via policies applicable to all republics.

In July 1944 Brazil was in the position of a woman who has given in to her lover, and can only trust that his intentions are honorable. Earlier that year, when the Brazilian transportation system was near collapse, Vargas had requested 3,500 trucks to keep it functioning. At the time the United States was anxious to continue to use the Brazilian bases after the war and Vargas could have asked for the trucks and much else as a *quid pro quo*.[92] Roosevelt wrote him that Brazil had an important role to play in securing the hemisphere and that it must be equipped to do so. "History will surely take note," he asserted, "that the turning point of the war in the European theater was coincident with the action of your government in providing bases and facilities which contributed so materially to the African campaign." Vargas and the Brazilian people should, Roosevelt said, "understand the appreciation of this Government and of the American people, for the very vital aid that Brazil has contributed to our common fight against the Axis powers."[93] Vargas and his advisors reacted so positively, and trusted Roosevelt so completely, that they relied on American "good faith and good intentions," and asked no *quid pro quo*.[94]

Aranha's letter of May 17 to Hull had not been answered throughout the air base negotiations, and the Brazilian government could only assume that the Americans agreed with Aranha's interpretation of their alliance. Finally, on July 17,

[91] Caffery, Rio, July 13, 1944, *Foreign Relations, 1944*, VII, 586.

[92] See *ibid.*, pp. 576–578, 585–586.

[93] Roosevelt to Vargas, Washington, n.d. (sent to Rio June 13, 1944), in *ibid.*, pp. 583–585.

[94] *Ibid.*, pp. 585–586.

Hull wrote that he and Roosevelt accepted as self-evident that the "extraordinarily close and fruitful cooperation" of the war years must continue in the postwar period. He wanted Aranha to come to Washington in August to discuss "a number of problems beginning to take shape," which included the "status and participation of powers like Brazil" in the United Nations, and the relationship of the Inter-American system to the world organization.[95] Perhaps if Aranha had gone to Washington and discussed the future role of Brazil and its relationship to the United States, he might have secured a more prestigious place in world affairs for his country. But he did not go because of the personal and political crisis that led to his resignation.

In mid-1944 Vargas was trying to reduce pressure for an early return to democratic government. In his May Day speech he reviewed all that his government had done for the laboring classes but declared that greater tasks lay ahead. After the foreign enemies were defeated it would still be necessary to conquer class discord, lack of social understanding, egotism, and the stubbornness of private interests. "Liberty, in the strict sense of political privileges," he warned, "was not enough to resolve the complex social problem." People could not stifle hunger with the right to vote, nor educate their children with the freedom of assembly. The workers would have to be economically secure in order to feel free to express their opinions. Brazil must right the imbalance between those who knew no limits to their profits and those who were trapped in a permanent struggle for subsistence. The interests of the entire society, he declared, must take precedence over the selfish pursuit of profits.[96] At the time the newspapers were full of complaints of artificially high prices and exorbitant profits, and stories about the government's struggle to control the situation. However, Vargas was also warning against a too precipitous reconstitutionalization that might give the worker the

95 Hull to Aranha, Washington, July 17, 1944, OAA.
96 Vargas, *Nova Política*, x, 287–293.

vote but leave him at the mercy of greedy capitalists. He was urging workers to form behind him to safeguard their economic and political well-being.

On July 5, 1944, the twenty-second anniversary of the Fort Copacabana uprising, Vargas appointed a new chief of police, Coriolano de Araújo Góes, a tough, professional policeman, who had served as Washington Luís' police chief and had imprisoned many of the revolutionaries of 1922 and 1924, including his three predecessors—Filinto Müller, Alcides Etchegoyen, and Nélson de Mello. Ambassador Caffery commented that his appointment would mean "a decided tightening of Government control in Brazil."[97] Coriolano worked closely with Benjamim Vargas and Minister of Justice and Labor Marcondes Filho to intimidate the regime's enemies and to destroy all opposition factions. The object was to eliminate organized opposition in order to smooth the way for Getúlio to be reelected president, with a congress and a functioning constitution; he could then go to the peace conference wrapped in an aura of democratic sanctity. Immediately upon taking office Coriolano suppressed four minor periodicals and one publishing house for alleged communist affiliations. In these actions he had army support; in fact his appointment may have been made at Dutra's behest, because the war minister believed that the communist danger was increasing. It should be noted, that army officers and members of the regime usually termed communist those who wanted a more democratic government—be that as it may, however, opposition to the regime certainly existed. Coriolano's appointment was met with consternation in São Paulo, where the previous November, as Secretary of Public Security, he had been responsible for breaking up student demonstrations. Two days after he took office students at the University of Brazil in Rio went on strike. And from the northeast came persistent rumors of antigovernment plots. The American em-

[97] Caffery, Rio, July 5, 1944, 832.00/7-544, NA.

bassy, however, seemed content that the new chief would "lay down a substantial foundation for the maintenance of public order" which would make postwar unrest controllable. The embassy's first secretary, Harold Tewell, considered Coriolano "more intelligent and more competent than any of his predecessors in the past ten years."[98]

On August 10, 1944, Coriolano closed the Society of the Friends of America, thereby precipitating the crisis that ended Oswaldo Aranha's chancellorship. The society, which was antifascist and prodemocratic, was headed by General Manoel Rabello of the Supreme Military Tribunal, long an enemy of Dutra.[99] Aranha, who had become the society's vice-president two years before in a public ceremony, had been reelected, and by law was required to go through a public installation which was scheduled for August 11. Aranha was not very much interested in the society, especially since many of its members seemed more concerned with Russia than with the United States, and he had told some of his friends to have nothing to do with it.[100] Yet he and his enemies would turn the society into a cause célèbre. When Coriolano informed General Rabello and Aranha that the announced ceremonies would be "inconvenient," Aranha agreed to postpone them. But cooperation was not the desired reaction. Marcondes, with whom Aranha had been competing for influence for some time, was out to humiliate him publicly. Coriolano sent police, who not only locked the society's rooms in the Automobile Club but ejected the Rotarians who were having their monthly lunch-

[98] Caffery, Rio, July 6, 1944, 832.00/7-644; July 7, 1944, /7-744; Harold S. Tewell (1st Secy. of Emb.), Rio, July 20, 1944, /7-2044; July 29, 1944, / 7-2944, all NA. The periodicals closed were: *Diretrizes; Mundo Médico; Renovação; Mensagens de N.S. do Menino Jesus;* the publishing house was *Editóra Calvino Ltd.* Tewell's estimation of Coriolano was in his July 20 report.

[99] For earlier Dutra–Rabello incidents see Caffery, Rio. Oct. 21, 1943, 832.20/554 and Oct. 28, 1944, /558, NA.

[100] Caffery, Rio, Sept. 4, 1944, 832.00/9-444, NA.

eon. The police then posted a notice that the building was closed.[101]

It had its effect; Aranha was insulted and decided that, although the incident was minor in itself, if Getúlio failed to back him he would have to resign. His prestige in the government was so low that when he recommended a man even for a porter's job it did not go through. He had always had a voice in distributing minor posts, as his files indicated, and he naturally resented losing it. But worse, Vargas had refused permission for him to accept Hull's invitation to go to Washington, and Dutra was preparing without Aranha's knowledge to visit the Italian front. Aranha identified Marcondes and Dutra as his principal enemies in the government. He later explained to Góes Monteiro that as the allied victory neared he became a greater threat to the *estadonovistas*, while at the same time the government's dependence on his direction of foreign affairs decreased. He recalled that he had not accepted the Chancellorship of the Itamaraty to serve the Estado Nôvo, but to serve Brazil and to keep his friend Getúlio from leading it astray. His attitude increasingly eliminated him from the formation of internal policy—indeed he was sometimes even excluded from business wholly within his ministry's realm. It was his conviction that "if Germany were winning, I would already have been shot, but from the front—as it is, being defeated, I was stabbed in the back."[102]

Aranha went to Dutra and suggested that they both resign. Dutra declined and urged him not to leave the government. Aranha met with Vargas, who gave him no satisfaction and suggested that the Aranhas hold a family council—undoubtedly he suggested this because in past crises the family had advised Oswaldo to stay in the gov-

101 These events took place Aug. 10, 1944. Gen. Manoel Rabello to Coriolano Góes, Rio, Aug. 13, 1944, OAA; Caffery, Rio, Aug. 11, 1944, 832.00/8-1144; Aug. 14, 1944, /8-1144; Aug. 15, 1944, /8-1544; Aug. 16, 1944, /8-1644; Aug. 17, 1944, /8-1744, NA.

102 Aranha to Góes Monteiro, Vargem Alegre, n.d., OAA.

ernment. Finance Minister Souza Costa, a close family friend, joined the Aranha meeting to advise against resignation, and Caffery warned Aranha throughout that his departure "would prejudice his country's interests."[103] But the family decided that he should remain only if Vargas took some action to increase his prestige at Marcondes' expense —they were confident that Getúlio could not afford to let Oswaldo resign. On the afternoon of August 21 Benjamim Vargas and General Oswaldo Cordeiro de Farias visited Aranha to review the whole controversy with Marcondes and Dutra. Afterward they went to tell Vargas that Aranha would resign unless the president acted against Marcondes. General Cordeiro returned with word that Getúlio wanted to talk, and that the president had asked if the police chief's dismissal would pacify Oswaldo. Aranha said that it would. Late on the 21st, Oswaldo and Getúlio had a long but unsatisfactory talk, in which the president failed to mention his offer to dismiss Coriolano. In the end they agreed that Aranha should leave, so he wrote a brief resignation saying the whole affair was "one more lack of consideration for a friend and Minister."[104] In conversation with Caffery he spoke darkly of the Brazilian Expeditionary Force veterans running Brazil after the war.[105] Two years to the day after Brazil had entered the war, and just as its forces were beginning to take their places in the European battlelines, the architect of the policy that had made it possible was forced out of the Vargas government.

Reaction was immediate. The Mexico City weekly news magazine *El Tiempo* was certain that Aranha's resignation, and especially Vargas' acceptance of it, placed Brazil's foreign relations "in a very dangerous phase." *La Nación* of Buenos Aires said that it signified the victory of those who favored continuing the Estado Nôvo over those who did

[103] Caffery, Rio, Aug. 19, 1944, 832.00/8-1944, NA.
[104] Aranha to Vargas, Rio, Aug. 21, 1944, OAA; Caffery, Rio, Aug. 21, 1944, 832.00/8-2144, NA.
[105] Caffery, Rio, Aug. 14, 1944, 832.00/8-1144, NA.

not. Another journal in the Argentine capital atributed Aranha's downfall to his *Yancofilo* foreign policy, which had proven too difficult for Brazilian patriots to tolerate. "Mr. Hull," it said, "has just suffered a great diplomatic defeat; and in a country that was supposed to be completely conquered."[106] The Brazilian press emphasized that the resignation would not affect the republic's foreign policy. Aranha told a reporter of the *Diários Associados* chain that "the foreign policy of Brazil will continue unalterably the same," and what he had done at the Itamaraty was only to follow the tradition of the Baron of Rio Branco.[107] Hull telegraphed that he was "deeply distressed" and asked that Aranha reconsider his decision. A few days later he wired his "deep personal regret" saying that Aranha's "constructive and enlightened leadership in the promotion of Inter-American solidarity is a bright page in contemporary history."[108] Caffery sent a short note thanking Aranha for his many kindnesses and cooperation, and saying "very few people indeed know, as well as I do, the brilliant part that you have played in the history of the Americas."[109] Many of Aranha's friends felt that he was "letting Brazil down." His successor as chancellor, veteran diplomat Pedro Leão Velloso Neto, who had represented Brazil in Italy and Japan, blamed Aranha's brothers, saying that they believed that Oswaldo "should be sitting in Getúlio's chair."[110]

Aranha had been the victim of what he termed a "Police Pearl Harbor" in the grand style of Estado Nôvo "jujitsu" politics.[111] Months later he wrote Sumner Welles that he

106 *El Tiempo*, Mexico City, Sept. 1, 1944; *La Nación*, Buenos Aires, Aug. 24, 1944; *La Fronda*, Buenos Aires, Aug. 25, 1944.

107 *Correio da Manhã*, Rio; and *Jornal do Comércio*, Rio, both Aug. 24, 1944. Papers in the *Diários Associados* chain carried the story the same date; *O Jornal*, Rio, Aug. 24, 1944.

108 Caffery to Aranha, Rio, Aug. 23, 1944 and Aug. 28, 1944, OAA.

109 Caffery to Aranha, Rio, Aug. 23, 1944, OAA.

110 Caffery, Rio, Aug. 28, 1944, 832.00/8-2844, NA. Velloso's remarks to Caffery made Aug. 27.

111 Aranha to Góes Monteiro, Vargem Alegre, n.d., OAA.

had been compelled to leave the government for reasons similar to Welles'—his presence was a threat to the ambitions and power-seeking of others who constantly sought to destroy him. He left his post, he said, only "when the victorious invasion of France would no longer give the recalcitrants opportunity to misdirect my country as they tried incessantly [to do] in the confused days produced by the German victories."[112]

Aranha's resignation, though rooted in personal vanity, Gaúcho stubbornness, and political expediency, had both short- and long-range consequences for Brazil. Most immediately, it added momentum to the upsurge of criticism of the Vargas regime. In mid-August Argentina had cut meat shipments to Brazil, which resulted in several meatless days per week. As a gesture to allay popular discontent Vargas replaced the heads of two agencies responsible for food supply.[113] Workers protested against such shortages, as well as against high prices, lack of transportation, housing, government health and medical care facilities, and delays in pension payments. Growing discontent and hostility at the lowest levels sent shocks up the social-economic scale, increasing the unity of the conservative middle and upper classes and making it difficult to preserve army support of the regime. Moreover, politicians correctly guessed that United States policy was shifting from maintaining Vargas to guaranteeing certain interests.[114]

Throughout the country and even among army officers there was increasing talk of the need for representative government. In official circles, Souza Costa, Benedicto Valladares, Francisco Campos, and Vargas' secretary, Luiz Vergara, were urging him to regularize the government be-

[112] Aranha to Welles, Vargem Alegre, May 24, 1945, OAA.

[113] Philip O. Chalmers to Shiras Morris (Div. of River Plate Republics, DS), Aug. 15, 1944, 832.00/8-344, NA.

[114] Cecil M. P. Cross (Consul General), São Paulo, Aug. 26, 1944, 832.00/8-2644, NA. Cross enclosed a report from the Sindicato de Fiação e Tecelagem em Geral (Spinning and Weaving) on conditions among its members. See also Cross, São Paulo, Sept. 6, 1944, 832.00/9-644, NA.

fore events got beyond his control.[115] Probably, if he had followed their advice, he would have stayed in office for several more years. But in late 1944 the general opinion was that in its current form the regime's days were numbered, and Aranha's withdrawal contributed substantially to that mood.

Washington feared that the resignation signified a rapprochement with Argentina. In fact, an exchange of visits between officers of the two armies had already been scheduled with Aranha's approval. He opposed Hull's harsh line against Argentina and was working to soften the differences between the Brazilian-American allies and the Argentines. His departure, if it had any effect, removed a calming voice that might have restrained Washington's actions against Perón. Foreign press criticism of the resignation made Brazilian authorities inclined to go even further than Aranha had, and perhaps without his caution, to show their friendship for the United States. The Brazilian generals hurriedly backed out of the exchange of visits. Dutra explained that the Brazilian army considered itself "identified" with the United States Army, and an entente with Argentina was "ludicrous." Vargas told Caffery that he was not happy about Aranha's departure and had tried to prevent it. It was "laughable," he said, to talk of the Brazilian and Argentine armies getting together. Aranha's resignation, he assured the ambassador, would not change Brazil's foreign policy.[116]

It was true that it did not change Brazil's policy, but it did make it less effective. In September 1944 the great powers met at Dumbarton Oaks to discuss the new world organization, but the Latin American republics had not been drawn into preconference planning. When Ambassador Carlos Martins told Undersecretary Edward Stettinius that they should have been consulted, Stettinius replied disparagingly that if they had been included the conference

115 Tewell, Rio, Sept. 27, 1944, 832.00/9-2744, NA.

116 Caffery, Rio, Aug. 25, 1944, 832.00/8-2544; and Aug. 26, 1944, / 8-2644, NA.

would not have been held on schedule. Martins asked if one of the republics would get a permanent council seat and Stettinius answered evasively that it was under study.[117] It was, of course, impossible to be certain that Aranha could have secured Brazil a seat on the Security Council, given the disappearance from the Washington scene of the men with whom he had influence. Welles was gone and Hull's health failed in late 1944, making it impossible for him to bear the strain of public service any longer.[118] Even Ambassador Jefferson Caffery, who had often been accused by some American officials of too readily accepting Aranha's point of view, was ordered home for "consultation" and then reassigned to the *de facto* French government in Paris. The United States economy was looking toward the coming peace and the dollar-a-year men and their allies, such as Stettinius, Rockefeller, Jesse Jones, James F. Byrnes, and Adolf Berle, were maneuvering to insure control of Latin American markets and raw materials. The American military were equally anxious to arrange postwar use of base facilities, and to establish arms-supply arrangements and training missions throughout the area. The desire of big business for a continued supply of strategic materials merged conveniently with military assessments of postwar national security requirements. After Roosevelt's death in April 1945 and the advent of Harry S Truman the drive for American domination accelerated. Truman's Secretaries of State, Stettinius and Byrnes, had limited knowledge of Brazilian-American relations and even less sympathy for Brazilian aspirations.[119]

[117] Edward Stettinius, Memo of Conversation w/h Carlos Martins (in home of Nelson Rockefeller), Sept. 27, 1944, 832.00/9-2744, NA. The various meetings at Dumbarton Oaks ran from Aug. 21 to Oct. 7, 1944.

[118] Theodore A. Xanthaky (Secy. Emb.) to Aranha, Rio, Dec. 15, 1944, OAA.

[119] For a study of United States policy toward Latin America in the last Roosevelt years and during the Truman administration see David Green, *The Containment of Latin America, A History of the Myths and Realities of the Good Neighbor Policy* (Chicago, 1971).

Aranha was dynamic where his successors were bland: he would undoubtedly have recognized that the shift in United States policy demanded that the Itamaraty assume a more protective stance. In November 1944 he publicly criticized Hull's Argentine policy, declaring that it might drag Brazil into an unwanted war with its neighbor.[120] Perhaps his statements prompted Vargas to send assurances to Roosevelt that "Brazil would follow the lead of the United States in all matters not only in the prosecution of the war but in political matters affecting this hemisphere and on all economic matters."[121]

Aranha could write Welles that his refuge in the countryside was "full of light and peace,"[122] but the political scene that he had left behind in the capital was full of shadows and confusion. Instead of peace, the end of the war would open a nineteen-year period of helter-skelter change that would exhaust the ability of the Brazilian political system to adjust, and would end in military dictatorship.[123]

[120] Stettinius to Stephen Early, n.p., Nov. 3, 1944, PPF 4380, FDRL.

[121] Stettinius to Roosevelt, n.p., Nov. 14, 1944, OF 11 Brazil 1940–45, FDRL.

[122] Aranha to Welles, Vargem Alegre, May 24, 1945, OAA.

[123] For a study of the postwar years see Thomas E. Skidmore, *Politics in Brazil, 1930–1964, An Experiment in Democracy* (New York, 1967). Aranha did not immediately join the opposition but remained out of the public eye for several months. Caffery speculated that he hoped that if he kept quiet Vargas would appoint him head of the Brazilian delegation to the peace conference. He may also have had financial reasons. Aranha had an expensive way of life complete with race horses, a "sitio" in the country, and a double family that he provided for lavishly. And for at least the period of his chancellorship, and perhaps before, his racing partner, Peixoto de Castro, ran the federal lottery under a government concession. Although at the last open bidding for the concession in May 1943 his partner had bid higher than one of the Marcondes clan, Aranha had gotten all bids cancelled and their own concession extended by presidential decree. A few days after his resignation Vargas issued a decree extending their concession for a year. Caffery wrote two reports concerning Aranha's lottery concession: Feb. 24, 1944, 832.00/4538 and Aug. 29, 1944, /8-2944, NA.

"They can go to Africa or Europe or Asia or wherever you want them to go."[1]

"We all look forward to the not-distant day when Brazilian and United States soldiers will be marching forward shoulder to shoulder on the field of combat."[2]

"The atmosphere surrounding the Brazilian Expeditionary Corps continues frankly indifferent and defeatist."[3]

12

The Cobra's Pipe

IF Brazil's war role was to be that of a supplier of raw materials and sites for foreign military bases its role in the postwar world was likely to be of a similar nature. If its belligerency was symbolic, its participation at the peace conference would be symbolic as well. But the war offered Brazilian leaders an opportunity to realize cherished dreams of international power and prestige, and they hoped that participation in the fighting would secure Brazil's postwar status. They had to show the world that their people were not merely a race of coffee-growing samba dancers but brave fighters who could defend their land and interests.

[1] Oswaldo Aranha's comment to Jefferson Caffery taken from Caffery, Rio, July 31, 1943, 832.20/540, NA.

[2] Roosevelt to Vargas, Washington, Sept. 14, 1943, PPF 4473 (Vargas), FDRL.

[3] Ministério de Guerra, Rio, Boletim de Informação No. 1, até Jan. 29, 1944, copy in OAA.

Underlying the desire to secure a solid position at the peace table was the fear that if Brazil did not present a strong, determined face to the world then perhaps the victors would divide it—like nineteenth century China or Africa. Unity and strength would avoid such a nightmare. The war provided a chance to rally the nation, still shaky from the turmoil of the previous years, around the green and gold banner. Troops abroad would provide a focal point for national unity. To discuss Brazil's preparation for combat overseas it is necessary to go back to the period just after its entry into the war, in August 1942, when Oswaldo Aranha was still foreign minister and the nature of the nation's participation in the conflict was as yet in doubt.

Various groups and individuals had their own reasons for seeking a more active war role. For Vargas armed participation meant time to restructure his government along more populist lines, while the people were distracted by military exploits. For the democratic camp participation was a pledge that the government that sent troops to fight Nazism-Fascism would restore democracy at home. For the military it was an unparalleled opportunity to become a modern fighting force of international stature, thereby strengthening its position in Brazilian society and vis-à-vis the armed forces of neighboring countries. And for some officers the war meant a purification of their former pro-Nazi images.

The idea of an expeditionary force and the desire for it developed in a haphazard way, buffeted by all the internal and external forces that had shaped Brazilian foreign policy in previous years. The army high command still contained a strong Germanophile element. Generals Dutra and Góes Monteiro were admirers of the German war machine, but they were also adept at survival in the army's internal politics and took a pro-allied stance rather than assume the ridiculous posture of favoring the losing side. They did not trust the United States, which already held bases on Brazilian territory, and they disliked the British, who had dominated the Luso-Brazilian world for so long. They were painfully aware of their military weakness and, although the American presence in the Northeast guaranteed support if the Axis attacked that region, the Brazilians understandably resented their dependence on the United States for war matériel. They became convinced that the only way to insure that the Americans would keep their promises to provide arms was to commit the Brazilian army to combat. But the practicality of sending an expeditionary force was debated heatedly. What worried the generals was the fantasy of Axis landings in Santa Catarina, where thousands of German and Italian immigrants of questionable loyalty could swell the invader's numbers and plunge Brazil into internal warfare. Such a situation would give Argentina an opportunity to attack, thereby opening a new front in the world conflict. This vision was not very convincing to allied officers involved in conventional warfare, but the Brazilian general staff had been nurtured on rebellion, civil war, and guerrilla campaigns. Their fears were not based on the events in Europe and North Africa as much as on the reality of Brazilian history.

A group of recent graduates of the army's General Staff School, centering on the former *tenente* Colonel Newton Estillac Leal and long-time supporters of the American alliance such as Oswaldo Aranha, generated a surge of enthusiasm for an expeditionary force. And in October and November 1942 some officers talked of an independent operation against Vichy's Guiana or Dakar. They were still smarting from the loss of friends and brother officers on the torpedoed *Baependi* (August 15, 1942) and dreamed of striking at those two supply-points for German submarines. And Guiana was indeed a center of German naval activity. In early November a Pan-American Airways pilot reported seeing six submarines moving up the Mana River in French Guiana, and, when a Brazilian steamer was sunk off the coast, French authorities suspiciously refused to receive the survivors. But American military authorities avoided a joint

occupation—they did not want to upset their delicate negotiations aimed at dividing the French in North Africa from
Vichy. Once that was accomplished the French could solve
the Guiana problem themselves.[4] Even so in December
pressure for active Brazilian participation increased almost
daily, especially as favorable reports rolled in concerning
the allied invasion of North Africa. Góes and Dutra exchanged ideas about an expeditionary force and the topic
was discussed in general staff circles.

Around mid-December Dutra asked a group of journalists to publish articles supporting the sending of a force to
North Africa. Shortly thereafter Foreign Minister Aranha
gave a speech asserting that Brazil should take a more active role in the war. The *Correio da Manhã* commented that
the time for street demonstrations against Nazi-Fascist ag-
gressions had passed, and that now Brazil was preparing
to do "what our North American allies are doing." Then
José Eduardo de Macedo Soares, in his *Diário Carioca* column, sounded the keynote in the rising chorus of dissatisfaction with Brazil's passive stance; the armed forces were
ready and willing to fight, he said, and were only waiting
for orders. On December 31 Getúlio told a group of officers
that the nation would not limit its activity to expeditions of
symbolic units, and that his government was ready to fulfill
Brazil's hemispheric obligations.[5]

So Brazil was going to the war. But desires are not reality
and decisions are not actions. The Brazilian army was
spread in units of regimental size from Amazonas and
Pernambuco to Minas Gerais, Mato Grosso, and Rio
Grande do Sul. Staging areas were nonexistent, as were
troop ships. And the army's hodgepodge of weaponry was

[4] Message, ATC Belém to ATC Atkinson, Nov. 7, 1942 as in History
SADATC, Part II, Chap. V, 114; SLC Minutes, Nov. 18, 1942, NA.

[5] *Correio da Manhã*, Rio, Dec. 23, 1942; *Diário Carioca*, Rio, Dec.
24, 1942; Getúlio Vargas, *A Nova Política do Brasil* (Rio de Janeiro,
1938-47), IX, 325. This was at an armed forces' luncheon at Santos
Dumont Airport in Rio de Janeiro.

needed to defend the home front. The general staff's problems in mounting an expedition were even greater than those which the American army had confronted in mobilizing for the war with Spain. In 1898 the Americans had a comprehensive railroad system, naval transports, a munitions industry, a sprinkling of combat veterans, and overflowing confidence—the Brazilians in 1942–1943 had none of these. If they were going to the front it would have to be in American vessels, with American weapons, and as it turned out even in American boots. Not only would the expeditionaries and their supporters have to struggle with detractors, defeatists, and fifth-columnists in Brazil, they would also have to gain the assistance and confidence of their American allies.

And it was not surprising that American leaders thought they could win the war without Brazilian troops. The American army was reluctant to clutter the field with small allied forces competing for glory. The Mexicans had wanted to send troops to North Africa, and the United States ambassador in Madrid was saying that Latin American units would strengthen the Spanish and Portuguese determination not to join the Axis. The State Department thought Latin American participation would convince the European governments that hemispheric solidarity was a reality. But the War Department turned down the Mexicans because, it claimed, of a lack of shipping and a variety of training and supply problems.[6]

The Brazilians could not be put off so easily because of the important United States bases on their soil, the close cooperation of their navy in the antisubmarine campaign, the vital natural resources they were supplying, and the need to keep their good will in case of conflict with Argentina. In November 1942 the Standing Liaison Committee considered the question of Brazilian participation. The army wanted to avoid even the sending of Brazilian liaison offi-

[6] SLC Minutes, Nov. 18, 1942, and Feb. 8, 1943, NA.

cers to General Dwight D. Eisenhower's headquarters; they had just turned down the Poles and were afraid of burdening their field army with a multiplicity of foreign officers. Eisenhower said his headquarters was already much too crowded. The army was willing to accept Brazilian observers, however, because observers could be accorded less attention than liaison officers. Sumner Welles said that the State Department was very much interested in treating "our Brazilian friends as though they were in the war with us, as they are facing that part of Africa." He did not think they would want to send mere observers when Vargas had expressed willingness to send troops. The army's attitude was that it could not use Brazilian troops in North Africa because it lacked shipping and the Brazilians did not have the type of personnel and equipment needed. With allied troops in North Africa the danger of a German invasion of northeast Brazil was decreasing steadily and with it the American desire to station combat troops in the northeast. The army's willingness to mollify the Brazilians was in direct proportion to what it wanted from them. The army already had the bases and the supplies were flowing, so why worry about the Brazilians? The aims and interests of Brazilian foreign policy were of little import to the American general staff. But in Welles' view the United States was committed to an alliance with Brazil which it should not take lightly.[7]

Direct presidential action and strong advice from American military representatives in Brazil would reverse the army staff's attitude in January 1943. Early in that month the military attaché in Rio reported that a large and growing group of officers, mostly recent graduates of the Gen-

[7] *Ibid.*; Dwight D. Eisenhower to George C. Marshall, London, Oct. 20, 1942, in Alfred D. Chandler and Stephen E. Ambrose, eds., *The Papers of Dwight David Eisenhower, The War Years* (Baltimore, 1970), pp. 628, 630. Anthony Eden, the British Secretary of State for Foreign Affairs, apparently supported the idea of a Brazilian mission being sent to the Allied Headquarters, see p. 630.

eral Staff School, wanted to organize a combat expeditionary force, they also wanted to remove from the government
all Axis sympathizers and "lukewarm" officials, including
Dutra, and they would accomplish this by peaceful persuasion of Vargas. The attaché warned that Brazilian enthusiasm for participation could not continue to be "dis-
missed in cavalier fashion without a harmful effect on the
attitude of Brazil toward the war and its allies."[8]

About two weeks later the Joint Brazil-United States Defense Commission (JBUSDC) recommended that the defenses
of north and northeast Brazil should be strengthened to
three infantry divisions, one motor division, one infantry
brigade, and appropriate coastal and antiaircraft artillery.
The equipment was to be supplied via the lend-lease program. These forces were greater than necessary for defense
of the region but, in the commission's words, they would
"constitute a force capable of being employed in other
operations in collaboration with American forces. . . ."[9]
With that recommendation the commission changed its
mission from planning the joint defense of the northeast to
lobbying for Brazilian participation in the fighting. Unless
the Brazilians actually fielded troops they could never hope
to pry from the Americans enough modern equipment to
outfit three infantry divisions.[10] The American members of
the JBUSDC were thus supporting the goals of the Brazilian
army against the position of the American general staff.

While the Americans were sorting out their attitudes,
Vargas flew to Natal to meet Roosevelt, carrying with him
Aranha's detailed review of Brazilian policy vis-à-vis the
war. Aranha did not think that the allies needed Brazilian

[8] W. N. Walmsley to Stephen Bonsal and Laurence Duggan, Memo
for DAR, Jan. 5, 1943, 832.20/515, NA.

[9] Col. Kenner F. Hertford (JBUSDC) to Orme Wilson (State Dept.
Liaison at War Dept.), Jan. 23, 1943, 832.20/488, NA. This was JBUSDC
Recommendation 14, Jan. 20, 1943.

[10] Stetson Conn and Byron Fairchild, *The Framework of Hemisphere
Defense* (Washington, 1960), p. 328.

forces, but even so Brazil should prepare as if it were going to enter combat immediately, in order to be ready if military action became necessary to support or defend Brazilian interests. "This preparation," he told Getúlio, "by itself, without our being called to battle, will be counted as one or more victories at the peace table."[11] Aranha believed, as did General Dutra, that a nation's voice was heard in direct proportion to the number of cannon it possessed. In the next months he came to realize that the Brazilian-American alliance by itself was not sufficient to obtain assistance from the United States. Washington was under the sway of men who gave precedence to short-range military objectives and to national interests rather than to broader alliances, or to Pan-American or world interests, and Aranha gradually came to understand that the Americans would supply only forces directly involved in operations of interest to the United States. This was disappointing; he would have preferred to build Brazil's military and industrial power without the expense of actual combat.

One of the objectives of Aranha's war policy was to gain greater ascendancy over Portugal and its possessions, which he referred to as "a patrimony that is hereditarily Brazilian." Indeed, he expected Brazil to play a key role in the whole question of European colonies, especially the Guianas.[12] During the meeting of the two presidents Brazilian and American desires conveniently appeared to converge. Roosevelt said that the United States military authorities preferred that Brazil, instead of sending troops to North Africa, arrange with Salazar for Brazilian replacement of Portuguese forces in the Azores and Madeira islands, thereby enabling Portugal to strengthen its home defenses. Vargas was willing to take up the question with Salazar, but re-

[11] Aranha to Vargas, Rio, Jan. 25, 1943, OAA; Vargas also had a memo from Dutra, written in early January, urging that any expeditionary force be a large one, see José Cão, *Dutra* (São Paulo, 1949), pp. 145–146.

[12] Aranha to Vargas, Rio, Jan. 25, 1943, OAA.

minded Roosevelt that he could not send troops "unless you furnish adequate equipment for them."[13] Roosevelt apparently committed himself to providing the necessary material because Vargas returned to Rio thoroughly pleased and enthusiastic, and, shortly after Roosevelt reached Washington, the War Department "reversed its position and supported the employment of Brazilian troops abroad."[14]

The Natal conference marked a shift in United States policy toward Brazil. Previously American interests did not appear to be tied to Brazil's war role, but after Natal Washington officials began looking toward peace, and thinking that if another American republic took part in the war it would strengthen the United States position as leader of and spokesman for the Americas in the postwar period. The national interests of Brazil and the United States drew closer together. General Dutra told the American military attaché to drop in any time, that it was no longer necessary to make an appointment. The intimate working relationship between the Itamaraty and the United States Embassy was now to be matched in the military sphere. Even Aranha began to think that Vargas had been right in keeping Dutra in the cabinet, because he was now cooperating wholeheartedly with "our side" and he had the virtue of lacking popularity. As Aranha expressed Vargas' attitude: "A popular Minister of War might get ambitious and cause us no

---

[13] Caffery, Rio, Jan. 30, 1943, 740.0011 EW 1939/27588, NA. The British invoked the old Anglo-Luzo Alliance to obtain use of bases in the Azores. In return Britain gave equipment to the Portuguese army, provided protection to Portuguese trade and shipping and "gave assurances about the maintenance of Portugal's sovereignty over all her colonies." Anthony Eden, *The Reckoning, The Memoirs of Anthony Eden* (Boston, 1965), pp. 392–393. For a full discussion of the question see Hugh Kay, *Salazar and Modern Portugal* (New York, 1970), pp. 165–170.

[14] Conn and Fairchild, *Framework*, p. 328.

end of trouble."[15] Gradually, Dutra's fascist coloring faded in American eyes.[16]

Even though the Portuguese operation did not materialize, the idea of a Brazilian expeditionary corps had taken hold in the minds of key policy-makers in both countries by April 1943. The zone of employment was unimportant, although at that time they were talking of North Africa. In mid-April the Brazilian representative to the JBUSDC in Washington, General Leitão de Carvalho, formally expressed to General Marshall Brazil's desire to form a three- to four-division corps. Marshall endorsed the proposal and forwarded it to the Joint Chiefs of Staff, who approved it in principle in the first week of May. But it was obvious to all the Americans concerned that equipping such a force would be a major problem.

On May 7 the JBUSDC, including Generals J. Garesche Ord (chief United States delegate and president of the commission) and Leitão de Carvalho, flew to Brazil to arrange the details of the Brazilian force's employment. At their stop in Miami they received news of the Axis surrender in North Africa, which eliminated the possibility of sending the expeditionaries there or to the Portuguese islands. In Brazil they encountered an unexpected difference of opinion as to which troops were to be employed, their staging area, and the amount of training material the United States was to provide. The commission's Recommendation No. 14 of January 20 had implied that the forces in the northeast were to be prepared for possible use abroad, and now that a German thrust from North Africa was no longer a danger a strong Brazilian garrison in that region was unnecessary. Therefore the Americans thought the northeastern units

[15] Caffery, Rio, Feb. 23, 1943, 832.002/215, NA. The reported conversation with Aranha took place on Feb. 22, 1943.

[16] Although Dutra became less suspect, some American officials, particularly in the State Department, harbored a continuing distrust of General Góes Monteiro. See, for example, comments in Walmsley to A. Berle, Washington, Jan. 21, 1943, 832.30/502, NA.

should form the expeditionary force. Some of the Brazilian army, however, suspected that the United States would attempt to keep the bases after the war—so it would be well to maintain sizable national forces in the north. General Dutra preferred to establish three new training centers in Rio de Janeiro, São Paulo, and the northeast. And he wanted the United States to provide each center with 50 percent of a division's normal complement of equipment. While General Leitão de Carvalho concealed his dismay at the impracticality of his chief's wishes, General Ord made clear that he could not see wasting the efforts already expended on training troops in the northeast, moreover Rio and São Paulo lacked facilities for training a division. And because the United States could supply only 50 percent of one division's gear he thought that they should follow up the start made in the northeast and establish a national training center there. The three divisions would be prepared successively: each division could use the allotted equipment and leave it for the next, as the troops would be reequipped when they arrived in the theater of operations. The careful planning of the JBUSDC was not to the liking of the Brazilian general staff. But at least Ord and Leitão de Carvalho could find hope for agreement in Dutra's request that his forces serve under American field commanders and not be placed with some other allied army. It was clear that Brazil would commit its troops, but the gap between Dutra's preferences on their training and supply and the Americans' suggestions could not be closed.[17]

Leitão de Carvalho and Ord watched maneuvers in the northeast and returned to the United States favorably impressed with the troops' state of training. Ord wrote Mar-

[17] Interview, Estevão Leitão de Carvalho, Rio, Sept. 9, 1965. Leitão de Carvalho thought that Dutra's passive resistance to the American alliance and his generally pro-Axis attitude caused Dutra to be unenthusiastic toward him. Their difficulty in working together comes across clearly in Leitão de Carvalho's *A Serviço do Brasil na Segunda Guerra Mundial* (Rio de Janeiro, 1952), pp. 298–320.

shall that Brazil intended to fight abroad, that its army would perform well after four to eight months of training with modern equipment, and that Vargas had agreed to accept the strategic direction of the United States for the employment of the Brazilian Expeditionary Force (FEB).[18] The JBUSDC arranged special training courses for Brazilian officers at various American installations: the three most important were the Command and General Staff School at Ft. Leavenworth, Kansas, the Infantry School at Ft. Benning, Georgia, and the Artillery School at Ft. Sill, Oklahoma. Eventually most of the key officers of the FEB would attend one or more of the courses. Brazilian officers had been taking various courses at American military schools since 1938, but after June 1943 the rate increased so that by the end of 1944 over 1,000 Brazilian military personnel had passed through such schools.[19]

[18] See Memos, Gen. Ord to Chief of Staff, June 7, 1943, and Ord to G-2, June 16, 1943, in OPD 336 Brazil, WWII RS, NA, as summarized in Conn and Fairchild, *Framework*, p. 328. Although I read all of the Brazilian material in the War Dept. papers in WWII RS, the security regulations would not allow detailed note-taking in quantity. The notes I took were reviewed by the Adjutant General's Office and after much delay returned with deletions. While doing the research I had determined that Conn and Fairchild's work contained faithful summaries of many of the documents that I wanted, so I have indicated the locations of various documents, both in WWII RS and in their book, against the day when the WWII records are fully declassified.

[19] "History of United States Army Forces, South Atlantic," pp. 13–17. This official command history was composed in General Walsh's headquarters in Recife. At this writing the copy in the Office of the Chief of Military History, Department of the Army, Washington, is still classified. Leitão de Carvalho discussed the training programs in *Serviço do Brasil*, pp. 358–363. Attendance at U.S. Army schools gave considerable prestige in Brazilian army circles. See comments in Floriano de Lima Brayner, *A Verdade Sôbre a FEB, Memórias de um Chefe de Estado-Maior na Campanha da Itália* (Rio de Janeiro, 1968), p. 54. By the war's end 259 Brazilian officers had taken courses at the Command and General Staff School at Fort Leavenworth, Kansas. They were the largest group from any one nation. The only ones close to them were the Chinese with 249 officers and the British with 208, while

Things appeared to be progressing nicely. Even such antagonists as Dutra and Aranha seemed to be getting friendly. When in July Vargas, with Dutra's approval, conferred the Order of Military Merit on Aranha, Dutra lauded the foreign minister as "a dedicated friend" of the army who understood its mission and role in national life, and a patriot who had realized "in the most intimate liaison with us" the ever-closer ties with the United States, "source of all our present resources and firm point of aid to our national defense."[20]

The Aranha-Dutra rapprochement, however, did not eliminate misunderstanding among Brazilians or Americans concerning the FEB's purpose. From a popular point of view it was to redeem the national honor for the German sinkings of Brazilian ships and to place Brazil in the midst of the great crusade to save civilization. On the official level, Aranha and Vargas had their eyes on the peace conference, and Vargas was extremely pleased with FDR's comment at Natal that he wanted Getúlio at his side at the peace table.[21] The Americans, on the other side, wanted to improve their image as leaders of the Western Hemisphere—if Brazil sent troops Washington's claim to speak for the American republics in allied councils would be enhanced. And if the Americans wanted Brazil to serve as a pro-American bulwark in South America, it was because of their own national interests. As for Dutra, he was obsessed with the need to increase his army's effective strength and ability to deal with any contingency, including possible difficulties with the Americans in the northeast, the Argentines, or the German immigrants. In March Vargas had stipulated that sending troops abroad would not eliminate the necessity of main-

---

the next largest groups from Latin America were the Venezuelans with 73, the Mexicans with 60, and the Argentines with 31. These figures are based on records at Fort Leavenworth.

[20] Eurico Dutra to Aranha, Rio, July 12, 1943, OAA.

[21] Caffery to Roosevelt, Rio, Feb. 9, 1943, PSF Brazil Folder, FDRL.

taining the defense of the northeast, albeit with comparatively minimum effectiveness. In mid-July, however, Dutra wanted as the condition for sending the expeditionary corps "the existence on national territory of equivalent and equally armed forces, to guarantee our sovereignty and the maintenance of order and tranquility here."[22] Many of the uncertainties that the FEB faced before reaching Italy in July 1944 were due to Brazilian inexperience with such large units, to shipping shortages, to American preoccupation with the great powers and a growing impatience with Brazilian slowness and hesitancy, and to the poor communications between the two allies and among the respective sections of their governments. But Dutra's unwillingness to send his troops off to war without simultaneously securing the home front was perhaps the key problem.

In August 1943 Dutra flew to the United States to work out an agreement on the proposed expeditionary corps. In previous weeks he had asked various generals to accept command of one of the FEB divisions. Apparently most of them declined, except for three officers including the com-

[22] Vargas to Leitão de Carvalho, Rio, Mar. 29, 1943 and E. Dutra to Leitão de Carvalho, Rio, July 17, 1943; both summarized and quoted in part in Leitão de Carvalho, *Serviço do Brasil*, pp. 310–311. Was Dutra truly worried about the Americans refusing to leave the bases after the war? It is true that the U.S. authorities began to think seriously of staying on in some fashion toward the end of 1943. The Argentine certainly worried Dutra's staff. It is, however, possible (if one follows the reasoning of General Nelson Werneck Sodré and others, that the post-1945 regime was the Estado Nôvo without Getúlio) to argue that Dutra wanted the army to maintain its force level in Brazil to insure the status quo. Could he have been worried in 1943 and 1944 that Getúlio would try to shift toward the left? After all, this is what happened in 1945, and the army quickly deposed the president. If national security vis-à-vis the Americans or the Argentines was paramount in the general's considerations why did he order dissolution of the FEB even before it returned from Italy and why was it disbanded the very day it disembarked in Rio de Janeiro? Some of these questions are dealt with below in Chapters 14 and 15. For Sodré see his *História Militar do Brasil* (Rio de Janeiro, 1965), pp. 289–304.

manding general of the São Paulo military region, João Batista Mascarenhas de Moraes, a short, quiet, intensely introverted, austerely rigid artillery officer, who was designated to lead the first division. According to Góes Monteiro, General Newton Cavalcanti, an extreme rightist and foremost military protector of the Integralistas, and General Heitor Borges, a respected officer, were to command the other two divisions, while Dutra was eventually to take charge of the full corps. Dutra, rather than first division commander Mascarenhas, selected the first division's staff, and issued a ministerial directive on August 9 designating units from four different military regions for integration into the division. This first and, as it turned out, the only expeditionary division was created in patchwork fashion, instead of ordering up one of the existing peacetime divisions. Unfortunately some units chosen were not the best of their type and had had no previous contact with one another. This mobilization of units scattered throughout Brazil underscored Dutra's determination not to use the northeastern forces. Perhaps, because the new division was to follow the American model rather than the Brazilianized French one, Dutra felt that only by mixing units and breaking their previous loyalties could he ensure their adjusting to the new milieu and developing a new esprit de corps.[23] At any rate, the basic organizational steps had been taken by the time Dutra arrived in Washington in mid-August.

Aranha had written him a long letter setting out what he hoped Brazil would gain from the endeavor. Asserting that the war had transformed the historic cooperation between the two countries into "a true alliance of destinies," he was

[23] Lourival Coutinho, *O General Góes Depõe* (Rio de Janeiro, 1956), p. 388. For the difficulties involved see Brayner, *Verdade*, pp. 16–52; for a platoon leader's view see Agostinho José Rodrigues, *Segundo Pelotão, 8a Companhia* (São Paulo, 1969), pp. 17–33. 8th Company was part of 3d Batt., 11th Infantry Regiment from São João del Rei, Minas Gerais. For the details of Mascarenhas' career see his *Memórias* (Rio de Janeiro, 1969), 2 vols.

certain that Dutra's visit would show him that Brazil had to adjust militarily, as it was already adjusting politically and economically, to American principles and resources. Although such adhesion carried grave dangers and even a "certain submission" incompatible with Brazilian national sovereignty and interests, it was necessary to accept the risks because Brazil by itself would not be able to protect its unexplored lands and riches. "The aggressive expansionism that characterized the xix and xx centuries did not threaten the existence of Brazil," he wrote, "because we never had economic autonomy nor even political-military existence." But now Brazil was gaining the attributes of a nation, and unless it allied itself "materially, morally, and militarily" to the United States "the future of Brazil will be everyone's except the Brazilians'." That was why he had worked since 1938 for approximation with the United States —it was a course of action that offered the greatest security and fewest risks. He was not speaking in absolute terms nor affirming that this policy would resolve all of their international problems. Far from it; it was the lesser evil, and they would have to maintain constant vigilance to avoid its pitfalls while striving to extract the hoped-for benefits. It was necessary that the Americans understand that the Brazilians having chosen their course and their companions for the journey, would not alter their route or hesitate in their advance. The Americans must not think that they were fakers seeking safety and comfort, but must believe that they were willing to share the tragic tests of war. Aranha obviously saw the expeditionary corps as the proof of commitment that the Puritan, crusading conscience of the United States demanded.

American assistance was essential to Brazil's industrialization—"the first defense against external and internal danger"—and everything "must be sacrificed to the necessity of truly installing basic war industries in Brazil." And Aranha, like Dutra, was preoccupied with the nation's lack of military preparedness. His solution was to use the expeditionary corps as a starting point for a wider collaboration that would involve a total reorganization and development of Brazil's military reserves and resources; moreover, he feared that if they restricted themselves simply to an expeditionary corps the Americans would abandon them. Finally, he reminded the minister of war that in the postwar world standing armies would be required for some time to insure order.[24]

On August 10 Góes Monteiro returned to his duties as chief of staff after a protracted leave for illness. American foreign service officers said that the illness was caused by Brazil's going to war with Germany, but such a view seems unduly harsh.[25] Góes sent a letter with Dutra for General Marshall, which recalled Góes' and Marshall's efforts in forging the preliminary military agreements in 1939 and expressed the hope that Marshall would give Dutra the means to increase Brazil's military contribution to the allied war effort. "You are very well acquainted," he wrote Marshall, "with our potentialities, our difficulties to equip, to transport and to supply an Expeditionary Force, no matter how small in size. . . . As you are aware our military organization, with regard to its command, administration and its very structure, as well as the training of the troops, is modelled upon the decadent French pattern. Thus to geographical and material obstacles will be added the difficulties of planning and understanding in a realistic way the type of modern warfare we should be called upon to face . . . I feel, however, that the most important point I should impress upon you is our wholehearted determination to throw in all our resources in joint cooperation with the

[24] Aranha to Dutra, Rio, Aug. 11, 1943, OAA. Aranha used the word order (*ordem*) not peace (*paz*). He wrote: "É necessario, Dutra, não esquercer de que o mundo futuro exigirá, para resguardar a ordem durante muito tempo, que as nações não voltem ao estado de paz, mas se mantenham no chamado 'pé de guerra.' "

[25] Caffery, Rio, Aug. 11, 1943, 832.20/542, NA; Walmsley to Berle, Washington, Jan. 21, 1943, 832.30/502, NA.

United States of America. . . ."[26] Dutra also bore a letter from Vargas to Roosevelt, stressing the Brazilian army's "very real desire" to take part in the European war.[27]

The Brazilian minister of war arrived in Miami on August 15, took part in a session of JBUSDC on August 21 in Washington, met with Marshall and other War Department officials, and then spent a month touring military installations. Marshall, who had supervised the military aspects of the American wooing of Brazil, could not help but be satisfied that his efforts were culminating in a Brazilian contribution of troops. Roosevelt termed Brazil's attitude "generous," and instructed Marshall to do all he could to facilitate matters. Eisenhower had stated that he could use up to three divisions, and the hope in the War Department was that the first would be sent overseas sometime in December. [28]

But Dutra and the Americans, indeed Dutra and the Brazilian military representatives in Washington, were still talking past each other. In an effort to get as much equipment into Brazil as possible, he insisted that the JBUSDC approve his wish to set up three separate training centers, one in the Recife area, and the other two near Rio de Janeiro and São Paulo. Not only did he want each to receive 50 percent of a division's full equipment complement, but he wanted the defense units in the northeast to continue receiving equipment. The American officials refused, insisting that the arms-supply situation could not permit such a large amount to be used needlessly in training troops. Very reasonably, they could not see why, since the divisions were to be trained successively, they should not be trained in the same place. Dutra had chosen the wrong time to push the

[26] Góes Monteiro to George Marshall, Rio, Aug. 9, 1943, OAA. The letter was sent with the official English translation quoted here.

[27] Caffery, Rio, Aug. 9, 1943, 832.20/541, NA.

[28] Roosevelt to Vargas, n.p., Sept. 14, 1943, PPF 4473 (Vargas), FDRL; Laurence Duggan to Berle and Edward R. Stettinius, DAR, Oct. 22, 1943, 740.0011 EW 1939/32096, NA.

establishment of permanent training centers at American expense. To make matters worse, his insistence on not using the already trained units in the northeast forced the cessation of arms deliveries to them, because the agreement covering deliveries stipulated that they would continue as long as the region was in need of defense, or until, by implication, the troops were to be used elsewhere.

Moreover, Dutra's cold treatment of his own representative, Leitão de Carvalho, a well-known supporter of constitutional government and of the American alliance, raised doubts in Washington about the sincerity of the Brazilian high command. American military intelligence agents and the United States Embassy and consular officers carefully watched and reported every twist and turn of Brazilian politics in the next two years. Photograph files and career histories of Brazilian officers were compiled. The basic questions seemed to be: who was friend and who was foe? would the FEB actually embark? and if Vargas were turned out of office would the succeeding government continue the alliance? But, confusing as the Brazilian scene may have been, after Dutra's visit Brazil's commitment to sending troops was sealed. Brazil's international prestige, not to mention national pride, the status of the Vargas regime, and the position of the Brazilian army depended on the FEB.

An interesting sidelight to Dutra's visit was that the agreements, reached while he was in Washington and later, did not project an independent Brazilian command or sector but a Brazilian corps serving as part of an American army. Even on an operational level the agreements permitted American superior officers to detach individual Brazilian units and place them under direct American control, or to assign American units to Brazilian operational control.[29] The Brazilians would have no seat on the allied war council, and no representatives at Eisenhower's headquarters. Their forces would be entirely dependent on the

[29] Leitão de Carvalho, *Serviço do Brasil*, p. 352.

American armed forces for transportation to the theater of operations, for equipment, training, and all manner of supply and servicing, including chewing gum and chocolate bars in their daily rations. Even their pay and mail systems were dependent.

Why was this? Partly from inexperience, partly from the bureaucratic weakness of the Vargas regime that encouraged individual officials to avoid responsibility or to minimize it, partly from humility, and a sense that the weak must seek the protection of the strong. Perhaps too the Brazilian leadership had lived for so long in a world where all was potential, where the smallest step was supermagnified, where dreams, words, and gestures counted as heavily as realizations, that they were overconcerned with the FEB's symbolism and underconcerned with the reality of war. Moreover, they displayed a poor understanding of American psychology. If participation was to win a strong voice in postwar councils and secure American assistance in transforming Brazil into a military power then the Brazilians would have to gain the respect and admiration of their allies—and not just that of Roosevelt, Hull, Welles, Marshall, and a few generals, but of the American people. In World War I, General John J. Pershing had refused to place the American Expeditionary Force under foreign operational control. In choosing the opposite course did the Brazilians expect admiration and respect? The military cannot be blamed entirely for this state of affairs, because Dutra took care to send Vargas and Aranha copies of the operational agreement in order to be certain that it was "in line with the highest interests of our foreign policy."[30] The Brazilian commitment to the military alliance with the United States was emphasized in November, when Vichy offered to send a former chief of the French Military Mission as military attaché so that he could help train the FEB. The Brazilians turned down the suggestion, saying they pre-

[30] Dutra to Aranha, Rio, Oct. 21, 1943, OAA.

ferred someone else and that the Americans were preparing the FEB.[31]

During these diplomatic moves the FEB was being organized. A Brazilian mission headed by General Mascarenhas de Moraes flew to North Africa and southern Italy, to establish liaison with American forces and presumably to study the front-line situation for planning purposes. But if the latter was done at all it did not filter back to those training the troops in Brazil. The chief of the FEB's staff, Colonel Floriano de Lima Brayner, was often disheartened by the lack of information on their future employment, and equally unhappy with the inexperienced, mediocre reserve officers sent by the United States to train the Brazilians. There were constant misunderstandings because of the language problem. One American, descendent of Azorian Portuguese, could speak their language, but with such a heavy Azorian inflection that he was difficult to understand. Among the other Americans a few spoke a little Spanish and the rest only English. The Brazilian officers, many of whom spoke French or Spanish, thought this indicated the Americans' low level of education and culture, as did their crude and uncordial behavior. Putting it mildly, Brayner said "they did not understand our people."[32]

The Axis propaganda machine and Brazil's collective paranoia combined to spread defeatist rumors that the FEB would never sail, or that it would be given antiquated weapons to fight crack German troops, or that once the troops had embarked the United States would use the bases to occupy Brazil. The regime's enemies began whispering and circulating handbills urging that the FEB stay home to overthrow the dictatorship.[33] Vargas was able to ignore

[31] Wilson (U.S. Consul), Algiers, Nov. 27, 1943, 832.20/564, NA.

[32] Brayner, *Verdade*, p. 50. Aguinaldo José Senna Campos, who as a major headed the 4th section of the division staff, described the tour of North Africa and Italy in his *Com a FEB na Itália, Paginas do Meu Diário* (Rio de Janeiro, 1970), pp. 30–54.

[33] Caffery, Rio, Nov. 10, 1943, 832.00/4500, NA.

such rumblings, or control them with police repression, but the so-called Minas Manifesto, calling for a return to constitutionalism after the war and signed by prominent Mineiros including former President Artur Bernardes, indicated that opposition politicians were beginning to stir. The army, however, except for some officers who opposed the FEB, was solidly behind the president. Observers, indeed, felt that if he had called elections at the end of 1943 he would have been reelected easily, because of his great popularity with the masses, especially urban labor.[34]

Uncertainty still held the FEB in its grip as 1943 came to a close. Not only had no sailing date been set, but the designated units were still in their scattered home barracks under the control of their respective regional commanders. The FEB staff could not properly conduct training, since it could not exercise command over the separated units. Local commanders even interfered with staff inspections, and merely getting the designated infantry regiments up to strength was a major task. The nine infantry regiments in the Rio de Janeiro-Belo Horizonte-São Paulo triangle were stationed in eight widely-separated towns, while the approximately 38,000 active army personnel in that region were based in some thirty-three different places. These men were intimately tied to the lives of their respective communities. Regimental personnel frequently came from the surrounding region and often lived in the town with their families, going to the barracks for duty the way their neighbors went to work in shops and factories. When a man was reassigned his family went with him. In normal times such moves were tolerable and infrequent, but when the 11th Infantry Regiment (IR) of São João del Rei, Minas Gerais, received 1,600 men from the 12th IR in Belo Horizonte and the 10th IR in Juiz de Fora, and when the 6th IR in Caçapava, São Paulo, received similar newcomers, the garrison

[34] "Ao Povo Mineiro," Belo Horizonte, Oct. 24, 1943, OAA; Walter J. Dowling (2d Secretary U.S. Embassy), Rio, Oct. 29, 1943, 832.00/4489, NA; Caffery, Rio, Nov. 5, 1943, 832.00/4495, NA.

towns were bursting at their seams.[35] And what was to be done with the families when the units converged on the FEB concentration around Rio de Janeiro? The government's improvised arrangements for waiting wives and families played havoc with troop morale.

A profile of the Brazilian army in 1942 showed that the officers came largely from the urban middle class, which was a much more restricted group than in the contemporary United States. It was fashionable for officers' sons and those of civil servants and merchants to seek admittance to the military academy (see Table 1). The old aristocracy and others of wealth avoided military service by joining shooting clubs, which provided periodic military drill and enabled them after a year to pass into the reserve. The enlisted personnel were conscripts drawn from the working classes and were often illiterate or poorly educated. They displayed low resistance to disease and their morale seemed to be unusually dependent upon the leadership of their officers, who could easily influence them to action or to indecision. Officers generally treated their soldiers as social inferiors, and they themselves seemed motivated more by self-interest than by a sense of duty or esprit de corps. Lack of incentive was so prevalent that, in the opinion of American military observers, when compared to European armies the Brazilian army had "a small percentage of good officers with the balance only fair."[36]

The salary scale reflected the distance between officers and the lowest-ranked soldiers. A major general received the equivalent of US $250 a month, a captain $105, a second lieutenant $65, a first sergeant $30, a second corporal

[35] Rodrigues, *Segundo Pelotão*, pp. 27–30, describes his experience during mobilization. Data on unit distribution came from U.S. Military Intelligence Service, War Department, "Survey of the Rio de Janeiro Region of Brazil," Vol. 1, Aug. 6, 1942, 54, 232–333. Declassified copy in author's possession. Note that Infantry Regiment will be IR, with sub-units such as Third Company, Second Battalion of the 6th being denoted thus: 3/II/6 IR.

[36] *Ibid.*, pp. 56, 60–61.

TABLE 1 Father's Occupation of the 1,031 Cadets Entering
Brazilian Army Academy, 1941–1943

Traditional Upper Class	No.	Middle Class	No.	Skilled Lower Class	No.	Unskilled Lower Class	No.
Land-owner	39	Business executive	32	Electrician	1	Domestic help	13
Ambassador	1	Military	219	Craftsman	8		
Doctor	44	Merchant & tradesman	265	Seaman	4	Worker	7
Lawyer	42			Machinist	2	Peasant	4
Engineer	41	Civil servant	163				
Dentist	23	Accountant	23				
Magistrate	7	Bank Clerk	19				
Rentier	7	Teacher	26				
		Druggist	19				
		Small farmer	15				
		Miscellaneous	7				
Total	204 (19.8%)		788 (76.4%)		15 (1.5%)		24 (2.3%)

Source: Alfred Stepan, *The Military in Politics, Changing Patterns in Brazil* (Princeton, 1971), p. 32. Stepan compiled these figures from the files of the *Academia Militar das Agulhas Negras*. Reproduced with the author's permission.

$11.40, and a nonspecialist private $2.80. By comparison, the minimum wage in 1942 for a worker in São Paulo or Rio de Janeiro was about $.48 (US) a day, or $14.40 for a thirty-day work month, while during this period the cost of living hovered around $11 a month.[37]

Prewar mobilization plans had called for drawing on the reserves to double the peacetime strength of existing units

[37] *Ibid.*, p. 57.

and to create new ones. Each state comprised a recruiting district, and each municipality had a draft board charged with supervising the compulsory service law. The Ministry of War estimated that basic mobilization could be completed within ninety days, and that thereafter replacements and troops for new units could be called at the rate of 20,000 a month. At the time Brazil entered the war there supposedly was sufficient equipment available to arm and equip 150,000 troops. But since 50 percent of expendable ordnance, principally artillery shells and small arms ammunition, would have to be imported, because of a lack of raw materials and manufacturing facilities, these troops would not be able to operate for an extended period without foreign assistance.[38]

As the mobilization went forward it became painfully obvious even to the most optimistic staff officers that they would be lucky to get one division on board ship, let alone three. FEB officers were puzzled as to the criterion that the war ministry used in choosing expeditionary units. It would be charitable to attribute some of the choices to nothing more malicious than poor planning. The most absurd case, according to division chief of staff Brayner, was the selection of the 9th Engineer Battalion based in Aquidauana, Mato Grosso, as the combat engineer unit. It was under strength, and what men it did have left much to be desired. It had to be brought all the way to Três Rios between Petrópolis and Juiz de Fora (somewhat over 2,100 miles) before it could be filled out.[39]

On arrival at the various training areas the soldiers found themselves in improvised, uncomfortable sheds (*galpões*) hurriedly constructed with minimum regard for hygiene, or squeezed into overcrowded barracks (*quartéis*). Unfortunately raw recruits, troublesome soldiers, reserve of-

[38] *Ibid.*, pp. 57–59.
[39] The foregoing is based upon informal conversations with FEB veterans; on Brayner, *Verdade*, pp. 33ff., 40ff., 112; Rodrigues, *Segundo Pelotão*, pp. 17–33.

ficers, and new graduates of the military school at Realengo were used to bring the units up to strength, instead of other regulars. Rumor had it that student opponents of the regime were being dragooned into FEB units. At least 302 of the 870 infantry line-officers were reservists, many of them professional men in civilian life, including some medical doctors and engineers. Now they suddenly found themselves at the head of infantry platoons readying for combat. It was not surprising that some of them suffered psychoses before their "grand adventure" was over, and at least one tried to commit suicide. The new military-school graduates were often much younger than their troops but, given their age and complete lack of experience with regular army units, they acquitted themselves well.[40]

[40] Democrito Cavalcanti de Arruda, *et al.*, *Depoimento de Oficiais da Reserva Sôbre a F.E.B.* (Rio de Janeiro, 1949), pp. 41–48. The figure, 302 reservists among 870 infantry line officers, was calculated from the lists of officers in Mascarenhas de Moraes, *A FEB Pelo Seu Comandante* (2nd ed., Rio de Janeiro, 1960), pp. 346–355. My figures include only Aspirantes-a-Oficial (a rank between Cadet and 2nd Lt.) to Majors. There were two classes of reserve officers: R-1, who were sergeants promoted to 2nd Lts.; and R-2, who were graduates of the Centros de Preparação dos Oficiais da Reserva (CPOR; somewhat like ROTC) and held commissions from Aspirante to Captain. The R-2 group is the one I refer to as reservists. In the FEB as a whole there were 452 R-2 officers, or 29.37 percent of the 1,539 total officer group, 130 R-1's or 8.45 percent, and 957 regulars or 62.18 percent. I have no data on their relative distribution in units, but memoirs indicate that most of the reservists were in the first three echelons, that is those that saw combat. At least three students from the University of São Paulo were forcefully enlisted and saw action in Italy; see Cecil Cross (Consul-General), São Paulo, Jan. 11, 1945, 832.00/1-1145, DSF. Brazilian military education was being reorganized in the midst of the war. Since 1911 the three-year Escola Militar, Brazil's West Point, had been at Realengo in the then Federal District. In 1938 construction began on new buildings at Resende, State of Rio de Janeiro, which were completed in early 1944. During that year, while the second- and third-year cadets continued at Realengo, the first-year men studied at Resende. At the end of 1944 Realengo closed. In 1951 the Escola Militar de Resende received its present name, Academia Militar das Agulhas

Many of the recruits, and indeed an embarrassing number of regular soldiers in the units called up, were found upon reexamination in Rio de Janeiro to be medically unfit. It seems that the medical selection boards in the military regions had been assembled hurriedly to examine hundreds and in some areas thousands of men. Usually the boards consisted of three doctors, two of whom handled administration while the third gave rapid inspections which, according to statistics gathered by Carlos Paiva Gonçalves of the Brazilian Army Health Service, rejected a low 23,236 out of a total of 107,609 examined. Poor teeth or poor physical condition were the most common reasons listed for rejection.[41] Even so the FEB dentists would find themselves overloaded with basic dental work in Italy, performing 16,015 examinations, 10,399 treatments, 9,071 extractions, and 8,329 fillings.[42] In the opinion of one medical doctor, who served in the 6th Infantry Regiment as an infantry platoon leader, the examinations given to his unit at Caçapava before moving to the staging area "could not have been more summary."[43] The reexaminations, though leaving much to be desired, turned up cases of tuberculosis, imbecility, hernia, color-blindness, parasites, circulatory and

Negras. A historical survey of the military school is in Umberto Peregrino, *História e Projeção das Instituições Culturais do Exército* (Rio de Janeiro, 1967), pp. 53–92. Gen. Nelson Werneck Sodré describes his cadet years at Realengo between 1931 and 1934 in *Memórias de um Soldado* (Rio de Janeiro, 1967), pp. 59–93. Graduating cadets received the initial rank of Aspirante-a-Oficial. According to Brayner those that were assigned to the FEB were promoted to 2nd Lt. on the day of departure; Brayner, *Verdade*, p. 112.

41 Carlos Paiva Gonçalves (Lt. Col. Medical Corps, Brazilian Army), *Seleção Medica do Pessoal da F.E.B., Histórico, Funcionamento e Dados Estatísticos* (Rio de Janeiro, 1951), pp. 67–142.

42 *Ibid.*, p. 104.

43 The M.D. was Massaki Udihara of São Paulo, a 1936 CPOR graduate, who was called to active duty in December 1942; see his "Um Médico na Infantaria," in *Depoimento de Oficiais da Reserva*, pp. 137–155. The quotation is from p. 151.

respiratory problems, and even two victims of leprosy. But despite efforts to correct flaws in the selection process there were cases of unhealthy men being sent abroad. Two extreme examples were a soldier suffering from epilepsy and an officer with chronic hepatitis, displaying periodic jaundice, who embarked in the first echelon.[44]

Psychological testing was not done, although medical authorities had tests in preparation that were to be applied to the second division which was never formed. Paiva Gonçalves observed that such testing might have avoided some of the 433 cases of mental disturbance which the FEB's health service treated in Italy.[45] None of the foregoing is intended to suggest that the FEB was composed of misfits or that it did not perform courageously; rather it emphasizes that its victories were gained in spite of deficiencies—and deficiencies that could have been avoided. At one point in the winter of 1944–1945 a FEB doctor reported that 400 out of 600 soldiers in one battalion required hospitalization. Higher command rejected his advice and the battalion was sent into the line facing Monte Castello. As a result the 4th Company, II Battalion of the 6th Infantry Regiment held the key position of Torre de Nerone with forty men, or one-fifth of its effective strength.[46] General Mascarenhas noted

[44] *Ibid.*, p. 145. He wrote: "Na 3a Companhia do mesmo Batalhão [1 Batt., 6 IR] um soldado, na lufa-luffa dos preparativos de embarque, teve um ataque epilético . . . Êsse soldado também embarcou." Further on he described the officer's case: ". . . havia um oficial [6 IR] com um processo hepático crônico que, periòdicamente, apresentava crises de icterícia." Although he was under the care of another infantry officer who was a medical doctor in civilian life, he was classified for inclusion in the FEB. During the voyage and after arrival in Italy he sustained attacks and was finally hospitalized. A colonel in the medical service told him that he should have stayed in Brazil but now that he was in Italy he could not remain in the hospital. However, he could not be sent home, so: "Agora tem que ficar aqui [Italy] por uma questão de patriotismo." *Ibid.*, p. 152.

[45] Paiva Gonçalves, *Seleção Medica*, p. 103.

[46] Massaki Udihara, "Um Medíco na Infantaria," *Depoimento de Oficiais da Reserva*, pp. 146–147.

that of the 11,617 casualties (*baixas*), between July 1944 and May 1945, 8,480 were due to illness.[47] Health problems represented a constant threat to morale, a drain on much-needed medical facilities, and a serious reduction of combat efficiency. Given the precarious physical condition of so many expeditionaries, their successes were nothing less than spectacular.[48]

The medical examinations were an interesting side-effect of the FEB, because they were carried out nationally and cut across socioeconomic class lines. They gave a depressing picture of Brazil's health situation: widespread malnutrition, poor physical development, tuberculosis, dental deficiencies, syphilis and related lesions and disfunctions of

[47] Mascarenhas, *FEB*, p. 402.

[48] Manoel Thomaz Castello Branco, who was a Captain in the 1 IR, commented in his *O Brasil na II Grande Guerra* (Rio de Janeiro, 1960), pp. 139–140: "Se os exames físicos deixaram muito a desejar, pior ainda foram os psicológicos, por cujas malhas passaram centenas de homens, inclusive oficiais, que não estavam em perfeitas condições para suportar as imenas responsibilidades que lhes caberiam na batalha" (p. 139). He noted that during the campaign the men suffered profoundly from the continuous strain, "sendo visíveis, em muitos dêles, sintomas de mêdo, ansiedade e fadiga, além de outras manifestações mais graves" (p. 140). Moreover, suggestions that such symptoms be treated with removal from the front and rest in the rear were met with resistance "dentro daquele conceito brutal, de que o homen deve ser superior ao próprio tempo" (p. 140). Such an attitude may have been engendered by the high casualty rate, because of illness and the unavailability of large numbers of trained replacements (see below Chap. 14), but it may have resulted in part from a desire to show their allies how tough they were; see Massaki Udihara, "Um Médico na Infantaria," *Depoimento de Oficiais da Reserva*, p. 153. By contrast, in the American army men were taught to expect fear; those who "developed incapacitating fear reactions in combat were labeled as medical cases," but the majority "were relieved of their symptoms after a few days of rest and medical care in the battalion aid station and were then returned to their company." The objective was to reduce "anticipatory anxieties about failing to maintain full emotional control in combat. . . ." This is from Samuel A. Stouffer *et al.*, *The American Soldier: Combat and Its Aftermath* (Princeton, 1949), pp. 196–198.

the cardiovascular system, and the prevalence of such viral disorders as trachoma. The examinations exposed one of the saddest aspects of underdevelopment—poor health and poor health care. They may have also convinced the general staff of the foolhardiness of continued mobilization.[49]

In January 1944, when the actual training program finally got under way, a rally was held at the Municipal Theater in Rio to commemorate the second anniversary of the break in relations with the Axis. Loud speakers carried the speeches outside, but few people stopped on the sidewalks of *Cinelândia* to listen. The official war ministry report cited the lack of popular enthusiasm as proof that "the atmosphere surrounding the Brazilian Expeditionary Corps continues [to be] frank indifference and defeatism."[50] It should be noted, however, that the division was not fully concentrated and organized until the second half of March. There was no reason why the man in the street should have been more enthusiastic than the army itself. "The Brazilian people," in Brayner's opinion, "believed more in Carnival and the football [soccer] Championship than in an Expeditionary Force to fight shoulder to shoulder with the allies and face to face with the Germans."[51]

General Mascarenhas later blamed the "alternating enthusiasm and dejection" on the confused political state of the government. He especially cited foot-dragging by "some officials close to the President who were known to be against the participation of Brazil in the war on the side of the United Nations"—unnamed officials who hampered the development of enthusiasm for the Brazilian war effort.[52] Thus in addition to truly grave physical problems con-

[49] Paiva Gonçalves, *Seleção Medica*, pp. 67–142.

[50] Ministério de Guerra, Rio, Boletim de Informação No. 1, Jan. 29, 1944, OAA.

[51] Brayner, *Verdade*, p. 49.

[52] Mascarenhas, *FEB*, p. 9. Even so, he said that he was convinced that Vargas supported the FEB and that ultimately the president's will would prevail.

nected with mobilization there were psychological and political difficulties. The nature of these problems was not well understood by the pro-FEB officers, some of whom, such as Mascarenhas, blamed officials around Vargas; others blamed the president personally, or the dictatorial form of government; still others saw incompetence in government bureaucrats, while some placed responsibility on pro-Axis military men. The Brazilian panorama did not engender confidence and enthusiasm in the FEB members.[53]

Plans called for the division to be shipped in echelon to North Africa for training and outfitting, and then to enter the line in Italy with the United States Fifth Army under General Mark Clark. War Department planners had refused to schedule a departure until the force was concentrated in one place and had received basic training and weapons familiarization. The American high command was too busy preparing the invasion of France to prod the Brazilians constantly, and naturally assumed that they would mobilize according to plan. But the Brazilian officers, hungry for encouragement, took the lack of urging as a sign of declining American interest in the project. Again they seemed to want others to display more enthusiasm than they did themselves.[54]

Possibly they could have been transported in February if they had been ready, but after that month and until planning for the Normandy invasion was completed no promises could be made. The FEB staff considered using the few small, slow-moving Brazilian-flag vessels, but soon realized their unsuitability—the question of maritime transport was only one of many factors not taken into account before the Vargas government had decided to enter the fray. Events were steadily proving correct Dutra's January 1942 estimate of Brazil's unpreparedness. By early May the Americans were sufficiently confident in the success of the coming invasion to commit themselves to transporting the Brazilian force in June. General Leitão de Carvalho sent the appropriate alert to the ministry of war, and the division began practicing embarkation procedures with a mock-up of a troop ship at Vila Militar. But the division's actual plans were known to such a small group of officers that even the head of the president's military household did not know that embarkation was imminent.[55]

The state of the troops' training was poor, and can only be explained by the Brazilian army's unpreparedness to fight a modern war. The cliché that building an American-style division from a French-style army caused great problems does not clarify the situation. Dutra gave Mascarenhas command authority over the "1st Division" only at the end of December while he was touring the Italian front, and the actual concentration, begun in January, was not completed until March, leaving only April and May for training as a division. Moreover, the Americans could take only 5,075 in the first echelon, necessitating segmenting the command and its various staffs, and they could not give the Brazilians any idea as to when the remainder of the division would follow. The combat equipment they were to use was unknown to officers and soldiers alike. Weapons such as the M-1 rifle, 60 mm. mortar, bazooka, .30 caliber light machine gun, Browning automatic rifle, 57 mm. antitank gun, and 105 mm. mortar had peculiar employment, maintenance, and tactical techniques that had to be taught and mastered. The communications apparatus of twentieth-century warfare such as field telephones and radio-telegraph were unfamiliar. The host of specialists necessary to service a field army, from tractor drivers and electricians to cooks and stenographers, had to be found or trained. Appropriate

[55] *Ibid.*, pp. 53–54; for Dutra's attitude on breaking relations with the Axis and the possibility of entering the war see above Chaps. 9 and 10; Eurico Dutra to Vargas, Rio, Jan. 27, 1942, AGV; Brayner quotes from this in *Verdade*, pp. 69–70; Leitão de Carvalho to E. Dutra, Washington, May 5, 1944, as in Leitão de Carvalho, *Serviço do Brasil*, p. 394; see also *ibid.*, pp. 398–401.

training manuals had to be prepared, printed, and distributed. Unrecoverable time was lost at every turn.[56]

A joke began making the rounds to the effect that Hitler was saying the FEB would sail the day Brazilian snakes took to smoking pipes. In a delightful example of Brazilian humor a smoking cobra became the symbol of the FEB. On May 20 the artillery units staged a fire-support demonstration, and on May 24 the entire division formed up on the Praça Paris and paraded before now cheering crowds. The international press began to make nasty comments about the Brazilians' ability to get headlines without fighting.[57] Brazil's pride and Brazil's prestige depended on the FEB seeing combat.

The need for secrecy as the sailing date approached was both obvious and impossible. German submarines were still attacking vessels along the coast but, given the exposed nature of Guanabara Bay, where every ship was visible from the surrounding mountains, it would be impossible to hide 5,000 men and their huge ship. To minimize the security risks, however, a maneuver was scheduled for the night of June 29–30 that started with the soldiers boarding closed trains for an unknown destination and ended with their rapid embarkation on the USS *General Mann*. They were distressed to find themselves en route to war without so much as a last goodbye to wives and sweethearts, and a bit confused when they realized that the security precautions did not apply to their American allies, who were given liberty in Rio. One of the reasons for the secrecy and the closed trains rumbling through the night was that the Brazilian staff feared desertion and evasion—and perhaps with reason. One rifle platoon in the 6th IR had had eight different commanders during its few months of training; all but one had arranged transfers out of the FEB. At least five of the regiment's nine companies had suffered a similar turn-

[56] Mascarenhas, *FEB*, pp. 12–13.

[57] See for example: ". . . the Near Future," *The Inter-American Monthly*, III, No. 7 (July 1944), 9.

over.[58] So many "daddy's boys" had avoided the call-up that the division's chief of staff admitted bitterly that "the great mass of those mobilized were there because they could not secure an escape."[59]

Dutra and Vargas came on board near midnight to wish the troops well, and the would-be heroes settled down to wait while the American crew enjoyed the delights of their city. The sailors' drunken return and the sight of some of them being dragged on board disturbed the Brazilians, who were already disappointed at the indifferent reception given them by the ship's personnel. Perhaps two and a half years of war had made the Americans apathetic, but Colonel Brayner attributed it to their race. He thought them cold, artificial Anglo-Saxons with an overwhelming superiority complex.[60] This would be only one of many disappointments in the Brazilians' relations with their American allies —although actually the ship's officers had urged the crew going ashore to learn a little Portuguese and not to be rowdy. The orders of the day for July 1st ended with a reminder and a plea: "They are Good Neighbors—Give them a break!"[61]

The embarkation was not without its tragicomic aspects. Brazilian marines had cordoned off Rio's dock area and detoured traffic. Suddenly a car, whose driver ignored signals to stop, smashed through a barrier and came to a halt only after the vehicle had been riddled with machine gun bullets. The driver turned out to be a Portuguese who had not understood the guards' gestures, and had not noticed the barrier. Dazed though unhurt, he was questioned all night by security officials, who turned him loose in the morning

---

[58] Brayner, *Verdade*, p. 74; Democrito Cavalcanti de Arruda, "Nossa Participação na Primeira e Segunda Guerras Mundiais," *Depoimento de Oficiais da Reserva*, p. 48.

[59] Brayner, *Verdade*, p. 74.   [60] *Ibid.*, p. 86.

[61] "Ordens Expedidas a Bordo do Navio *Gen. W. A. Mann*," July 1, 1944, Arquivo da FEB, Ministério de Guerra, Rio de Janeiro.

without a word as to why all this had happened.[62] And because there was a ban on newspaper publicity presumably he did not find out why until the FEB arrived in Naples.

On Sunday, July 2, at 6:30 A.M., the *General Mann* weighed anchor and steamed with its apprehensive cargo for the mouth of the bay. As they passed the fortresses of Laje and Santa Cruz they could see the garrisons lined up on the walls, with flags flying in a farewell salute. Not since Salvador de Sá led the successful expedition against the Dutch in Angola in 1648 had Rio seen its sons sailing to do battle in the eastern hemisphere. Above and to the right the mists swirling around Corcôvado cleared, to reveal the statue of Christ bathed in the morning sunlight. With three Brazilian destroyers providing escort and an American blimp patrolling above, the *General Mann* headed for the open sea. As the white ribbon of Copacabana beach slipped from view the chaplains prepared to sing the FEB's first Mass.[63] If the cobra was not yet smoking, at least it was lighting its pipe.

[62] Brayner, *Verdade*, p. 83.
[63] *Ibid.*, pp. 97–100; Mascarenhas, *Memórias*, I, 141–143.

". . . there is no question but what Brazil has the biggest industrial potential of any nation in Latin America."[1]

13

War and Development

WHEN IT went to war in 1942, Brazil was an economic dependency of Europe and the United States with foreign capital investment totaling $2,242,200,000 (US). Of that amount 48 percent was British, 25 percent American, 18 percent Canadian, and 9 percent from a variety of other sources. Foreign control extended to a wide range of business enterprises. The situation in Rio de Janeiro was painfully typical of the country as a whole. Brazilian Traction, Light, and Power Co., Ltd. of Canada provided electric power, artificial gas, and streetcar service. A British concern, Wilson & Sons, Ltd., imported most of Rio's coal from Wales and West Virginia, while Standard Oil, The Caloric Co., The Texas Co., and Anglo-Mexican Petroleum provided oil from fields in Venezuela, Mexico, and the United States. Food processing and supply, when not foreign-owned, depended on imported equipment, while Standard Brands provided canned goods. Three of the four flour mills in the Rio area were foreign-controlled; one of them—Moinho Fluminense—by Bunge and Born of Bueno Aires. Ice and cold storage plants depended on American, French, and German equipment, and of the six principal plants two had German management and one had British. Though Rio was 98 percent self-sufficient in cement, the only plant in the city (one of six in Brazil) was 100 percent American (Portland-Lone Star). Many of the tugs, launches, and

[1] "Brazil—A 20-Year Boost," *Business Week* (Nov. 18, 1942), p. 18.

barges in the great harbor were owned by such firms as Rio
de Janeiro Lighterage Co., Wallace & Co., and Herman
Stoltz & Co. Telegraphic communication with the rest of the
world went over the cables of the British Western Tele-
graph Co., the American All-America Cables and Radio,
Inc., and the Italian *Compagnia Italiana dei Cavi Tele-
grafici Sottomarini.* Foreign investment had even turned a
profit in sewerage; the British Rio de Janeiro Improvement
Co., Ltd., had evacuated sewage from the older sections of
the city since 1857. A municipal agency utilized foreign
equipment to dispose of waste in the newer districts of
Urca, Ipanema, and Leblon.

'I'he Brazilian navy could not put to sea without petroleum from American oil companies and, before the war,
coal from England, nor could it engage an enemy without
imported projectiles and powder. The army's equipment
was a mixture of German, British, Czechoslovakian, American, and Italian items. In 1942, supposedly there was sufficient equipment to arm and equip 150,000 troops, but to
expand to a war footing at least 50 percent of all expendable ordnance would have to be imported. Eighty percent
of the air force's 220 aircraft (only about 30 were fighter
craft) were American-made; the remainder came from
Britain, France, Germany, and Italy. The great majority of
spare parts and all the necessary fuel and oil were imported.

In the field of entertainment the great Hollywood studios,
such as Paramount, RKO, and Twentieth Century-Fox, dominated the silver screens, and more often than not in their
own theaters. The American firms went so far as to have the
State Department exert pressure on the Vargas regime to
refrain from taking contemplated measures to protect the
barely nascent Brazilian cinema industry, with the result
that few local films were made and those that were could
not find outlets in the foreign-owned theaters. Of the
twenty-one newspapers then functioning in Rio the British
subsidized the *Correio da Manhã*, while the German embassy supported *Meio Dia, A Pátria, O Imparcial,* and *A*

Nação. The only sources of news from abroad were the foreign wire services—Associated Press, United Press, Reuters, and the German Trans-Oceanic—and all newspapers were dependent on imported newsprint.

The German submarine campaign against Brazil raised the specter of total economic collapse and, in the event of German supremacy on the high seas, the impossibility of repelling an invasion. Even such a basic part of the diet as salt—two-thirds of which came from Rio Grande do Norte and could be shipped south only via sea—could be eliminated with a few well-aimed torpedoes.[2]

Although the war cruelly exposed the extent of Brazil's dependency on foreign investments, imports, and markets, it also provided an unparalleled opportunity to build an infrastructure to support economic development under national control. With Europe in flames Brazil was more dependent on the United States (for example, prior to 1940 Europe had absorbed 40 percent of Brazil's coffee exports), but it was also freed from the necessity of compromising goals to suit both European and American interests, now that it could bargain comprehensively with one government. While this presented obvious dangers to national sovereignty it should be recognized that the United States desperately needed various Brazilian products. Brazil was, for example, the sole available source of quartz crystals, which the rapidly expanding American military forces needed for their radio sets; it was a simple matter of no crystals, no radios, no field communications. Iron ore and rubber were likewise of tremendous strategic value. To insure continued Brazilian military cooperation in permitting

[2] U.S. War Dept., "Survey of the Rio de Janeiro Region of Brazil," (s 30–772), Aug. 6, 1942, Vol. 1. Declassified mimeographed copy in author's possession. The study dealt with Rio de Janeiro, Niterói, São Paulo, Santos, and Vitória and adjacent areas. There is a similar study of the states of Pará, Maranhão, and Piauí: U.S. War Dept., "Survey of the Pará Region of Brazil," (s 30–770), June 6, 1941, Vol. 1. Declassified mimeographed copy in author's possession.

unhampered functioning of the air and naval bases, the United States was willing to go to great lengths to placate the Brazilians. It was also in the American national interest to lessen Brazilian dependency on the United States as a source of supply, for the simple reason that it needed its scarce shipping for other things besides carrying coal, oil, newsprint, and spare parts to Brazil. Thus the war offered Brazil a chance to reduce its dependency and, at least until 1944, forced the United States to assist it in doing so.

After Finance Minister Souza Costa signed the Washington Accords in March 1942, the Board of Economic Warfare (BEW) proposed sending a mission of technical experts to Brazil to analyze the economy and to suggest ways to achieve the following: 1) replacement of imported American commodities with Brazilian-made items so as to save shipping space; 2) to decrease Brazilian industry's dependence on imported raw materials through development of those locally available; 3) to maintain and improve the transportation system; 4) to provide Brazil with a foundation for long-range industrial growth.[3] Columnist Drew

[3] Press Release, Sept. 1, 1942, OF 11 Brazil 1940–45, FDRL; "Brazilian Economy Revolutionized," *The Inter-American Monthly*, I, No. 10 (October 1942), 46; *Monitor Mercantil*, Rio, Oct. 21, 1942; Alex Taub to Members of Mission, n.p., Sept. 1, 1942, Cooke Papers, Brazilian Mission, 0283, FDRL. There is some question as to whether the Brazilians or the Americans proposed the mission. Henry Wallace and Cordell Hull said in a letter to Roosevelt that it was formed "at the request of the Brazilian Government"; Aug. 26, 1942, of 11 Brazil 1940–45, FDRL. But it is possible that the idea originated in BEW as part of a general program to survey the Latin republics; see David Green, *The Containment of Latin America* (Chicago, 1971), p. 203, and 338 FN 42. The relationship between the Cooke Mission and the 1942 economy planning survey, conducted by American specialists under Alex Taub at Brazilian request, needs clarification. For the Taub group's report see Conselho Nacional de Política Industrial e Comercial, *A Planificação da Economia Nacional, Estudos e Ante-Projecto* (Rio de Janeiro, 1945). Commenting on the Taub survey Robert T. Daland said: "This group produced a plan of investment for a ten-year period to cost a total of four billion dollars. The interest of the United States in this activity was to use Brazil as a

Pearson reported that the State Department had attempted to ignore the proposal, and that BEW head Milo Perkins had gone to Ambassador Carlos Martins, suggesting that the United States send its idle machinery to Brazil to produce many items then taking up cargo space, and that a mission of experts could work out the details. Pearson maintained that thereafter the "Brazilians did all the pushing."[4] Actually, Foreign Minister Aranha was skeptical of the whole idea and was beginning to tire of American experts. To avoid criticism, and any suspicion that the mission was an intelligence-gathering force for Wall Street, Aranha and Caffery insisted that its members should not have any direct or indirect business interests in Brazil.[5] Thus in the crucial days of July and August 1942, as Brazil slid closer to war, the United States was pressing for import substitution and construction of a transportation infrastructure to reduce the drain on its own economy, while encouraging the Brazilians to believe that the United States would aid their postwar industrial development.

The members of the American Technical Mission were sincere about making a thorough study and formulating useful recommendations. President Roosevelt named as chief of the mission Morris Llewellyn Cooke, former head of the Rural Electrification Administration, chairman of the Shipbuilding Stabilization Committee, and recently a key personality in arranging settlement of the Mexican oil compensation dispute.[6] The other members included a chemical engineer, an industrial relations specialist, an economist, a geologist, a lawyer, and fuel and power, metallurgical, transportation, and production technicians. These men

---

pilot area to test modern methods of industrial development." From Daland, *Brazilian Planning, Development, Politics, and Administration* (Chapel Hill, 1967), p. 27.

[4] Drew Pearson, "Merry-Go-Round," *Washington Post*, Sept. 13, 1942.

[5] Caffery, Rio, July 14, 1942, 832.60/10, NA.

[6] For a biography of Cooke see Kenneth E. Trombley, *The Life and Times of a Happy Liberal* (New York, 1954).

knew little if anything about Brazil, but their advisory staff included knowledgeable specialists from the War Department, BEW, the Office of Strategic Services, the State Department, and the Office of the Coordinator of Inter-American Affairs.[7] And Aranha assigned a couple of his bright young men at the Itamaraty—Vasco Leitão da Cunha and José Jobim—to act as Cooke's advisers. The coordinator of the Brazilian economic mobilization program, João Alberto Lins de Barros, headed the group appointed by Vargas to work with the Americans. Among its members were Valentim Bouças, Edmundo de Macedo Soares e Silva, director of Volta Redonda, and Napoleão de Alencastro Guimarães, head of the Central do Brasil.

Over and above Washington's desire to use the Cooke Mission for propaganda purposes, the members of the Mission sought permanent benefits for the Brazilian economy—not just emergency measures. Their basic philosophy was that the United States should share its technical knowledge in order to increase Brazilian productivity and prosperity. And because trade increased between rich nations, not between rich and poor ones, the establishment of a prosperous Brazil was in the national interest of the United States. The objective was, in Cooke's phrase, to build up the Brazilians' "power to purchase."[8] It was an extension of the basic open-door philosophy that would underlie much of American postwar foreign policy.

In the mission's view increased production would result in greater profits which would allow higher salaries, thereby enlarging the consumer sector and permitting lower

[7] These advisers included: Emilio Collado, Special Assistant to the Undersecretary of State; Laurence Duggan, Adviser on Political Relations, Department of State; Col. Kenner F. Hertford, Head Brazil Desk, War Department; Col. Lemuel Mathewson, Chief, Latin American Theater, OGD, War Department; Dewey Anderson, Chief, American Hemisphere Division, BEW; Maj. Preston James, Chief, Latin American Sector, OSS; Berent Friele, Director, Brazilian Division of OCIAA.

[8] Morris L. Cooke, *Brazil on the March, A Study in International Cooperation* (New York, 1944), p. 4.

prices; this in turn would encourage consumption and ever-rising production. As the mission's report expressed it: "Only as the output and the pay per individual worker is increased will there be more cash available for expenditure by the average citizen. Temporary booms [are] stimulants which in the end may have no long-term beneficial effect. It is the steady drive for a constantly increased and balanced output, rationally distributed, which lifts a people from a lower scale of living to a higher one."[9] The era of a colonial economy was at an end, and Brazil would attain industrial maturity through hydro-electric energy, air transport, and light metals. An official news release trumpeted optimistically: "The technological revolution now confronting the civilized world promises to change Brazil as rapidly as England was altered by the Industrial Revolution of the 18th Century."[10]

After a couple of months of study and travel the mission produced extensive joint reports on the proposed use of cargo planes and gliders, ground transportation, fuel, petroleum, electric energy, textiles, paper, mining and metallurgy, the chemical industry, commercial associations, food production, markets and prices, education, translation of books into Portuguese, industrial financing and sources of credit, manufacture of electrical equipment, and economic mobilization. Cooke, who was a conservation enthusiast and a believer in regional planning with experience on the Mississippi Valley Committee, promoted a study of the potential use of the São Francisco river valley. The voluminous documents were bound in handsome leather and submitted to the two presidents in December 1942.[11] The basic theme

[9] Morris Cooke and João Alberto to F. D. Roosevelt and G. Vargas, n.p., Dec. 1, 1942, Cooke Papers, 0283, FDRL.

[10] News Release, Dec. 1, 1942, in *ibid.*; Memo: "Summary of Preliminary Report of Joint Brazil-United States Technical Mission," DAR, Dec. 4, 1942, 832.20/480, NA.

[11] These are in the Cooke Papers, 0283, FDRL. A Brazilian edition appeared in 1949; *A Missão Cooke No Brasil*, Relatório dirigido ao

of the reports was that the immediate demands of wartime production and the requirements of long-range growth could be joined in a carefully planned development program that utilized electrical power, light metals, and the airplane to replace coal, steel and heavy industry, and the railroad. Their immediate impact was frustratingly slight. The Brazilian press eagerly reported and editorialized on the mission's objectives and activities, raising hopes to a new high that Brazil's day was about to dawn.[12] The so-called revolution of rising expectations began during World War II and not in the late nineteen-fifties. The United States actively encouraged the belief that industrialization, education, housing, electrification, and trade would be the immediate results of allied victory, thereby bribing the Latins to stay in the American camp. The postwar disillusionment of Latin America that culminated in Richard M. Nixon's fateful 1958 tour of South America and the Cuban-Russian alliance must be seen against the backdrop of unkept American promises.

Cooke and his collaborators earnestly attempted to avoid becoming "just another mission," and after returning to the United States prodded the State Department to take action to implement their proposals. What was done, however, was done piecemeal—without coordination and, it seems, without reference to the mission's work. Cooke warned the unresponsive bureaucracy that "any failure to make a delivery commensurate with the promise inherent in our publicized instructions will react unfavorably not only in Brazil but elsewhere in Latin America. . . ."[13] As part of his campaign to stimulate interest and support, he edited portions of the mission's reports and published them under the title

Presidente dos Estados Unidos da América pelo Missão Técnica Americana enviada ao Brasil (Rio de Janeiro, 1949).

[12] There is a large collection of clippings from the Brazilian press on the mission in 832.60/52, NA.

[13] Cooke, Memo, June 1, 1943, Cooke Papers, 0283, FDRL.

*Brazil on the March—A Study in International Coopera-
tion.* Although unable to obtain action, he kept undimin-
ished faith in "what may be accomplished for Brazil and
ultimately for the United States in the free passage of our
technology as an essential element in the industrialization
of Brazil."[14]

Walter Walmsley of the Division of American Republics
most aptly expressed the attitude prevalent in the State Department when he commented that Cooke's report contained "captivating excursions into fantasy," and that Cooke
seemed infected with the enthusiasm about Brazil's natural
resources and future that prompted "so many otherwise
normal American visitors to imaginative thinking."[15] The
Department had favored the mission as a means of reducing Brazilian pressure on shipping space and only secondarily as an advisory body on developmental policy. The
few projects resulting from the mission's studies—equipment for the Bahian oil fields and railway maintenance,
coal-washing apparatus for Santa Catarina mines, items for
a number of power plants and transmission systems, and
books for schools in Ouro Prêto and Pôrto Alegre—could
well have been carried on without the ballyhoo, expense,
and unkind stimulation of Brazilian expectations.

Although its objectives were not fulfilled, the Cooke mission did have some long-range results, the most important
of which was that it sketched the pattern for postwar
United States policy toward underdeveloped regions. Be-
lieving that American prosperity was related to economic
growth in those areas, Cooke drafted an important fifty-
page memorandum entitled: "Promotion of the Development of the Brazilian Economy as a Pattern for Hemispheric Economic Relations—The Long View." He argued
that postwar international relations would utilize a new

[14] Cooke to Miguel Álvaro Ozorio de Almeida and Samuel Wainer,
n.p., June 30, 1943, Cooke Papers, 0283, FDRL; Cooke, *Brazil on the
March.*

[15] W. N. Walmsley, DAR, Dec. 8, 1942, 832.20/480, NA.

type of balance of power based on economics and divided into three elements: 1) securing raw materials to sustain military operations and civilian populations; 2) cooperation in development programs to strengthen economies of friendly nations and to tighten political ties; 3) the supervision of individual commercial transactions to insure their compatibility with (1) and (2). Furthermore, the United States government needed an agency in the Department of State "to direct and promote the development of the economy of other nations through an exchange of facilities, technical skills and commodities." Years later the Agency for International Development (AID) would fulfill that objective. He also urged a basic reform of the Department to prepare for the new diplomacy. "It must," he urged, "expand its *institutional mind* to a breadth and reach of vision that embraces on the one hand economic objectives on a new and higher plane of international policy and ethics, and on the other hand a full realization of the varieties of expertness involved in the execution of plans."[16] The Department's officers at the time, though willing to admit deficiencies in the economic area, were cool to Cooke's suggestions, asserting that he failed to appreciate many of the practical problems inherent in the operation of a foreign office. But willing or not, time and events would bring them to adopt Cooke's point of view.

The mission provided the basis for the 1948 John Abbink Mission and the 1953 Joint Brazil-United States Economic Development Commission, as well as the rationale adopted for the Alliance for Progress in 1961. And—perhaps a more significant achievement—it confirmed the Brazilian government's tendency toward centralized economic planning and helped convince Washington of its utility.[17] It also injected the American government into Brazilian economic affairs in the most intimate fashion. Thus Brazil was the testing

16 Cooke to Welles, Washington, Mar. 9, 1943, 832.60/75, NA.

17 See Daland, *Brazilian Planning*, pp. 26–35, for a summary of planning from Vargas to Juscelino Kubitschek.

ground for postwar United States economic policy and the Cooke Mission was the beginning of a process still underway at the beginning of the 1970's.

While the Cooke Mission was conducting its studies the two governments were taking steps to implement provisions of the Washington Accords of 1942 regarding rubber supply. With the Far Eastern plantations in Japanese hands the United States was forced to turn to the home of natural rubber, the Amazon basin. As late as mid-July 1941 the Germans and Japanese had been buying such large quantities of crude Brazilian rubber that tire manufacturers in São Paulo were experiencing a supply shortage,[18] and with the disruption of normal trade it seemed as if there would be a new Amazonian rubber boom. Even if the United States had not needed rubber it would have been forced to take some action to prevent the Brazilians from selling to the Axis. Aranha's approximation diplomacy, however, and Brazil's entry into the war made the United States the sole buyer.

The Reconstruction Finance Corporation established the Rubber Reserve Company (later called the Rubber Development Corporation) to procure supplies in Latin America, principally in Brazil. To cooperate with the Rubber Reserve Company Vargas set up a Special Commission for the Regulation of the Washington Accords, under the direction of Finance Minister Souza Costa and with a team of specialists that included Valentim Bouças. Vargas also created the Rubber Credit Bank, which established branches in Belém and Manaus to buy crude rubber. Unfortunately, aside from the largely unsuccessful efforts of Henry Ford to cultivate rubber on planatations, the trees grew wild and were separated from one another—as was the population. The Amazon basin covered an area of roughly 1,845,500 square miles and contained a population of about 1.5 million persons. Of those 250,000 were in Belém and about 90,000 in

[18] "Rio Rubber Crisis," *Business Week* (July 12, 1941), pp. 78–79.

Manaus, while five other towns, the largest of which was Santarém, ranged in size from 15,000 down to 5,000. This provided a population distribution of about five persons for every four square miles of territory. Not only would the trees have to be hunted but workers would have to be imported.

Two agencies—the National Department of Immigration and the Special Service of Workers' Mobilization—were set up to recruit latex gatherers from the drought- and poverty-ridden states of Ceará, Piauí, Rio Grande do Norte, and Maranhão, to transport them to the Amazon, and to establish them in the rubber zones. This ambitious colonization program, which originally aimed at 50,000 workers and their families, was the sort of idea that made a great deal of sense in a ministerial conference room in Rio de Janeiro or Washington but disintegrated before the harsh realities of the Northeast and the Amazon. Many of those recruited, when examined at encampments near Belém, were found to be afflicted with various diseases. Others withered away from the constant fight with nature in isolated shacks miles upstream on the many tributaries of the great river. To supply food and provide medical care for the workers, and to transport the rubber, the Brazilian government created three agencies—the Supply Service of the Amazon Valley, the Navigation Service of the Amazon, and the Special Public Health Service. The number of persons recruited, transported, and established as collectors was variously reported as between 24,000 and 35,000 by 1945. The government established price levels for food, but local suppliers often charged exorbitant prices and reduced some of the rubber collectors to a condition bordering on slavery.[19]

[19] The foregoing was based largely on a comprehensive memorandum by the Rubber Development Corp.'s Rio director: C. A. Sylvester to Aranha, n.d. (probably 1944), Rio, OAA. For an interesting contemporary account see Henry A. Phillips, *Brazil, Bulwark of Inter-American Relations* (New York, 1945), pp. 37–98. For the number of those transported see Valentim F. Bouças, *Estudos Econômicos e Financeiros*, II

The lonely gatherers tapped the trees along the trails in the jungle near their shacks and coagulated the raw latex over a smoky palm-nut fire. Slowly, layer by layer, they built the twenty-five pound balls which they turned over to the local trader, who "owned" the area and provided their supplies on credit. The gatherers were frequently months, if not years, behind in settling debts. The trader had obtained his supply items—machetes, hammocks, canned goods, candles, kerosene, knives, manioc farina, dried fish, cloth, and clothing—on credit from an import-export firm in Manaus or Belém which deducted the value of the accumulated rubber from the trader's account. There were few, if any, exchanges of cash. The firm then sold the rubber to the Rubber Credit Bank, which channeled it either to the American Rubber Reserve or to production plants in southern Brazil. The gatherers' bimonthly trips to the trading post, the arrival of the company steamer, or a locally popular saint's day enlivened the dull, weary days. The patron-client system of relationships based on credit had developed during the great rubber boom in the first decade of the century, and the relatively rapid expansion of rubber gathering during the war failed to produce a suitable replacement. Indeed, the public health service found the system extremely useful in the distribution of free antimalaria tablets (Atabrine). Officials feared that if the drug were distributed through normal commercial channels it would not reach collectors isolated on high tributaries, and they wished to avoid encouraging black-market trade. The health service gave the drug to the import-export firms with the understanding that they furnish it free of charge to the trader and through him to the gatherer.

Attempts failed during the war to short-circuit the traditional system of commercial relationships and to sell supplies directly to the trader or to set up government-sponsored collectors. The long-standing credit and social relationships between trader and company, and trader and collector, were too firmly embedded to be readily replaced. The formation of cooperatives and the extension of credit directly to the gatherer would do away with the trader and eliminate the security he provided, but the Amazonian or the transplanted Northeasterner was not yet ready to replace a flesh and blood patron with an impersonal government agency. After all, government agencies did not have saints' days or birthday parties! The anthropologist Charles Wagley, who spent the war working in the Brazilian north and northeast with the health service, concluded after studying this commercial system that it could be helpful in introducing innovations. "New ideas, new forms of technology, and new instruments may be introduced," Wagley suggested, "through the city firms, to their traders, and finally to the collectors and farmers in distant areas of the Valley."[20] During World War II, however, government-sponsored attempts at basic change were ill-conceived and of minor effect.

The predicted recruitment and transportation of 50,000 Northeasterners by June 1943 was absolutely unrealistic. By mid-April of that year only some 264 persons had been moved onto collection sites and production figures were naturally far below original estimates. The Rubber Reserve Corporation had planned to build some twenty air fields throughout the Amazon to fly supplies in and rubber out. But so little construction was actually done that in late 1943

[20] Charles Wagley, *Amazon Town, A Study of Man in the Tropics* (New York, 1953), p. 99. The above account is based on Wagley, pp. 96–100. After a tour of the rubber zone in mid-1943 a U.S. Embassy representative recommended "closer cooperation with business firms in Manáus in respect to the sale and distribution of foodstuffs and the handling and distribution of crude rubber"; Caffery, Rio, May 29, 1943, *Foreign Relations, 1943*, v, 669.

the number of fields was reduced to two, one at Manaus and one at Iquitos, Peru, and air transport of rubber was committed to Brazilian civilian lines, principally *Panair do Brasil.* The wide gap between planning and execution was, according to Ambassador Caffery, "due principally to lack of equipment and labor but not, it would seem, to lack of 'experts.' "[21]

Walter Walmsley, then Second Secretary of the United States Embassy, was harsher than his chief or Professor Wagley in his condemnation of the "Amazon Rubber Program." After touring the area he wrote that he was deeply impressed with the "futility of reform by outsiders. Foreigners, and by this I also mean non-Amazon Brazilians, are helpless in the face of the problems of distance, of scarcity, of hunger and disease." He wisely observed that Belém, Manaus, or even Pôrto Velho and Santarém were not the real Amazon, but "comparatively luxurious islands in an endless morass" where the struggle between water and land was still unsettled. He then analyzed the "fundamental errors" and "endless" mistakes which well-intentioned but ignorant outsiders committed in trying to develop Amazonian rubber production. Walmsley wrote:

> No darker picture exists anywhere of what in more progressive countries we choose to call corruption and exploitation. Yet the established society, with its century-old tentacles stretching up all the thousands of tributaries, was totally ignored in our earlier rubber program. The river trade is the bloodstream of this feudal social organization. We have attempted to cut across these arteries expecting that the body would not only survive but would also be useful to us. We have failed to consult those who, through long experience have accumulated the only accurate knowledge of the region. We have entered someone else's property and ignored the owner. We

[21] Caffery, Rio, Apr. 19, 1943, *ibid.,* pp. 667–668; other aspects of the rubber program are discussed pp. 664–684.

have made decisions not only in Belém and Manaus, which is bad enough, but also in Rio and Washington, which is worse, on problems with which we have not the faintest familiarity. Despite our recent concessions to them, both local business men and local officials continue suspicious and sullen. . . . The Amazon is a hierarchy of middlemen feeding on the body of the *seringueiro* [collector]. . . . Cash means little to a *seringueiro* buried in his pest-ridden barracão [shack]. What he needs is food and medicine to keep him alive and alcohol to keep him from despair. What difference is it to him if he gets out of the red and can't eat. If a *seringueiro* is credited with a higher price for his rubber, he is debited with a higher price for his supplies. Neither the Rubber Bank nor the RDC [Rubber Development Corporation] nor any other entity without the river organization of the commercial firms, has anything to offer the *seringueiro* in return for added rubber production. The inducement can only follow the normal line through the commercial firms. . . . It is useless as sorry as we may feel for the *seringueiro*, for us to try to reach him direct. . . . We have planned in a vacuum, on a large scale, without knowledge of local conditions and somehow expecting that a man whose right hand we cut off will offer us his left.[22]

The administrators sent from the United States to oversee the rubber program discredited themselves one after the other, wasting incalculable amounts of money on supplies, homes for staffs, the migration program, uninventoried equipment and graft. And with it all they had been unable to increase rubber production. American authorities eventually decided, in an effort to reduce costs, to turn the functions they had assumed over to Brazilian organizations. Walmsley thought that this would result in a wider distribution of funds, make more people happy, and might even produce more rubber.

[22] Walmsley, Rio, n.d. (Oct. 1943), *ibid.*, pp. 680–681.

Production figures may not be trustworthy but the 1942 estimates for the next three years were not met. In 1943, instead of the predicted 35,000 tons, Brazil produced 22,000 tons; the following year the total was 28,000; and in 1945 it reached 40,000. Of this approximately 10,000 tons was required for the 136 Brazilian factories manufacturing rubber products ranging from tubes and tires to shoe soles and rainwear. The Brazilian government's Coordinator of Economic Mobilization limited products by type and percentage of rubber content to keep consumption low. And all rubber over and above domestic needs was sold to the Rubber Development Corporation at 45 to 60 cents a pound. Brazil developed a profitable trade in rubber goods with the other South American countries, principally Argentina and Chile. An active contraband trade also grew up, with Chilean buyers at one point outbidding the Americans at $1.75 a pound.[23]

Washington's efficiency experts decided in 1944 that Brazil's war effort would be more effective if the United States provided technical data to set up synthetic and reclaimed rubber plants in Brazil. The Brazilians sent a technical mission, at American expense, to visit tire factories in the United States to learn how to utilize synthetics. The objective was to reduce Brazil's natural crude rubber consumption to below 8,500 tons a year (the surplus would then be exported to the United States), and "to encourage the maximum practical utilization of reclaimed rubber, synthetic rubber and similar plastics . . . in place of natural crude rubber."[24] In order not to destroy the rubber collecting trade immediately, which would have had unhappy political consequences, the United States agreed to extend rub-

23 *Ibid.*, pp. 664–684; Bouças, *Estudos Econômicos*, ii, 247–258; Anapio Gomes, *et al., Economia de Guerra no Brasil, O Que Fêz a Coordenação da Mobilização Econômica*, v and vi (Rio de Janeiro, 1946), 7–29.

24 Douglas H. Allen (President, Rubber Dev. Corp.) to John H. Neumann (Field Rep. of RDC), Washington, July 31, 1944, *Foreign Relations, 1944*, vii, 609.

ber price controls until March 31, 1946, to keep the bottom on the market. But it made clear that it would buy all the synthetic rubber tires Brazil produced, over whatever was needed for domestic use and export to other Latin American countries.[25]

This seemed like a fine idea to the Brazilian rubber manufacturers, who would be able to modernize by going synthetic. Interestingly enough, the two largest tire producers were the American *Companhia Goodyear do Brasil* and *Indústria de Pneumáticos Firestone S.A.* But if local industry reduced its dependence on natural rubber, and if the United States discontinued buying after the war, and the Far Eastern plantations filled European demands, what would happen to the struggling Amazonian natural rubber industry? The answer was painfully simple, and pressure from Brazilian industrialists and the American government forced Vargas to acquiesce in abandoning Amazonian development although it was one of his fondest dreams. A percentage of the Rubber Credit Bank's reserves had been earmarked for such development, but the Americans and Vargas interpreted development differently, as can be seen in a statement by Douglas H. Allen, president of the Rubber Development Corporation: "In connection with the utilization of the development fund, we wish to emphasize that our primary interest lies in measures designed to bring about immediate stimulation of rubber production rather than in long-term plantation projects . . . but it may not be wise to oppose the use of any part of the fund for such long-term projects, particularly in view of President Vargas' interest in such projects."[26]

Some Brazilians may have hoped that the new synthetic plants would free southern Brazil from dependence on the backward north, but for a time after the war the plants would still depend on imported ingredients, such as a par-

[25] *Ibid.*, pp. 603–606, 610.
[26] Allen to Neumann, Washington, Sept. 16, 1944, *ibid.*, p. 613.

ticular consistency of wood resin, which could be had only from the United States. As the war ended Brazilian industry was seeking nationally made substitutes.[27]

The second rubber boom subsided as the war drew to a close. Like the first it failed to develop either Brazilian rubber production or the Amazon, and did not even have the virtue of leaving splendid monuments, such as the 1910 boom left behind in Manaus. Opera houses and palaces in the jungle at least attract tourists.

A proposal that could have produced major changes in the Amazon, in fact in the whole interior of the South American continent, faded once the Axis submarines had been driven from the sea-lanes. In 1942, when the attacks and sinkings had forced ships under the Brazilian flag into port and were playing havoc with the tenuous system which linked Brazil to its sources of supply, the governments of the United States, Brazil, and Venezuela seriously considered dredging the upper Orinoco and the Rio Negro and opening the Casiquiaré "Canal" that linked the two rivers at various times of the year. This would allow water transportation from the Caribbean into Amazonia. By using the Madeira-Mamoré rivers vessels could then enter Bolivia, and via the Tapajós-Juruena-Rio do Sangue and a connecting canal or road to the upper Paraguai they would be able to travel the Paraná-Paraguai system into Paraguay and Argentina, and ascend the Tocantins and Araguaia to the head of navigation; cargoes could then go by road to Goiânia and thence by railroad to São Paulo and Rio de Janeiro. This route would have allowed Venezuelan oil to reach the southern portion of the continent without danger, and would have stimulated economic development and trade. The United States sponsored a couple of feasibility studies of navigation on the Orinoco and Rio Negro and even prepared a draft of an agreement with Brazil, but then Ad-

[27] Anapio Gomes, *et al., Economia de Guerra no Brasil*, v and vi, p. 24.

miral Ingram's forces drove the submarines from the south Atlantic and the idea was forgotten. The exciting scheme became another victim of the short-sighted war effort.[28]

Another project of high developmental potential was the "Basic Economy Program" which aimed at improving food supply, and health and sanitation facilities. The propaganda for the program gave it the appearance of pure altruism, limited only by the desire to display "the tangible benefits of democracy . . . to people who are illiterate or lack media of communications."[29] In truth the program originated in a suggestion in November 1941 by Nelson Rockefeller (then Coordinator of Inter-American Affairs), that the United States engage in large-scale public works construction at "strategic and focal points" for emergency use by the American armed forces. The army suggested that such construction should be concentrated in Northeast Brazil, and Rockefeller discussed the details of the program with General

[28] Berent Friele to Cooke, n.p., Nov. 28, 1942, Cooke Papers, 0283, FDRL; the proposal was discussed in *A Noite*, Rio, Oct. 23, 1942. The idea of opening an Orinoco-Rio Negro-Amazon navigation route via the Casiquiaré was not new; see Charles M. Pepper, "South America Fifty Years Hence," *The National Geographic Magazine*, XVII, No. 8 (August 1906), 427–432. The Hudson Institute has recently made a similar proposal, but using a series of dams and artificial lakes. The Brazilian government commissioned Montreal, a São Paulo and Rio de Janeiro construction and research company, to do a developmental program for the Amazon. Montreal's studies, completed in 1966, also called for increased water transportation using canals and lakes. See Superintendência de Desenvolvimento da Amazonia, *Resumo do Programa de Ação Para 1967–1971* (São Paulo, November 1966). The government has also recently opened roads to Pôrto Velho on the Madeira, and from Brasília to Belém, and at this writing (1972) is constructing a "Transamazonic Highway" from the Brasilia-Belém road westward; see Robert G. Hummerstone, "Cutting a Road Through Brazil's 'Green Hell,'" *The New York Times Magazine*, March 5, 1972, pp. 31ff. Trucks, buses, goods, and people are now flowing over those roads and the kind of development envisioned in 1942 is taking place, but two and one-half decades later.

[29] Basic Economy Report, 1942–43, Box 1, OF 4512, FDRL.

Marshall in early 1942. In February Roosevelt provided some $25,000,000 from the President's Emergency Fund to finance a health and sanitation program throughout Latin America, and a month later Rockefeller's office set up the Institute of Inter-American Affairs (directed by General George C. Dunham of the Army Medical Corps) to supervise the programs.[30] The three major objectives were: 1) safeguarding the lives and health of American military forces and of their allies stationed in strategic locations; 2) improving health conditions and food supply for workers in order to increase production of strategic and critical materials; 3) to maintain the stability of the republics whose economies the war had upset.[31]

In its initial phases the Basic Economy Program was linked to the efforts of the Office of the Coordinator and the Board of Economic Warfare, to prevent the Axis from obtaining vital raw materials in Latin America. The army was intimately involved via Secretary Henry L. Stimson's membership on the BEW, and through the Board's American Hemisphere Division which was headed by an army officer. Rockefeller's office also aided the army in the collection and dissemination of information and propaganda in and about Latin America. Army interest faded once it became apparent that large-scale defense of Latin American territories would be unnecessary, but the programs in Brazil preserved the three objectives stated above.[32]

With those guidelines the American and Brazilian governments inaugurated a series of health and sanitation projects, and an ambitious food-supply program based on agreements reached in the second half of 1942. Unlike other joint ventures the emphasis was on a low American profile. Some forty United States nationals worked with 412 Brazil-

[30] Stetson Conn and Byron Fairchild, *The Framework of Hemisphere Defense* (Washington, 1960), pp. 196–197.

[31] "Annual Report, Basic Economy Department, Office of Coordinator of Inter-American Affairs, 1942–43," Box 1, OF 4512, FDRL.

[32] Conn and Fairchild, *Framework*, pp. 197–198.

ian technicians from the Special Public Health Service and the Ministry of Agriculture and about 1,700 lesser personnel. The projects were concentrated in the Amazon to support rubber collection, in the northeast to safeguard health in the vicinity of the air bases, and in the south along the route of the Vitória-Minas Gerais railway. The reason for the last project, according to the program's official report, was that the route through the Rio Doce valley had to be made habitable for the workers repairing the railway line because "upon the rehabilitation of the railroad, manganese is expected to move in large volume from Itabira to the port of Victoria [*sic*] for overseas shipment to the United States."[33]

In the Amazon region an imaginative and extensive health program utilized floating dispensaries to reach isolated settlements and families. The health teams made a major effort to eliminate malaria by distributing a million tablets of Atabrine a month as described above, and official estimates claimed a 90 percent reduction of malaria incidence among those using it. Elsewhere efforts centered on improving water and sewage systems, as in Governador Valladares, Minas Gerais, leprosy control in Belo Horizonte, training of doctors and nurses in Belém, Bahia, and Rio de Janeiro, and construction of a hospital in Rio Branco.[34]

The food-supply program had its origins in the Brazilians' fear that the American troops would eat up the scarce foodstuffs in the areas surrounding the air bases, and in the need to feed the rubber gatherers and to reduce dependence on ocean transport. Axis propaganda played on this fear and the food program was the American response. Separate from the program but providing an obvious example was Admiral Ingram's vegetable farm near Recife, which his command established to provide foodstuffs for

[33] Basic Economy Report, 1942–43, Box 1, OF 4512, FDRL.
[34] For a list of the projects see Appendix B in *ibid.*

the Fourth Fleet and to alleviate the local food shortage. Under a September 1942 agreement the Institute of Inter-American Affairs contributed $2,000,000 to a two-year program, while the Brazilians promised to make available $250,000 in funds and $1,750,000 in services and equipment to bring 1,450,000 acres under culvitation in Mato Grosso, Acre, Amazonas, Pará, and the nine northeastern states from Maranhão to Bahia. Over 100,000 hand tools, thousands of tons of seed, and hundreds of tons of insecticides and fungicides were distributed to farmers and potential growers of beans, rice, corn, mandioca, fruit, vetegables, and peanuts.[35]

The program eased conditions in middle- and upper-class urban areas in the north and northeast, but, because the vast majority of Brazilians lived on a bare subsistence level in which starvation and malnutrition were commonplace, it did little to alter either the basic diet or the patterns of food distribution. Middle-class households continued to have adequate supplies, while the poor majority in the slums, backlands, and rubber zones subsisted on a small quantity of black beans and rice.

Although the program failed to reach its acreage quota or change Brazilian diets it had tremendous propaganda utility for the United States. Roosevelt told Rockefeller that the Basic Economy Report was "extraordinarily interesting." Genuinely impressed with the program's potential, he wrote: "What we need most of all are some colorful stories for public consumption of the type that can be printed in Liberty, Collier's or even the Saturday Evening Post. I do want to get across the idea that the economic and social welfare of Jesus Fernandez in Brazil does affect the economy and social welfare of Johnny Jones in Terre Haute, Indiana."[36]

[35] *Ibid.*

[36] Roosevelt to Nelson Rockefeller, n.p., June 11, 1943, Box 1, OF 4512, FDRL.

Roosevelt undoubtedly believed that the program would improve Jesus Fernandez' economic and social welfare, and he probably did not realize that other United States programs would tend to minimize the possibility of increasing the average Brazilian's food consumption. The Office of Economic Warfare, the Commodity Credit Corporation, and the British Ministry of Food arranged in late 1943 to buy Brazil's surplus rice. Theoretically, local needs would be satisfied before any grain was offered for export but, given the artificially low level of consumption due to poverty, the sales agreement necessarily supported rice prices at a level that would discourage increased domestic consumption. Guaranteed prices and the prospect of developing a profitable export market encouraged producers to sell to the allied purchasers; while the additional foreign exchange encouraged the government to use past, poverty-determined consumption levels in deciding the tonnages required for home use.[37]

Probably such conflicting efforts were neither intentional nor malicious. The United States was at war and every action was somehow related to and justified by the war effort. American officials, if they thought about it at all, probably assumed that the Brazilians would look out for their own national interests. Unfortunately, however, the Brazilians seem to have been overwhelmed by the scope of the war and the steadily growing might of the United States. The multiplicity of programs affecting Brazilian interests and of American agencies operating in Brazil were difficult to correlate or to control. By the end of 1942 there were some fifty Brazilian "desks" in various Washington agencies busily duplicating each others' work, and sending such swarms of representatives to Brazil that the Brazilians nicknamed them "parachute troops" and began nervously joking about the American invasion. The Brazilians were irri-

[37] For the negotiations and agreements see *Foreign Relations, 1943*, v, 709–719.

tated by so many experts knowing so much and dispensing their knowledge in a patronizing manner: the Americans appeared to think that the Brazilians could do nothing for themselves.

The foreign ministry, notably those close to Aranha, began to worry that the United States might take advantage of wartime economic activities to impose American ideas and business methods—to exploit Brazilian resources without contributing to industrialization. Volta Redonda was still more promise than reality. They feared that American tactics were drifting toward those used in the days of the "big stick." Ambassador Caffery warned that "unless something is done about this, trouble looms ahead."[38]

The war offered Brazil an opportunity to secure assistance in developing its economy, but the combination of its leaders' ineffectiveness and American policies often limited or negated potentially profitable efforts. By the end of the war Brazil still had not achieved economic independence or large-scale development.

[38] Walmsley, DAR, Dec. 30, 1942, 832.60/51½, NA; "The Wooing of Brazil," *Fortune*, XXIV, No. 4 (October 1941), 100; Walmsley, Memo of Conversation with José Nabuco, DAR, Nov. 9, 1942, 832.00/431½; Caffery, Rio, Nov. 30, 1942, 711.32/149; and Dec. 24, 1942, 711.32/150, NA.

"O Brasil esta presente."[1]

"Our presence on the battlefields of this war will lend us prestige in the concert of the United Nations, as a military power, and give us the right to occupy a post of honor at the peace table."[2]

14

The Smoking Cobras

BEGINNING July 18, 1944, the press in Brazil burst out in joyous headlines announcing the safe arrival in Naples of the first FEB contingent two days before. Political commentator José Eduardo de Macedo Soares proclaimed it the greatest day in Brazilian history since independence. Brazil was in Europe, he said, to defend the Christian civilization that it had received from there. "Our Army offers its blood for the liberation of humanity. Our cause is that of the free democracies."[3] Numerous columns and editorials throughout the country heralded the nation's unselfishness and idealism in seeking to do combat with the Nazi-fascist barbarians, and portrayed Brazil as rising to the defense of democratic institutions and freedom. Before the troops had even fired a shot the press was telling Brazilians that their sons were winning Brazil the right to take part in the postwar reconstruction of international society. While many people undoubtedly believed that the brave boys of the FEB were performing an act of pure generosity, the irony of a dictatorship sending its army across the seas to liberate op-

[1] *Jornal do Brasil*, Rio, July 19, 1944.
[2] *Diário Carioca*, Rio, July 19, 1944.
[3] José Eduardo de Macedo Soares, "O Maior Dia da Nossa História," *Diário Carioca*, Rio, July 19, 1944.

pressed peoples did not escape them. For many the FEB was a guarantee that Vargas would keep his 1943 pledge to return the country to constitutional rule.

News stories made repeated references to Brazil's position as leader of Latin America at the side of the great world powers. Basking in the reflected limelight of those powers, Brazilians began to feel that they were indeed contributing to the coming victory. *O Jornal* boasted that Brazil was fulfilling its historic destiny and was playing "a role equal to its reality as a great power." The FEB was proof that the nation was "prepared to assume full responsibility of alliance with the United States." *O Globo* expressed confidence that in the hands of the *praçinhas*, as the soldiers were popularly known, the Brazilian flag would not be disgraced, while the *Diário da Noite* explained the purpose of the FEB with the hopeful assertion that "with the presence of these troops we break forth as a great nation among the free powers."[4] Many, however, hesitated to believe the stories of the FEB's successes until the very end of the war, for fear that they were somehow being deceived.[5] The national inferiority complex fed whisperings to the effect that the troops were not really fighting but only having a holiday in Italy. How preposterous to think that Brazilians could defeat Hitler's experienced, well-equipped soldiers! But underneath the doubts were hopes that somehow it was true.[6]

[4] *O Jornal*, Rio, July 19, 1944; *O Globo*, Rio, July 19, 1944; *Diário da Noite*, Rio, July 19, 1944.

[5] In August 1945 the American Consul General in São Paulo commented that when the FEB was formed there was a definite "undertone of anxiety" among Brazilians, who nourished "a very deep lack of confidence in their troops and were afraid that they would cover themselves with ridicule and that their effort would be a complete fiasco. This inferiority complex manifested itself in jokes and criticism, as well as a large amount of unfavorable comment to the effect that the government's policy in sending such a force was nothing less than an absurdity." Cecil Cross, São Paulo, Aug. 3, 1945, 832.20/8-345, DSF.

[6] See for example: *A Notícias*, Rio, July 18, 1944; *Folha Carioca*,

For the FEB the arrival in Italy was not quite so pleasant. After fourteen days in the cramped quarters of the *General Mann*, eating strange food, worrying about submarines, and being seasick, the Brazilians disembarked into the ruins of Naples.[7] They were shocked at the destruction and not a little overcome by the blatant power of their allies. En route from Rio the allied command had switched their destination from North Africa, where there were outfitting depots and training areas, to southern Italy where none were available. The FEB had no kitchen equipment, no tenting, no sleeping gear, no weapons, no vehicles, in short none of the things necessary for an independent existence. Neither the American command nor the Brazilian liaison officers had done anything to prepare an initial bivouac area. The FEB's first night in Italy was spent unsheltered and shivering in a staging area located in the dusty crater of the extinct volcano Astronia. Morale plummeted with each hour, and with remembrance of the hostility with which the people of Naples had greeted them. Marching unarmed and in olive-green uniforms they were mistaken for Nazi prisoners. Their reception was hardly a heroic one.

Their superior officers seem to have been afflicted with cultural shock, and their dependent position affected their ability to function and to make decisions. Their uncertainty as to the limits of their own responsibilities and rights aggravated their malaise. They had not been briefed adequately on the terms of the agreements with the United States, and only after arriving in Naples did they comprehend the extent of their unpreparedness. "We were badly

---

Rio, July 18, 1944; *Jornal do Brasil*, Rio, July 19, 1944; *Diário Carioca*, Rio, July 19, 1944; *O Jornal*, Rio, July 25, 1944. For a sampling of stories originating with the government news agency (DIP) see *Os Brasileiros Chegam ao "Front"* (Rio de Janeiro, 1944), pp. 66–77.

[7] For interesting, humorous comments on problems related to feeding the troops see Ubirajara Dolácio Mendes, "Soldado Com Fome Não Briga," in Demócrito Cavalcanti de Arruda, *et al.*, *Depoimento de Oficiais da Reserva Sôbre a F.E.B.* (Rio de Janeiro, 1949), pp. 263–274.

uniformed, badly shod and badly equipped. And above all unarmed."[8] Very few officers spoke English and the Americans would not deal in any other language. They became dependent upon interpreters, the most popular and successful of whom was Vernon Walters, a tall young officer who spoke Brazilian Portuguese without a trace of foreign accent and who was a practicing Catholic. He smoothed the way as much as a foreign officer could, and won the enduring esteem of the Brazilian officer corps. But he was, after all, an American.[9]

During training near Naples the poor quality of the Brazilian uniforms and boots became embarrassingly apparent. Rain gear proved not to be waterproof, the colors ran in the shrinking uniforms, and the boots fell apart. The Joint Brazil-United States Defense Commission (JBUSDC) agreements said that the United States would provide helmets and armament, but personal uniforms were the Brazilians' responsibility. It was not a question of tropical uniforms being unsuitable for an Italian winter; it was obvious that they would need help when the snows came, but now it was still summer and their uniforms could not stand the rigors of combat training. It is likely that some contractors made a healthy profit at the FEB's expense.[10]

[8] Floriano de Lima Brayner, *A Verdade Sôbre a FEB, Memórias de um chefe de Estado-Maior na Campanha da Itália* (Rio de Janeiro, 1968), p. 115.

[9] Vernon Walters had a way with languages, reportedly speaking eight. After the war he frequently traveled as interpreter with American generals and during the 1950's he often accompanied President Eisenhower on trips abroad. He was with Vice-President Nixon during his ill-fated Latin American tour in 1958. In 1964 he was military attaché in Rio de Janeiro when many of his former FEB friends overthrew the João Goulart administration. His tentmate from the Italian campaign, Humberto de Alencar Castello Branco, became the first president of the military regime.

[10] All of the memoirs speak bitterly of the uniforms and the indignity of fighting in American clothing. See for example: Elber de Melo Hen-

Reluctantly, General Mascarenhas accepted the suggestion of the American liaison officers that he request American uniforms for his troops. He and his chief of staff went to the nearby supply base expecting an immediate remedy. Mascarenhas tried to explain his problem but the American general cut him short and asked sharply "What did you bring to fight with?" His tone and question hit the two Brazilians like a slap in the face, and they seemed to sink deeper into the soft cushions of the general's sofa. The American interpreter, a Captain J. Russo, who had lived in Recife, did not translate the remark and attempted to prevent further comments by saying: "General, I want to inform you that General Mascarenhas was the Brazilian commander who organized the defense of the Brazilian northeast for America!" Without waiting for an interpretation Mascarenhas, who had understood, declared vehemently: "For America, no! For the threatened world!" The American general softened and said he was not censuring Mascarenhas and would see what he could do. But the damage was done. The Brazilians saw all too clearly how things stood. They were only a drop in the human ocean that was sweeping over Europe. Chief of Staff Brayner wrote: "We should not have come. That was the cold truth. If we came, for example, like the South Africans, or Canadians, or New Zealanders, who brought everything from their country, including transport and maritime escort, the Americans would have received us with a number 1 (one) smile. But, we were there only with cannon fodder and the great loyalty typical of Brazilians."[11]

Shocked and disappointed at the lack of importance the Americans attached to their presence, the Brazilian command struggled to gain the approval and confidence of

riques, *A FEB Doze Anos Depois* (Rio de Janeiro, 1959), pp. 223–225; and Paulo Dumangin Santos, "Observações de um Oficial de Informações de Batalhão," in *Depoimento de Oficiais da Reserva*, pp. 299-302.

[11] Brayner, *Verdade*, pp. 117–120.

their Anglo-Saxon allies. Their determination to succeed became overriding, and was rooted not in confidence but in abhorrence of the consequences of failure. Not only did their individual careers depend on success, but the honor and the future position of Brazil were at stake. The crushing sense of responsibility rested most heavily on Mascarenhas, who at sixty-one was the oldest general in the Fifth Army, a man who disciplined himself and his charges with equal severity. He had spent his life in the Army of Caxias,[12] in which the gulf between officers and troops was not only that of rank, but of social and economic position, education and opportunity. The Army of Caxias was composed not of "citizen-soldiers" spread through the ranks from private to general but of two distinct military castes, the officers, who considered themselves the army, and the soldiers (not including one-year draftees), who were from the poorest, least literate levels of society. The basic concept of duty was simple; superiors gave orders and inferiors carried them out. There was no discussion, no exchange, and little concern for morale.

The stiff, formal relationships of the army in Brazil, an army that had not engaged a foreign adversary since the War of the Triple Alliance (1865–1870), were soon shaken in the ranks of the FEB. Instead of illiterates, officers found college students in their companies, and colonels found reservists serving under them who were doctors, engineers, and lawyers, as well as former sergeants promoted to lieutenants. And all around them was the powerful example of the egalitarian American forces, with their fine distinctions of when, where, and how formal military courtesies were to be rendered or forgotten. Cut off from Brazil and faced

[12] So called in memory of the hero of the Paraguayan War (1865–70) and principal military figure of the imperial period, Luis Alves de Lima (1803–80), the Duke (Duque) of Caxias. After his death the "Iron Duke" was raised to the level of a military saint; he was the patron of the army whose life was held up for emulation.

with the harsh realities of modern warfare the FEB soon became something very different from the Army of Caxias.[13] For Mascarenhas the adaptation to new methods of command was difficult, and complicated by the multifaceted problems facing him—arming and training his troops, dealing with foreign superior officers whose language he did not speak, keeping an ear cocked for adverse political activity among his officers and on the home front, not to mention the necessity of fighting what he considered the world's finest army.

Mascarenhas' stern image and his earnest desire to gain the Americans' confidence regardless of the cost to his troops were illustrated in the following incident. On November 2, 1944, the Second Battalion of the 6th Infantry Regiment (IR), after a solid month and a half of combat in the Serchio valley, moved 120 kilometers to the Reno valley to replace an American unit at the most exposed point in the Fourth Corps line, the Torre de Norone salient, on the night of November 3rd. The Americans had taken the position in a hard fight the week before and had weathered five German counterattacks in the days since. After their rapid transfer and previous weeks of combat the men of the Second were nearly exhausted, were short of basic equipment such as machine guns, mortars, ammunition, and lacked radios and telephones. The Second's commander supposedly arranged with the Americans for a twenty-four hour delay so that the unit could gather equipment and rest a bit. But when the suggestion of delay was presented to Mascarenhas he rejected all excuses, demanding to know "Didn't each soldier receive a knife?" If the officers were unwilling to lead the Battalion, he and his staff would do so! The Second moved into the American positions but the

[13] The fullest discussion of the clash between the mentality of the FEB and that of the Army of Caxias is José Góes Xavier de Andrade, "Espírito da FEB e Espírito 'De Caxias,'" *Depoimento de Oficiais da Reserva*, pp. 311–391.

American officers refused to withdraw until the Brazilians were properly supplied—some forty-eight hours later.[14] When this incident occurred Mascarenhas had just assumed the field command of the division and was anxious for all to go well. He would improve, but throughout the campaign the spirit of Caxias and the spirit of the FEB would be at odds.

At Bagnoli near Naples some training was carried out, the most significant being the courses in combat leadership and mine warfare given to a small group of English-speaking personnel, but without arms and transportation equipment large-scale training could not be undertaken. The United States Army's bureaucratic procedures frustrated and confused the Brazilians, who could not understand why they could not be given some of the material visible in the

[14] Demócrito Cavalcanti de Arruda, "Impressões de um infante sôbre o comando," in *ibid.*, pp. 72-75. He wrote that Mascarenhas gave a pathetic "pep" talk on "the name of Brazil, the prestige of Brazil, the Flag of Brazil, the honor," etc. When one of the officers attempted to explain their view of the situation, he said: "Cale-se! O Sr. não tem nada a dizer." When they continued to object on grounds of not being supplied, Mascarenhas said: "Os Srs. não têm facas? Cada soldado não recebeu uma faca? A munição irá depois. De qualquer forma, o batalhão subira hoje, porque, se for preciso, eu assumirei o comando do batalhão e os meus oficiais de Estado-Maior, o comando das companhias" (p. 75). The battalion held the Torre de Norone from November 3, 1944, to March 5, 1945, and left 77 percent of its dead and sustained 72 percent of its wounded there. Mascarenhas' knives were not soon forgotten. In his account Brayner said that Mascarenhas treated the officers roughly and threatened them with drastic measures; see *Verdade*, p. 218. The reserve officers' criticism stung Mascarenhas, who defended himself with statements, collected from the American commander of the unit being relieved and from General Willis Crittenberger, to the effect that the substitution was necessary and that Mascarenhas had acted probably in seeing it through. See letters from Col. Lawrence R. Dewey and Gen. Crittenberger to Mascarenhas de Moraes in his *A FEB Pelo Seu Comandante* (2nd ed., Rio de Janeiro, 1960), pp. 98-104. But Mascarenhas missed the point of the criticism. The officers were more disturbed about his treatment of them than about the correctness of his decision.

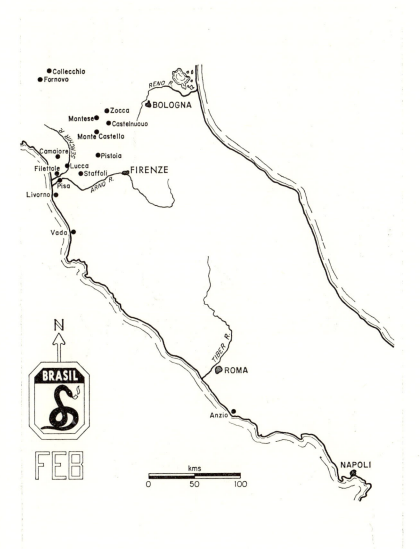

Collecchio
Fornovo

Zocca
Montese
Castelnuouo
Monte Castello

BOLOGNA

RENO R.

Camaiore
Pistoia
Filettole
Lucca
Pisa
Staffoli
FIRENZE
Livorno

SERCHIR R.
ARNO R.

Vada

N

BRASIL

FEB

TIBER R.

ROMA

Anzio

NAPOLI

kms
0   50   100

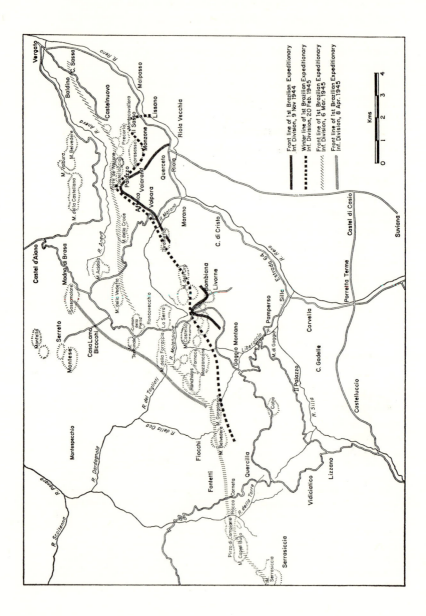

Front line of 1st Brazilian Expeditionary Inf. Division, 9 Nov 1944

Winter line of 1st Brazilian Expeditionary Inf. Division, 20 Feb. 1945

Front line of 1st Brazilian Expeditionary Inf. Division, 6 Mar. 1945

Front line of 1st Brazilian Expeditionary Inf. Division, 8 Apr. 1945

Kms

0 1 2 3 4

vast supply area. For the Americans the reason was simply that a ship was en route with the equipment designated for the FEB. An example of the misunderstandings that arose concerned the type of rifle the *praçinhas* were to receive. The American supply people determined that rifles were not being shipped from the States, and that they could give the FEB's first contingent 5,000 M-1903 Springfield rifles (5 rounds, 30 caliber, bolt action). Mascarenhas had the idea that they were to receive new M-1 Garrand (8 rounds, 30 caliber, semiautomatic) rifles, and balked at the suggestion that his men use the older weapons. After the Americans agreed to include some M-1's and to provide more later, Mascarenhas reluctantly accepted the Springfields.[15] Since his troops were not proficient in the use of either rifle, his insistence struck the Americans as odd. Of course the general wanted to obtain the latest equipment for his troops, but he would soon realize that training was more important than new equipment.

For their part the American officers were disappointed, if not alarmed, at the physical and medical condition of the Brazilian troops. Dozens of expeditionaries, including a few officers, had dental problems that were nearly incapacitating. About two hundred soldiers were found to have ailments related to poor hygiene. Both American and Brazilian sources emphasized the deplorable state of sanitation and hygiene, a situation directly attributable to inexperience in dealing with such large troop concentrations.[16] Mas-

15 Lt. Col. Nathan S. Mathewson, "History and Training of the 6th Combat Team Until its Entrance into Combat," Report on the 1st. Infantry Division B.E.F. in Italy, OCMH, DA (microfilm copy in author's possession). There is another copy of this document in 301 (BEF)-833, WWII RS, NA but it carries a classification that would not permit its being copied. Mathewson's report is one of several subparts of the general report on the FEB which is described in the bibliographical essay below. The general report will hereafter be cited as Report 1/Inf. Div. BEF, OCMH. For the Brazilian side see Brayner, *Verdade*, pp. 122–123; Mascarenhas, *Memórias* (Rio de Janeiro, 1969), I, 146–148.

16 Capt. Frank T. Cameron, "Historical Report of the Brazilian

carenhas commented after the war that "the U.S. medical authorities' impression of the physical value of our first expeditionary contingent was not very flattering."[17]

After the FEB moved north of Rome, "a veritable mountain of varied and complex war material" was transferred to it and an intensive three-week training program began under the guidance of American combat veterans.[18] The training followed the sequence of familiarization with the firing of weapons (shortness of time did not permit attaining proficiency), unit tactical training in offensive and defensive measures, and, finally, a combat team in the attack exercise with full artillery preparation and support. At this point the FEB became part of the United States Fifth Army, then under the command of Mark W. Clark. This young, energetic general instantly won the trust and admiration of the Brazilians. He was a good diplomat who understood that the performance of the FEB was "important politically as well as militarily," and he was eager "to give them every chance to make a good showing."[19]

August 25, the anniversary of the death of the Duke of Caxias, was the Brazilian army's Soldier's Day; it was also the day that Paris fell to the allies. General Clark was in attendance as the Brazilian troops paraded on their camp grounds at Vada. In a sense that day at Vada was a watershed in the FEB's experience and in Brazilian history. Before Vada the FEB was afflicted with uncertainty and difficulty, afterwards it grew in confidence and was eager for battle. In a larger framework Vada was symbolic of the

Replacement Depot," Report 1/Inf. Div. BEF, OCMH; Clovis Garcia, "Como Um Combatente Viu os Serviços Médicos," *Depoimento de Oficiais da Reserva*, pp. 287–296.

[17] Mascarenhas, *FEB*, p. 35.   [18] *Ibid.*, p. 36.

[19] General Mark Clark, *Calculated Risk* (New York, 1950), p. 389. Clark came from an army family, was graduated from West Point in 1917, served in World War I, and rose from Lt. Col. in 1940 to Major General in October 1944.

shift from French to American preeminence in the intellectual and cultural life of the Brazilian army and society. On the review platform next to General Clark stood General Chadebec de Lavallade, last chief of the French Military Mission to Brazil, who had flown from France for the ceremonies. His gesture of friendship pleased the Brazilians and reminded them of the old ties with France, but at the end of the review the Brazilian troops broke into a rousing chorus of "God Bless America" in English. Perhaps the post-facto symbolism of such an event should not be made too much of, but it is true that in the years after the war France did not regain its former influential position.[20]

At Vada, Clark told the assembled troops that their presence was "but another indication of the solidarity of purpose which exists between our two great nations." And that with their fighting spirit great days lay ahead.[21] In the same hopeful tone *A Manhã* of Rio analyzed the situation two days later. Brazil had made, it said, immense contributions to the allied cause with raw materials and foodstuffs and now the FEB was helping to consolidate the victory. "We have thus conquered undeniable rights to sit at the peace table and to defend our interests in the reorganization of the future world, as well as in the distribution of economic, military and political power in South America."[22]

Fortunately, Mark Clark appreciated the political dimension of the FEB's role in Italy. "It was always," he wrote in his memoirs, "in our minds that a set back for these troops would have an unhappy political reaction in the Americas."[23] For their own reasons, the Americans wanted the FEB to cover itself with a portion of the glory. When they

[20] Mascarenhas, *FEB*, p. 40; Clark, *Calculated Risk*, pp. 393–394; Brayner, *Verdade*, p. 144.

[21] Address by Mark Clark, at Vada, Aug. 25, 1944, Boletim 10, Sub-Pasta 2, Pasta 201, Armário 4, AFEB.

[22] *A Manhã*, Rio, Aug. 27, 1944.

[23] Clark, *Calculated Risk*, pp. 389–390.

completed their training as a combat team, the first contingent of *Febianos,* as they began to refer to themselves, moved to a staging area near Pisa, and formed as a special detachment under the command of Brigadier General Euclydes Zenóbio da Costa. This exuberant, confident native of Mato Grosso loved danger and the direct command of troops in the field. Among the FEB's four generals—Mascarenhas, Oswaldo Cordeiro de Farias, chief of artillery, Olympio Falconieri da Cunha, FEB inspector general and head of supply—only Zenóbio was a confirmed infantryman and only he had requested assignment to the expeditionary force.

The allied armies were moving against the heavily fortified Gothic Line; their objective was to reach the Po Valley and Bologna before Christmas. Fifth Army welcomed the new troops and hoped that the rest of the division and succeeding divisions would arrive soon, because the Fifth had been depleted to furnish forces for the invasion of southern France in July.

Fifth Army was divided into three corps areas, with the United States Fourth on the left and the United States Second and British Twelfth on the right, while on Fifth Army's right flank was the British Eighth Army. Because Fourth Corps had contributed the largest number of units to the French invasion force it was spread thinly along the front and was incapable of a sustained offensive. Fifth Army strategy called for the Second to spearhead the attack with the Fourth immobilizing and harassing enemy units facing it. Clark assigned the FEB detachment under Zenóbio to the Fourth Corps, commanded by General Willis D. Crittenberger,[24] because its sector was comparatively quiet and would allow the Brazilians time to adjust to combat with a minimum of losses.

[24] Willis D. Crittenberger was a tall, ramrod-straight native of Indiana, who was a member of the Class of 1915, U.S. Military Academy. Plain spoken and candid, it took time for him to adjust to the Brazilians. Once he did he became their lifelong supporter.

On September 15 the detachment entered the line in the Serchio River basin near the resort town of Viareggio, which overlooks the western coastal plain twenty-five miles north of Pisa. The next forty-five days were marked by rapid advances against light resistance from the Germans, who were withdrawing to the prepared Gothic Line positions further north. The Brazilians' confidence grew as they nipped at the heels of the retreating enemy. The Germans harassed the advancing Brazilians with mortar and artillery fire, but actual contacts were slight. When they did occur, for example at Monte Prano (September 23–26), the Brazilians succeeded in taking the enemy positions only after the Germans withdrew. Indeed, during Zenóbio's command of the detachment, blown-up bridges, rain, and mud were bigger obstacles than the German army.[25]

That is not to say that the Brazilians did not do well or that the initial experience was pointless—far from it. Zenóbio proved himself to be very active in moving his men forward rapidly, even personally directing traffic at times. However, the Brazilians perceived their advance as forcing the German retreat and, taking light casualties (108 for the period of September 16 to October 31) in their first month and a half, they became overconfident. The inevitable reverse took place during the night of October 30–31. After a day-long fight up steep rocky slopes in a heavy cold rain the Brazilians took the Lama di Sotto-Monte San Quirino ridge line that formed the defenses for the city of Castelnuovo di Garfagnana, a German communications center of major importance in the Gothic Line which lay four kilometers from the new Brazilian positions. The ridge had been held by the Fascist Italian Monte Rosa Division, which had recently replaced the German 232 Division, and which, from the large number of prisoners taken, did not seem disposed to a determined struggle. The grand affair was witnessed by some sixty-four new officers recently ar-

[25] Combat Diary, Report 1/Inf. Div. BEF, OCMH.

rived from Brazil, all the FEB generals, and a representative of the Fourth Corps.

At nightfall one battalion, comprising four companies, was perched on a series of hills separated by deep gulleys along a four-and-a-half-kilometer front, with little or no linkage between positions. The men were cold, wet, and extremely tired. The nature of the terrain, the lateness of the hour, the unaccustomed weather, the poor communications between units and with the rear headquarters, the lack of mules to carry supplies to forward positions, and the fact that the men had never suffered a sharp reverse contributed to a poor defensive posture. Soldiers huddled around fires to warm themselves and to dry out clothing. Instead of digging foxholes and trenches and carefully setting out fields of fire they sought shelter in shell holes, behind rocks, in natural depressions, and in scattered buildings.

With the cry of "Heil Hitler" Nazi S.S. troopers, who had replaced the Italians for the assault, launched a series of counterattacks, beginning at 2:30 A.M., against the 3rd (1/6 IR) and 7th (III/6 IR) Companies, and attempted to encircle them. The Germans, after having lost a position, typically used the tactic of a forceful counterattack at narrow points. They used it with such regularity and success in the Italian campaign that the allied forces had come to expect it, but the Brazilians had not yet experienced it. They learned the hard way. The besieged companies fought back stubbornly until noon on the 31st. Low on ammunition and with no relief in sight they withdrew in orderly fashion, the 3rd Company having suffered four dead, five wounded, and fifteen, many of whom were wounded, taken prisoner by the Germans.

Their resistance had been so forceful that it had consumed the entire German effort; only in the late afternoon were the Germans able to turn their fire on the two remaining companies. Of these the 1st Company (1/6 IR) took the brunt of the onslaught, but held its ground until all its ammunition had been expended. Once it began to withdraw the 2nd Company (I/6 IR) had no choice but to do likewise.[26]

The acrimony resulting from the reverse continues to the present day. Mascarenhas blamed the troops for not taking careful precautions and, according to an officer of the 3rd Company, he reprimanded them strongly and accused them of being "cowards fleeing before half a dozen, before one patrol of demoralized enemy."[27] In his *Memoirs* the general said *the troops* had underestimated the enemy, but he failed to say why he did not suggest or General Zenóbio did not insure that the positions were properly secured and that a reserve had been deployed in preparation for the counterattack which he implied he expected.[28] To attack and to hold a position of importance to the enemy without careful investment and a reserve would be foolhardy in any case, but to do so in this instance was sheer negligence on the part of Zenóbio and Mascarenhas, because on the afternoon of the 30th an aerial artillery observer reported heavy German reinforcement of the units facing the Brazilians.[29] It is, of course, impossible to be certain that the four companies would have held even with preparations, given the Germans' determination, but it appears that they did as well as possible in the circumstances—especially when one considers that the Americans,[30] who replaced the Brazilians when

[26] See entries for Oct. 30–31 in *ibid.*; José Alfio Piason, "Alguns Erros Fundamentais Observados na FEB," *Depoimento de Oficiais da Reserva*, pp. 103–107. Piason was subcommander of the 3rd Company I/6 IR and a doctor in civilian life. Mascarenhas, *Memórias*, I, 183–188.

[27] Piason, "Alguns Erros," *Depoimento de Oficiais da Reserva*, pp. 105–106.

[28] Mascarenhas, *Memórias*, I, 186–188.

[29] Mello Henriques, *Doze Anos Depois*, pp. 72–74.

[30] This was the U.S. 92nd Infantry Division, composed of Negroes and nicknamed the Black Buffalo. Because of their low combat efficiency and because the Negroes were segregated into a separate division the *Febianos* held them in disdain. For a discussion of the 92nd's performance see Samuel A. Stouffer, *et al.*, *The American Soldier: Adjustment During Army Life* (Princeton, 1949), pp. 586–595.

they moved to the Reno valley, were likewise unable to secure the Lama di Sotto-Monte San Quirino ridge, which remained in German hands for the next five months.[31]

The incident was an unhappy end to Zenóbio's command of the FEB detachment, and coincided with General Clark's decision of October 30 at the command conference at Vada to bring the whole 1st Division of the FEB into action in the Reno Valley. The second and third echelon had arrived from Rio and had undergone some training at Filettole. The reports of American training officers emphasized in no uncertain language the problems experienced in outfitting the Brazilians and the low level of preparation that these troops had received before arrival in Italy. Supply difficulties caused near-paranoia among the Brazilian staff officers[32] and frustrated their American colleagues. Evidently the FEB was to be equipped under an outdated table of equipment, with the bulk of the material coming from the States, while shortages were to be filled out of stocks available in the theater of operations. This resulted in confusion exacerbated by the late arrival of cargo vessels, mixed shipments, incorrect marking of crates, nontactical loading, and several gales which delayed unloading. The Brazilians had expected new equipment and were mortified to find that they were receiving secondhand gear, often with the last user's name on it. There were no carbines or forty-five Colt sidearms, so the officers carried Springfields and hand machine guns. The two regiments in training had to be given differ-

[31] The most objective account of the affair at Lama di Sotto-Monte San Quirino is Manoel Thomaz Castello Branco, *O Brasil Na II Grande Guerra* (Rio de Janeiro, 1960), pp. 206–214. For a map of FEB dispositions see p. 208. Brayner said that the troops were the least to blame and that the heaviest responsibility fell on Zenóbio's staff and his immediate adviser at the time, the Division G-3, Lt. Col. Humberto de Castello Branco. But because there is an undercurrent of hostility in Brayner's book toward Humberto de Castello Branco his comments must be weighed carefully.

[32] Brayner, *Verdade*, pp. 178–179.

ent arms, which created problems of instruction, supply, and fire power.

Once equipped, the 1st IR (the Sampaio from São Paulo) and 11th IR (São João del Rei, Minas Gerais) went through a rapid one-week tactical training program which revealed that they were "not sufficiently trained for heavy combat." They were "not thoroughly familiar with care and cleaning of equipment, mechanics of weapons and techniques of fire." They were in good physical condition, however, and displayed a great willingness to learn. According to the senior American adviser, the officers had "high confidence in American leadership and in American weapons." But he warned that the soldiers displayed faults that could not be overcome in a few days' training, because they were so basic. As he assessed the two regiments: "The majority of the troops are intelligent and not lazy and should, in time, make good hardened soldiers. Enemy contact is a great teacher and these troops will learn and assimilate many lessons the hard way. But until these lessons are learned, they will not secure the results that are necessary to effect a decisive defeat upon a well seasoned enemy such as now confronts them."[33]

With that prophetic evaluation the 1st and 11th regiments joined the 1st Division FEB for the assaults on Monte Castello. That mountain brought the FEB its greatest frustrations, exposed glaring flaws in its training and command structures, and offered bloody lessons. On five different occasions the Brazilians threw themselves against the German fortifications—November 24, 25, 29, December 12, and February 21—the first two times as part of an American operation, and the last three under their own green and gold banner. Nearly four out of their nine months' combat were spent under the guns of Monte Castello.

[33] Lt. Col. David J. Colyer, Senior Adviser's Report to Hdqs. IV Corps, quoted in Lt. Col. Nathan S. Mathewson, "Training of the 2d Echelon of the 1st Infantry Division, BEF," Report 1/Inf. Div. BEF, OCMH.

In the attacks on November 24 and 25, the Brazilians were attached to an American task force, in spite of the fact that they had been in combat sixty-eight straight days without rest or replacements and were displaying extreme fatigue and low morale. They faced the veteran German 232 Grenadier Division entrenched on the 987-meter Castello and the surrounding heights, which ranged from 1,120 to 1,140 meters. The Germans had established interlocking fields of fire and had a complete view of the approaches. The first attempt on the 24th was thrown back with heavy casualties, some of which were sustained when a battalion of the United States 92nd Division on the left flank of the III/6 IR withdrew without notifying the Brazilians, thereby exposing them to withering fire. At 8.00 A.M. on the 25th the III/6 returned to the attack, without rest and with numerous gaps in their lines because of casualties and the lack of replacements. The Germans had been reinforced, and counterattacked strongly. After a day-long seesaw battle the heights remained in German hands.

At a tense conference on the morning of November 26, Mascarenhas heatedly demanded of General Crittenberger that *Febianos* not be placed under American command again. Crittenberger declared that he was there to employ the troops assigned to the Fourth Corps and that he had nothing to do with diplomacy, but because Mascarenhas felt his responsibility to the Brazilian government required that the entire FEB remain under his command at all times, he would "pass the ball to him." Mascarenhas replied: "I take the ball, but in very bad condition."[34]

In order to prove themselves, the Brazilian command was determined to carry the mountain. Mascarenhas had noted that the American commanders relied heavily on their operations officer, and so he departed from the Brazilians' traditional integrated staff approach to operations planning and

[34] The incident was reported in full by Brayner, who was present. He prints Mascarenhas' undelivered memo to Clark and Crittenberger, see *Verdade*, pp. 245–252.

gave full charge to the division G-3, Lt. Col. Humberto de Castello Branco. They scheduled an attack for November 29, using the same frontal assault tactics. Units available to fill out the ranks were some distance away, and had to march rapidly through freezing weather struggling with ice and mud. One battalion, the III/II IR, was pulled out of training at Filettole, still poorly equipped, and rushed into position during the night some two hours before the start of the assault. The soldiers had not eaten, or had time to make a careful reconnaissance, and once day broke they were in full view of the Germans.

The lessons of the three previous months seemed lost. The two battalions (the I/1 and III/11) were to operate independently with no functional reserve, because the reserve designated, the III/6 IR, had been so battered on the 24th and 25th that it was in no condition to support anyone. Also the inclement weather made aerial direction of artillery fire impossible. The brunt of the enemy's reaction fell on the I/1 IR. Its 3rd Company was cut to pieces and immobilized and its commander received a grave head-wound while trying to rally his men. The 2nd Company's captain was so shocked by the massacre that he refused to continue, and ceded his post to a lieutenant in the midst of battle. Fragmentation grenades did their bloody work with terrifying success. At one point a single grenade killed nine men. Explosions shook the earth and screams mingled with a constant staccato of machine gun and rifle fire. One wounded soldier yelled hysterically: "Mother, I'm going to die . . . Oh! my mother . . . For the love of God! Get me out of here lieutenant . . . I don't want to die . . . I can't stand the pain."[35] Another remembered that while he lay, covered with mud and blood, his right hand mangled, he watched a friend vomiting blood nearby and felt strangely indifferent

[35] Agostinho José Rodrigues, *Segundo Pelotão, 8a Companhia* (São Paulo, 1969), p. 91. Rodrigues was a platoon leader in 8th Company, 3/11 IR. He describes the events of November 29 in vivid detail, pp. 81–95.

to the chaos around him and immensely happy at being alive.[36] The III/11 IR made it closer to the top, but after almost twelve hours its progress too was paralyzed and at nightfall all returned to their lines. The results were cruel. The 1/1 IR suffered 157 casualties, destroying its offensive utility, while the III/11 IR was comparatively lucky in losing only twenty-eight. But even in its deplorable state the 1/1 IR managed to beat back a German assault that reached its forward positions the next day.[37]

The effect on FEB morale was extremely depressing. On the night of December 2 the remainder of the 1st and 11th regiments nervously entered the line, fresh from the Filettole training area. They had heard the horror stories of the III battalion. Late in the evening when the Germans began aggressive patrolling panic spread through the ranks. Under an artillery and mortar barrage several companies broke and fled toward the rear. If the Germans had swept through they could have moved down an open highway (No. 64) to the FEB command-post in Porreta-Terme and endanger, if not capture, the Fourth Corps headquarters at Tavino, four kilometers behind the FEB positions. Fortunately the Germans were unprepared to take advantage of the gaping hole, and the FEB artillery soon laid down such fierce fire that German offensive action was impossible. By daylight the line was restored. The Brazilians were learning that there was more to replacing front-line troops than issuing orders.[38]

[36] Joaquim Xavier da Silveira, quoted in Mello Henriques, *Doze Anos Depois*, p. 99.

[37] Entries for Nov. 29 and Nov. 30 and Summary for November, Combat Diary, Report 1/Inf. Div. BEF, OCMH; Brayner, *Verdade*, pp. 253–264; Castello Branco, *Brasil na II Grande Guerra*, pp. 245–256; Mello Henriques, *Doze Anos Depois*, pp. 93–108; Gentil Palhares, *De S. João del-Rei ao Vale do Pó* (São João del-Rei, Minas Gerais, 1951), pp. 231–241.

[38] Mello Henriques, *Doze Anos Depois*, pp. 109–113; Palhares, *De S. João del-Rei*, pp. 242–261; Brayner, *Verdade*, pp. 264–270; Castello Branco, *Brasil Na II Grande Guerra*, pp. 253–256. The Brazilians were

Incredible as it seems, the Brazilians staged a fourth frontal assault on Monte Castello on December 12. The two attacking battalions—the II and III of the I IR—were to surprise the Germans by moving out at dawn without prior artillery preparation. But when firing broke out unexpectedly the III battalion leaped forward precipitately, while the II battalion was held down by pre-set German artillery and mortars for nearly two hours. A cold, bone-chilling rain had been falling for two days, and the objectives were covered by dense fog and low-lying clouds which impeded regulation of allied artillery fire. The Germans had every advantage, and exploited each mercilessly. By mid-afternoon the attack was given up with no objectives reached and 145 casualties sustained.[39]

The Germans were amazed at the stubbornness of the Brazilians. A German captain at Monte Castello told a captured Brazilian lieutenant: "Frankly, you Brazilians are either crazy or very brave. I never saw anyone advance against machine-guns and well-defended positions with such disregard for life. . . . You are devils." That day the Germans lost only five killed and thirteen wounded.[40]

The Brazilians' lack of success was repeated all along the Fifth Army front—Bologna and the Po Valley would remain in German hands for one more Christmas. And now the FEB had to fight a political battle on the homefront. In late September, when Minister of War Dutra visited the troops, he sounded out Mascarenhas' reaction to possible promotion to Lieutenant General, a rank not then in use in the Brazilian army, and assignment to a "higher" post in

---

mortified, but the American "Combat Diary" for that date read simply: "The attack was supported by intense artillery and mortar fire and at 0350 A, a penetration had been made between the 1st and 3rd Battalions, with the right of the 1st Battalion and the 9th Company withdrawing slightly."

[39] Brayner, *Verdade*, pp. 278–281.

[40] Emílio Varoli, "Aventuras de um prisoneiro na Alemanha Nazista," *Depoimento de Oficiais da Reserva*, p. 447.

Brazil. Mascarenhas declined what he took to be a move to replace him as commander of the FEB. Now that the cobras were carrying smoking guns the hangers-back and *pessimistas* in Rio wanted to get into the limelight. With the help of the Americans Mascarenhas later sidetracked another Dutra suggestion that troops be rotated after six months duty in Italy. From the Ministry of War on the Praça da Republica in Rio it probably seemed like a good idea for as many troops and officers as possible to have combat experience. And Dutra's brief tour, which included a few days playing at field commander, may have given him the erroneous impression that combat operations were not very different from practice maneuvers. But the last thing the FEB needed was a constant stream of inexperienced men relieving its veterans, so Mascarenhas presented his problem to the Fifth Army's new commander, Lucian K. Truscott.[41] Fortunately, Truscott's approval was necessary for the Air Transport Command to fly the proposed replacements from Natal to Italy, and he declined to give it.[42]

After the unsuccessful assault of December 12 on Monte Castello, Mascarenhas considered resigning his command and returning to Brazil to defend himself from the criticism of the armchair officers and to explain the FEB's situation to Getúlio Vargas. His staff persuaded him not to resign and to send his chief of staff, Colonel Floriano de Lima Brayner, to explain things at home. Brayner arrived in Rio de Janeiro on January 12 and found the incessant rumor-mill of the fifth column creating a pessimistic attitude toward the FEB, so he did his best in newspaper interviews and private conversations to give a more encouraging view. He told Dutra that, given the tremendous problems which they had encountered in equipping one division, Mascarenhas

---

[41] Truscott was commissioned via ROTC at Cleveland Teachers Institute in 1917, was a WWI veteran, and commanded a division in Tunisia, Sicily, Salerno, and a corps at Anzio. Commander of Fifth Army from December 13, 1944 to June 1945.

[42] Mascarenhas, *FEB*, pp. 56–57 and *Memórias*, I, 237–238.

preferred that the 4,500-man contingent which had arrived in Naples on December 7 be the last. The FEB staff feared that, even if they could get two more divisions into the war zone, they would not be formed into a Brazilian Corps under Mascarenhas but divided according to the needs of Fifth Army; they had seen this happening to the Indians and to liberated Italian units. On February 22, however, one more detachment did reach Italy, most of whose members received rigorous training but did not enter combat.

On January 25 Brayner went to the Catete Palace for a long conference with Vargas, who was alarmed that the news from the front had turned from good to bad. The sudden change in the FEB's fortunes and the reports that the fights at Monte Castello were massacres upset him. Brayner explained that the *Febianos* had entered the line before they were ready because Mascarenhas could not adequately explain to the Americans, without suffering a loss of prestige, their lack of preparedness. During the October 30th conference at Vada, when Clark asked Mascarenhas to commit his division, he felt that Brazil's honor demanded that he comply. Brayner emphasized the difficulties and misunderstandings caused by the lack of men in the FEB who spoke English and the absence of Brazilian liaison officers at Fifth Army and Fourth Corps headquarters. And the misunderstandings extended to the lowest levels—a company-grade officer had requested lubricating oil for his weapons and received cans of tomato juice.[43]

Getúlio was deeply moved at Brayner's description of the determination with which the troops faced their hardships, and he probed carefully for the colonel's opinions of each of the FEB generals. They had many enemies in the army, who were commenting pejoratively on events and spreading rumors of impending disaster. Moreover, the FEB colonels would probably be promoted rapidly after the war, ahead of many who had alleged one excuse or another for

[43] Paulo Dumangin Santos, "Observações de um Oficial de Informações de Batalhão," *Depoimento de Oficias da Reserva*, pp. 302–303.

not going to Italy. It was clear that the stay-at-home, politically-oriented, ponderous Army of Caxias was growing uneasy about its strange stepchild. It is interesting that Getúlio himself did not seem uneasy about it, although it was to become commonplace to say that the FEB signed the death-warrant of the Estado Nôvo. Perhaps he hoped that the FEB would transform the Brazilian army from a praetorian guard into a nonpolitical professional force. Whatever his thoughts were, he gave his word that Mascarenhas would not be relieved.[44]

Getúlio knew that Mascarenhas was nonpolitical, respected legal authority, and took deep pride in his "old habit of discipline." In 1901 they had been cadets together at the Preparatory and Tactical School of Rio Pardo in Rio Grande do Sul, and they were both *Florianistas*.[45] Once, when the school's commandant ordered the cadets not to attend ceremonies honoring Marshal Floriano's memory, Getúlio's political sentiments took precedence and he attended with the majority of the cadets, but Mascarenhas obeyed the order.[46]

In January 1945 snow began to pile up, to the mixed delight and dismay of the Brazilians. The command took advantage of the comparative lull in the fighting to give the *Febianos* ski training, as well as rest and recreation in rear

[44] Based on Brayner's account *Verdade*, pp. 312–327; Mascarenhas mentioned thoughts of resignation after the December 12 defeat in *Memórias*, I, 227.

[45] Followers of deceased marshal and president Floriano Peixoto. For a discussion of *Florianismo* see Nelson Werneck Sodré, *História Militar do Brasil* (Rio de Janeiro, 1965), pp. 162–177.

[46] As Mascarenhas told the story, when the commandant discovered that most of the cadets had disobeyed and gone to the ceremonies he sounded assembly. Mascarenhas, running to the patio, was the first to arrive, he looked around and saw Getúlio coming in from outside the school. They were the first two to form up. The incident showed Getúlio's willingness to give the appearance of compliance while actually doing what he wanted, while Mascarenhas followed the simpler rule that an order given was an order obeyed. Mascarenhas, *Memórias*, I, 14, 104–105.

areas. A number of men utilized their leaves to marry Italian women, while others visited Rome, Pisa, and Florence, but for most of the troops the winter meant dangerous daily patrols, ducking for cover during the continuous German artillery harassment, worrying about trench foot, and re-reading untold times the last letter from Montes Claros, Pôrto Alegre, Campo Grande, Fortaleza, or Pindamon-hangaba.

Mail from Brazil was censored and often arrived at the front only after a long interval. During the FEB's first days in Italy there was a period of about a month without mail. Darcy Vargas, the president's wife, wrote Roosevelt asking that he arrange transportation, and immediately the Air Transport Command began ferrying mail from Brazil.[47] But when it finally reached the troops, they found attached to each letter instructions from the Ministry of War that they advise their correspondents to write clearly on one side of a page, and that they were to do likewise to speed censorship. In one case an officer's wife was expecting a baby when he embarked, and after a long anxious wait a letter from her arrived saying that she had had a girl "but . . ." and there followed a long blank ending with *abraços.* Imagine the poor fellow's state of mind until the next letter came saying that all was well![48] Receiving censored mail did not help morale or increase the *Febianos'* love of the Vargas regime, which they blamed for it, but of course such censorship was general in the allied armies.

American authorities discouraged the Brazilians from sending packages, and those that were sent often arrived open and half-empty.[49] The front-line troops thought that such treatment compared unfavorably with the American

---

[47] Darcy Sarmanho Vargas to Roosevelt, Rio, Dec. 29, 1944, PPF 4473 (Vargas) and FDR to Darcy S. Vargas, Washington, Mar. 31, 1945, of 11-A, FDRL.

[48] Dumangin Santos, "Observações," *Depoimento de Oficiais da Reserva,* pp. 304–305.

[49] *Ibid.,* p. 305.

army's mail system but the Americans suffered similar inconveniences. The American army, however, did place higher priority on troop well-being and morale than did the Army of Caxias.

Nowhere did the spirit of Caxias and the Americanization of the FEB clash with more force than in the division's replacement depot. Before December 1944 the FEB had no replacement system because it had no replacements. When the last two echelons (the 4th and 5th), of approximately 5,000 men each, arrived in December and February they were formed into a training and replacement command of twenty companies near Staffoli, between Pisa and Florence. The colonel in command consistently ignored the advice of the Fifth Army team sent to assist him. Sanitation, supply, maintenance, the assignment system, and training operations were all adversely affected by his arrogant determination to do things his way. Although the Mediterranean theater command refused to approve his proposed table of organization, he put it into effect anyway. American advisers called it a "monstrosity"; compared to American replacement depots twice the number of officers and enlisted men were used for administrative tasks, and of the 2,053 officers and enlisted men assigned to the command only fifty-five were directly under the training officer (s-3) and available as instructors. This was entirely inadequate.

The overabundance of personnel naturally led in good Brazilian fashion to a superabundance of red tape. So much "unnecessary paper work" was being done that no one bothered to see if the training companies and individual soldiers actually received requisitioned equipment. After three months of operation only one and one-half gallons of water was available per man, instead of the five gallons per man recommended for a semipermanent camp without plumbing, because many companies had not received their proper allotment of storage facilities (water cans, lister bags, etc.). The full allotment of soap and fatigue uniforms was not distributed, so the troops often appeared sloppy and dirty.

And because footwear was not fitted, inspected, or re-paired, the soldiers marched about in the wrong-sized boots in all stages of deterioration.

A motor pool was not established until mid-March, and until then vehicles were kept in company areas or parked in front of the user's tent. Vehicles entered and left the de-pot with no records kept. Joyriding was common and main-tenance abominable. As elsewhere in the allied forces, "midnight requisitioning," particularly of jeeps, was a de-fensive necessity, but one which the Brazilians enjoyed. Many accounts, including Mark Clark's, refer to the large number of accidents, which American advisers attributed to inadequate driver training.

No system was established for classifying personnel in re-lation to the division's needs, so the FEB headquarters could not set up a replacement system based on skills required; it merely called for numbers, often receiving untrained offi-cers and troops. Until the beginning of March 1945 "almost no training facilities such as ranges, infiltration courses, bayonet courses, etc. existed; there was a great lack of train-ing equipment; and instructors were insufficient as well as poorly trained. Replacements being sent into combat in in-fantry units never saw 60 mm. mortars or Browning Auto-matic rifles, because the Depot had none."[50]

In February the Fifth Army sent a team of Portuguese-speaking instructors to the depot to supervise training. The depot commander reduced the recommended training pe-riod from eight to six weeks and always had an excuse when men missed training sessions. At least, however, he did ap-prove expanding the work week to forty-eight hours. Co-operation between the senior officers at the depot and their American advisers was less than complete. The training offi-cer (S-3), Colonel Archiminio Pereira, was, in the opinion of American observers, "the only senior Brazilian officer

[50] Capt. Frank T. Cameron, "Historical Report of the Brazilian Re-placement Depot," Report 1/Inf. Div. BEF, OCMH. Declassified microfilm copy in possession of author.

TABLE 2. DATA ON FEB

1. 239 days of continuous contact with enemy units September 6, 1944 to May 2, 1945.

2. Troop Strength

1st Echelon	5,075
2d & 3d Echelons	10,375
4th Echelon	4,691
5th Echelon	5,082
Arrived by air	111
TOTAL	25,334

3. Troops in Front-line units 15,069
   Troops attached to personnel depot and
   other noncombatant organizations 10,265

4. Casualties and Prisoners of War
   a. Killed

Officers	13
Enlisted	444
Officers of Brazilian Air Force (1st Fighter Squadron 12 U.S. Army Air Force)	8
	465

   b. Wounded and Accident Victims

Wounded in combat	1,577
Combat-connected accident victims	487
Non-combat accident victims	658
	2,722

   c. Brazilians Taken Prisoner

Officers	1
Enlisted	34
	35

   d. Regimental Deaths

1st IR	154
6th IR	108
11th IR	134
	396

5. German and Italian Prisoners Taken

Generals	2
Officers	892
Enlisted	19,679
	20,573[1]

6. Victories

Camaiore	Montese
Monte Prano	Zocca
Monte Castello	Collecchio
Castelnuovo	Fornovo

7. Casualty Figures

1944	July	316
	August	130
	September	215
	October	519
	November	901
	December	2,016
1945	January	1,474
	February	1,537
	March	1,978
	April	1,963
	May	568
	TOTAL	11,617[2]

[1] Most of these were from the 148th Infantry Division, the 90th Motorized Division, and the Italia Division.

[2] Of these an estimated 8,430 were due to sickness. The remainder were killed, wounded, missing in action, or injured in accidents. Data from: Mascarenhas, *FEB*, insert opposite p. 26, & pp. 402–403.

responsible for the success of the infantry training." From March 19 until May 15 American personnel supervised every hour of such training, producing the only fully trained troops in the FEB; and these troops never saw combat. "The Depot never approached 100% efficiency, but it was able to rid itself of almost complete paralysis."[51]

Men risking their lives in the front lines understandably

[51] *Ibid.*

resented those who sought the safety of the personnel depot. The latter echelons apparently had many officers who wanted the distinction of serving in the FEB to further their careers, but who had joined the outpost of the Army of Caxias at Staffoli rather than the FEB facing Monte Castello. The *Febianos* sang in their trenches and foxholes with considerable resentment about those "heroes of the rearguard" who lived the good life without ever seeing Germans. They also sang "Lili Marlene," as did their allies and opponents. On the way over on the ships they had sung of the need to hurry to the front before the war was over and of what they were going to do to the *tedescos* (Germans). On the front their songs were both serious and frivolous: one urged the *tedescos* to surrender because their cause was lost, while another compared the German machine guns (called *Lourdinhas*) to a rapid-tongued girl friend. One of Dorival Caymmi's sambas (*Que é que a baiana tem?*) was reworded to describe the glories of Brazil (*No Brasil Tem*), where everything existed that people could want.[52]

In spite of feeling backward in comparison to their allies (indeed in their minds Brazilian country folk compared unfavorably to the industrious Italians around them), the *Febianos'* self-criticisms were balanced by a growing pride in Brazil and a determination to develop it according to the standards they saw on every side. These noisy, gregarious soldiers who painted names and sayings on the bumpers of their jeeps and trucks, listened to German propaganda broadcasts of sambas, soccer, and news, in Portuguese, and read mimeographed newspapers called *Zé Carioca* and *É a*

[52] "Herois da Retaguarda," written by soldier Pieri Junior, a member of the Sampaio Regiment (1 IR) musical group. The group formed before embarkation in 1944 and re-formed in 1965 to make a record of FEB songs: "20 Anos Depois: Expedicionários em Ritmos," Chantecler Records, São Paulo, release CMG 2397; interviews with Seraphim José de Oliveira, group leader, Rio, Sept. 1965; Dumangin Santos, "Observações," *Depoimento de Oficiais da Reserva*, p. 382.

cobra fumou, would return home greatly changed from the men who sailed from Rio de Janeiro. And by no means the least element affecting them was the egalitarian atmosphere of the front-line units, where lieutenants and captains listened respectfully to advice from sergeants and corporals.[53]

Such exchanges may have helped avert another suicidal frontal attack on Monte Castello when the Fifth Army renewed the offensive against the Gothic Line in late February. For the Fourth Corps to advance it had to sweep the Germans off Monte Belvedere, Monte Gorgolesco, and Monte Castello. On February 19 the United States 10th Mountain Division, specially trained for this type of warfare in the Rocky Mountains, began attacking Belvedere and Gorgolesco to the east of Monte Castello. Once those heights were secured the Brazilians were to take Castello and move on toward Montese. Strong resistance and counterattacks prevented the 10th from reaching the point which was to signal the FEB's advance until February 20. Next day at dawn the Sampaio Regiment (1st IR) moved out to attack Monte Castello's flanks, this time avoiding the disastrous frontal assault. As the 10th Mountain and the Sampaio advanced with heavy patrols to the front, one of the American units wandered into the Brazilian zone and, mistaking the Brazilians for Germans, opened fire on one of the Sampaio companies, killing a soldier and wounding several others. Only Mascarenhas' direct intervention prevented one of the Sampaio's battalion commanders from "teaching a lesson" to the Americans.[54] Meanwhile, many German soldiers in front of the Sampaio took advantage of the confusion and fled from their positions to avoid capture. The incident cast a shadow on an otherwise glorious day.

Late in the afternoon Generals Crittenberger, Clark, and Truscott visited Mascarenhas' command post. Crittenberger wanted to know why the FEB's reserve had not gone into

---

[53] Joel Silveira, *As Duas Guerras da FEB* (Rio de Janeiro, 1965), pp. 62–64.

[54] Brayner, *Verdade*, p. 357.

action. Mascarenhas said it was not yet opportune. Irritated and impatient, Crittenberger pointed at his watch and said: "It is 1600 hours. Nightfall is imminent. And Monte Castello, nothing, once more!" General Clark reminded him that Mascarenhas was in charge and had not asked for any assistance. After they left Mascarenhas said he agreed that the Sampaio was moving too slowly and sent Brayner to tell General Zenóbio, who was supervising the maneuver from the Sampaio's command post, about the Americans' visit and that he wanted the crest reached while it was still daylight to allow maximum artillery support. "We will not lose the confidence of the American commanders," Mascarenhas declared.[55]

At the Sampaio command post Zenóbio was also becoming impatient. With considerable emotion the regimental commander, Colonel Aguinaldo Caiado de Castro, excused the slow advance, saying that he was trying to avoid an "exaggerated sacrifice, aggravating the losses that we are suffering." "But my dear fellow," Zenóbio asked sarcastically, "do you want to conquer Monte Castello with men or with flowers?"[56]

At 4:20 P.M. the FEB artillery concentrated all of its guns on the German positions in a long rapid-fire bombardment. An hour and a half later (5:50 P.M.) the telephone rang in Mascarenhas' command post, and from the other end of the line General Zenóbio was shouting excitedly that the mountain was theirs. The FEB had proven itself! Crittenberger's acid question of December 12 as to whether the FEB had "an offensive capability" was answered affirmatively.[57] Monte

[55] *Ibid.*, p. 358: "Não percamos a confiança dos Chefes americanos."

[56] *Ibid.*, p. 359: "General, meu único intuito, cercando-me de precauções, é evitar o sacrifício exagerado, agravando as perdas que estamos sofrendo." "Mas, meu caro, você quer conquistar Monte Castello com homens ou com flôres?"

[57] For this comment see the exchange of letters between Mascarenhas and Crittenberger, Dec. 13, 1944 in Mascarenhas, *FEB*, pp. 133–136. For a description from the perspective of Gen. Cordeiro de Farias' artillery command post see Silveira, *Duas Guerras*, pp. 98–103.

Castello was the barrier that stood between the FEB and maturity as a fighting force. Other difficult battles lay ahead, but the fight for self-confidence and for the respect of the American field commanders had been won.

The songs of the troops said it best. They had come from Brazil to show the greatness of their people (*grandeza de nossa gente*) by doing their duty in the fight for liberty. When the Sampaio took Monte Castello at bayonet point it had "conquered glory and shown the fiber of the Brazilian army." With relief, joy, and confidence in victory they sang of these things at a show on the slopes of Monte Castello on February 16.[58]

In Brazil the press heralded the victory as the apex of the FEB's campaign. It predicted that Brazil would be invited to join the big five in the Supreme Allied Council, thus advancing Brazil to great-power status. As *A Manhã* editorialized: "This position—in which we will be able to participate directly in the political and economic reconstruction of the world—was conquered by the dedication of Brazil to the cause of the United Nations, by its firm antitotalitarian posture, by the sacrifice of our people and, above all, by the heroism of our expeditionaries. Monte Castello already is a legend. The young Brazilians who implanted the Brazilian banner on its summit will conquer for Brazil the place that it merits in the world of tomorrow."[59]

It would take more detail than is warranted here to treat the rest of the campaign. Suffice it to say that on March 5, 1945, Castelnuovo fell to the FEB, followed by Montese on April 16 after a grueling four-day battle with 426 casualties,[60] and finally Fornovo on April 29. Then came the heady experience of fighting to a standstill the German

58 The above is based on the following songs: "Capitão Iedo comandou"; "Parabéns à FEB"; "Presente"; taken from recording "20 Anos Depois, Expedicionários em Ritmos," see note 52 above.

59 *A Manhã*, Rio, Feb. 27, 1945.

60 Ruben Braga, "Brasileiros na Guerra," *Realidade*, IV, 40 (July 1969), 53; Newton C. de Andrade Mello, *A Epopeia de Montese* (Curitiba, 1955).

148th Division and remnants of the Fascist Italian Monte Rosa, San Marco, and Italia Divisions, which surrendered to General Mascarenhas on April 29–30. In the space of a few days the Brazilians trapped and accepted the surrender of two generals, 800 officers, and 14,700 enlisted men.

With the German surrender the FEB changed from a fighting force into a political force. As the political tempo increased in Brazil with each allied victory many saw the FEB as a guarantee that the Vargas dictatorship was finished. At the end of 1944 even Vargas was talking publicly about elections,[61] and such stalwart *estadonovistas* as Góes Monteiro and Dutra were calling, in the phrase of commentator Macedo Soares, for a revival of a "free political life under legitimate democratic institutions."[62] *O Jornal* opined that in the coming peace conference Brazil "should play a part that measures up to the responsibilities we have assumed and the sacrifices we have made during this war." It warned Brazilians, however, that they could not do so "with the full force of our prestige, if in our country we have not put completely into practice the democratic principles for which we fight."[63] *Diário de Notícias* editorialized that if Vargas were to be a candidate he could not preside over the elections.[64] And on February 23 eight Rio de Janeiro newspapers came out in support of the candidacy of Air Force Brigadier Eduardo Gomes. *Correio da Noite* exclaimed: "His name yesterday whispered as a rumor is today pronounced freely. . . . A reviving breath of democracy is breathed."[65]

Mascarenhas had tried faithfully to control his officers' political activity during the campaign, and he himself had kept quiet. But he could not prevent the Brazilian press,

61 *O Globo*, Rio, Jan. 2, 1945.

62 *Diário Carioca*, Rio, Feb. 3, 1945.

63 *O Jornal*, Rio, Feb. [ca. Feb. 6], 1945.

64 *Diário de Notícias*, Rio, Feb. 23, 1945.

65 *Correio da Noite*, Rio, Feb. 23, 1945. The other newspapers were *Diário Carioca, O Jornal, Correio da Manhã, Diário de Notícias, O Globo, Diário da Noite, A Notícia.*

once domestic censorship had been lifted, from using the FEB and the generals' names. Anti-Vargas publisher Assis Chateaubriand sent heated cables to his man in Italy, Jöel Silveira, demanding that he get the generals' opinion about Gomes' candidacy and the political situation. Mascarenhas passed the word that the rule was "no comment," but even so the *Diários Associados* chain carried the story in late February that Generals Cordeiro de Farias and Falconiere and Colonel Nélson de Melo supported Gomes.[66]

In March the FEB's newspaper, *O Cruzeiro do Sul*, began carrying summaries of political news from home. One issue mentioned that Oswaldo Aranha was supporting Gomes, that Dutra was the official government candidate, that the Brazilian Press Association (ABI) had formed a committee to seek liberation and amnesty for political prisoners and exiles, and that Carlos de Lima Cavalcanti, Brazil's ambassador to Mexico, was resigning to support Gomes.[67] On March 26 Mascarenhas made it clear to his special services chief that he did not like such reporting, and ordered a strict set of guidelines prepared. The resulting prohibitions forbade comments on political parties, local disturbances, or any mention of political figures—especially, regardless of their nature, no references were to be made to communist leaders. The FEB press was "to limit itself to information of a general order on decrees, codes, or measures taken by the government and to a cold exposition on the evolution of the political situation."[68] Thereafter the column *O Que Vai Pelo Brasil* (What's Happening in Brazil), which had carried

[66] *O Jornal*, Rio, Feb. 27, 1945; Silveira discussed political activity among Febianos in his *Duas Guerras*, pp. 29–31. Col. Nélson de Melo was corresponding with Virgílio de Melo Franco, a leader of the anti-Vargas forces; see Carolina Nabuco, *A Vida de Virgílio de Melo Franco* (Rio de Janeiro, 1962), pp. 159–160; see also Mascarenhas, *FEB*, p. 305.

[67] *O Cruzeiro do Sul*, FEB, Mar. 22, 1945, AFEB.

[68] Maj. Reynaldo Ramos Saldanha da Gama, Chief of Special Services, to Commanding General 1st. Inf. Div. FEB, Florence, Mar. 26, 1945; and Maj. Saldanha da Gama to Colonel, Chief of Staff [Brayner], Florence, Mar. 26, 1945, in Serviço Especial 28 and 29, Pasta 22, Armário I, AFEB.

most of the political news, confined itself to harmless items such as a recent fire on the Rio docks.[69] By late April the editor became bold enough to report that Vargas had decreed amnesty for political exiles.[70] But that was the limit.

Even without detailed news from home and without official interviews, however, the FEB officers talked a good deal "off the record" to the effect that the Estado Nôvo, like the German army facing them, was living its last moments. Many a bottle of Italian wine was opened to "celebrate the victories of the second front, of the internal front."[71] Everyone thought that the FEB's return would somehow transform Brazil. The *Febianos* had seen the power of their allies at first hand, had seen the sturdy industriousness of the Italians, the dogged determination and superb organization of their opponents; above all they could not deny that, while Brazil might have everything, Brazilians enjoyed very little of their land's wealth. Recognition of this unpleasant truth brought a commitment to change, to development, which would sooner or later lead the *Febianos* more as a unified spirit than as a physical group into the struggle for political power.

In mid-May the Brazilian press was concerned over the Trieste situation, and possible involvement in an allied struggle with Marshal Tito's Yugoslavs. The *Correio da Manhã* urged immediate withdrawal of Brazilian troops—they had accomplished their purpose and "no more Brazilian blood must flow."[72] The government agreed and Mascarenhas requested early shipment home. On May 11 in Alessandria's cathedral the FEB honored its 457 dead at a solemn Requiem Mass.[73] They buried their comrades at

[69] *O Cruzeiro do Sul*, FEB, Apr. 1, 1945, AFEB.

[70] *Ibid.*, Apr. 22, 1945.   [71] Silveira, *Duas Guerras*, pp. 30–31.

[72] *Correio da Manhã*, Rio, May [ca. May 16], 1945.

[73] Of the 457 total, 396 were from the three infantry regiments (1, 6, 11), some 14 were beyond identification and two were never found. Their remains rested in the Brazilian cemetery at Pistoia until 1960 when they were entombed in the crypt of the World War II monument in Rio, a short distance from the old Praça Paris where they lined up

Pistoia, where the Brazilian flag still flies, and gathered at Francolise amid the memories, the dust, and the sympathetic whores to await the troop transports. The atmosphere was melancholy and the troops were oppressed with a sense of being marginal. They deeply resented being forced to surrender the captured German guns, trucks, and horses. But the American request that they turn in their weapons and equipment was particularly shocking and degrading, especially because Brazil was willing to pay in hard currency for what the troops felt they had already earned with their blood. Did the Americans not feel gratitude for their efforts? How could they return home as naked as they had come? Mascarenhas turned aside suggestions that they form part of the armies of occupation, to avoid the uneasy feeling that they were mercenaries. An understandable attitude, but one that caused Brazil to miss a singular opportunity to expand its wartime role into one of greater influence in peacetime. Of course the Brazilians could not imagine in June and July of 1945 that in the months ahead the mammoth American forces would be rapidly demobilized and that a full combat-trained division in occupied Europe would count for a great deal more than it had during the war. The diplomats arranged for the FEB to keep its weapons and therewith its pride.[74] But the return to Brazil would be marred by further deceptions and bitternesss when their own countrymen extinguished the cobra's fiery pipe.

---

for review in May 1944. The Pistoia cemetery still contains the remains of one unknown discovered at Montese, and the FEB's memory is honored with a large monument cared for by a *Febiano* from Rio Grande do Sul who is married to an Italian woman. It is a curious accident that Pistoia was and is a stronghold of the Italian Communist Party. For a current description of the battlegrounds see Ruben Braga, "Brasileiros na Guerra," *Realidade*, IV, 40 (July 1969), 29–58. The FEB's total battle casualties were 3,187, with another 8,430 evacuated to rear areas at one time or another because of accidents or illnesses.

[74] Memo of Conversation between State and War Departments Representatives, May 25, 1945, 832.24/2545, DSF.

Three Brazilian and three American vessels returned the FEB to Rio in echelon. Ironically and prophetically, the Brazilian ships were the *Duque de Caxias*, the *Pedro I*, and the *Pedro II*. The very day the USS *General Meigs* steamed out of the Naples harbor with the first echelon of 4,931 expeditionaries, Minister of War Dutra issued orders demobilizing the FEB immediately upon arrival in Rio de Janeiro and setting an eight-day limit on use of the FEB uniform and the Smoking Cobra and Fifth Army shoulder patches. The order of July 6 also forbade the forming of veterans' groups, commenting on the campaign, or even reading the poetry the men had written. The regime was afraid that Dutra or Gomes would use the FEB to overthrow it, because 80 to 95 percent of the officers were reportedly opposed to the dictatorship. It is also likely that Gomes' popularity with those same officers made Dutra more than willing to see the FEB disassembled rapidly, to prevent it from being used in a pro-Gomes coup d'état. Supposedly Dutra, who stood to gain more than Vargas by eliminating the FEB as a pawn in the political chess game,[75] had been making strategic transfers and arranging the retirement of officers who might oppose him. Actually the vast majority of *Febianos*, although they recognized the need for political reform, were more concerned about returning to their homes and families than about politics. Dutra's orders, however, were to have an effect opposite to that desired—striking at the FEB and depreciating their sacrifices would politicize them rather than distract them from the political scene.[76] In the opinion of FEB Chief of Staff Brayner "it was an integral victory for the 'Fifth Column,' that had caused so much trouble during the campaign."[77]

[75] Adolf A. Berle, Rio, July 10, 1945, 832.00/7-1045; Memo, Views on Brazilian Situation, Rio, May 28, 1945, 832.00/5-2845, DSF.

[76] See comments in Castello Branco, *Brasil na II Grande Guerra*, pp. 539-544.

[77] Brayner, *Verdade*, p. 520; for one officer's personal difficulties see Dumangin Santos, "Observações," *Depoimento de Oficiais da Reserva*, p. 307.

On July 18, as the *Meigs* passed Sugar Loaf Mountain, the cannons of the old fortresses fired salute upon salute; hundreds of boats escorted the troopship toward its moorings while the great bells of Rio's many churches pealed and crowds gathered in the streets. Rio de Janeiro was in *festa!* Generals Clark and Crittenberger and other American officers were on the reviewing stand with Mascarenhas, as General Zenóbio led the troops past cheering throngs who soon broke police lines and reduced the victory parade to carnival chaos. The *pracinhas* shouldered their way single-file through their jubilant countrymen, eventually reaching the paymasters' tables. Meanwhile, on the docks, less patriotic citizens were busy looting the veterans' duffle bags.[78] Before nightfall the *Febianos* were out of Rio, scattered to units all over Brazil, and some were demobilized and returned to civilian status that very day.[79]

Mammoth victory celebrations were held in São Paulo, Belo Horizonte, and Pôrto Alegre when units from those towns reached home. Following the example of Rio, crowds swarmed into the parading soldiers, pounding their backs, giving them abraços and kisses, and carrying them on their shoulders "with all the effusiveness usually reserved for immediate friends and relatives." In São Paulo, the demonstrations surpassed "the wildest carnivals."[80] The American generals were amazed at the outpouring of emotion, which in staid, conservative Belo Horizonte reached such a pitch that the crowd literally picked General Clark off his feet and carried him to his hotel.[81]

But when the cheering died down the *Febianos* were ignored, if not entirely forgotten. The first legislation awarding veterans' benefits did not come until 1948. Many veterans languished in an emotional void, in the absence of

---

[78] *Ibid.*, pp. 307–308.
[79] Berle, Rio, July 10, 1945, 832.00/7–1045, DSF. This is a report of debarkation plans.
[80] Cecil Cross, São Paulo, Aug. 3, 1945, 832.20/8–345, DSF.
[81] Clark, *Calculated Risk*, pp. 450–451.

a comprehensive program, unable to find their niche in civilian society. The rough, rapid demobilization generated "a sense of anguish among those who had committed the ugly crime of . . . being *febiano*."[82]

The vague resentments of the *Febianos* would deepen with the years, would change focus and direction, even as Brazil changed. They knew, better than their fellow countrymen, how underdeveloped their land was, and how useless was talk of grandeur without organization and will power. Even though their deeds in Italy fed the expanding nationalist myths, they were confirmed internationalists, confident in their American ally's sincerity. As one ex-FEB officer expressed it: "In the War the United States had to give us everything: food, clothes, equipment. After the War, we were less afraid of United States imperialism than other officers because we saw the United States really helped us without strings attached."[83] The ex-officers of the FEB would struggle against what they considered the exaggerated nationalism of their army colleagues, and would blame the ineptness of the civilian elite for the nation's underdevelopment.

[82] Brayner, *Verdade*, p. 521; Castello Branco, *Brasil na II Grande Guerra*, pp. 539–544; Newton C. de Andrade Mello, *Causas e Consequências da Participação do Brasil na II Grande Guerra* (Rio de Janeiro, 1958), pp. 47–49; Luciano Alfredo Barcellos, "A Flagelação dos Ex-Combatentes," in José Louzeiro, ed., *Assim Marcha a Família* (Rio de Janeiro, 1965), pp. 145–159.

[83] Edson de Figueiredo, as quoted in Alfred Stepan, *The Military in Politics, Changing Patterns in Brazil* (Princeton, 1971), p. 242. General Figueiredo was a captain during the campaign and was decorated by the American, Italian, and Brazilian governments.

> "History and time shall speak for me. . . . The work-
> men, the humble . . . the people—will in the end
> understand me."[1]

15

End of an Era

THE YEAR 1945 ended an era in Brazilian history
that had begun with the consolidation of civilian control of
the central government in 1898. During that forty-seven
year period, although the military establishment was the
ultimate source of power and legitimacy, politicians dominated and managed the officer corps to suit political goals.
The military did not adhere to one political ideology, although they tended toward the conservative, gradualist
politics of the middle classes from which most of the officers
came. Perhaps the most distinctive political tendency in the
thinking of the officer corps was a shallow, but continuous,
undercurrent of *Florianismo* (from President and General
Floriano Peixoto, 1891–1894), which sought to replace the
conservative, rurally-based, upper-class government with
a middle-class regime that extended a degree of participation to the vaguely defined Brazilian people.

The *tenentes* of the 1920's seem to have absorbed elements of *Florianismo*, and the reformist ideology of the
Revolution of 1930 showed its influence. The army that
overthrew Washington Luís, however, and delivered the
presidency to Getúlio Vargas, acted to avoid civil war and
not out of political identification. It was the turmoil of the
1930's—the Paulista uprising of 1932, the resurgence of di-

[1] Getúlio Vargas' resignation note published in *O Jornal*, Rio, Oct.
30, 1945. See note 100 below.

visive regional oligarchies, the Integralista and communist attempts to mobilize the middle and lower classes—that convinced the military of the bankruptcy of the liberal principles underlying the Republic.

Before 1937 the military viewed the chaos in society from their barracks, and generally accepted civilian interpretations of events. During the Estado Nôvo, however, the officers acted as interventors, industrial managers, censors, and propagandists, served on economic study commissions with civilian leaders, negotiated agreements with foreign officers, trained in the United States, prepared for war with Argentina, became increasingly involved in internal anti-subversive activities, and managed a combat division in Italy. The sum of these experiences produced an officer corps more aware than before of political forces and technocratic methods, and thoroughly committed to national development. At the same time they shared the middle-class fear that politicization of the masses would be a basic threat to their security, which they identified with national security. Moreover they were coopted by the old elite, which intimidated the officers with its apparent savoir-faire and luxurious way of life. This cooptation was especially widespread among general officers, who were economically and socially nearer the top of the social scale than the bottom, and who tended regardless of background to absorb an upper-class view of society and of national needs and priorities. Thus the officer corps in 1945 was intellectually different from what it had been before 1937 and was committed to economic development as a means of insuring national security, but it had not yet formulated its own body of doctrine. Such formulation was retarded by the officers' lack of appreciation for the complexity of creating an industrial society out of one that was predominantly agricultural, and nearly half of whose population was illiterate and living on a subsistence level. The officers' desire to be accepted by the victorious Americans and Europeans also prevented them from designing indigenous developmental formulae. Social reform on the communist model or mass mobilization of the Perón type were rejected because neither was acceptable to the Brazilian elite or to the Americans. The need of the officer corps to be accepted by those two groups, plus their own uncertainty as to what was best for Brazil, led them into a nervous coup d'état against Vargas. In the process they prevented establishment of a constitutional government under civilian aegis, and fully repossessed the role of the moderator of the political system which they had shared with Vargas. World War II raised the military professionalization of the officer corps but it also intensified its politicization. While the coup of October 29, 1945, removed the civilian dictator, it also insured military participation in the postwar political process and contributed to the establishment of military rule in 1964 by obviating the politicians' need to behave responsibly. Brazil would have "democracy" at bayonet point.

Dutra and Góes Monteiro gave Getúlio dictatorial powers in 1937, when such powers were fashionable, and took them away when the mode changed. Góes, who was an admirer of Napoleon Bonaparte, liked to play the grand role. After Aranha resigned he threatened to do likewise (because of his friendship with Aranha, rather than for political reasons), but Getúlio wished to keep him out of the opposition camp and ordered him home from Montevideo. En route to Rio de Janeiro regional commanders told Góes of the unrest and the general feeling that, because the war was ending and Brazilian blood had been shed for freedom, it was time for the dictatorship to end as well. A brass band, guard of honor, and a constellation of generals welcomed Góes to Rio, on November 1, as if he were the man of the hour. Later that day Dutra told him that because they had been chiefly responsible for "the situation created in 1937," and since Getúlio had kept silent for seven years about submitting the constitution to a plebiscite and about elections, it was their duty to force him to clarify his intentions. Before going to a luncheon in his honor, Góes sounded out

Aranha and opposition leader Virgílio de Melo Franco, and found them anxious for a change and talking of Air Force Brigadier Eduardo Gomes as a presidential candidate. At the luncheon at the Rio Yacht Club an anti-*Getulista* general, who normally opposed Dutra, toasted the Minister of War. Dutra responded with a prepared address, reviewing his ministry in what appeared to be a presentation of accounts. General Firmo Freire, chief of Vargas' military staff, turned to Góes Monteiro to ask what this meant. Góes answered playfully: "The cobra is smoking. . . ."[2] He might just as well have said that the chameleon was adapting its color to its new surroundings.

That afternoon Góes told Getúlio that he had returned to end the Estado Nôvo, as the mood in the country and the coming allied victory demanded. Getúlio was not impressed with Góes' advice to call a constitutional convention to decide the nation's course. Apparently he preferred a solution based on implementation of the 1937 constitution which would safeguard his numerous decree-laws. At any rate he promised Góes that Minister of Labor and Justice Marcondes Filho would consult with the generals as he drew up plans to restore constitutional rule.[3]

On the last day of December 1944 Vargas addressed a gathering of ranking officers at a luncheon in the Automobile Club. He said that the internal situation and the course of the war would shape the problems of political organization, and that "premature agitation" and "threats to the public tranquility" would only make things difficult. Political and social changes should occur within the "processes of gradual evolution, under the imperium of law and order." Every effort would be made, he promised, to secure a "pacific atmosphere" in which to freely and fully consult public opinion. He did not use the word elections but the

[2] Lourival Coutinho, *O General Góes Depõe* (Rio de Janeiro, 1956), pp. 401–405.

[3] *Ibid.*, pp. 406–407.

Rio newspapers and foreign observers interpreted his statements that way. He did say that the "consultation" (con-
sulta à opinião) would take place "shortly" (brevemente).[4]

It was significant that he made the annoucement in a
speech to the principal military officers—although he was
building organized support among the working classes he
knew that the army was the key pillar supporting the regime. At the same time he had hopes of distracting them
from the political game by increasing their participation in
economic sectors. In Vargas' schema the military would
have the twofold role of supplying trained technicians and
providing discipline. "Unity of purpose and unity of action"
were necessary to avoid a dispersion of effort in the postwar period.[5]

Dutra echoed the president's plea for continued military
support the next day at the New Year's reception for generals at the Ministry of War. It was their duty, he declared,
to preserve internal order and to prevent the end of the war
from having "great social repercussions." And they could
best do that by remaining above the political struggles.[6]
Ostensibly, Dutra was concerned because the anti-Vargas
forces were attempting to split the officer corps and involve
it in the campaign. Opposition leaders had met in Rio at the
end of December to promote Brigadier Eduardo Gomes as
their candidate. He had a heroic image as the survivor of
the 1922 *tenente* revolt at Fort Copacabana, and a democratic reputation because he had resigned his command to
protest the 1937 coup d'état and because of his supposed
closeness to Americans in the northeast. Such an image
suited the antifascist, pro-allied attitudes of many young

4 *O Globo*, Rio, Jan. 2, 1945; Vinton Chapin (1st Secy. Emb.), Rio,
Jan. 2, 1945, 832.00/1-245, Department of State Files. State Dept. documents for period after Jan. 1, 1945 are, at this writing, located in the
central files of the department (DSF).

5 *O Globo*, Rio, Jan. 2, 1945.

6 *Correio da Manhã*, Rio, Jan. 3, 1945.

officers, especially those in the FEB, who were anxious that
Brazil be welcomed in the victors' councils.

The Division of Brazilian Affairs of the Department of
State, which was following the situation, predicted: "If
President Vargas loses the support of any substantial portion of the Army, his government is not likely to survive."[7]
Throughout the next months Getúlio had two objectives:
first, to build a viable political structure that would survive
the Estado Nôvo and preserve his influence; second, to keep
the army either neutral or supportive. His wealthy industrial backers planned to finance a campaign to keep Getúlio
in the presidency, because "any other Administration would
cause the loss of the ground already won by industry and
would annul the place which we are trying to win for the
future."[8] Minister Marcondes Filho had a Paulista lawyer,
Benedito Costa Neto, working on a sweeping additional act
to the constitution. Under the plan, which Marcondes had
concocted with Benjamim Vargas and the industrialists,
elections would be held but before that secret agents would
instigate a series of strikes, culminating in a general strike.
Then, at the peak of the agitation, a new constitution would
be issued. Marcondes depended "a great deal on the support of the industries and on the suddenness of the measures" in preparation. Euvaldo Lodi wrote Roberto Simonsen that Marcondes was convinced that there was "not the
slightest risk of a disagreeable surprise" in the elections, but
Lodi had his doubts; he warned that in order not "to lose
the game, we are going to spend about one hundred million cruzeiros." Interested industrialists in Rio de Janeiro
and São Paulo were being asked to contribute.[9]

[7] Randolph Harrison to Philip O. Chalmers, Division of Brazilian
Affairs, Jan. 27, 1945, 832.00/1-2745, DSF.

[8] Euvaldo Lodi to Roberto Simonsen, Rio, Jan. (n.d.), 1945, 832.00/
4-945, DSF. In addition to Lodi and Simonsen others involved were
Guilhermo de Silveira, Rocha Faria, and members of the Seabra family.

[9] *Ibid.* There was no indication in DSF of how this letter was obtained
but it appeared to be genuine. Cr. 100,000,000 equaled about $5,000,000.

The opposition's only recourse was to gain sufficient support in the officer corps to split its ranks and to launch a coup before the elections. Subsequent strategies all called for forcing Getúlio out of office—obviously the opposition's main objective—and also for constitutional government. Both the pro- and anti-Getúlio elements needed the army to carry out their plans. But the Marcondes group depended on labor to fill the ballot-boxes in order to provide democratic sanction, and the necessary political mobilization of the working classes panicked the opposition and frightened the army. The result was a military solution that eliminated both Vargas and the chance for eventual stable democratic government.

Getúlio's personal desires and attitudes in the midst of the plots and counterplots of 1945 were vague and seem to have fluctuated with events. He was genuinely tired and repeatedly expressed the wish to retire; but he was also concerned that his efforts to develop the country would be undone and, until Roosevelt died, he was anxious to take his place with him at the peace conference. He probably encouraged Marcondes' plots to increase his own options. Evidence that Getúlio was planning a coup d'état à la 1937, this time with active labor support and army acquiescence, was circumstantial but not conclusive. Certainly his fifteen years in power had taught him that an attempted coup would fail without the backing of the army high command.

In January the graduation ceremonies of the various *faculdades* (constituent colleges) of the University of São Paulo developed into open political demonstrations against the regime. At the polytechnical school ceremonies the principal speaker criticized the government; afterward the police called him in for questioning and a reprimand, although when students gave similar speeches at the medical school ceremonies shortly thereafter the police did nothing. The commencement speaker at the philosophy faculty cited Vargas' past statements favoring freedom of speech, elections, and the press, and then complained of the gap between promises and actions. The audience leapt to its feet, applauding vigorously. State officials on the platform, especially the police representative, were obviously ill at ease but remained silent. The indulgence in free speech reached its peak at the law school commencement on January 10. This time, to avoid embarrassment, state officials did not attend, and, despite police warnings, the class patron called for freedom of the press, the holding of elections, and a return to democracy. There were several outbursts of organized cheering, especially for the FEB, and each cheer was punctuated with "Down with the Estado Nôvo!" Three members of the class, who had been drafted into the FEB for taking part in student agitation in 1943, received their degrees in absentia and prolonged applause followed the reading of their names.[10]

From all over the country came reports that the left and the right were moving toward agreement on abolition of the dictatorship and return to constitutional government. A consensus seemed to be forming that unless Vargas took definite steps toward elections by the end of March there would be open revolt.[11] On January 26 the First Congress of Brazilian Writers demanded free speech and direct elections. A few days later Góes Monteiro commented that censorship was justified only in war or for national security, and implied that the time had come to end it. Newspaper editorials followed the persistent theme that Brazil must change its political system to attain international acceptance. *O Jornal's* presentation during the first week of February was typical: "The moral and political atmosphere of the world has been decisively transformed with the defeat of the totalitarian states and the triumph of the democratic systems. . . . The peace conference is drawing near; a con-

10 Cecil Cross, São Paulo, Jan. 11, 1945, 832.00/1-1145, DSF.

11 Donald W. Lamm (Vice-Consul), Recife, Jan. 12, 1945, 832.00/1-1245; and R. Harrison to Philip O. Chalmers, DBA, Jan. 27, 1945, 832.00/1-2745, DSF.

ference in which we should play a part that measures up to the responsibilities we have assumed and the sacrifices we have made during this war. We could not, however, take our place at the conference table with the full force of our prestige, if in our own country we had not put completely into practice the democratic principles for which we fight."[12]

On February 2 the new American ambassador, Adolf A. Berle, Jr., reported that the coming electoral law would provide for political parties and freedom of the press. Discussion of the impending liberalization was so open that the *New York Times* correspondent filed a story about it on February 9.[13] Seven days later Secretary of State Edward Stettinius arrived in Rio from Yalta, en route to the Inter-American Conference in Mexico City. Ostensibly, he had come to take Foreign Minister Velloso to Mexico, but according to the rumor mill he came to tell Getúlio that democracy was the order of the day. Wags said that Stettinius' gift, a radio, was to enable Vargas to find out what was happening in the world. Actually he had come to talk of Brazilian recognition of the Soviet Union, to muster Velloso's aid at Chapultepec, and to smooth any feathers ruffled by Washington's quashing of the Inter-American conference scheduled to meet in Rio in October. Now that it was safe to do so the anti-Vargas politicians came forward to strike their blows for freedom. José Américo de Almeida, a presidential candidate in 1937, issued a call for elections and declared that he, Vargas, and the other 1937 candidates should be ineligible. On February 23 eight Rio newspapers came out for Gomes, and the *Diário de Notícias* editorial-

12 *O Jornal*, Rio, Feb. (1 to 7), 1945, as quoted in Vinton Chapin, Rio, Feb. 7, 1945, 832.00/2-745, DSF. For a report of Dutra's fears of a split in the army see Walter J. Donnelly (Chargé), Rio, Jan. 16, 1945, 832.00/1-1645, DSF.

13 Adolf A. Berle, Rio, Feb. 2, 1945, 832.00/2-245, DSF; *New York Times*, Feb. 21, 1945. The *Times* story was datelined Rio, Feb. 9.

ized that Vargas' candidacy would not be compatible with his presiding over the elections.[14]

For the United States the events in Brazil in early 1945 were peripheral, of much less interest than news from the fighting fronts of Europe and the Pacific. But a small core of observers in the Department of State monitored the developing situation. Ambassador Berle, formerly an assistant secretary of state, filed voluminous and well-written despatches, but he lacked the rapport Caffery had enjoyed with Vargas and had no Aranha to provide inside information. The question Brazilians were asking was what attitude would the United States adopt toward Vargas? When Stettinius suddenly appeared in Rio, the opposition was afraid it signified Washington's approval. Some argued that Roosevelt's fourth-term election necessarily meant that the White House would not oppose Getúlio's staying in office if a legalistic way could be found. Actually Vargas' willingness to continue to cooperate, rather than a commitment to democratic government, would determine the American attitude. Berle was much concerned with maintaining the United States commercial supremacy in the Brazilian markets, and with implementing the June 1944 agreement providing for joint use of the northeastern air bases.[15] And during 1945, especially after Roosevelt's death in April, the Americans moved to disassociate themselves from Vargas and sought to insure a friendly, cooperative government in postwar Brazil. Admittedly there was a very practical consideration—if the DBA's January assessment that the Vargas regime "may be losing its grip" proved true, then the United States might be caught supporting the losing side in a revolution. One DBA official warned that there was "a tendency in the Department to take Brazil too much for

[14] *Diário de Notícias*, Rio, Feb. 23, 1945. The other newspapers were *Diário Carioca, O Jornal, Correio da Manhã, O Globo, Correio da Noite, Diário da Noite, A Notícia.*

[15] Berle, Rio, July 20, 1945, WPD 452.1 Brazil, WWII RS, NA; and *Foreign Relations, 1945*, IX, 623–638.

granted . . . we should not allow ourselves to be lulled, into a false sense of security." And while he considered an immediate revolt unlikely, "the trend of events in Brazil is such that we must be prepared for any eventuality."[16] Preparation included making clear to the opposition that rumors of United States intervention to prevent Vargas' deposition were false, and that Washington would not get involved in internal Brazilian politics.[17] The State Department's principal concern was to determine the opposition's attitude toward the United States. Early in 1945, one analyst noted that opposition leaders Virgílio de Melo Franco and Gomes were "very friendly to the United States so that any government which they headed might be expected to continue satisfactory cooperation with us."[18] Later when Dutra entered the lists as the government candidate he quickly announced that he favored "the strong and indestructible ties of friendship" that linked the two countries and that he would continue to collaborate "without restrictions."[19] By mid-1945 it appeared that, barring the sudden emergence of new forces or the "influence of international propaganda," and regardless of who won the presidency, the United States position in Brazil would be politically secure. There would be no need for intervention. As Berle put it, "both our short and long-range interest, as well as our moral integrity, requires continuance of the classic policy of non-intervention, accompanied by encouragement of the steady development of democratic institutions."[20] Later,

---

[16] Philip O. Chalmers to Mr. Warren (American Republics Affairs), Jan. 27, 1945, 832.00/1-2745, DSF.

[17] Berle talked with Juracy Magalhães and Oswaldo Aranha; see Berle, Rio, Feb. 10, 1945, 832.00/2-1045; and Feb. 15, 1945, /2-1545, DSF. Aranha came out for Gomes in late February, saying that "no other Brazilian, at this juncture, corresponded better to the necessities and aspirations of Brazil." See *O Jornal*, Rio, Feb. 25, 1945.

[18] Harrison to Chalmers, DBA, Jan. 27, 1945, 832.00/1-2745, DSF.

[19] *O Globo*, Rio, Apr. 3, 1945.

[20] Berle, Rio, May 9, 1945, 832.00/5-945, DSF.

Berle would discover that the Brazilians did not define "encouragement" and "intervention" the same way he did.

The favorable consensus regarding the American alliance allowed the United States government relative freedom to concentrate on insuring hegemony over Brazil's economic and military sectors. As the war in Europe came to a close Brazil was dependent on the United States market for the disposal of nearly all its exports, save for small amounts going to other South American countries and to South Africa. It also depended on American oil, coal, finished steel products, newsprint, and wide varieties of machines. Brazilian textile mills, especially, were anxious to keep their wartime boom going by importing new machinery. American private businessmen sensed the opportunity for production companies to unload secondhand machinery that they wished to replace, and for equipment firms to establish themselves in a foreign market ahead of the British. Businessmen put pressure on United States government agencies to allot them scarce shipping space, arguing, as did the president of a Philadelphia company specializing in machinery for bleaching and finishing cotton cloth, that "one of our allies is very anxious to control this market in our class of machinery. . . ."[21]

Meanwhile wartime agencies, such as the Foreign Economic Administration and the War Production Board, under the control of dollar-a-year Wall Streeters, sought to keep Brazilians dependent on United States products in such areas as petroleum, railroad equipment, and aircraft. When the Joint Brazilian-Bolivian Commission requested drilling rigs to sink ten wells in Bolivia, the DBA commented that, considering the scarcity of shipping to Brazil and the chaotic internal transportation situation, "it would be little short of madness to go out of our way to support" the equipment request. In like manner, the Foreign Economic

[21] Harry W. Butterworth, Jr., to Dept. of State, Philadelphia, Mar. 23, 1945, 832.24/3-2345, DSF.

Administration (FEA) and the War Production Board (WPB) could not give the *Companhia Brasileira de Material Ferroviário* the necessary ratings to get materials needed to maintain deliveries from its car assembly plant and to complete its maintenance foundry, because of the "substantial quantity of critical materials" involved and the changed strategic situation.[22] This last meant that because the war was going well the United States could afford to say no; earlier Washington had encouraged the projects and given high priority to necessary shipments.

The FEA likewise attempted to cripple a plant turning out aircraft engines for the Brazilian military. The Wright Company in the United States, which had been supplying the castings, notified the Brazilian plant that it was changing over to a new type of engine and would no longer provide castings. The Pan-American lend-lease officer at FEA informed the DBA that the American members of the Joint Brazil-United States Defense Commission and the Navy Department were "unfriendly to the project," and had requested that it not be included in State Department discussions with FEA and WPB. The officials involved were all aware that Vargas was much interested in having the plant operational, and that both Sumner Welles and Army Air Force chief General Arnold had originally backed its construction.[23] At the same time the American government was rushing to sell aircraft to Brazil in order to keep the British out of the market. Ambassador Berle, sometime aviation ex-

[22] The oil well equipment was discussed in R. F. O'Toole to Farriss, DBA, Mar. 30, 1945, 832.24/3-2145; the railroad equipment in Edmund E. Levin (Company Rep.) to Nelson Rockefeller, New York, Apr. 5, 1945, 832.24/4-545; and attached document, Harrison to Levin, Washington, Apr. 14, 1945, same number, all DSF. A similar case involved TNT and nitrates for the Pernambuco Powder Factory, see Berle, Rio, Apr. 13, 1945, 832.24/4-1345, DSF.
[23] O'Toole to Chalmers, DBA, June 18, 1945, 832.24/6-1845, DSF; and Chalmers, Memo of Conversation (Acting Secy. of State Joseph Grew, Ambassador Martins, and Chalmers), June 13, 1945, 832.24/6-1345, DSF.

pert who had represented the United States at the 1944 Chicago Aviation Conference, warned Washington that there was more at stake than just the Brazilian market.[24] The issue was whether Britain or the United States would eventually dominate internal transportation in South America. He warned that "a long hold on the situation will likely be held by the first in the field."[25] To be fair, however, it should be noted that the Brazilian airlines and military were not aiding the cause of their nascent local industry by seeking only foreign models. Instead of negotiating for at least partial independence by establishment of local factories, they attempted to play the Americans and British against each other to secure better terms and rapid deliveries of finished aircraft.[26]

The prevailing American attitude was bluntly summed up in a State Department despatch dealing with "possible moves now and in post-war period by Brazil to place controls on export of raw quartz." Brazilian producers had naturally increased exports during the war because, as a 1942 army intelligence report noted, Brazil was "practically the only source in the world of quartz crystals for use in radio equipment" to control the wave length of transmitters.[27] Brazilian businessmen approached Berle about obtaining quartz-cutting equipment to prepare semifinished and fin-

[24] For the Chicago conference see *International Civil Aviation Conference* (Chicago, Ill., Nov. 1 to Dec. 7, 1944), *Final Act and Related Documents* (Washington, 1945). It was especially important in that the final agreement recognized the principle that routes should follow "a reasonably direct line out from and back to the homeland of the State whose nationality the aircraft possesses"; pp. 91–95 summarize results of conference.

[25] Berle, Rio, July 20, 1945, WPD 452.1 Brazil, WWII RS, NA.

[26] See discussion of British efforts in DuWayne G. Clark (Commercial Attaché), Rio, July 31, 1945, 832.20/7-3145, DSF.

[27] U.S. War Dept., "Survey of the Rio de Janeiro Region of Brazil," (S 30-772), Aug. 6, 1942, Vol. I. Declassified mimeographed copy in author's possession. U.S. dependence on Brazilian quartz is also mentioned in History SADATC, Part 3, VI, 14.

ished products for export. After discussing the question with the WPA and FEA, the State Department instructed Berle to warn prospective manufacturers that the postwar market for such products "may be substantially smaller" than during the war. And the war procurement agencies were "interested in the possibility of obtaining assurance that the Brazilian Government will not interfere with export of raw quartz to the United States and that no effort will be made to require importation of semi-fabricated or fabricated quartz units along with raw quartz."[28]

American military policy toward Brazil had three principal aspects in 1945: 1) to insure Brazilian military superiority over Argentina, to allow the United States to deal by proxy "in strong ways" (Roosevelt's words) with that republic; 2) to maintain use of United States air bases in Brazil; 3) "to prevent European powers from providing arms and military missions to Latin American republics." This last would be achieved by supplying Brazil's neighbors with American arms and military missions.[29]

The linkage of American military and foreign policy with private business was clearly spelled out in a Navy memorandum which said that, among other purposes, the United States Naval Mission to Brazil was to assure the "predominance of the United States in Brazilian and Western Hemisphere affairs"; and ". . . to introduce the use of United States material in the Brazilian Navy *in order to promote American trade . . .*"[30] (italics added).

American failure to obtain a security council seat for its faithful ally and Washington's general depreciation of Bra-

[28] Joseph Grew (Acting Secy. of State), Washington, June 1, 1945, 832.24/6-145, DSF.

[29] Brig. Gen. John Weckerling (Dep. CS, Army, G2) to Maj. Gen. Clayton Bissell (ACS, G2), n.p., June 6, 1945, OPD 336 Brazil, WWII RS, NA.

[30] Memo: Background of Naval Mission Functions, Enclosure A (Functions USN Mission-Brazil), NS, ND, QC/EF12, A14-5 Documents US 4th Fleet, Naval History Division, Dept. of the Navy. For a fuller summary of the memo see Chap. 11, p. 328.

zilian prestige paralleled American economic and military efforts to keep Brazil subservient. Hull claimed that he and Roosevelt had favored a permanent seat for Brazil and had proposed it at Dumbarton Oaks, but that "both the British and the Russians emphatically opposed our view."[31] If that was indeed the case the United States owed Brazil an honest explanation, but it was never given. Washington allowed the Brazilian government to continue in the expectation that its efforts would be rewarded, and when the Brazilians were disgruntled after the San Francisco Conference the Americans affected surprise and puzzlement. In January 1945 Foreign Minister Velloso said: "We did not enter this war in order to exact rewards. . . . But our allies will be the first to realize that such action presupposes the admission of Brazil among the powers. . . ."[32] Constantly the Brazilian press emphasized that the FEB, the air and naval bases, the strategic materials, and Brazil's diplomatic efforts were earning it an important place at the peace conference, in the world organization, and among the powers. Instead of greatness, however, its reward was subservience.

In June, Berle and Acting-Secretary Joseph Grew discussed with President Truman the decline in the Vargas regime's willingness to cooperate. The air base agreement, for example, was not being implemented. Truman told Berle that he was "more anxious to have good relations with Brazil than any other country in Latin America." It is interesting that Grew noted that the deterioration began about the middle of April—when Roosevelt died.[33] The State Department urged Truman, who was about to meet with Velloso, to assure the foreign minister that "the new Administration is fully de-

[31] Cordell Hull, *The Memoirs of Cordell Hull* (New York, 1948), II, 1678.

[32] *A Noite*, Rio, Jan. 4, 1945.

[33] Grew, Memo of Conversation (Truman, Berle, Grew), June 13, 1945, 711.32/6-1345; and Grew, Washington, June 27, 1945, 711.32/6-2745, DSF.

termined to maintain Brazilian-United States relations on the same cordial and friendly basis as in the past."[34]

Meanwhile the political situation in Brazil had been moving along rapidly. In late February the regime issued an Additional Act to the Constitution of 1937 abolishing the president's right to choose the candidate to succeed him (Art. 75), and stating that within ninety days the election date would be set.[35] In ministerial circles debate had raged over whether the presidential election should precede or follow a constitutional convention, and even whether a new constitution was necessary. Getúlio had no great love for the 1937 document, except that it gave sanction to his decree-legislation which he naturally wished to protect. Close advisers, such as his secretary Luiz Vergara, argued that a national convention should prepare a new charter before the electorate chose a president and congress; otherwise they would have to function under the Estado Nôvo constitution, which would produce opposition and accusations that they were attempting to continue the regime. Vergara also objected to the electoral law's provision that state interventors could not be candidates, which he called a blow against the team which had assisted Vargas in administering the country. Marcondes' opposite position won out, but the issue of whether elections should precede or follow the constitutional convention continued to unsettle the administration. Getúlio apparently was uncertain, and decided to let events determine the outcome. His lack of leadership was regrettable because it further clouded his intentions, and allowed supporters to frighten the opposition into near-

[34] Nelson A. Rockefeller to H. S. Truman, n.p., July 2, 1945, 832.021/7-245, DSF.

[35] Benedicto Valladares, *Tempos Idos e Vividos, Memórias* (Rio de Janeiro, 1966), p. 234. The act appeared on Feb. 28, but had been in preparation at least since late January; see Berle, Rio, Feb. 2, 1945, 832.00/2-245, DSF. An extended and heated debate over the electoral rules was going on in the government; see Luiz Vergara, *Fui Secretário de Getúlio Vargas* (Rio de Janeiro, 1960), pp. 159–165.

panic when they took to the streets with cries of *Constituinte com Getúlio* ("Constitutional Convention with Getúlio"). Partly out of dissatisfaction with Marcondes' handling of the electoral law, Getúlio took away his portfolio as minister of justice, which he had held jointly with that of minister of labor, and gave it to the interventor of Pernambuco, Agamemnon Magalhães, whom he trusted and who had the additional virtue of being close to General Dutra.[36] A joke making the rounds had Getúlio asking: "How is it, Senhor Marcondes, that you are not doing anything for me? I have lived in this house 14 years and they want to throw me out in the gutter!"[37]

The opposition crystallized around Eduardo Gomes and formed itself into the *União Democrática Nacional* or UDN (Democratic National Union), which attracted conservatives and anti-*Getulistas*. Whom would the government propose? Would Vargas run? On March 2 newsmen asked the president that question, and he avoided a clear response. A few days later several thousand persons gathered in a drizzling rain in front of Rio's Municipal Theater, to hear former Gaúcho leader Flôres da Cunha and others call for complete restoration of political rights. Paulo Silveira, president of the *União Nacional dos Estudantes* (UNE, National Student Union), which sponsored the rally, drew loud applause and cheers with his declaration: "The nation is fed up with dictatorship." A similar UNE rally in Recife led to violence which claimed the lives of two students. Staff members of several government-controlled newspapers resigned, in protest over stories and editorials that they said sought to create confusion to benefit the regime. Several ranking generals apparently told Vargas that he should either announce that he was not a candidate or, if he was going to run, immediately resign to insure free and open elections.[38]

[36] *Ibid.*   [37] *O Globo*, Rio, Apr. 3, 1945.

[38] The UNE rally was Mar. 7; Vinton Chapin, Rio, Mar. 8, 1945, 832.00/3-845, DSF. Seventeen from *Folha Carioca*'s editorial staff resigned,

At that juncture Governor Benedicto Valladares of Minas Gerais and the new Minister of Justice Agamemnon Magalhães, realizing that Getúlio would never permit Gomes and the reactionary UDN to win the election, put forward the "high constable" of the Estado Nôvo, General Dutra, as the government candidate. Getúlio was not enthusiastic about Dutra, and in the ensuing months suggested to others, such as Góes and Valladares, that they would be better choices. But he accepted the basic logic behind Dutra's candidacy; that he could insure the army's loyalty until a more suitable candidate came forward—perhaps Getúlio himself—or if elected could be depended on to preserve the basic elements of the Estado Nôvo. As Getúlio explained to Góes, because his enemies had threatened him with a sword, he responded in kind.[39]

Increasingly, with news of each FEB victory, the opposition described Brazil's war effort as a commitment to democratic government. Rio's *Diário da Noite* quoted a letter from Sgt. Willy Schmaltz of Ipameri, Goiás, saying that the FEB was fighting "for democracy and the liberty of tomorrow."[40] The *Diário Carioca* quoted Major Reinaldo Saldenha, chief of the FEB's Special Services, as writing in the division's *Cruzeiro do Sul* that: "The Army to which we belong is not Brazilian, British, American, or Russian; it is the Allied Army, the Army of the free world."[41] On March 20 *O Globo* carried a headline, "On the 'Front' They Are Already Counting on Redemocratization of Brazil," and an

---

six left *A Noite*, and the editor of the *Estado de São Paulo* quit; Paul C. Daniels (Chargé), Rio, Mar. 6, 1945, 832.00/3-645, DSF. The report on army pressure did not name the generals involved, but Marcondes had discussed the electoral law in detail with Góes Monteiro and Dutra; see Chapin, Rio, Mar. 6, 1945, 832.00/3-645, DSF; and Coutinho, *General Góes*, pp. 408–411.

[39] Valladares, *Tempos Idos e Vividos*, pp. 235–243; Coutinho, *General Góes*, pp. 411–412.

[40] *Diário da Noite*, Rio, Feb. 15, 1945.

[41] *Diário Carioca*, Rio, Feb. 15, 1945.

interview with Colonel João Segadas Vianna, who had commanded the 6th Infantry Regiment until shortly before. He said that the *Febianos* hoped the regime would be democratized and elections set before the war ended.[42] Three days earlier *O Globo* had pointed to the victory at Monte Castello as verification that Brazil had entered "the ranks of the great powers, who are going to direct the world."[43] The FEB victories provided an excuse for rallies, such as the one in Rio on March 23, that tended to be antiregime. Speakers hailed the brave soldiers defending democracy, Christianity, and liberty; they declared that there was no liberty in Brazil, called for amnesty for political prisoners, and warned that danger existed of a new "10th of November." Getúlio should resign, a speaker shouted, and turn the government over to the president of the Supreme Federal Tribunal.[44]

But Getúlio was not without support. Separate public opinion polls taken in Rio in late March and early April indicated reserves of popularity. The Brazilian Institute of Public Opinion and Statistics asked a few hundred Cariocas two questions: 1) Whom do you wish to be elected President? 2) As between Gomes and Dutra which would you favor? The responses were tabulated as follows:

> Question 1: 30% Vargas
> 20% Gomes
> 10% Luís Carlos Prestes
> 5% Dutra
> 5% Various Others
> 30% No idea
> Question 2: 50% Gomes
> 20% Dutra
> 30% No opinion

It is interesting that those favoring Vargas were largely government employees, while those for Prestes, the Com-

---

[42] *O Globo*, Rio, Mar. 20, 1945.   [43] *Ibid.*, Mar. 17, 1945.
[44] *Gazeta de Notícias*, Rio, Mar. 24, 1945.

munist Party chief, were the best educated. *O Globo* polled 438 medical doctors in Rio and discovered the following: 200 were for Gomes; 99 for Vargas; 49 for Dutra; 5 for Prestes; and 85 expressed no opinion.[45]

If similar polls had been made in working-class districts the percentages and numbers of Vargas would probably have been higher. About the same time that the surveys were made a wave of strikes swept the country. Marcondes' Ministry of Labor controlled the unions, and observers doubted that the union leaders would call their people out unless they had official encouragement or sanction. Marcondes may have wanted to give the impression either that the workers were striking in support of Getúlio or that the communists were behind the strikes; in the process he hoped to rally the army to the regime. The Brazilian economy, however, was on the verge of chaos—inflation had begun to skyrocket toward the end of February. By June 1945 roughly 22,000,000,000 cruzeiros would be in circulation representing more than a 350 percent increase since 1940.[46] The success of a recent dock strike in Santos, and acute conditions in which workers' wages were too low to feed and clothe their families, were sufficient motivation for the strikes, "without," as Ambassador Berle observed, "dragging in political intrigue."[47] Even so some of the walkouts were government-instigated. At one São Paulo plant when the workers went out, the managers asked them to indicate the leaders who would carry on negotiations. The workers raised a huge picture of Vargas and cried: "This is our leader." At another plant where there was a similar incident, the workers shouted: "40 percent [raises], Vargas, and the National Flag." In both cases the men returned to

[45] The results of the institute poll were in Berle, Rio, Mar. 23, 1945, 832.00/3-2345, DSF; *O Globo*, Rio, Apr. 3, 1945.

[46] William Sherwood, Memo: "Brazilian Economic Conditions . . . ," in George L. Bell (Dir. Pan-Am. Br. FEA) to John C. McClintock (Spec. Asst. to Rockefeller), July 11, 1945, 832.24/7-1145, DSF.

[47] Berle, Rio, Apr. 12, 1945, 832.00/4-1245, DSF.

the factories after the demonstration without making any further demands.[48]

The release of Prestes

On April 16 Vargas ordered the head of the Communist Party, Luís Carlos Prestes, released from jail, where he had been since 1935. Before the order João Alberto, a fellow *tenente* from the revolts of the 1920's, visited Prestes and possibly obtained his pledge to back Vargas. But it should be noted that his release came slightly more than two weeks after Brazil and the Soviet Union had agreed to establish relations, and may well have been a Soviet *quid pro quo* or a Vargas gesture of good will. It certainly increased Vargas' popularity on the left but when Prestes spoke, boosting Vargas, before some 50,000 people at Vasco da Gama stadium on May 23 the results were mixed. He alienated much of the left, especially the intellectual communists, with a call for temporary acceptance of low living standards, urging the workers to do without even available conveniences such as refrigerators and radios. After asking the American consulates to check local reactions, Berle reported that, in urging resignation to existing conditions and cooperation with bosses, Prestes appeared "more reactionary than the Vatican."[49] Whether Prestes took this stance from conviction or because of a deal with Vargas was not clear. Indeed, others besides the president may have helped influence him toward a moderate, nonradical approach. Roberto Simonsen, president of the national manufacturing association, also negotiated with Prestes to insure the proper development of the situation. As part of their arrangement Simonsen financed the communist newspaper *Tribunal Popular* (Rio)[50] —the Brazilian industrialists seemed to be placing bets on all the contenders. Prestes thereby eliminated himself as a political option for the left, leaving it with the choice of throwing over ideology to back one of the two generals or

[48] Cross, São Paulo, May 30, 1945, 832.00/5-3045, DSF.

[49] Berle, Rio, May 24, 1945, 832.00/5-2445; and May 30, 1945, /5-3045, DSF.

[50] Berle, Rio, May 28, 1945, 832.00/5-2845, DSF.

of forgetting the past and joining Getúlio's popular procession.

Dutra, meanwhile, was carrying on a lackluster campaign that reflected his bland personality. He favored all the right things: amnesty for political prisoners, free speech, free elections, relations with the USSR, continuation of the American alliance, in short the Estado Nôvo without Getúlio. Aranha wrote Welles that he was supporting Gomes because the Brigadier had always been anti-German and had worked for Brazilian-American unity, whereas Dutra had refused to attend the closing of the Rio Conference as a protest against Brazil's break with the Axis. He did not think Dutra had changed, but he admitted sadly that without guarantees the official candidate would win.[51] Dutra, who had spent his life in the Army of Caxias and whose circle included those officers least democratic in their views, was now talking like an ardent democrat. His candidacy, however, did prevent the Gomes group from considering a coup d'état. They were determined not to submit to an election as long as Getúlio held power.[52] But to mount a coup they needed the army and as long as Dutra was minister of war that was impossible.

At mid-year a new element appeared which further complicated the confused situation. Even though Getúlio had publicly said he was not a candidate, his brothers, Benjamim and Viriato, Marcondes, and others mounted what was supposedly a spontaneous campaign to keep him in office. It began with posters and painted walls proclaiming *Queremos Getúlio* (from *querer*, to want), and progressed to mass rallies and processions. The *Queremistas*, as they were soon called, aimed at September 3, the last date for candidates to announce themselves before the elections, now scheduled for December 2. Their noisy activities plus the

[51] Aranha to Welles, Vargem Alegre, May 24, 1945, OAA. Aranha made a statement of support for Gomes in "Elections Will be Held in Brazil at an Early Date," *Brazil*, XIX, No. 4 (April 1945), 5.

[52] Harrison, Washington, Apr. 19, 1945, 832.00/4-1945, DSF.

return of the FEB may well have caused Getúlio to have second thoughts about running. Although the *Febiano* officers might be pro-Gomes and opposed to the president continuing in office, the cheering throngs that greeted Vargas during the victory celebrations moved FEB commander General Mascarenhas to say that Vargas' popularity was "incredible."[53] Góes Monteiro thought he noted a change in Getúlio after the victory parades. The president wanted to identify himself with the Smoking Cobras by taking Mascarenhas into the cabinet as minister of transportation, but the appointment did not materialize. Vargas' growing popularity and obvious political strength, however, undoubtedly troubled the opposition.

Although Dutra was Gomes' opponent, the UDN expended most of its efforts attacking Vargas and the Estado Nôvo. Its central committee charged that the government had not taken advantage of the war to mobilize the nation's resources efficiently, or to create an infrastructure for future growth. Brazil, according to a UDN spokesman, was "a body without muscles" that had accomplished only "a descent from poverty into misery."[54] The fact that Dutra had been a key figure in the government responsible for this state of affairs did not prevent Gomes from offering to withdraw if Dutra would remove Vargas, take power, hold elections—in which the minister would be the winning candidate—and above all repress the drift to the left. The propertied and industrial classes were upset by a recent decree aimed at controlling trusts, and they believed rumors that other radical decrees were in preparation which would spread profits among the workers, require an employee on every board of directors, and distribute all unused land within a hundred kilometers of any town among those willing to develop it. The upper classes in São Paulo were so alarmed at the

[53] Robert F. Corrigan (Vice-Consul), Natal, Sept. 22, 1945, 832.00/ 9-2245, DSF. Corrigan talked with Gen. Mascarenhas the day before.

[54] *Correio da Manhã*, Rio, June 8, 1945. Interview with UDN central committee member Gen. Olintho Mesquita Vasconcelos.

growth of political consciousness among the masses and their apparent disposition to rally behind Vargas and Prestes that some of the elite gathered arms in their homes.[55] The situation was serious enough for the Church to feel compelled to clarify its position as moderately reformist. Acting as its spokesman, Dom Carlos Carmelo, Archbishop of São Paulo, said that the Church opposed all totalitarian systems, whether of the left or the right; both Dutra and Gomes were worthy of Catholic votes; relations with the Soviet Union were exclusively a state concern; strikes were justified as a last resort; and the Church opposed continuance of latifundia landholding.[56]

In early July a poll of 1,000 literate Cariocas showed that 86 percent had not joined either the UDN, the PSD (Dutra's party, largely government employees—*Partido Social Democrático*), or the PTB (basically pro-Vargas, drawn from labor—*Partido Trabalhista Brasileiro*), because those parties did not have objective programs to solve Brazil's problems.[57] It was becoming increasingly apparent that there were huge reservoirs of political power waiting to be tapped. Even the Brazilian Monarchist Party nurtured hopes that the pretender, Prince Pedro Enrique Orleans e Bragança, might be called upon to save the country from the republican quagmire and to restore the Empire.[58]

Ambassador Berle believed that if there were "fair, free and open elections and if Vargas were to be a candidate, probably he would be elected by popular majority."[59] Ad-

[55] Cross, São Paulo, July 3, 1945, 832.00/7-345, DSF.

[56] *O Jornal*, Rio, June 24, 1945.

[57] The *Instituto Brasileiro de Opinião Pública e Estatística* (IBOPE) conducted the poll. The results were summarized in U.S. Embassy Memo, Rio, July 16, 1945, 832.00/7-1645, DSF.

[58] John G. Mein to Chalmers, DBA, Aug. 23, 1945, 832.00/8-2345, DSF. The monarchists could not participate in the elections because in 1936 the Supreme Electoral Tribunal had ruled that the Constitution of 1934 prohibited parties advocating abolition of the federated republican form of government.

[59] Berle, Rio, July 17, 1945, 832.00/7-1745, DSF.

herents in both the Gomes and Dutra camps realized this, and continued to talk of a coup to eliminate Vargas—thus revealing themselves as antipopulists. They wanted "democracy" but not democracy based on the will of the people or majority rule. It was to be a restoration of the classical, elite-dominated society of pre-Getúlian Brazil.

Into this confusion came the FEB, home from the war against fascism, with reportedly 80 to 95 percent of its officers opposed to the regime and many favoring Gomes. The first contingent of 5,000, which arrived in Guanabara Bay on July 16, was held aboard ship until the next day, then disembarked, formed up for a tumultuous victory parade, filed past paymasters, and immediately scattered to barracks all over Brazil. The lame excuse for the rapid dispersal was that there were no facilities for so many troops in the Rio area. But what facilities were needed for hardened veterans who had been living in the field for months? They could have formed the core of many training units to modernize the Brazilian army and to preserve the lessons of the war, the Smoking Cobra was sacrificed to political expediency—Vargas and Dutra each had their reasons for wanting it eliminated.[60]

In August Dutra resigned from his ministry, so as to be eligible to run in the December 2 elections, and his alter ego Góes Monteiro replaced him. The march to October 29 now entered its final and decisive phase. *Queremos Getúlio* signs were everywhere and demonstrations were constant; it was obvious that Vargas would not let the *Queremistas* go to such lengths if he did not have some purpose. They had even propounded the idea that the Constitution of 1937 did not prevent the incumbent from succeeding himself, and did not require that he resign to stand for elections. It appeared that when the moment was right, Getúlio might suddenly change the electoral code to allow his candidacy.

[60] See U.S. Military Attaché Col. Ben. W. Barclay's comments in Berle, Rio, July 10, 1945, 832.00/7-1045, DSF. See Chap. 14 above.

If the *Queremistas* could keep the pressure on they might frighten both the army and the opposition into accepting such an action, in which event Getúlio's election would be assured.[61]

Shortly after taking over as minister of war, Góes, who supposedly favored a constitutional assembly followed by either direct elections or election by the assembly as in 1934, quietly alerted army units to stand ready for quick action in the event of an unspecified emergency. His bulletins, according to General Newton Estillac Leal, who commanded a brigade in Rio Grande do Sul, contained vague allusions to the political situation. General Estillac was convinced, after a conversation with Góes, that he was preparing "something serious" and was deliberately trying to heighten the confusion in the country. Estillac sent a warning to Vargas' aides. In retrospect, Vargas' secretary Luiz Vergara would point to the episode as "evidence that the 'coup' was already planned and awaited only the pretext to be carried out."[62]

But Getúlio let the deadline for declaration of candidacy go by and even a large, noisy demonstration in the palace grounds on September 2 did not wring a clear statement from him. An estimated 25,000 persons literally thundered for the cancellation of elections and the calling of a constitutional convention with the short, smiling Getúlio presiding. He had suffered, he told them, from the abuse of those "who thought only of themselves, and never of the common man." "*Viva a constituinte!*" they shouted back. He paused as if in deep thought, then said, in almost a stage whisper: "I shall preside over the elections, and afterward I would like to go back to my little farm in Rio Grande and leave the responsibilities of state to the duly-elected representatives

[61] For an excellent, detailed report on the situation at the end of August see Chapin, Rio, Aug. 27, 1945, 832.00/8-2745, DSF.

[62] Vergara, *Fui Secretário*, pp. 199–200. He recounts conversations with Gen. Estillac.

of the people." Then he added, as an afterthought: "If you ever need me, you have but to call on me. I shall always be at the service of my people."[63] What did he mean, "you have but to call on me?" They had called on him and he had said no. Or had he?

General Oswaldo Cordeiro de Farias and other FEB officers let it be known that they would use force against any attempt to postpone the elections.[64] Pro-Vargas military officers, such as FEB commander Mascarenhas, were kept away from Rio, either on inspection tours, or, like the old general, on ceremonial trips abroad. Mascarenhas, for one, thought that the Gomes forces were treating Getúlio unfairly with their excessive criticism. He did not care for Dutra, attributed Getúlio's equivocal behavior to his distaste for both Gomes and Dutra, and suggested that a compromise candidate such as Minister of Aeronautics Salgado Filho, who enjoyed the confidence of both Getúlio and the military, would be better.[65]

Instead of declining, the *Queremista* agitation in favor of a constitutional assembly with Getúlio increased in tempo, apparently building toward an October 3rd climax—the fifteenth anniversary of the 1930 Revolution. A countermovement called *Resistência* began placarding walls and trees. Day by day the Gomes and Dutra factions cooperated more closely in persuading the military to guarantee elections. The extreme left—Prestes' communists, Marcondes' unions, Hugo Borghi's PTB, and the *Queremistas* who included elements of all these groups—and the dictator were

[63] Edward Tomlinson, "Dictator's Choice," *Collier's*, CXVI, No. 21 (Nov. 24, 1945), 76–83. Tomlinson was in Rio at the time and witnessed the Sept. 2 rally.

[64] Military Attaché's report summarized in Berle, Rio, Sept. 20, 1945, 832.00/9-2045, DSF.

[65] Corrigan, Natal, Sept. 22, 1945, 832.00/9-2245, DSF. He talked with Mascarenhas and his staff the day before, when they stopped at Natal en route to Salzburg. Mascarenhas was out of Brazil for most of the time from July until Nov. 5, 1945; see João B. Mascarenhas de Moraes, *Memórias*, II, 436–450.

in alliance against the conservative upper and middle classes and the military. Getúlio had detached himself from the groups that had put him in power and had formed a new political base. The situation that had pertained in 1937 had been reversed. Often the very people who had backed Vargas then were opposed to him now, and those who had opposed him were shouting in his favor. The resulting alliances were odd indeed. Prestes, whom Vargas had imprisoned and whose German-born wife the regime had deported to her death in a Nazi concentration camp, now spoke in Getúlio's favor. Liberal democrats such as Aranha found themselves allied with conservatives such as Melo Franco and Gomes, and with militarists such as Dutra. The common people, little concerned with electoral niceties, were in the streets shouting for their benefactor, while the elite and middle classes huddled in conspiracies and hoped to use the disguise of liberalism—political rights and democratic elections—to cover continued suppression of the Brazilian masses.

The attitude of American officials changed suddenly in September from a watchful neutrality to an anti-Vargas position. On September 3 Berle wrote that progress was being made toward constitutional government, and there was "no reason as yet to assume change of circumstances or take for granted" that Vargas would not keep his pledge of elections. The ambassador then detailed circumstances that would justify United States interference:

> Representatives of the United States may be compelled to express their views as Ambassador Braden is doing now in Argentina, and as Mr. Sumner Welles did in Cuba in 1933. Such occasions should be rare, and should be last-resort measures, whose justification rests on the fact that the government attacked has threatened the peace of the hemisphere, or has violated the standards of civilized nations, or has failed in complying with the obligations which the American group of nations have mutually

assumed. Only by straining the present facts, or acting on suspicion of future events, could such action be taken in Brazil now.[66]

The next day Berle explained the Brazilian situation in a letter to President Truman, repeating that the political campaign was completely open and free, that voters were being registered honestly, that any Brazilian could form a committee, hire a hall, get up a party, put out a newspaper, and campaign against the government in safety. He did not think that Perón and Vargas were comparable. After all "Vargas kept his obligation to the hemisphere and was our most active ally. Argentina and Perón did the opposite." As long as Vargas continued to lead the country toward democracy, Berle thought that the best policy was "quiet encouragement." If Vargas changed course, or did something violent then they could reexamine their position. Such an attitude would "satisfy everyone except a few who have come to believe that there is virtue in being belligerent." He then made this assessment: "All hands agree that if Vargas were to run, all lower classes and some of the upper would vote for him. His government is almost as corrupt as Pennsylvania. It is inadequate economically, but has done more for the masses than its predecessors. Brazilian people may be misplacing their confidence; but he has it." Truman replied that he thought "it would be disastrous to interfere with the internal affairs of Brazil at the present time." It seemed to him that things were going as well as they could want. "Vargas," he commented, "certainly has been our friend."[67] On September 7, at Independence Day cere-

---

[66] Berle, Rio, Sept. 3, 1945, 832.00/9-345, DSF.

[67] Harry S. Truman to Dean Acheson (Asst. Secy. of State), White House, Sept. 19, 1945, 832.00/9-345, DSF. The Berle letter to Truman is attached to this document. Truman replied to Berle on Sept. 13; he then sent Berle's letter with the president's reply to Acheson for his information.

monies, Vargas said again that he would preside over honest elections and that he was not a candidate.[68]

But eleven days later Berle again raised the question of making some sort of statement. He admitted that he did not know if one would be needed, or even if it was wise, but he wanted the Department of State to consider it so that they would be ready if the need arose. In the Division of Brazilian Affairs there was "considerable skepticism of the wisdom of making any statement at all."[69] Upon reflection, however, the DBA decided that a statement should be made, with the caution that timing was extremely important to avoid charges of intervention. DBA officials thought it would be best if the Secretary of State made it at one of his press conferences, perhaps in reply to a planted question. They thought that the statement should be made in Washington, to make it appear less like intervention, and to avoid compromising Berle's position in Rio. They recommended that Berle draw up a draft immediately.[70]

Whether sudden insight, or as yet unavailable secret reports, or the politics of bureaucratic survival overcame the DBA's skepticism is not revealed in the State Department files. But the division's rapid conversion to the kind of "crack-down policy" then in effect against Juan Perón's nationalist-oriented Argentine government suggested strongly that self-preservation rather than conviction had been the prime motivation.[71] In August Republican Nelson A. Rockefeller had been forced out of the position of assistant secretary of state. He had favored working through Perón to

[68] Getúlio Vargas, *A Nova Política do Brasil* (Rio de Janeiro, 1938–47), XI, 183.

[69] Chalmers to Berle, Washington, Oct. 2, 1945, 832.00/9-2945, DSF.

[70] Daniel M. Braddock and Mein to Chalmers, DBA, Sept. 21, 1945, 832.00/9-1845, DSF.

[71] For an excellent, lengthy discussion of the policy then in effect against Argentina see John M. Cabot (Chargé) to Ellis O. Briggs (Dir., Office of American Republics Affairs), Buenos Aires, Nov. 17, 1945, in *Foreign Relations, 1945*, IX, 426–434.

safeguard American interests in Argentina, rather than taking an aggressive stance against him. His successor, the then ambassador to Argentina, Spruelle Braden, on the other hand, favored a head-on clash. Both Rockefeller and Braden "accepted the strategic premise that Argentine political and economic nationalism must be undercut. They differed only with respect to tactics."[72] The DBA's acceptance of open intervention against Vargas coincided exactly with Braden's appointment as assistant secretary with responsibility for Latin America. If Argentine nationalism and Perón's mobilization of mass support was a threat to the American vision of hemispheric solidarity, then Brazilian nationalism and Getúlio's activities were an equal threat. It took some agile mental gymnastics to ignore the differences in the two cases, but the DBA, Braden, and Berle were nimble indeed.

[margin note: Impact of Argentinian politics on US perception of Brazilian situation]

On September 23 Braden stopped in Rio, to confer with Berle before going on to Washington to take up his new post. He agreed that a statement was necessary, and approved Berle's idea of including it in an address he was to deliver to a group of journalists in Petrópolis on September 29. Braden may have feared that Perón and Vargas would make common cause against the United States. Years later, Berle justified his decision by saying that if Vargas canceled elections and Gomes' people revolted the American troops in Brazil would be left in a delicate situation.[73] Meanwhile the *Queremistas* stepped up their propaganda and were plotting a coup, which naturally troubled Góes and Dutra. Góes told Vargas if he, the president, were behind it and had changed his mind about holding elections Dutra would withdraw from the race and Góes himself would resign. Getúlio said that he never intended to be a

[72] David Green, *The Containment of Latin America, A History of the Myths and Realities of the Good Neighbor Policy* (Chicago, 1971), p. 252.

[73] John W. F. Dulles, *Vargas of Brazil, A Political Biography* (Austin, 1967), p. 268.

candidate, and that he did not sympathize with those who were trying to organize the *Queremista* movement into a coup d'état. Dutra, relieved, went off to São Paulo to give a speech and Góes continued as minister of war.

On Friday evening, September 28, Berle took his speech to Guanabara Palace for Getúlio's approval. The president said again that he would not be a candidate, either in the December 2 election or in a constitutional assembly vote, for two reasons: 1) he had given his word; and 2) if he left power soon he would do so "with acclaim and gratitude of the people"; he did not want to stay until he left with their hatred or indifference.[74] Berle reported that Vargas had had no objections to the speech, and afterwards had discussed it with advisers, one of whom called the ambassador to say they were pleased with the whole idea. Vargas would later claim to have been sleepy and to have paid little attention to Berle's poor Portuguese—therefore he was not certain that the speech he had approved was the one hailed by the opposition.[75] Vargas may not have known that the intended audience were journalists; because the majority of newspapers were antiregime, his later remark that Berle had addressed the opposition could well have been sincere.[76]

Berle's words seemed harmless, but they publicly injected the United States into the situation. He declared:

> The solemn promise of free elections in Brazil, scheduled for a definite date by a government whose word the United States has always found inviolable, was acclaimed with as much satisfaction in the United States as in Brazil. The Americans do not agree with those who try to represent these promises and solemn declarations as insincere or mere empty words. . . . The leadership which Brazil

[74] Berle, Rio, Sept. 29, 1945, 832.00/9-2945; Oct. 1, 1945, /10-145, DSF. The latter provided a chronology of Berle's activities.
[75] Coutinho, *General Góes*, pp. 431–432.
[76] *Ibid*.

enjoys has already shown itself to possess the greatest wisdom, having taken steps to carry through the elections without in any way impeding the reorganization of its constitution by means which the people may indicate.[77]

The opposition press loudly acclaimed the speech, while the *Queremistas* sank into gloomy anger. Vargas irritatedly asked Góes Monteiro what the army intended to do about this breach of national sovereignty. Góes reminded him that Berle had cleared the speech in advance.[78] The army would do nothing. One of Vargas' brothers said "if President Roosevelt were living, it wouldn't have happened"; and Senhora Vargas told an assistant military attaché: "We assume this is the official stand of your government. Naturally we are surprised, hurt, angry. Our Ambassador in Washington does not take sides in your politics. We consider it undiplomatic and unfriendly."[79]

If October 3 were the target date for a *Queremista* coup d'état, or a buildup to one, the speech may have acted as a restraint, but it may well be that the demonstrations on that day were merely poorly planned and executed. As Berle assessed it, the speech "did contribute materially to stabilizing [the] situation." Remarking on the oddity of the alliance between the "substantially fascist group and the extreme left," he said that the *Queremistas*, notably those around Viriato Vargas, and the communists were upset but unable to formulate an attack because the speech appeared to praise government policy. They were especially frustrated, he thought, because their plans for October 3 aimed at creating an atmosphere favorable to a "palace revolution," to calling off the elections and substituting in their place a constitutional convention "really designed to perpetuate Vargas' dictatorship without benefit of elections." If a palace coup d'état had occurred the opposition would certainly

---

[77] *Correio da Manhã*, Rio, Sept. 30, 1945.
[78] Coutinho, *General Góes*, p. 432.
[79] Chalmers to Berle, Washington, Oct. 2, 1945, 832.00/9-2945, DSF.

have revolted, in which case the position of the United States and "of this Embassy," Berle wrote, "would have been extremely difficult." Vargas' "good sense," with American prodding, had saved the day.[80]

On October 3, fifteen years after taking office, Vargas paced about the palace considering a dramatic resignation before the crowd that would assemble later in the day. He thought of blaming reactionary forces for keeping him from satisfying the people's wishes and then going down among them to add his "voice to the majority of Brazilians."[81] But Góes Monteiro, Agamemnon Magalhães, and João Alberto dissuaded him from such a drastic step. When the approximately 15,000 demonstrators, who for the most part had come to Rio in special free trains, marched noisily to the garden of Guanabara Palace he told them that they had the right to demand a *constituinte*, and that if their will was frustrated there would be agitation for "disorder and revolt." He assured them that he relied on their support but urged them to stay within the law. He reaffirmed that he was not a candidate, and that he only wanted to preside over the elections and to deliver the government to his legally-chosen successor. Then, reaching the high point of the speech, he cried that there were "powerful reactionary forces, some hidden, some open, opposed to the calling of a *constituinte* . . . [but] as far as things depend on me, the people can count on me."[82] Similar demonstrations failed to come off in São Paulo because the army commanders there warned that they would not tolerate trouble.

The press accused Vargas of equivocation. Assis Chateaubriand, in a column entitled "The Blue Fly," commented that the presidency was "a sublime sweetheart" which everyone wanted and looked upon coveteously—but that

[80] Berle, Rio, Oct. 1, 1945, 832.00/10-145; Oct. 4, 1945, /10-445, DSF.

[81] "A Vida de Getúlio Contada por Sua Filha, Alzira Vargas, ao Jornalista Raul Guidicelle," *Fatos e Fotos*, Brasília, Aug. 3, 1963.

[82] Vargas, *Nova Política*, XI, 191. Berle described events in his Rio, Oct. 4, 1945, 832.00/10-445, DSF.

it was time for a new lover.[83] On October 10 Vargas further muddied the waters by giving in to continuous pressure from the state interventors to schedule the state and municipal elections concurrently with the presidential election on December 3. The opposition was stunned. Their strategy had called for winning the presidency, then replacing state and local officials with their people before the lower elections, but Vargas had beaten them to it. It was a simple matter: whoever controlled the government controlled patronage, votes, and the counting of ballots. Incumbent governments had a way of winning elections in Brazil and neither side was reformist enough to want to change that fact of political life; the Gomes people only wanted their turn at controlling the electoral machinery. Governor Valladares, for example, had been constantly replacing and shuffling local officials in the past few months, seeing to it that many of his relatives, *compadres*, and confidants were holding the reins of local power. The army chief of staff, General Cristovão de Castro Barcelos, and leading generals such as Álcio Souto, who commanded the tank forces in Rio, were livid; they demanded Góes' interference to persuade Vargas to nullify the decree.[84]

The Department of State considered asking President Truman personally to encourage Vargas to hold the promised elections. This time the DBA officers stood their ground, perhaps aware that their former chief Sumner Welles considered Berle's speech "disastrous."[85] They argued forcefully that another statement was not needed, and that the

> projection of the President of the United States into the Brazilian political scene at this crucial time, however carefully it were managed, would most certainly lead to

[83] "A Mosca Azul," in *O Jornal*, Rio, Oct. 7, 1945.

[84] Jay Walker (Consul) to Walter J. Donnelly (Chargé d'Affaires in Rio), Belo Horizonte, Jan. 8, 1945, 832.00/1-845, DSF; Coutinho, *General Góes*, p. 438.

[85] Welles, *Where Are We Heading?* (New York, 1946), p. 219.

the charge of intervention, which is already being made as a consequence of Ambassador Berle's speech. . . . Brazil, large, friendly, and cooperative as it is, has shown itself to be hardly less sensitive to intervention than have some of our smaller neighbors. Brazil is of paramount importance to us in our relations, both in the continent and in world councils. It would be deplorable to risk forfeiting the friendship and confidence of Brazil by attempting to influence the outcome of its private internal affairs. Even those elements which would stand to gain most at the moment from our intervention would, in the long run, be likely to resent our having intervened. . . . It is our view that the United States should scrupulously refrain from exerting, or appearing to exert, any pressure on Brazil in connection with its progress toward redemocratization.[86]

Perhaps Perón's triumphal return to power the day before the DBA officers wrote the memorandum above convinced them that Braden's style of diplomacy was not only dangerous but could well backfire.

Getúlio was following the events in Buenos Aires via detailed letters from Ambassador João Batista Luzardo. The president spoke enthusiastically to Góes of the power of the masses, possibly recalling the *vivas* he had received during the victory parades. But Góes, cutting him short, pointed out that the Argentine masses had carried Perón to power only because of army support. Góes noted that Getúlio did not care for his observation, but "fell silent and didn't touch on the subject again."[87]

Vargas was not feeling well when the workers of the Light and Power Co. marched to the palace to demonstrate their esteem on October 18. After Marcondes Filho addressed the crowd in the president's name, they applauded

86 Braddock and Mein to Chalmers, DBA, Oct. 18, 1945, 832.00/10-1845, DSF.

87 Coutinho, *General Góes*, p. 439.

and called for him to speak. He did so briefly: "Workers of
Brazil. Today my voice is silent. But this silence has a significance that should be interpreted thus: the president is
with the people."[88] Some commentators said he was encouraging the *Queremistas*; others said he was not. José
Eduardo de Macedo Soares critically reviewed Getúlio's recent speeches, and said that the president realized it was
time to stop such pronouncements. "The Carnival was lasting too long; Ash Wednesday was due. So Senhor Getúlio
Vargas spoke only to indicate that the comedy was over."
His silence was that of the "victim sacrificed on the altar of
the 'people.' "[89]

Góes Monteiro called the generals to the Ministry of
War's council chamber on the 22nd. After deliberation they
sent Vargas a vigorous threat: they would take action if he
attempted to stay in power. Góes issued a statement to the
Folha Carioca that Vargas would preside over the elections.
Góes was trying, as he himself described it, with "super-
human effort" to prevent the army from taking precipitous
action and to keep Getúlio from succumbing to the blan-
dishments of the *Queremistas*.[90] But he could not stop the
heightening of political suspense, which was increased
when several important interventors, including Governor
Valladares of Minas and General Pinto Aleixo of Bahia,
suddenly arrived in Rio. Indeed, Góes may deliberately
have fostered suspense to place himself at the center of decision. The activities of the PTB also contributed to the
rapidly rising tension. The party's secretary general, José
de Segadas Vianna, and wealthy speculator and leader of
a Paulista PTB faction, Hugo Borghi, were openly active in
the *Queremista* movement. Parenthetically, it should be
noted that Borghi was accumulating a fortune in the cotton
market through speculations which he financed with loans
of dubious legality from the Bank of Brazil. He and other

[88] *O Jornal*, Rio, Oct. 19, 1945.
[89] *Diário Carioca*, Rio, Oct. 21, 1945.
[90] Coutinho, *General Góes*, p. 442.

Queremistas quite possibly had a financial stake in the continuation of the regime. Finally, Federal Police Chief João Alberto's adherence to the PTB and Vargas' appeals for workers to join the party added to the generals' alarm. Rumors gained currency that a rally scheduled for October 26, under the sponsorship of the "Committee for the Candidacy of Getúlio Vargas," would set the scene for the feared coup d'état. Vargas' agents, according to the rumors, had readied the necessary decrees, and had prepared a general strike and other disorders to create confusion and thereby to justify Vargas' continuance.[91] Something was indeed afoot. By October 25, Vargas had secretly planned for Rio's mayor, Henrique Dodsworth, to become foreign minister or ambassador to Portugal, with Police Chief João Alberto succeeding to the key mayoralty post, and brother Benjamim Vargas taking over as head of the police. Getúlio, who probably planned to announce these changes at the rally, deliberately kept Góes Monteiro uninformed.[92] On October 24 the pro-Vargas *O Radical* carried the banner headline: "The people know the route that leads to the ballot-boxes—a motto: CONSTITUINTE WITH GETÚLIO VARGAS!" The paper called on the public to march to Guanabara Palace on Friday the 26th "to hear the command of President Getúlio Vargas."[93] The same day *O Globo* asserted that "anything could happen," but that on December 2 the slogan "*constituinte* with Getúlio" would win, implying that the mass swing to the PTB would result in a conclusive write-in vote on election day for a convention under Vargas' direction.[94]

Meanwhile, the Gomes camp was preparing a counter-coup, and Góes Monteiro, attempting to maintain order, put

91 Chapin, Rio, Oct. 25, 1945, 832.00/10-2545, DSF.

92 Dulles, *Vargas of Brazil*, p. 271; Coutinho, *General Góes*, pp. 441–443.

93 ". . . rumar ao Guanabara para ouvir a palavra de ordem do presidente Getúlio Vargas"; in *O Radical*, Rio, Oct. 24, 1945.

94 *O Globo*, Rio, Oct. 24, 1945.

the army on standby alert on the night of the 25th. He applied pressure on the *Queremistas* to postpone the meeting scheduled for the next day and apparently got Gomes to suspend the revolt, which *A Noite* charged was also set for the 26th.[95] The same day Philip O. Chalmers of DBA talked with Berle via intercontinental telephone and found that the embassy was having trouble securing information and "in trying to draw an understandable picture."[96]

It was now the weekend and Rio settled into a deceptive calm for the last two days of Getúlio's rule. The Estado Nôvo lived out its last moments as it did its first—quietly. On Sunday evening Vargas decided to go ahead with the change of positions among Henrique Dodsworth, João Alberto, and Benjamim Vargas, and authorized João Alberto to inform Góes Monteiro. Early on Monday morning João Alberto rode from Copacabana to the Ministry of War with a furious Góes, who felt that Getúlio had committed an unpardonable breech of faith. His own account does not charge the president with plotting a coup but with neglecting to keep him in his confidence. He deeply resented Vargas treating him, the central prop of the regime, as a lackey who could simply be informed of such a pregnant decision. For Góes it was not a question of Vargas' plans but that he had not been consulted. He could not have confidence, he told João Alberto, in a man who treated him in such fashion. It nullified his pledge to maintain the regime in power because it was such an "inconceivable and inadmissible" blow and that "as a soldier, I would prefer to die than submit to a humiliation that would be the negation of my past and would cast me into disgrace."[97] João Alberto unsuccessfully tried to calm his friend and to convince him that he could change Getúlio's mind.

95 *A Noite*, Rio, Oct. 26, 1945. In an editorial, "Revolução," it charged that Gomes had only suspended, not cancelled, the revolt. *A Noite* was government-controlled.

96 Chalmers, DBA, Oct. 26, 1945, 832.00/10-2645, DSF.

97 Coutinho, *General Góes*, pp. 442–443.

Between eight and nine A.M. Góes prepared a proclamation to the people and the army declaring his resignation as minister; he ordered all regional commanders to execute the prearranged antisubversion plan, placed the First Military Region, which included the capital, on alert, and told the armor commander to ready his tanks; he called in the naval liaison officer to alert the navy, and summoned the ranking generals to his office. The latter agreed to the suggestion of General Gustavo Cordeiro de Farias that, because Vargas had lost their confidence and therefore no longer held authority, Góes should prevent chaos or civil war by assuming command of the armed forces and taking charge of the nation's destiny. Góes, who was suitably attired in civilian clothes, agreed and proceeded to depose his old chief and collaborator.

The events of the day moved slowly but inexorably. It appeared for a time that Getúlio and Góes might both back down, but the anti-Vargas generals and the Gomes forces saw their opportunity to let Góes direct their coup for them. Gomes and Dutra agreed to cooperate—so did the navy. Even so, Dutra attempted a last negotiation with Getúlio and received three alternatives that would have left the president in office, but Góes maintained that they had gone too far to back down without resolving anything. Tanks already blocked the approaches to Guanabara Palace and troops controlled the communications centers, so Vargas wisely rejected Prestes' offer to launch street demonstrations.[98]

That evening Góes sent his reluctant chief of staff, the former commander of the FEB artillery and long a friend of Vargas, Oswaldo Cordeiro de Farias, to Guanabara with the military's ultimatum calling on Getúlio to resign. The president said that he preferred to die fighting against this unconstitutional coup d'état, leaving Góes and the army with the responsibility for the massacre of those in the pal-

[98] *Ibid.*, pp. 454–455; Dulles, *Vargas of Brazil*, p. 272.

ace. The general replied that they had nothing that extreme in mind; instead they would cut off the palace's water, power, and food supplies until he gave up. The last thing Vargas wanted was to look ridiculous, so in return for guarantees that he and his entourage would be allowed to leave Rio in safety he agreed to resign. Reportedly he told General Cordeiro: "I would prefer that you all attack me and that my death remain as a protest against this violence. But as this is to be a bloodless coup, I shall not be a cause of disturbance."[99]

The next day the Chief Justice of the Supreme Tribunal, José Linhares, was sworn in as interim president at a brief ceremony in the council room of the Ministry of War. Getúlio issued a restrained statement saying that he had resigned to save the country from "greater evils and irrevocable damage. . . . History and time shall speak for me, determining responsibilities. . . . I have no reason to complain of the glorious Armed Forces of my country, to whom I always attempted to give prestige. . . . I shall not hold hatred. . . . The workmen, the humble . . . the people—will in the end understand me."[100] Then he boarded an air force plane to return to his ranch near São Borja, Rio Grande do Sul. Góes Monteiro prevented the victors from imposing sanctions on his ex-chief, while the new government showed its upper-class bias in repealing the antitrust law, and revealed its determination to control the elections by naming new state interventors. The December 2 vote was limited to the presidency and the national legislature, and state and local elections were postponed until after the constitutional convention.

[99] As quoted in Dulles, *Vargas of Brazil*, p. 274. Cordeiro's gesture in going to Vargas was a friendly one and not the betrayal of a friend. His intention was to see that no harm came to the president.

[100] *O Jornal*, Rio, Oct. 30, 1945. Vergara said that Vargas wrote out two versions of the resignation note, one of which bitterly attacked the "*generais golpistas*," but that João Alberto convinced the president not to use it, and told Vergara that "*é preciso que a outra não seja conhecida*"; in *Fui Secretário*, pp. 183–188.

Dutra won the election, assisted by a last-minute word of support from the former dictator, while Vargas himself, without being a candidate and because of his immense popularity, was elected senator from two states and federal deputy from seven. He chose to represent his home state of Rio Grande in the Senate but he rarely appeared; for the most part he confined himself to his *estância* for the following years. At the end of 1945, a State Department official correctly observed: "It is not beyond the realm of possibility that Mr. Vargas may, within a short period, again be the Chief Executive of Brazil."[101] He was re-elected president in 1950, but the example of 1945 would irresistibly lead to the civil-military crises that were to produce his suicide in 1954 and the subsequent decade of unrest that ended with the establishment of military rule in 1964.[102]

As the Panama *Star and Herald* remarked after the October 29 coup d'état, the entry of the Brazilian army into "the field of militant politics" had "decidedly ominous potentialities for the future."[103] The army was not only again the moderator of the political game but was now a player of such preponderance as to nullify chances for a system based on the free and open choice of the people. The army would eventually formulate its own political and social-economic doctrines and would seek to insure conformity to them. Góes Monteiro puzzled reporters in December 1945 when he interpreted Dutra's election as approval for the army's action, both in supporting establishment of the Estado Nôvo in November 1937 and in overthrowing it in October 1945.[104] During the next nineteen years, as crisis followed crisis and as the military became steadily more

101 Mein to Chalmers, DBA, Dec. 13, 1945, 832.00/12-1345, DSF.

102 For a detailed study of 1945–1964 see Thomas E. Skidmore, *Politics in Brazil, 1930–1964* (New York, 1967); and for an analysis of the military's role see Alfred Stepan, *The Military in Politics, Changing Patterns in Brazil* (Princeton, 1971).

103 *Star and Herald*, Panama, Oct. 31, 1945.

104 *O Jornal*, Rio, Dec. 13, 1945.

embroiled in politics, the reporters' puzzlement would turn to understanding. The articulate middle and upper classes who cast the election ballots would favor military rule to protect their interests from the majority of their poor, illiterate, undernourished, and propertyless countrymen. Vargas and his populist successors conjured up a vision of social-economic change and Brazilian politics has struggled to deal with it ever since.

Note on Sources and
Supplementary Bibliography

THIS ESSAY and bibliography are not intended to be an exhaustive listing of materials on the Brazilian-American alliance or on Brazil's wartime role but an indication of the most important sources used in this study. Other items will be found in the footnotes. By far the most important information came from archives in Brazil and the United States. Rather than discuss them in order of importance it might be of interest to the reader if I retraced the research trail from its beginning in the fall of 1964 to its conclusion in the summer of 1970.

Early in 1963 I applied to the Office of the Adjutant General, United States Army, for clearance to use the army files in the World War II Section of the National Archives. After nearly a year that office extended a secret clearance which allowed me to see everything in the War Department's War Plans Division and Operations Plans Division, except Top Secret documents. The army restricted my note taking, and the Adjutant General's Office held my notes for lengthy reviews before releasing them. In the case of one group of less than one hundred note sheets the process took more than a year and a half, during which portions of some notes were deleted and others were not cleared for unspecified reasons. In several cases, such as the Góes Monteiro–Marshall correspondence, from which the Adjutant General held back parts of documents, I found unrestricted copies of the same letters in Brazilian archives. As a result of such hindrances

I have cited in the notes the official army history, Stetson Conn and Byron Fairchild, *The Framework of Hemisphere Defense* (Washington, 1960), which gives accurate summaries of the documents. In each case I read their summation against the original document. The most valuable papers for studying policy formation were those of the War Plans Division (WPD), which was responsible for developing hemispheric defense measures prior to Pearl Harbor. Its papers were well organized and had an excellent index. Despite the restrictions the army records provided many ideas and clues as to topics that could be investigated. The military intelligence reports, which I was not allowed to cite, were especially valuable for assessing American attitudes toward particular Brazilian officials.

An example of the inconsistency of the operation of the classification system was my experience with the valuable "Report on the 1st Infantry Division Brazilian Expeditionary Force in the Italian Campaign from 16 July 1944 to the Cessation of Hostilities in May 1945." This document was marked "Secret" in the WWII RS, while an exact copy in the Office of the Chief of Military History had been declassified. When I pointed out this discrepancy, officials at WWII RS still declined to declassify the original but agreed to make for me a microfilm of the copy at OCMH. Later during my army tour it became clear to me that the Adjutant General's office had no one with sufficient historical training or knowledge of Brazilian-American relations to pass intelligently on the security content of my notes. As late as 1968–1969, when archivists in the WWII RS maintained that all the Brazilian material could be declassified if they had adequate staff to remove the markings, the Adjutant General still deleted portions of my notes on 1944–1945 documents. Fortunately, as a result of the furor over the Pentagon Papers, President Richard Nixon issued Executive Order 11652 on March 8, 1972, lifting most of the restrictions described here. Even the military intelligence files, which contain a wealth of detailed information on wartime Brazil, are in the process of being cleared. Future work will be hampered less by restrictive controls than by the sheer mass of papers.

The Department of State files, which up until the end of 1944 are housed in the National Archives, were less restricted. At the outset of research they were open to the end of 1943 but after the *Foreign Relations* volumes for 1944 and 1945 appeared, the material for those years was also released. The 1945 files are still located in the Central Files of the State Department building. The Historical Office of the Department cleared my notes rapidly. To my knowledge the only items to which I was denied access were reports originating in the Justice Department and the Federal Bureau of Investigation; the latter was apparently involved in intelligence and counterintelligence efforts. The most important State Department files were those concerning political events in Brazil (832.) and United States relations with Brazil (711.). There were special files relating to World War II (710.0011 European War 1939) to Inter-American conferences (710.Consultation) to the German compensation trade (632.), to Getúlio Vargas (832.001 Getúlio Vargas), and to Oswaldo Aranha (033.3211 Aranha). Clippings from Brazilian newspapers were of particular interest. From 1940 to 1945 the Rio embassy regularly compiled news summaries complete with annotated clippings (832.9111). These indicated which newspapers the State Department considered noteworthy and which ones would be useful during research in Brazil. The minutes of the Standing Liaison Committee provided one of the few high-level sources on prewar policy planning. For that period there was an absence of documents indicating how the State Department formulated policy, but from 1943 on there were more intramural memoranda. The documents in the *Foreign Relations of the United States* for the years 1937 to 1945 are both representative of the various file groups and useful. The work of the Office of the Coordinator of Inter-American Affairs can be traced in many unclassified reports, and its general history in the National Archives. The research in the foregoing was carried out for 1937 to 1943 before going to Brazil in 1965, and the remaining two years were studied in 1968 and 1969.

The United States Navy records had fewer restrictions and a more liberal and rapid declassification system; an officer removed hindering classifications as a seaman wheeled the documents into the research room. I consulted the papers of the United States Fourth Fleet under its various designations. The most helpful items were the operations reports, the "War Diary: Commander South Atlantic Force," and Admiral Jonas Ingram's reports to the Chief of Naval Operations. Most of the collection was well summarized in an unpublished fleet history by Charles Nowell: United States Navy, "Commander South Atlantic Force, United States Naval Administration in World War II." The Navy Library kindly provided me with a microfilm copy.

After the security-conscious surroundings in Washington the minimal restrictions of the Franklin D. Roosevelt Library were a pleasure. Hyde Park gave me new insights. The atmosphere of the library, the museum, the knowledgeable staff, and Roosevelt's home provided something intangible that cannot be documented or listed in a bibliography. I half expected FDR to come wheeling into the room. Although the documents on Brazil were not extensive they were helpful in determining how the government developed its policies. The President's Personal File (PPF) had material on Vargas, Aranha, Caffery, Welles, and others. The President's Secretary's File (PSF) and the Official File (OF) provided information on a variety of subjects, including the Office of the Coordinator of Inter-American Affairs, Brazilian economic development, the lend-lease agreements, and aviation policy. A valuable guide for determining what records exist is the two-volume U.S. National Archives, *Federal Records of World War II*, Vol. I: *Civilian Agencies* (Washington, 1950), and Vol. II: *Military Agencies* (Washington, 1951).

The records of Pan-American Airways supplemented and amplified State and War Department sources. The airline's files are stored with a commercial archivist in New York, but through the intercession of the company's legal department the files of the Airport Development Program were brought to the PanAm Building for my use. Although the airline's records are extremely valuable for the history of aviation they are not generally open to researchers. It would be well if the Civil Aeronautics Board encouraged airlines to deposit their files in the National Archives. The Office of the Chief of Military History provided a microfilm copy of the "Official History of the South Atlantic Division, Air Transport Command," which traced the growth of the ADP and American military policy toward Brazil. It was a command history written at Natal from documents in the headquarters files. Its appendices contained several documents which were classified in the World War II Section of the National Archives. William A. M. Burden's *The Struggle for Airways in Latin America* (New York, 1943) was a thorough study based in part on material given Burden's researchers by Cauby C. Araújo, former president of Panair do Brasil. During late 1965 Dr. Araújo, who was primarily responsible for the Brazilian ADP, graciously opened his files and library. Since he had written many of the ADP reports that I had read earlier in the Pan-American Airways papers our conversations were of great value. A tour of former American bases in the Brazilian northeast, in May 1965, was helpful in giving me a "feel" for conditions there. At Recife, with a congenial naval lieutenant as a guide, I roamed the former Fourth Fleet base (located next to a seventeenth-century Dutch fort) talking to repair-shop mechanics, various officers, including the commanding admiral, and the officers and crew of the scout destroyer, *Bracuí*, formerly U.S.S. *McCann*.

It took from 1965 to 1969 to gain access to the foreign ministry files housed in the Itamaraty palace in Rio de

Janeiro. In 1965 the Brazilian Embassy in Washington sent a strong request that I be given access and several young diplomats, headed by sometime poet Francisco Soares Alvim Neto, actively backed it, but discussion was ended abruptly in August when President Humberto de Castello Branco issued a decree closing the diplomatic archives to foreigners back to the beginning of this century. Fortunately, in 1969 President Artur Costa e Silva opened the papers to the end of 1940 to individuals whose requests had been approved by the *Comissão de Estudo dos Textos da História do Brasil* (Decreto #64,122, February 19, 1969). For this study access was granted and the research supervised by a committee composed of historian José Honório Rodrigues; head of the archive, Martha Maria Gonçalves; and Ambassador Álvaro Teixeira Soares. I was allowed to read through correspondence between Rio and Berlin, Washington, and London. The ambassador then decided which documents might be microfilmed. Although the process was slow and it took a year to obtain the microfilm, the wealth of data more than repaid the effort expended. The high quality of the Brazilian diplomats' reporting, especially from Berlin, made for exciting reading. The cause of history would be greatly served if more of this material could be published.

Through the good offices of reporter-historian Hélio Silva the son of Foreign Minister Oswaldo Aranha, Euclydes Aranha Neto, gave me complete access to his father's archive and spent a considerable amount of time in his office and home answering my questions. The Aranha archive, located over a garage on family property in Cosme Velho, contained the minister's correspondence, scrapbooks, and numerous reports. It spanned the years from the Revolution of 1930 down to Aranha's presidency of the General Assembly of the United Nations. As should be evident from the footnotes this study owes much to that collection. Although the two rooms containing the file cabinets were without functioning electric lights, when I worked there in November 1965, the beautiful garden below the window, the spectacular view of Corcôvado mountain above, and the excellent bread from the bakery down the street were adequate compensation for the dim light. Curiously enough there were only a few unimportant notes to and from the German and American embassies—even though Aranha was in almost daily contact with Ambassador Jefferson Caffery. Probably most of their exchanges were verbal. The Brazilian "Green Book" (Ministério das Relações Exteriores, *O Brasil e a Segunda Guerra Mundial*), 2 vols. (Rio de Janeiro, 1944), issued to explain Brazil's entry into the war, contained some interesting documents not found in the Aranha collection.

Euclydes Aranha interceded with Alzira Vargas do Amaral Peixoto, daughter and sometime secretary of Getúlio Vargas, to allow me to use her father's papers. Although she agreed to do so in late 1965, she went to Petrópolis to escape Rio's summer heat and the disastrous rains of January 1966 prevented her return. In the months before my return to the United States, in June, she was in Europe. I passed her apartment building, where the papers were located, almost every day, but there was no way to gain access without her presence. My dissertation "Brazil and the United States and the Coming of World War II, 1937–1942" (Indiana, 1967) had to be written without having seen the Vargas papers. Finally, in the summer of 1969, thanks to the support of Colonel Amos Jordan, head of Social Sciences at West Point, I was given leave from my military duties to return to Brazil. Dona Alzira received me graciously in her apartment overlooking Guanabara Bay and spread her father's papers on the dining-room table. There, surrounded by Vargas memorabilia, she answered my questions about people and events mentioned in the documents. She, more than anyone else, gave me a sense of what it must have been like to be president of Brazil in those years. I believe that she showed me everything I asked to see. She had arranged the documents in chronological binders each of which had a numbered table of contents. From them one can follow the decision-making process as viewed from the pinnacle. Obviously based on her father's papers, as well as her own recollections, is her sympathetic, but highly useful, *Getúlio Vargas, Meu Pai* (Pôrto Alegre, 1960). It is especially good for insights into Vargas' personality and for the struggle to control the Estado Nôvo. Likewise of great use were Vargas' speeches, interviews, and reports, published in eleven volumes entitled *A Nova Política do Brasil* (Rio de Janeiro, 1938–47).

Other books that provided different perspectives on the regime's political operation were Luiz Vergara's knowledgeable *Fui Secretário de Getúlio Vargas* (Rio de Janeiro, 1960); and governor of Minas Gerais, Benedicto Valladares' all too concise *Tempos Idos e Vividos, Memórias* (Rio de Janeiro, 1966), which covers in short vignettes the years from the Paulista revolt of 1932 to the deposition of Vargas in 1945. Valladares is one of several Getulistas of whom a biography would be immensely helpful. Articulate opposition views are expressed in the third volume of Afonso Arinos de Melo Franco, *Um Estadista da República* (Afrânio de Melo Franco e seu Tempo) (Rio de Janeiro, 1955); and in Carolina Nabuco, *A Vida de Virgílio de Melo Franco* (Rio de Janeiro, 1962). A study of both the *Estado Nôvo* and its opponents is needed. A competent contemporary study by a foreign observer that is still useful is Karl Loewenstein, *Brazil Under Vargas* (New York, 1942). There is an important compilation of documents from the Aranha and Vargas papers, with chronologies and commentary, in Hélio Silva's continuing series *O Ciclo de Vargas*; especially *1937, Todos os Golpes Se Parecem* (Rio de Janeiro, 1970) and *1938 Terrorismo em Campo Verde* (Rio de Janeiro, 1971). A first-rate study based on the Aranha, Vargas, and other archives is Robert M. Levine, *The Vargas Regime, The Critical Years, 1934–1938* (New York, 1970), which I used both in manuscript and published form. Helpful information on the relationship between the Paulista indus-

trialists and the Estado Nôvo is in Warren Dean, *The Industrialization of São Paulo, 1880–1945* (Austin, 1969).

The *Biblioteca do Exército* and the *Arquivo da Força
Expedicionário Brasileiro* in the *Ministério de Guerra* (Rio
de Janeiro) enabled me to observe the nerve center of the
Brazilian army while studying its involvement in World
War II. My initial contact with the Brazilian officer corps
had been in Washington where Colonel Newton C. de
Andrade Mello, assistant military attaché and a Febiano, devoted a good deal of time to discussing the FEB with me. His
two "conferencias," *Causas e Consêquencias da Participação
do Brasil na II Grande Guerra* (Rio de Janeiro, 1958) and
A Epopeia de Montese (Curitiba, 1955), were among the
first Brazilian items I read on the expeditionary force. In
succeeding years I talked with and got to know a goodly
number of officers and a lesser number of enlisted men.
Many of my ideas on the prewar Brazilian army are based
on these rather random friendships, conversations, and
encounters.

Two American officers gave me the benefit of their ex-
perience in dealing with the Brazilian army: Lt. General
Willis D. Crittenberger, the commander of Fourth Corps,
Fifth Army, which included the FEB; and Major General
Vernon A. Walters, who served as liaison officer with the
FEB and who, during my first two stays in Brazil, was
United States Military Attaché in Rio. Walters not only discussed my project with me but successfully interceded on
my behalf with the Brazilian navy and army authorities to
grant me access to their archives. Both responded affirmatively, but in the end the navy conceded only limited access
to documents on wartime cooperation, while the army
matched the promise with the deed. Marshal João Batista
Mascarenhas de Moraes, commander of the FEB and subsequently chief of the general staff of the Brazilian armed
forces, gave me an interview, an autographed copy of his
command diary, *A FEB Pelo Seu Comandante* (Rio de
Janeiro, 1960), and sent his aide-de-camp to present me to

the director of the *Arquivo do Exército* with the message that I should be allowed to use the *Arquivo da F.E.B.* The latter was then headed by Captain Seraphim José de Oliveira, who had been a corporal in the 3rd Company of the Sampaio (1 IR) during the Italian campaign. Captain Oliveira guided me through the collection, which obviously had serious gaps. Apparently many battalion-level records were kept by individual officers, not to speak of sectional records of division staff, intracorps communications, and unit combat diaries. It was easier to construct day to day division-level operations from the American liaison reports in Washington than from the FEB materials in Rio. Though Oliveira was aware of this he had neither the facilities nor the authority to search out and secure the numerous small collections in private hands throughout Brazil. As he has now retired from the service and, since Mascarenhas' death, the FEB archive's special status has been abolished, the staff reassigned, and the collection absorbed into the *Arquivo do Exército*, it is unlikely that a complete collection will ever be assembled. And because the directorship of the archives is a normal duty tour that may fall to any field-grade officer regardless of his background the rules of access are constantly in flux. With so much turbulence at the top the career functionaries have not been able to develop the archives into a research facility. But as always in Brazil, a *jeito* is possible for a researcher with patience, tact, and determination. Fortunately for this study the problems were minimal, thanks to Oliveira's cheerful assistance.

He regaled me with tales of life in the Brazilian army before and during the war, and he introduced me to the music of the campaign as performed by his *conjunto* of veterans in their album *20 Anos Depois, Expedicionários em Ritmos* (Chantecler Records, CMG 2397). These contacts and informal ones with other veterans provided a variety of impressions that do not fit into scholarly footnotes but are nonetheless important.

At Marshal Mascarenhas' suggestion I sought an interview with Marshal Estevão Leitão de Carvalho, who represented Brazil on the Brazil–United States Military Defense Commission during the war. He played a key diplomatic role in the formation of the FEB. Leitão de Carvalho's *A Serviço do Brasil na Segunda Guerra Mundial* (Rio de Janeiro, 1952) and his *Memórias de um Soldado Legalista*, 3 vols. (Rio de Janeiro, 1961, 1962, 1964) were especially good for his views of the internal workings of the army hierarchy. Likewise General Pedro Aurélio de Góes Monteiro gave his version of the inside story to journalist Lourival Coutinho, who mixed it with his own running commentary in *O General Góes Depõe . . .* (Rio de Janeiro, 1956). Though it must be used with care because of the manner in which Coutinho ran his own comments and questions into Góes' statements, it is a key source because of Góes' intimate role in the rise, operation, and overthrow of the Estado Nôvo. His biography should be written.

Publications on the FEB itself have been limited thus far to diaries, reports, memoirs, and combat histories. A devoted student of Brazilian military history, Colonel Francisco Ruas Santos, whose army career unfortunately has prevented him from writing his history of the FEB, has done other scholars a great service with his *Fontes para a História da FEB* (Rio de Janeiro, 1958). It is a detailed annotated bibliography. Typical of the diaries are Newton C. de Andrade Mello's *Meu Diário da Guerra na Itália* (Rio de Janeiro 1947); Elber de Mello Henriques, *A FEB Doze Anos Depois* (Rio de Janeiro, 1959); Gentil Palhares, *De São João del-Rei ao Vale do Pó* (São João del-Rei, 1951); and Aquinaldo José Senna Campos, *Com a FEB Na Itália, Páginas do meu Diário* (Rio de Janeiro, 1970). In a class by itself is Agostinho José Rodriques' exciting, well-written *Segundo Pelotão 8.a Companhia* (São Paulo, 1969). It is more memoir than diary, but obviously closely based on notes made in the field, and deals with his assignment to the

FEB and the first of two platoons that he commanded during the campaign. Rodriques was a reserve officer with the 11th Infantry Regiment. Also well written but lacking the front-line intimacy of Rodriques' work are two books by wartime correspondents—Rubem Braga, who reported for *Diário Carioca*, and produced *Crônicas de Guerra (Com a FEB na Itália)* (Rio de Janeiro, 1945 and 1964), and Joel Silveira of the *Diários Associados*, who wrote *Histórias de Pracinha (Reportagens de guerra)* (Rio de Janeiro, 1945). Silveira re-issued it in simplified form after the Revolution of 1964 under the title *As Duas Guerras da FEB* (Rio de Janeiro, 1965). Part one dealt with the coup d'état against João Goulart and was entitled "A FEB no Poder," while part two contained the 1945 stories with the title "A FEB na Guerra de Verdade." His dismay at the turn Brazilian history had taken is caught in three sentences (p. 6): "hoje, no poder, novamente a FEB vez por outra faz lembrar o antigo exército germânico. Mas a semelhança agora não é de farda. A semelhança agora, mais triste, é de mentalidade e de pro-cessos" ("Today, in power, once again the FEB reminds one of the old German army. But the similarity now isn't the uniform. The similarity now, more sadly, is one of mental-ity and actions").

Of the various reports the most valuable was the one pre-pared by the American liaison staff, the "Report on the 1st Infantry Division Brazilian Expeditionary Force in the Ital-ian Campaign from 16 July 1944 to the Cessation of Hos-tilities in May 1945." I have already discussed the docu-ment's classification. Copies of it are in WWII RS, NA and the Office of the Chief of Military History. Only slightly less useful was the biting and often bitter collection of reports by reserve officers who served with the FEB; Demócrito Cavalcanti de Arruda, *et al.*, *Depoimento de Oficiais da Reserva Sôbre a F.E.B.* (Rio de Janeiro, 1949). Many of their comments and analyses cut close to the bone of the regular officer corps. Although their special perspective must be considered carefully their *Depoimento* is a mandatory source. Formation of the FEB is dealt with in many of the above, but none displays so graphically the health problems involved in raising a modern army in Brazil of the 1940's as Carlos Paiva Gonçalves, *Seleção Médica do Pessoal da FEB, Histórico, Funcionamento e Dados Estatísticos* (Rio de Janeiro, 1951). The Brazilian air force's expeditionary contribution was a fighter squadron, which I did not deal with in this book, but which was discussed with good prose and good humor in Luiz F. Perdigão, *Missão de Guerra, Os Expedicionários da FAB na Guerra Européia* (Rio de Janeiro, 1958).

An illuminating and sometimes disgruntled memoir was Floriano de Lima Brayner's *A Verdade Sôbre a FEB, Memórias de um Chefe de Estado-Maior na Campanha de Itália* (Rio de Janeiro, 1968). When the FEB was formed, its staff was organized in the French style with a chief of staff coordinating its efforts and responsible only to the commander. In Italy Mascarenhas, without changing the staff structure, shifted to the American procedure of the commander dealing directly with his operations staff officer (G-3), who was Lt. Colonel Humberto A. de Castello Branco. This left full-Colonel Lima Brayner with a substantially reduced operational role. He remained stubbornly loyal to Mascarenhas, but he was obviously annoyed at his loss of prestige and Castello Branco's rise. Since his book appeared after Castello's death the ex-president's friends arranged publication of Mascarenhas' two volume *Memórias* (Rio de Janeiro, 1969), with a preface by General Carlos de Meira Mattos (a captain in the FEB) stressing Mascarenhas' reliance on Castello during the campaign.

The best combat history is Manuel Thomaz Castello Branco, *O Brasil na II Grande Guerra* (Rio de Janeiro, 1960). Though it is not footnoted it is based on material in the FEB archive. It is a necessary source for studies of the war period, but the author avoided political commentary. Just the opposite is Nelson Werneck Sodré's *História Militar do Brasil* (Rio de Janeiro, 1965) which gives the

FEB rather short shift, but does set the war years in the perspective of Brazilian military history. Also valuable is Sodré's *Memórias de um Soldado* (Rio de Janeiro, 1967), which provides a view from the lower ranks of the army. The development of military education can be traced in Umberto Peregrino, *História e Projeção das Instituicões Culturais do Exército* (Rio de Janeiro, 1967). A more detailed history of this sort is badly needed. The effects of the FEB experience on the army have not been studied. A short, depressing sketch of the treatment FEB veterans received is drawn by Luciano Alfredo Barcellos in "A Flagelação dos Ex-Combatentes" in Jose Louzeiro, ed., *Assim Marcha a Família* (Rio de Janeiro, 1965), pp. 145–159.

Two recent books by Americans, Ronald M. Schneider, *The Political System of Brazil, Emergence of a "Modernizing" Authoritarian Regime, 1964–1970* (New York, 1971), and Alfred Stepan, *The Military in Politics, Changing Patterns in Brazil* (Princeton, 1971), also provide insights into and information about military personalities in the war period.

Brazilian foreign policy has not received the attention it deserves. The best one-volume summary is Carlos Delgado de Carvalho, *História Diplomática do Brasil* (São Paulo, 1959). The general outlines of twentieth-century diplomacy are traced in José Honório Rodriques, *Intêresse Nacional e Política Externa* (Rio de Janeiro, 1966). And foreign policy is subjected to a geopolitical analysis in J. O. de Meira Penna, *Política Externa, Segurança and Desenvolvimento* (Rio de Janeiro, 1967). There is an essay by Jaime Pinsky, "O Brasil nas Relações Internaciones: 1930–1945," in Carlos Guilherme Mota, *Brasil em Perspectiva* (São Paulo, 1969). Monographic studies thus far are few, but fortunately scholars have begun to span this century at least chronologically. E. Bradford Burns looks at the turn of the century in his *The Unwritten Alliance, Rio-Branco and Brazilian-American Relations* (New York, 1966). The only study that treats the period between the Rio Branco and Vargas eras is a dissertation by Lewis House, "Edwin V. Morgan and Brazilian-American Diplomatic Relations, 1912–1933" (Ph.D. Dissertation, New York University, 1969). A study of Brazilian diplomacy in that same time frame would be valuable. Donald W. Giffin chronicled American policy vis-à-vis Brazil in "The Normal Years, Brazilian-American Relations, 1930–1939" (Ph.D. Dissertation, Vanderbilt University, 1962). And by far the most solidly based study of pre-World War II Brazilian foreign policy is Stanley E. Hilton, "Brazil and the Great Power Trade Rivalry in South America, 1934–1939" (Ph.D. Dissertation, University of Texas at Austin, 1969). Hilton used many of the sources mentioned above and has provided a good amount of new material. Likewise John Wirth provides some interesting summations in *The Politics of Brazilian Development* (Stanford, 1970), and Thomas Skidmore quickly reviews the political events of 1930–1945 in the first chapter of his *Politics in Brazil, 1930–1964, An Experiment in Democracy* (New York, 1967).

Studies of German, British, Italian, and French relations with Brazil are lacking. For Germany, the most useful published material is in the United States Department of State, *Documents on German Foreign Policy, 1918–1945*, Series D (Washington, 1949–). Also helpful is William N. Simonson's "Nazi Infiltration in South America, 1933–1945" (Ph.D. Dissertation, Fletcher School of Law and Diplomacy, 1964). Alton Frye's *Nazi Germany and the American Hemisphere, 1933–1941* (New Haven, 1967), though based on the unpublished German records, did not provide new insights or information on Berlin's relations with Brazil.

For United States policy toward Latin America in this period there is no solid, comprehensive study. A good summary is in Donald M. Dozer, *Are We Good Neighbors? Three Decades of Inter-American Relations, 1930–1960* (Gainesville, 1960). The best account by far is still that of William L. Langer and S. Everett Gleason, *The Challenge of Isolation, 1937–1940* (New York, 1952) and *The Undeclared War, 1940–1941* (New York, 1953). Cordell Hull's *Memoirs,* 2 vols. (New York, 1948) and Sumner Welles' *The Seven Decisions That Shaped History* (New York, 1950) continued their feud without result, but presented some useful information. Probably the most provocative study on United States Latin American policy is David Green's *The Containment of Latin America, A History of the Myths and Realities of the Good Neighbor Policy* (Chicago, 1971), in which he contends that American postwar policy aimed at suppressing independent nationalism in the region. This naturally placed Washington at odds with Vargas in 1945 and with Juan Perón's regime in Buenos Aires in the 1950's.

Of the many Brazilian newspapers cited in the notes the *Jornal do Brasil* and the *Correio da Manhã* were the most accessible because their offices had complete sets of back issues and small work areas. The *Biblioteca Nacional* also has back issues but they are not as convenient to use. The Department of State, as mentioned above maintained a clipping file from 1940 to 1945 (832.911), and the Oswaldo Aranha Archive had a collection of clippings on Aranha's career (Lux Jornal).

The following supplementary bibliography is arranged alphabetically and lists some helpful items.

I. Published Works:

A. Books:

Alexander, Robert J. *Communism in Latin America.* New Brunswick, 1961.

Amado Jorge. *O Cavaleiro da Esperança, Vida de Luís Carlos Prestes.* Rio de Janeiro, 1956.

Barros Gomes, Jayme de. *Exposição Sucinta dos Trabalhos Realizados Pelo Itamarati nos Últimos Doze Meses, 1938–1939.* Rio de Janeiro, 1940.

———. *A Política Exterior do Brasil, 1930–1942.* Rio de Janeiro, 1943.

Bello, José Maria. *História da República*. São Paulo, 1964.

Bemis, Samuel Flagg. *The Latin American Policy of the United States*. New York, 1943.

Blum, John M. *From the Morgenthau Diaries: Years of Crisis, 1928–1938*. Boston, 1959.

———. *From the Morgenthau Diaries: Years of Urgency, 1938–1941*. Boston, 1965.

Borges Fortes, Heitor. *Velhos Regimentos, Ensaio Sôbre a Evolução da Artilharia de Campanha Brasileira de 1931 a 1939*. Rio de Janeiro, 1964.

Calmon, Pedro. *Brasil e América*. Rio de Janeiro, 1944.

———. *História do Brasil*. Vol. vi: *A República e o Desenvolvimento Nacional*. Rio de Janeiro, 1959.

Campos, Francisco. *O Estado Nacional*. Rio de Janeiro, 1941.

Cooke, Morris L. *Brazil on the March, A Study in International Cooperation*. New York, 1944.

Craven, Wesley F. and James L. Cate. *The Army Air Forces in World War II*. Chicago, 1948.

DeJong, Louis. *The German Fifth Column in the Second World War*. Chicago, 1956.

Doenitz, Karl. *Memoirs, Ten Years and Twenty Days*. Cleveland, 1959.

Donahoe, Bernard F. *Private Plans and Public Dangers: The Story of FDR's Third Nomination*. Notre Dame, 1965.

Duggan, Laurence. *The Americas*. New York, 1949.

Gordon, David L. and Royden Dangerfield. *The Hidden Weapon: The Story of Economic Warfare*. New York, 1947.

Greer, Thomas H. *What Roosevelt Thought: The Social and Political Ideas of Franklin D. Roosevelt*. East Lansing, 1958.

Guerrant, Edward O. *Roosevelt's Good Neighbor Policy*. Albuquerque, 1950.

Gunther, John. *Inside Latin America*. New York, 1941.

Henriques, Affonso. *Vargas, O Maquiavélico*. São Paulo, 1961.

Herring, Hubert. *Good Neighbors: Argentina, Brazil, Chile, and Seventeen Other Countries*. New Haven, 1941.

Hill, Lawrence. *Brazil*. Berkeley, 1947.

————. *Diplomatic Relations Between the United States and Brazil*. Durham, 1932.

Horowitz, Irving L. *Revolution in Brazil*. New York, 1964.

Inman, Samuel Guy. *Inter-American Conferences, 1826–1954: History and Problems*. Washington, 1965.

International Military Tribunal. *Trial of the Major War Criminals Before the International Military Tribunal*. Vols. v, xiii, xiv, xviii. Nuremberg, 1948.

Johnson, John J. *The Military and Society in Latin America*. Stanford, 1964.

Joint Brazil-United States Economic Development Commission. *The Development of Brazil*. Washington, 1953.

Josephson, Matthew. *Empire of the Air: Juan Trippe and the Struggle for World Airways*. New York, 1943.

Leitão de Carvalho, Estevão. *Dever Militar e Política Partidária*. São Paulo, 1959.

————. *Discursos, Conferências e Outros Escritos*. Rio de Janeiro, 1965.

Lieuwen, Edwin. *Arms and Politics in Latin America*. New York, 1961.

Lissitzyn, Oliver J. *International Air Transport and National Policy*. New York, 1942.

Macdonald, Norman P. *Hitler over Latin America*. London, 1942.

McMurray, Ruth E. and Muna Lee. *The Cultural Approach: Another Way in International Relations*. Chapel Hill, 1947.

Morison, Samuel E. *The Battle of the Atlantic*. Boston, 1947.

Palmer, Thomas W. *Search for a Latin American Policy*. Gainesville, 1957.

Peterson, Harold. *Argentina and the United States, 1810–1960*. New York, 1964.

Pogue, Forrest C. *George C. Marshall: Education of a General.* New York, 1963.

Pratt, Julius W. *Cordell Hull.* Vols. XII and XIII in Robert H. Ferrell, ed., *The American Secretaries of State and Their Diplomacy.* New York, 1964.

Rauschning, Hermann. *The Voices of Destruction.* New York, 1940.

Roosevelt, Elliott. *F.D.R.: His Personal Letters, 1928–1945.* New York, 1950.

Salgado, Plínio. *O Integralismo Brasileiro Perante a Nação.* Lisbon, 1946.

Shepardson, Whitney H. *et al. United States in World Affairs.* New York, 1938–1943.

Silva Py, Aurélio da. *A 5ª Coluna no Brasil, A Conspiração Nazi no Rio Grande do Sul.* Pôrto Alegre, 1942.

Stimson, Henry L. and McGeorge Bundy. *On Active Service in Peace and War.* New York, 1948.

Tavares de Sá, Hernane. *The Brazilians, People of Tomorrow.* New York, 1947.

United States Navy, Office of Naval Intelligence. *Fuehrer Conferences on Matters Dealing with the German Navy.* Washington, 1947.

———, Bureau of Yards and Docks. *Building the Navy's Bases in World War II.* Washington, 1947.

Vianna, Hélio. *História Diplomática do Brasil.* São Paulo, 1958.

Watson, Mark S. *Chief of Staff: Prewar Plans and Preparations.* Washington, 1950.

Welles, Sumner. *The Time for Decision.* New York, 1944.

Willems, Emílio. *Assimilação e Populações Marginais no Brasil.* São Paulo, 1940.

Wood, Bryce. *The Making of the Good Neighbor Policy.* New York, 1961.

Young, Jordon M. *The Brazilian Revolution of 1930 and the Aftermath.* New Brunswick, 1967.

B. Articles:

Beals, Carleton. "Totalitarian Inroads in Latin America," *Foreign Affairs*, xvii, No. 1 (October 1938), 78–89.

"Brazil: the New Ally," *Fortune*, xxvi, No. 5 (November 1942), 104–109.

del Villar, Frederico: "Brazilian Air Chief," *The Inter-American Monthly*, ii, No. 8 (August 1943), 15–17.

———. "Life and Death of Brazilian Fascism," *The Inter-American Monthly*, ii, No. 6 (June 1943), 16–19.

Hall, Melvin and Walter Peck. "Wings for Trojan Horse," *Foreign Affairs*, xix, No. 2 (January 1941), 347–369.

Leite Linhares, Maria Yedda. "Vargas: A Tomada do Poder," *Tempo Brasileiro*, iv, No. 8 (February 1966), 39–55.

Maack, Reinhard. "The Germans in South Brazil: a German View," *Inter-American Quarterly*, i, No. 3 (July 1939), 5ff.

Monbeig, Pierre. "The Metallurgical Industry in the State of Minas Gerais," *Brazil*, x, No. 118 (August 1938), 6–10.

Murkland, Harry Banta. "Brazil Fights Subversive Elements," *Current History*, iii, No. 16 (December 1942), 334.

Murphy, Charles. "Letter from Recife, Intrigue on the Bulge," *Fortune*, xxiii, No. 6 (June 1941), 36ff.

Nasht, John. "Brazil's Year of Change," *The Inter-American Monthly*, ii, No. 5 (May 1943), 27–29.

Rodriques, José Honório. "The Foundations of Brazil's Foreign Policy," *International Affairs*, xxxviii, No. 3 (July 1962), 324–338.

Sevareid, Eric. "Where Do We Go From Rio?" *Saturday Evening Post*, ccxiv, No. 39 (March 28, 1942), 27ff.

Sharp, Walter R. "Brazil 1940—Whither the New State?" *Inter-American Quarterly*, ii, No. 4 (October 1940), 5–17.

Stuart, Graham H. "The New Office of American Republican Affairs in the Department of State," *The American Political Science Review*, xxxiv, No. 3 (June 1945), 483–484.

"War Projects for Brazil," *Fortune*, xxvi, No. 5 (November 1942), 216–218.

II. *Unpublished Material*:

American Technical Mission to Brazil. "Report to the President of the United States." December 1942. FDRL.

Burden, William A. M. "Latin American Air Transportation." Report prepared for the Coordinator of Commercial and Cultural Relations Between the American Republics. June 1941. Pan-American Airways Library.

Matthews, Charles. "Sidelights on the History of Parnamirim Field." Report to Historical Office, SADATC. n.d. Charles Matthews Papers, Natal.

Miller, Beatrice R. "Brazil Enacts its Benefits." Unpublished Master's Thesis, Indiana University, 1945.

Pratt, Curtis G. *et al.* "Construction of Certain Latin American and Caribbean Air Bases Built by the United States." Report submitted to the Under-Secretary of War. January 25, 1946. Records of Army Service Forces. Office of the Chief of Military History.

Simpson, Richard P. "History of Airport Development Program—Brazil." November 11, 1943. Office of the Chief of Military History.

Taylor, Philip Bates, Jr. "The Relations of Brazil with the United States since 1937." Unpublished Master's thesis, University of California, 1947.

Woodward, Paul B. "Brazil's Participation in the Second World War." Unpublished Master's thesis, Georgetown University, 1951.

Index

Abbink Mission (1948), John, 387
Ação Integralista Brasileira, 31.
 See also Integralistas
Additional Act to Constitution
 of 1937, 459.
Administrative Department of
 Public Service, 26
Aeronautics, Ministry of, 218, 226,
 293
Aêropostal Brasileira, Cia., 227
Africa, 6, 125, 192-193, 242, 306,
 308, 346, 348, 352, 373, 405
Agency for International Develop-
 ment, U.S., 387
Agriculture, U.S. Department of,
 127, 265
aid, U.S., 126-130
Airport Development Program,
 217, 221-239, 269-270, 274, 275;
 Brazil and the war, 240, 292;
 security, 233-234, 242, 246,
 260. *See also* army, U.S.; foreign
 policy, U.S.–aviation; Panair do
 Brasil, Pan-American Airways
air force, Brazilian, 134, 270, 293,
 379; U.S., 145
Air France, 215-216, 227, 232, 236
Air Transport Command, 424,
 427. *See also* Airport Development Program; army, U.S.
Aleixo, Pedro, 315
Alemanha antártica, 114
Alencastro Guimarães, Napoleão
 de, 383

Allen, Douglas H., 395
Alliance, Brazilian-American,
 5-10, 61, 67-69, 75-76, 112, 118,
 267, 304, 309, 314-315, 319-321,
 325-328, 330-332, 342, 348, 350,
 357-359, 453-454
alliance, Cuban-Russian, 385
Alliance for Progress (1961), 387
alliance, Inter-American, 330
Alliance, Liberal, 13
Alliance, National Liberation, 29
Amapá, 287
Amaral Peixoto, Ernani, 255, 279,
 280, 289
Amazon, 119; Brazilian govern-
 ment agencies for, 388f; devel-
 opment, 264-265, 268, 276, 306,
 388-396; and Northeast, 389
American-Anglo relations, 306
American Council of Learned
 Societies, 249
American Technical Mission, *see*
 Cooke Mission
Américo de Almeida, José, 36-37,
 41, 45, 58, 451
Andrade, Antônio Carlos de, 35
Angola, 377
anti-trust decree, 466
Approximation Policy, 5-7, 10, 68,
 74-76, 129, 133, 140, 159, 302,
 304, 310, 330-332, 358, 388
Aranha, Adalberto, 40, 59, 61-63
Aranha family, 70-71, 101-102,
 336-337

Aranha, Luís, 62
Aranha, Luiza de Freitas Valle, 70
Aranha, Manoel, 101-102
Aranha, Oswaldo: alliance and
policy, 250, 304-307, 331; arms
supply, 43, 204-205; aviation,
220, 226, 228, 233, 330; Caffery,
266, 281, 452; chancellorship,
73-76; characterized, 51-52, 116;
defense, 269-271; development,
195-196, 197, 198; elections, 312,
315, 351-352, 355, 465; Estado
Nôvo, 9, 28, 33, 35-36, 38-41,
59-72, 75; expeditionary force,
344-346, 349-351; Fournier incident, 101-102; Friends of
America, 311; Góes Monteiro,
139, 142, 331; hemispheric security pact, 106-122; mentioned,
201, 202, 382, 402, 437; Mission
(1939), 123-133, 147, 193-194;
resignation, 319-320, 324-325,
333, 335-342; Rio Conference,
250-258, 263-264; Ritter, 86-87,
96, 99-100, 103-104, 166-167,
176-178; trade, 155, 158-159, 166-
169; United Nations, 297-298;
U.S. policy, 158-159, 247, 326-
327, 332-333; Sumner Welles, 52,
87, 112-113, 319-320; World
War II, 144, 179-180, 182, 184,
189, 209, 289-290, 357-359
Argentina, 5, 6, 43, 68, 69, 88, 91,
106, 110, 113, 116, 186, 188, 203,
210, 291-293, 300; Axis, 323;
Bolivia, 310-311; Brazilian fear
of, 139-140, 176, 331, 345, 355,
444, 457; foreign policy, 284;
Lima Conference, 117-121; military, 320-324, 327, 340, 394;
Rio Conference, 252-260; U.S.
treatment, 281-284, 473-474
armed forces, see army, military
arms supply, 106, 110-111, 119, 139,

143-147, 184-185, 187-188, 195,
204-211, 241, 272, 308; domination, 328-330, 341; German
purchases, 111-113, 168, 174, 177,
182, 200, 205, 241, 255-256, 258;
Góes Monteiro visit, 139-143;
FEB, 345, 350-351, 406-407, 410-
411, 418; isolationism, 143, 184;
Italy, 181, 209; Northeast Brazil,
135-136, 141, 242; Siqueira
Campos Affair, 209-211, 302;
Souza Costa Mission, 259-263,
267-270; staff agreements,
330-331
army, Brazilian: approximation,
131-147; attitudes toward
Americans, 113, 208, 241, 361-
363, 376, 406-408, 410-413, 419;
Caixas, Army of, 408-410;
described, 346-347, 364-367, 369,
379; effect of FEB demobilization, 468; English, 302, 344-345;
jurisdiction, 237; strategic
views, 133-134, 138, 140, 147, 245,
272-274, 277, 295, 345; training,
272, 353-354, 360-364, 374-375,
410-412; war plans, 296-297;
misc. 180, 205, 226. See also
arms supply, expeditionary
force, military
—, German, 132, 135, 178, 183,
188, 363
—, United States: Air Transport
Command, 217, 228, 234-238, 260,
270, 294-295; Basic Economy
Program, 397-398; Brazil, 133,
135-141, 266, 271, 272, 365; FEB,
347-349, 351, 362, 419, 428-429,
431; Latin America, 108-109;
Northeast Brazil, 135-136, 138,
141, 145, 147, 201-209, 242-246,
270-271, 295, 452; Pan-American
Airways, 213-217, 220-239;
training centers, 354n; misc.,

183, 250, 261. *See also* Airport
Development Program, Pot
of Gold
Araújo, Cauby C., 224-227, 229-
230, 240
Araújo, Góes, Coriolano de, 325,
334-335
Arnold, Harold, 235, 455
Ascension Island, 274
Aski marks, *see* compensation
Assis Chateaubriand, Francisco de,
30, 437, 477-478
assistance program, 267
Asunción, Paraguay, 214, 224, 310
asylum, 101-102
Atlantic Airways Ltd., 235
Atlantic Charter, 305
Auslandsorganization (AO), 98,
103
Austria, 74-75, 82, 85
aviation, 5, 214-221, 330, 455-456
Axis, 4, 124-125, 134-135, 146, 176,
191, 202, 204, 213, 230, 244, 280
Azores, 308, 350, 352

Bagnoli, 410
Bahia, 287
banks, 129; Bank of Brazil, 132,
150, 153, 157, 165-167, 173, 181,
200, 310, 480; Central Bank, 128-
129, 131-132; Export-Import,
68, 127, 128, 168; Federal Reserve, 127; Reichsbank, 171, 173;
Rubber Credit, 268
Barber, Henry A., 271
Barcelos, Cristovão de Castro, 478
Barreiras cut-off, 199, 224, 229
Barron's, 32
Barros Cámara, Don Jaime de, 317
base agreement (1944), 452
bases, U.S., 110-111, 135, 138, 140,
202, 380-381; ADP, 217, 221-239,
242, 246, 260, 269-270, 274, 275,

Basic Economy Program, 397-401
292, 332; postwar, 330, 341, 355,
363, 452
Belém, Pará, 134, 203, 214, 217,
227, 229, 233, 238, 246, 288, 295,
388ff
Belo Horizonte, Minas Gerais, 137,
181-182, 198, 288, 315, 441
Berle Jr., Adolf A., 341, 451-458,
463, 464, 467, 471-477; speech,
475-477, 478-479, 482
Berlin, 125, 167, 174, 182
Bernardes, Artur, 315, 364
bilateral military agreements, 330
blockade, 173, 179, 192, 205, 216,
247, 274, 294; *Siqueira Campos*,
209-211
Blumenau, Santa Catarina, 151,
180
Board of Economic Warfare, 381,
398
Bolivia, 43, 252, 282-283, 310-311,
321, 323, 327, 454
Bologna, 414, 423
Bonaparte, Napoleon, 445
Borges, Heitor, 357
Borghi, Hugo, 470, 480
Bouças, Valentim, 131, 226, 264-
266, 383, 388
Braden, Spruelle, 471, 474, 479
Brady, E. E., 293
Braga, Odilón Duarte, 46, 315
Bragança, Pedro Enrique Orleans
e, 467
Brayner, Floriano de Lima, 363,
367, 372, 376, 407, 424-425, 434,
440
Brazil: described, 16-22, 134; Germans in, *see* immigrants; experience compared with U.S., 32;
penetrated political system,
25-26, 161, 169-170, 387; stra-
tegic importance, 4; University
of, 334; vice president, 312

Brazilian Academy of Letters, 317
Brazilian-American Association, 127
Brazilian-American relations, 43, 65, 123-147, 193-201, 215-238, 271, 281-284, 296-297, 332, 340, 342
Brazilian-Argentine relations, 110, 113, 119-121, 139-140, 281-284, 292-293, 320-324, 340
Brazilian-German relations, 77-83, 86-91, 94-101, 115-116, 182, 252; affair of the ambassadors, 103-105, 176-178; Caffery, 285-286; trade, 128, 129, 132, 190-193, 199-201
Brazilian-Italian relations, 90-91, 181, 184
Brazilianization, 77, 90, 178
Brazilian liaison mission, 363
British aircraft, 235; Foreign Office, 209-210. See also England
Buenos Aires, 183, 214, 248, 254
bulge, see Natal; Northeast Brazil
business, 151, 157-158, 316-317
Byrnes, James F., 341

cacao, 163, 166, 170
Caffery, Jefferson, 46, 53-54, 87, 93, 136-137, 159, 184-188, 190, 194-195, 197, 202, 204-207, 237, 255, 261, 266, 269, 279, 311, 337; Amazon planning, 392; Aranha, 338, 341, 382, 402, 452; entry of U.S. troops, 246, 270-271; evaluated, 284-286, 294; Natal, 307-308, 309-310, 311, 337
Caiado de Castro, Aguinaldo, 434
Caldeirão, Ceará, 22
Camoçim, Ceará, 227
campaign of 1937, 34-42
Campos, Francisco, 11, 33-34, 41, 44-45, 46, 56, 62, 65-66, 69-73, 82, 89, 131, 280, 314, 339

Capanema, Gustavo, 71
Cape Verdes, 244
Carioca, Zé, 248, 299
Cantillo, José Maria, 117, 121
Carmelo, Dom Carlos, 467
carnival, 18, 85
Casablanca Conference, 304, 309
Casa Rosada, 320
casinos, 299
Castello Branco, Humberto de, 421
Castelnuovo, 435
Castelnuovo de Garfagnana, 415
Castillo, Ramón, 260, 292-293, 320
Catete Palace, 46, 57, 92, 94, 425
Catholic Church, 17-18, 317, 467
Cavalcanti, Newton, 57, 59, 357
Cavalcanti de Albuquerque, Pompeu, 59
Caxias, Army of, 408-410, 426, 428, 432, 465; Duke of, 412
Caymmi, Dorival, 432,
Ceará, 20, 22
censorship, 174, 427-428, 450
Central America, 161
Chaco war, 108, 119
Chalmers, Philip O., 482
Chapultepec Conference, see Inter-American Conferences
Chile, 88, 252, 321, 323, 394
China, 326
Ciano, Count, 184; Edda, 137
Cicero, Padre, 22
citizenship, German view of, 78
Civil Aviation, Department of (DAC), 227
civil service, 313-314, 316
Clark, Mark, 373, 412-413, 418, 425, 429, 433-434, 441
coal, 160, 172, 194, 198
Coelho dos Reis, José, 280, 315
coffee, 23-24, 63-64, 161-162, 166, 167, 170, 190, 192, 195, 196, 380
Cohen Plan, 38
Collado, Emilo, 265

collective security pact, *see* Lima Conference

Colombia, 161-162

Columbia Broadcasting System, 107-108

colonies, 306, 350

Companhia Brasileira de Material Ferroviário, 455

compensation trade, 111, 128, 129, 131-132, 152-155, 157-160, 164-165, 168, 170-172; explained, 150

Commerce, U.S. Department of, 127

communications, 266

Communist Party, Brazilian, 14, 28-30, 335, 444, 464-465, 470

Condor, 215-221, 230

Congress, Brazilian, 46; of Brazilian writers, 450; U.S., 141, 146

Constituent Assembly (1933), 27

Constituinte, *see* Constitutional Convention

Constitutional Convention, 446, 459-460, 469

Constitution of 1934, 27; of (Nov. 10) 1937, 8, 34, 41, 46, 55-56, 314, 446, 459, 468

Cooke Mission, 381-388

Cooke, Morris Llewellyn, 382

Coordinator of Economic Mobilization, 394

Corcôvado, 11, 17, 377

Cordeiro de Farias, Gustavo, 483

Cordeiro de Farias, Oswaldo, 72, 82, 92, 137, 337, 414, 437, 470, 483-484

Costa, Fernando, 46

Costa Neto, Benedito, 448

cotton, 153, 162, 166, 167-170, 190, 192, 196

coup d'état 1930, 13-14

Crittenberger, Willis D., 414, 420, 433-434, 441

Cruzeiro do Sul, Serviços Aêreos, 220

Cuba, 108

cultural relations, 107-108, 247-249

Curitiba, Paraná, 137, 214

currency, 132, 161, 175, 281

Czechoslovakia, 91, 111, 113

Daltro Filho, Manoel de Cerqueira, 39, 72

Dakar, French West Africa, 133, 221-222, 242, 245, 308, 345

Danzig, 143

debt, 61, 63-64, 70, 126, 132, 175

defense, 124, 129, 132-146, 222, 242, 246, 277, 286

degermanization, *see* foreign policy, U.S.–aviation

democracy, 31-32, 301, 344

Department of State, *see* State Department

dependency, 5, 120, 163, 175, 180, 265, 282-283, 345; description (1942), 378-381; efforts to avoid, 194, 196, 302, 305-306, 320, 358; FEB, 405-407; rubber, 394-396, U.S. policy, 454-457

depoliticization of military, 303-304

depression, 7, 23-25

destroyer transfer, 113, 188

development, 61, 68, 73, 74, 180; Aranha Mission, 125ff; Amazon, 388-397; Cooke Mission, 381-388; dependency, 454-457; health, 371-372; military, 321, 444-445; resources, 268-269, 283, 314, 341, 343, 394-396; Souza Costa Mission, 264-269; trade, 148, 160-161, 172, 180-181; transportation, 396-397; UDN criticism, 466; Volta Redonda, 193-

development (*cont.*)
  199; World War II, 305-306,
  322, 358-359, 380-402
Diário Oficial, 45, 228
dictatorship, 30, 32-33, 342
disease, 20, 236
Disney, Walt, 247, 299
Division of American Republics
  (DAR), 106-107, 327, 386
Division of Brazilian Affairs
  (DBA), 448, 452-453, 454, 473-
  474, 478-479
Division of Cultural Relations,
  107-108
divisions, army: 10th Mountain,
  U.S., 433; 92nd, U.S., 420; 148th,
  German, 436; 232nd, German,
  415, 420; Monte Rosa, Italian
  Fascist, 415, 436
Dixie Clipper (PAA), 307
Dodsworth, Henrique, 311, 481,
  482
dollar-a-year men, 341
Dorsch, Ernst, 82-83
Duck, Donald, 299
Duggan, Laurence, 265
Dumbarton Oaks, 340, 458
Dunham, George C., 398
Dutch, 133, 163, 377; Guiana, 244
Dutra, Eurico Gaspar, 9, 34, 42, 45,
  57, 71, 92, 101-102, 137, 181, 188,
  200, 204, 207, 211, 240-241, 244,
  270, 273, 325, 335-337; Aranha,
  351-352, 355; arms, 360-361;
  Axis, 254-257, 280-281; candi-
  date, 437, 447, 453, 461, 462,
  465-468; coup Oct. 1945, 445,
  446, 483-486; plots, 301-302

economic orthodoxy, 25
economic nationalism, 149, 161
economic policy: Brazil, 61, 63-64,
  148-175, 305-306; Germany, 90,
  148-175; U.S., 90, 123-133, 148-

175, 195, 206-207, 261-267, 282-
  284, 341, 381, 394-396, 452-459.
  See also foreign policy; trade
economic planning, 387
economy, Brazilian, 79, 174, 275,
  300, 378-402, 463
Ecuador, 119
education, 18-19
Egypt, 169
Eighth Army, British, 414
Eisenhower, Dwight D., 348, 360
electrification, 160, 172
elections, 41, 301, 311-312, 314-315,
  335, 339, 364, 446-447, 459, 460,
  466-469, 472-473, 478, 480, 485
elite and opposition to Vargas,
  466-467
embargo, 275-277
emergency, state of, 30. *See also*
  war, state of
Emmons, Delos C., 145-146, 201,
  222
England, 111, 113, 124, 172, 178,
  179, 182-184, 187-189, 192; and
  Brazil, 112, 147, 148, 152, 174,
  203-204, 217, 235, 240-241, 282,
  302-303, 321, 326, 458; *Siqueira
  Campos* Affair, 209-211; trade
  competition with U.S., 455-456
Engineer Battalion, 9th, Brazilian
  (Aquidauana, Mato Grosso),
  367
espionage, 247, 260-261, 266
Estado Nacional, 300
Estado Nôvo, 46-51, 53-55, 62-63,
  68, 71-73, 75, 114, 334, 337, 338;
  anniversaries, 250, 300-301; end,
  450-452, 482-486; example of
  decree method, 225-228; FEB,
  363, 426, 438; Integralistas and
  Nazis, 77-105; military, 444-448,
  461; U.S., 139, 159. *See also*
  Vargas, Getúlio
estadonovistas, 336

Estância Itú (São Borja, Rio Grande do Sul), 40
Estillac Leal, Newton, 345, 469
Etchegoyen, Alcides Gonçalves, 280, 334
European influence & U.S. arms supply policy, 329-330
expeditionary force (FEB), 3, 297, 317, 324, 337 development, 343-371: American view of, 347-349; commanders, 356-357, 361-362; departure, 373-377; equipment, 374; General Staff School, 345, 348-349; JBUSDC, 352-354; popular support, 372, 375, 404; problems, 347, 356; purpose, 355-356, 404; selection of troops, 365, 369-372; training, 353-354, 362-364, 374-375; Italy, 405-439: Americans, 433-435, 439; Corps, 425; data, 430-431; described, 431-433, 438-439; equipment, 406-407, 410-412, 424-425, 428-429, 439; great power status, 435, 462; health, 411-412; invasion of France, 414; mail & censorship, 427-428; music, 432, 435; R & R, 427; replacement depot, 428-429, 431; training, 410-412, 418-419, 421, 426, 428-429, 431; post-campaign: demobilization, 439-442, 468; ex-officers & U.S., 442; occupation role rejected, 439; politics, 436-438, 440, 442, 447-448, 450, 461-462, 468, 470; return, 438-442, 466, 468; veterans, 441-442
expeditionary force (U.S.) for Northeast Brazil, 141, 201, 203-204, 208; World War I, AEF, 362. See also Pot of Gold

Fairbanks, Douglas, Jr., 247
Falconieri de Cunha, Olympio, 414, 437
Farley, James A., 241
Farrell, Edelmiro J., 324
favelas, 17, 20
fazendeiros, 16, 22
Fôrça Expedicionária Brasileira (FEB), see expeditionary force
Febianos, see expeditionary force
Federação 25 de Julho, 81
Federal Bureau of Investigation (FBI), 117
Federal Communications Commission, 107
Fernando de Noronha Island, 140, 145, 201
ferrying operations, see Air Transport Command
Fifth Army, U.S., 373, 412, 414, 423, 424, 425, 428, 429, 433
fifth column, 191, 230
Filettole, 418, 421-422
Financial Reconstruction Corporation, U.S., 127
Finletter, Thomas K., 265
First World War, 152, 295, 329
Flôres da Cunha, José Antônio, 35, 37-39, 95, 460
Florianismo, 443. See also Florianistas; Floriano Peixoto
Florianistas, 426. See also Florianismo; Floriano Peixoto
Fluminense Football Club, 92
Flying Fortresses, 143, 145
food supply, see Basic Economy Program
Fontes, Lourival, 199, 280
Ford Company, 268; Ford, Henry, 388
foreign companies & investment, 378-379
Foreign Economic Administration (FEA), 454-455

foreign policy, *Brazil*: alliance
formula, 112, 267; Argentina,
110, 113, 119-121, 139-140, 281-
284, 324-327; effects of Aranha
resignation, 338, 340-341; Germany, 9, 94-100, 103-105, 143,
170, 176-180, 182, 190-193, 196-
197; hemispheric security, 112-
122, 245, 250; methods, 158, 260-
268, 271, 275, 332; military relations, 133-144, 186, 195; neutrality, 114-115, 184; Rio Conference, 250-258; role in South
America, 119-120, 252, 310-311;
situation 1940, 176-180, 212;
trade, 148-150, 153-175, 190;
U.S., 5-7, 9, 54-55, 60-61, 64-69,
74-76, 87; U.S. aid, 127-132, 193-
198; war aims, 306, 357-359;
World War II opportunities,
343-345, 358-359, 362, 380-381;
Germany: 69-70, 80-81, 94-
100, 103-105, 106, 182; economic
importance of Brazil, 115-116,
162-165, 169, 190-193; trade,
150-175; view of Brazil, 160, 170,
192-193;
United States: alliance, 325-
328; arms supply & hegemony,
328-330, 341; aviation policy,
213, 215-221; Brazil & Argentina,
8, 281-284, 323-324, 342, 347,
457; Brazilian development, 61,
67-69, 126-130, 193-199, 262-269;
dependency, 381, 394-396, 452-
459; characterized, 126-127, 139,
159; cross-purposes, 243; cultural
relations, 247-249; economic relations & political cooperation,
195, 206-207; experts, 401-402;
hemispheric security, 106, 122;
intervention, 453-454, 471-477;
Latin America, 7, 265, 331-332;
methods, 266, 271, 478-479;

Open Door philosophy, 383;
personalities, 320, 325-326, 341,
452; postwar policy for under-
developed regions, 386-388;
trade, 148-175; Vargas, 67-68,
159, 207, 269, 278-279, 339, 452-
454, 471-477; view of Brazil,
160, 248
Foreign Relations Council, 127
Fornovo, 435
Fort Copacabana, 334, 447
Fort Knox, 130
Fort Leme, 92
Fortaleza, Ceará, 227, 233, 287
Fortune, 222
Foster, Paul, 293
Fournier, Severo, Incident, 101-102
Fourth Corps, U.S., 409, 416, 420,
422, 425, 433
Fourth Fleet, U.S., 274, 293
France, 113, 119, 125, 172, 178, 183,
184, 190, 202, 373, 414
Friends of America, 311, 335
Freitas Valle, Cyro de, 144, 172,
174, 190, 192, 193, 211
French Foreign Office, 184; mili-
tary mission, 190; influence,
356, 359, 362, 374, 413
Freire, General Firmo, 446
Freyre, Gilberto, 12
friendship, diplomats' need for,
104
Funck, Walther, 170

Gallup Poll, 184
gaúcho, *see* Rio Grande do Sul
general officers, elite cooptation of,
444
General Mann, USS, 375, 377, 405
German National Socialist Party,
see Nazi
Germany, 68, 108, 124, 135, 143,
146, 166, 169, 171-174, 189, 216,
241; Argentina, 321-322; post-

war plans, 192-193; trade, 148-175

Gestapo, 69

Gibraltar, 197, 209

Góes Monteiro, Pedro Aurélio de, 8, 26-27, 29, 33, 35, 38, 42, 56-57, 59, 70, 72, 82, 91, 177, 190, 200, 210, 225-226, 230, 240-241, 270, 280; Aranha, 130, 142, 318-319, 336, 338, 445; Axis, 254-255; coup 1945, 445-446, 450, 468-469, 474-477, 480-486; development, 322; FEB, 344, 346, 357, 359; Spanish America, 331; U.S., 123, 132-133, 137-143, 145, 187-189, 202, 204, 207, 208, 321; Vargas, 318-319; war "plans," 296-297

Goering, Hermann, 178

gold reserves, 300

Gomes, Eduardo, 59, 218-219, 233, 270, 311, 436-437, 440, 446-448, 451, 453, 460, 462, 465-469, 470-471, 481-486

Good Neighbor Policy, 7, 67-68, 127, 159, 188, 194

Gothic Line, 414, 415, 433

Graça Aranha, Themistocles, 143-144, 177

Graf Spee incident, 182

Grande Hotel (Natal), 231, 236

Great Britain, see England

greenshirts, see Integralistas

Grew, Joseph, 458

Guanabara Bay, 375; Palace, 40, 45, 47, 91-92, 93, 137, 288-290, 293, 477, 481, 483

guaraná, 236

Guatemala, 108

Guiana, British, 294, 306; Dutch, 244; French, 345-346, 350

Guinle, Guiherme, 195, 197

Guilhem, Henrique Aristides, 41, 85

Havana Conference, see Inter-American Conferences

health, 365, 369-372, 390, 399, 411-412. *See also* Basic Economy Program

Helena, USS, 201

Himmler, Heinrich, 69

Hitler, Adolf, 32, 78, 79-81, 83, 98, 114, 124, 133, 143, 144, 151-153, 172, 173n, 177-178, 184, 190, 277-278

Hollywood films, 11, 379

Hopkins, Harry, 308

Horne, Frederick J., 309

Hull, Cordell, 109, 127, 186, 194, 250, 319-320, 323-326, 362, 458; Aranha resignation, 333, 336, 338, 340, 341; Lima Conference, 117-122; Rio Conference, 252-258

Humboldt, USS, 307, 308

Hyde Park, New York, 15, 309

ideology and Vargas, 66, 105, 114, 149

immigrants, 19, 77-79, 87, 90, 97, 134, 151, 176, 180, 187, 191, 345, 355

imperialism, American, 264

India, 169

industrialists, 27, 448

inflation, 463

infantry regiments: 1st (the Sampaio; São Paulo), 419, 421-422, 433; 6th (Caçapava, São Paulo), 364, 369, 370, 375, 409-410, 421-422, 462; 11th (São João del Rei, Minas Gerais), 364, 419

Ingram, Jonas H., 274, 276-277, 293-296, 300, 302, 307-309, 323, 399-400

Inheritance of 1835, 38

Institute of Public Opinion and Statistics, 462

Institutional Act, 1964, 34
Integralismo, see Integralistas
Integralistas, 8, 14, 30-31, 36, 38, 44-45, 54, 59, 77, 83-86, 91-96, 105, 134, 182, 233, 243, 314, 444
Inter-American Affairs, Institute of, 398, 400; Office of the Coordinator of, 108, 247, 249. See also Rockefeller
Inter-American Conferences, 107; Buenos Aires, 8, 115, 118; Chapultepec, 451; Havana, 189, 196, 207; Lima, 106, 117-122, 123; Panama, 146, Rio, 104, 250-258, 318, 320
intervention, 116, 453-454
interventors, 26, 39, 46, 58, 72, 82, 279, 478, 480
Iran, 169
Ishii, Itaro, 253
Itabira, Minas Gerais, 268
Italian Fascist Divisions, 436
Italy, 111, 116, 124, 135, 137, 144, 178, 181, 183-184, 205, 209, 403-442, 444
Itamaraty, 12, 73, 76, 117-118, 121, 144, 174, 178, 179, 191, 209, 248, 257, 288, 290, 322, 324, 336, 338, 342, 351

João VI, 182
Japan, 68, 116, 124, 135, 146, 210, 253, 388
Jobim, José, 383
Joint Army and Navy Advisory Board on the American Republics, 328-329
Joint Board for the Defense of Northeast Brazil, 272-273
Joint Brazilian–Bolivian Commission, 454
Joint Brazil–United States Defense Commission, 261, 271-273, 297, 349, 352-354, 360, 406, 455

Joint Brazil–United States Economic Development Commission, 1953, 387
Joint Chiefs of Staff, 352
joint defense agreement, 269-273. See also Joint Brazil–United States Defense Commission
joint staff agreement, 1941, 246
Jones, Jesse, 194, 196-197, 341
Jouett, USS, 307
Juazeiro, Ceará, 22
Juiz de Fora, Minas Gerais, 42
Justo, Agustín, 292

Kibon ice cream, 299
Kimberly, Allen, 145, 189
Knox, Frank, 284, 295-296
Krupp, 111-112, 141, 177, 193, 195, 197, 200, 209, 241

labor, 301, 313-317, 339, 364, 365, 479-480; Amazon, 389-393; political mobilization, 444, 449, 466-467; strikes, 463-464
LaGuardia, Fiorello, 185
Lama de Sotto-Monte San Quirino, 415
Lampião, 22
language problems, 237, 363, 376, 406, 425, 429
Lati (Linee Aeree Transcontinentali Italiane), 215-216, 220-221, 236
Latin America, 68, 98, 106-122, 297-298, 329
Lavallade, Chadebec de, 413
League of Nations, 170, 298
lebensraum, 152
Leitão de Carvalho, Estevão, 137, 188, 273, 352-353, 361, 374
Leitão de Cunha, Vasco, 383
lend-lease, 262, 268, 272, 328
Leme, Dom Sebastião Cardinal, 17
Lévi-Strauss, Claude, 19, 21

Lili Marlene, 432
Lima Cavalcanti, Carlos de, 437
Lima Conference, *see* Inter-
American Conferences
Linhares, José, 484
Lins do Barros, João Alberto, 26,
92, 383, 464, 477, 481, 482
Lippmann, Walter, 129-130
Lloyd-Brasileiro, 125
Lodi, Euvaldo, 316, 448
Lourenço, José, 22
Low Countries, 182, 202
Lufthansa, 214-216, 220, 226
Luftwaffe, 183
Lusitania, 185
Luzardo, João Batista, 479

Macedo Soares e Silva, Edmundo,
193, 383
Macedo Soares, José Carlos de,
34-35, 42, 45
Macedo Soares, José Eduardo de,
346, 403, 436, 480
Maceió, Alagoas, 227
Maciel Júnior, J. S., 309
Machado, "Widow," 232
Madeira, 308
Madrid, 347
Magalhães, Agamemnon Sérgio
Godoy de, 33, 45, 460-461, 477
Magalhães, Juracy, 26
Magalhães Barata, Joaquim, 26
Manaus, Amazonas, 288, 388ff
Marcondes Filho, Alexandre, 280,
312, 315, 317, 325, 334-336, 337,
446, 448, 449, 459, 460, 463,
465, 479
Marshall, George C., 123, 125, 133,
136-138, 140-141, 143, 145, 202,
205, 207, 210, 223, 225, 242,
352-354, 360, 362
Martins, Carlos, 183, 185, 195, 297,
340-341, 382
Mascarenhas de Moraes, João

Batista, 233, 357, 363, 370-371,
372-373, 374, 407, 408-411; de-
tachment Zenóbio, 417-418, 420,
423-426; candidates, 470; FEB
& politics, 436-437; Monte Castello, 433-434; return to Brazil,
438-439, 441; Vargas, 424-426,
466
Mato Grosso, 283
Matthews, Charles, 231
McKee Co., Arthur J., 194
Melo, Nélson de, 334, 437
Melo Franco, Afrânio de, 118, 121,
311, 315
Melo Franco, Virgílio de, 315, 446,
453
Memphis, USS, 323
Mendonça Lima, General, 311
Mesquito Filho, Júlio de, 34
Mexicans, 347
Mexico, 108, 279
Miami, Florida, 214
middle class, 365-366, 400
military academy, Brazilian,
365-366, 368n
Military Appropriation Act
(1940), 222-223
military assistance, *see* foreign
policy, U.S.
military attaché, 108-109
military, Brazilian: break with
Axis, 254-258; coup of 1937,
35-45, 58-59; depoliticization,
303-304; development, 444-445;
politics, 312, 318, 443-445, 476,
477, 485-486; press, 240-241;
South America, 321; trade, 168,
181; Vargas, 26-27, 94-95, 176,
187-189, 194, 211, 225-226, 240-
241, 243, 259, 303-304, 312, 316,
318-319, 364, 443-448, 461, 480,
483-486; World War II opportunities, 344-345. *See also* army,
Brazilian; expeditionary force;
Vargas

Military Brigade (Rio Grande do Sul), 39

military cooperation, *see* arms supply; army, Brazilian; army, U.S.; defense; dependency; foreign policy

Military Mission, U.S., 145

Miller, Lehman, W., 138, 187, 204

Minas Gerais, 13, 180-182, 198-199, 315; *Minas Gerais* (Brazilian battleship), Vargas' speech on, 185-190

Mineiro Manifesto, 315-316, 364

Minister of Navy, *see* Guilhem, Henrique Aristides

Minister of War, *see* Dutra, Eurico Gaspar

Miranda, Carmen, 248

missions, U.S. Army, 107-108

mobilization, 366-375

moderator, 445

Modern Art Week (São Paulo, 1922), 21

modernization, necessity of, 23

Monarchist Party, 467

Moniz de Aragão, José Joaquim de Lima e Silva, 97, 103-104, 167

Monroe Doctrine, 122, 135, 182, 189, 206

Monte Castello, 3, 10, 370, 419-425, 432-435, 462. *See also* expeditionary force

Monte Prano, 415

Montese, 435

Montevideo, Uruguay, 318, 323, 445

Moore-McCormack Lines (SS *Argentina*, SS *Brazil*, SS *Uruguay*), 108

Morínigo, Higínio, 310

Morison, Samuel E., 294

Müller, Filinto von Strubling, 34,

45, 92, 99, 200, 247, 280, 301, 334

Munich, 113, 115

music, 18, 22, 432, 435

Mussolini, Benito, 32, 124-125, 137, 178, 184

Naples, 403, 405, 425, 440

Nashville, USS, 136, 138, 143

Natal, 4, 29, 133, 134, 140, 145, 201, 203, 210, 214, 215, 220-222, 227ff, 246; conference, 304-310, 349-351, 355; Stimson, 262, 278, 294

National Broadcasting Company, 107

nationalism, 82, 314-315, 474

national security, 9, 114, 115-122, 160-161, 256; council, 227; development, 125, 306, 314-315, 444-445

natural resources as leverage, 179

naval diplomacy, U.S., 276-277, 293-296

Naval High Command, German, 277

Naval Mission, U.S., 270, 328, 457

navy, Brazilian, 42, 276, 295, 300, 328, 379

—, U.S., 245, 291, 293, 295-297

—, U.S. Department of, 107, 109, 127, 129, 243, 455

Navicert (Passport System), 174. *See also* blockade

Nazi Party, 72, 77, 79-83, 86-91, 98-101, 103, 104, 116, 134; anti-Nazi decree (1938), 89, 97; trade, 151-152, 169-170

Negrão de Lima, Francisco, 41

Neurath, Konstantin von, 78

neutrality: Argentina, 323-324; Brazil, 9, 144, 174, 181-182, 187, 189, 192; ADP, 230, 235, 242, 250-251, 252, 267; German view of, 277-278, 291-292; U.S., 141, 146

New Amsterdam, 124

New Deal, 126-127

New Dealers & "dollar-a-year" men contrasted, 264

newspapers: *Berliner Boersen Zeitung,* 89-90; *Chicago Daily News,* 284; *Correio da Manhã,* 75, 114, 131, 240-241, 299, 346, 379, 438; *Correio da Noite,* 436; *La Crítica* (Buenos Aires), 49, 186; *La Crónica* (Lima), 49; *O Cruzeiro do Sul* (FEB), 437, 461; *Diário Carioca,* 75, 240-241, 269, 299, 309, 346, 461; *Diários Associados,* 30, 338, 437; *Diário da Noite,* 114, 404, 461; *Diário de Notícias,* 299, 436, 451; *Deutsche Allgemeine Zeitung,* 95-96; *Deutsche Diplomatische Korrespondenz,* 88; *É a Cobra fumou* (FEB), 432-433; *Essener National Zeitung,* 89; *O Estado de São Paulo,* 34; *Folha Carioca,* 480; *Gazeta de Notícias,* 288; *O Globo,* 125, 404, 461-462, 463, 481; *La Hora* (Santiago de Chile), 49; *O Imparcial,* 30, 379; *O Jornal,* 54-55, 67, 89, 114, 404, 436, 450-451; *Jornal do Brasil,* 250-251; *A Manhã,* 269, 309, 413, 435; *Meio Dia,* 199, 288, 379; *Il Messaggero* (Rome), 50; *El Mundo* (Buenos Aires), 49; *A Nação,* 379; *La Nación* (Buenos Aires), 49, 337; *La Nación* (Santiago de Chile), 49; *New York Times,* 50, 129, 130, 186, 451; *A Noite,* 309, 482; *A Pátria,* 379; *O Radical,* 481; *Star and Herald* (Panama), 485; *El Tiempo* (Mexico City), 337; *Tribunal Popular,* 464; *A Vanguarda* (Belém), 287; *Zé Carioca* (FEB), 432

Nixon, Richard M., 385

Niteroi, 279

Northeast Brazil, 20, 133-136, 138, 140-141, 145, 147, 213, 242-246, 272-274, 345, 348-349, 352, 389. *See also* ADP; army, U.S.; Natal

Nôvo Hamburgo, Rio Grande do Sul, 151

Old Republic (1891-1930), 25

Olds, Robert, 270

Open Door, 149, 168, 171, 175; philosophy, 383

opposition, 315-316, 318, 447, 449, 453, 459-462, 465, 478. *See also* União Democrática Nacional

oranges, 170

Ord, J. Garesche, 352-353

Ortiz, Roberto M., 121

Paiva Gonçalves, Carlos, 369-370

Panagra, 214

Panama Canal, 138, 201, 239. For Panama Conference & Declaration, *see* Inter-American Conferences

Panair do Brasil, S.A., 93, 214-218, 220, 224, 226-230, 232, 236, 392

Pan-American Airports Corporation, 223-224

Pan-American Airways, 199, 213, 214-215, 217-239, 345

Pan-Americanism, 67-68, 189, 304

Pan-American Conferences, *see* Inter-American Conferences

Papacy, 28

Paraguay, 5, 43, 186, 252, 310-311, 321, 323

Paraná, 78, 90

Parnamirim, 220-222, 231-232, 235-239, 307-308

Partido Social Democrático (PSD), 467
Partido Trabalhista Brasileiro (PTB), 467, 480-481
Paulista, *see* São Paulo
Peace Conference, 309, 344, 350, 355, 413, 458
Pearl Harbor, 136, 220, 233, 235, 246, 250
Pearson, Drew, 381-382
Peixoto, Floriano, 443, *see* Florianismo
Pena Jr., Affonso, 315
Peñaranda, Enrique, 311
Pereira, Archiminio, 429-430
Perkins, Milo, 382
Perón, Juan, 321, 324, 331, 340, 445, 472, 473-474, 479
Pershing, John J., 362
Petrópolis, 83, 131, 225
Peru, 117, 119, 323
Pimentel Brandão, Mario de, 83, 107, 110
Pinto, Francisco José, 92, 136, 225, 226, 227
Pistoia, 439
Pittman Resolution, 144-145
plots, 86, 91-94, 116, 180, 183, 189, 203, 256, 279, 301-302, 315-316, 323, 335, 468
Poços de Caldas, 42
police, 33, 280, 301-302; chiefs listed, 334
political alliances, 1945, 470-471
Political Defense, Emergency Advisory Committee for, 318
political parties, 58
politics, 1930's, 12-14, 26-48; post-1943, 311-319, 324-325, 333-340, 342
Poland, 116, 142, 146, 172, 178, 348
population, 16-17
Porreta-Terme, 422

Pôrto Alegre, 71, 85, 137, 180, 214, 287, 441
Portugal, 209, 241, 244, 306, 350
postwar, 297-298, 333, 342, 343, 350, 359, 362, 383, 385, 403, 452; U.S. development policy, 386-388
Pot of Gold, 203. *See also* army, U.S.; expeditionary force for Northeast Brazil
Potengi River (Natal), 234, 238, 307
Po Valley, 414, 423
poverty, 17, 401
pracinhas, 404. *See also* expeditionary force (FEB)
Prado, Paulo, 22
press, 177, 179, 182, 186-187, 200, 222; Aranha, 129-131, 337-338, 340; Berle speech, 475-476; Brazilian, 95, 98-99, 249, 379-380; Cooke Mission, 385; Estado Nôvo, 49-50, 54, 450-451, 460-462, 477-478, 480, 481-482, 485; FEB, 403-404, 413, 432-433, 435-438; foreign policy, 66-67, 74, 250; German, 88-90, 95-96, 98; Marshall, 137; military, 240-241; Munich, 114; Natal, 309; peace conference, 458; Souza Costa Mission, 269
Prestes Column, 21n
Prestes, Júlio, 293
Prestes, Luís Carlos, 29, 462, 464-465, 483
propaganda, 107, 182, 191, 247-249, 363, 383, 397-401, 432
Press and Propaganda, Department of (DIP), 85, 199, 240, 280, 315
Press Association, Brazilian, 437
Prüfer, Kurt Max, 177-178, 187, 190-191, 193, 196-197, 200

public opinion, Brazil, 462-463,
467; U.S., 184

quartz, 380, 456-457
Queremista campaign, 465-466,
468-470, 474-477, 479-482

Rabello, Manoel, 311, 335
railroads, 180-181, 262, 268, 282-
283, 310-311, 399, 455
Rainbow Plans, 201, 203, 245-246
Ramírez, Pedro P., 324
Rauschning, Herman, 80
Realengo, *see* military academy
Recife, Pernambuco, 20, 29, 134,
214, 227, 233, 243, 246, 287, 294
Reichsdeutsche, 80
Reno Valley, 418
representative government, 339-
340. *See also* elections
Resistência, 470
reservists, 368n
revolution of rising expectations,
385
Revolution of 1930, 443
Ribbentrop, Joachim von, 169
Ridgway, Matthew B., 138, 141,
145, 206, 242, 271
Rio Branco, Baron of, 5, 298, 338;
Avenida, 11, 136
Rio Conference, *see* Inter-Ameri-
can Conferences
Rio de la Plata, Viceroyalty of,
322, 327
Rio de Janeiro, Federal District,
11, 17, 20-21, 29, 36, 54, 67, 134,
136, 137, 203, 214, 248, 251-258,
298-299, 378-379, 441
Río de Janeiro, State of, 198
Rio Grande do Sul, 13, 17, 35-39,
51, 71-72, 78, 82, 90, 137, 180,
273
Riograndense, *see* Rio Grande do
Sul

Rio Negro, Palace (Petrópolis),
225
Rio Pardo, Preparatory & Tactical
School, 426
Ritter, Karl, 69, 83, 86-87, 89,
91, 94, 96-100, 103-104, 158,
167-168, 170, 176-178, 191-192
river systems & transportation
development, 396-397
Rockefeller, Nelson A., 247, 264-
265, 341, 397-398, 400, 473-474
Rodrigues Alves, José de Paula,
292
Rome, 253
Rommel, Erwin, 229, 235
Roosevelt administration, 65, 67-
68, 127, 135, 149, 159, 207, 325,
341
Roosevelt, Franklin D., 52, 65,
178-179, 184, 187, 190, 200-203,
247, 262, 265, 286, 288, 292, 398,
400-401, 427, 452, 458; Argentina, 323; death, 341; Iceland &
Greenland, 243-344; hemispheric
security, 107, 115, 119, 122-124,
127, 139, 143, 145-146; Munich,
124-125; Natal, 304, 307-310,
349-351, 355; postwar, 297-298;
"turning point of the war," 332;
Vargas, 7-9, 15-16, 32, 67-68,
128, 145, 241, 250, 263, 303-304,
342, 355; Welles, 319, 320, 362
Rothschilds, 5, 129
Rosas, Juan Manuel de, 322
rubber, 129, 163, 264, 268; program, 388-396; Credit Bank,
268, 388, 390, 395; Development
Corporation, 268, 394, 395;
Reserve Company, 268, 388;
synthetic, 394-396
Rumania, 179
Russia, 170, 178, 208, 279, 326,
335, 451, 458, 464, 467
Russo, Captain J., 407

Sabará, 198
Saican, Rio Grande do Sul, 180
salary-wage scale, military & labor
    compared, 365-366
Salazar, Antonio de Oliveira, 244,
    350
Saldenha, Reinaldo, 461
Sales Oliveira, Armando de, 34, 37,
    45, 58, 317
Salgado, Plínio, 30, 44, 55-58,
    84, 314
Salgado Filho, Joaquim Pedro,
    226, 244, 470
Salvador, Bahia, 134, 214, 215, 227,
    243, 274, 287, 295
Salvador de Sá, 377
Santa Catarina, 78, 90, 180, 194,
    198, 345
Santos, São Paulo, 137, 310
São Francisco River Valley, 125,
    384
São Paulo, 13, 26, 42, 78, 137, 180,
    181, 288, 312, 316, 335, 441, 443
São Paulo (Brazilian battleship),
    85; São Paulo, University of,
    19, 449-450
Schmaltz, Willy, 461
Scotten, Robert M., 56, 75
Second Corps, U.S., 414
secretary of state, see Byrnes, Hull,
    Stettinius
Segadas Vianna, José de, 480
Segadas Vianna, João, 462
Senate, U.S., Military Affairs
    Committee, 124
Serchio River, 415
Sergipé, 287
seringueiro, 393
sertão, 20
Seventh Artillery Group, Brazil-
    ian, 287
ships sunk: Anibal Benévolo, 287;
    Arará, 287; Araraquara, 287;
    Baependí, 287, 345; Buarque,

276; Cairú, 275; Itagiba, 287;
    Jacira, 287
siege, state of, see war, state of
Silva Py, Aurélio, 82
Silveira, Jöel, 437
Silveira, Paula, 460
Siqueira Campos Affair, 209-211,
    225-226, 240
Simonsen, Roberto, 316, 448, 464
smoking cobra, 375
social change and the military,
    444-445
Sola, Ugo, 181, 252-253
South Africa, 300
South Atlantic Force, see Fourth
    Fleet, U.S.
South Atlantic Wing of the Air
    Transport Command, see army,
    U.S.
Souto, Álcio, 478
Souza Costa, Artur de, 62, 64, 68,
    91, 130, 193, 219, 337, 339, 381,
    388; German trade, 153, 155,
    158, 196; Mission, 259-269
Soviet Union, see Russia
Spanaus, Karl, 81
Spanish America, 6, 322, 331;
    Spanish Civil War, 108
San Francisco Conference, 458
Spaatz, Carl, 235
speeches: Berle, 475-476; Dutra,
    446-447; Góes, 189-190; Roose-
    velt, 184; Vargas: continental
    solidarity, 250; constituinte,
    477; democracy, elections,
    labor, 300-301; elections,
    446-447; 469-470; Estado
    Nôvo, 47-48, 56; labor, 313,
    333-334, 480; natural resources,
    314; neutrality, 181-182; Siqueira
    Campos, 211; sovereignty, 114,
    180, 289-290; Welles, 67

spheres of influence, 193; and arms supply, 328-330
S.S. troopers, 416
Staffoli, 428, 432
Standard do Brasil, 220, 237
Standing Liaison Committee (SLC), 109-110, 278, 309, 347-348
Stark, Harold R., 201-202
State Department, U.S., 88, 107-109, 122, 124, 127, 129, 145-146, 182, 186, 194, 203, 207, 243, 248, 265, 324, 347, 379, 448, 485; Aranha criticism, 327-328; Cooke Mission, 382, 385-387; postwar, 297-298; shifting policy, 452-459
Stettinius Jr., Edward R., 329, 340-341, 451, 452
steel, 172, 179; Steel Corporation, U.S., 194. *See also* Volta Redonda
Stimson, Henry L., 185, 208-209, 262, 398
strategic materials, 245, 268-269, 283, 341, 343, 398; internal security, 329; as bargaining tool, 380-381; rubber, 388-396
students, 19, 279, 316, 318, 335, 368, 449-450, 460
submarine warfare, 258, 275, 277-281, 286-290, 345, 375, 380; and development, 396-397. *See also* ships sunk
sugar, 165,
supply problems, 279-280, 281-283, 286-287, 300, 348
Supreme Allied Council, 435
Supreme Federal Tribunal, 230, 462
Sweden, 179, 192

Tavino, 422
taxes, 318
technology, transfer of, 383, 386

tenentes, 13, 26, 311, 443, 447, 464
Tennessee Valley Authority, 125
Tewell, Harold, 335
Time magazine, 137
Tiradentes Palace, 251
tobacco, 162, 167, 170
Torre de Nerone, 370, 409-410
Trade: aid, 126-130; arms supply, 131, 168, 181, 328-329; balance 1942, 300; Brazilian policy, 148-149, 157-158, 171; British, 455-456; and development, 148, 160-161, 172; Germany, 128, 129, 132, 150-175, 190-193; German-U.S. competition, 148-175; neutrality, 192; practices, 145-146, 150, 152, 156-157, 161-162, 165, 171; Reciprocal Trade Agreement, 149, 154-157
Trans-World Airways, 237
Transportation & Public Works, Ministry of, 227
Trieste, 438
Treasury, U.S. Department of, 127
Três Rios, State of Rio de Janeiro, 367
Triple Alliance, War of (1865-1870), 310, 408
Trippe, Juan T., 216
Truman, Harry S, 341, 458, 472, 478-479
Truscott, Lucian K., 424, 433
Twelfth Corps, British, 414

United States Armed Forces, South Atlantic, *see* army, U.S.
United States Engineering Department, 238
União Democrática Nacional (UDN), 460-461, 466. *See also* opposition
União Nacional dos Estudantes (UNE), 460. *See also* students

United Nations, 297-298, 305, 308, 311, 329, 333, 341, 372, 457-458
Uruguay, 88, 116, 182, 203, 252, 321, 323

Vada, 412-413, 418, 425
Valladares, Benedicto, 36, 41-42, 58, 198, 339, 461, 478, 480
valorization, 24, 63-64. *See also* coffee
Vandenberg, Arthur, 185
Vargas do Amaral Peixoto, Alzira, 12, 36, 92, 255, 266, 279, 297
Vargas, Benjamin, 315, 325, 334, 337, 448, 465, 481, 482
Vargas, Darcy, 102, 427, 476
Vargas, Getúlio Dornelles:
Aranha, 62, 101-102, 124-128, 132, 304-307, 335-342; attitudes 1945, 449, 459, 477; auto accident, 278-279, 312; aviation, 219, 224-227; Berle speech, 475-477; business, 316-317, 448; deposition, 319, 481-486; described, 13-16, 312; development, 61, 175, 180, 193-199, 455; diplomats, 285, 297; elections, 301, 312, 335, 446-447; embargo, 275-277; entry into World War II, 286, 288-289, 293; Estado Nôvo, 33-48, 54-76, 267, 269; FEB, 344, 346, 348, 349, 354-356, 360, 376, 424-426, 436; *futebol*, 100; government, 26-32, 125-126, 128, 160-162, 172, 339-340; ideology, 66, 105, 149; Ingram, 293-296, 300; Integralistas, 44-45, 55-59, 77, 83-86, 91-96, 105; labor, 313-317, 333-334; Lima, 118-122; methods, 227-228, 247, 263, 297, 313-316, 332; military, 26-27, 35-45, 94-95, 176, 180, 187-189, 194, 211, 225-226, 240-241, 243, 259, 303-304, 312, 316, 318-319,

364, 443-448, 461; military cooperation, 110-111, 140-141, 250; Navy Day Speech, 185-190; Nazi Party, 82-83, 106; Prestes, 464-465; pro-German followers, 200; Queremistas, 474-475; Rio Conference, 253-257; Roosevelt, 7-8, 15-16, 32, 67-68, 128, 145, 241, 244-245, 263, 303-304, 342; senator, 485; Souza Costa Mission, 259-269; sovereignty, 114, 148; support for, 460, 462-465; trade, 148, 162, 190-191; U.S. & Germany, 175, 193, 196, 200, 217, 241-242
Vargas, Getúlio Jr., 177, 307
Vargas, Luther, 177
Vargas, Manoel do Nascimento, 102
Vargas, Viriato, 465, 476
Varig (Viação Aêrea Rio Grandense), 215-221
Vasp (Viação Aêrea São Paulo), 215-221
Velloso Neto, Pedro Leão, 338, 451, 458
Venezuela, 161-162
Vergara, Luiz, 339, 459, 469
Vichy, 242, 245, 346
Vila Militar, 374
Vitória, Espirito Santo, 228
Volksdeutsche, 80, 81, 98
Volta Redonda, 4, 193-199, 217, 262, 297, 314
Von Cossel, Hans Henning, 81, 99, 100, 103

Wagley, Charles, 391, 392
Wakama incident, 182
Wall Street, 264, 382
Walmsley, Walter N., 312, 386, 392-393
Walsh, Robert, 295
Walters, Vernon, 406

War College, U.S. Army, 125, 133, 135

War Plans Division, War Department, 141, 206

War Production Board, 454-455

War Shipping Administration, 282

war, state of, 30n, 38, 39

War, U.S. Department of, 107, 109, 119, 127, 129, 138, 145, 204, 207, 219; ADP, 221-223, 229, 239, 243, 246, 261-262, 271-272; Caffery, 285; FEB, 360, 373

Washington Accords (1939), 128-130, 147; (1942), 267-269, 381, 388. *See also* Aranha and Souza Costa Missions

Washington Luís, 334, 443

Washington Press Club, 127

Wehrmacht, *see* army, German

Weizsäcker, Ernst, 97

Welles, Sumner, 41, 51-53, 65-66, 68, 75, 87-88, 107, 110, 112, 117, 159, 179, 183, 187, 196, 199, 202, 207, 210, 241, 455, 471; Argentina & Brazil, 282-284; arms supply, 259-262; Aranha Mission, 124, 127-129; Aranha resignation, 338-339, 342; attitude contrasted with Hull's, 325-326; Berle speech, 478; FEB, 348, 362; PAA importance, 215-216; postwar, 297-298; resignation, 319-320, 324; Rio Conference, 250-258; Vargas, 278-279

Western Prince, 69, 70

Wilhelmstrasse (German Foreign Office), 88, 89, 90-91, 97, 100, 103, 167, 169, 173, 178, 200

Willkie, Wendell, 331

wool, 163

World War II, 5, 144, 172-174; Argentina, 320-324; development, 305-306, 322; entry, 288-297; opportunities, 343-345, 391, 402, 466

Yalta Conference, 451

Young, Evan, 223

Zenóbio da Costa, Euclydes, 414-418, 434, 441